P9-CDV-846

THE
UNIVERSITY
OF
CALIFORNIA
1868-1968

THE
UNIVERSITY
OF
CALIFORNIA

1868-1968

A Centennial Publication of the University of California

by Verne A. Stadtman

McGRAW-HILL BOOK COMPANY

NEW YORK   ST. LOUIS   SAN FRANCISCO   LONDON   SYDNEY
TORONTO   MEXICO   PANAMA

FIRST EDITION   60615

Preface

THE UNIVERSITY OF CALIFORNIA has enjoyed international eminence for nearly three-quarters of its life, and, by 1964, Californians were no longer the least bit self-conscious when they called it "great." Writing about its enrollment (79,609), newspaper reporters rounded the figure to the nearest thousand; writing about its endowment ($152,873,330), or its annual expenditure ($563,758,040), they rounded the sums to the nearest million. Impartial national studies had proclaimed the University's ranking among the top three universities in the United States on the basis of the distinction of its departments, the size of its library collections, and the performance of its graduate divisions. Its faculty included 15 per cent of all of the Americans who had ever won a Nobel Prize and scores more who had received other international honors or had been elected to the nation's most prestigious scholarly societies. One of its former students, Earl Warren, was Chief Justice of the United States; three more, Robert S. McNamara, Dean Rusk, and William Wirtz, were members of the President's Cabinet; and another, Ralph Bunche, held the Nobel Peace Prize. The University's president, Clark Kerr, had only recently delivered the famous Godkin Lectures at Harvard on "The Uses of the University" and had done it so lucidly that he became, almost overnight, one of America's foremost statesmen in higher education.

At this point in the University's history (July, 1964), preparation of this book began. In the planning stages, it was called a "chronological history," a description that took the University's eminence for granted and seemed to call for a fairly simple recitation of the highlights of the past.

Within three months after my work began, traumatic events at Berkeley made a reappraisal of the assignment necessary. The shock of student rebellion was all the more severe because the University's history as then understood prepared neither the public nor the University community for seeing the revolt in proper perspective. Knowing this, I found it necessary to probe a little more deeply than I originally intended into forces that affect the internal authority structure of the University and that have shaped student life at the University for nearly a century.

It was also clear that the development of new campuses at San Diego,

v

Irvine, and Santa Cruz, which together will accommodate more than a third of the University's student body within the next three decades, could not be perfunctorily treated as just a segment of a concluding chapter. Their beginnings nearly coincide with the start of the University's second century and their planning benefits from all of the hindsight found on early pages of the narrative.

In the course of preparing this work, I have discovered that continuous growth and expansion may well be the central theme of the University's history and I have tried to indicate, as best I could, the impact of that theme upon the institution's organization and the interrelationships of its human components—students, faculty, administrators, and Regents.

What is offered here, therefore, is something more than a simple chronology, or a remembrance of significant occasions. On the other hand, emphasis has been selective. Some forces in the University's development are treated more thoroughly than others. The author accepts responsibility for this emphasis and, at the same time, disclaims all pretensions to having written a definitive account.

Readers should know that I have been inhibited by only two factors in the research and writing of this volume—the short period of time allowed for its completion and an early decision to hold it to a length comfortable in a single volume. I have had access to abundant records from the archives and current files of the University. For this, I am grateful to former President Clark Kerr; former Acting President Harry R. Wellman; President Charles J. Hitch; Miss Marjorie Woolman, secretary of the Board of Regents, and members of her staff; Mrs. Mary Cove, senior administrative assistant in the president's office; Arthur E. Hutson, secretary of the Academic Senate; Mrs. Dorothy Randolph, senior administrative assistant in the Secretariat of the Academic Senate; and the public affairs and public information officers on the various campuses. I am especially indebted to the staff of the Bancroft Library, and, among these, particularly to Mr. J. R. K. Kantor, archivist at Berkeley, for indispensable assistance that included a sympathetic and helpful review of the entire manuscript.

Notes and documents gathered between 1954 and 1960 by Professor Walton Bean and his assistants were made available to me and proved to be invaluable. I must also acknowledge the services of the hundreds of faculty members, administrators, and the dedicated staff who participated in the preparation of *The Centennial Record of the University of California*. That compendium of factual information remained open on my desk almost constantly while this book was being written.

For their confidence in my ability to undertake this work, I am deeply thankful to Vice-president Earl Bolton and former President Clark Kerr. For his consistent protection of my independence, I am indebted to former Vice-president Thomas C. Sorensen.

One of the most treasured benefits of writing this book has been the opportunity to enjoy the frequent good company of John D. Hicks, Morrison Professor of History Emeritus, at Berkeley, upon whom I have always been able to count for sound advice and friendly encouragement. It was a great thrill to work closely with a man I first came to admire at some distance nearly twenty years ago when I was one of his undergraduate students. I have similarly enjoyed working with James D. Hart, chairman of the Department of English at Berkeley, who, along with Professor Hicks, read every chapter and supplied suggestions that spared me inevitable embarrassment and vastly improved the clarity of the text.

I have been fortunate throughout the preparation of this book to have the services of an excellent staff, whose members have amassed information, reviewed chapter drafts, suggested approaches and revisions, typed manuscripts, verified sources, and performed many other essential chores. My gratitude to all of them is unqualified, and it is a pleasure to acknowledge the substantial contributions of our secretary, Mrs. Katherine Jacobs; her predecessor, Mrs. Mary Roberta Orme; and our editors and assistants: Mary Anne Stewart, Richard H. Colton, Susan Howard, Victor Fischer, Edward Franklin, Robert Read, Carol Agee, Michael Otten, and Stephen Brier. Miss May Dornin, formerly University archivist, joined the staff at its inception in 1964 and continued to render services on a voluntary basis long after her official retirement. This loyalty to the University and to its Centennial Editor is of a rare and moving quality that deserves recognition far beyond my simple but sincere "thank you."

In acknowledging the assistance of all of those whom I have named, as well as scores more who have reviewed portions of the manuscript to verify factual information, I must make clear that I do not intend that they share anything but whatever credit may be due the work we have done together. Although the Regents and administration of the University have sponsored my efforts, they have permitted me full latitude of judgment in using the information available to me. Accordingly, for the accuracy and point of view of this narrative, I accept complete and sole responsibility.

The four years that culminate with the completion of this book have been full and short ones for me. I know that they have sometimes seemed to be dull and long ones for my wife, Jackolyn, and our children: Kristen, Rand, Judith, and Todd. I hope they find this book to be worthy of the sacrifices they have made because of it. I also hope that they will share my pride in the

University whose story I have attempted to tell. The quality of life that they and their children will lead in the next century depends, in more ways than can be counted, upon the uninterrupted growth and development of the University of California and the institutions that will successfully emulate its achievements.

VERNE A. STADTMAN

Contents

x   CONTENTS

THE
UNIVERSITY
OF
CALIFORNIA
1868-1968

I

The Foundations

INSTITUTIONS that began on America's Western fron-
tier tended to burst into full bloom before anyone noticed that they had been
in bud. That, apparently, happened to the University of California.

The men who organized the territory of California into a state in 1849
and 1850 took for granted that someday there would be a public university
there and they provided for it in the first constitution. Their assumption was
based on neither invention nor foresight. They only knew that older states
had provided for universities and guessed that California would do the
same.

That a university built on the Pacific Coast would, in its genesis, be further advanced in design and function than its Eastern prototypes at a similar
stage was, of course, inevitable. It was, fundamentally, an import. Some of it
came around the Horn in the minds of men like Henry Durant. Durant was
an alumnus of Yale, an institution which, during his student days, was
America's leading conservator of the classical curriculum and an approach
to instruction that relied upon textbook, lecture, and recitation to fill the
empty heads of society's future leaders. Durant brought much of this tradition to his work as the first principal of Contra Costa Academy, founded in
Oakland in 1853. That academy eventually became the College of California, an evolutionary antecedent of the University. Durant subsequently became the first president of the University. Some elements of the University
were prescribed from Washington in provisions of the Morrill Land Grant
College Act of 1862, which stipulated that the institutions it intended to

1

support were to teach, among other subjects, agriculture and the mechanic arts in order to promote "the liberal and practical education of the industrial classes in the several pursuits and professions in life." Still other elements in the University of California design were borrowed from such well-established state universities as those in Michigan, Wisconsin, and Minnesota. Twenty years after Durant's arrival in California, another Yale alumnus, who was also an admirer of the German universities, assumed the presidency of the University of California. He was Daniel Coit Gilman, whose influence upon the University is still felt although he was its leader for less than three years. For it was Gilman who defined for the people of California the new kind of institution that they had made by adapting to their needs the oldest traditions of American higher education with such refinements as were suggested by the experiences of the state universities in the Midwest, the provisions of the Morrill Act, and the examples of the great German universities.

In borrowing from so many sources for the design of their University, Californians rejected ideas that had led other American college- and university-builders into difficulties. The nonsectarian character of the University of California was established in the law that created it. Religion, as a consequence, never became an issue serious enough to rend the institution. Nor was there much tolerance for interference with the University on the basis of party-oriented political ideology. Tuition was abandoned early and any effort to brand the University a "rich man's school" was made somewhat tenuous as a result. Women were admitted in 1870, two years after the University's establishment, without significant controversy.

By design, the University of California was also intended to be apolitical. In reality, it could not be. It was the creature of the people of the state. Right or wrong, they would exercise their right to criticize or applaud the institution they regarded as the capstone of their public education system. In the early 1870s organized workingmen and farmers challenged the notion that the people of California were served as well by the comprehensive University that had been established as they might be by a more narrow type of institution offering instruction in agriculture and the mechanic arts. They proposed amendments to the legislation creating the University that would have separated these subjects from its curriculum and torn it asunder. Under the relentless criticisms of the workingmen and the farmers, every aspect of the University's management, organization, and aspiration was flayed open to public exposure. As a result of the thorough scrutiny the controversy made possible, California's citizens could see more clearly the comprehensive work and plan of their University and they came to realize that, while it must always be possible to criticize the University, it must be made more difficult for that criticism or some enthusiasms of the day to alter the purpose and character of the institution in a fundamental way. In 1879, therefore, they approved, as a part of a new constitution of the state, provisions that made the act of the legislature creating the University of California in its then existing form a part of the highest law of the commonwealth.

Chapter 1

THE COLLEGE-BUILDERS

MOST OF THE men who built colleges in pre-Civil War America were religious missionaries. They regarded their struggling institutions as frontier outposts of New England culture and the Christian faith. They built colleges to satisfy regional pride; they built colleges to meet denominational competition; they built colleges to train ministers; and they built colleges to keep up with the ever-elusive frontier.[1]

In May, 1849, the American Home Missionary Society, a cooperative agency of the Congregationalists and the "New School" Presbyterians, reported: "This year, we have also found the FAR WEST; which had been here, and there, and every where, and yet we had not been able to reach it. . . . Fifty years ago, it seemed to be in Central New York; forty years ago, in New Connecticut; twenty years ago, in Indiana and Illinois; and fifteen years ago, to be meditating the passage of the Upper Mississippi. But, this year, it has made its permanent settlement on the shores of the Pacific. . . ."[2] The same report announced that early in the year a twenty-seven-year-old graduate of Dartmouth, Rev. Samuel H. Willey, had left New York to represent the American Home Missionary Society in California. He would spend much of the next two decades as one of the builders of a college that was a direct antecedent of the University of California.

When Willey arrived in Monterey on February 23, 1849, he found that most of the male population of the town had gone to the gold fields and that the women who stayed behind were too "connected with the Catholic church"[3] to help him start a Protestant congregation. The young missionary made the best of his disappointment by teaching school, serving as chaplain to the Monterey army post, interesting himself in the efforts of the Californians to establish a civil government, and making friends with leading citizens.

In April, Thomas O. Larkin, a prominent Monterey merchant and land-owner, sought Willey's advice. As one of three proprietors of the town of Benicia, Larkin had received a deed that was already signed by his partners. It conveyed land for "the foundation of a school to be called Benicia university." [4] The school would be founded and operated under the auspices of the "Old School" Presbyterian Church, a purist branch of the denomination which, in 1837, withdrew from the cooperative relationships with Congregationalists that had been activated by a "Plan of Union" in 1802. Congregationalist Willey advised Larkin not to sign the deed until advice could be received from men at well-established Eastern colleges. Willey's own opinion was that California needed one well-endowed college rather than several "crippled all the time for want of means." [5] Larkin first expressed a favorable disposition toward the Benicia University plan, and the only recorded advice from the East warmly endorsed it,[6] but for reasons no longer known, he did not sign the deed, and the project was aborted.[7]

On a visit to Sacramento eight months later, Willey learned that a group of "New School" Presbyterians and Congregationalists were well along in plans for the establishment of a college in San Jose. To further these efforts, Willey abandoned plans to make a missionary trip to the mines and went to San Jose instead to proceed with negotiations to acquire a college site.

The most important feature of the proposed college was that it was to be undenominational. Theoretically, it would thus have a fund-raising advantage in a territory where the population represented many denominations, but where no one denomination had enough members or money to support a college. The secular cast of the enterprise was further emphasized by proposing that the governor and state superintendent of schools be ex-officio trustees and by planning to locate it in San Jose—the city that everyone expected to become California's permanent capital. An attempt of the founders to preempt the name "University of California" was foiled by a legal opinion that use of that name was reserved in the constitution to the state.[8] In internal organization and courses of instruction, features of the best-known Eastern colleges would be incorporated. These older institutions were well represented by graduates participating in the California venture. One leading figure in the movement was Sherman Day, a son of Yale's president Jeremiah Day.[9]

By May, 1850, an offer of land for a site and pledges of $30,750 in donations were in hand.[10] On June 27, a request for a charter for the "College of California" was submitted according to procedures then set forth by law to the California Supreme Court. The plan collapsed in December, when the court denied the college's petition on grounds that the tracts of land available for its site in San Jose had not been sufficiently described.[11] The court also questioned true value of pledges of money that had been made to the college men.

Where the Congregationalists and "New School" Presbyterians failed, others succeeded. The Methodist Episcopal Church chartered California Wesleyan College (which became the University of the Pacific) in San Jose in 1851. In the same year, rudimentary beginnings of the University of Santa Clara were made in the Santa Clara Mission buildings. In Benicia, the Benicia Young Ladies Seminary, the antecedent of Mills College, began in 1852.[12]

The failure of the College of California men at San Jose had its compensations. The leaders gained experience. A band of loyal supporters became known, and would return to the cause when a new opportunity arose. Perhaps most important of all, those active in the college movement who were truly interested in education were freed for labor in a more urgent endeavor —the building of California's public school system.

Less than a score of schools of any kind existed in California between 1846 and 1851.[13] Most of these were makeshift, short-lived ventures associated with pioneer churches or set up in tents, shanties, or private homes. In 1850, Samuel Willey and John C. Pelton, San Francisco's pioneer schoolmaster, led a street march of one hundred children to demonstrate that San Francisco had enough prospective pupils to warrant establishment of public schools. Another College of California supporter, Colonel Thomas Nevins, wrote the ordinance to establish them and later became San Francisco's first school superintendent.

The first state public school laws were passed in 1851. That year, California's superintendent of public instruction reported an enrollment of 1,846 students in all of the schools of the state. These represented about one-fifth of the children between the ages of four and fifteen in the California census. By 1852, the superintendent was able to report the existence of thirty-two schools in the state. The number of students enrolled had not quite doubled; the census of school-age children had tripled.[14] By 1852, a few private academies and colleges offered the equivalent of an Eastern high school education, but there were no public high schools in California until 1856. In that year, one was established in San Francisco and another in Sacramento. No more would be established until 1862.[15] A somewhat common form of early preparation for college in California was that of Josiah Royce. That famous philosopher prepared to enter the University of California's class of 1875 under the tutelage of his mother, who conducted a private school for her own and other children in Grass Valley.[16]

By failing to wait for the adequate development of elementary and secondary schools in California, the state's college-builders of 1849 and 1850 had merely observed an irrational, unwritten law of early American college-founding.[17] By diverting some of their efforts to the cause of public schools in 1850 and 1851, they demonstrated a better understanding of California's educational priorities and pursued a more patient and deliberate college-building pace.

A TIMELY ARRIVAL

Although Samuel Willey came to the college movement just when it had been initiated by others,[18] its momentum became geared to the cycle of his personal interest and involvement. Men with their own churches and businesses to tend were content to entrust him with the extensive correspondence, travel, and negotiation college-building required. As a young missionary without a congregation, Willey was able to perform such coordinating functions with enthusiasm in 1849 and early 1850. But he regarded his "main work of life" to be the Gospel ministry,[19] and he was able to get on with that mission in August, 1850, when he started the Howard Street Presbyterian Church in San Francisco. Thereafter, someone else would have to give college-building the demanding service Willey had rendered before.

Such a man, fresh from the ship, knocked on Samuel Willey's door on the morning of May 1, 1853. Tall, spare, intense, and twenty years Willey's senior, he was Henry Durant, Yale '27, most recently a teacher at a select high school in Byefield, Massachusetts, but also described in letters of introduction as an exceptionally learned former pastor of a church in the same place.[20] He had come, he said, to work for the establishment of a college. Willey was delighted, for, as he said forty-three years later, "to have a man, a trained educator, come of his own accord to build a college in a country such as this was at that time a surprise and a wonder." [21]

About ten days after his arrival in San Francisco, Durant went with Willey to Nevada City for a joint meeting of the Congregational Association of California and the Presbytery of San Francisco ("New School"). One full day of the meeting was given over to a discussion of educational matters. At the conclusion of these deliberations, a committee was appointed to cooperate with Durant "to determine the expediency of establishing an institution of learning and if it be expedient, to proceed to form a plan for its establishment." [22] The committee was empowered to constitute itself as the nucleus of a board of trustees for the institution and to represent the Presbytery and the Association in obtaining land and endowment. The members of the committee were Willey; Joseph A. Benton, Sacramento; S. B. Bell, Oakland; and Timothy Dwight Hunt, San Francisco. All of them except Bell were veterans of the college-building effort of 1849–1850.

A few months earlier, Willey had written to the Home Missionary Society about an area on the east shore of the San Francisco Bay that was called Contra Costa. It was, he said, somewhat "a speculator's town," but nevertheless "a good place to open a boarding school; and may by and by be a good place for an academy." [23] The town was incorporated in 1852 as "Oakland," named for the thousands of oak trees that grew at 40- to 60-foot intervals throughout the area. The year before, the town had seventy-five registered voters.[24] To reach it from San Francisco, one took "a wheezy little steamer [that] had got into the habit of crossing the bay three times a day to carry passengers. It was pretty regular, except that it was liable to get stuck on the bar now and then." [25] The town itself had "one street, Broadway, extending from the landing toward the hills—with a few buildings here and there on either side and a few houses scattered about among the trees." [26]

It was in this town, where Bell was pastor of the First Presbyterian Church, that the committee of clergymen appointed at Nevada City held its first meeting to help Durant plan a school. It was here, also, that Durant began the work he came to California to do. In a letter written on the nineteenth and twenty-fourth of May, 1853, Durant told his wife that he had rented a building for "our residence, and the High School." [27] The rent was $150 a month. The building, a vacant dance hall and boardinghouse, was located at what is now Broadway and Fifth Street.[28] It would be ready for classes by the first week in June.

To secure a student body, Durant wrote to ministers encouraging them to "think well of our undertaking and make an effort to bespeak for it the public favor." [29] An advertisement for the school in the *Pacific* identified it as a "Scientific and Classical School at Contra Costa." The text called it a "Family High School for Boys." The same announcement said, "The branches of study to be pursued will comprise, besides those usually taught in High Schools, the Latin, the Greek, and if desired, the French, German and Spanish languages. The price for board, washing, domestic care, and school instruction will be $12.50 per week, payable monthly in advance; for tuition alone, $10 per month. Each boarder will provide his own chamber furniture." [30]

Only thirty-seven days after Durant's arrival in California, the new school opened with three pupils. On June 14, 1853, eight days after the school opened, a Board of Trustees was formally organized with Willey as president and Bell as secretary. The Congregational members of the planning committee, Hunt and Benton, were elected trustees. So were Edward B. Walsworth, a Presbyterian minister in Marysville, and Horace Carpentier, a proprietor of the town of Oakland. The formal organization of Contra Costa Academy (the name finally chosen) was legally recorded on June 20, 1853.[31]

The practical affairs of the school were Durant's responsibility completely. He collected the student fees, paid the bills for food and supplies, taught the courses, and kept for himself such funds as might be left after expenses. This was very little. Within the first two months, Durant was behind in monthly payments of $150 to the couple who were hired as housekeepers. They sought redress by settling in the lower part of the house, advertising for boarders and lodgers, and offering alcoholic drinks for sale on the premises. Durant somehow managed a meal for his students and then set about packing up the couple's belongings so that they could be put out. When the husband resorted to physical restraint, he suddenly became "pale as a cloth," realizing to his horror that his employer was a minister who, quite possibly, was as consecrated as his own priest.[32] The matter was soon settled cordially, but the incident dramatized the precariousness of a school that depended upon small fees from a very small student body to meet such heavy fixed expenses as rent and housekeeping, totaling $300 a month. The rent payments, at least, could be saved if a subscription was made to buy a proper site and building outright.

Durant located just such a site at the edge of town and began negotiations to acquire it. One day, to his dismay, he found a large group of squatters gathered at the north end of Broadway, all preparing to make claims in the vicinity of the blocks he had chosen. Durant worked his way into their midst and pleaded the cause of the college he hoped to build on the parcel of land they were admiring. In response, the squatters voted on the spot to reserve four blocks of land for the new college.[33]

The site Durant selected is now bounded by Twelfth and Fourteenth Streets, and Harrison and Franklin Streets in downtown Oakland. Contributions were obtained to meet the purchase price of the land, to fence it, and to begin construction on the first building. The building had been roofed, but not completed, when Durant encountered still another strange business practice of the frontier. He learned that the contractor planned to sell the unfinished schoolhouse to a third party for the amount still owed for its completion ($600–$700). On the advice of a lawyer, Durant took a friend to the building one night, installed tables, chairs, and other furnishings in the one finished room, and went to bed. When the contractor arrived the next morning, Durant explained that he had decided to move into his new home a little early. The contractor went away, and so did Durant's friend. When the contractor returned, he was accompanied by two "burly fellows." At this point, Durant realized that his only means of defense was an axe that was under the bed. Even so, he warned his visitors that if they had come to evict him, he did not intend to leave the room "in a sound condition," and that, by harming him, they would "commit a crime, as well as a trespass." [34] Though some contemporaries described Durant as "tall and spare," none of them recorded an estimate that would suggest he was a physical match for three ruffians. He had another quality, however, "a moral sublimity in his appearance," [35] and it was believed that his real power existed in "his very presence. You could not resist it, because you did not wish to." [36] Faced by such a man (or his argument), the contractor and his companions departed, leaving Durant peacefully in possession of the school building. The school moved to the new location in 1854.

Henry Durant was a man apart from his fellow college-builders in California. He shared their vision and enjoyed their respect, but his methods ignored the principles of long-range planning and financing that were carefully observed by the trustees. He preferred to make the best of whatever opportunities might arise. For example, the Oakland ground had not yet been fully paid for when Durant entered a bid on an adjoining plot of ground across Twelfth Street, leaving the trustees and the school's friends the problem of finding money to buy it. The land was eventually occupied by the institution's chapel. When the trustees were making campaign plans to secure many thousands of dollars for an endowment, Durant was "out begging" [37] for money to pay off some pressing debt or to finance an immediately necessary improvement. He bought a bell on credit from a San Francisco hardware merchant. A year later, a group of students had to raise the money (almost the entire balance from the time of purchase) to save the bell from repossession.

Whatever financial strain may have been put upon the school's treasury by Durant's management was apparently endured by the trustees with little rancor. They had no choice, really. As Bell would comment many years later, "All other seminaries of learning have been commenced by rearing structures; we, with the living man. . . . Nothing in all the world, but THE MAN!—Henry Durant." [38] There were many months when his salary could not be paid. There were times when he was deeply in personal debt. Ironically, there were also instances when his own pledges of financial support were at least equal to those of more affluent citizens. Finally, whether he intended to or not, Durant forced the college-builders to stretch their interest, energies, and resources to keep up with the commitments he made in the institution's behalf. The result was tangible progress—enough progress so that on April 13, 1855, petitioners organized by the trustees of Contra Costa Academy were granted a charter for a College of California. The property of the Contra Costa Academy was transferred to the college, but, as the "College School," the academy continued to operate. Its immediate responsibility was to prepare a Freshman college class by 1860.

BUILDING AGAINST THE ODDS

The 1850s were not ideal times for college-building in California. In 1851 and again in 1856, San Francisco's citizens resorted to vigilantism to tame their wild, violent, crime-ridden city. People thus preoccupied could not be expected to give the founding of a college full attention. To make matters worse, California had its first financial depression in 1854. Josiah Royce described the economic collapse as the natural result of "continuous over-confidence in the rapid development of the wealth of the country." More specifically, he said: "The production of the mines began to fall off, immigration decreased, many people left the land, the consumption of food diminished, interest and rents declined in San Francisco, and 30 per cent of the warehouses were empty." [39] Businesses that served a transient, temporary population dependent upon the Atlantic seaboard for supplies and comforts had been a stabilizing influence in California's economy since the Gold Rush. Now, the American families began to settle down—raising their own food, beginning to manufacture their own furniture and tools, becoming generally more self-reliant. During the time when California was adjusting to these changes, its economy was bound to falter.

Why, then, did the College of California builders charter their institution in these uncertain times? In public addresses, some college supporters tended to emphasize that recession and civic turbulence were the just wages of a people negligent in providing ample educational opportunities for their sons and daughters. But there was more rhetoric than reason in such pronouncements. The real reasons for the decision to start the college in unsettled times had nothing to do with the state's economic and social condition. In the first place, Durant and his colleagues had intended to build a college, not an academy, when they began their work two years earlier. The year 1855 found the academy to be self-supporting, owning its own land, and owing only $5,000 on its buildings. The institution was ready, then, to make the change. In the second place, word had come from the East the year before that "religious leaders" there were advocating incorporation of the college as a center to provide training for an educated ministry in California.[40] That was an important consideration indeed, for, in the third place, the college-builders were pretty well agreed that their institution could not be sustained without Eastern philanthropy.

The California college-builders could not have known that the Eastern philanthropy that had helped to build frontier colleges all of the way to the Mississippi during the 1830s and 1840s was playing out by 1855. Willey was vacationing in the East when the College of California was incorporated. At the request of the college's trustees, he called upon several prospective Eastern donors. From them he learned the discouraging truth about Eastern philanthropy. He was told that the colleges founded on the older frontiers were still relying on Eastern patrons either to sustain a precarious existence or to finance expansion. The same patrons were being asked to support the even more substantial expansion and development of well-established New England colleges in their own back yards. A flurry of New England church-building was calling forth still other appeals for contributions. Then, too, the mortality rate of frontier colleges was so high that many generous but practical men had long ago lost their enthusiasm for building colleges. Finally, Willey could not convince his prospects that the streets of California were not paved with gold. Willey's fund-raising triumph was a gift of $5,000 from the Pacific Mail Steamship Company. It would be matched several years later by the same company, but its amount as a single gift would never be exceeded in the complete history of College of California fund-raising.

THE SEARCH FOR A NEW SITE

When Horace Bushnell, the famous Congregational theologian, came to California for his health in 1856, he let it be known that he would welcome any constructive activity that would keep him out of doors and benefit the college. The trustees had just the job for him. The city of Oakland was crowding in around their grounds, and a more desirable location for the college was needed. So, on horseback, by steamer, by stage, and on foot, Bushnell visited sites near Oakland; at Martinez; in the Petaluma and Sonoma Valleys; in the valley "owned by Señor Suñol, back of the Contra Costa Chain"; at and near Mission San José; at San Pablo; and in the Napa Valley.[41] He personally helped survey possible sites, made inquiries concerning their availability, and measured their water supplies. After nine months, he recommended a site at Napa.

Bushnell's site recommendation was never followed, but his activities made the college better known throughout a large, well-populated section of the state. With a visitor's insight, he was able to sense the mood of California in the 1850s and to identify the building of a great university—already the College of California's announced objective—with pioneer efforts to create a good and prosperous life out of such raw stuff as the state then offered. His widely publicized "appeal" to the people of California, written just before he returned East in January, 1857, was an eloquent statement of the college's case. If he erred at all, it was in underestimating the prospects of a state-supported university and in setting fund-raising goals too high. He urged Californians to create a private college endowment of between $300,000 and $500,000 when the college had yet to open its doors to a Freshman class, and when $100,000 would work college-building wonders. But Bushnell contended: "It is vain to imagine that we are going to impoverish or unreasonably distress California by asking for a sum, such that if only we had every twentieth cigar consumed in the state, it would more than fill the contribution." [42]

By the time the College of California could begin negotiations for property, the Napa site had been sold. One by one, other sites favored by Bushnell also turned out to be unavailable or inadequate. Late in the summer of 1857, reconsideration was given to a site Bushnell and the college trustees had liked, but rejected because they believed its water supply was insufficient. The place was known to many of the trustees as early as 1855 and located about four miles north of Oakland and adjacent to a ranch owned by a retired sea captain, Orrin Simmons. It was he who suggested to Durant that the spot might be a good location for the college. A more careful estimate proved the availability of an abundance of water there, and the trustees took steps in November, 1857,[43] to obtain 124 acres of land from five different settlers.

The entire site was located within a crude triangle formed by the intersecting north and south forks of Strawberry Creek, closed at the top by an eastern boundary roughly coincident with today's Piedmont Avenue, and a shorter line along what is now Hearst Avenue between Piedmont and the north fork of the creek.

Though terms of acquisition were agreed upon in 1857, other pressing matters would delay actual possession for several years. For one thing, "the school grounds in Oakland were in peril—a mortgage of 2,000 dollars on it—a judgment of 2,000 dollars more against it. . . ." Another claim against the college for some $1,200 was "unsettled and urged for payment." [44] Furthermore, in March, 1858, the trustees found it necessary to raise $10,000 for improvement of existing buildings and to construct a new building at Oakland for the College School to use after the college itself opened its doors. Willey's list of contributions to this project totals less than $7,000, but the construction was completed during the summer of 1858, fully funded or not.

The trustees acquired the new site in parcels. One part was bought outright for $1,200. Another part was donated. The others were transferred to the trustees by deed, on the condition that $2,000 would be paid within eight months. By 1861, sufficient progress had been made in acquiring the land to permit the trustees to dedicate it officially to the eventual use of the college. This ceremony took place at Founders' Rock, a large outcropping at the foot of the hills.

In May, 1866, with some other trustees and friends of the college, Frederick Billings revisited this rock. Looking across the gentle slopes and grain fields to the great bay and the Golden Gate, he recalled lines from a poem by George Berkeley, Bishop of Cloyne:

> Westward the course of empire takes its way;
> The four first acts already past.
> A fifth shall close the drama of the day;
> Time's noblest offspring is the last.

The author of these lines was an Irish philosopher and patron of colleges (especially Yale, the alma mater of several California college-builders). With that in mind, Billings was inspired to suggest that the college grounds and their immediate environs be called Berkeley. At a meeting held the same afternoon, May 24, 1866, the trustees concurred.

THE BLUEPRINT

In 1859, a year before the College of California would receive its first class, what Willey called a "breeze of opposition" blew across the enterprise. [45] Among its leaders was one of the "Old School" Presbyterian ministers who had hoped to start the Benicia university until that project quietly died in Thomas Larkin's pocket in 1849. Its contention was that "Old School" Presbyterians should withdraw any support they were giving to the College of California and give it, instead, to a denominational college of their own. The suggestion was particularly embarrassing to two prominent trustees of the College of California, Billings and Rev. W. C. Anderson, both of whom were "Old School" Presbyterians. Both men publicly repudiated the idea of a denominational college and urged Californians to give their support to the institution that would very soon be under way at Oakland.

The effect of the controversy was to force the College of California men to be more articulate about their precise plans. They prepared a document called the "Organic Basis" of the College of California. It begins:

> The College of California is an Institution designed by its founders to furnish the means of a thorough and comprehensive education, under the pervading influence and spirit of the Christian religion.
>
> The bonds which unite its friends and patrons are, a catholic Christianity; a common interest in securing the highest educational privileges for youth; the common sympathy of educated and scientific men, and a common interest in the promotion of the highest welfare of the State, as fostered and secured by the diffusion of sound and liberal learning.
>
> In accordance with these considerations, and in order that the Institution may never come under the control of Church or State, or any branch of the one denomination or of the other, they adopt the following Organic Rules. . . ." [46]

The rules themselves required that the trustees be so elected as to "fairly and equally represent the patrons and contributors to the funds of the Institution. . . ." They further required that while a majority of the trustees should always be members of evangelical Christian churches, only one-fourth could be members of the same Christian denomination. In the hiring of professors, preference would be given to men "of Christian character," and the president and a majority of the faculty had to be members of evangelical Christian churches. The trustees avoided unhappy incidents that had occurred at other young colleges by making it possible for founders of professorships—"subject always to the acceptance of the Board of Trustees"—to prescribe the religious beliefs of the incumbents. [47] Students would be required to attend morning prayers and church on Sundays with some religious congregation.

In addition to the "Organic Basis," the trustees adopted the "Laws of the College" on December 15, 1859. These laws entrusted the government of the students and the internal management of the college to the "President, Vice President, Professors, and Instructors, who shall be called the Faculty of the College." They required that a student be fourteen years of age for admission to the Freshman class. He must also pass an examination in the following studies, or their equivalents: "Latin Grammar; Latin Reader;

Caesar's Commentaries, first five books; Cicero's Select Orations; Virgil's Bucolics, and the first six books of the Aeneid; Latin Prosody and Composition; Greek Grammar; Greek Exercises; Xenophon's Anabasis, first five books; Greek Testament, the two Gospels, Luke and John; The Greek Accents; English Grammar; Elements of Rhetoric; Geography; Higher Arithmetic; Algebra to Quadratic Equations; and the Rudiments of French and Spanish." In general, these requirements closely paralleled those that had been required of many of the college-builders at their New England schools. The laws of the college also decreed that "every student is expected to conduct himself as becomes a gentleman; and is particularly required to avoid intemperance, profaneness, gaming, and all indecent, disorderly behavior, and disrespectful conduct to the Faculty, and all combinations to resist their authority." Parents of students might also have been reassured by those laws that required faculty approval of living accommodations for all students, notice of a student's plans to leave town overnight, and a periodic check to discover "extravagant habits or outlays." [48]

The formulation of the "Organic Basis" and the "Laws" anticipated the admission of the College of California's first Freshman class in July, 1860. It also helped to dampen some of the opposition from the college's detractors in the Bay Area. Moreover, extracts from the "Organic Basis," accompanied by testimonials from leading American educators and divines, documented the case for the college when a second effort to obtain funds from the East was made in the second half of 1860 and the early months of 1861.

The college's unhappy emissary in the East this time was Martin Kellogg, a former Congregational minister in Grass Valley, who had accepted a professorship in mathematics at the college the previous year. Over his vigorous protests of inexperience in such matters, Kellogg was asked to raise $25,000 from Eastern donors. If Willey's fund-raising efforts in the East in 1855 were disappointing, Kellogg's efforts in 1860–1861 were humiliating. He encountered all of the familiar resistance to philanthropy for a college in California. In addition, he discovered that the timing of his trip was bad. It took place precisely during the months when the nation was deciding whether Abraham Lincoln should become President of the United States, and anxiety for the soundness of the Union was mounting. As a result of his inexperience, the new indifference of Eastern philanthropy to frontier college-building, and the political distractions of the time, the professor from California obtained no substantial gifts. On one occasion, he visited a "flourishing farming town" where he "preached in three parishes" and brought away $20 for his trouble. The total income of his campaign, only $1,132.58, was so embarrassing that Kellogg insisted on paying his own expenses for the trip.

THE COLLEGE WORK BEGINS

At the same meeting of the trustees in 1859 that resulted in Kellogg's appointment as professor of mathematics, Henry Durant was named professor of languages. In his new position, Durant would relinquish the principalship of the College School to Rev. Isaac Brayton, who would purchase the school's building and two blocks of property from the college trustees in 1864. From that time on, Brayton and his wife operated the school under an agreement that made the trustees of the college also trustees of the school "without, on the one hand, absolute control or on the other, pecuniary or other responsibility. . . ." [49]

College instruction began while Kellogg was in the East. Durant assumed most of the teaching responsibility, but the catalogue also listed Isaac Brayton as professor of rhetoric, *belles lettres,* and the English language; William K. Rowell as teacher in mathematics; Charles L. Des Roches as teacher in French; and Jose Manuel Ibanes (one of the Freshmen) as teacher in Spanish.

The full academic program was published for the first time in the catalogue for 1861–1862. Students had no electives until the Junior year. Courses in Greek and Latin language and literature were required during the first two years. In mathematics, students were taught algebra and geometry as Freshmen; analytical geometry as Sophomores; and trigonometry and calculus as Juniors. English composition, reading, and declamation were taught through the Sophomore year. Elocution was required in the second term of the Freshman year, and rhetoric was a required full-year study for all Sophomores. Science was served by courses in elementary physics, chemistry, mineralogy, astronomy, navigation, geology, anatomy and physiology, and meteorology. Of these science courses, only navigation was introduced before the Junior year. Courses in logic, ancient literature, intellectual philosophy, natural theology, general history, moral philosophy, political economy, the Constitution of the United States, and international law were introduced in the Junior and Senior years. The most controversial feature of the curriculum was the attention given to the modern languages—Spanish, French, and German. In 1860 and 1861–1862, French and Spanish (in addition to Latin, Greek, and English) were required courses for Freshmen and Sophomores. Sherman Day, son of Yale's president Jeremiah Day and a trustee of the college, criticized this emphasis as "not a very profitable discipline of the mind." Furthermore, he observed: "A college that cannot support its Latin and Greek Professor [Durant] because all the income has been absorbed by the teachers of modern languages, or vice versa, is no College at all. . . ." [50] Such protests were apparently satisfied by the decision that the teaching of French and Spanish be eliminated in the Freshman year. The college then offered French in the Sophomore year and German in the Junior year. Spanish became an elective offering for Seniors.

WANTED: A PRESIDENT

Letters of introduction that preceded Durant to California in 1853 pronounced him as one who "would help man a college, though not perhaps exactly the man to be at the head of it." [51] When no one else was able or willing to undertake the college-building labor as a full-time occupation, Durant arrived to make a beginning. He filled the principalship of the Contra Costa Academy and the College School with an unselfish dedication that earned him the affection and admiration of many Californians. But there was general agreement that Durant would not be the president of the new college. Beginning in 1858, the trustees began to exercise increasingly more control over the daily affairs of their institution. Their main agent in such matters was Samuel Willey, who had been the secretary of the trustees since at least January, 1856.

Shortly after the college opened, it became plagued with financial problems. In March, 1861, Durant found himself more than $900 in debt, even though "the college owes me enough to pay all this amount." [52] At this time Durant was beginning to doubt his ability to remain in the college's service without more financial security.

There was no one to take charge of the institution's business affairs until 1862 when Willey announced that he was retiring as pastor of the Howard Presbyterian Church, with plans to return to the East for the restoration of his failing health and for assuming ministerial work in an "older society." The trustees took advantage of this turn of events on March 27, 1862, and elected Willey vice-president of the college with responsibilities of president, until "that indefinite time in the future when the College would be able, as it had been hoped for from its inception, to command the services of some man of eminence in the East." [53] In yet another resolution, Willey was made financial agent and manager of the institution. All of these new titles and authorities would be added to his continuing ones as secretary of the trustees. Willey accepted, saying: "I have neither experience in work like this nor fondness for it and nothing but a commanding motive, such as the upholding of this College presents, would induce me to undertake it." [54] His acceptance probably added several years to the precarious life of the institution.

The College of California would never have a president. Bushnell had been offered the position when he was in California in 1856, but he never encouraged those who sought him for it. Frederick Billings also declined in favor of his law practice and business interests. In 1863, a $25,000 endowment was raised to insure the salary for William G. T. Shedd of Union Theological Seminary, if he would accept the presidency. He declined. A similar endowment was raised to back up an offer to Roswell D. Hitchcock, also of Union Theological Seminary. He also declined.

Under Willey's business leadership and Durant's academic guidance, the College of California gamely persisted for seven more years. The main difficulties were financial. On the anniversary of the college in 1862, Willey reported: "Your Agent finds no money in the Treasury." [55] Outstanding debts at that time included $1,300 owed to members of the faculty and staff and totaled $3,800. Tuitions for the coming year were expected to yield $860 against contemplated expenses of $36,300. The assets of the college consisted of the Oakland campus, its three buildings valued at $18,000, and the Berkeley site, valued at $18,600. A campaign for an endowment to relieve the college was moderately successful. It involved large contributions that could be paid off in three annual installments. Its returns sustained the college through the war years. In 1863, Willey raised $7,500 for a new building to house a chapel, classrooms, and a library. The next year, the sale of the College School building and two blocks of Oakland property to Isaac Brayton for $10,000 also helped keep the college solvent.

Horace Bushnell was critical of state universities when he made his famous appeal for support of the College of California in 1857. On the other hand, the College of California builders, by resisting any suggestion of denominational control and by publicly identifying their institution at every opportunity with the destiny of the state of California, quite transparently bid for support from the public treasury. But their overtures never were successful, and they remained dependent on their own meager resources to the end.

ACTIVITY AT BERKELEY

In 1864, there were fifteen students enrolled in the College of California. Three years later, there would be twenty. The reputation of the college was good and its circle of friends was widening. But its financial problems defied solution. Such funds as were contributed for endowment had to be spent almost immediately to meet current obligations. Under these precarious circumstances, the education work of the college was bravely carried on at Oakland.

The denouement of the story of the College of California, however, would transpire at Berkeley. The Berkeley site had always given the College of California men a tangible hold on dreams for the building of a great university. Its gentle slopes, spectacular views, rushing streams, and venerable oaks were always described with reverence. Its very possession was an achievement of respectable order.

Before the site could be occupied by the college, however, its water resources would have to be secured from diversion or abuse by neighboring landholders. To acquire this insurance, the trustees resolved to buy the Simmons Farm, that adjoined the campus site to the east. To raise the $35,000 purchase price, Willey devised a plan that, if successful, would not only result in college ownership of the desired property but also would hasten the development of a college community. To effect the plan, trustees and friends of the college would buy, in addition to the Simmons Farm, an additional 160 acres south of the campus grounds. This additional property, available for $33,000, would be given to purchasers of "shares" in what was to be incorporated as the "College Homestead Association." Loans were obtained, and negotiations for the purchase of the Simmons Farm and the homestead sites were completed in the late summer of 1864.

Shares were sold for $450 to $500, payable in twenty monthly installments of $25 each. Since 128 lots had been plotted, the total anticipated income from the transactions would be at least $64,000. This was only $4,000 less than the amount needed to liquidate the mortgages on all of the new Berkeley properties. If all of the shares had sold quickly, the plan might have worked. But they did not sell soon enough for the trustees to avoid high interest payments ($9,600 by December, 1866) on the money they borrowed to make the deal. To make matters worse, the funds available from the endowment created in 1862 were running out and Willey and the trustees were so engrossed in salvaging the homestead operation they could not undertake a fund-raising campaign to replenish it. By the end of 1866, the trustees had spent $26,000 from the homestead share revenues just to keep the college going. The debt on the Simmons Farm was paid off by the end of 1865, so college control of the water supply was achieved. But the transaction that was to be so profitable found the trustees $42,000 in debt by the beginning of the calendar year 1867.

By the end of 1866, the trustees had transferred their hopes for financial salvation as offered by the homestead plan to a new scheme. They now controlled the water in Strawberry Creek. Somehow, they had also gained control of Wild Cat Creek to the north of the Berkeley site. If they could supply water to the homestead lots, they would sell more briskly. Even more exciting was the possibility of serving the water needs of the city certain to rise in Berkeley and, perhaps, even Oakland. The trustees of the college incorporated themselves into a new company, "The College Water Company," acquired all legal rights needed for their objective, borrowed $5,000 from the college's library fund, and built a reservoir in Strawberry Canyon.

To celebrate the completion of the waterworks, a public "rural picnic" was held on the college grounds on August 24, 1867. The spectacular finale of this event was the opening of valves that sent plumes of fresh water as much as 70 feet into the air on the college site and in various locations on the homestead tract.

The triumph of the trustees in adding to the college grounds and in developing their waterworks must not be underrated. But within only two months they would find that the destiny of their institution was linked not so much with white sprays of water as with new efforts of the state to create a public institution of higher learning.

Chapter 2

CALIFORNIA'S UNIVERSITY COMMITMENT

THE DELEGATES WHO convened in Monterey in 1849 to write California's first constitution were in a hurry to complete the business at hand.

To speed their labors, they borrowed extensively from constitutions of other states. The newest, framed in 1846, was the constitution of Iowa.[1] Article IX, ii, Section 5, of that constitution required Iowa's general assembly to "take measures for the protection, improvement, or other disposition of such lands as have been or may hereafter be reserved or granted by the

United States, or any person or persons to this state, for the use of the university. . . ." [2] The provision protected federal land grants already made to Iowa and twelve other states according to precedent established in the Northwest Ordinances of 1785 and 1787. California was entitled to similar benefits when it acquired statehood.[3] So the delegates at Monterey asked Congress to set aside public lands for a California university and, with minor changes, made the Iowa constitution's Article IX, Section 5, the California constitution's Article IX, Section 4. One change of wording made by the Californians prophetically referred to "such branches of the university as the public convenience may demand." [4] The provision was approved at the convention without debate and without opposition.[5]

From that time on, California was considered constitutionally pledged to create a state university. As early as February, 1850, State Senator Thomas J. Green announced plans to submit a bill to establish an institution modeled after Mexico's Collegio de Mineria, in which "minerals and mining should be the leading branch." [6] With this proposal he intended to make "the preliminary move . . . for the organization of our State University. . . ." [7]

A more substantial proposal was made by General Guadalupe Vallejo the same year. Along with other lands and buildings, this colorful California pioneer offered to contribute 20 acres of land and $36,000 for a state university,[8] if the legislature agreed to move the state capital to the city bearing his name. The general's offer was accepted in 1851 [9] but rejected in 1852 and the scheme that might have started early university-building in California thus became part of the rubble of his ensuing financial disaster.

THE SEMINARY-OF-LEARNING GRANT

The commitment to create a university that was implicit in California's first constitution was reinforced in March, 1853, when Congress granted 72 sections, or 46,080 acres, of land to the state for a "seminary of learning." It was widely assumed that this land would be located in the gold country, and Governor Bigler confidently announced that it would sell for $15 an acre, or a total of $691,200. That amount, Governor Bigler asserted, would be enough to establish not one, but two, institutions of higher learning in California, one north and one south of San Francisco.[10]

In almost every ensuing session of the legislature at least one bill was introduced for the establishment of a new college or for the use of the federal grants for the support of existing incorporated colleges.

To create a financial endowment for education in California, the seminary lands and 500,000 acres of other lands granted by the federal government to support common schools were ordered sold for $1.25 an acre in 1858. At this low rate, the seminary lands sold quickly for a total of $57,000. Michigan received a somewhat smaller seminary grant from the federal government but managed it so astutely that it eventually yielded almost ten times that much.[11]

In 1858, Samuel B. Bell, one of the early College of California trustees and a member of the state senate, introduced a bill that would have divided California's resources for higher education among chartered colleges loosely confederated under the name of "the Regents of the University of California." [12] His measure died after the Assembly Education Committee denounced it as calculated to "engender sectarian strife and unseemly jealousies among the various colleges united under this mongrel incorporation and destroy all laudable competition, establish an odious system of centralization, antagonistic to the spirit of our free institutions and prejudicial to the interests of education." [13]

Between 1857 and 1861, a proposal to create an institution of higher learning patterned after a military academy had the strong backing of California's superintendent of public instruction, Andrew J. Moulder. The idea was actually the brainchild of W. C. Kibee, California's adjutant general, but Moulder kept it alive. He contended that California wanted no "pale and sickly scholars," [14] and praised the military scheme as conducive to good student discipline and the development of manliness. He also proposed that the institution favor instruction in the professions and practical pursuits. To that extent his views rather faithfully echoed those of other nineteenth-century educational reformers who urged universities to give more attention to science and technology and less to the traditional classical curriculum.

The nearest Moulder's plan came to materialization was in a bill introduced by Assemblyman D. B. Bailey in March, 1860. Bailey's bill created a "University of California" [15] governed by a board of regents elected by the legislature from each judicial district. The governor, lieutenant governor, and judges of the supreme court were to be ex-officio members of the board. These regents were empowered to prescribe the course of study. "At their discretion," they could organize an agricultural department, a department of the mechanic arts, and the departments of law and medicine.[16] They were also authorized "to organize the University on the military plan, after the system pursued at the U.S. Military Academy at West Point." [17] Bailey's bill was discussed and amended, but was still in the Assembly Education Committee when the eleventh session adjourned.

THE STAKES GET BIGGER

Those who supported legislation to create some kind of California university, college, institute, or seminary between 1850 and 1861 were troubled by conflicting considerations. Article IX, Section 4, of the state constitution of 1849 could, indeed, be interpreted as a state commitment to create a university. Acquisition of the seminary-of-learning grant did, indeed, provide wherewithal for such an undertaking. But the constitutional provision did not, in any way, place high priority on the establishment of a university, and the seminary-of-learning grant did not provide nearly enough money to make a university self-supporting. Moreover, there was little pressure from the general public. Even in 1862, there were only two public high schools in the whole state, and existing colleges had no difficulty accommodating as many students as demanded entrance.

When Governor Leland Stanford called for the establishment of a seminary of learning or university in 1862, he stressed that the seminary lands had all been sold and that the old "objections . . . arising from want of funds to commence the work . . . cannot now be urged." [18] But a select committee of the assembly responded:

> . . . We find the funds at our command so small, and the State Government in so embarrassed a condition at present, that we think it more wise to loan the University Fund [as the proceeds from seminary land sales were called] to the State, thus accumulating by interest, and adding other sources of revenue, until the fund shall be sufficient to found a University that shall meet the expectations of Congress, by whom the land was donated, and of the framers of our State Constitution, who very wisely provided in that instrument that the funds received from the lands donated, and from all other sources, shall be inviolably set apart for the endowment and support of a University; by which, we understand, a separate and distinct institution, which shall give the most complete instruction in all the principal sciences, and shall prepare the student for immediate entrance upon the practice of any of the learned professions, which shall *really* be a University in the proper sense of the term, a worthy rival of the world-renowned European Universities, placing California where she should be, at the educational centre of the States bordering on the Pacific.[19]

The committee's advice was heeded, and a pending bill to create the university was referred to committee without further consideration.

Financial considerations were not the only ones that restrained efforts to fulfill California's university-building commitment. Despite their isolation from it, Californians in 1862 shared the national preoccupation with the Civil War, and the tendency to postpone decisions on all but the most urgent matters was a part of their wartime mood.

That mood was cracked, though hardly shattered, by Justin S. Morrill, United States Congressman, son of a Vermont blacksmith, and persistent advocate of establishing colleges to prepare large numbers of young men for successful lives on the farm, in the factory, and in the pursuits of commerce. State legislators and other congressmen had introduced petitions and bills that sought to achieve similar goals before Morrill did. Morrill's contribution was tenacity. In 1857 he introduced a congressional act "to offer an opportunity in every State for a liberal and larger education to large numbers, not merely to those destined to sedentary professions, but to those needing higher instruction for the world's business, for the industrial pursuits and professions of life." [20] The bill passed both houses over heated opposition and by narrow margins, only to be vetoed by President Buchanan. Morrill introduced the bill again in 1861, steered it around hostile committees, and again saw its passage by both the House and the Senate. This time, on July 2, 1862, it was signed into law by Abraham Lincoln.

The Morrill Act, sometimes called the Agricultural College Land Grant Act, or simply the Land Grant College Act, gave each state 30,000 acres of public land for each of its senators and congressmen. The land was to be sold and the proceeds invested in government or other safe securities to yield interest for "the endowment, support, and maintenance of at least one college where the leading object shall be, without excluding other scientific and classical studies, and including military tactics, to teach such branches of learning as are related to agriculture and the mechanic arts, in such manner as the legislatures of the States may respectively prescribe, in order to promote the liberal and practical education of the industrial classes in the several pursuits and professions in life." [21] That California would accept the new grant was not questioned. The problem was to decide how to use it.

Some states had simply turned the grant over to their most prominent existing institutions. According to this precedent, the College of California trustees created a "Mining and Agricultural College" as a department of their institution in 1864 and notified the legislature that they would gladly hold California's college land grant in trust for their new enterprise.[22] A bill incorporating the College of California's proposal was actually prepared, but the legislature adjourned before it could be enacted. Announcements of this mining and agricultural department were printed by the college each year between 1864 and 1867, but each one contained the melancholy report that there had been an "unexpected delay" in the organization of classes.

In 1863, the legislature discussed a proposal for the establishment of a mining college and another to create a state agricultural college and farm. But these measures were forced to the background when the legislature decided to entrust the whole question of organizing a state university to a commission consisting of Professor J. D. Whitney (for whom Mount Whitney was named), state geologist; John Swett, state superintendent of public instruction; and J. F. Houghton, state surveyor-general. In April, 1863, they were asked to report to the legislature upon the feasibility of establishing a state university, "embracing an Agricultural College, a 'School of Mines,' and a Museum—including the Geological collection of this State." [23]

THE MUSEUM PLAN

Whitney dominated the work of the commission to plan a university. Its final report, issued in December, 1863, drew heavily upon ideas he had expressed in an address for the sixth anniversary of the College of California on June 6, 1861. In that address, he introduced the novel idea that the various sectarian colleges in California adequately met the needs of the state for undergraduate instruction. The university, he suggested, should be "the supplement of the colleges, made up of the various schools of law, medicine, philosophy and the arts, all propelled around one center, aiming at a high standard of acquirement, supported by liberally endowed libraries, museums, and galleries of art." [24] This idea became one of the main features of the report of the Board of Commissioners. Another was that federal grants then available to the state were too small to support more than one institution. Consequently, educational programs for agriculture and mechanic arts should be combined with those of the university, which actually should be called a "School of Science and Art" or "California Polytechnic School," having for its purpose "the professional training of young men in the exact and natural sciences and their application to arts, manufactures, mining and agriculture." [25] Rensselaer Polytechnic Institute was cited as a "general Guide" for the school's organization. The commission judged establishment of distinct colleges of mechanical arts or agriculture premature in 1863, but noted that they might be established later.

The Whitney scheme became known as the "Museum Plan" because its third major idea was that a museum, particularly one that would house the collections of the California Geological Survey, should be the "incipient part" of the university. The report asserted that "the establishment of the Geological Survey was in fact the first step towards the production of a State University. Without the information to be obtained by that Survey, no thorough instruction was possible on this coast, either in geography, geology, or natural history; for the student of these branches requires to be taught in that which is about him, and with which he is brought into daily contact, as well as that which is distant and only theoretically important." [26] Upon this rationale the commission based its recommendation that the university's first structure house a museum, with "room for a Library, a Laboratory and the necessary offices for the Geological Survey, and also a lecture room, in which instruction may be given at such time as may hereafter be deemed advisable, so that the institution shall be sufficiently complete in itself to answer the purposes of a Scientific School, in case that from any cause, impossible now to foresee, nothing further should ever be done towards establishing the State University." [27] The commissioners thoughtfully drafted a bill "to Establish the State Museum of California, and to Provide for the Establishment of a School of Practical Science as a Branch of the State University." [28] But the bill provided only for the building of the museum and further study to determine organization of a "State Polytechnical School in connection with the State Museum."

The bill drafted by the commissioners was not politically sound. Californians might find a state museum a nice thing to have, but its creation to satisfy the intent of the Morrill Act would require an explanation so oblique as to tangle their tongues. It specifically favored San Francisco as a location for the museum and gave other cities a chance to offer sites only if San Francisco declined to do so. It disappointed Californians who wanted a new Harvard, Yale, or Dartmouth built within commuting distance of their homes. It also disappointed agricultural and mining interests by its lack of serious attention to practical education for life on the farm or in the mines.

CALIFORNIA'S FIRST LAND-GRANT COLLEGE

The bill drafted by the university commission was never introduced, but in 1864, the California legislature formally accepted the college lands offered by passage of Morrill's Agricultural College Land Act. The next step was to establish a college. According to the law, that step had to be completed by July, 1866.

On March 31 of the deadline year, the legislature created the Agricultural, Mining and Mechanical Arts College. The bill that did the job was innocent of pretensions. It stated that the college was created "to carry out in good faith the provisions of an Act of Congress, passed July second, eighteen hundred and sixty-two, granting to the State lands for maintaining an Agricultural and Mechanical Arts College. . . ." [29] Its provisions carefully avoided the political snags of the museum bill. Agricultural and mining interests were represented almost equally on the Board of Directors; specified procedures for selecting a location permitted any area to place itself in contention. The course of instruction was to "embrace the English language and literature, mathematics, civil, military, and mining engineering, agricultural chemistry, mineralogy, metallurgy, animal and vegetable anatomy and physiology, the veterinary art, etymology, geology, technology, political, rural and household economy, horticulture, moral and natural philosophy, history, bookkeeping, and especially the application of science and the mechanical arts to practical agriculture in the field and mining." [30] Almost no interest was left out.

The act placed all of the federal grants made to California for higher education purposes since 1853 at the new college's disposal. It also blasted all hopes that any existing private college might share in the federal largesse by requiring that the Agricultural, Mining and Mechanical Arts College "not be united to or connected with any other institution of learning in this State." [31]

Governor Frederick Low, self-educated merchant, former congressman, and friend of the College of California, was elected chairman of the new college's Board of Directors when they met for the first time in San Francisco's Occidental Hotel on June 20, 1866. At this same meeting, the directors authorized solicitation of offers "for the sale or donations of lands for an Agricultural College and Farm." [32] By September, the directors had received seven proposals from individuals and citizen groups in Sacramento, San Jose, El Dorado County, Santa Clara County, Napa County, Sutterville, and Alameda County. The most numerous of these came from Napa, where the citizens and taxpayers promised not only to provide land but also to tax themselves to donate $20,000 for other needs of the college. [33]

The most significant offer came from Henry Durant. He offered "a most desirable farm in Oakland township, consisting of two hundred acres situated much like the site [Berkeley] of the College of California; commanding about the same prospect, having the advantage of similar climate, with the best sorts of soil and exposure; sufficient water; near a steamboat landing, and touched on one side by the prospective Railroad from Oakland (San Francisco) to Martinez, connecting with the interior system of the State." The directors' minutes record that "no price is mentioned in connection with the proposal." [34] The land in question was undoubtedly Durant's own. He had purchased large sections in the vicinity of the College of California property from two different parties in 1858 and 1859.[35]

When a delegation of the Agricultural, Mining and Mechanical Arts College directors arrived in Oakland to make an inspection of the site, Durant had arranged for red-carpet treatment from city officials and leading citizens. The delegation was first shown a site that was probably Durant's property. They liked it. Durant then showed them part of the property of one Napoleon Bonaparte Byrne.[36] Byrne had come to California in 1859 from Missouri, where he had been a plantation owner. In 1860 and 1861, he bought a total of 827 acres of land in what is now north Berkeley. His holdings extended over the ridge of the hills to the east and below what is now Live Oak Park.[37] Their southern boundary was shared for about half a mile by the northern boundary of Durant's land. The visiting delegates liked this site even better than they liked Durant's. Before they went home, they were also shown the "University site" owned by the College of California. This site impressed them as "a gem," [38] and they expressed a wish that their college could locate there.

There was no further action on site selection until the following summer, though the minutes of the Board of Directors of the Agricultural, Mining and Mechanical Arts College record the reading of a letter from Byrne at their meeting of March 14, 1867.

Governor Low had taken great interest in the location of the new state college and had been a member of its delegation to visit the Durant, Byrne, and College of California sites. He visited Oakland again on June 6, 1867, to take part in observances of the College of California's commencement and sixth anniversary. The oration for this occasion was delivered by Dr. Benjamin Silliman, Jr., professor of applied chemistry at Yale. The burden of his message was that creation of California's Agricultural, Mining and Mechanical Arts College had been hasty and ill-advised. He believed the courses prescribed for the new college were deficient, even for an agricultural and mechanical arts school. He found the organization of the institution "subject to the fluctuation of party politics, than which nothing can be more fatal to the well-being of an institution of learning." In his final judgment, California was "still without any provisions for the establishment of a University. No merely polytechnic or trades school—no simply professional school—is a University. Such schools if wisely ordered are extremely useful, and the pressing demand which is felt in this State for a good Mining, Mechanical, and Agricultural College may very likely for a time keep back the development of a State University, and obstruct the plans of those who seek to establish literary and scholastic institutions of a higher grade, like the College of California." [39]

CREATING THE UNIVERSITY OF CALIFORNIA

Among those impressed by Dr. Silliman's ideas was Governor Low. Low wanted very much to be the governor of California when her state university was founded, and the establishment of the Agricultural, Mining and Mechanical Arts College seemed at first to fulfill that wish. Now, he had misgivings. Speaking to the College of California alumni on the evening of the commencement of 1867, he said: "You have here in your College, scholarship, organization, enthusiasm, and reputation, but not money; we, in undertaking the state institution, have none of these things, but we have money. What a pity they could not be joined together." [40]

Six days later, by a narrow margin, the directors of the Agricultural, Mining and Mechanical Arts College voted, on third ballot, to fix the location of their institution in Alameda County. They also appointed a committee to negotiate for acquisition of a specific site.

It was generally known that although the whole of Alameda County was theoretically under consideration, the directors of the Agricultural, Mining and Mechanical Arts College were really negotiating for one of the Berkeley sites. Durant believed that the directors favored the Byrne property, but that Low refused to establish the college there. The governor wanted the College of California site instead. To get it, and to make of the state university a more respectable institution in the bargain, he began to urge that the act of 1866 be revised, so that the Agricultural, Mining and Mechanical Arts College would be augmented with other departments of instruction. According to Durant, Low proposed as follows: "We will get a University of the State organized. We will get that created. And we will have the agricultural school a department of the University, and we will have the College of California a department of the University as the College of Letters; and so we will really bring into existence a University. You can reach all the ends you propose in that way. The College of California can accomplish all its ends a great deal better than it could alone." [41] Between June and October of 1867, the friends and trustees of the College of California would deliberate on this proposition.

There were many things to consider. Such gifts and tuition as they had been able to raise were inadequate even for the day-to-day support of their college. In addition, they were neck deep in the soggy bog of the homestead-lot and water schemes designed to secure and improve their Berkeley site. They had deliberately insisted upon an undenominational stance in order to attract the broad, undifferentiated support of California's general public only to find, in 1867, that no particular constituency had their welfare at heart. Finally, by creating a state institution, the legislature had deprived them of any unique claim to the support of the people at large. For years they had been talking about building a university, and Durant often referred to the Berkeley grounds as "our university site." To make that promise good to the people of California would require more than modest philanthropic support. To make it good with a state college competing for friends and students and funds—possibly next door—would require commitment to a long, tedious, and perilous effort. To make it good by following Governor Low's advice was the only responsible alternative.

The trustees of the College of California came to this conclusion at a special meeting on October 8, 1867. They so advised Governor Low, who joined them for part of the discussion, and then adjourned until the following day when an official resolution could be voted upon.

At noon the next day, John W. Dwinelle, chairman of the drafting committee, read the following resolutions:

> *Resolved,* That the President and Board of Trustees of the College of California hereby offer to donate and convey to the State Board of Directors of the Agricultural, Mining and Mechanical Arts College one hundred and sixty acres of land in the township of Oakland, Alameda County, including the lands between the two ravines commonly known as the California College site, for the site and farm of the said State College.
>
> *Resolved,* That in making this donation the College of California is influenced by an earnest hope and confident expectation that the State of California will forthwith organize and put into operation upon this site, a University of California, which shall include a College of Mines, a College of Agriculture, and an Academical College, all of the same grade, and with courses of instruction equal to those of Eastern Colleges.
>
> *Resolved,* That the President and Secretary of this Board be authorized to enter into a contract on behalf of this corporation with the State Board of Directors of the Agricultural, Mining and Mechanical Arts College, to the effect that whenever a University of California shall be established as contemplated in the next preceding resolution, then the College of California will disincorporate and after discharging all its debts pay over its net assets to such University.[42]

The directors of the Agricultural, Mining and Mechanical Arts College accepted the College of California offer on November 7, 1867. The two boards took different routes, however, towards establishment of a university. The directors of the Agricultural, Mining and Mechanical Arts College seemed to feel that the work could be accomplished by mere amendment of the legislation that established their college in 1866. In a report to the legislature on behalf of the directors, the secretary of the Board contended that the 1866 legislation "appears to contemplate the establishment of a university which shall combine under one management, schools or colleges in which shall be taught all the higher branches of learning." He then recommended such amendments as would "more clearly define the intent of the legislature." [43]

In December, 1867, Governor Low reported to the legislature. He too urged that the aim of the March 31, 1866, legislation creating the agricultural college be "more clearly defined." [44] He also asked for the establishment of a state university on the Berkeley site under the existing agricultural-college directors. This recommendation had been endorsed in February, 1867, by the full Board of Directors of the Agricultural, Mining and Mechanical Arts College.

Meanwhile, the delegates from the Agricultural, Mining and Mechanical Arts College had barely left the fateful meeting of the College of California trustees on October 9, when a committee composed of Rev. James Eells, Henry Durant, Samuel Willey, and John Dwinelle was appointed to draft a new law to create a University of California.

Willey's record of the development of the law that eventually created the University indicated that a first draft was prepared by Dr. Eells. A more complete draft was developed by Dwinelle, and his thinking dominated the final version. This was only proper because in November, 1867, the College of California men and other citizens of Alameda County succeeded in electing him to the state assembly with presentation of the University bill as a priority assignment.

THE UNIVERSITY BILL

The assembly bill that created the University of California was carefully composed. Its phrasing in almost every section displayed that John Dwinelle and his advisers were aware of the history of California's college-building, that they were familiar with mid-nineteenth-century trends in American higher education generally, and that they were alert to the political pressures that an infant state university must avoid. The bill deftly balanced references to practical versus classical studies so as to qualify the University for federal agricultural-college land grants, while permitting the immediate introduction of courses in letters and pure sciences. From the act that established the Agricultural, Mining and Mechanical Arts College two years previously, the new bill borrowed the intriguing provision that made the secretary of the Regents a sort of one-man university extension, preserving information on practical farming, collecting seeds and cuttings, and distributing agricultural information and samples to California farmers on request. From the same source, the act took the idea of adding to the Board of Regents the governor and the presidents of the State Agricultural Society and the Mechanics' Institute as ex-officio members. To balance this obvious nod to practical-education advocates and to provide an even stronger demonstration of the University's secularity, the bill added the lieutenant governor, speaker of the assembly, and the superintendent of public instruction to the list of ex-officio Regents. Because the College of California had never been able to hire a president and survive, the authors of the University bill could see no reason not to give strong powers to the University's Regents and their secretary. To insulate academic affairs from politics and unprofessional meddling, the bill entrusted these matters to an Academic Senate, composed of the members of the faculty. From the old "Museum Plan," the bill borrowed the idea of giving the specimen collections of the State Geological Survey to the University. In the hands of a run-of-the-mill lawmaker, a measure with so much detail and miscellany tucked among its general provisions might be vulnerable. In Dwinelle's hand, with Willey and others helping out behind the scenes in Sacramento, the measure appeared to offer legislators nothing less than an historic opportunity to perform finally their constitutional duty to establish a university on terms conspicuously advantageous to the state.

The University bill was introduced on March 5, 1868. Its only opposition came from Senator Charles Maclay of Santa Clara County. Senator Maclay had a bill of his own pending which would create a central School of Science supported by half of the federal land-grant funds. The other half would be used to support existing colleges.[45] At least part of the senator's opposition, however, derived from his understanding of an early version of the University bill that called for election of eight of the Regents by the University's alumni as soon as they numbered one hundred. Another provision made all alumni of the College of California alumni of the University upon passage of the bill. As a staunch supporter of the Methodists' University of the Pacific, Senator Maclay feared that these provisions perpetuated control of the University by the Presbyterians and Congregationalists who (with their nondenominational policies put aside) were so prominently identified with the

College of California. When he was satisfied by an amendment changing the method of selecting the Regents, he withdrew his objections. The bill was passed by the legislature on March 21, 1868, and signed by the governor on March 23, 1868. Frederick Low, who so fervently desired to see a state university established during his administration, was denied that honor. In the same election that brought Dwinelle to Sacramento to present the University's Organic Act, Low was defeated for reelection by Henry Haight, a Democrat who had not been prominently identified with California's higher-education efforts before, but who had supported the University bill from the first.

The act that Governor Haight signed into law on March 23, 1868, created a completely new institution. It was not, as is sometimes asserted, a merger of the College of California and the Agricultural, Mining and Mechanical Arts College. It was, more accurately, the child of this very brief association in the fall and winter of 1867. From the College of California the new University inherited a collegiate tradition, a site, and facilities. From the Agricultural, Mining and Mechanical Arts College, the new University inherited the challenge of serving popular demand for practical, as opposed to classical, higher education in California and eligibility for federal assistance. But these inherited tasks, traits, and privileges were combined into the work and character of a new and distinct institution—the University of California—which the Agricultural, Mining and Mechanical Arts College had never intended to become, and which the College of California, despite two decades of effort, was unable to become.

Chapter 3

—————————

BY THE AUTHORITY OF THE REGENTS

IN THE BEGINNING, the University of California consisted of a state law, 160 acres of land in Berkeley, a modest state university fund, immodest expectations, and six ex-officio Regents.

The six Regents were the governor, lieutenant governor, speaker of the assembly, superintendent of public instruction, and the presidents of the Mechanics' Institute of San Francisco and the State Agricultural Society. A second group of Regents was to be appointed by the governor with the consent of the senate, and a third group was to be elected by the fourteen appointed and ex-officio Regents. Only after this board was complete would it be possible to hire a faculty, build buildings, organize courses, enact rules and regulations, and begin instruction.

To smooth the way for an early opening of the University, the Organic Act permitted the governor to appoint the first eight Regents after the 1867–1868 legislature adjourned and without the consent of the state senate. Governor Haight took full advantage of that provision. For one thing, the eighteenth session adjourned on March 30, 1868, just a week after the University bill became law. For another, the senate majority did not belong to the governor's party.[1] For still another, securing the proper balance of interests and experience among members of the Board required time and deliberation. It was not until mid-May that the governor finally announced his appointees. Among them were four lawyers, a railroad company officer, a mine owner, a doctor-builder-real estate developer, and a Unitarian minister.

On May 23, 1868, an advertisement in the San Francisco *Examiner* announced: "The Board of Regents of the STATE UNIVERSITY are requested to assemble at the office of J. Temple, Esq., No. 510 Jackson street, San Francisco, on Thursday May 28th, at 11 A.M. to complete the organization of the Board. . . ." [2] If this meeting was held, it was informal. No record was made of the proceedings. The first recorded meeting was held on June 9. At that meeting, and in compliance with the Organic Act, lots were drawn to determine the length of the terms of the first appointed Regents. These terms ranged from two to sixteen years, and were staggered to allow a governor to appoint no more than one new Regent every two years. With their respective terms of office determined, the Regents then proceeded to elect the eight "honorary" Regents. The terms of these Regents would also be determined by lot. Their authority and privileges were in every way identical to those of the appointed and ex-officio Regents. The term "honorary" denoted only the manner of their selection.[3]

As finally constituted, the Board included four state officials, eight lawyers, two doctors, a railroad vice-president, a Unitarian minister, a nurseryman, two farmers, a gas company president, a manufacturer, and a former state superintendent of public instruction. One of the lawyers was former Governor Low. Another was S. F. Butterworth, who figured prominently in

Abraham Lincoln's ill-advised attempt to confiscate California's rich New Almaden mine in 1863.[4] Through legal shrewdness, Butterworth's own Quicksilver Mining Company eventually gained ownership of that operation. Charles Reed, president of the State Agricultural Society, was, of course, a farmer. He was also a miner and former president of the Sacramento Irrigation and Navigation Canal Company. Andrew Hallidie, president of the Mechanics' Institute of San Francisco, joined the Gold Rush at the age of sixteen, was a builder of suspension bridges and mining machinery at the age of nineteen, and at the time of his appointment to the Board of Regents was only thirty-two and engaged in cable manufacturing. Four years later he would invent San Francisco's famous cable cars. Andrew Moulder, stubborn advocate of the military institute plan for a university when he was superintendent of public instruction, was elected as one of the honorary Regents. The two doctors, Samuel Merritt and Augustus Bowie, were also successful real estate speculators. Merritt was particularly well known as a builder.

Politically, the appointed and honorary Regents were almost equally divided between Republicans and Democrats.[5] This balance was upset, however, by the fact that the governor, lieutenant governor, speaker of the assembly, and superintendent of public instruction—four of the six ex-officio Regents—were Democrats.

The religious complexion of the Board is indicated in a complaint by Samuel Willey that the first eight Regents "turned out to include Roman Catholics, Jews, and indifferents or Skeptics—but—no minister of the Gospel (but one Unitarian) and not one of the characterizing and efficient friends of the College, which had given the University its existence. . . ." [6] In general, Willey was correct. The Board was secular in character. Governor Haight deliberately avoided denominational favoritism. Willey overlooked the fact, however, that in addition to Horatio Stebbins, who succeeded the famous Thomas Starr King as pastor of San Francisco's Unitarian church, O. P. Fitzgerald, the state superintendent of public instruction, was a Methodist minister who had served congregations in San Francisco, Santa Rosa, Sonora, and San Jose.

Stebbins was also one of two Regents who had been prominently associated with the College of California. The other was John Dwinelle, author of the University's Organic Act.

All efforts to characterize the first Board of Regents as the product of Governor Haight's political and religious favoritism were ultimately belied by the Board's well-balanced representation of economic, religious, and political interests of the state. The Regents were probably better educated, as compared to any random group of twenty-two men in the state, because four of them had been to a college or university. But in other respects they had been drawn, as Regents have been drawn ever since, from the ranks of Californians who had reputations for astuteness in business or for contributions to the cultural development and general prosperity of the state. That was considered qualification enough for men who became the hand and the voice of the people in the management of the state's University. To them were entrusted the institution's property and records. They were empowered to receive lands, moneys, bonds, securities, or other property given to the University and to manage these gifts under such provisions as the donors required. They were to "supervise the general courses of instruction, and on the recommendation of the several Faculties prescribe the authorities and text-books . . . and also to confer such degrees and grant such diplomas as are usual in Universities, or as they shall deem appropriate. . . ." [7] They were responsible for constructing buildings, enacting laws for the government of the University, electing a president and professors, hiring other instructors and employees, and determining the "moral and educational qualification of applicants for admission to the various courses of instruction." [8] In short, they were the supreme power in the University. For two years, they were the only power in the University.

RULE BY COMMITTEE

At Cornell, Michigan, and a few other American centers of learning in 1868, the university idea was taking hold as an alternative to New England collegiate forms. Many men in the country understood the tempo and direction of this trend, and such a man, with sufficient stature to command the confidence of the Regents and the people, might have been more sure-footed in the initial organization of the University than the Regents were. But the Regents were relatively young men (only five were over fifty years old), and they were accustomed by their frontier experiences to the need to undertake work in which they were not experts. To such men, the building of a university was an irresistible challenge.

First at Governor Haight's offices in San Francisco, later in rented quarters over a bank, the Regents met once a week throughout June and early July, 1868. Between meetings of the full Board, special committees met.

On June 12, a committee was appointed to prepare the rules and by-laws of the Regents. The draft was prepared within a few days and was adopted on June 19.[9] These by-laws called for regular, quarterly meetings of the Board. Special meetings could be held on call of the president or any three members. In the absence of the governor, Regents in attendance at a meeting were authorized to call any fellow member to the chair as presiding officer.

The by-laws divided the work of managing the University among ten standing committees. These were the Committees on Finance and Accounts, Grounds and Buildings, Library, Building, Supplies, Instruction, Agricultural College Lands, Endowments, Degrees, and Annual Reports. Jurisdiction would conflict from time to time, but the length of the committee list considerably limited the things that could go on in the University without Regental notice. For instance, no bill or claim against the University could be paid without examination by the Finance Committee and endorsement by its chairman. No salaries could be paid without the endorsement of the governor as president of the Board. The responsibility of other committees was comparably detailed.

The exemplary speed with which the Committee on Rules and By-Laws acted was matched two weeks later by a special committee on the organization of the colleges of the University. The sequence in which the colleges were to be established was already specified in the Organic Act. The College of Agriculture was to be established first, followed by the Colleges of Mechanical Arts, Mines, Civil Engineering, and Letters. Because only the College of Letters could offer more than one year of instruction during the initial year and because the instruction for all colleges during the initial year would be essentially the same, the committee decided that a very small faculty would be needed at the outset. Even so, much remained to be done before students could be accepted. The organization of the Regents had to be completed with the election of a secretary and a treasurer; buildings had to be started at Berkeley; the details of courses of the five colleges had to be determined; a faculty had to be selected; and a president had to be found. To do all that, the Regents needed ample time. The legislature; the people of California; the trustees, students, and faculty of the College of California; and the Regents themselves anticipated the opening of University classes in September, 1868, but the committee discouraged the Regents from attempting such an early start. "To announce the University of California in ninety days would be like extemporizing a pyramid," [10] the committee advised. So the Regents reluctantly postponed the opening of the University for one year.

TRANSACTIONS IN OAKLAND

To accommodate those students who would be ready for University instruction in September, 1868, the Regents asked the trustees of the College of California to keep their school open until summer, 1869. The trustees reluctantly complied with the request only after receiving a $10,000 loan from the University to help meet the unanticipated expense.[11]

Freed of the pressure of an early opening date, the Regents continued the slow work of organizing the University. They elected Andrew Moulder secretary of the Board and then elected State Senator John Hager to fill Moulder's place as an honorary Regent. They also elected William Ralston, "The man who built San Francisco," [12] treasurer of the Board. Following that, they began the search for a president and faculty members and sent one of their first faculty appointees, Robert Fisher, formerly with the Sheffield Scientific School, to New York, London, and Paris, with authorization to spend $15,000 on books, teaching exhibits, and laboratory apparatus for the University. Meanwhile, under the supervision of Regents' committees, the Berkeley site was cared for and buildings were planned.

By April, 1869, the Regents had made sufficient progress to remind the College of California that in October, 1867, it had promised to disincorporate when the University was ready to carry on the college's work. In accordance with that pledge, the trustees were asked "now to conclude the transactions by which their institution and its effects are to be transferred to the University." [13]

Some of the college trustees considered the Regents' proposal premature and even confiscatory. Samuel Willey was among them. Had there not been an inopportune slump in the East Bay real estate market, and if he had not suffered from a long, grave illness soon after the University was created, Willey would have long before tried to make a financially advantageous disposition of the College of California assets. Without building or students, the University hardly appeared to be ready to offer instruction. Besides, he and other trustees of the college were having second thoughts about the legality of their transfer to the state of properties acquired through private benefaction.

Advised of the concern of the College of California trustees for their authority to donate their property to the state, the Regents immediately suspended plans for the development of the Berkeley site. Regent John B. Felton, an Oakland resident and an attorney, was asked to undertake further negotiation with the college trustees. In this role, he persuaded the trustees to engage in a "friendly suit" before the California Supreme Court. The College of California brief, prepared with Felton's help, argued the trustees' inability to transfer their properties from private control to state ownership. Felton was also on hand when the case was heard in July, 1869. The court decided that, despite the philanthropic origin of some of the College of California's assets, the trustees had authority not only to give away the University site, but also, if it so desired, to disincorporate and give the rest of its properties to the University.

Willey felt betrayed by this decision, because Felton had given him and other trustees the impression that the case would only settle the title to the Berkeley site. By settling the question of disincorporation as well, the decision destroyed the most practical argument against immediate dissolution of the college. From the summer of 1869 on, the relationship between the College of California and the University it had helped to create was bitter. Willey was so disenchanted that it took forty years and the solicitous personal diplomacy of a University president to convince him that the University was a deserving heir to the College of California's legacy.[14]

Even after the court's decision, the College of California trustees insisted that they be permitted to superintend their own dissolution. They would give nothing to the Regents, they said, until their indebtedness was cleared. In response, the Regents took a tough line in the exercise of an option given by the college trustees early in 1868, involving 32 acres of land that squared off the northwest corner of the University site. The college trustees had lost enthusiasm for the transaction by 1869, but were moved to sell the 32 acres and all of their Berkeley water rights when the Regents agreed, in return, to remit $6,500 still owing on the loan to the college by the University in 1868 and to assume some $23,500 indebtedness on the property.[15]

As the fall of 1869 approached, however, the Regents were still unsuccessful in their attempts to acquire the college's property in Oakland as part of the spoils of disincorporation. They rented the property in time to accept the University's first students in September, 1869, but did not actually acquire it until May, 1870.[16] By this time, it consisted of one building owned by the college, another very small one owned by Henry Durant, and one block of land. By withholding it while offering the Regents various parcels of unimproved land in Berkeley, the college trustees made the Oakland property seem all the more precious. Only when it was included, along with 230 acres of hill lands east of the University site and about 82 acres of unsold College Homestead lots, were the Regents willing to consider purchase. The price

agreed upon was an amount equal to the college's total indebtedness—
$54,430.

In 1870, to accommodate a preparatory department and an anticipated
increase in University enrollment, the Regents also bought the old College
School that was operated by Isaac Brayton between 1860 and his death in
1869. Brayton had purchased these three blocks from the College of California in 1864. The Regents acquired the two blocks on which the main
buildings of the school were located by transferring to Brayton's widow all
of the Berkeley hill and homestead properties that had been acquired from
the College of California the previous May. This trade was accepted in full
payment of the $80,000 Mrs. Brayton asked for her Oakland property.
Later, the Regents paid her another $20,000 for the last of the four original
college blocks not in their possession.[17]

By the end of 1870, then, the Regents owned school buildings and the
four college blocks in Oakland, the 160 acres given to the state as the University site in 1868, 32 additional Berkeley acres purchased from the College of California, and about 10 Berkeley acres acquired by gift from
George M. Blake, an early Berkeley settler, in 1869. To acquire these
holdings (excepting the University site and the 10-acre gift), they spent
$107,045 in cash and traded away about 300 acres of Berkeley hill and Col-
lege Homestead properties.

BUILDING AT BERKELEY

The temporary location of the University in Oakland was specifically permitted by the Organic Act, but when the College of California agreed to
accept students for an additional year, beginning in the fall of 1868, some
Regents held the short-lived, but exciting, hope that the University might
actually begin exercises the following year in its own buildings in Berkeley.

Unfortunately, the Regents could not move quickly enough. They could
not decide whether the first buildings should be constructed of wood, stone,
or brick. Three different standing committees claimed jurisdiction for campus planning. Then, after several weeks were consumed in the resolution of
these difficulties, it suddenly became clear that less money would be available for building than was first expected.

The question of jurisdiction, at least, was settled when the whole matter
of building, planning, and construction was entrusted to the Regents' executive committee, with power to act. The members of this committee, created

on January 16, 1869, to serve as the "executive head" of the University until a president could be elected, were a remarkable trio. One was the professionally ruthless Samuel F. Butterworth. Another was the unworldly Rev. Horatio Stebbins. The third was the flamboyant plunderer of the Comstock, William C. Ralston, whose next big venture would be the construction of San Francisco's elegant Palace Hotel.[18]

To Stebbins fell the job of inviting San Francisco architects to submit plans for the first several buildings at Berkeley, one of which was to be large enough to serve temporarily the faculty and students of all the colleges. The committee authorized Stebbins to say that awards would be made in the amounts of $1,000 for the best design, $750 for the second best, and $500 for the third best.[19] Only four designs were submitted, and when Diaper and Saeltzer, fourth-place architects, protested that they had not been informed that, instead of receiving a commission, they were in a competition, the Regents generously paid them $250.[20]

But the winning architects, Wright and Saunders, declined their award, when they were told it was full payment for their plans and that the Regents intended to pay only $1,500 more for specifications. The 5 per cent of building costs that was the customary architect's fee would not be paid.[21]

The Regents did not accept the next-best design. Instead, on August 31, 1869, they entered into an agreement with the firm of Kenitzer and Farquharson.[22] Under this agreement, the architects furnished all services, including supervision, for a flat fee. The buildings covered by the agreement included an agricultural building, an academic building, a magnetic observatory, a president's office, seven houses for professors, and two outbuildings.[23]

By this time, so much delay had been caused by the questionable validity of the University's title to the Berkeley land and by controversy over building materials and committee jurisdiction that the Regents were forced to begin instruction in buildings rented from the College of California in Oakland.

Meanwhile, the building and grounds committee had been busy seeing to the general improvement of the Berkeley site. Dr. Samuel Merritt, who practiced medicine in Oakland only a few years before entering the real estate and building business, was the committee's most active member and eventual chairman. Under his direction, caretakers were hired, trees were planted by the hundred, fences were built, and, at the end of the road connecting the University site with Oakland, a bridge was constructed across Strawberry Creek.[24] This work began in the fall of 1868 and continued until May 10, 1870, when construction began on the agricultural college building (later known as South Hall). The basement of this building was almost finished when the Regents discovered that income from the college land grants and state endowment was insufficient to complete the work. Also, the legislature's 1870 requirement that labor for public buildings had to be paid on an eight-hour-day rate, instead of on contract, had added unexpectedly to the building's expense. Construction stopped in January, 1871.

In April of the following year, the legislature appropriated $300,000 for University construction and the Regents were favored by special legislation exempting the University from the day-rate compensation laws. Building activities resumed in June. David Farquharson, the architect, continued to supervise construction of the agricultural college building, but his plans for the College of Letters building (later known as North Hall) were adapted for wood construction under the direction of the building committee, now headed by Dr. Merritt.

Dr. Merritt's reputation as a builder in Oakland was well known to the Regents. His favorite contractors, Power and Ough, had also been employed many times for small construction projects on the University site, apparently to the Regents' satisfaction. But the Regents could not risk any taint to their handling of the building affairs of the University and, on June 26, 1872, passed a resolution "that no Regent shall be interested, directly or indirectly in furnishing labor or any kind of material for building the different structures of the University at Berkeley."

The measure did not deter Dr. Merritt. Not only was the College of Letters contract awarded (after bids were held in his custody overnight) to Power and Ough, at a price just $150 less than that of the next lowest bidder, but also much of the lumber and cement for the building came from Merritt's own lumber company. Some of it had been ordered before bids were opened, a fact known only to Merritt and Power and Ough. On February 7, 1873, the Regents gave Merritt broad powers to complete and equip the College of Agriculture and College of Letters buildings. In the latter project, his committee was authorized to retain Farquharson "or not, as they might see proper." They saw proper not to.

On April 1, 1873, the contract for the College of Letters was awarded to Power and Ough for $83,750, "subject to such alterations as the Building and Advisory Committees may suggest." [25]

By this time, the Regents were anxious to have the buildings completed as soon as possible, and Dr. Merritt obliged by keeping his reports to them short, making alterations in the plans as he went along, and by finishing the College of Letters building within six months. Dr. Stebbins was so grateful that, on September 6, 1873, when the building was officially accepted, he introduced a resolution "that the special thanks of the Board be given to Dr. Samuel Merritt, for the devotion of a great amount of time, experience and business ability, without any compensation, to the plans and construction of this building."

Dr. Merritt expressed his personal triumph in a resolution submitted at the same meeting. It warned the contractor for the College of Agriculture, built precisely to specifications under the watchful eye of its architect, that if he could not complete his project within three weeks, he would be liable for damages.[26]

MONEY AND THE COLLEGE LAND GRANTS

When the Regents began their work, they counted among their assets the University site, valued at $80,000; seminary and public building funds, $100,000; property (in addition to the University site) coming from the College of California, $40,000; and prospective receipts from sales of tidelands, $200,000, besides "the proceeds of the 150,000 acres of Agricultural College Lands." [27]

The accounting was too optimistic. The University site, whatever its worth, was not a liquid asset. Instead of getting $40,000 worth of Oakland and outlying Berkeley property from the College of California as a gift, the Regents found out they would have to buy it. On March 26, 1868, the legislature transferred $44,000 from the California School Fund to the University Fund.[28] This was only part of the seminary and public building funds available to the Regents. In all, the University received $72,831 (not the expected $100,000) from this source by the end of 1869.[29]

The $200,000 expected from the sale of salt- and tidelands was appropriated in the last days of the 1867–1868 session of the legislature.[30] The only problem was that no money was available until the lands were actually sold. By December 12, 1869, $100,000 of this appropriation had been received. The other $100,000 was not received until the following year.

The most hopeful financial expectations of the Regents were placed on the 150,000 acres of agricultural college lands made available to the state by the Morrill Act. Their committee on organization estimated that the yield from the sale of these lands would be as much as $1,000,000.[31]

To amass an endowment of that magnitude taxed the ingenuity of even the most shrewd businessmen on the Board. For one thing, land selection under the Morrill Act was limited to surveyed lands proclaimed for sale, and surveyors could not work fast enough to keep up with the rate at which public land was being transferred to private hands in California. Moreover, by 1868, 580,572 acres of public land had been entered in California by purchasers of agricultural college land scrip issued by Eastern states that received Morrill Act benefits although they had no public lands of their own to sell.[32] This further depleted the available surveyed land. There were other limitations, too. The least amount of land that could be selected by a purchaser was 160 acres. Selections previously granted to railroads were counted double; that is, every acre of this land selected was counted twice as a deduction from the total 150,000 acres available to the state. Finally, no mineral lands and no lands preempted by squatters or homesteaders could be selected.

In most states receiving agricultural college land grants, the appropriate state officers selected the number of acres allotted by the Morrill Act and disposed of them at the best price they thought they could get. The Organic Act specified that California's land grants "shall be located and sold under the direction of the Board of Regents, and for such price, and on such terms only as they shall prescribe." [33] It was a wise provision.

One of the honorary Regents, Isaac Friedlander, became chairman of the college lands committee when the Regents were organized.[34] It was an obvious choice. Using agricultural college scrip of other states, Friedlander had acquired 196,000 acres of his own in California, and at the time he was elected Regent, he was said to have a virtual monopoly of the trade in grain between California and Europe.[35] His experience with the land grants made him acutely aware of their limitations.

This awareness was shared by Governor Haight, who had warned the legislature in 1868 that surveyed lands in California had been so picked over that the state should seek from Congress a liberalization of the Morrill Act to permit entry into reserved sections within railroad grants and to make selections on unsurveyed land. Congress not only made such dispensations, but later reduced the minimum on acres of agricultural college lands that could be purchased from 160 to 40.[36]

The Regents actively sought these liberalizations, of course. By so doing, they obtained what amounted to a near-exclusive franchise for the sale of unsurveyed public lands in California.[37] The advantage of this arrangement was so attractive that Isaac Friedlander resigned from the Board in order to offer to buy the entire 150,000 acres.[38] His offer was $3.50 an acre, $50,000 of which was to be paid in cash with the remainder payable on time at 7 per cent interest. The Regents had originally set their price at $5 an acre, and declined Friedlander's offer. Later, one A. W. McPherson offered to buy 20,000 acres at $5 an acre, paying 20 per cent in cash and the remainder at

10 per cent interest. The offer was not only accepted, but similar terms were also made to subsequent purchasers. Paul Gates, in his study of California's college lands, charitably concedes that the Regents may not have been aware that McPherson was acting in behalf of one of their number, Samuel Butterworth.[39]

At first, the University's own agents located land to offer for sale. As time passed, however, people who were interested in buying desirable parcels of unsurveyed public land came to the University land agent to have the land "located." The result was that most of the land patented under Regental management was of prime value. It formed a part of the large timber holdings of companies in Plumas, Butte, Tehama, Humboldt, Mendocino, and Santa Clara counties. It rounded out the holdings of such large land and ranch operations as those of Miller and Lux, the Kern County Land Company, and Flint, Bixby and Company.[40] Some of the land eventually was abandoned because it was found to be occupied by squatters, because it proved useless to the buyer, or because payments could not be met. A few hundred of these acres were a part of the Regents' holdings as recently as 1966.

Almost all of the agricultural college lands had been sold by the Regents by 1900, and by 1966, the total income from the sales had exceeded $770,-000 ($5.17 an acre). Few states fared better, and most fared worse. The average yield throughout the country was only $1.65 an acre.[41]

For the management of California's agricultural college lands, the early Regents had special talent, experience, and the temperament. Their success in the matter was, in many ways, their best achievement during the University's formative years.

The profitable management of the land grants did not, however, improve the cash position of the Regents very soon. In the first place, all of the revenue from land-grant sales did not come at once. As has been noted, disposition of the grant took almost thirty years. Even if the proceeds had been available at once, they could not have been used. By law they had to be invested in government or other secure bonds as an endowment. Only the interest on this investment could be used for operations. None of the endowment income could be used for buildings.

By 1870, the University was feeling the pinch of its financial condition. In January of that year, the entire Board of Regents met in the assembly chamber in Sacramento "by invitation of the Legislature." [42] During the meeting, Secretary Moulder reported on the financial condition of the University, and five members of the Board spoke of the need of additional assistance. In a meeting of the Board held in conjunction with this session, the Regents requested that the legislature donate all of the tidelands about the Bay of San Francisco to the Regents for the support of the University. The legislature did not go quite that far. It did, however, vote to donate so much of the proceeds from the sale of the bay tidelands as would yield $50,000 a year in income for the University.[43]

The legislature's help would not be realized, of course, until the tidelands were actually sold. In the meantime, Professor John LeConte, Secretary Moulder, and the University's land agent voluntarily forfeited part of their salaries, and building operations were delayed.

These conditions persisted for two years. On January 9, 1872, Secretary Moulder reported that the University had $10,827.30 on hand, with fixed expenses of $3,800 per month for salaries.[44] Another appeal was made to the legislature. This time, the legislature provided more direct assistance. It agreed to appropriate up to $6,000 a month to cover deficiencies between the University's expenses and its income from endowment and other sources.[45] But legislation was intended only to provide support until the University could take care of itself. It was self-terminating in 1874. Another appropriation in 1872, already mentioned, was $300,000 for University construction.[46]

It is probable that both the Regents and the legislature suffered under similar financial illusions. For decades, founders of state universities and colleges in America believed that given sufficient endowment from land revenues, taxes, philanthropy or some other source, their institutions would go into perpetual motion without further assistance from the public treasury. After 1872, California's legislators spent several decades looking for the formula by which the University could be made self-sustaining. But in the critical first years they also made certain that no one could accuse them of letting the young University fail for want of the one more financial push it needed.

SELECTING A PRESIDENT

On July 2, 1868, the Regents' Committee on Organization of the Colleges of the University advised that: "The President of the University is its chief executive officer, has large powers confided to him, and is in fact the central pivot of the whole mechanism of the Institution. Without him no one of the Colleges is complete, and in view of the very great assistance a competent President could render the Board in all the details of organization and development of the University, and giving it a proper initial direction, it is well worthy of consideration whether one of our first steps towards the establishment of the Institution should not be the selection of that officer." [47]

The election of a president finally took place in November, five months after the Committee on Organization gave its report. In a shameful display of partisanship, Regent Richard P. Hammond, 1841 graduate of West Point and a prominent Democrat, nominated General George B. McClellan. The general's qualifications for a university presidency were not immediately evident and he still was known best as a general fired twice from the command of the Union armies; as the Democratic opponent of Abraham Lincoln in the contest for the Presidency in 1864; and as an advocate of peaceful compromise with the Confederacy. To prevent his election as president of the University, the Republican Regents suggested three candidates: Joseph Henry of the Smithsonian Institution; Regent Horatio Stebbins; and Frederick Law Olmstead, the famous planner of New York's Central Park and the author of early plans for development of a college on the Berkeley site. It was a weak field. Of the Republicans' candidates, only Joseph Henry had anything resembling experience in administering an educational institution. Besides, the Republicans and Independents were plainly outnumbered. When the vote was taken, McClellan received twelve votes, Stebbins received five, and Henry and Olmstead each received one. Former Governor Low immediately resigned from the Board in disgust. Andrew Hallidie, thirty-two-year-old president of the Mechanics' Institute, whose Republicanism was practiced with a heroic fervor, was not present when the vote was taken, but when he arrived, he insisted that his opposition to McClellan's election be recorded in the minutes of the meeting. Dwinelle showed his displeasure by voting "no" on a courtesy resolution inviting and encouraging the general to accept the position when it was offered. Later, many newspaper editors dealt out verbal punishment to the Regents. Some conceded that no one really knew whether McClellan would make a good president or not, but even those who were thus uncommitted could not excuse the Regents for their political indiscretion.

After all the furor, McClellan did not accept. His decision was read to the Regents at their meeting of January 5, 1869, and seven new nominations were made immediately. No election was held, however, and Regent Butterworth suggested that the members of the Board elect three Regents to be an "executive head" of the University until a president could be chosen. His suggestion was followed at the following meeting, and Regents Butterworth, Stebbins, and Ralston were elected to the committee thus provided.

There was no further action on the University presidency until June,

1869. On the fourteenth of that month, Regent John Felton, then mayor of Oakland, was nominated and declined. Elections were again postponed, but the Regents voted to request John LeConte, the senior faculty member, to assume the duties of the presidency "in addition to his other duties as Professor of Physics—and that his salary be fixed for the time being, at that already named for the Presidency." That amount was $6,000 a year.[48] Even after this action, however, the Executive Committee of the Regents remained in existence and LeConte's responsibilities were restricted to faculty and student affairs. This arrangement was continued for a full year.

A new list of nominees was drawn up in June, 1870. It included General George Stoneman; General Benjamin Alvord; Dr. John S. Hart, principal of the New Jersey State Normal School; W. J. Lucky, principal of the California State Normal School; General Gibbon, of the United States Army; a Professor Trowbridge;[49] Regent Butterworth; and the Acting President's younger brother, Joseph LeConte. The star name on the list, however, was that of Daniel Coit Gilman, who was then secretary of the Sheffield Scientific School and who was rumored to be the standard-bearer of a faction of the Yale faculty seeking to replace the retiring President Woolsey with a man more attuned to new ideas concerning the nature of universities. Regent Tompkins was Gilman's discoverer and champion. Even before Gilman knew he was a candidate, the Regents elected him. That was on June 21, 1870. Advised of his election, Gilman responded promptly that he could not accept. He was too deeply involved in the affairs of Sheffield Scientific School at a critical time. Moreover, his wife had died only two months before, and he considered it important that, for the time being, his two daughters be cared for by relatives in the East.[50]

On August 16, two weeks after Gilman's message was read to the Board, the Regents tried again to select a president. This time, the nominees were W. J. Lucky, Regent Tompkins, and, for the first time, Henry Durant. Durant was sixty-eight years old and in retirement, but his seventeen years of labor with the Contra Costa Academy and the College of California had become legendary. They were also the closest thing to experience in university administration that the Regents had immediately at hand. He received thirteen of the Regents' votes. Lucky received one vote, Tompkins received one, and there were two blanks.

Durant lived just across the street from the University buildings in Oakland and was able to begin the work of the presidency immediately after his election. In November, the Regents abolished their executive committee, but, after almost two years of managing the University without a president, they found the exercise of administrative functions an ingrained habit. Durant's presidency, therefore, was not much more demanding than LeConte's acting presidency was.

Durant resigned in 1872 at the age of seventy. Later, he served as mayor of Oakland for two terms and engaged in real estate transactions. He died suddenly on January 22, 1875, in the midst of a speech he was delivering before a literary society. He left only scattered, fragmentary papers and reports. None of them suggest that he was responsible for any outstanding achievements of the University. On the other hand, it must be remembered that, between them, the legislature and the Regents had done most of the work that a founder of the traditional sort would do. Durant could only supply what was missing. He did that simply by being there, for through his personal involvement he identified the University with the sacrifice, the courage, and the enlightened spirit that had characterized his earlier labors with the College of California. Such was the first faint glimmer of a University spirit worthy of honor.

Chapter 4

TEACHERS AND SCHOLARS

EXACTLY ONE WEEK after the Regents had chosen General McClellan to be the University's president, they began to elect members of the faculty. The professorships to be filled were advertised in local newspapers, and applications for positions were made by letter. Some applications were sent to the secretary of the Regents. A few went directly to the governor. There were few, if any, personal interviews, and the endorsements of a candidate's friends, colleagues, and prominent acquaintances were given considerable weight.

John LeConte, the first professor hired for the University, and his brother Joseph, another member of the pioneer faculty, were endorsed by such famous scientists as James Pierce and Louis Agassiz at Harvard; Joseph

Henry of the Smithsonian Institution; and Benjamin Silliman at Yale. The reputations of the two brothers had been earned as faculty members of several Southern colleges and they were both professors at South Carolina College when the Civil War broke out.

During the war, John LeConte was superintendent of the Confederate government's Nitre and Mining Bureau, and his brother was a chemist in the same agency. When the war was over, they found their old college in the hands of carpetbaggers and their private fortunes depleted. New England prejudice against men who had served the Confederacy kept the doors to colleges and universities in the North closed to the LeContes and there was no place for them in the South. They were considering emigrating to Mexico, South America, or England when Joseph learned about the impending opening of the University of California. Through a friend, General Barton S. Alexander, then on duty in San Francisco, Joseph LeConte got the promise of a prominent Union party man, Regent John W. Dwinelle, that LeConte's politics "will never be considered by the Regents when his name comes before them." [1] John LeConte was elected professor of physics at the University of California on November 17, 1868. Joseph LeConte was elected professor of geology, botany, and natural history two weeks later.

In addition to Joseph LeConte, two other professors were chosen on December 1. One was Martin Kellogg, the only member of the College of California faculty immediately carried over to the University staff. He was elected professor of ancient languages. The other was Robert A. Fisher, formerly associated with the Sheffield Scientific School, who was named professor of chemistry and metallurgy.

There were no further faculty elections until the following summer, a little more than a month before the University enrolled its first students. Paul Pioda, a principal of a young ladies' seminary in Santa Cruz, who advertised himself as "confident that I could fill to the satisfaction of your honorable Board a chair requiring a liberal education and a polyglot knowledge," [2] was elected professor of modern languages on July 7, 1869. William Swinton, on the same date, became professor of English language and literature, and Ezra S. Carr became professor of agriculture, agricultural chemistry, and horticulture. Both Swinton and Carr were endorsed by impressive sponsors. Swinton claimed United States Secretary of State Seward as a reference. Carr's principal endorsement came from Colonel John G. McMynn, a Regent of the University of Wisconsin. [3] If the Regents knew that Swinton, former literary critic and war correspondent of *The New York Times,* had barely missed execution on orders from General Burnside for journalistic spying on the activities of commanding generals of the Union

Army,[4] they did not hold the episode against him. Apparently they were also completely unaware that, before he came to California, Carr was often the central figure in turmoil at the University of Wisconsin, where he was frequently in dispute with his colleagues, members of the Board of Regents, and politicians.[5] Carr failed to win reelection to Wisconsin's faculty in 1867.[6]

By contrast, the Regents investigated the first professor of mathematics very carefully. He was William Thomas Welcker, a native of Tennessee, who had ranked fourth among the forty-two members of West Point's class of 1851. He was an attractive candidate because he indicated that, in addition to teaching mathematics, he was prepared to give any military instruction.[7] The Regents were worried, however, by the fact that Welcker had never taught at a college or university before. They finally elected him to the professorship on August 10, 1869. But on the same day, as though to cover their bets, they named another West Point graduate, Frank Soulé, Jr., as assistant professor of mathematics.

The Regents devoted ten months to the election of the nine professors and an instructor in drawing who formed the original faculty. A few of their choices soon proved to be unwise. On the other hand, four of them—the two LeContes, Martin Kellogg, and Frank Soulé—were still giving distinguished service to the University twenty years later. Two of them—John LeConte and Martin Kellogg—became presidents of the University. Without experience in academic recruitment, and relying entirely upon their own intuition and such documentation as was volunteered by the candidates and their supporters, the Regents could have done far worse.

THE ACADEMIC SENATE OF THE SEVENTIES

All ten of the first faculty members were automatically members of the Academic Senate. This body was created by the Organic Act and was responsible for "conducting the general administration of the University and memorializing the Board of Regents; regulating in the first instance, the general and special courses of instruction, and to receive and determine all appeals counted in respectful terms, from acts of discipline enforced by the Faculty of any College." [8]

The senate was also expected to advise the Regents in the development of courses of instruction, selection of textbooks, and the conferral of degrees and diplomas. Its membership consisted of the president, all professors, lecturers, and instructors of the University, but only the president and professors could vote.[9]

By the time the Regents' Committee on Instruction began to develop courses of instruction for the University, there were only four members of the faculty elected—the LeContes, Fisher, and Kellogg. So there was no Academic Senate to advise them in their early work. Instead, John LeConte, as senior faculty member, came to California in March, 1869, to help the Regents' committee develop the prospectus of the University's courses of instruction. In that work and in the subsequent work of devising statutes and regulations for the University, LeConte functioned alone in the exercise of the senate's responsibilities.

The first meeting of the Academic Senate was held on December 6, 1869, twenty months after the University was created. The business transacted was routine.[10] A week later, the Regents adopted rules of order and general regulations that required the Academic Senate to meet once every two weeks. The Regents also empowered the senate "to try offences committed by the students . . . determine their relative standing . . . adjudge awards and punishments . . . and make . . . regulations of their own proceedings." [11]

The president of the University was, and still is, president of the Academic Senate. At first, the actual administrative leadership of the faculty was exercised by Professor Fisher, who had been appointed dean of the faculty by the Regents. After 1870, the dean of the faculty was an elective office, and until 1885 it was held by Martin Kellogg. The duties of this office were enumerated by Kellogg to support his request for clerical assistance: The dean had to be present at all senate meetings, take the minutes, and later enter the minutes in the record books along with records of communications from the Regents and copies of all reports. The dean compiled a monthly report of attendance, entered the names of all new students in the "great Register" of the University, received the professors' reports for each term, and posted one copy on the bulletin board. At the end of the term, the dean added up all of the students' grades and entered their averages in the students' record book. He also conducted all correspondence relating to the terms of admission and courses of study. In addition, he was secretary of the alumni association, "with its correspondence, preparation for meetings, editing of proceedings, etc." [12] Managing all of this in the days before typewriters was a tall order for the University's only full professor of Latin and Greek, who also had "complete responsibility for the whole classical department." [13]

Though the dean of the Academic Senate was overworked, the senate itself was restricted in its deliberations to matters of student discipline, course and schedule planning, and textbook evaluation. More than fifteen years would pass before the Regents would delegate further responsibilities to the faculty.

THE FACULTY AND REGENTS DISAGREE

In December, 1869, the Regents asked the legislature for permission to buy the Brayton buildings on the old college blocks in Oakland as an accommodation for a University preparatory department. This permission was no sooner granted [14] than the faculty advised the Regents that they considered operation of preparatory classes by the University to be inexpedient. Besides, they believed that such an undertaking rightfully belonged to the high schools of the state.[15]

The Regents persisted. On April 12, 1870, Regent O. P. Fitzgerald, California's superintendent of public instruction, introduced a resolution of the Regents that the faculty be requested to organize "a fifth class or otherwise, which shall bring the different University schools into direct relation with the Grammar Schools of the State." [16] In May, Dean Fisher indicated that the faculty had retreated slightly from its original stand. Now, he advised Regent Fitzgerald, the Academic Senate found it desirable that a fifth class "of the nature of a preparatory class" be established on a temporary basis and on condition that the University admissions requirements would not be disturbed.[17] No faculty plan for a fifth class was immediately forthcoming, however, and Regent Tompkins grew impatient. As the state senator who had introduced the legislation enabling the University to start a preparatory department, he had political face to save. As the attorney for Mrs. Brayton, he had a professional interest in the matter. On May 25, he suggested that the Regents' Executive Committee and Committee on Instruction present a plan for a preparatory department for consideration at the next Regents meeting. This suggestion that the Regents take the preparatory school matter into their own hands went unheeded, and the whole question was temporarily set aside.[18]

Meanwhile, the Regents found themselves at odds with the faculty on another matter. No students had enrolled in the University's College of Mechanics in the first term. This was a poor showing, indeed, for "Land Grant colleges" were obligated to hold as "leading objects" the teaching of "such branches of learning as are related to agriculture and mechanic arts." [19] The Board of Trustees of the Mechanics' Institute diagnosed the difficulty as one of location. On January 26, 1870, they suggested to the legislature that the University's Colleges of Agriculture, Mechanical Arts, Mines, and Engineering all be moved from the isolation of the proposed site in Berkeley to the centrality of San Francisco. In their estimate, location of the campus in Berkeley would tend to exclude boys who could not afford the expense of the long commute across the bay or the even more costly convenience of living near campus. The Mechanics' Institute trustees reasoned that boys who could afford such expenditures would so naturally prefer academic or literary courses that "the colleges of applied science, if located in Berkeley, would become practically useless to the public." [20] The legislature did not agree, but the president of the Mechanics' Institute, Andrew Hallidie, was an ex-officio Regent, and he used his position to engineer the creation in San Francisco of a branch of the University's College of Mechanic Arts. To make it work, the faculty was requested to organize "a preliminary course of one lecture per week" to be "commenced immediately," and "continued at the Lecture Room of the Mechanics' Institute." [21]

Through Acting President LeConte, the faculty protested to Governor Haight that the mechanic arts college scheme was impractical. The resident professors, LeConte said, "will be occupied with their regular duties in the University during six days of the week, from 9 o'clock in the morning until 2 o'clock in the afternoon. . . . It is respectfully submitted, whether the night lectures in San Francisco would not so far exhaust their vital energies as to render the professors unfit for their performance of their regular duties of the University." [22] As an alternative, he suggested hiring nonresident professors to give the San Francisco lectures.

The Regents were so deeply committed that they would accept no such compromise. In August, Regent Dwinelle appeared before the Academic Senate. He introduced his remarks with a brief statement of the financial condition of the University and then "addressed the Academic Senate upon the necessity of 'popularizing' the institution, by the establishment of a fifth class (preparatory) and by giving the proposed course of lectures before the Mechanics' Institute of San Francisco; to which (the speaker said) the Board of Regents had committed themselves." [23] When he withdrew from the room, the faculty immediately passed resolutions to the effect that they were ready to lecture before the Mechanics' Institute.[24] Furthermore, they resolved "that in pursuance of the power conferred by the Board of Regents, the faculties of the University hereby establish a Fifth Class in the nature of a preparatory class to continue during the pleasure of the Board of Regents." [25]

When Durant assumed the presidency in November, 1870, he found the faculty still chafing, though reconciled. "The Faculty *yielding to the views of the Board of Regents*," [26] Durant reported in December, "decided in favor of the adoption of both these measures and proceeded immediately to take the steps necessary to put them into execution. The Fifth class and the course of Lectures in question were inaugurated in due time and both with the most flattering prospects of success." [27]

In the first year of operation, the fifth class enrolled 55 students in Oakland under the supervision of George Tait, formerly a teacher at the College School. Of the University's 65 Freshmen entering in 1871, 54 were "fifth class graduates." In the same year, 149 students, only two less than were enrolled in the University itself, were enrolled in preparatory classes.[28] Unfortunately, however, many students enrolled in the fifth class without paying the required fees. The resulting deficit, problems of discipline, and a growing feeling that the department really was inappropriate to the University after all, forced the Regents to close the fifth class in August, 1872.[29]

The Mechanics' Institute lectures were continued for at least four years. As many as five hundred people attended. They could hear Professor Carr on "What We Breathe" and "What We Drink, and What We Eat"; John Le-Conte on "The Distances and Activities of the Stars"; Martin Kellogg on "Homer, and the True Homeric Poems"; and Swinton on "Books, and the Use of Books." [30] There were one hundred men on the waiting list for enrollment the first year.

The University's success with the Mechanics' Institute lectures and its brief experience in preparatory education would be no more than historical curiosities except for the fact that both programs were developed in spite of formal protest and dissent on the part of the faculty. For decades thereafter, the Academic Senate was seldom consulted on matters of general policy.

By August, 1872, faculty organization at the University was changed. The University *Register* referred to "the two faculties [College of Letters and the Colleges of Science] closely cooperative with each other and usually meeting as a single body." By February of the following year, the president of the University (Gilman) raised the question as to whether the faculties should not be more formally separated into "the Departments of Science and Letters." [31] That idea barely came to the surface before the cohesion of the faculty was sundered by the establishment of a medical department of the University in San Francisco. The notion that the doctors of the faculty in the city could have much to contribute to the deliberations of the teachers at Oakland was not very realistic. Moreover, the medical department was under the control of its own faculty to a much greater extent than the departments at Oakland were. The intrusion of Oakland professors would neither be useful nor welcome. Yet the Organic Act declared all members of the faculty to be members of the Academic Senate.

The solution finally agreed upon was to organize the academic staff into three distinct faculties—one for the College of Letters, one for the sciences, and one for the medical school.[32] The members of all three faculties were members of the Academic Senate, although they met infrequently in that capacity from 1874 to 1885. The arrangement made faculty members strong in questions involving instruction, curriculum, and student conduct. But they were too divided to play a forceful role in the development of general University policy, to influence their own working conditions, or to safeguard fair treatment in the recruitment and dismissal of their colleagues.

THE PROFESSORS' LOT

Paul Pioda, professor of modern languages, heard twenty hours of recitation every week by Freshmen, Sophomores, and Juniors. In addition, he taught languages in the preparatory department.[33] Henry Durant, when he became president of the University in 1870, gave six and a half hours of instruction a week in mental and moral philosophy without slighting his administrative duties.[34] Durant, the LeContes, Kellogg, Welcker, Pioda, Carr, and Swinton gave a total of forty lectures to the Mechanics' Institute in San Francisco by 1871. Since there were few agricultural students on the campus, Carr was encouraged to lecture elsewhere in the state in order to familiarize rural California with the agricultural work of the University.[35]

To lighten these burdens and to add illustrious names to the faculty roster, the Regents named several "honorary" professors. One of these was the well-known mining engineer William Ashburner; another was George Davidson, of the United States Coast and Geodetic Survey; a third was United States Supreme Court Justice Stephen J. Field. These men did not meet classes regularly, but they did consult with other members of the faculty and gave periodic lectures.

A more practical relief for the overburdened resident faculty was provided by a corps of young instructors recruited in the 1870s from the ranks of University graduates. Some of these young men later became respected scholars and teachers in their own right. George C. Edwards, '73, was one of them. He was hired as an instructor in mathematics and served as commandant of the military battalion. At the time of his death in 1930, he had been a full professor for twenty years. Josiah Royce, '75, taught English at Berkeley as one of the young instructors of the 1870s, but his fame came later when he was a philosopher at Harvard. Joseph C. Rowell, '74, served the University as librarian for almost forty-five years. Edmund O'Neill, '79, became a highly respected professor of chemistry. William Carey Jones, '75, who started his University career as recorder of the faculty, eventually became professor of jurisprudence.

Salaries for University instructors and professors were not far out of line with those paid at other institutions in the 1870s, but there were curious inconsistencies in salaries within the same rank, and a man's salary tended to be fixed indefinitely at his starting rate. Young instructors received between $75 and $100 a month. Professors were paid $200 to $300 a month. Only two assistant professors were appointed during the first decade of the University's history; one was paid $150 a month, and the other was paid $175 a month. The rank was completely abandoned in 1877, appeared again briefly in 1881, almost immediately disappeared, and was not used thereafter until 1886. The first associate professor was hired at $200 a month in 1890. The previous year, the average salary of the University's professors reached $2,000 a year for the first time.[36]

THE INSECURE FACULTY LIFE

In October, 1870, no less a personage than Robert Fisher, professor of chemistry and dean of the faculty, read about his dismissal from the faculty for reasons of "economic retrenchment" the day after it happened—in the newspaper. He did not receive formal notice of the action from President Durant until twenty days later. When he asked the Regents for a hearing so that he could silence "vile slanders against my character that are assigned as the true cause of the late extraordinary action on the part of the Board," [37] the Regents passed a resolution claiming that they "deem it only necessary to say that there have been no charges against Dr. Fisher at any time before the Board and that nothing in the action of the Board, in abolishing the chair he occupied was intended to reflect on his character." [38] At the same meeting, a motion to reinstate Professor Fisher failed by a vote of two to eleven.

The fate of a University of California faculty member rested less upon the will of the entire Board of Regents (although the full Board acted on all personnel matters) than it did upon a relatively few Regents who were members of a dominant committee of the Board. At first, this was the three-man Executive Committee of the Regents. When that committee was abolished in 1870, its work was transferred to the Regents' Advisory Committee. This committee was intended to be advisory to the president of the

University, but it usually met without his presence. It made all recommendations concerning hiring and firing of professors until June, 1880, when it was superseded by the Regents' Committee on Instruction and Visitation. Horatio Stebbins had served on all three of these committees and was chairman of both the Advisory Committee and the Committee on Instruction and Visitation. His power became so entrenched that a fellow Regent claimed that "at his frown every Professor in the University trembled in his boots." [39]

LIVING IN BERKELEY

When the University was still located in Oakland, its professors found living quarters for themselves and their families in the surrounding community. They anticipated the move to Berkeley with misgivings. In 1873, according to President Gilman, Berkeley had "no school, no practicing physician, and but few and indifferent stores. The walks and roads are in bad condition most of the year, and the inconveniences of family life are great." In recognition of the University's isolation, the Regents originally planned to build faculty homes on the University site. The plan collapsed for want of money and under the force of Regent Hallidie's argument that no one could design one house to suit the taste and needs of ten different professors.[40] Besides, some professors bought Berkeley lots and were building homes of their own at about the time the Regents were concluding their long debates on the housing problem.

After the University opened at Berkeley, some professors remained in residence in Oakland, and the Regents arranged to provide special horsecar service for them so that they could get to classes on time. A few of the young instructors were allowed to rent rooms on the top floor of North Hall. At President Gilman's instigation, several cottages were built on the Berkeley campus in 1875 for rental to student residence clubs. Because this plan failed to work, the cottages were offered for rent to the staff and faculty. They were not very satisfactory for this use either. Joseph LeConte had to replace the entire floor in the cottage he rented. Another professor found that his chimney "smokes so dreadfully as to prevent us kindling the fire." [41] The saddest tenant of all, however, was Professor Welcker. He began corresponding with the secretary of the Regents in May, 1877, concerning his cottage's shortcomings. First, about a square yard of ceiling plaster fell into his dining room.[42] The plumbing in his kitchen was faulty. The plumbing in his washhouse was so bad that his washing woman was sick several times, and he reported, "I am afraid that I cannot get her to continue to work at it." [43] A few months later, the Regents undertook wholesale reconditioning of all of the cottages. Eventually, these buildings were used exclusively for academic purposes, and the faculty moved off campus.

THE BEGINNING OF RESEARCH

For several decades, the University of California faculty had little time and virtually no facilities for research. Even so, both John and Joseph LeConte published results of scholarly investigations as early as 1871. John LeConte's work was entitled "Limiting Velocity of Meteoric Stones Reaching the Surface of the Earth." Joseph produced two reports. One was called "Some Phenomena of Binocular Vision"; the other was "Law of Circulation in Nature." These two men continued to make investigations and to publish their findings throughout their careers at the University. In 1872, Martin Kellogg published "Ars Oratoria." Three years later, Bernard Moses, professor of history and political science, published "Georg Stjernhjelm, the Father of Swedish Poetry." A year later, he published "The Beginning of Modern History."

Frederick Hesse, the first professor of industrial mechanics, began devising implements to test the strength of Pacific Coast timbers soon after his appointment to the faculty in 1874.

Next to the LeContes, the most productive research scientist at Berkeley in the early decades was Eugene Hilgard, who succeeded Ezra Carr as professor of agriculture in 1875. He was already known for his "analysis of soils and for the light he has thus thrown on some of the most intricate problems of agricultural science" at the University of Mississippi when he came to Berkeley via the University of Michigan. On the University grounds, he almost immediately embarked on studies of the effects of various fertilizers and the depth of plowing on the fertility of Berkeley's soil. Five years later, the legislature appropriated $3,000 for a University investigation in the field of viticulture under Hilgard's direction.

Despite these beginnings, research would not progress significantly until the people of California accepted it as part of the proper work of the University. "College" and "university" were popularly regarded as the same thing, and professors of either institution were believed to have but one responsibility: however limited their knowledge might be, they had to make it somehow useful to students in their classrooms. These overriding public expectations considered, the surprise is not that research effort was so meager in the University of California during the 1870s, but rather that it was made at all.

Chapter 5

THE ARRIVAL OF
DANIEL COIT GILMAN

DANIEL COIT GILMAN, who turned down the University of California presidency in 1870, was a contemporary of Presidents Charles William Eliot of Harvard, Andrew D. White of Cornell, and James B. Angell of Michigan. All of them were aware that the familiar American college, with its rigid curriculum and religious foundations, was an incomplete answer to the higher education needs of a maturing nation. To the best features of the college they were adding diversified instruction in the sciences and the professions; they were encouraging a pursuit of truth to the ultimate point where curiosity could be sustained; and they were assembling companies of wise and stimulating scholar-teachers. They were, in short, building universities —institutions new to America.

For the work of building an American university, Gilman was especially well prepared by study and experience. He became familiar with the American collegiate tradition as a student at Yale when that college was still stubbornly committed to classical forms. In 1853, a year after his graduation, he was able to compare this prototype with other systems during an extended visit to Europe. While there, he made careful studies of European universities and was particularly interested in those of Germany, where the sciences flourished and where high honors came to men successfully engaged in the independent search for new knowledge. His observations and insights concerning higher learning abroad became a part of the prospectus he wrote in 1855 on behalf of the Yale Scientific School. This forerunner of the famous Sheffield Scientific School was just being organized when Gilman returned to the United States and he played a leading role in raising funds for it. Gilman became assistant librarian at Yale in 1856 and librarian in 1858. His habit of writing down his observations and ideas concerning any interesting experience in his life yielded, in 1860, an article on the history of Yale's library and a complete description of its facilities. He resigned the librarian-ship in 1865 to seek a more challenging endeavor.

Gilman's understanding of educational problems increased during his service as acting school visitor for New Haven, Connecticut, beginning in 1856. It was a part-time job, but Gilman pursued the work assiduously. He held office hours to consult with teachers and citizens on school problems, helped organize the city's first high school, and, characteristically, wrote down his observations and philosophies concerning elementary and high school education for the guidance of others. The true character of the position is revealed by the fact that his successor was appointed on a full-time basis with the title of Superintendent of Schools. In 1865, his competence in matters of education was recognized by the State Board of Education in Connecticut, which elected him secretary—or principal executive officer.

In 1863, Gilman was one of three representatives from Yale who success-fully urged the Connecticut legislature to accept the benefits of the Morrill Land Grant Act for the Sheffield Scientific School. In subsequent negotia-tions in Washington, Gilman became personally acquainted with Senator Morrill himself. Their relationship was sufficiently familiar that in 1867,[1] when the Senator paid a visit to Yale, he stayed in Gilman's house. On that occasion, he gave Gilman what amounted to a private seminar on his inten-tions in introducing the Land Grant College Act of 1862. As a result, years later when Gilman's adversaries in California attempted to interpret the act according to their own desires, he had the advantage of first-hand informa-tion. He kept abreast of the effects of the act by corresponding with land-grant-college administrators throughout the country. Foremost among them was his Yale schoolmate and European travel companion Andrew White, who led in the establishment of Cornell. In the 1870s he became more famil-iar with such institutions by virtue of visitations made at the request of the United States Commissioner of Education.

Gilman's interest in the Sheffield Scientific School persisted despite his other assignments at Yale and his work on behalf of the public schools of New Haven and Connecticut. In 1863, on the basis of his scholarly writing in the field, he was appointed professor of physical and political geography at the Scientific School. In 1866, he was elected secretary and for the next six years gave that position prior concern. Though it was identified with Yale College, the school was virtually autonomous, and Yale gave it no financial support. Raising funds for an endowment, for a library, for labora-tory apparatus, and other necessities became vital work for the entire fac-ulty. With his ability to observe, analyze, and explain, Gilman was ideally suited to the task of helping the public understand the values of science and the nature and purpose of the Sheffield Scientific School. After several lean years, the fund-raising began to succeed, and between 1870 and 1872 the impressive sum of $250,000 was obtained for the school's endowment.

As the Sheffield Scientific School began to prosper, as Gilman's writings on educational subjects became widely known, and as his acquaintances at American colleges and universities grew in number, he became a prime candidate for the presidency of an American college or university. The University of Wisconsin bid for him in 1869 and was turned down. California was next, in 1870. He was not yet ready to move and also turned that offer down. A faction of his colleagues at Yale hoped and worked for his selection as the successor to President Woolsey in 1871, but the Yale Corporation made a more conservative choice.

In 1872, Gilman traveled again under the auspices of the United States Commissioner of Education to study American scientific colleges. This time, his travels brought him to California. During his visit, representatives of the Regents told him that Henry Durant wanted to retire, and asked him if he would be willing to have his name considered again for the University of California presidency. Because his work at the Sheffield Scientific School and at Yale had reached a stage where it no longer challenged him as it had in the beginning, and because his younger daughter was in poor health and might find California's climate salutary, Gilman consented to be considered a second time. Soon after Gilman returned to New Haven, word reached him that, on July 30, 1872, at the age of forty-one, he had been elected president of the University of California.

ONE YEAR OF GLORY

If Gilman had not spent another day as president of the University of California, his contributions on the day of his inauguration, November 7, 1872, would have earned him a significant place in the institution's history. In his inaugural address, he showed Californians their University as they had never perceived it before. He put it in historical focus, noting that it had been created precisely at a time when interest and activity in university-building was intensified throughout the world. He sharpened their vision of the University that he believed should be developed for California:

> First it is a "University," and not a high-school, nor a college, nor an academy of sciences, nor an industrial-school, which we are charged to build. Some of these features may, indeed, be included in or developed with the University; but the University means more than any or all of

them. The University is the most comprehensive term which can be employed to indicate a foundation for the promotion and diffusion of knowledge—a group of agencies organized to advance the arts and sciences of every sort, and to train young men as scholars for all the intellectual callings of life. . . .[2]

It is not the University of Berlin nor of New Haven which we are to copy; it is not the University of Oakland nor of San Francisco which we are to create; but it is the University of this State. It must be adapted to this people, to their public and private schools, to their peculiar geographical position, to the requirements of their new society and their undeveloped resources. It is not the foundation of an ecclesiastical body nor of private individuals. It is "of the people and for the people"—not in any low or unworthy sense, but in the highest and noblest relations to their intellectual and moral well-being.[3]

Gilman also used his inaugural address to define the work of the University of California: "It is to fit young men for high and noble careers, satisfactory to themselves, and useful to mankind; it is to bring before the society of to-day, the failures and successes of societies in the past; it is to discover and make known how the forces of nature may be subservient to mankind; it is to hand down to the generations which come after us, the torch of experience by which we have been enlightened." [4]

He called upon the faculty to provide the *"genius loci,* the spirit of the place." [5] He asked the Regents to be "the power behind the throne. . . . Upon their wise choice of instructors, their careful guardianship of moneys, their construction of buildings, their development of new departments and schools, their mode of presenting the University to the public, will depend the confidence and liberality of the community." [6] From the state authorities, he wanted "steady, munificent, and confiding support. 'Quick to help and slow to interfere' should be their watchword." [7] The ministers and the press of the state could be of assistance, too, by granting the University understanding and encouragement.

He also talked about the place of the natural sciences, history and social science, language, and religion in a university education.

His enthusiasm was contagious; his personality was magnetic. Within a few months of his arrival in California, he had no trouble at all in gathering together a group of leading citizens, Regents, and professors who enjoyed stimulating discussion and conversation. They were constituted as the Berkeley Club, a western echo of an organization that Gilman had belonged to in New Haven. The Berkeley Club furnished the new president with learned company, respected counsel, and strong support throughout his stay in California. He widened such associations by joining several other social, literary, and cultural societies in the Bay Area.

The Regents of the University were so impressed by him that he was officially invited to attend their meetings and participate in their deliberations. As soon after his arrival as possible legislation was introduced and passed so that the president of the University would serve ex officio as a member of the Board of Regents.[8] Gilman first sat in this capacity in 1874.

Regent Edward Tompkins, who had engineered Gilman's election to the presidency in 1870, showed his enthusiasm and confidence in Gilman in 1872 by becoming the University's first important donor. In September, he arranged to give some Oakland properties to the University so that they could be used as an endowment for the establishment and perpetuation of a professorship of Oriental languages. Tompkins never saw his professorship established, nor did he see, for long, his young president-protégé in action. He died just a week after Gilman was inaugurated.

In fund-raising, Gilman had been schooled in the competitive environs of New England. A University alumnus, Dr. H. M. Pond (A.B. '76, M.D. '80), remembered Gilman for astuteness in such endeavor. Pond recalls that a press was installed in the top floor of North Hall in 1874 to print the student newspaper, college announcements, and the like. In addition, the printing operation provided part-time employment for the students. On Charter Day, 1874, Gilman told the printing superintendent to get all of the boys on his payroll into the print shop and to engage them in labor of some kind immediately after the day's exercises. "At the appointed time," Pond says, "every man who knew a composing rule from a monkey wrench was at a stand going through the motions of setting type. Webb Pierce was working the old Washington Press. I was inking the forms. As the crowd of invited guests whom President Gilman had selected for that day filed in through the doors, Webb in his excitement and hurry broke the press, but we laid aside the fragments and went through the motions with great energy.

"President Gilman made a little speech about self-supporting students, about the opportunity for them, about how hampered the effort was because of lack of equipment, and secured twenty-five hundred dollars on the spot." [9]

In March, 1873, ownership of a medical college in San Francisco founded by Dr. H. H. Toland was conveyed to the University, with Gilman handling many details of the transaction. It became the University's Medical Department and its first professional school. Three months later, the year-old California College of Pharmacy was affiliated with the University and was the beginning of the present School of Pharmacy on the San Francisco campus.

Work on the buildings in Berkeley was in progress when Gilman arrived in California to take up the University presidency. In May, he participated in the laying of the cornerstone for North Hall. In July, he presided over the first University commencement in Berkeley, even though the buildings were not yet complete. The academic procession began at the University buildings in Oakland and marched to the new campus. One participant later recalled: "The students, about one hundred strong, marched in uniform led by their drum corps, three in number, and preceded by a number of carriages filled with distinguished guests, including our own professors. . . ." [10] Other alumni would remember the message of President Gilman to the graduates: "The University sends you forth the first of its four-year classes. You are twelve in number,—be jurors, sworn to declare the truth as you find it; be apostles, bearing everywhere the Master's lessons. Young gentlemen, as we part, I invoke upon you the blessing of Almighty God; I bid you welcome to the responsibilities and the opportunities of educated men; I warn you against dishonesty, selfishness and sloth; and in the name of this band of instructors, who have watched for four years the unfolding of your characters, and who will ever be your friends, I bid you, with mingled hopes and fears, an affectionate farewell." [11]

The commencement in July, 1873, and the move to the Berkeley campus the following September were events marking high points in Gilman's popularity in California. With justification, he was regarded as somehow stronger and more vital than the institution he led. His presence was reassuring to California's intellectuals. Every Gilman achievement pointed up, by contrast, the amateurish planning and administration of the University before he came, but those most responsible for the old order—the Regents and men like Henry Durant and John LeConte—were happy enough to have Gilman set matters right. They remained his boosters throughout his California years.

Unfortunately, Gilman did not please everybody. Many Californians honestly misunderstood what he was trying to do. Others, within the University, had been more comfortable when the University's leadership was less able and the awkwardness and imperfections of the place hid their own incompetence.

SLINGS AND ARROWS

There was no lack of petty issues for Gilman's foes to rally around. Some of them emerged in response to the public, secular character of the University. Others involved differences of opinion concerning the very nature of a university presidency.

The cultivation of a respectable level of philanthropic support traditionally has been one of the major assignments given to American university presidents. To carry it out, Gilman had to wait patiently upon California's men of wealth and influence. For his pains he received little money and drew the charge that he and the University favored the sons of wealth over those of the working classes. Gilman deserved the charge less than most college and university presidents. His concern for the education of boys from poor homes led him to work quietly with Regent Hallidie for the establishment of a privately supported vocational school in San Francisco. The plan was almost ready for implementation when it became general knowledge that James Lick, an eccentric, wealthy ex-cabinetmaker, had left money in his will for a similar project. Under the impression that the Lick provision took care of the matter, supporters of the Hallidie–Gilman project lost interest and the plan failed.

Gilman's reorganization of University instruction, announced in a "provisional" circular of information for 1873, recognized the student demand for literary courses and the need to combine instructional resources in the mechanical arts and sciences. All that he actually did was to organize two "departments" at Berkeley and a third, a medical department, at San Francisco. One of the departments at Berkeley was to be a department of letters. The other was to be called the Department of Sciences, and was subdivided into courses in agriculture, chemistry, engineering, and mechanical arts. These "courses" were called "colleges" in the register of 1874, probably in deference to the language of the Organic Act.

Gilman's critics claimed that he was really intent on deemphasizing the mechanical arts to the greater glory of language, history, and literature. They also capitalized on the popular concept of a "college" as something with a building and staff to itself, and suggested that Gilman's plan was intended to hide the fact that the mechanical arts colleges required by the Organic Act did not exist at Berkeley. This argument became so troublesome that the Regents eventually made it a specific duty of members of the faculty to help dispel the public misconception of what a college, as the term was used by the University, was supposed to be.

Religious and political discrimination in University matters was prohibited by law. California's political code required that "no sectarian, political, or partisan test must ever be allowed or exercised in the appointment of Regents, or in the election of professors, teachers, or other officers of the University, or in the admission of students thereto, or for any purpose whatsoever; nor must the majority of the Board of Regents be of any one religious sect or of no religious belief." [12] No stance toward religion would have satisfied everyone, of course. The stance imposed by law disappointed those who anticipated that the University would evangelize. To these, the University was "Godless."

Gilman encountered their hostility after the commencement of 1873, when a minister wrote an article claiming that during the exercises, "the name of God was not spoken; no prayer was offered; nor was any reference made in any of the young men's speeches to moral or religious ideas. Now, even an atheist does not desire his boy to be trained a materialist." [13] Gilman's rebuttal was easy. The minister apparently was not in attendance at the exercises. If he had been, he would have heard the Episcopal bishop of California open and close the program with prayer, and he would have heard Gilman himself invoke the blessings of "Almighty God" upon the University's "twelve apostles" graduated that day.

Gilman's alleged favoritism for the rich, his alteration of the University's courses of instruction, and the University's "Godlessness" were not, in themselves, issues of critical proportions. They were troublesome, though, and they were a prelude to controversy that involved the integrity of the Regents; the security of the University from political plunder and economic starvation; and the ability of the institution to excel in liberal and comprehensive instruction and research. These bigger issues rose to the surface in the second year of Gilman's presidency.

Chapter 6

SURVIVING THE POLITICAL TURBULENCE OF THE 1870s

BY THE TIME Daniel Coit Gilman came to California, the Regents had organized the University according to provisions of the act that created it in 1868. The courses of study had been worked out, and the rules for internal government had been enacted. There was even a tradition of sorts, inherited from the old College of California. Upon these beginnings, Gilman wanted to build a comprehensive university, offering instruction in many fields of knowledge and encouraging research in every promising direction. The only trouble, as his biographer notes, was that "very few persons in the community comprehended in any degree, as he did fully, the whole round of university work." [1]

Many of the features of the emerging American university could be found in 1872 as innovations and experiments associated with several institutions of learning. Gilman would integrate the best of these features into a single university. Conservative men who knew only the old New England colleges were skeptical. Men who had known no college at all were easily content with the University as it was when Gilman found it. Still others, caught up in the social unrest of the 1870s, when California's farmers and workingmen were challenging established wealth, established authority, and established intellectual values, found the University, even as it then existed, too rich for the needs of the common man. To them, the best education for Californians was one that taught young men the practical arts of farming, building, and manufacturing. Everything else was a waste of time. Men of this persuasion could be found among the members of the Mechanics' Deliberative Assembly, an early labor organization, and the secretly organized Granges in the rural areas of the state. In their councils, the University was heatedly criticized because, for several years, none of its students pursued a course exclusively devoted to agriculture or the mechanical arts.

The anger of the Grangers was often fed by one of the University's own professors, Ezra S. Carr, the professor of agriculture. To stimulate interest in the University's offerings and programs in his specialty, as directed by the Regents, he gave an average of two public lectures every three weeks. His meeting hall and audience were often provided by the Grangers. Personally charming and rhetorically clever, Carr acquired an extensive rural following. He used subtle references to his influence with the farm people to try to extort concessions for the College of Agriculture from president and Regents. When the Regents complied too slowly to satisfy him, their failure was made known to the state's powerful agricultural leaders. As the list of Carr's unfulfilled requests lengthened, he spoke more openly in behalf of a plan that would, in effect, divert California's benefits from the Morrill Land Grant Act of 1862 from the University to the exclusive support of practical training in farming and the mechanical arts.

Since it was new, the University had some immunity to such proposals; the public was perfectly willing to give it the benefit of all doubt. But in 1874, the University was touched by scandal, and, forever after, was vulnerable to the mischief of whatever enemy or detractor might come forth.

THE HOUSE THAT MERRITT BUILT

The cause of the scandal that broke around the University in 1874 was the impatience of the Regents in building the campus at Berkeley. By entrusting supervision of the construction of the College of Letters (North Hall) to one of their own number, Dr. Samuel Merritt, instead of an independent architect; by allowing him considerable latitude in changing specifications; and by acquiring special legislative exemption from the 1870 statute that required work on public buildings to be done by the day and under the eight-hour system, the Regents stepped on many toes. Those offended included professional architects and contractors; the workingmen for whose benefit the "eight-hour" law had been passed; Merritt's competitors in the building and building-supply business; and social reformers who could not resist an opportunity to embarrass the University and its Regents as representative of the Establishment, and Dr. Merritt as a 6-foot, 3-inch, 340-pound personification of the acquisitive rich. The San Francisco *Evening Post,* edited by the inventive economist and social reformer Henry George, began suggesting as early as January 6, 1874, that wrong-doing was involved in the building of the College of Letters. A few weeks later, it protested: "If we are to have a State University, we want one whose buildings will not be monuments of corruption and rascality. . . ." [2]

On January 8, 1874, the assembly authorized its public-building committee to investigate the University's management of the construction work at Berkeley. It began taking testimony in San Francisco in the middle of January and continued its hearings through March 3. The Regents met almost daily during this same period. Hundreds of pages of testimony were taken. Broadly reviewed, the charges were that Merritt and some friends in the building industry had taken advantage of Merritt's unusual authority in the supervision of the building of the College of Letters; that Merritt himself had profited financially in the venture; and that the University had acquired a building of inferior quality at an exorbitant cost. When the investigations [3] concluded, the assembly committee announced its finding that the College of Letters building cost $24,000 more than it was worth.[4] Almost all of the blame was placed on Dr. Merritt. The rest of the Regents were scolded only for making a "gross blunder" [5] in giving Merritt too much power in building matters and for their "clannishness" [6] in supporting him when his mismanagement of their trust and the public's funds became evident.

Dr. Merritt resigned from the Board of Regents in June, 1874, and in

October refunded to the University $867 in profits earned by his Oakland Lumber Yard when the College of Letters was under construction.[7]

ATTACK FROM ANOTHER SECTOR

While the College of Letters investigation was in process, legislators were pondering a "Memorial of the California State Grange and Mechanics' Deliberative Assembly." This document was prepared by a joint committee of the two organizations to advise lawmakers in Sacramento that the University was not carrying out in good faith the "leading object" of the Morrill Land Grant Act, which was "without excluding other scientific and classical studies, and including military tactics, to teach such branches of learning as are related to agriculture and the mechanic arts, in such manner as the Legislatures of the States may respectively prescribe, in order to promote the liberal *and practical* education in the industrial classes *in their several pursuits.*" [8]

The memorial charged that only one-twentieth of the University's expenditures was devoted to the agricultural department and that only one professor was discharging all of the work in that subject. Furthermore, no technical instruction in the mechanic arts had been given. By way of remedy, the committee suggested an appropriation sufficient to support a long list of agricultural programs, including "a plain, convenient, and commodious frame house, with suitable outhouses, to be occupied by the Professor of Agriculture or some practical farmer to act under his direction." [9] The memorial also asked for appropriations sufficient to secure the *"practical* instruction in the mechanic arts; to provide blacksmiths', carpenters', cabinet, and machine shops, and printing press under the supervision of competent persons." [10] This recitation of specific needs was suspiciously similar in content and wording to the unrequited demands Professor Carr had made upon the Regents from at least 1872 on to the time of the hearings.

Moving to more general recommendations, the memorial suggested that the University should be placed in charge of a state board of education, which would also have charge of a state normal school and other public schools. The board would consist of fifteen Regents, including the six who were already ex-officio members of the University Board of Regents and the master of the state Grange. Eight of the new Regents would be elected to four-year terms from each congressional district. The University's independent Board of Regents would be abolished.

The memorialists further suggested that the University's management of the federal land grants be investigated, and they concluded with a request that the legislature "order that black letters be prepared and placed upon the east and west faces of the main building [South Hall] of the University, marking it for all time with the words, AGRICULTURAL COLLEGE OF THE UNIVERSITY OF CALIFORNIA." [11]

The Regents of the University were confident that their management of the University could bear scrutiny. They welcomed an inquiry into the questions raised by the Mechanics and Grangers, proposing on February 17, 1874, that the inquiry concern:

1st. What instruction has been given in Agriculture and the Mechanic Arts in the University of California; whether the same has been defective or not; and if defective, wherein such defects consist, and what is the cause as well as the remedy of such defects.

2nd. What has been the management by the Regents of the University of California, of the 150,000 acres of agricultural lands donated by Congress to the State of California, and by the State to the University; whether the same has been defective or not; and if defective, wherein such defect has existed, and what is the cause, as well as the remedy, of such defects.

3d. Whether or not the Regents of the University have properly administered the funds of the University which have been entrusted to them; and if not, in what particulars. [12]

On February 23, 1874, a newly appointed joint committee of the senate and assembly met with the Regents in Sacramento. The committee chairman announced that an inquiry into the management of the University would be made beginning on March 3, a week away and the day after the College of Letters investigation was closed. To the three subjects suggested by the Regents, a fourth, more sweeping topic was added:

4th. Also upon any other matters relating to the University upon which in the opinion of the committee, further information may be of use to the Legislature or the public. [13]

The University's answers to the questions under the legislative inquiry were prepared in advance by President Gilman, with the help of the faculty; by the secretary of the Regents; and by the University's land agent. These documents constituted the case for the University's defense. They pointed out that the agricultural college land grant received from the federal government was only one of six sources of the University's original endowment.

Others included the old Seminary of Learning grant, a smaller public building grant made by the federal government, property donated by the College of California, certain grants made by the California legislature, and gifts from private donors. The authors of the University documents also pointed out that Senator Morrill's act of 1862 did not require institutions benefiting from its provisions to emphasize the mechanic arts and agriculture to the exclusion of other subjects. By establishing a College of Agriculture as the first unit in the University of California, the Regents had observed the spirit of the Morrill Act and the letter of the University's own Organic Act of 1868. They contended further that the agricultural students at the University received full advantage of all of the University's resources and offerings. The authors submitted a description of the special course in agriculture that was written by Professor Carr himself. According to that description, agricultural studies included "in the Junior year, the chemical composition of agricultural plants; the plant, as an organism, adapted to perform certain work; the material when wrought; the forces by which the work was accomplished; the relation of the plant to the atmosphere (agricultural meteorology) and to the soil; the nature, origin and composition of the soil. The Senior studies will include tillage, irrigation, drainage, reclamation of land, field crops, sheep and cattle husbandry, forest and arboriculture, sericulture, fruit and other special cultures, household and rural economies; together with a part of the lectures mentioned under the preceding year." [14] The authors of the defense documents also submitted a list of needs of the University for agricultural facilities that available financial resources could not meet. This list was also prepared by Professor Carr. It included facilities for scientific and practical experiments in agriculture and horticulture, instruction in economic botany and zoology, and instruction in applied mathematics. It also mentioned the desirability of employing experts in special cultures, "as the vine, silk, fish, in Veterinary Science, Agricultural Entomology; and the Mechanics of Agriculture, to give from three to fifteen lectures annually." Finally, the accounting of unmet needs included the recommendation that a farmers' institute be held at the University each year.[15]

With respect to the other mechanic arts, the University's case stressed that the engineering studies of the University "are closely related" to mechanic arts.[16] It also reminded the legislators that men eminently associated with the University, Regent Hallidie and President Gilman, had demonstrated their sympathy for vocational education by raising funds to begin a vocational school in San Francisco. That plan had been set aside only when it was learned that James Lick, the wealthy, eccentric former cabinetmaker, was leaving enough money in his will to provide for such a school without the help of other donors.

The entire history of the management of California's land grant under the Morrill Act was included in the University's case statement. It pointed out that steps had been taken to protect settlers and to discourage irresponsible exploitation of timber land. It showed that under the management of the Regents, California's land grants were sold for a higher price than those of all but one other state. In all, a principal of $114,000 was acquired by 1874. Of that amount, $79,710 was in the Bank of California earning 6 per cent interest. The remainder was temporarily invested in the purchase of the four "college blocks" that originally belonged to the College of California in Oakland. Between 1868 and 1874, the Regents received $32,221.57 in interest from the investment of Morrill land-grant revenues. This interest, the only income from the Morrill Act land grants that could be used for operations, averaged out to about $450 a month. The University authors took care to note that the salary of the professor of agriculture "alone" was $300 a month.[17] That point alone shattered arguments that the University had usurped the Morrill land-grant income for purposes other than support of instruction in agriculture and the mechanic arts.

The University's answer concluded with a completely audited financial history and reports on plans for the future development of the Berkeley site and increased service to California agriculture.

THE CASE FOR THE PROSECUTION

The prosecution was represented by two star witnesses. One was Professor Carr. The wording and detail of his requests to the Regents for support of the College of Agriculture had turned up in portions of the memorial of the Mechanics and Grangers that inspired the investigation. He could not disavow the memorial, therefore, without losing face with those who had seen fit to become his champions in the legislative arena. Nor could he openly charge the University with gross misconduct without putting his job on the line, and without exposing the institution to public abuse for which he would have to accept responsibility if his charges should fall under heat of inquiry. His testimony was masterfully noncommittal.

The other star witness was William T. Swinton, the first professor of the English language, English literature, and history at the University. Swinton was a friend of Henry George, the editor of the San Francisco *Evening Post,* which, it will be recalled, took editorial relish in salting the Regents' wounds during the College of Letters investigation in January and February of 1874. But Swinton's hostility toward the Regents was personal, and possibly unrelated to his friendship with Henry George. The Board, apparently on Gilman's recommendation, refused to allow Swinton to take a prolonged leave of absence to edit some school geographies he had written and which were being published in New York. The refusal led to Swinton's resignation from the faculty on March 2, the day before the legislature's investigation of the general management of the University began.

Swinton had no reason to follow Carr's moderate example. Asked for suggestions for improvement of the University, he responded: "As a measure of economy, I should say that the abolition of the office of President would be a desirable measure." [18] He claimed that Gilman had "put the Board of Regents in a sort of tacit attitude of antagonism to the wishes of the people of the State in regard to certain phases of practical education." [19] He also asserted that the students lacked confidence in Gilman. The students were surprised to find that out and wrote to the legislature to disclaim Swinton's estimate of their attitudes and to declare "President Gilman is our true friend." [20]

THE VERDICT

After study of the Grangers' and Mechanics' memorial, the Regents' case statements, a lengthy written deposition volunteered by Professor Swinton, and the information yielded in testimony at the hearings, the joint committee issued its report. It said that "the Regents and Faculty of the University have done as well as any reasonable citizen could expect. Our state is young, and the University is in its very infancy. We could not, therefore, reasonably expect, at this date, any great results. We do not gather ripe and luscious fruit from very young trees. . . ." [21]

Gilman reported the results of the investigation to his friend President Andrew White of Cornell, in these words:

> The legislature refrained from all adverse legislation, made the Pres. an ex-officio member of the Board of Regents, and gave us all the pecuniary help we had asked for. So we stand today. But the peril to the Univ. has been great. The Grangers were determined to capture the concern,—up to the last moments were endeavoring to abolish the Board of Regents, and substitute a Board chosen by popular election—two from each congressional district. Dr. Carr, who appears to

have instigated the whole movement, at the last of it backed down, testified that he had never heard any complaint! That as far as indoor instruction was concerned, the Univ. compared favorably with any institution in the country, etc., etc.! The whole battle had its droll as well as its provoking side.[22]

Gilman's relief that the University had not been severely damaged by the investigation was overshadowed by his fears that the political climate of California was hostile to the development of a "true University." [23] On April 8, 1874, he wrote to the Regents about his apprehensions:

The University of California is now organized on a comprehensive and liberal basis. Its plans are in accord with the best experience of modern institutions in other States and countries. I believe in it as it stands, rejoicing that in so short a time so much has been done. . . . I am heartily in sympathy with the introduction of science into higher educational establishments and eager to see also the wide diffusion of technical instruction. But because I cannot assent to some of the radical demands which would overthrow the University, abolish the Regents, and entirely change the present course of study, I am exposed to censure.[24]

Later, in the same letter, he declared: "For University fighting I have no training; in University work I delight. I therefore beg of you to release me from the post I hold, at the earliest day you can consistently do so." [25]

Gilman was persuaded to withdraw his resignation, but the idea of leaving the University was not dismissed from his mind.

ANOTHER LOOK AT PROFESSOR CARR

During and after the investigations of the University in early 1874, discreet inquiries were belatedly made to men who had known Professor Carr's work before he came to California. The most revealing reply came from Paul Chadbourne, who had been chancellor of the University of Wisconsin when Carr left it. In a letter to a friend in California, Chadbourne said: "If he [Carr] (or rather his wife, for she is the guiding power), has begun to play the Wisconsin role in Cal. . . . there will be mischief enough, unless Pres. Gilman has the good fortune to know as much of him as I did . . . he was not fit for his place and he knew it—and *he knew that I knew it.* . . ." [26]

Gilman's personal compilation of Carr's record contained a long, damning list of particulars. Carr was "behind hand" in his knowledge of agriculture; he could not make a proper chemical analysis; he had never made any experiments or researches in any department of agriculture; he was negligent in attendance at faculty meetings; he was frequently absent from his recitations and lectures; he had made the agricultural college "notoriously 'easy' " for the students; many letters sent out by him were actually written by his wife, though his name appeared as signator; he had attempted to marshal public opinion against the University and its Board of Regents; and his proposal for additional expenditures in the department of agriculture included items for his personal advantage (that model farmhouse in which the professor of agriculture would reside, for instance).[27]

Beyond these specific grievances, Gilman was concerned about a serious conflict in educational philosophy between Carr and himself. Carr believed that the farmer would be raised to professional status if he could show a diploma proving that he had been taught how to plow, sow, and reap at a university. Gilman believed that a university could teach such subjects no better than a farm parent or a good foreman could. He also believed that the farmer's station in life would be improved to whatever extent the methods of science could be applied to agricultural problems. Gilman saw no shame in having only one student enrolled in the University's agricultural course as long as that student was learning how to uncover new truths that all of the state's farmers could use. Carr, on the other hand, considered it disgraceful to have a student body at the University in which the proportion of agricultural students bore no relationship to the proportion of farmers in the total population of the state.

Because of this difference of opinion on basic policy, as much as the imposing evidence of his incompetence, Carr was asked to resign. When he refused to do so, he was dismissed on August 11, 1874.

Carr's friends rallied just as soon as he was seen to be in difficulty. On August 8, three days before Carr was dismissed, the Grangers, Mechanics' State Council, and Mechanics' Deliberative Assembly sent a series of resolutions to the Regents, opposing the impending action against Carr, and demanding that both the agricultural and mechanical departments of the University "each receive as much money and as much attention as the College of Letters." [28] This document did little more than arouse further public controversy.

California's newspapers took sides. The *Daily Evening Post* said that "every one of the Regents who voted for the resignation of Professor Carr is either a rich lawyer or a capitalist. . . ." [29] The San Jose *Mercury* called Carr's removal "treachery to the people." [30] Carr's friends clipped newspaper stories that criticized his dismissal and sent them to editors who had not yet been heard from. When the editor of the *Grass Valley Union* received such a selection, however, he advised his readers that they had been sent so that "Professor Carr and his circumstances may be kept before the public." [31] He then said: "We have to say that we are not one of the newspapers that is jumping stiff-legged because Professor Carr was invited to resign his chair, and, failing to accept the invitation, was incontinently ousted by the Board of Regents. These Regents are at the University for the purpose of governing the institution, and we presume that they are doing their duty to the best of their ability." [32]

Professor Carr put together his own defense in a pamphlet entitled *The University of California and its Relation to Industrial Education*. In it, he recapitulated the original charges of the Grangers and the Mechanics, published the full testimony of William Swinton before the joint legislative committee the previous spring, and included a long introductory article in which he blamed the University's problems on the Regents because they had "unfortunately, placed too much power in the hands of the President, a person without experience in Government, without knowledge, interest or sympathy in industrial education, and who had obtained a recognized position among the obstructionists." [33]

Carr's most sensational revelations appeared in a section headed "ARE THE REGENTS HONORABLE MEN?" [34] There he reported that A. Higbie, chairman of the assembly committee on education, had secured from Regent John Dwinelle a pledge of immunity for Professor Carr, if a pending bill transferring management of the University from the Regents to an elected state board of education were killed. According to Higbie, Dwinelle specifically promised that Carr would not be publicly associated with the Grangers' charges against the University and that Carr would be fired "only for such causes as would remove a Professor from any Chair." [35] The bill died. So did another calling for the election of the president of the University by the faculty.

Carr's story of this incident was published in September, 1874. In that same month, Dwinelle attended his last meeting of the Board of Regents. The exposure of his transaction with Higbie, made inevitable by the dismissal of Carr, left him no alternative but to resign. He had been, on the whole, one of the most thoughtful and articulate members of the Board. If Gilman had understood the University as a doctor might understand a patient, Dwinelle had understood it as a father might understand a son. Even the desperate act that brought about his resignation was one of loyalty to the institution that his pen and his advocacy had brought into being six years before.

GILMAN RESIGNS

The ease with which the California legislature could be moved into the service of popular political causes frightened President Gilman. He wrote:

> The University of California is . . . nominally administered by the Regents; it is virtually administered by the legislature. The Political Code, which went into operation on the first of January 1873, placed the Regents in the position of a commission of the legislature liable "to be sponged out" in a single hour of partisan clamor; and the mode of procedure during the last session of the legislature, although it resulted in nothing which was openly harmful, showed clearly what might have happened if the legislature had been composed of a more hostile element.
>
> Moreover, the revelations of that session were such that five gentlemen, whose names I could give were it not for the confidence with which all such communications should be regarded, each of whom had contemplated large gifts to the University informed me that they could not now bestow their gifts upon an institution which might be swept away in any hour.[36]

Plagued by all of these reservations about the future of the University of California, Gilman gave serious attention to possibilities of returning East. Throughout the fall of 1874, he considered an opportunity offered to him by the trustees of the Johns Hopkins University of Baltimore. It involved nothing less than creating a new institution without restriction of precedent or the interference of political manipulators. It was so perfectly suited to his abilities and his temperament that he would have been tempted away even if his experiences in California had been more pleasant. He submitted his resignation to the Regents December 9, 1874. This time he could not be persuaded to withdraw it. Among those who understood his decision best was John Dwinelle. "Of course you will accept the Baltimore appointment," Dwinelle wrote. "We have not furnished you the entertainment to which you were invited. We are on the eve of a contest where the Board of Regents is to be assailed by falsehood, malice and every kind of nastiness from the outside, aided by treachery from within. We did not invite you to this, and you have the right to retire from it, particularly when the mode of retirement comes in the form of accepted reward of well-doing—promotion." [37]

Dwinelle's prophecy was near the mark. Carr was no sooner dismissed than his supporters called for the election of legislators pledged to help abolish the Regents, reserve the agricultural college land grants for practical instruction, and transfer the University to the control of an elected board of education, thus making it a part of the common school system. On February 8, 1876, the speaker of the assembly, Gideon J. Carpenter, introduced a bill to achieve all of these ends. One provision of his bill was especially distasteful to some of the Regents. It made the superintendent of public instruction the secretary and member of the executive committee of the proposed board.[38] The man elected to this potentially dominant position in 1875 was the deposed professor of agriculture, Ezra S. Carr.

Carpenter's bill was passed by the assembly on March 9, 1876, but consideration of it was indefinitely postponed in the senate on March 29. At the next session of the legislature, the measure was revived by Senator N. Greene Curtis (who became a Regent a few years later). Curtis made two minor revisions in the old Carpenter bill. One made the president of the University, as well as the superintendent of public instruction, an ex-officio member of the executive committee of the board of education. The other provided that "colleges would be located in various parts of the state to provide practical instruction in agriculture and the mechanical arts." [39]

In February, 1878, fourteen Regents signed a memorial to the legislature pointing out the "Disastrous Effects" of the passage of the Curtis bill. They contended, first of all, that if the constitution of California had intended that the University be a part of the common school system it would not have devoted a separate section to provisions anticipating its establishment. They also asserted that by abolishing the corporation of the Regents, the legislature would forfeit the gifts from the College of California, Regent Tompkins, and others, since these had been made to the Regents or had been made under the assumption that the University would remain an independent institution beyond political control. The Regents also stated that the elected members of the proposed board of education would have so much of their time taken up by other educational matters and would be so scattered throughout the state that they could not efficiently attend to the work of the University. Their clinching argument was that "in the history of all institutions of the higher education, it has been found that they owe their prosperity, and the valuable endowments they receive, to the commanding fact that they are organized upon a principle indestructibly uniform, though progressive, and that they are organically exempt from the disturbing effects of political intervention. In such a position it was the purpose of its founders to place the present University. If that purpose should fail, the State will have to charge itself with the entire maintenance of the institution, as no foundations, endowments, donations, or bequests, will ever be made in the future, after a change in its organization so absolute has been effected." [40] The Curtis bill was withdrawn on March 6, 1878.

THE NEW CONSTITUTION

These were difficult times. The state had not recovered fully from the financial panic that came to the whole nation earlier in the decade. Drought in 1876–1877 deprived the farmers of their harvests and incomes. Men were out of work everywhere. The workingmen, led by Dennis Kearney and others, formed a political party to work for reforms that might bring more jobs, better education for their children, and tighter regulations on big business and monopolies of all kinds. As an instrument of reform, a new constitution, revised to suit the needs of California after almost thirty years of population growth and economic, social, and political change, was advocated by the new party and many other Californians as well. In response to these sentiments, a Constitutional Convention was called in Sacramento in September, 1878.

Those delegates who still favored the point of view of the Grangers toward the University took advantage of the convention to attempt to write a boiled-down version of the Carpenter and Curtis bills into the constitution. Other delegates worked equally hard to preserve the management of the University in its original form. The debates between the two factions were a grand recapitulation of every controversy that had touched the University since 1873.

The University's interests were well served by eight delegates who were, or who recently had been, Regents.[41] They defended the University against attack and corrected the record when hostile delegates inaccurately described its management or circumstances. They were so effective that two delegates who had come to the convention prejudiced against the University's management concluded, as one of them said, "that a great deal of the clamor and prejudice is . . . unfounded." [42] Another loyal University supporter was Jacob R. Freud, '76, the only University alumnus among the delegates. He proved the quality of the education he had received at Berkeley in an oration that made up in embellishment what it lacked in brevity. "Election of Regents involves the destruction and ruin of the University," [43] he warned. "Political prejudices and conspiracies creep into the institution and poison its best blood, and vitiate its highest energies. It sets the University adrift upon the boisterous sea of politics, sure to wreck to pieces on the rocks of partisan strife and party contention. A careful research into this matter has thoroughly convinced me that no surer and quicker way could be devised to strangle our young University than thus to hurl it into the cesspool and whirlpool of politics." [44]

The most strategically placed University supporter was a San Francisco lawyer, former president of that city's school board and, since 1875, a Regent of the University—Joseph W. Winans. Winans was named chairman of the convention's education committee, through which any provision altering the management of the University would have to pass. On the same committee was another Regent, J. West Martin, a banker and president of the Oakland Gaslight Company.

Suggestions for the section of the new constitution dealing with the University included abolishing it in favor of an institution teaching only the mechanical arts and sciences, and one proposal that would place it under the direct control of the legislature. The classic argument favoring legislative control was presented by Joseph C. Brown of Tulare County:

> What has been given and donated to that institution [the University] cannot be taken away by the Legislature. I am under the impression that we may safely lodge with the Legislature power even to remove the Regents, if it shall become necessary. Why should not the Regents be amenable to Legislative authority when they do anything amiss? I cannot see anything wrong in it. Now, if there is anything in this section [the proposal to give the control of the University directly to the legislature] that is contrary to the Act of Congress, I have not seen it. I have heard it asserted, but I cannot see it; neither is there anything antagonistic, except it be antagonistic to say that the Regents shall not be superior to the law.[45]

The counter argument was offered by Winans: "There are men in this state who are anxious to make donations to this institution the moment it is placed on a permanent basis. But so long as it is made subject to Legislative caprice; so long as it can be made to subserve sectarian and political designs, it never will flourish. . . ." [46]

The measure finally incorporated into the constitution as Article IX, Section 9, was a victory—narrowly won—for those who followed Winans' reasoning. The provision declared the University to be a "public trust," and provided that its organization and government should

> . . . be perpetually continued in the form and character prescribed by the Organic act creating the same . . . (and the several Acts amendatory thereof), subject only to such legislative control as may be necessary to insure compliance with the terms of its endowments and the proper investment and security of its funds. It shall be entirely independent of all political or sectarian influence, and kept free therefrom in the appointment of its Regents and in the administration of its affairs; provided, that all the money derived from the sale of the public

lands donated to this State by Act of Congress, approved July second, eighteen hundred and sixty-two (and the several Acts amendatory thereof), shall be invested as provided by said Act of Congress; and the interest of said moneys shall be inviolably appropriated to the endowment, support, and maintenance of at least one College of Agriculture, where the leading objects shall be (without excluding other scientific and classical studies, and including military tactics) to teach such branches of learning as are related to scientific and practical agriculture and the mechanic arts, in accordance with the requirements and conditions of said Acts of Congress; and the Legislature shall provide that if, through neglect, misappropriation, or any other contingency, any portion of the fund so set apart shall be diminished or lost, the State shall replace such portions so lost or misappropriated, so that the principal thereof shall remain forever undiminished.[47]

The constitutional provision also contained the statement that: "No person shall be debarred admission to any of the collegiate departments of the University on account of sex." [48] Except very briefly at an affiliated school, admission to both men and women had been available at the University since 1870. The sentence nevertheless pleased the delegates who wanted to do something for the ladies. It also made it possible for a disgruntled delegate to say: "The section relating to the government of the State University is not viewed with much favor. Its adoption was secured, not on its merits, but by an alliance between its supporters and the advocates of women's suffrage." [49]

The constitution submitted to the people in 1879 was regarded as too radical by those who were politically and economically conservative. It was regarded as too conservative by the workingmen and the farmers who had sought revision of the old constitution as a means of reform. Winans and three other Regents were among those who believed that the constitution went too far in its reforms. They eventually voted against it. The people in the Granger-dominated rural areas figured most prominently in the approval of the constitution by a narrow 11,000-vote margin in popular election. The University's protection from "pernicious political influence" [50] was won, therefore, from precisely the sector most responsible for political interference in the preceding tumultuous decade.

II

The Structure Rises

❧❧❧❧❧❧

THE UNIVERSITY of California gained maturity much faster than many people realize. Before it was twenty-five years old, it stood among the highest ten universities in the country ranked according to such quantitative criteria as enrollment, size of faculty, income, and number of graduate students. Before it was fifty years old, it was judged to be among fifteen great universities of the United States.

Reasons for such a rapid rise to eminence are hard to find within the University. For fifteen years after Gilman's departure, the University was under the nominal leadership of conscientious but inexperienced and unqualified presidents. For another nine years, the conservative, sound, but unspectacular Martin Kellogg was the University's chief executive. Throughout the whole twenty-four years between 1875 and 1899 the Regents of the University were the real managers, giving attention to the most minute details of operations, hiring and firing faculty members and presidents with the same care and sensitivity they might use in dealing with bank tellers or ranch foremen. The original financial support of the University was scandalously inadequate, and based, unbelievably, on nothing more than the relatively small state and federal endowments that were created in 1868.

These internal shortcomings were counterbalanced by impelling influences from the outside. Foremost among them was the tremendous, rapid, and diversified growth in California's population and economy. Between 1870 and 1900, the population nearly tripled, going from 560,000 to 1,485,000. The economy that was once tied to agriculture (or gold if you

85

went back far enough) now embraced food processing, transportation, manufacturing, and commerce. There were more jobs that required people with an education, and there were more young people going to college. Between 1870 and 1900, the enrollment of the University rose from 40 to 2,550. A second outside influence was philanthropy. Gilman had inspired such men as James Lick, Dr. Hugh Toland, and Edward Tompkins to make gifts of (1) the world's largest telescope, (2) a medical school, and (3) a chair of Oriental languages to the University. Later philanthropy resulted in the creation of an affiliated law school and an institute of art in San Francisco; a college of commerce at Berkeley; and a site for medical, dental, and pharmacy education on Sutro Heights. Phoebe Apperson Hearst made the University the object of generous and remarkable philanthropy that provided a handsome architectural scheme for the campus at Berkeley, and fostered activities leading to the establishment of a department of anthropology and museum of vertebrate zoology. Annie Alexander provided support for work leading to the creation of a department of paleontology. Down at La Jolla, E. W. and Ellen Browning Scripps provided the subsidy for studies of marine biology that developed into a comprehensive institution for the study of oceanography. A prominent attorney in Sacramento, Peter J. Shields, made no large gift, but almost single-handedly, and without University support to speak of, secured passage of legislation creating a University Farm in Yolo County. The significance of such action and generosity is found less in the monetary value of the gifts received than it is in the fact that they pushed the University into new endeavors and made it reach out beyond its existing limits. A third factor is competition. Until the twentieth century, the University had little competition from public colleges. But when Leland Stanford Junior University, "the most richly endowed private institution in the West," began instruction in 1891, the University's virtual monopoly on university-level endeavor came to an abrupt end. Stanford University was excellent from the start, and the faculty and Regents of the University of California looked over their shoulders more than once to see what Stanford had done in selecting presidents and teachers, or expanding its programs. Competition from the public institutions, especially the junior colleges and state normal schools, became a factor in University planning and policy by 1915. The development of these institutions in southern California, where the University's service was indirect and inadequate, created the spectre of a second, duplicate university, vying with the University of California for support in Sacramento. To avoid such an ominous advent, the Regents extended the University to Los Angeles with the creation of a southern branch. In doing so, they set the precedent for the multi-campus system that became the University of California's most definitive characteristic in the ensuing half-century. Finally, there was the benevolent interest of alumni, including two governors, an unknown number of legislators, and seven Regents. They had a special interest in the University's welfare and prosperity and helped, in many ways, to keep the public's enthusiasm for their alma mater at a high level.

It was a University that was being shaped and fostered largely by external influences, therefore, that Benjamin Ide Wheeler came to lead as president, in 1899. He was badly needed, for the University had developed largely without plan or object. The time had come for someone else to do what Gilman had started to do in 1875—tell Californians what kind of institution they had built, consolidate its strengths, and build toward new greatness. The twenty years that Wheeler gave to these tasks marked one of the golden eras of University of California history.

Chapter 7

THE ERA OF POWERLESS
PRESIDENTS

THE MOST INJURIOUS result of the University's involvement in political controversy in the early 1870s was the resignation of President Gilman. By va-
cating the presidency when the Regents and many leading citizens wanted
him to stay, he left the University leaderless and invited conjecture that the
office was not substantial enough for a man of eminence. By resigning after
the University's vulnerability to political interference was exposed, he invited further conjecture that the office might even be untenable.

Either because they were aware of the shortcomings of the office, or because they were, themselves, weary after long months of political crisis, the
Regents had little enthusiasm for president-hunting after Gilman was gone.
Instead, they settled for several presidents of less than national stature as
educational statesmen and, the better to protect the University from any future charge of mismanagement, assumed direct control over its administration. Under this arrangement, the president was still nominally to blame for
misfortunes befalling the University that could not be explained in any other
way. But he had direct authority only in the areas of student conduct, making a good impression on the public, fund-raising, and maintaining a comfortable relationship between the Regents and members of the faculty. If he
failed in any of these capacities to a degree that aroused criticism outside the
University, his job was in jeopardy. Four presidents discovered as much for
themselves in the fifteen years between 1875 and 1890.

In March, 1875, the Regents called John LeConte back from the classroom to be acting president, and during the fourteen months that he served
in an "acting" capacity the authority and duties of the presidency were
gradually eroded. Some of them were granted to the secretary of the Regents, R. E. C. Stearns. Others were exercised by the Regents themselves,

88

particularly through their Advisory Committee, headed by Regent Stebbins, and the Finance Committee under the chairmanship of Andrew Hallidie. In a memorandum still preserved in the University archives, J. Ham Harris, assistant to Secretary Stearns, wrote: "Under the present regime, the Acting President is but little more than the President of the Academic Senate— not being consulted as to the management of the grounds and buildings or the employees of the University." [1] LeConte became the full-fledged president of the University in June, 1876. But the change in title did not significantly increase his authority.

During LeConte's second administration, the University received such famous gifts as the Lick Observatory, the old Bacon Art and Library Building, and a badly needed gymnasium. Negotiations for the establishment of the University-affiliated Hastings College of the Law in San Francisco were also concluded. But most of these benefactions were a response to the excitement that Daniel Coit Gilman had generated for the University's upbuilding during his brief sojourn in California. LeConte was unable to generate anything like it on his own. Regrettably, this failure was not fully discerned until the University faced impending financial crisis at the end of the 1870s.

LeConte's ability to deal with students was tested in 1879 and 1880. The first test was provided by the secret societies (fraternities) that had, by 1879, a strong foothold at the University with influence that dominated the better-established student activities. Rivalry between students who were privileged to belong to fraternities and those who were not became bitter in 1878. To put an end to this divisive element in the student body and, in the same action, to curtail shameful and excessive behavior reputed to be typical of the fraternity man at leisure, conservative Regents and faculty members decided to abolish secret societies. Formal action for this purpose was taken by both the Board of Regents and the Academic Senate, but, in the face of immediate protests from parents of students and prominent alumni, they were forced to retreat. Because he was president at the time, John LeConte took much of the blame for the University's embarrassment when the policy was officially rescinded in 1880. The second incident involved publication of what, in those days, was regarded as an obscene parody of the Junior Class Day Program. In righteous indignation, President LeConte suspended most of the Sophomore class for complicity in the affair. The suspensions were big news and the newspapers treated them accordingly. The public lined up in two camps: one made up of those who were shocked because the University's discipline permitted such an indecent occurrence in the first place, and another made up of those who considered LeConte's penalty too arbitrary and severe. The case was especially sensitive because the sons and relatives of several prominent Californians (including a Regent) were among those suspended.

President LeConte's popularity declined rapidly after the student discipline incidents of 1879, and his position was further weakened because he was unable to head off financial difficulties that befell the University beginning in 1880 and 1881. Explaining that LeConte lacked administrative ability, Stebbins' Advisory Committee, under the new name of Committee on Instruction and Visitation, recommended in May, 1881, that the office of president and the chair of physics be declared vacant.[2]

The rationale for the Stebbins committee report was the need for economy. Thus, the recommended dismissal of LeConte was coupled with recommendations that the chair of mathematics, the offices of instructor of physics and mechanics, instructor in Spanish, and one office of instructor of chemistry should also be declared vacant. A reduction in faculty salaries was also proposed.[3] The Regents postponed action on these recommendations for one week, and on the eve of the meeting at which final action was to be taken, LeConte wrote out his letter of resignation from the presidency. The next day, June 7, contrary to the recommendation of the Stebbins committee, the Regents voted to allow LeConte to retain his professorship in physics.[4]

LeConte had influential friends. So did William T. Welcker, the dismissed professor of mathematics. So their dismissals brought forth a hue and cry. The *Wasp,* a San Francisco periodical, claimed that the dismissal of LeConte was due to the Regents' need of a scapegoat, notably for "the secret society fight and the Sophomore expulsion." [5] To charges that LeConte was an incompetent administrator, Regent Winans responded, "I am satisfied that the President administered the affairs of the University with as much ability as a President can, unless he is made an executive officer." [6] Another Regent anonymously told a San Francisco *Examiner* reporter, "The fact is, that if he had the executive ability of a Wellington and Napoleon combined, he has no chance to use it. Stebbins runs the committee and Stearns runs Stebbins, and between them they manage or mismanage all of the affairs of the University to the minutest details." [7] Stearns' dislike of LeConte was well known and is easily documented in some of his letters to Regent Davidson, with whom the secretary enjoyed a very close friendship during this period.[8] Davidson, incidentally, was identified by alumni in newspaper accounts of the dismissals as the man who visited Welcker's class for a half-hour and then advised the Stebbins committee that the methods of the professor were out of date.[9] About fifty alumni of the University, meeting in the Pioneer Hall in San Francisco, complained that the investigation of Welcker's com-

petency had been inadequate and passed a resolution demanding his reinstatement. Members of the class of 1881 also petitioned the Regents for a
reexamination of the charges against LeConte and Welcker, alleging that
their dismissals were part of an intrigue by Bernard Moses, professor of history and political economy, and Edward Rowland Sill, professor of the English language and literature, to acquire power for themselves. The petition
went so far as to allege that the two professors had tried to bribe the fraternities "to use their influences to this object." [10]

Charges that the move was politically inspired came out almost as soon as
the Advisory Committee recommendations were public knowledge. Regent
Winans made the charge first, in his interview with a San Francisco *Examiner* reporter on June 4.[11] But the fuel for the charge existed as early as January, when the *Examiner* pointed out that Governor Perkins, a Republican,
had replaced Regents Casserly, Bowie, and Archer, all Democrats whose
terms expired in 1880, with Republicans, despite the fact that all three retiring Regents were "eminently worthy of being reappointed." [12] The result
was that the appointed members of the Board consisted of eleven Republicans and four Democrats,[13] with one seat vacant. Possibly in the heat of
these charges, Perkins filled the vacancy by appointing former State Senator
N. Greene Curtis, a Democrat, to fill the remaining vacancy. By the time of
the LeConte–Welcker dismissals, then, the Board of Regents consisted of
eleven appointed and five ex-officio Regents who were Republicans and
four appointed and one ex-officio (LeConte) Regents who were Democrats.
Despite this alignment, Welcker, who like LeConte was not only a Democrat but a former servant of the Confederacy, told the Oakland *Tribune*'s
reporter that the reason for his dismissal "may or may not be a political one;
but I think not." [14]

By the end of June, 1881, the victims of the Regents' action—LeConte,
Welcker, and the dismissed instructors—were no longer the center of controversy. Instead, it was the powerful Advisory Committee which had recommended the firings that came under attack. Its opponents were in the
minority on the Board, mustering only from six to eight votes, depending on
the point at issue. Three of them were Democrats, including J. West Martin,
in his tenth year as Regent; Judge John Hager, a Regent since 1868; and
Judge William Wallace, a Regent since the beginning of LeConte's presidency in 1875. Others were the president of the State Agricultural Society,
James McMillan Shafter; John Beard (on some issues), the first alumnus to
serve on the Board of Regents; Judge Winans, who had worked so hard to
free the University from political influence during the Constitutional Convention of 1878; and, surprisingly, Governor Perkins. On June 5, 1881,

Judge Hager was quoted as saying that the Advisory Committee was "usurping the functions of other committees and of the President and violating the law. . . . No such power as they exercised had been delegated to them, and their silent, secret course of action towards a gentleman so well known and highly esteemed all through the world of letters as President LeConte was not only good evidence of destitution, so far as the possession of magnanimity was concerned, but also indecent and deserving of the severest censure." [15]

The Committee on Instruction and Visitation and the Regents who supported it were soon labeled "The Stebbins Ring," and charged with plotting to capture the University and run it as they pleased. The minority Regents found damning evidence to support this theory when they learned that Harvard's Charles Eliot had written a testimonial letter for Stebbins' candidate as LeConte's successor more than a month before Stebbins' committee recommended that the presidency be vacated.[16]

THE RING'S CHOICE

The subject of that correspondence was William T. Reid. A son of Harvard, he had been a high school principal in Rhode Island and Massachusetts before coming to California in 1875. In June, 1881, he was thirty-eight years old and in his sixth year as principal of the Boys' High School of San Francisco. He was first nominated for the presidency of the University by Regent Stebbins on the same day that President LeConte's resignation was accepted. At the same meeting, other Regents nominated Professor Martin Kellogg, General George Stoneman, Judge W. C. Belcher, and Regent J. M. Shafter. Later the name of Bishop E. O. Haven was placed before the Board. Regent Shafter was president of the State Agricultural Society and the favorite candidate of Regents opposing the so-called ring. He promised that if he was elected he would serve only until a more suitable person could take the position. His strategy failed. On June 28, after five ballots, eleven votes were cast for Reid and seven were cast for Shafter.[17]

Reid's selection disappointed the friends of John LeConte, and they included most members of the faculty. Some of the Regents who resented Stebbins' influence on the Board and opposed his presidential candidate refused to attend Reid's inauguration. The students had read, and believed, that under Reid's principalship the Boys' High School of San Francisco had become a Harvard "stuffing school" and were prepared to mistrust their new president's loyalty to California. On Junior Day, 1881, a compliment to Le-

Conte "evoked loud applause" from the students while an expression of good wishes to Reid "was received with solemn and ominous silence. . . ." [18]

President Reid was sure that if the faculty, the students, and the people of. California gave him a chance he could overcome the prejudices that had built up against him. All he needed to do was to restore confidence. To do that, one of his first jobs would be to reverse the downward trend of the University's enrollment. It had dropped from 332 in 1878–1879 to 268 the next year. In 1882–1883 it sank still further to an embarrassing low of 215.

He could not do much about the prevailing economic recession that accounted for part of the decline. But he was eminently qualified to do something about another significant cause. That was the almost total abandonment, after enactment of the constitution of 1879, of community efforts to build public high schools. The farmers and workingmen of the 1880s generally believed that keeping young people in school longer than necessary to prepare them for life on the farm or work in the factory was a waste of time and money, and they carried that belief into the new state constitution by making no provision for state support of high schools. The problem posed for the University by this omission was to maintain reasonably high requirements without enough schools where students could prepare to pass the entrance examinations.[19] In 1882, President Reid said, "As nearly as I can determine, out of the fifty-two counties in the State but seven offer opportunities for preparation for the University at the public schools, and under the operation of the new Constitution the number of High Schools has already diminished by one. In other words, our boasted free University is free to those who can afford to pay for preparatory education, but practically cut off from those who are not able to incur this preliminary expense—the very persons whose education it is of especial interest to the State to secure." [20]

Reid encouraged the Regents and the faculty to provide incentive for local school boards to create public high schools even if state financial support was unavailable. His strategy was to keep the University's admissions requirements high and to force school boards to initiate instruction that would meet them. To make it easier for local school officials to know what the University's standards of admission were, he induced the faculty to substitute written entrance examinations for the old oral ones. Performance on these examinations could be measured objectively and uniformly. Furthermore, once used, examination questions could be distributed to school officials as examples of the level of competence expected from entering students. The first written examinations were given in Los Angeles, Berkeley, and Marysville in 1882.

President Reid then refused to be panicked by declining enrollment as long as the University's standards were not diluted. "A scholarly atmosphere is not created by numbers," he said, "but by a learned Faculty and a body of students, small though it may be, of good ability, good attainments, and enthusiastic in their studies." [21] The only honorable way to increase enrollment was to make it necessary for local communities to provide adequate high schools to prepare their children for the University. He recommended that there should be at least one such school in every county. To realize this goal, he and members of the faculty joined other leaders of California education in meetings with school boards, legislators, and civic groups. They encouraged establishment of local high schools, and mustered political support for some kind of statutory redress of the inadequacies of the new constitution's provisions for education. They were partially successful in 1883, when a state law was passed to permit payment of premiums to schools that offered instruction to "fit and prepare students therein to enter the scientific departments of the University. . . ." [22]

In the following year, the Regents resolved that "upon the request of the Principal of any public school in California whose course of study embraces in kind and extent the subjects required for admission to any college of the University a committee of the Faculty will visit each school and report upon the instruction there given. If the report of such committee be favorable, a graduate of the school upon the personal recommendation of the Principal accompanied by his certificate that the graduate has satisfactorily completed the studies of the course preparatory to the college he wishes to enter, may at the discretion of the Faculty be admitted without examination." [23] The plan was not new. It was borrowed from the University of Michigan, where it was instituted in 1871. Nor did the plan originate with the Regents. The faculty announced it as the policy of the University in 1881, and, ironically, William Reid, then still principal of Boys' High School in San Francisco, was one of two principals who sought to take immediate advantage of it. President LeConte had the visiting committees already appointed, but the idea collapsed when the Regents' Committee on Instruction and Visitation, reluctant to give up the traditional entrance examinations, failed to endorse it. President Reid revived faculty interest in the plan late in 1883 and won the Regents' approval of it in March, 1884.

Before the following June, five schools applied for faculty visitation and two were immediately admitted (the term soon became "accredited"). A third was admitted when it replaced a textbook that the University's visitors judged inadequate. A high school accredited by the University gave a community prestige and, in 1885, three more schools applied for faculty visitations. That same year, enrollment at the University began to rise again.

President Reid's work to encourage high school development did more than increase University enrollment. It also protected the University's high standards for admission and made it unnecessary for the faculty to offer too many remedial or elementary courses. Furthermore, the whole program depended upon faculty cooperation. By relying on faculty advice, assistance, and initiative in this important matter, President Reid probably took one of the most important steps since the writing of the Organic Act to give meaning to the work of the Academic Senate as an instrument of University government. Because of this same relationship, President Reid also was able to nudge the University into modern times by insisting that modern languages receive greater prominence in the curriculum.

An opportunity to make the University of California the object of former Governor Leland Stanford's philanthropy during Reid's presidency foundered. Stanford was one of three men nominated for membership on the Board of Regents by Republican Governor George C. Perkins while the legislature was not in session in 1881. Stanford told Reid on one occasion that he "intended to do something for education" and left the President with "the impression that he had the University in mind." [24] Unfortunately, President Reid never had the chance to find out for sure. After the 1882 elections, the Democratic legislators caucused and voted to reject out-of-hand all interim appointments of Governor Perkins that were awaiting senate confirmation. The names of Stanford and the two other Perkins nominees for the Regency were withdrawn from consideration to avoid the embarrassment of their bearers if they were rejected. One of them, Isaias Hellman, was subsequently renominated by Governor Stoneman and was confirmed, but Stanford was lost to the University's cause forever after.[25]

Despite his backing by the Stebbins majority, President Reid enjoyed no more familiarity with the work of the Board of Regents than had President LeConte. The secretary of the Regents continued to be the closest administrator to the Board. Secretary Stearns resigned as secretary of the Regents to accept another position at about the same time that Reid became president. His successor was Rev. J. H. C. Bonté, one of the most remarkable men in the University's history. Bonté studied law in New York and practiced in Ohio for several years as a young man. But the law did not satisfy him as a career and he entered the theological school of Kenyon College. Two years before his graduation, he became an ordained Episcopal minister. He was rector of churches in Georgetown and Oswego, New York, while he was still in his thirties. In 1870 he came to Sacramento to become rector of what was then Grace Church and remained there until his election in 1881 as secretary of the Regents of the University.[26] Bonté's concern for the University frequently drove him to exhaustion from overwork. He was privy to most of the Regents' deliberations and personally attended to the details of the University's business management. President Reid, on the other hand, was held primarily responsible for the academic endeavor of the University and for student discipline. He was also assigned such time-consuming chores as reporting meteorological and magnetic observations at the University to the Smithsonian Institution, and compiling monthly reports on the hours each professor or instructor gave to class duties each day.[27] When he asked to be relieved of such routine duties so that he could attend to more pressing matters, the Regents turned him down.

Until 1883, President Reid shared his responsibilities in academic matters with Stebbins' Committee on Instruction and Visitation. That division of authority ended when all but two of the ex-officio positions on the Board of Regents were filled by new men as a result of a Democratic victory in the 1882 state elections. One of the new Regents was William T. Welcker,[28] who had lost his professorship at the University only two years before on the recommendation of the Committee on Instruction and Visitation. Welcker had already received partial revenge in the elections when he defeated a member of that committee, F. M. Campbell, in the contest for the office of state superintendent of public instruction. He carried his revenge farther on May 28, 1883, when he led the Regents in action that abolished the committee itself.

The students never trusted Reid. His words to them during his inaugural address were both condescending and tough: "I believe," he said on that occasion, "that, as a rule, students have manly instincts and manly inclinations, and that they may be relied upon to follow these better inclinations if they are made to feel that manly action is expected of them. The exceptions to this rule do not deserve consideration and should be summarily sent from the University as soon as discovered." [29] The students reacted with defiance. They could not forget that Reid had been a high school principal before assuming the presidency of their University and believed that he "was trying to govern the lives and the public morals of university 'men' as he had those of his schoolboys." [30] To demonstrate their disagreement with that position a group of students met outside the President's window one night, thrust a long ladder through a front window, and "to the chant of obscene songs, swung it back and forth, up and down, round and round, till everything breakable within sounded broken and the drunken indignation outside was satisfied or tired." [31]

In 1884, Reid's efforts to tame the University's wild student element took a new turn. In that year he offered a resolution to the Board of Regents that requested the cooperation of Berkeley officials in stricter enforcement of laws prohibiting the sale of liquor within a mile of the campus. These efforts won Reid few friends among Berkeley tavern owners and prompted press criticism that he had a narrow interest in "bossing the boys," and was undermining the public's confidence in the University by statements that tended to advertise the misbehavior of a minority of its students.[32]

In late December, 1884, the new anti-Stebbins majority on the Board of Regents was reported to be "determined in their own minds that a radical change must be made; in other words, that President Reid must be removed." [33] A month later, President Reid submitted his resignation, "to take effect at the close of the present academic year, August 1, 1885." [34]

JUDGE HAGER'S CHOICE

When President Reid resigned in 1885, John Sharpenstein Hager, one of the Regents who was most critical of the Stebbins "ring," was about to make a trip to the Atlantic Coast on business. Aware of his impending departure, the Board resolved to appoint him as a committee of one to interview such potential presidents as might be found in Eastern colleges and universities. He was an impressive emissary. Elected to the Board in 1868, his tenure as a Regent was exceeded only by Hallidie and Stebbins, and by them for only a few weeks. He was an attorney by profession, but was best known for a distinguished record of public service as state senator, district court judge, United States senator, and member of the Constitutional Convention in 1879.

Regent Hager discovered that even in the East, where colleges and universities were plentiful, potential university presidents were scarce. Those that were available were weighing several propositions at once. But, at the Washburn Observatory at Madison, Wisconsin, he found Edward S. Holden, "pleasantly situated, engaged in a field of labor suited to his tastes, with a first-class and well equipped observatory at his command." [35] Then forty-five years old, Holden was a graduate of Washington University at St. Louis and of West Point, had served as a professor of mathematics at Annapolis, and had been connected with the Naval Observatory at Washington. He made it clear to Regent Hager that he was primarily interested in being an astronomer and that when the Lick Observatory, with the largest telescope in the world, was completed, he would like to become its director. If the Regents would appoint him to that post he would consent to serve the University, temporarily, as president.[36] His competency as an astronomer was attested to not only by Regent Hager but also by President Eliot at Harvard and President Gilman at Johns Hopkins. Hager had no difficulty, therefore, in securing Holden's election on October 20, 1885, as president of the University and director of the Lick Observatory.

Much of the new president's time was spent in supervising construction of the telescope on Mount Hamilton. He had little authority for anything else, and the temporary character of his leadership did not favor the initiation of long-range academic developments. It is not too surprising, under these circumstances, to find that the inauguration of a rudimentary teacher-placement service for alumni was probably his most significant presidential achievement.

Holden attempted to avoid difficulties. He warned the Freshmen against doing anything "thoughtless" that he would have to excuse to the citizens of the state; he said that he did not want to see "any silly stuff in the college publications about the 'coeds' "; and he outlawed the annual "rush" between Sophomores and Freshmen. That event traditionally had involved loosely regulated, and frequently bloody, bodily contact that, as one writer said, earned boys more friends in a few hours than they could normally acquire in six months.[37] Holden's edict did not end all student violence, however. In November, 1886, about a month after his lecture to the Freshmen, a boy's face was badly burned by either acid or fire in a fraternity hazing incident. The President took no action against the offending society because it assured him that initiation rites would be changed so "no injury to the University shall result." He did, however, issue a statement assuring hazing victims that they would have the full backing of the University president and the Academic Council if they ever decided to press charges against their tormentors in police court.[38]

Another well-publicized incident involving Holden and students took place in June, 1887, as a part of Class Day observances. As "dispensator" for the occasion, Julius Wangenheim (many years later president of the Alumni Association and an ex-officio Regent) performed a mock marriage ceremony and "by his levitous conduct outraged the feelings of the spectators and made a mockery of a sacred ceremony." [39] It was tame stuff, actually. Even according to the taste of the times, the stunt was considered no more offensive than those that were a part of prior Class Days. But Holden and the faculty decided to hold up presentation of Wangenheim's degree as punishment. The entire Senior class threatened to boycott the Commencement exercises on June 29 if the Academic Council did not relent,[40] but the threat was not carried out, even though the Academic Council considered Wangenheim's explanation of the affair insufficiently apologetic to warrant pardon. The young man received his diploma several days after Commencement.[41]

On Commencement Day that year, the students' appraisal of President Holden was reported in the San Francisco *Evening Post*. "When ex-President Reid retired," the article said, "the students cordially welcomed President Holden, whose administration they knew could not fail to be an improvement. In this they were right, and now they will as cheerfully welcome whatever successor the Regents may select, knowing that the only chance of missing a still more gratifying improvement would be to go back to Reid." In further analysis of Holden's failing, the report said, "He does not understand young men, nor sympathize with them. Their harmless escapades are crimes to one in whom the reverence for order and precision is so rooted as in this inflexible combination of martinet and astronomer." [42]

That summer, Holden began to think about a return to scientific pursuits, and notified the Regents of his intention to resign the presidency, effective "from the day when the Lick Observatory is formally accepted by the Regents of the University. . . ." [43] In January, 1888, the Regents amended the resignation by adding to the original effective date, "or upon the election and installation of a President of the University, if elected and installed prior to that day." [44] A successor was named a month later.

THE PROMISING MR. DAVIS

The Regents made informal inquiries concerning possible successors to Holden as soon as his resignation was in hand. Among those contacted was ex-President Gilman, even though one newspaper was touting the rumor that he was also being sought to head the new university that former Governor Stanford was building down the San Francisco Peninsula.[45] By January, 1888, the list of possible candidates was thirty names long. It included many distinguished educators outside of California, several personal friends of the Regents, and a few men identified with the University itself. Candidates associated with the University seemed, at first, to have an edge. They included Martin Kellogg; Frank Soulé, professor of civil engineering and astronomy; Regent Welcker; and former Regent Fred M. Campbell.[46] But none of these men were as prominent or popular as Horace Davis. A Harvard alumnus, Davis sailed around the Horn to join his brother who was already in California and engaged in coastal shipping operations. When he arrived in the Golden State, Davis worked briefly as a lumber surveyor, then as a purser for a steamship line, and later as a librarian. In 1860, he and his brother came into possession of the Golden Gate Flour Mill and their operation of this property made them both wealthy men.

Davis was elected to Congress in 1876 and contributed to one of the most fascinating chapters of California history by introducing the famous Chinese exclusion bill in 1878. After two terms in Congress, he returned to California, where his business interests continued to expand.[47] Even before former Congressman Davis was officially elected president, the Berkeley *Advocate* predicated that "Under President Davis we see no reason why our University should not enter upon a career of progress and prosperity similar to that which attended Harvard upon the advent of President Eliot." [48] The era thus heralded began officially on February 7, 1888, when Davis was unanimously elected to the University's presidency by the Regents.[49] But the advertised glories to come from his administration did not materialize.

Immediately after his election, President Davis asked for three weeks' leave to settle his business affairs and move from San Francisco to Berkeley. But the move was never made. Before long, he asked for another six weeks' leave to consult with a New York specialist concerning the illness of his wife. While he was in the East, he visited several colleges and universities to study trends in higher education in the country.[50] As his absences from Berkeley became prolonged and frequent, the Regents became more and more insistent that he move to Berkeley. The more insistent the Regents became, though, the more reluctant Davis was to move. He told them that he was at Berkeley by about ten every weekday morning and did not leave before three in the afternoon. Moreover, he considered his presence among socially and financially prominent people in San Francisco advantageous to the University.

Like his predecessors, President Davis cultivated good relationships between the University and the elementary and secondary schools of the state and became an advocate of establishing a department of pedagogy at the University. He also attempted to surround the University with informal religious centers of all denominations. Some of them would provide housing as part of their physical accommodations. All of them would exert a continuous religious influence that the University, by law, could not itself provide.

Davis was making remarkable progress in his work with the churches, particularly with the Methodists, until in December, 1888, a Unitarian minister included in his sermon one Sunday favorable comment on a novel called *Robert Elsmere*. This book chronicled one man's disaffection and separation from his early faith. A Presbyterian minister in Oakland, Francis Horton, was shocked. He condemned the book and the Unitarian minister who praised it. He then took occasion to note that one of the University's most prominent Regents, Horatio Stebbins, was also a Unitarian minister and that President Davis was not only a member of Stebbins' congregation but the husband of the daughter of Thomas Starr King, the most famous of all the early California ministers, and Stebbins' predecessor at the First Unitarian Church in San Francisco. In these intricate relationships and circumstances Horton discerned a plot within the University directed against "revealed religion" and "favorable to the most ultra type of rationalistic Unitarianism. . . ." [51] "The University is set to educate the youth of the State," he insisted, "but not to destroy their foundations of religious belief by inculcating a skeptical philosophy. . . . This is a serious problem and should be taken in hand by the State with vigor, beginning with a resignation or two from the Regents." [52]

Horton's sermon touched off a controversy that eventually involved the ruin of President Davis's work with the local churches, and attacks on certain members of the faculty. Joseph LeConte, who was known to have accepted the theory of evolution, was one of them. Another was George Holmes Howison, the first to fill the D. O. Mills Chair of Intellectual and Moral Philosophy and Civil Polity at the University, who allegedly believed in no God at all.[53]

By the beginning of 1889, the tempest stirred up by Horton had finally been dissipated, but only a few months passed before President Davis was in the middle of another storm. This time, the trouble came from the faculty.

In June, 1889, Regent J. West Martin, chairman of a special Committee on Salaries, introduced a new salary scale for members of the faculty. The object of the committee was to restore to some of the older faculty members a loss of income they incurred in 1882 when, in the interests of economy, Stebbins' Committee on Instruction and Visitation obtained Board approval of cuts that reduced professors' salaries from $3,600 a year to $3,000 a year. Martin's committee, counting on income from a penny tax levied by the legislature in 1887, set up a range of $3,000 to $4,000 for professors' salaries. But it only provided actual salaries of $3,300 for professors who did not hold endowed chairs. Under the new formula, then, the "old time" professors were paid $300 less than they were before the cuts of 1882.

While they were adjusting the professors' salaries, the Martin committee members also decided to correct abuses of a long-standing practice of the

Regents in appointing only professors and instructors, and seldom anyone at intervening ranks, at wildly fluctuating pay rates. As a partial solution to this problem, the committee recommended the creation of the rank of associate professor. Then, with President Davis's acquiescence (and some believed that it was on his initiative), several well-known and well-liked professors were reduced to the new rating and a popular assistant professor was reduced to instructor.[54] The basic reason for the reductions was to spread the limited funds over as many positions as possible, and there is no record of any criticism of the work of the faculty members involved. Their plight was no less severe by reason of this fact, however, and the reaction of the students and faculty to the demotions was bitter. On November 12, 1889, the Regents received petitions signed by 32 out of 39 members of the faculty and 65 out of some 400 students, requesting that all four of the demoted men be restored to their former ranks.[55] Action on the matter was delayed until January 18, 1890, but the Regents finally acceded to the petitioners' demands.

Apparently believing that the incident would not have become so bitter if the Regents were in more direct contact with faculty matters, Regent Hallidie secured the establishment of a new Committee on Internal Administration at the same meeting that restored the four demoted faculty members to their earlier ranks. The duties of the new committee would be "to consider and report on questions affecting appointments, promotions, transfers, and the compensation of professors and others on the educational staff of the University, and to confer with the President of the University on matters affecting the government of the various departments of the University." [56] It was nothing less than the old Committee on Instruction and Visitation under a new name, but, as it turned out, the same old leadership. The three members were Horatio Stebbins; George Marye, an attorney who took Stanford's place on the Board in 1883; and D. M. Delmas, another attorney, who was appointed to the Board by Governor Stoneman in 1885.[57]

Establishment of the Committee on Internal Administration was a clear sign that President Davis had lost the confidence of the Board of Regents. Speculation that he would soon resign or be eased out of office found its way into the newspapers by mid-March, 1890.[58] The lever was new action by the Regents to require that the president and professors of the University live in Berkeley. On April 4, Davis submitted his resignation, giving as his reasons inability to move to Berkeley as he had originally planned, because of personal circumstances beyond his control. The Regents accepted his resignation, effective September 1, at their May meeting.[59]

A DAWNING AWARENESS OF THE FLAW

Davis's reasons for resigning were not accepted everywhere at face value. The requirement that the president reside in Berkeley seemed petty when scores of students commuted to the campus from San Francisco as a matter of course every day. But no other reasons were any better. Horton's blasts at Stebbins involved President Davis only in a peripheral way. The President's hand in setting new faculty salaries in June, 1889, might not have been as firm as many supposed. Rumors that he was unpopular with the faculty and students were vague and unspecific. Yet, something, obviously, was seriously wrong.

Milicent Shinn, the first woman to earn a Ph.D. from the University, and the first person to write a serious history of it, thought she knew. In 1892 she wrote:

> Of the successive presidents [presumably after Gilman], every one was an able man, and most successful in his own special work,—not one was primarily a college president; not one had had training inside any great university elsewhere within recent years, nor followed the developments of university administration. Not one was first carefully chosen by the Regents—with reference to his *special* qualifications for the place and with full regard to the wishes of the faculty,—and then strongly supported by them. This experimental way of treating the presidency grew, I believe, from that same underrating of the importance of this part of the work that was visible from the first. The names that have been put in nomination for the presidency first and last make instructive reading. The early regents nominated each other; they nominated military men whom they admired; normal school principals; personal friends. For many years after President Gilman went away a large minority of the regents were possessed with the idea of disregarding scholarship and knowledge of universities altogether, and choosing a man for industrial success or enthusiasm for the industrial arts. The recurrent fear that some such destructive blunder would be made—though in fact it never was—has injured the relation of the faculty to the regents, lowering its confidence in them as a body.[60]

Because they appointed men with inadequate qualifications for the presidency, the Regents reserved to themselves and their secretary authority over even routine transactions. In a letter to D. O. Mills, Reid complained after his resignation: ". . . the Regents have so encroached upon the province of the Faculty and have so hedged the President about with restrictions as to make it impossible for him to carry out a vigorous individual policy, and it is useless for a man to hope to conduct an institution of learning to a successful issue if he is to be guided by, or subject to, the varying views of a body that is, and from its very constitution must be, more or less, heterogeneous and unacquainted with the details of the work the President is chosen to direct." [61] In a similar vein, Holden observed that "the law had given the University three presidents—the president *eo nomine,* the secretary of the Regents, and the professor of agriculture." [62] Then, almost two weeks before his resignation was accepted, President Davis was quoted in the Oakland *Daily Evening Tribune* as saying that "the Regents give altogether too much attention to the smaller details of management at the University, both in the scholastic and the business department. He [the president] can hardly get a chair varnished that he does not have to apply to some committee of the board for permission to do so." [63]

The possibility that there was something organically wrong with the relationship between the University of California's president and its governing board was appreciated by some of the Regents. A "Special Committee on matters relating to the President" was appointed just before President Davis resigned, and after the resignation was announced the Regents did not rush to fill the office immediately. Instead, they named Martin Kellogg, whose faculty leadership extended back into the old College of California days, acting president. In November, 1890, they demonstrated the seriousness of their concern by asking their Committee on Internal Administration "to report to this Board a series of regulations defining the authority of the President of the University conferred by law and that which it may be deemed expedient to confer upon him by this Board." [64]

The Committee on Internal Administration kept the subject of the president's authority under study for three months while factions formed over the issues in question. Columbus Bartlett, who had been chairman of the special committee on the presidency just before Davis resigned, led the bloc that favored generous delegation of authority from the Board to the Regents' chief executive. The faction that desired to reserve to the Regents as much authority as possible was led by Regent Stebbins.

On his own initiative, Regent Bartlett offered a series of resolutions on January 13, 1891, designed "to prevent any misunderstanding or conflict of authority between the President and Secretary." The proposal, in effect, transferred to the president, from the secretary, authority to care for and control the University grounds at Berkeley, and employ, dismiss, and regulate the duties of the janitors and watchmen.[65] His proposal neatly tidied up preexisting orders that divided these responsibilities between the president and the secretary.[66] Even Bartlett believed that the Regents should not be left out of administrative matters completely, however, and he also proposed that the Regents appoint a superintendent of grounds and buildings at Berkeley who would be jointly responsible to the president and the Regents' own Committee on Grounds and Buildings.[67]

Bartlett's resolutions were referred to the Committee on Internal Administration of which Regent Marye was still chairman and Regent Stebbins a forceful member. The third member, since January, 1890, was Columbus Bartlett. Thus constiuted, the committee could offer nothing but a compromise to the Bartlett resolutions. So on May 12 it offered a resolution giving all of the authority over grounds and buildings to the secretary of the Regents "subject to the direction of the President." The Regental faction favoring a strong presidency rejected the compromise, however, and, by amendment, restored the resolutions to essentially the form Bartlett had offered them three months earlier.[68] In separate action, Martin Kellogg, as acting president, was expressly charged with exercise of the newly granted powers.[69] This action embittered the incumbent secretary, J. H. C. Bonté, against Kellogg throughout his remaining years.

Stebbins succeeded in clouding the whole issue again at the next meeting of the Board when he secured passage of a resolution that "the duties devolved upon the President by the recent amendments to . . . the Regents Manual be exercised by him at his pleasure through the Secretary of the Board of Regents and through such other officer or officers as may be appointed by the Board of Regents or selected by the President for the performance of such duties." [70]

No further move to strengthen the presidency was made for nearly a year. Then it was again made by Regent Bartlett in his capacity as chairman of the Regents' committee to select a permanent president. His resolutions were:

1. The President of the University shall be a member *ex-officio* of every standing and special Committee of the Board of Regents.[71]
2. All appointments, removals and promotions of professors, instructors and other members of the University, and increase or decrease of their salaries shall be made on the recommendation of the President of the University only.
3. All communications from the Academic Senate, from any Faculty or other organizations of the University and from professors and instructors and other members of the University to the Board of Regents, shall be through the President of the University only.
4. The Secretary of the Board of Regents is subordinate to the Pres-

ident and should he become *persona non grata* to the President, he
shall be relieved.
5. The President may give instruction in some subject to be chosen
by himself.
6. Contiguous offices shall be provided for the President of the University, Secretary of the Board of Regents and Dean and Recorder
of the Faculties at Berkeley.[72]

Upon the insistence of Bartlett that no competent president could be obtained without the Board's concurrence, all six of the above resolutions were
passed on April 12, 1892.

Chapter 8

THE PROVIDERS

IN SOME UNDATED notes written in 1870 or early 1871, Andrew J. Moulder,
first secretary of the Board of Regents, said: "We cannot now count certainly on the means to sustain the University later than December 1, 1871.
Its support, after that, depends upon the contingency of Mr. Richardson's
donation. That failing, it will require sharp financiering to provide the necessary ways and means." [1]

The Benjamin Richardson upon whom so much depended amassed a fortune in the Gold Rush, invested it in a Missouri quarry and New York City
real estate, and died a man "whose great wealth, stirring history, queer attire, great beard, and collection of Revolutionary relics made him one of the
best-known characters of New York." [2] Some of the Regents of the University believed he had the means to become California's John Harvard or Ezra
Cornell, and he was counted upon for at least $1,250,000 to erect buildings
in Berkeley. He disappointed them by giving the University nothing. Until
income from the land grants came in, therefore, the Regents were at the
mercy of the legislature, where Moulder feared the University's appeals
"would not only be refused, but, in my opinion, would provoke an attack

upon the existence of the University itself." [3] Fortunately, Moulder's fears were not realized. In 1872 the legislature gave the University $300,000 to construct buildings at Berkeley and passed another bill that provided emergency financial assistance until 1874.

No one anticipated that the legislature's generosity had set a precedent. Most Californians believed that the endowments being amassed with the proceeds of federal and state land grants would, in due course, sustain the University comfortably. With its basic sustenance thus made certain, the gifts that rich and enlightened Californians would bestow in addition would make the University prosperous beyond any institution of learning known to the history of man. Surely many Californians of means would step forward to do what Mr. Richardson would not.

THE FIRST BENEFACTIONS

The 160-acre site at Berkeley was part of the evidence. That land, after all, once belonged to the College of California, an institution created and sustained for more than two decades by private donors. When the land was given to the University in 1868, it was, in a sense, given in its benefactors' names. Later, donations of books for the library and items for the museum trickled into the University as Regents, professors, and other friends of the University watched for book bargains during their travels and made available Indian relics and assorted specimens of flora and fauna from the California countryside.

On September 18, 1872, Regent Edward Tompkins became the first big donor to the University when he conveyed to the Regents 47 acres of land at the junction of Broadway and University Avenue in Oakland. He instructed the Regents to dispose of the land as soon as it could be sold for $50,000 and use the money to establish an endowed professorship of Oriental languages and literature. The gift expressed not only Tompkins' affection for the University, but also his conviction that "The child is now born that will see the commerce of the Pacific greater than that of the Atlantic." [4] He asked that the professorship be called the Agassiz Professorship of Oriental Languages, in honor of the distinguished Harvard scientist Louis Agassiz, who was then visiting in California. The Regents could not dispose of the property for the price Tompkins specified until 1887. Then, they refused $50,000 for the entire plot, subdivided it, and, by 1895, realized $87,629.45 from the property for the Tompkins endowment.

Tompkins' gift was made two months before the inauguration of Daniel

Coit Gilman. In his inaugural remarks, Gilman praised Tompkins' generosity and spoke generally of the role of philanthropy in the University's development. "It is true," he said, "the State has been, and is likely to be, liberal in its appropriations; but a great University requires almost unlimited means for its support." [5] While the legislature could be relied upon for the "most essential things," Gilman said, "we must look to men of wealth to provide the richer and more complete endowments which will place our University by the side of her older sisters at the East. The rich Californians, who have made this wilderness rejoice and blossom like a rose, who have built these banks and warehouses, these railroads and steamships—the men who by their enterprise have made a University desirable and possible, and who now need it for their children—must make it actual by their munificence." [6]

Gilman followed up his plea for philanthropic support with personal cultivation of donors. When James Lick, the eccentric cabinetmaker whose investments made him a multimillionaire, decided in 1873 to build the world's most powerful telescope, Gilman was one of his advisers. Originally, Lick intended to leave his observatory to the California Academy of Sciences. In 1875, he changed his mind and decided to give the $700,000 installation to be built atop Mount Hamilton in Santa Clara County to the University. [7]

Gilman was also instrumental in obtaining the donation of facilities for the University's medical department. The building and facilities of the Toland Medical College, founded in 1864 by Dr. Hugh H. Toland, were first offered to the Regents in June, 1870. [8] The offer was accepted [9] and a faculty for the department was appointed by the Regents, [10] but acceptance was withdrawn after Toland demanded, in November, that the new department be called the "Toland Medical Department of the University of California." [11] Three years later, negotiations were reopened and successfully concluded. The Toland Medical College became the Medical Department of the University of California and the founder's name was perpetuated through a professorship. The University thus began education in the higher professions at an early date. It also acquired property valued at about $100,000, consisting of a large building and an adjoining lot on Stockton Street near Chestnut in San Francisco. [12]

Gilman also promoted the University library as an object of public philanthropy. He was so successful that the 1,036 volumes inherited from the College of California were increased twelvefold by the time he left California in 1875. Some of the new acquisitions were purchased by the University, but many came from donors. In 1873, F. L. A. Pioche, of San Francisco, left his library of 1,500 books to the University. [13] In the same year,

Gilman learned that an important private collection of books on economics and politics was for sale in the East. He gave the story to the San Francisco newspapers in hopes that someone would buy the collection for the University of California. On March 28, 1873, his strategy paid off: Michael Reese, a prominent San Francisco banker, sent a draft for $2,000 with instructions to use it in purchasing the library described in the papers.[14] Thus began a warm relationship between Reese and the University. When he died, Reese left $50,000 as a special endowment for library acquisition.[15]

Reese's bequest to the University might have been even more generous if he had not feared that Granger-inspired legislative investigations of 1874 would impair its ability to withstand political interference.[16] If other major philanthropists were inclined to contribute between 1874 and 1877 they, too, waited to see how well the University survived the political maelstrom. The gifts of this period were small and the typical donor was a Visalia man who wrote to the secretary of the Regents to say that near his home there was an old battlefield with "quite a number of human skeletons lying yet on the surface." If "in a scientific point of view" one of them was needed, he saw "no harm in boxing up one of these unknown uncared for remains and sending them to the University." [17]

Two years after this offer, the roster of gifts to the University included "a skull from the West Berkeley Shell Mounds," "two snakes," and a "species of bat." [18] In the same year the University received a bust of Henry Durant from the Oakland Ladies Relief Society; a framed, watercolor drawing of a hydraulic engine from a Benicia man; and money to purchase a presidential gown and chair from "several ladies in Oakland." [19] Such gifts were gratefully received. Some of them provided modest comforts and ornaments the University could not afford out of ordinary revenues. The others, equally difficult to obtain without the help of donors, provided materials that could be used directly in teaching and research. Partly as a result of large numbers of donations, the library and museum collections grew more rapidly than anticipated.

President LeConte placed the need of a new library and museum at the top of his lists of "wants of the University" in 1877.[20] On December 13, 1877, Henry Douglas Bacon, of Oakland, answered this "want" with an offer to donate his personal library and art collection and $25,000 in cash to pay for the "first subdivision" of a building to house both a University gallery and a library.[21] In 1878, the legislature matched Bacon's $25,000 with a special appropriation,[22] and the Bacon Art and Library Building was constructed about 100 yards east of South Hall. It was dedicated on August 23, 1881, and served as the main library at Berkeley until 1911, when a larger library was constructed. It then housed the geology and geography departments until it was razed in 1961 to make way for a new physics building, Birge Hall.

Another major "want" of the University (it stood second on President LeConte's list in 1877) was a building to serve as an "Auditorium, ... Gymnasium, and a Military Drill-room." [23] This need was satisfied when A. K. P. Harmon, whose mercantile profits during the Gold Rush were invested in the Rich Washoe mining enterprises in Nevada, simply built an octagonal-shaped gymnasium on the campus and presented it to the University on January 20, 1879.[24] As the campus enrollment grew, the building was expanded by means of additions in 1886, 1897, and 1900. It was torn down in 1933 when a modern gymnasium was built to take its place.[25]

THE UNIVERSITY'S LIMITED RESOURCES

The early benefactions bestowed upon the University were mixed blessings. They had considerable monetary value and they met desperate needs. But they also required maintenance. Books had to be catalogued, shelved, and protected. Museum specimens and art works had to be identified and properly stored. Buildings had to be kept clean and in good repair. Such activity increased daily operating costs.

To meet its normal expenses, the University could charge tuition and other student fees, could receive gifts of money, could draw upon interest earned on state and federal endowments, or could ask for legislative appropriations. The alternatives did not offer equal yields and some of them were feasible only hypothetically or with expenditure of inordinate amounts of time on the part of University officials. One was rejected in December, 1869, when the Regents abolished tuition to insure that this would not be a financial barrier to prevent any California youth from entering the University.[26] The first gifts to the University were more likely to be books, rocks, shells, and small animals than big money. And the original endowment of the University could produce no income until the federal and state lands from which it was derived were all sold. Until that time (expected to arrive by 1876), the legislature was willing to make up reasonable deficits in the Regents' budget. It also provided a few appropriations for special projects, such as the Viticultural Laboratory, that served important segments of the state's economy.

In 1874, the Regents had to borrow $25,000 to meet expenses for the last four months of the fiscal year.[27] For 1877–1878, the secretary of the Regents reported an anticipated deficit of some $4,000 and warned, "It is very evident that expansion in any direction is inadmissible, and the most rigid economy, even to the point of contraction, is required." [28] The mood of the Regents became one of austerity. The budget had to be cut back drastically, and the Committee on Instruction and Visitation was asked to examine the general efficiency of the University. As a result of the work of this committee, John LeConte was forced to resign from the presidency to avoid being fired as an inadequate administrator. Another result of this committee's work was a cutback in salaries and expenses by $6,384.90 at the beginning of the fiscal year for 1881–1882.[29]

THE PERPETUAL ENDOWMENT

Some of the Regents' restiveness concerning the University's financial prospects was caused by concern for the security of the University's endowments. Until 1878, there were actually five different endowment funds. One consisted of the proceeds from the 150,000 acres granted to California by the first Morrill Act. Another consisted of proceeds of the sale of the "Seminary of Learning" grant in 1853. A third consisted of proceeds from sales of California salt- and marshlands, invested under terms of an 1870 state law for the purpose of yielding $50,000 annually for the University. Finally, there was the income from the sales of Brayton property in Oakland. In 1878, the California legislature passed a bill creating the "Consolidated Perpetual Endowment Fund of the University of California," consisting of all the University's endowment funds then extant. The law stipulated that the principal could never be diminished and that investments from it had to be in government bonds "or other safe stocks or bonds" yielding at least 5 per cent a year.[30] On May 22, 1878, the Regents turned $386,500 in endowment funds over to the custody of the state treasurer, as was required by the act.[31] The fund was not complete because all of the Morrill land grant had not yet been sold. Moreover, some of the "Seminary" grant revenues had found their way into county school districts before the University was created and would not be retrieved for the University for some time.

A few years after the Consolidated Perpetual Endowment Fund was created, it was found to have a flaw. The wording of the law that established the fund allowed the state treasurer to prohibit removal of any part of the endowment for any purpose, including reinvestment, unless the money taken out was immediately replaced by bonds or cash of equal value. This insured that the endowment was undiminished at all times. But when some of the first bonds purchased by the university matured, the Regents discovered that the funds they yielded could not be reinvested without a warrant by the state controller, and unless they could find money from friends or loaning agencies to deposit temporarily until the reinvestment was made. As Regent Winans reported in 1883, "D. O. Mills, treasurer of the University, has frequently come to their [the Regents'] relief, but he declines longer to be victimized by the stupidities of legislation. . . . The counties are calling in their bonds very rapidly, and it is probable that within the next two years there may be not less than a half million dollars of University funds lying in the State Treasury, as wholly unproductive." [32] To prevent this unpleasant prospect from coming true, the Regents requested legislation in 1883 that gave them full control over investment and reinvestment of the Perpetual Endowment Fund, without any interference from the state treasurer. At the same time, they sought modification of the requirement that investment of the endowment be in government or other bonds yielding 5 per cent interest. This provision had been established as a part of the Morrill Land Grant Act of 1862 to govern investment of land-grant revenues. When the Perpetual Endowment Fund was created, the Morrill Act restrictions on investment were simply applied to the entire fund.[33] By the 1880s interest rates were falling, even on government bonds, and the Regents were finding it difficult to invest so as to insure the minimal 5 per cent return. In 1883 the state legislature gave the Regents almost unlimited flexibility in the investment of the University's endowment, and parallel legislation was obtained from the federal government. Thereafter, the Regents were free to invest not only in bonds, but also in mortgages and real estate, including the profitable ownership of two office buildings in San Francisco.

A NEW FACTOR IN THE FINANCIAL FORMULA

The income from the University's endowment covered operating expenditures only twice—in 1876–1877 and 1877–1878. Thereafter, the Regents made up the difference from such diversified sources as rental of the student cottages, sale of water to the University's neighbors, loans, and fees charged for the execution of documents related to land-grant sales. Between 1876 and 1885, further income was provided by out-of-state students, who paid $25 matriculation fees and a nonresident tuition fee of $50 a year. As long as the University was in an enrollment slump, as it was for about six years, beginning in 1879, its own resources were adequate to cover a very austere budget. But there was no margin in the University's income to pay for a renewal of worn-out facilities, for growth in services, or for improvement of equipment and techniques of instruction. By 1882, President Reid indicated that more help from the legislature was required. Requests were granted the following year for about $57,800, most of which was earmarked for special work in agriculture and the departments of mechanics, mines, engineering, and viticulture. In the same year, 1883, a new secretary of the Regents, J. H. C. Bonté, suggested that the legislature make an automatic appropriation of $40,000 each year to be spent at the discretion of the Regents. In addition, he urged that "a certain percentage of the annual taxes of the State be devoted to the University for a series of years." [34] In 1884, President Reid took up Bonté's idea and recommended to the Regents that the people of California enact a law to give "the sum of one-tenth of a mill on each dollar of taxable property" to the University.[35]

President Holden took up the same cause in 1885. In his annual report, he questioned the advisability of asking the legislature only to provide buildings and funds for specialized activities. "Special appropriations for buildings, etc., while absolutely necessary," he said, "add seriously and almost fatally to the demands upon the General Fund. The building must be cared for, incidental expenses must be incurred, an additional force must be employed, and, in due time, without an increase in the General Fund, the Regents may not be able to accept as a donation a building that may be really necessary in itself.

"The Legislature, therefore, while not withholding appropriations for new buildings, should add to the General Fund, either by increasing the capital, or by a small tax for a period of years. The appropriation of $20,000 per annum, to be expended in payment of current expenses, and in educating promising students, would be of inestimable value to the State." [36]

Holden repeated his recommendation in his biennial report for 1886, advocating a tax of one cent on each $100 assessed valuation that ". . . produces an income which is proportional to the value of the State's wealth, and thus keeps the University income abreast with the wants of the State without perpetual adjustments and readjustments." [37] In addition, he favored enactment of a law that would require the legislature to make an automatic appropriation of $60,000 a year for the permanent support of the University.

The use of taxation, either alone or in combination with annual appropriations of consistent size, to keep state colleges and universities in perpetual motion without constant legislative attention was not original in California. The idea had been employed at Michigan and Minnesota in the 1870s, and other states adopted various versions of it in the 1880s. The President and the Regents of the University of California embraced the general principle as a way out of a condition in which income derived from endowments for operations could never grow fast enough to meet the demands of rapid growth.

The man who was almost fanatically dedicated to this scheme was Dr. John Harmon C. Bonté. In due time, he became not only secretary of the Regents, but also superintendent of grounds and buildings, land agent, and professor of legal ethics. He fiercely guarded his prerogatives in all of these capacities. There were proprieties, rules, and procedures that he expected to be observed. He observed them meticulously himself. Only those who did not know him or who had skins thick enough to withstand the heat of his eloquent wrath evaded his dicta. To a man thus disposed to orderliness and certainty, the unreliable nature of the University's financial resources was almost unbearable.

In 1886, with the full approval of the Board of Regents and the President, Bonté and the Regents' legal counsel, John B. Mhoon, drafted a bill that would give the University one cent for every $100 worth of taxable property in the state. This draft was then worked over by E. W. Maslin, the politically sophisticated secretary of the State Board of Equalization.[38] In its revised form, it was then presented in the senate by Henry Vrooman, self-educated leader of the Republican minority, whose home district was Alameda County. In the assembly, the bill was introduced by University alumnus Charles O. Alexander, also an Alameda County Republican. Bonté spent considerable time lobbying for the measure in Sacramento, cheered on by periodic messages of encouragement from President Holden in Berkeley. In the senate, the bill was passed with virtually no opposition. In the assembly, however, amendments requiring that half of the measure's revenues be used for permanent improvements of the University were defeated only on Bonté's assurances that the intent of the amendments would be observed whether they were written into the bill or not. By February 10, the mission in Sacramento was all but accomplished and President Holden wrote to Bonté: "From what I have heard in various places and in various ways, I am satisfied that this has been an extremely difficult task which you have accomplished and the University will always be indebted to you for it." [39] The thanks of the Regents went to Senator Vrooman, who was also honored with an alumni banquet, and the bill became popularly known as the Vrooman Act.

Before long it made little difference who deserved or got the credit. The "penny tax" fell far short of its goal of supporting the University of California indefinitely and painlessly in a manner consistent with its need.

TOO MANY STUDENTS

In 1884, the University began to recover from an enrollment slump that had started five years before. The new growth was attributed in part to California's immigration boom of the 1880s, and in part to policies of the legislature and Regents that gave encouragement to the development of district high schools. By the time the penny tax was enacted, enrollment was rising at a rate of between 10 and 15 per cent a year. In contrast, the state appropriations to the University fluctuated wildly, shooting up by $69,000 in one year and dropping down by $25,000 the next. In 1888, when the first penny-tax proceeds were received by the University, state appropriations totaled $103,000. Ten years later, they totaled $124,000, just $21,000 more. Over the same period, enrollment increased from 477 to 2,066.

Under these circumstances, Bonté's promise to the assembly that penny-tax revenues would cover special appropriations items previously requested from the legislature for permanent improvements began to look like an unprofitable bargain.

The report of the Regents' Finance Committee in 1889 pointed out that the special appropriations between 1868 and 1883 had averaged $50,000 a year. If that sum were to be taken out of the penny-tax revenue, "The natural growth of the University will more than swallow up the difference." [40] By 1893, the Regents had spent $145,000 of penny-tax revenue for buildings and equipment and contemplated further expenditure of $70,000 to complete work in progress. To provide a badly needed classroom building, the Finance Committee recommended, for the first time since 1887, asking the legislature to appropriate $500,000 to be spent over two years.[41]

The special appropriations that had favored the College of Agriculture were also terminated with passage of the penny-tax law in 1887. Fortunately for the University, Congress passed a law in the same year that appropriated $15,000 annually to states that could maintain experimental agricultural stations. This amount precisely offset the amount lost from the special agricultural appropriations the University received from the state legislature in the past. In 1891, however, Congress extended federal help with the Morrill College Aid Fund, which gave gradually increasing assistance to land-grant colleges for instruction in agriculture, the mechanic arts, the English language, and other subjects "with special reference to their applications in the industries of life." [42]

The Regents were forced into drastic economies despite federal windfalls. In 1893, there were 815 students at Berkeley alone and only 60 staff members to teach them. By December of that year, the financial outlook of the University was so poor that the Regents reduced faculty salaries. The range of pay for professors, formerly $3,000 to $4,000, was reduced to $2,700 to $3,300; instructors, who had received $1,200 to $1,700, were dropped to between $900 and $1,500 a year. Ranks in between were dropped by $300 a year at the beginning levels only, giving associate professors $2,100 to $2,700 and assistant professors $1,500 to $2,100.[43]

The following year, enrollment at Berkeley reached 1,124, and there were 72 members of the faculty. President Kellogg protested that "The University has outgrown its present resources. . . . Its class-rooms are overcrowded, its laboratories are becoming insufficient. Some of its departments are badly housed. The Museum is choked with undisplayed treasures. The health-giving Gymnasium has but half the needed space and appliances. There is no fit Armory, and no drill-room. The Faculty records are insecure in a wooden building. The hundreds of young women have for a day-home only one room in a basement. There is no assembly room for public gatherings." [44] The Regents thought darkly of imposing a $25 annual tuition fee but rejected the idea even though its supporters included the formidable Andrew Hallidie and the joint membership of the Finance and Internal Management Committees.[45] An alternate suggestion of a $10 annual incidental fee was also rejected by the Board.[46] To balance the budget for the coming year without the additional revenue he had hoped to obtain from the students, Hallidie and his committee trimmed out expenditures totaling $17,979.22. Among them were such items as fuel, $500; equipment, $500; repairs, $500; painting buildings, $2,000; reservoir, $2,000; and University site improvement, $1,500.[47]

REGENT REINSTEIN'S CAMPAIGN

In October, 1895, Jacob Reinstein, a 5-foot, 4-inch, forty-two-year-old San Francisco attorney "whose brain is in inverse ratio to his inches," [48] became a member of the Board of Regents. Like Governor James E. Budd, who appointed him, Reinstein was one of the "twelve apostles" who made up the University's first four-year class. On May 12, 1896, he was elected chairman of a special Regents' Committee on Ways and Means. The committee was supposed to find a way to avoid a $13,000 deficit that would confront the University in July and surely get bigger in subsequent years unless more income could be found. Reinstein saw that such income would have to come from the legislature and that, in order to get it from that source, any prejudices against the University that might exist had to be removed.

The first instrument of Reinstein's attack was a brilliant public relations document in the guise of an analysis by his committee of the University's financial difficulties. The report's statement of the University's needs was both accurate and emotional: "Some instructors are rendering efficient service for the wages of a cash boy. There are no useless or high-salaried professors, . . . and hardly one whose University duties do not require his attention for more hours than the common laborer works. There is no money to care for the grounds . . . buildings have been unpainted for several years. . . . With no money for lighting the grounds or library, and a student roll which overtaxes the physical accommodations and the time and energies of the teaching force at the University, it is no wonder that the feeling is general that the youth of the State are turned away from its highest institutions of learning to other colleges, where not only do we believe they will receive a less excellent instruction, but *they will lose the patriotism, love, and pride for the State of California* which will result inevitably from their additional obligation to their State, as the donor to them of the benefits of higher education." [49]

In an appeal to state pride, the report noted that the liberality of the states of Missouri, Wisconsin, Michigan, Minnesota, Nebraska, and Indiana in the support of state universities exceeded that of California. Such precedents "we believe will not only justify, but move, the State of California to take such steps that this State shall not suffer by an invidious comparison with any other State in this Union." [50]

Far from being the result of mismanagement, the University's difficulties, as made clear in the report, were due to its success and the confidence of California parents: "Within the last five years the number of students at the State University at Berkeley has trebled, and is at the present writing, 1,336, while in the entire University, including its affiliated colleges, the number is 2,047, while the indications are that the next Freshman class will outnumber all before it. The income of the University from this Act [the penny tax of 1887], however, so far from doubling, has increased only an insignificant amount within the last five years, and is actually less in 1895 than in 1894 or 1893." [51]

Reinstein and his committee were almost diametrically opposed to Hallidie's Finance and Audit Committee concerning solutions to the University's problems. Hallidie's committee had insisted that the University live entirely within its means. If it could not cover expenses with revenue currently available, it should find some. The source they favored was some kind of student fee, a prospect abhorred by the Governor and narrowly defeated by a vote of the entire Board. Reinstein took the audacious position that the University should spend what it needed to spend in order to do its work in accordance with high standards. If a deficit resulted, the legislature either must cover it or accept the responsibility for letting the University slide. The legislators' choice could be weighted in the University's favor by making it even more indispensable and attractive to California's citizens than it already was.

CHANGING THE IMAGE

The legislators' choice could also be influenced by freeing the University of certain prevailing misconceptions about its work. In the politically powerful rural areas, for instance, it was still generally believed that the University's concerns were with impractical matters. To correct that impression, Reinstein sought and obtained $3,500 from the Regents for sponsorship of fifty meetings throughout the state.[52] At these meetings, members of the College of Agriculture faculty and staff talked about new farming techniques and new world markets for California's products. They not only succeeded in winning University friends in California farm areas but also succeeded in establishing a continuing demand for such meetings and further development of the Farmers' Institute programs of the University.

On February 27, 1896, the little Regent marshaled 800 students into a labor crew to work at campus landscaping and road-building. This small army not only got some needed work done but demonstrated what Reinstein wanted to show—that students at the University were not all indolent sons of wealth who were afraid of manual labor. The Regents had photographs taken of the students in their working clothes.[53] And the event was so much fun that it was repeated as the traditional "labor day" every leap year for three decades thereafter.

MRS. HEARST HELPS IMPROVE THE LOOKS OF THE CAMPUS

It took a more loyal than average Californian to be inspired by the appearance of the University in the early 1890s. Even Milicent W. Shinn, who in 1898 became the first woman to receive a Ph.D. degree at the University, complained, "The buildings are most of them good, though none compare in beauty with the Leland Stanford Jr., University [opened 1891], and there is no comprehensive plan among them; they are even of unpleasantly differing shades of brick. The affiliated schools being in San Francisco, the Observatory at Mount Hamilton, and the buildings at Berkeley scattered over a considerable tract of ground, they make a less display than those of most universities of equal importance." [54] Reinstein shared Miss Shinn's misgivings about the face the University showed to the world. So did a young instructor of architectural drawing, Bernard Maybeck, with whom he conferred at length. In April, 1896, at a special meeting held for that purpose, the Regents heard Reinstein give an "extended report" on the "urgent necessity" of adopting a permanent plan for the improvement of the University's grounds and buildings. A significant feature of his idea was University sponsorship of a competition whereby "designs & plans might be secured from the best architects of this country & Europe." [55] The Regents agreed to the extent of authorizing their Committee on Grounds and Buildings, the President, the Academic Council, and Maybeck to work out the details of such a scheme. In October, the project acquired a benefactress. She was Phoebe Apperson Hearst, widow of the distinguished senator, and mother of publisher—editor William Randolph Hearst. Mrs. Hearst wrote to Regent Reinstein to tell him that she had been informed of the Regents' interest in developing a comprehensive building plan and offered to pay the expenses for the competition. More than that, she implied that completion of a suitable plan would also result in further contributions for the erection of buildings she had contemplated donating to the University.[56]

Mrs. Hearst's offer was, of course, accepted and eventually cost her $200,000. Its value in making possible the orderly development of the campus was incalculable. It had an important side-benefit, too, because it called international attention to the University of California and its needs. Newspaper stories all over the world told of the beautiful building site at Berkeley and of the spectacular contest being held to decide how it should be developed. Californians were caught up in the excitement. When, in September, 1899, the plan of a Frenchman, Henri Jean Emile Bénard, was selected from the original field of more than 100 entries, there was general expectation that old South Hall, North Hall (the house that Merritt built), and assorted other buildings would be razed immediately to make way for the gleaming Italian Renaissance structures that Bénard had designed. In the face of the University's sudden rise to international attention, the legislature could not easily fail to give adequate support.

THE SECOND PENNY TAX

When the legislature convened in 1897, the University was overcrowded. Tents donated by Mrs. Hearst were housing classrooms and students. Governor Budd, on January 4, warned "The University must have aid, or it will be compelled to apportion the students hereafter throughout the State in accordance with population, and thus deprive many of its splendid privileges." [57] Two Alameda County legislators, Assemblyman H. E. Wright and Senator F. S. Stratton, answered the call for aid with sponsorship of a bill to double the University's income from the state by adding to its revenue an additional one cent on each $100 of taxable wealth of the state. Secretary Bonté was too ill to take an active role in the bill's support, but it had stellar champions in President Martin Kellogg, Professor Bernard Moses, and Regent Reinstein. There was virtually no serious opposition to the bill and the only proviso included in it was that one-half of the income derived from the added penny tax should be used for permanent improvements.

When the bill was passed, on February 18, 1897, University alumni who were members of the assembly staged a victory rally, yells and all, on the floor of their chamber. That night, the chambers of both the senate and assembly were decorated with blue and gold and Governor Budd was given a blue-and-gold pen to sign the new law. In Berkeley, President Kellogg declared a half-holiday during the ensuing week and a review of the cadets was held in honor of the legislature.[58]

Polled for their reactions, one Regent speculated that more professors would be hired with the new income. Another said buildings would be expanded. Regent Hallidie predicted that the University still needed more money than the bill furnished.[59]

ANOTHER FIGHT OVER TUITION

Hallidie's prediction proved correct within a year. By 1899 he reported to the Regents on behalf of the Committee on Finance and Audit: "Ten years ago the University had no surplus income. Since then its income has increased only thirty-three per cent. In these ten years the number of students at Berkeley has increased 460 per cent. . . .

"It is a mathematical impossibility to go on increasing this way, with no increase of income. The possible limit was reached, we thought, several years ago; and the added one cent tax did not by any means do away with the discrepancy." [60] In early May, plans for the 1899–1900 budget anticipated a deficit of nearly $48,000.

On May 9, Regents Hallidie and Miller, along with Martin Kellogg, who had retired from the presidency in March, recommended that the deficit be met by charging students an "incidental fee" of $20 per term.[61] Students on scholarships would be exempted. "The dilemma is this," they said, "either cripple all the Departments of instruction, or collect from the students a very small fraction of the total expense of their education. Tuition proper is not the only cost to the State. The cost of the grounds; the care of buildings that house nearly 2000 students; the equipment of class-rooms and laboratories; the using up of materials in the laboratories, and of books in the Library; all the wear and tear of buildings, furniture, machinery, etc.,—such items in so large a University community amount to more than the sum proposed in an incidental fee. The State would still be furnishing actual tuition gratis." [62]

On May 12, the Finance Committee, under Hallidie's direction, submitted four alternatives to the Regents. The first involved a 12½ per cent across-the-board reduction of all budget items, including salaries. The second suspended the office of president, transferring his duties to a president of the Academic Council; left the office of secretary of the Regents (made vacant by the death of Bonté in 1896) unfilled; and cut the budget of the College of Commerce by $4,200, the Department of German or Romance [languages] by $7,200; the Lick Observatory by $18,000; the examination-of-schools program by $2,000; the library by $2,000; and the University Printing Office by $1,500. The third proposal was the same as the second except that the Farmers' Institutes were sacrificed instead of the presidency. The fourth proposal was to charge students an incidental fee of $20 a term. Regent William T. Wallace, a prominent Democrat, former chief justice of the California Supreme Court, and judge of the Superior Court in San Francisco, moved adoption of the across-the-board cuts. Hallidie immediately moved to substitute his incidental-fee plan. Hallidie's motion was lost and the whole matter was deferred until the next regular meeting.[63]

A special faculty conference committee on finances was appointed to join five Regents in further budget deliberations. By pruning courses and increasing the size of some classes, this committee reduced the anticipated deficit to about $30,000. It sought a further reduction by recommending a $4,000 cut in the budgeted salary for the as yet unnamed successor to Kellogg as president, and by leaving the office of secretary of the Regents unfilled to realize another $7,000 payroll saving. The "Retrenchment Committee," as it was also called, then proposed that a "registration fee" of $10 per term be charged every student, laboratory fees (ranging from $5 to almost $32 depending upon the course involved) be simultaneously cut in half, and that the $10 deposit students paid for their diplomas be abolished. These recommendations brought the budget very nearly in balance. By a vote of ten to five, the Regents decided to keep the president's salary at $10,000. They also voted to cut laboratory fees and abolish the diploma fee. When the question of imposing a registration fee "only during the next academic year" was put before the Board, John Budd, the former governor's younger brother, who was named a Regent in 1896, unsuccessfully sought to avoid consideration on the parliamentary grounds that the failure of Hallidie's substitute motion on fees at the previous meeting was tantamount to the expression of the Board's "determination not to charge a fee of this kind." Despite his argument, the measure passed by a vote of eleven to four.[64]

Governor Henry T. Gage was not in attendance when the Regents adopted the registration fee, but he let it be known afterward that he was disappointed and that, moreover, he considered the new rule to jeopardize the University's chances to obtain legislative assistance in the future. He called for a special meeting of the Regents to reconsider the matter, explaining: "I do not believe that if the tax [on students] stands the University will ever rally from the effects of the blow. The tax will, in my opinion, inure to the advantage of other institutions. I am decidedly in favor of free schools, from kindergartens to the graduating class of the State University, and I will never countenance any proposition that will compel an admission tax to schools which should be free and open." [65]

It soon became evident that the Governor would have ample support. The San Francisco *Examiner* stressed the effects of the fee on students: "It is one of the glories of the University of California that for the most part its students are poor. It is carrying out the purpose of its foundation—to put the children of citizens of small means on the same footing in the opportunities for education as the children of the rich. The unavoidable expenses of support and books and current expenses are difficult enough to meet, and the majority of the students have to think of the nickels in order to make their allowance cover their expenses. To this large class the additional expense of $10 a term will be a sore infliction." [66]

Three Regents who were alumni openly opposed the fee and indicated their intention to vote against it when it was reconsidered. They were John E. Budd (called the "Champion of the Students" by the San Francisco *Bulletin*), George Pardee (who would succeed Gage as governor), and Arthur

Rodgers. The voluble Regent Reinstein went to some trouble to explain that he stood with his fellow alumni in opposition to tuition at the University as a matter of principle, although he had voted for the fee as a way of equalizing for all students the burden of expense then carried only by those taking laboratory courses.[67]

On the faculty, Martin Kellogg, Armin Leuschner, Joseph LeConte, and Eugene Hilgard all supported the fee proposal, partly in absence of any other available income source, and partly as an extension of the principle that students should pay something for the wear and tear on University facilities. Charles Mills Gayley, of the English department, was a particularly articulate advocate of the student tax. His argument had as its essence "He who pays, appreciates." In elaboration he urged, "We must be careful not to encourage our young men and women to feel that the world owes them a living." [68] In this view he was seconded by Regents Hallidie and Albert Miller. Miller went so far as to invoke the example of President Garfield, who, he said, "gave private lessons to enable him to pay the moderate fee required by his alma mater and if I am correctly informed split wood for his poor widowed mother in his leisure hours, principally at night. May our boys do as well." [69]

At the special meeting held on July 1, 1899, thirteen Regents voted to rescind the fee established two weeks earlier. Two voted in opposition, and the University's unhappy financial affairs were referred back to committees.

THE SEARCH FOR NEW INCOME

Somehow, the University managed to complete the 1899–1900 fiscal year with a deficit of only $5,000. Savings were realized by getting by with the equipment at hand and by allowing classes to grow large. Eight classes containing over 100 students each were in operation during the year. There were also fifteen classes containing between 75 and 100 students and thirty-three classes containing between 50 and 75 students. These large classes helped the University keep the cost per student to a very low $134. This was $28 less than the year before when, according to a study made by Professor Leuschner, of the astronomy department, Harvard's cost per student was $307 and Columbia's was $524.

Governor Gage was well aware that his stand on what he called a "student tax" had cut off income that the University needed. He also sensed that the whole "penny tax" idea might be unsound. In his biennial address of 1901 he suggested that the University was in some ways better off before 1887 when "The condition of the University was . . . exhibited directly to the representatives of the people, and became thereby a subject of public discussion and concern. By this method the people were brought in touch with the management of the institution. By contrast [,] under the laws of 1887 and 1897, the real condition of the University is found only in its biennial reports to the Governor . . . [which] do not receive the general attention of the people." Without making a specific recommendation, he observed, "in the light of the past history of the University, . . . standing taxes for its support are not as productive of benefit to that splendid crown of the common schools as appropriations passed by each Legislature, according to its increased or diminished necessities." [70]

In line with this spirit, the Governor proposed that in 1901 funds earlier appropriated for a governor's mansion be used to alleviate the University's financial burdens. To provide still more help, he proposed legislation that would allow the Regents, for the current year, to use for general support that portion of the two-penny tax that the law required to be set aside for permanent improvements. This latter suggestion was made particularly feasible by Mrs. Hearst's announcement of plans to provide funds for some of the new structures to be erected under the new comprehensive building plan.[71]

None of these solutions were permanent, of course, and the University would continue to have financial difficulties through the next few decades. Governor Gage was probably right in declaring the penny taxes a mistake. They did seem to perpetuate the myth that if one found the right source of income it should keep up with the University's needs forever. And they did absolve the legislature and, to some extent, the Regents from the onerous responsibility of financing the University according to its needs instead of its resources. But they had an important virtue. Their introduction was an acknowledgment by the legislature and the people that they no longer expected the University to sustain itself on income from gifts and its original endowments. Once freed of that notion, the Regents and the legislature could begin to evolve a more reasonable approach to meeting the University's financial needs.

Chapter 9

SAN FRANCISCO DEPARTMENTS AND AFFILIATES

WHEN THE UNIVERSITY of California was established, Americans were even less certain than they are now about what a university should do. As a minimum, there was agreement that a university ought to do what colleges do, but do it better. Before 1868, there was further agreement that a university should provide education for those entering the "higher" professions of medicine and law. Beyond these assignments, many academicians and politicians held universities responsible for the cultural and intellectual development of the people they served. To fulfill those functions, the legislature authorized the Regents to organize all instruction and to enter into affiliation with "any incorporated College of Medicine or of Law, or other special course of instruction now existing, or which may hereafter be created, upon such terms as to the respective corporations may be deemed expedient. . . ." [1] In compliance with this provision the University of California had departments of medicine and law within a decade of its establishment. It had a department of dentistry by 1881. A college of pharmacy was affiliated with the University as early as 1873 and a college of veterinary medicine in 1894. By affiliation and trusteeship, the University was also allied to an art institute and an industrial school for boys before the turn of the century. All were in San Francisco.

DR. TOLAND, DR. COLE, AND THE UNIVERSITY MEDICAL DEPARTMENT

Since the authors of the University's Organic Act were College of California men, the principle of "affiliation" may have been inspired by offers made to the college in 1863 and 1864 by Dr. Hugh H. Toland.[2] Dr. Toland followed the lure of gold to California in 1852. Soon disenchanted with mining, he opened a practice of medicine in San Francisco. He saw private patients in the morning and as many as one hundred clinic patients in the afternoon. All patients filled their prescriptions in his drugstore. Miners and isolated ranchers described their symptoms by mail and Dr. Toland diagnosed and treated them the same way. He was an excellent bone surgeon and was noted for six successful plastic facial operations. Out of an income reported to be about $40,000 a year, he was taking money to build a medical college on Stockton near Chestnut Street.

At that time, the College of California trustees were organizing a mining and agricultural college that would qualify as a recipient of California's Morrill land grant. Dr. Toland was also founding a college, and offered space for the mining and agricultural college in the structure he was building in San Francisco. A year later, 1864, he offered to accommodate a medical school as well, if the College of California wanted to create one. Such an association would have benefited Dr. Toland if the College of California trustees had been successful in obtaining the financial support and recognition they sought from the state of California and the federal government.

When the Toland Medical College opened in 1864, its faculty was derived from two sources. One group was recruited directly by Dr. Toland. The second group came from Cooper Medical College, founded in 1858, which was subsequently affiliated with the University of the Pacific in San Jose, but was forced to close its doors in 1864.[3] The University of the Pacific faction withdrew in 1870 when Dr. Thomas Bennett, dean of the newer school, wrote, with Toland's blessings, to the Regents to say that if they "should deem it expedient to accept Toland Medical College as the Medical Department of the State University—the Trustees of the College will convey by Deed their entire property to the Regents on behalf of the University." [4]

The assumption that the state University should control the quality of professional practice in California lay beneath the proposal of the Toland College trustees that the University's medical department faculty and five other practicing physicians approve the granting of degrees in medicine. The old Cooper College faction of the faculty, which reassociated itself with the University of the Pacific after breaking with Toland, concurred in the idea that the University of California should protect the quality of the M.D. degree, but suggested that it should do so "independent of all medical schools, through which all candidates for graduations, from whatever school, shall receive the diploma of the Medical Department of the University of California." [5]

The advice of the University of the Pacific's doctors notwithstanding, the Regents not only set up the Board of Medical Examiners but accepted the Toland Medical College. In the fall of 1870, the Regents named a Board of Medical Examiners. On November 10, this board nominated five candidates for the M.D. degree.[6] The names of the University's medical school "graduates" appeared in the University of California *Register* in 1870, therefore, despite the fact that negotiations for the transfer of the Toland Medical School to the Regents subsequently, and temporarily, collapsed.

Failure of the move occurred when Dr. Toland imposed, as a condition of signing over the deed to his property, the proviso that the new department should be called the " 'Toland Medical Department of the University of California' and that should the name be changed or the Building used for any other purpose, then the property shall revert to myself or my heirs." [7] The Regents found this provision unacceptable and, on December 6, 1870, rescinded their acceptance of the Toland College of Medicine.

Faced with the prospect of continuing operation of the college on his own with reestablished competition from the University of the Pacific, Dr. Toland enlisted the aid of another famous San Francisco physician, Dr. R. Beverly Cole. Politically astute, Dr. Cole was outgoing where Dr. Toland was withdrawn and gruff. He made important friends and kept them in the same way that Dr. Toland made money and kept it. They complemented each other well, despite the fact that in 1857 Dr. Cole had taken the witness stand in the famous trial of James P. Casey for the murder of James King of Williams, editor of the San Francisco *Daily Evening Express,* to say that the famous journalist had not died of the bullet from Casey's gun, but from improper treatment of his wound by Dr. Toland.[8] The ensuing enmity between the doctors did not end until they joined forces in the medical school.

Dr. Cole became the dean and professor of diseases of women and children at the Toland Medical College. In this capacity he was the principal representative of the college when he and Dr. Toland decided to renew discussions of an association with the University. The University's representative in these deliberations was President Daniel Coit Gilman. This time, Dr. Toland attached no strings to his offer, and, on March 4, 1873, the Regents accepted not only Dr. Toland's lots and buildings on Stockton and Chestnut Streets in San Francisco, but also "a fair beginning of a library and museum, with the collections of materia medica, plates and diagrams, philosophical and chemical apparatus, and other helps to medical instruction." [9]

When the Medical Department was accepted by the Regents, the University was in financial difficulty and unable to spend much money on their new acquisition. It was financed entirely from income provided by student tuition and fees. In bad years, there were assessments on the faculty of the department to meet expenses. In the good years, profits were shared. One of the good ones was 1875, when each faculty member received $350.[10]

The medical faculty governed the department in all of its internal affairs. The entrance requirements they set were so low that any young man or woman of good character who could put together $5 for the matriculation fee and $130 for tickets to the lectures and demonstrations for a year was admitted.[11] Anatomy was stressed. The announcement for the school boasted in 1875: "Indeed the opportunities for prosecuting the study of practical Anatomy, in this city, are superior to those of any known region of the globe. Independent of the advantages in climate, material for dissection . . . is abundant and cheap, and our salubrious breezes not only preserve the cadaver for an indefinite length of time, but secure the health of the student from injury in consequence of the effluvium. . . ." [12] Clinical material was available at the county hospital, city receiving hospital, county jail, city branch jail, house of correction, and San Francisco Benevolent Society.[13]

Courses offered by the department in the early years included principles and practice of medicine, anatomy, physiology, surgery, chemistry, materia medica, clinical surgery, clinical medicine, pathology, midwifery, diseases of women and children, clinical diseases of women, clinical midwifery, ophthalmology, and otology. Because of "the increasing ratio of insanity to population" and "the many casualties, injuries, and deaths . . . in this State involving medico-legal investigation," a chair of mental diseases and medical jurisprudence was added in 1877.[14]

In 1879 an effort was made to upgrade the general level of work in the department. A third year was added to the course (though students still paid only for two), and yearly, graded examinations were instituted.[15] Five years later, standards were further raised by admissions requirements more nearly the same as those at Berkeley and by extending the length of the course from five to nine months, effective February 1, 1885.[16] In the 1890s, the Medical Department faculty decreed that entering students without credentials that would admit them to the academic college of the University would have to pass an examination.[17] They also extended the course of instruction to four years. The first could be spent at Berkeley or any other college for study of chemistry, physics, botany, comparative anatomy, and comparative physiology.[18]

Despite this gradual tightening of standards, enrollment increased steadily. It had reached 50 in 1879–1880, 97 ten years later, and 153 by 1900.[19]

To provide opportunities for postgraduate studies in medicine, the Regents entered into an affiliation with the San Francisco Polyclinic in 1892.

Unlike the Toland Medical College, the San Francisco Polyclinic retained its own property. The affiliation ended after the destruction of many of the Polyclinic facilities in the earthquake and fire of 1906.

MATTERS OF MANAGEMENT

Dr. Toland died in 1880 and Dr. Cole assumed full control of the University's Medical Department, first as dean, later as president of the faculty. The Regents approved the faculty's nominations of new instructors and professors and granted the M.D. degree to the department's graduates in accordance with the faculty's recommendations but they carefully avoided all financial involvement. In December, 1886, the medical faculty petitioned the Regents' Finance Committee for relief from annual expenses for maintenance items "such as repair of building, gas, water, fuel, janitor, laboratory expenses and apparatus." These expenses were barely covered, according to the professors, by the student fees originally intended to provide faculty salaries.[20] The Regents answered with an expression of their appreciation to the Medical Department faculty for its sacrifices, but denied the petition for financial assistance and asserted that the Regents' agreements of affiliation "were purposely drawn to make the financial affairs of the affiliated colleges independent of the control of the Board of Regents." [21] This position of the Regents was not challenged for another decade.

On March 28, 1898, in a letter to the secretary of the Regents, Professor A. A. D'Ancona pointed out that Dr. Toland's gift of his buildings and equipment was unconditional. Moreover, the departments had no trustees, and "management of the institution passed directly from the Board of Trustees of the Toland Medical College to the Board of Regents of the State University. In other words whatever differences exist between the control by the Board of Regents of the Medical Department and any other department of the University are due solely to the action of the Board of Regents, neither shared in nor desired by the Medical Department. The abolition of such differences rests entirely and solely with the Board of Regents, the Medical Faculty neither claiming nor desiring any voice in such control." [22] A special Regents' committee concerning the relationship between the Medical Department and the University reported on June 14, 1898, that they considered a change of status to be in the best interest of the University, its Medical Department, and the profession of medicine.[23] The committee's recommendation was approved on August 9, 1898.[24]

THE COLLEGE OF PHARMACY

For the education of future pharmacists, the California Pharmaceutical Society incorporated the California College of Pharmacy in August, 1872.[25] Two months later, on the initiative of President Gilman,[26] affiliation of the California College of Pharmacy with the University was approved by the Regents.[27] As an affiliated institution, the college retained its own board of trustees, appointed its own professors, established its own courses, and held its own property. Degrees were conferred by the University on the recommendation of the college's own examiners as approved by a committee of the Regents.

Instruction under the new agreement began on July 8, 1873, in rented quarters at 728 Montgomery Street in San Francisco.[28] The following year, the college presented its lectures in the Toland Medical College building on Stockton Street.[29] The year's course included lectures in pharmacy, chemistry, materia medica, and botany.[30] Because most of the faculty members had their own practices and many of the students worked during the day, the lectures were given on Tuesday and Friday nights.[31]

Entrance requirements were not specified in the beginning, although any student who had not studied Latin was urged to do so "to enable him to read prescriptions and pharmacopoeias." [32] In 1875, the faculty anticipated that some kind of entrance examination would be required eventually and advised pharmacists of "the desirability of taking for apprentices such youths only as have the advantage of a liberal education." [33]

Because the terms were not too long (seven months), and lectures were only offered twice a week, the lecture tickets were sold for $50 a year. There was also a $2.50 matriculation fee.[34]

In 1875, Emlin Painter, secretary of the college, reported that the class of 1874 had consisted of 23 students.[35] By 1879 the college was sufficiently prosperous that it began paying its faculty a small stipend. Two years later, thanks to private contributions, a lot was purchased on Fulton Street, near Polk. The college constructed its own building there, finishing it in 1883.[36]

Study of pharmacy at the college was made more attractive by the legislature in 1876, when it provided that any young man who had completed four years of apprenticeship and could produce a college of pharmacy diploma was eligible for registration as a pharmacist without submitting to examination.[37] By 1877, enrollment reached 37 and by 1881 it had risen to 67.[38] At this point, the faculty of the college began to require that students admitted to College of Pharmacy lectures be at least as well qualified by education as were freshman high school students.[39] Tests were given at the end of the first year to weed out students who would be unable to complete the course required for graduation.[40] As a result of these new standards, enrollment dropped to a low of 46 in 1885–1886 but rose again to a high of 114 in 1895–1896. A further tightening of entrance requirements, addition of courses, and decreasing financial rewards received for the practice of pharmacy contributed to another enrollment decline in 1896.[41] The school did not see 100 students at one time again until 1913.[42]

THE FIRST COLLEGE OF THE LAW

In the University *Register* for 1870, the appointment of Justice Stephen J. Field of the United States Supreme Court as nonresident professor of law was announced "as the first step toward the full organization of the College of Law." [43] The second step was not taken until 1878, when Judge Serranus Clinton Hastings set a new course in law school development.

Judge Hastings had been a schoolmaster in his native New York; a journalist, lawyer, and state legislator in Indiana; and a congressman and chief justice of Iowa before making the overland journey to California at the age of thirty-five in 1849. A few months after his arrival, he was named chief justice of California. After two years in that office he was elected state attorney general. Leaving state politics, he entered private practice and undertook banking and business activities that soon made him one of the wealthiest men in the state.[44] In 1878, he announced that he intended to establish a law school and affiliate it with the University of California.[45]

By creating California's first law school, Judge Hastings fulfilled a personal desire to diffuse knowledge of the law throughout society, elevate the general standing of the bar, and perpetuate "the purity and dignity of the Bench." [46] With the help of Regent William T. Wallace, an old friend and at that time chief justice of California, Judge Hastings drafted legislation authorizing him to establish a college of law. His bill empowered a board of directors to manage all business of the college and to appoint its officers. The chief justice of the California Supreme Court was designated, ex officio, as president of the board. One of the founder's heirs would be a member at all times. When the act passed, Judge Hastings was required to deposit $100,000 in the state treasury. Thereafter, 7 per cent in annual interest on his endowment would be paid directly to the college's board of directors. Judge Hastings' bill also directed that the new law college affiliate with the

University, that the faculty of the University confer diplomas on the college's graduates, that the dean of the college be, ex officio, one of the faculty of the University, and that the University provide a room for the college's use at Berkeley.[47] Whether the Regents desired it or not, enactment of the Hastings College bill on March 28, 1878, now affiliated the college with the University. Thus Hastings College of the Law is, itself, a legal curiosity. It is especially so because the law that created it was the last valid legislation to alter the form of the University. After ratification of California's second constitution in May, 1879, the University's organization and government were frozen in the forms described in the Organic Act and its amendments and could be changed only by the Regents. Because the Hastings College Act was regarded as one of the amendments to the Organic Act it, too, enjoyed constitutional sanction. Ironically, this status later prevented the school from becoming a regular department of the University.

Three prominent attorneys, William Wallace, Samuel McKee, and Joseph Winans, were on the committee of the Regents appointed to work out an affiliation agreement. None, apparently, questioned the way the University's relationship to the Hastings College of the Law came about. Almost a year to the day after "Hastings Law Department of the University of California" began operations under that name,[48] the Regents accepted the affiliation. Their action was unnecessary, however, and was probably taken only to demonstrate compliance with the Hastings College Act of 1878.

Judge Hastings was the first dean of the college, but took little part in its instruction. For that work, he hired a prominent New York attorney, John Norton Pomeroy. Pomeroy was a graduate of Hamilton College and had studied law privately with successful attorneys in Cincinnati and Rochester, New York. Between 1864 and 1870 he was professor of law in the University of the City of New York. When Judge Hastings asked him to come to California, Pomeroy was practicing law in Rochester and working on *Equity Jurisprudence,* one of several important books that he wrote for the benefit of students of his profession.[49]

In planning the instruction for the new college, Professor Pomeroy and Judge Hastings made no compromise with the frontier character of California. Entrants had to "possess sufficient knowledge and culture to enable them to profit by the course of study." [50] In practice, that meant a high school education or its equivalent, and by 1892 the entrance requirements were described as demanding "a full university matriculation, such as would admit to the college of Berkeley." [51] Students had to be at least eighteen years old. In these requirements, the Hastings College of the Law exacted higher standards than any other of the "higher" professional schools of the University and most of the nation's law schools, including Harvard's.[52]

In 1879, two women, both certified for the practice of law in California, applied for admission and were rejected. One of them, Mrs. Clara Short-ridge Foltz, carried her claims for the right of admission to the State Supreme Court. That body ruled in her favor and gave as its opinion that when Hastings College of the Law affiliated with the University it "became an integral part of it, and in our opinion became subject to the same general provisions of the law as are applicable to the University; and the same general policy which admitted females as students of the University, opened to them as well the doors of the College of the Law." [53] The judgment illuminated not only the rights of women in the University's professional schools but also some of the implications of affiliation.

What was already called the "case system," introduced at Harvard, was adopted by Pomeroy as the pattern for instruction at Hastings, with the significant difference that he extended the time required for the course to three years. Except for a series of lectures on legal ethics the first year, Professor Pomeroy gave all of the instruction until 1880, when an assistant was hired to direct the Junior class. In 1885, Pomeroy died and his professorship of municipal law was assumed by Charles W. Slack, a future judge, Regent, and dean of the college, who graduated from the University in 1879 and from Hastings in 1882.[54]

The Hastings College Act required that the Regents set aside a room for the college at Berkeley and that the city of San Francisco provide it quarters as well. The school never located in Berkeley despite these provisions. It began exercises in the old Pioneer Hall on Montgomery Street, but moved fifteen times within the next seventy-five years before locating permanently in its own building at Hyde and McAllister Streets in San Francisco.[55]

BEGINNING THE DENTAL COLLEGE

There was virtually no limit to the number of professional affiliates the University of California could accommodate. They were no drain on the University treasury, required little attention from the Regents or faculty at Berkeley, yet gave the University instant identification with professional education in the state. Affiliation was attractive to the founders of professional schools because it meant that their ventures would enjoy the moral, if not financial, backing of the state.

With a desire to do for dentistry what Judge Hastings had done for law and Dr. Toland had done for medicine, Henry Cogswell sought to start a dental college that would be affiliated with the University. A dentist who arrived in California in 1849, made a fortune in mercantile and real estate transactions and retired early, Cogswell broached his idea to the Regents in a letter dated April 11, 1879. About a month later, he deeded a lot and building to the Regents with the stipulation that one floor be occupied by a dental school and that the rest of the building be so managed as to provide income for the school's support. When they could, the Regents would be required to expand the building to acquire income for student aid and for the endowment of a chair of moral and intellectual philosophy.[56] The plan was too complicated to succeed, and although the Regents announced intention to open "Cogswell Dental College" in 1879–1880 they later decided to put the whole idea aside and wait for more promising opportunities to serve the dental profession.

Bay Area dentists prevailed upon faculty members in the University's Medical Department for help in getting a school started. In response, the Medical Department faculty informed the Regents that they were willing to select a faculty to teach dentistry and to provide space in the Toland building, free of charge, for dental instruction.[57] The Regents accepted the proposal and approved organization of the Department of Dentistry on September 7, 1881.[58]

As the first dean of the department (also referred to as a "College" in some early University records) the medical faculty and the Regents chose Samuel William Dennis. Dennis, who was the son of a Maine farmer, sought his fortune in the gold fields ten years too late, arriving in California by ship on May 18, 1859. Discouraged after three years of labor in the mining areas, he entered the office of a San Francisco dentist as an apprentice and studied medicine in his spare time. By 1863, he was able to open his own dental office. He was a founder of the San Francisco Dental Association and later served as president of the State Dental Association.[59]

The faculty of the University's Dental Department consisted of the dean and two other dentists, augmented by Medical Department faculty members teaching physiology, chemistry, anatomy, and surgery.

In its first year, the Dental Department offered a preliminary four-week term in April and a five-month term beginning on June 1. Entrants had to be at least eighteen years old and of good moral character. Fees totaled $165 a year. To win the degree of Doctor of Dental Surgery required attendance at two full courses, satisfactory performance on oral and written examinations, an original thesis, and demonstration of ability to treat patients and make dentures.[60] In 1884, the department became the second in the country to offer a nine-month course of lectures. Two years later, it was the third dental school in the country to require three years before graduation.[61] By the end of the nineteenth century, its admissions requirements admitted only students with three years of high school (including a year's study in Latin).

The faculty of the Dental Department obstinately guarded the integrity of the University's D.D.S. degree. Men who had practiced dentistry for thirty-eight years were refused the degree unless they met the entrance and graduation requirements. At least one member of the faculty could not get the degree without further study, and some of the department's students were men who wanted the D.D.S. degree so badly they enrolled after as many as twenty-two years as practitioners in the profession.[62]

Dr. Cogswell's gift was eventually withdrawn, and the Dental Department remained in its Toland building location until 1891, when its bulging enrollment forced it to move to larger quarters at Market and Taylor Streets.

Like the Medical Department and the California College of Pharmacy, the University's Dental Department was administered by its faculty. Professors were paid out of whatever money was left from tuition income after maintenance and other expenses were met. For the entire first seven years of the department's existence, that share amounted to only $500 for each professor.[63] This state of affairs persisted for some time. In 1894, the dean of the department reported, "The policy of the Faculty has been to devote almost the entire income to educational purposes, which has resulted in our having, probably, the best equipped dental college in the country. . . ." [64] But the same report suggested that the department's record would be a still greater credit to the University if the faculty could be paid fixed salaries, if more central accommodations were found, and if the department enjoyed a closer relationship with the academic parts of the University.

THE CALIFORNIA VETERINARY COLLEGE

The University of California acquired its first veterinary college by affiliation in 1894. The president and secretary of the California Veterinary College wrote to the Regents in November of that year to propose the merger [65] and the Regents agreed to the affiliation on December 11.[66]

Throughout its existence, the California Veterinary College was located at the corner of Post and Fillmore Streets in San Francisco. It had eleven

Freshmen in 1895–1896 and managed to award three D.V.M. degrees in 1897. But its enrollment never exceeded that of its maiden year. Beset with financial worries, charges of mismanagement lodged by the California State Veterinary Medical Association, and faculty discouragement, the school was discontinued in 1901.

THE AFFILIATED COLLEGE BUILDINGS

When Dr. Toland built his medical college in 1864 it was an ample struct-ture. In 1881 it was still large enough to accommodate the University's newly acquired Dentistry Department. But in 1886, the once-commodious building was overcrowded. Enrollment had grown. So had the science of medicine. The need for special laboratories and a library that were not an-ticipated in 1864 was suddenly urgent. The building was also twenty years old and had received only minimum maintenance since its completion. In 1889, the faculty officially asked the Regents to help them get an appropria-tion from the legislature for a new building.[67] Relief came for the Medical Department when the dental faculty moved out of the Toland building in 1891, but the vacated space was soon filled and the need for more room be-came as acute as ever.

In 1893, the dean of the Dentistry Department reported that despite its new location, better accommodations elsewhere had to be secured before the beginning of another session. A total lack of laboratories hampered the College of Pharmacy and kept it out of serious competition with other phar-macy schools in the country. Hastings College of the Law had not been per-manently located since its creation.

Because the needs of all of the professional departments of the University became acute at about the same time, efforts were made to solve all of them at once. The first attempt was made in 1890, when the Regents asked the legislature for funds to build professional-school accommodations. The leg-islature obliged, but the governor vetoed the appropriation. In 1895, a new plan to seek legislative appropriations for professional-department build-ings was placed before the Regents. This time an alumnus, James E. Budd, was governor, and the legislature's appropriations were fully endorsed.

The special needs of the medical center governed the location of the pro-fessional schools in early deliberations. With these needs in mind, Regent Reinstein led a group of Regents who preferred a site on Potrero Street, which was near the San Francisco City and County Hospital. Local authori-ties in San Francisco encouraged selection of this site by indicating a willingness to permit the University to operate the county receiving hospital in the basement of its professional-school buildings.[68] The Regents were also offered a site at the corner of Central Avenue and Geary Street for $55,-000.[69] The most attractive offer, partly because it was to be a gift, came from Mayor Adolph Sutro on September 5, 1895. Mayor Sutro owned several thousand acres of property in the hills south of Golden Gate Park. On one section of the property he planned to build a library. Another large section he offered to the University. Its distance from the center of the city would be overcome, Sutro promised, with the early extension of electric streetcar lines to the area.[70] The Sutro site was favored by Dr. Cole and, later, by a special committee representing all of the affiliated and professional departments involved. It was the ultimate choice of the Regents, as well.

Four major buildings, constructed out of stone quarried by state prisoners at Folsom, were built on the Sutro site. The Department of Medicine moved into its new quarters in October, 1898, but the other departments delayed moving until they could afford the necessary furnishings and equipment they would need in their new location. Until the earthquake and fire, both the Medical and Dental Departments continued to maintain clinic facilities in downtown San Francisco.

Called the "Affiliated Colleges" on San Francisco maps and in University usage for many years, the Sutro Heights complex only accommodated one affiliated unit—the California College of Pharmacy. The California College of Veterinary Medicine forfeited its quarters there. Hastings College of the Law also declined the use of its building, and the space was made available as an exhibition hall for great quantities of archaeological material collected under the sponsorship of Mrs. Phoebe Apperson Hearst. This building was also the home of Ishi, the famous last survivor of the Yana Indian tribe, who was brought to the University to be a "technical expert" on the ways and languages of his people for the University's anthropology department.

For many years, the Regents preferred to regard the professional schools in San Francisco as affiliated institutions regardless of their actual legal status. That way, they avoided financial responsibility for their operations. With the arrival of Benjamin Ide Wheeler as president of the University in 1899, however, the Regents were made increasingly aware of their responsibility for maintaining high standards in any school or department bearing the University name. Within a decade, they began to make all of the professional schools integral parts of the University. In 1934, the College of Pharmacy acquired such status. It was the last of the early professional affiliates to do so. Hastings College of the Law, partly by preference, and partly because of its unique organic character, retains its affiliated status at the present time.

The idea of "affiliation" made it possible for the Regents and independent schools or associations to share the risk in launching new endeavors in education. The University would never have developed professional schools as early as it did, if that procedure had not been followed. The affiliation principle also invited speculation that any worthwhile endeavor for cultural improvement and public enlightenment might well be through some kind of association with the University. Precisely that kind of thinking led in the 1890s to the University's affiliation with an art institute and its trusteeship for a vocational school.

SERVING THE ARTS

At about the time the University first opened, public interest in the arts was cultivated by the San Francisco Art Association, which, in 1874, founded the California School of Design.[71] The art enthusiasts who were members of the association sponsored exhibitions and supported instruction in leased quarters on Pine Street. The University of California became identified with this work in 1893, when Edward F. Searles gave the Mark Hopkins mansion to the Regents in trust, on condition that it be used "for the exclusive uses and purposes of instruction in and illustration of the Fine Arts, Music and Literature or any of them including the maintenance of galleries, reading rooms, and other suitable means of such instruction and illustration." [72] Mark Hopkins, one of the Central Pacific Raiload's "Big Four," spent between $2,000,000 and $3,000,000 building the house and left it to his wife when he died. Mrs. Hopkins later married Searles. Upon her death, he inherited the mansion, a San Francisco landmark on Nob Hill. As a part of the transaction giving the fabulous structure to the Regents, articles were drawn up to effect an affiliation between the San Francisco Art Association and the University. Under the terms of this agreement, the association was given use of the building in return for the responsibility of maintaining it. The association also retained its own board of trustees and faculty. The association's school was renamed the "Mark Hopkins Institute of Art." The Regents retained ownership of the building and authority to grant certificates to the institute's students and graduates. In 1899, Mr. Searles built an annex on the property and called it the "Mary Frances Searles Art Gallery," in memory of his wife, the former Mrs. Hopkins. It provided badly needed exhibition facilities.[73]

The mansion and its outbuildings were burned in the great fire of 1906, and the San Francisco Art Association constructed a new building and called it the San Francisco Institute of Art. In 1916 it was renamed the California School of Fine Arts. The site was sold to the Mark Hopkins Hotel in 1926 and a new building was built on the northeast slope of Russian Hill. There, under the name of the San Francisco Art Institute, the school still occupies property held by the Regents and gives instruction to more than 750 students as an institution affiliated with the University of California.

MR. WILMERDING'S BEQUEST

The public's imperfect understanding of the functions of the University of California was demonstrated in 1894 when J. Clute Wilmerding, a prosperous San Francisco liquor merchant, died and left the Regents $400,000 with which to establish and maintain a trade school for boys. It is true that, after teetering at the financial precipice, weak colleges and universities throughout the country had sometimes made themselves solvent by lowering admissions requirements and devoting at least a part of their effort to vocational education. The Regents had never advocated such a course, however, and the faculty would have resented it if they had. On the other hand, the Regents had been subjected to public condemnation twenty years earlier because they appeared unresponsive to the need for an adequately educated industrial class. Furthermore, $400,000 was too much money to turn down, even when the work it was to support would be only incidentally identified with the University. Nor were the Regents inclined to frustrate Wilmerding's last wishes to provide for young boys an education "fitting them to make a living with their hands, with little study and plenty of work." [74] The Wilmerding bequest was therefore accepted and in 1899 construction of the school began in San Francisco across the street from "The California School of Mechanical Arts," which had been established in 1895 with $540,000 bequeathed for that purpose by James Lick.[75] Before work on the Wilmerding school building was completed, the man the Regents had chosen as principal died and in 1900 George A. Merrill, principal of the Lick School, was prevailed upon to direct operations at both schools. In 1915 boys were admitted concurrently to what inevitably became known as the "Lick Wilmerding School." [76]

Over the years, the work of the school became less and less oriented to education in the trades and by 1941 the Regents and Lick trustees had created a joint Lick–Wilmerding administrative board to govern the institution. Twenty years later, realizing that the University's continuing relationship with the school was inappropriate to its functions, the Regents asked for and were granted discharge from their responsibility for the Wilmerding Trust.

ANOTHER LOOK AT AFFILIATION

In 1897, the Regents were besieged with invitations to affiliate with existing institutions of one kind or another. Cooper Medical College and the College of Physicians and Surgeons of San Francisco asked for an agreement whereby their students would be given bachelor's degrees after three years of premedical study at the University. The Board of Trustees of Hahnemann Hospital Medical College requested an agreement of affiliation similar to that enjoyed by the old Toland Medical School.[77] The requests of the Cooper Medical College and the College of Physicians and Surgeons were denied on the grounds that, according to law, bachelor's degrees could only be conferred after examination by members of the University faculty. The Hahnemann Hospital request was more difficult to handle because it was a homeopathic institution with some important public support, even though its affiliation was opposed by most medical practitioners and by many scientific societies in the state. On September 14, 1897, the regents voted against the Hahnemann Hospital affiliation by a vote of fourteen to four.[78] In 1915, the Hahnemann Hospital trustees renewed their request for affiliation. This time, although there was no affiliation agreement, the Regents consented to make instruction in homeopathic medicine by members of the Hahnemann faculty available to the University's medical students on a purely optional basis.[79]

All things considered, much of the stature that the University of California acquired in the first decades of its life came with the emergence of the professional departments and affiliates in San Francisco. That fact is particularly remarkable because the incentive for these developments came inevitably from outside the University. Not only that, but those professional departments that survived did so without benefit of much more than the Regents' blessings and plenty of hard work on the part of the practitioners who joined the faculties. They gave of their time. When the books wouldn't show black ink, they responded to assessments. They put up with inadequate equipment, cramped, ill-designed classrooms and laboratories, and Regental unconcern. They kept their entrance requirements at least as high as comparable schools elsewhere in the country, even when doing so meant an inevitable loss of enrollment, tuition income, and money for faculty salaries. They served the University, perhaps, but they also served young people who wanted the education they were willing to give, and Californians everywhere who would someday benefit from the skills of the doctors, lawyers, dentists, druggists, and other professional men they taught. In the end, they served the University as well. Certainly it was far better and more complete by 1900 than it could ever have been without them.

Chapter 10

EUGENE HILGARD RESCUES THE COLLEGE OF AGRICULTURE

ANY COLLEGE OF agriculture created out of the benefits of the Morrill Land Grant Act of 1862 had built-in partisans among farmers and the politicians who represented them in state legislatures. These people expected that the agricultural colleges in America's land-grant institutions would soon be teeming with students who would be taught in buildings that were monuments to the dignity of the rural life and would spent pleasant hours each day in character-building toil on model farms.

When John Dwinelle drafted the Organic Act creating the University, these expectations were already vested in the Agricultural, Mining and Mechanical Arts College that had been established as California's beneficiary of the land grants only two years before. Establishment of that college would have to be nullified if the Morrill Act land grants were to be redirected to the University of California. The problem was to do it in such a way that the agrarian interests of the state would not feel betrayed.

Partly to insure compliance with terms of the Morrill Act, and partly to allay the farmers' fears, Dwinelle loaded his bill with what amounted to promises that the University of California would give agriculture special consideration. His act provided that of all of the colleges of the University, the College of Agriculture would be established first.[1] Students were to have the opportunity to participate in a "system of moderate manual labor" in connection with that college.[2] The secretary of the Regents was required by the bill to be a "practical agriculturalist by profession, competent to superintend the working of the agricultural farm." [3] He was also charged with responsibility for correspondence with agricultural societies and practical farmers, "with view of eliciting information upon the latest and best modes of culture of the products, vegetables, trees, etc., adapted to the soil and climate of the State, and also on all subjects connected with field culture, horticulture, stock raising, and the dairy." [4] He was further required to collect seeds and cuttings of as many of the world's plants, shrubbery, and trees "as may be adapted to our climate and soils, or to purposes of experiment therein." [5] If he received more than he could use on the University grounds, he was required to distribute the excess to any private farmer who would cultivate the seeds and cuttings properly and render reports on the results.[6]

The Regents carried out the agricultural provisions of the Organic Act as best they could. They created the agricultural college first, even though there could be no actual planting in Oakland and no one was too certain how much demand for agricultural education existed. The first building at Berkeley was intended for the College of Agriculture and originally so designated, even though it would have to be shared with other departments for a while. It later became South Hall. As it was being built, Regent Hallidie, eager to fulfill the University's obligations in agriculture, urged construction of a wooden structure at Berkeley that would be "suitable for the immediate requirements of the College of Agriculture." [7] In the same spirit, Regent Bolander urged in April, 1872, the appointment of a special committee of the Board to "consider and report upon the best means for the early practical opening of the College of Agriculture, and Horticulture." [8]

Later that year, President Gilman reported that the University's agricultural college "offers a most complete course of instruction, running through the full period of four years necessary to obtain a degree. Those who may be unable to remain so long, or who do not desire to graduate, may take a 'special course.' " [9] But very few students applied for admission to the college, and resident Gilman directed the professor of agriculture to use his time to make the University better known by "agriculturists of the State," through lectures in "all the agricultural counties and centers of population . . . and in every convenient neighborhood where accommodations can be obtained." [10]

Ornamental planting was started at Berkeley before the first buildings were completed. After the move to the new campus from Oakland, fifty-one students were employed in further planting and landscaping, thus meeting the "modest manual labor" provisions in the Organic Act.

In 1874, with funds specially appropriated by the legislature and under the supervision of Regents' Secretary Robert E. C. Stearns, the northwest sector of the campus was developed for agricultural use. A barn was built where the chancellor's house now stands. Propagating houses and work-sheds were constructed. For ornamental purposes, 10,000 eucalyptus trees, 5000 acacias, 200 species of native and foreign conifers, 112 varieties of roses, 13 varieties of azaleas, 12 varieties of camellias, and 6 varieties of magnolias were produced.[11] Orchards, vineyards, and gardens to correct the nomenclature of fruits then in cultivation and "for furnishing hereafter scions and plants for distribution through the State" [12] included 141 vari-eties of apples, 14 of crab apples, 57 of plums, 82 of cherries, 89 of peaches, 22 of apricots, 2 of quinces, 15 of nectarines, 73 of grapes, 7 of blackberries, 8 of gooseberries, 35 of strawberries, 3 of filberts, 1 of asparagus, 16 of rhu-barb, 6 of mulberries, "and all the species of walnuts and chestnuts." Sev-eral varieties of oranges, lemons, and limes were also procured.[13]

The plantings, on land now occupied by Wellman, Giannini, and Hilgard Halls, provided one of several subsurface issues over which Professor of Ag-riculture Ezra Carr later disputed with the Regents. He expected to superin-tend the agricultural operations on the campus himself, and resented the secretary's intervention. His disapproval of the orchards was echoed in 1918 by E. J. Wickson, who became the first director of the University's institutes for farmers and later became dean of the College of Agriculture. According to Wickson ". . . the trees were mostly grubbed out in 1895, long in advance of need for building space, because of unthrift and because, being planted by a 'very competent English gardener' chosen by the secre-tary, they were grown with trunks four or five feet high and were laughed at by visiting California growers as a 'frightful example of how not to do it in this country,' this being about the only instructional purpose they served." [14]

Wheat and oats were grown on the University grounds for several years, first by private farmers who leased acreage for that purpose, and then by the University for experimental planting and for feed for its work horses. In 1875, the wheat crop (about forty-one tons) was not needed by the Univer-sity and was sold.

A SHIFT IN DIRECTION

Under Ezra Carr, instruction in agriculture was liberally salted with refer-ences to the historical, social, and political aspects of farming. According to Wickson, Carr's instruction began "with a thorough course on fruit growing in the Garden of Eden, passing spiritedly to grain growing in Egypt and the conditions surrounding the corner in sorghum which Joseph contrived for Ramses II, pausing to look carefully into the dairy practices of the Scythians, and was rapidly approaching the relatively modern cabbage growing of Cincinnatus when, as tradition declares, both instructor and pupils fell asleep while pursuing dry-farming by the encyclopedestrian method of teaching." [15] With this approach, Carr attempted to tie the study of agriculture to the fields of learning that were more traditionally a part of collegiate education. As though to keep agriculture from soaring completely out of sight at this elevation, Carr anchored it to the soil by insisting that, when all was said and done, no instruction in the subject was worthwhile unless it was put in practice on a college farm. This ambivalent approach satisfied neither the faculty, who could not accept plowing or hoeing as exercises worthy of University credits, nor the farmers, who could not understand how Carr's academic lectures would be very useful to their sons at planting time. Unable to reconcile these two attitudes, Carr eventually revolted against the academic tradition and cast his lot with the farmers and practical education. This strong coalition forced the Regents and the president to defend the University's broader objectives and management before a legislative inquiry. It also led to a reappraisal of Carr's professional competence and his dismissal from the University in 1874.[16]

Carr's successor was Bavarian-born, European-educated Eugene Woldemar Hilgard. In 1855, Hilgard began geological explorations in Mississippi and became state mineralogist there in 1858. Like the LeConte brothers, he performed chemical services for the Confederacy during the Civil War. When the war was over, he joined the University of Mississippi faculty as professor of geology, zoology, and botany. Publication of his work on the soils of Mississippi as state mineralogist and subsequently as a professor of the university there stood as the most authoritative reference on the subject for many years. In 1871 he was named professor of experimental and agricultural chemistry. A year later he became a member of the National Academy of Sciences. In 1873, Hilgard joined the faculty of the University of Michigan. On the recommendation of Gilman, the LeContes, and other members of the scientific faculty, the Regents called him to the University of California in 1874 as Carr's successor.

Hilgard did not try to make agriculture look respectable to the scholars at Berkeley. He took its importance for granted and assumed that any thoughtful person on the faculty would do the same. But where Carr had talked about "practical" agriculture, Hilgard talked about "rational" agriculture. He urged his colleagues and the farmers to consider what might lie ahead for the profession of agriculture if it were conducted less by instinct and tradition and more in accordance with scientific principles. At Berkeley, he devised courses that relied heavily upon the scientific background provided by other departments. While he awaited the time students would come to take them, he devoted his energies to research.

Hilgard considered the University's failure to attract large numbers of agricultural students right away as a natural condition of most American colleges of agriculture. The history of American higher education proves him right. Moreover, he was confident that when land was no longer abundant in California and farmers had to make the most of what they had, they would not only begin to send their sons to the University for science-oriented study of agriculture, but also would make sure that local schools provided adequate preparatory training for such studies.

In the meantime, he offered instruction to the "special students" Gilman had described in 1872 who could not meet University entrance requirements and did not intend to receive a degree but wanted to learn more about agriculture. Two-year courses, covering the agricultural subjects normally taught only in the Junior and Senior years of the regular course in the College of Agriculture, were also offered in the 1880s.

THE EXPERIMENT STATIONS

Hilgard also used these formative years to build up a body of scientific knowledge about California's climate, soils, and practices in irrigation and cultivation. In this work, he carried out the intent of Gilman's announcement in 1873 that "the University domain is being developed, with a view to illustrate the ability of the State for special cultures, whether of forests, fruits, or field crops, and the most economical methods of production. It will be the station where new plants and processes will be tested, and the results made known to the public." [17]

In the 1870s Hilgard made detailed observations of Berkeley's climate and soils and tested the effects of various fertilizers and different depths of plowing on the cultivation of wheat on the University grounds. In one corner of the basement in South Hall, he set up his chemical laboratory. His research was initially supported by the University at an expense of $250 a year. Later, it was supported on a year-to-year basis by special legislative appropriations. In 1878, experimentation in viticulture and wine-making began at the University. This work attracted enough legislative support in 1880 to finance excavation of a fermentation cellar under the carpenter's shed on campus and convert half of the structure into a viticulture laboratory. Four years later, the College of Agriculture occupied the entire building for experimental work.

In 1877, Hilgard published a bulletin describing how soil samples should be taken for scientific analysis, and had it distributed throughout the state. Farmers and other interested persons were urged to submit specimens from their own home regions so that a general profile of California's soil characteristics could be developed. This effort was aided by the Southern Pacific Railroad Company in 1880 when it assigned one of its engineers the job of traveling over the company's lines within the state for the express purpose of collecting soil samples. More than four hundred specimens were gathered in this way.[18] In all, twelve hundred samples were analyzed by Hilgard and were reported in the Tenth Census of the United States as a monograph on "The Physical and Agricultural Features of California."

OUTLYING RESEARCH STATIONS

The University's experiments in agriculture were further extended after passage of the Hatch Act by Congress in 1887. This act appropriated $15,000 a year to existing land-grant colleges for the purposes of establishing and maintaining agricultural experiment stations. The benefits of the act became available in the spring of 1888 and some of them were put to use immediately to build a new Agricultural Experiment Station Building on the site of the old carpenter shop in Berkeley. This building, for all practical purposes, became the main agriculture building at the University and served in that capacity until it burned down in 1897. The building was immediately rebuilt and renamed Budd Hall in 1912, honoring James E. Budd, the first alumnus of the University to become governor of the state and one of the University's first two graduates in agriculture.

Berkeley's soils and climate were hardly typical of the state's principal agricultural regions. Hilgard and the Regents therefore agreed that the bulk of the Hatch Act funds should be used to support outlying experiment stations. To that end, Hilgard divided the state into four main climatic regions, and sought out donations of land and buildings by farmers and communities in each one. Such donations were obtained near Jackson, in Amador County; near Paso Robles, in San Luis Obispo County; and in Tulare, in the San Joaquin Valley. In 1890, a fourth station was built at Pomona. Operations in these stations were supported by the annual congressional appropriations made under the Hatch Act. General supervision and expertise were provided by the agricultural staff at Berkeley, which became known as the "central station."

At the four "sub-stations," foremen under Hilgard's direction collected data on soils, climate, and water. They also submitted reports on the ability of the station to support a wide variety of crops and alerted Hilgard when neighboring farmers introduced new plants or experimented with promising techniques in cultivation.

Because the sub-station foremen were not scientists they did not function as reliably as it was originally hoped they would.[19] In fact, reports submitted to Hilgard by private farmers were often as valuable as those sent from the University's "sub-stations." When it became clear in 1903 that Hatch Act funds were insufficient for all of the activities first contemplated, it was decided to close the stations at Jackson and Paso Robles and take increasing advantage of private farmers' willingness to cooperate with the University by conducting experiments on their own property, using their own labor and equipment. A few years later, the other two of the original sub-stations were also closed.

An immediate effect of the closing of the sub-stations was the diversion of funds to support experiments of the central station at Berkeley. These experiments became more extensive and more sophisticated as a result. Another result was the generation of heavy farmer demands on the legislature for appropriations to support University research on special problems. Thus, in 1903, when growers and canners of asparagus feared the destruction of their crops by asparagus rust, they brought Professor Ralph E. Smith from Amherst to conduct investigations. The treatment he devised was so effective that farmers menaced by other blights raised money to keep him in the area and convinced the legislature to provide funds for the establishment, in 1905, of the Southern California Pathological Laboratory at Whittier, with a branch at Riverside. The Riverside branch of this laboratory evolved into the University's famous Citrus Experiment Station. On request of poultry farmers of the Petaluma region in 1903, the legislature also appropriated funds to establish a station "to ascertain the causes of disease, the relative value of poultry foods, methods of sanitation and liberally to promote the poultry interests of the State." [20] This work was conducted at Petaluma between 1904 and 1909 and was subsequently continued at the University's farm at Davis. In 1905, the legislature joined California millers and grain dealers in providing the financial support for University experiment stations in the Sacramento and San Joaquin Valleys, where the possibility of growing a native wheat rich in gluten could be explored. If the possibility could be proved, California would no longer have to import such wheat to mix with its own in making flour.

By 1890, the University's scientific expertise was so generally respected in the state that Hilgard was able to tell President Davis: "While we are not, as yet, given opportunity to impart instruction to farmers' sons as much as we could wish, we are actually giving a very large amount of information and instruction directly to the farmers themselves, both through our publications and (to an extent often amounting to serious inconvenience) by a heavy and constantly increasing correspondence." [21] By 1903, circulation of Agricultural Experiment Station bulletins had reached 10,000 copies, including many that were sent out of state. In addition, correspondence with individual farmers concerning their professional problems involved as many as 15,000 letters a year.[22]

THE FARMERS' INSTITUTES

In-person conferences with farmers accelerated after Hilgard's arrival in 1874. He knew that he could not be effective in California if he did not enjoy the rural loyalties that Ezra Carr had developed. He also knew that Carr's dismissal would hardly guarantee the new professor of agriculture an enthusiastic welcome in farm communities. His technique in overcoming this hostility is suggested by Wickson, who, as editor of the *Pacific Rural Press,* attended a meeting where Hilgard was confronted by an audience made up of prominent agriculturists intent on snatching the College of Agriculture from the grasp of the "classical institution" located in Berkeley. Hilgard's manner was friendly. He expressed pleasure at being at the meeting; he spoke of his conviction that nothing much could be done for farming without having personal knowledge and support of farmers; he noted his awareness of their political points of view and said he hoped they could talk more about them when they became better acquainted; he stated that he had a great interest in California's climatic diversity and that he had a desire to understand its agriculture better. Drawing upon his boyhood experiences on his father's farm in Illinois, he began to talk about the soils he had encountered there. Then he began to talk about soils in general, how they were formed, and how they could be irrigated and enriched. Throughout his discussion, he carefully avoided scientific language so that his remarks sounded like "straight farming talk about soils and plants." At the end of his talk he asked if any soil in California was as hard to handle as the gumbo soil he had found in the Mississippi Valley. Several farmers immediately nominated troublesome soils on their own farms and asked Hilgard to come and see them. After a brief discussion, the meeting was over and one of the leaders of the anti-University forces whispered into Wickson's ear, "My God, that man knows something!" [23] That meeting was typical of hundreds that followed, and California farmers became accustomed to attending them to learn the newest agricultural information.

In 1890, the college became a beneficiary of a new act of Congress which supplemented federal support of land-grant colleges. With a portion of this money, and at the request of the California State Grange, the University's leadership in organizing educational meetings on agriculture was made formal. The Farmers' Institutes were created, and E. J. Wickson, who had become a lecturer in the College of Agriculture in 1880 and was lecturer in practical agriculture at this time, was placed in charge of the program. In the first three years of the program, thirty-five institutes were held in ten counties.[24]

In 1901, an average of eighty-two institutes reaching 20,000 people were held each year.[25] Instruction by correspondence began in 1903. Wickson and others within the University had adopted a generic term, "agricultural extension," for this total effort, though it did not have that official title until many years later. As important and successful as it was, however, it threatened to be the tail that wagged the College of Agriculture dog. In his report to the president of the University in 1902, Hilgard complained that the demand for institutes was so great that the most valuable members of the college were losing time from their classes and research. Over 25 per cent of the time assigned to certain courses was lost in this way.[26]

He called for assistance in the form of funds to hire assistants who could carry on lecture courses when the professors in charge were on institute duty. The best solution, he suggested, "would be the adoption by this State of the same policy that prevails in almost every State in which Farmers' Institutes are in regular operation, namely the direct appropriation by the State of a sufficient amount to defray the expenses of these meetings. Such appropriation should not be less than $6,000 per year ... rendering it possible to employ competent outside lecturers when obtainable, and also to employ the needful assistance for the home work during the necessary absences of the regular staff." [27]

In 1903, the legislature considered Hilgard's proposal and appropriated $12,000 for the support of Farmers' Institutes during the next two years. Six years later, the annual appropriation for the program was increased to $10,000.[28]

THE UNIVERSITY FARM

Most farmers and many University officials took for granted the need of a farm for the College of Agriculture. In May, 1870, Ezra Carr recommended the establishment of such a farm on the Berkeley campus. His proposal called for the development of 75 acres for the purpose, and provided that he, as professor of agriculture, would be responsible for the farm's planting, exhibition, and financial management. A corollary to his proposal was that he move to Berkeley to begin his work even before the main University buildings were constructed. He asked that the Regents provide a house on the University site for his immediate occupancy.[29] The validity of Carr's proposals was marred by what President Gilman and some of the Regents considered to be an implicit bid for extraordinary personal privileges and benefits (i.e., the farmhouse). They also were made at a time when the Regents' financial resources were very low. No action was taken on them until after Carr's dismissal in 1874.

Although the planting that took place at Berkeley in 1874 was recommended by Carr four years earlier, its instructional value was marginal. Its supervision was entrusted to the secretary of the Board of Regents instead of a professor of agriculture. Students who helped cultivate and maintain it were not formally engaged in any laboratory work in practical agriculture. They were, instead, earning the twenty cents an hour University employment paid for manual labor.

Hilgard took exception to the idea that a farm in connection with the College of Agriculture should illustrate "the best local practice" [30] in farming. Such exemplary practice could be observed directly at any number of good farms in the state, and seriously interested students would derive more benefit from working on such farms as apprentices than they would from studying one operated by the University. Surprisingly, he also had reservations about an experimental farm, which might impart to the younger students "an unsound taste for experimenting," [31] even though it was very useful for the guidance of experienced farmers. If a farm was to be established at all, Hilgard believed that it should be a "model as regards the kinds of operations, crops, stock, etc., showing the best of its kind in everything, without any reference to local profitableness, or adaptability to climate or local circumstances. It is to the student of agriculture what the laboratory and cabinet of minerals, models, etc., are to the mining and metallurgical student." [32] He deemed even this kind of farm infeasible because "such an establishment embraces a great variety of objects and appliances, such as no sane man would think of accumulating on his premises for commercial purposes. Like all other appliances for educational purposes, it is an expense— it cannot be lucrative, or even self-sustaining, except at the expense of the students." [33]

Since the ideal farm was infeasible, Hilgard suspected that alternate proposals were nothing less than attempts of the old advocates of "practical" education in agriculture to undermine the "rational" approach to farming that he championed and cherished for thirty years at the University. Moreover, because Berkeley's soil and climate were not suited to first-rate farm operations, serious effort along such lines would have to be pursued somewhere else and there was danger that the ultimate effect of establishing a University farm distant from the main campus would be the separation of the College of Agriculture from the other branches of learning at the University.

Just before Hilgard's retirement as dean of the College of Agriculture in 1904, Peter J. Shields, a determined young lawyer in Sacramento, undertook what was almost a one-man effort to create a University farm. Until the age of fourteen, he had lived with his family on a farm near Hangtown Crossing. Even though he spent most of his life in the legal profession and as a powerful friend and confidant of politicians in the state capital, he never lost his love for farmers and for the rural values.

In 1899, Shields was named secretary of the California Agricultural Society. In that capacity he learned, for the first time, that other agriculturally important states taught young men and women how to judge the quality of dairy products and other useful agricultural subjects on farms operated by colleges of agriculture. In subsequent investigation, he learned of the work of Hilgard and his assistant (and later his successor), E. J. Wickson, at Berkeley and the outlying experiment stations. He also carried on extensive correspondence with deans and professors at agricultural colleges elsewhere in the country. In 1901 and 1903, he persuaded legislators to introduce bills which he wrote for the purpose of creating a University farm in California. His first bill did not pass in the legislature and his second was vetoed by Governor Pardee, who, according to Shields, said the bill was "too narrow." [34] In 1905, a bill with the same general intention was passed by the legislature and signed into law. It created a commission to locate and buy land for a University farm. Upon purchase, the land was to be conveyed to the Regents, who were made responsible for offering instruction under the College of Agriculture for all persons "who desire instruction in agriculture, horticulture, viticulture, animal industry, dairying, irrigation and poultry raising." The farm was also to be used for agricultural experiments and for the teaching of "short courses" in such subjects as might be offered to "provide for popular attendance and general instruction in agricultural practice." [35]

The state senator who sponsored the bill was Marshal Diggs of Yolo County, and a rider to the bill outlined criteria for the farm site that automatically eliminated many locations but were easily met in Senator Diggs' home district.[36] After looking at fifty sites scattered across central California from the Coast Range to the Sierra Nevada, the commission chose 779 acres of a farm once owned by Jerome C. Davis and located near what was then called Davisville, in Yolo County. In 1906, the land was purchased for $103,290.[37]

One of the sites under consideration in 1905 was a portion of the property owned by M. Theo. Kearney of Fresno. Kearney offered as much land as the commission might need free of charge, if they chose to locate the University Farm there. While the commission's decision was still pending, he had a will prepared that gave his entire estate to the University as endowment of local instruction and experimentation in agriculture. He died in a ship disaster in 1906 after the Davis property had been purchased, but without changing his will. Thus, in 1906, President Wheeler reported that the University had not only recently come into possession of a farm at Davis, but an estate of 5,400 acres valued at over $1,000,000 in Fresno. Only its distance from Berkeley prevented location of a second University farm on the Fresno site in 1906. Instead, the University operated the Kearney property for a few years to earn income sufficient to meet claims on the estate. Most of the property was later sold to provide the endowment funds for the Kearney Foundation for Soil Science. The principal balance of that endowment is now valued at $2,945,633.

Buildings were constructed on the University Farm at Davisville as soon as practicable. In October and November of 1908, short courses were taught there, and in 1909 the University Farm School opened, offering a three years' course to which students who had finished grammar school were eligible for admission.[38]

In view of the fact that the University Farm's admissions requirements were not any higher than those of a high school, it is remarkable that the Berkeley faculty did not object to its association with the University. Instead, President Wheeler gave reluctant support to Shields' efforts, and Ernest W. Major, the assistant professor of animal industries, helped Shields by supplying technical advice. Hilgard opposed the creation of the farm, and Wickson, because of his association with Hilgard, was regarded as "vaguely opposed to it." [39] If Wickson actually did oppose the farm, he changed his mind before 1918 when he wrote that it was fortunate that no effort to arouse faculty opposition had been made. He believed that such effort would have so alienated Shields and his supporters that they would have attempted to set up a "rival institution" to compete with the University for appropriations and farmer approval.[40] By accepting the farm, even with its low admissions standards, the University avoided hostility and unnecessary competition. In the bargain, it won space and facilities for work in animal husbandry; good soil and climate in which to grow typical California crops for teaching and research; and a new public interest in the University's agricultural activities.

THE SUCCESS OF HILGARD'S STRATEGY

Hilgard was no longer dean of the College of Agriculture when the University Farm was created. He had retired the year before. His opposition to the project may have been short-sighted, but it was compatible with principles of agricultural education to which Hilgard had adhered since arriving in California. He believed that experience was an important part of the successful practice of agriculture, but could not be taught, even on a practice farm where techniques were adapted to specific, well-understood, natural conditions. He believed that, in addition to experience, successful farming required a thorough understanding of the true nature of plants, animals, soils, climate, and water, and the complicated ways in which they react to one another. These truths could be learned through scientific investigation. Once learned, they could also be taught, and teaching them was appropriate work for the University. Because it was based upon the established sciences, this approach won for Hilgard the respect of his academic colleagues at Berkeley and gave them confidence in the college of agriculture he built.

Hilgard's prediction that farmers would be more interested in sending their sons to agricultural colleges when land was less abundant came true. In the 1880s, real estate promoters and the railroads sponsored intensive campaigns to lure people from the East and Midwest to California as tourists and settlers. Between 1880 and 1890, the population of the state increased from almost 865,000 to more than 1,213,000.[41] As the new settlers arrived, many of them began farming, and the amount of land per farm in the state naturally declined.[42] At the end of this decade, the enrollment in the University's College of Agriculture began a steady increase from nine in 1889–1890, to thirty-one in 1899–1900, to one hundred and ten in 1904, the year Hilgard retired.[43]

Hilgard's work in collecting information about the characteristics of soils, water, and climate in various regions of the state and then observing the success of many different crops in each region yielded basic information that was of practical use in the successful diversification of agriculture in the 1890s. In bulletin form, the information was available to the new settlers when they arrived. Later in the decade, farmers could get first-hand information from visiting experts at the University-conducted Farmers' Institutes.

By 1900, the annual value of California farm products exceeded $130,000,000.[44] Included were "horses, cattle, sheep, wheat, barley, sugar beets, wine, brandy, raisins, oranges, lemons, alfalfa, dairy products, figs, prunes, peaches, other deciduous fruits, almonds, walnuts, poultry, and an endless list of other products." [45] The great value and diversity of these crops was in considerable measure the yield of Eugene Hilgard's work in the University of California's College of Agriculture. By developing the Agricultural Experiment Station and its sub-units throughout the state he proved the value of research in a subject long dominated by hand-me-down knowledge and tradition. By taking out to the farmers the knowledge few of their sons would come to Berkeley to get for themselves, he placed the University in a new and unexpected role. Public service, for the first time, became as much a part of the University function as teaching and research. By maintaining distinguished standards in all of the College of Agriculture's activities, Hilgard fit it comfortably into University life and made it eminently deserving of every penny of support it received through the Morrill Land Grant Act and subsequent state and federal appropriations.

Hilgard's deanship did not remove the College of Agriculture entirely outside the line of public criticism. The notion that such a college was divisible and, perhaps, lost within the broader work of the University died hard. But Hilgard made the University's College of Agriculture a friend the farmer could not do without. The farmers came to know it. Legislators from rural districts of the state knew it too, and as long as these districts dominated the state senate, the University was assured of support there for any reasonable activity. To that degree, Hilgard's work brought more than fame to the University. He also brought tangible support that benefited every department.

Chapter 11

THE STUDENTS

THE FRESHMAN CLASS that entered the University of California when it opened in 1869 included several future faculty members and three future Regents, including one future governor of the state.[1] They paid a $20 entry fee and $20 more in tuition for each of the three terms that comprised an academic year.

Their Freshman instruction included a modern language (French, German, Spanish, or Italian), history, algebra, drawing, rhetoric, English composition, geometry, physiology and hygiene, natural history, trigonometry, and mensuration. In addition, students who enrolled in the College of Letters were required to take Greek and Latin. Most of these subjects were taught in the mornings. Afternoons were left open for compulsory military instruction for all students at one o'clock on Mondays and Fridays, and laboratory practice and electives for more advanced students.

When the members of the pioneer Freshman class began their second year, prospects had brightened. For one thing, tuition had been abolished. For another, on October 3, 1870, the Regents voted to admit women students "on equal terms, in all respects, with young men." [2] Seventeen young ladies registered for classes in 1870–1871, but only eight were in attendance at any one time. The course work of the pioneer class was again loaded with requirements that year. They continued to attempt mastery of a modern language and to acquire the skills of rhetoric and English composition, studied physics, chemistry, botany, drawing, navigation and surveying, mechanics, and zoology, and attended laboratory demonstrations. Laboratory practice was made available on an optional basis. Students in the College of Letters still had to take Latin and Greek.

When they became Juniors, the members of the pioneer class got a little more variety. All members had to study a modern language, mental philosophy, mechanics, mineralogy, and zoology, and, again, the students in the College of Letters had to study Latin and Greek. But students in the Colleges of Arts (agriculture, mining, and civil engineering) were offered specialized work in analytical chemistry, surveying, mechanical drawing, topographical survey, and metallurgy.

President Gilman was at the University for the Senior year of the class of 1873 and he boasted that the University's elective system "permits any person to receive its instruction in any branch of study at any time when it is given in due course, whether he wishes to study anything else or not." [3] In practice, this policy applied only to special students who did not intend to graduate or take an advanced degree. Regular students had little elective opportunity since they were required to study physics, geology, a foreign language, and linguistics at least, and most of them also had to attend mandatory classes or lectures on moral philosophy, meteorology, mineralogy, law, modern history, political economy, ancient literature, Greek and Roman archaeology, and hygiene. The old "Colleges of Arts" were now listed in the *Register* under the heading, "Colleges of Science and Arts," and Juniors and Seniors enrolled in them received special instruction in their chosen subjects. This special work was demanding. In chemistry, for instance, Seniors were required to spend twenty-four hours a week in the laboratory.

The general subject pattern of instruction at the University remained unchanged for many years after the class of 1873 graduated. By 1881, students may have had a little more flexibility in determining the order in which they took their courses, but the requirements were similar to those of 1872, and a minimum of sixteen hours of instruction a week was required for the bachelor's degree. In 1893 there were more faculty members and more courses available. That year, the *Register* announced that completion of 125 units (weekly instruction hours) was required for a bachelor's degree. Seventy-one of those had to be selected from a list prescribed by the student's college. Another twenty-four had to be chosen from one of several lists of "group electives," specified by the college. These "groups" contained from four to ten courses. The remaining thirty units were to be selected from "free electives" chosen by the students. The total 125 units could be easily amassed by students who attended class at least sixteen hours a week.

A sixteen-hour week does not, on the face of it, seem overlong. But it should be kept in mind that many students spent from three to four hours a day commuting to the University from homes in Oakland or San Francisco and still others (about 50 per cent of the students in 1874) worked at manual labor on the University grounds, at San Francisco trades, or in the service of private families to help put themselves through college.[4] In 1891 a "Free Employment Bureau" was established to help students find work at "typewriting, copying, tutoring, gardening, carpentering, etc. . . . to earn a part, or all of the funds to carry them through college."[5] The University paid twenty cents an hour to students who helped with gardening or landscaping, maintained the heating apparatus, or worked in the printing office on the campus.

University officials were proud of their working students and pleased that the student body was not composed of idle young men of means. "One of the best characteristics of the American colleges," John LeConte said in 1875, "is the bringing together on terms of equality, free from artificial and conventional distinctions, [of] young men of different pecuniary conditions. The sons of the rich and of the needy grow up side by side, and the honors which they receive from one another and from the Faculty are bestowed without any reference to the homes from which they come."[6]

ROOM AND BOARD

Some parents considered the education of their children so important that they packed up and moved from wherever they were to the Bay Area in order to be close to the University. The father went to work in Oakland or San Francisco. The mother opened extra rooms to lodgers. This pattern of adjustment to the economic crisis represented by an offspring's going to college could be one of the reasons why, in 1897, a sixth of the University's students lived at home in Berkeley, and almost half lived in boarding houses.[7]

Twenty years earlier, when the University was still located in Oakland, the percentage of students taking board and room in private homes was much greater. Such accommodations were the only ones available for students whose family homes were very far away. Dormitories were suspected by many mid-nineteenth-century educators and moralists of being incubators of student disorder, and the University's Organic Act succinctly declared: "The dormitory system shall not be adopted."[8] Instead, the Regents relied upon the initiative of private citizens to meet student housing needs.

The situation was bad enough in Oakland. For a while, it was worse in Berkeley. When President Gilman announced that the University would definitely move to Berkeley in the fall of 1873, a writer for the student newspaper expressed a genuine and widespread student concern in two poignant lines:

I'm sure we'll have no place to slape
And what shall we do for something to ate.[9]

When classes convened the following September, about twenty students were housed in buildings on the University grounds.[10] The top floor of North Hall and two very small wooden structures were made available for this purpose. The rest of the students lived either in Oakland or Temescal (a village midway between Oakland and the University), or made the two-and-a-quarter-hour commute by ferry and horsecar from San Francisco.

In 1874 a town had begun to develop around the campus. Among its establishments were the University Hotel, the Berkeley coffee saloon and lodging house, and the "Antisel House, a spacious three-story building, with restaurant attached, kept by Mrs. Murphy." [11] There were also several boarding houses, but they were considered expensive and their proprietors tended to select their tenants at random, a practice that failed to promote cordial student associations.

While the University was still in Oakland, a group of students from Healdsburg got together to develop an alternative to public accommodations as an answer to their housing needs. They obtained a house near the University, hired a Chinese cook and houseboy, and shared expenses of provisions. They called themselves a club and had prescribed rules and regular meetings. A writer in the student newspaper observed that they lived "quietly, cheaply, and well." [12] When the University moved, the club, called the "Bach Club" (for bachelors) or "Healdsburg Club," also moved, and occupied a building adjacent to the University Hotel. A second club was organized and occupied the bunkhouse originally built for the construction workers who put up North and South Halls. Members of this club paid their rent to the state through President Gilman. The two organizations reduced their members' living expenses to "sixteen or seventeen dollars per month, for each person, including rent, food, washing, lights, fire, and service." [13]

President Gilman was so impressed by the success of these *ad hoc* clubs that he convinced the Regents to build cottages on the campus and to lease them to student clubs for $300 a year. Eight cottages were built in 1875, including five in the southwest sector of the campus between Strawberry Creek and what is now Edwards Track Stadium, and three (for women) located more or less along the creek in the eastern sector of the campus. The cottages had four bedrooms, each accommodating two students. In addition, there were a parlor, dining room, kitchen, and servant's quarters.

But what had been done by students on their own initiative could not, apparently, be done by them under the University's aegis. Some of the clubs economized so drastically in the hire of servants that they forfeited proper day-to-day maintenance of their quarters and adequate meals. A few of the cottages were so abused that the Regents refused to lease them to men students any longer and they were offered, instead, to members of the faculty and staff of the University.[14]

The "club" arrangement might have been more successful if other developments affecting the need for living accommodations had not occurred before they were long under way. More hotels and lodging houses opened in Berkeley. The town's citizens were fitting out spare rooms and setting extra chairs at the dining table to accommodate student boarders. Transportation from Oakland and San Francisco was made faster. The pokey "bob-tail" car on the Choate (Telegraph Avenue) route to the University from Oakland was replaced by a steam-powered train. The improvement cut travel time over the route by almost two-thirds. A steamboat began to keep a regular schedule between San Francisco and "Jacobs' Landing" at the foot of what is now University Avenue. At the landing, busses picked up passengers and brought them to the vicinity of the University.[15] In 1876, a railway connection was made between the Oakland wharf and a "Berkeley Terminus" at what is now Shattuck Avenue and Center Street.[16] The commute on this route still required three hours a day for students who ferried over from San Francisco and more than two hours a day for students living in Oakland. But it was convenient enough for the 45 per cent of the University's students who lived in those two cities as late as 1888.[17]

Commuters and other students who were unable to eat at home could not find enough places to eat in Berkeley. For those who brought food from home, a lunchroom was outfitted in the basement of North Hall, but it became a campus disgrace. Benches were broken in roughhousing, walls were stained in evidence of fiercely fought apple-core battles, and other equipment in the room was in general disarray. Sermons by student leaders and campus newspaper editors brought no improvement.

An adaptation of the residence-club idea solved the problem for many students. Six eating clubs with such names as The Ghouls' Retreat and the Pi Eta Hash Club were listed in the 1877 *Blue and Gold*. Some of them had slogans, such as "Sic Semper Turkeybus" and "Lettuce have Pease." [18] Two years later, only one eating club continued to exist.

In 1894, on the initiative of some of the students, the University Dining Association, open to faculty members and students alike, began operations in one of the old student cottages in the eastern part of the campus. It became decreasingly popular with the students at about the same rate that it became increasingly popular with the faculty members. Eventually, it survived only as the nucleus of the Faculty Club on the Berkeley campus.

Women students found the shortage of adequate housing and eating places particularly difficult. In about 1898, the situation became so bad that a group of them took their problem to Dr. Mary B. Ritter, the women's medical examiner. Dr. Ritter had helped women students obtain limited access to the gymnasium on an earlier occasion and they thought she might champion their cause on housing matters. To gather facts, Dr. Ritter visited every girl enrolled on the campus. What she found was deplorable: ". . . not all of the residences by any means, had been connected with [city] sanitary systems. Outhouses still existed and sometimes nearby wells supplied the drinking water. In such houses bathing facilities were either definitely inefficient or entirely lacking. I also found that where conditions were the worst, the boarding-house keepers were the most reluctant to let me inspect them." [19] One by-product of her survey, incidentally, was a University regulation that students of the two sexes must live in separate houses. Another was that houses that did not meet local sanitary codes were reported to city authorities.

The solution Dr. Ritter worked out was very much like the old "club" plan of the 1870s. Through the generosity of Phoebe Apperson Hearst two clubhouses, to be occupied by a house mother and fifteen girls, were outfitted. Then the students took over, sharing expenses of rent, maintenance, and food on a pro rata basis. These first two clubs were so successful that in 1903 President Wheeler appointed a committee of faculty members and faculty wives to develop others, "in order to help those who at present are living in an unsanitary way: some in garrets, some in sheds in back yards, and many doing their own cooking and not supplying themselves with wholesome food." [20] The committee raised money for furnishings and utensils and then lent it to student groups prepared to develop residence clubs. As these loans were paid off, money was offered to other groups. During the thirty years that the committee was in existence, it helped to establish forty-two clubhouses—twenty-three for women and nineteen for men. Some of them eventually became sororities or fraternities.[21]

In 1908 and 1910 private entrepreneurs announced ambitious plans to build dormitories for students. Most of these schemes failed to materialize, but one, College Hall, a large boarding house located across Hearst Street from Founders' Rock, provided student housing until it was destroyed by fire in the mid-1920s. Attempts during the 1900s to raise dormitory construction funds by public subscription failed, and the University had to wait until 1928 before anyone would come forward to build a student dormitory of respectable size at Berkeley.

FRATERNITIES AND SORORITIES

The most enduring achievements in providing food and lodgings through student organization were made by the "secret societies" or fraternities. Only a year after the University opened, six young men met in Oakland's Newland Hotel and formed the Iota Chapter of Zeta Psi fraternity. Chartered the following year, 1871, the chapter became the first college secret society on the Pacific Coast.

It was more than a mere residence or eating club. Its aim was "to gather a company of manly, sympathetic students, whose union would tend directly to the promotion of zeal in study, the formation of warm and lifelong friendships, and whose combined influence should be exerted in the college ever in the direction of progress." [22]

The members of the fraternity took an active part in all student activities on the campus and made their influence felt in some of the most prestigious organizations. The main one was the Durant Rhetorical Society, named for the University's first president, which held discussion meetings and debates and published the *University Echo,* the first student newspaper. The Zetes also formed the first boat club and the first dramatic club at the University. After the move to Berkeley, the fraternity occupied a farmhouse near the campus for a year and then leased the Humboldt Park Hotel in Temescal. There, members not only had commodious rooms for sleeping, studying, dining, and chapter functions, but also had a 10-acre garden, a skating rink, bowling alley, and a shooting gallery at their disposal. After a year in this luxury, the fraternity moved to a rented house on Dwight Way near the University in 1875 and, in 1876, built their own chapter house on a lot just east of the University grounds (site of the present School of Law). Constructed by ex-Regent Samuel Merritt, this three-story wood house stood until 1911, when it was replaced by a more substantial and handsome one made of brick.[23]

The success of the Zeta Psis invited attempts at duplication. By 1879, therefore, there were five fraternities at Berkeley and the faculty and some of the Regents were beginning to wonder if such organizations should be encouraged. For one thing, their development tended to divide the student body between men who were in and men who were out of fraternities. The ability of a secret society to take over the traditional campus organizations was considered a threat to the rights of all students to participate equally in the life of the University. Moreover, whenever there was riotous, noisy, or offensive conduct on the part of students, members of the "secret societies" were frequently found at the core of it. To halt further development of such organizations, the faculty, with the approval of the Regents, voted in 1879 to require all Freshmen to sign a pledge that they would not join any secret society during their association with the University. By thus shutting off the supply of future members, the faculty intended to pronounce a death sentence on the fraternities.

The faculty's action caused an angry uprising of fraternity men and fraternity alumni throughout the state. They claimed that the faculty had acted in response to complaints of jealous non-fraternity men who not only slandered the societies but framed the Zeta Psis for producing an "incredibly vulgar" number of an ephemeral publication called the *Scylla*.[24] The members of the fraternity hired a detective to "ferret out" the real authors and asserted later that the slander alone "conclusively" proved them innocent of the accusation.[25] Under mounting pressure from alumni, the Regents declared the matter to be entirely under the faculty's jurisdiction and the faculty backed down.

With a more hospitable attitude toward secret societies prevailing, the University's first sorority, Kappa Kappa Gamma, made its appearance the following year. But student opposition to fraternities continued and no other sororities were established for another decade.

The fraternities controlled the *Berkeleyan,* a student newspaper that, in 1874, merged the old *University Echo* and the *Neolaean Review,* which had been launched in March, 1873, by a Sophomore debating organization similar to the Durants. The *Berkeleyan* had opposition from the *Occident,* a successor to the anti-fraternity newspaper that helped arouse faculty opposition to the fraternities in 1879. In the first number of its 1882 edition, the *Occident* openly declared itself to be "an anti-fraternity paper." [26] It explained that its aim would be to tell "the unvarnished truth" about the fraternities but promised also that "whatever in them or their conduct is upright and good will be shown up as far as we are able." [27] The editors found little that was upright and good and much that was not. One of its more vituperative stories appeared in 1889 and claimed that "the drunkenness, the debauchery, riotry, cheating in examinations, and what there was else of [University] crime was shown to exist in the fraternities almost entirely. . . ." [28]

Some fraternities and some fraternity men fully deserved the denunciations that the *Occident* vented. On the other hand, members of these mysterious "secret societies" were commonly found among the leaders in student publications, athletics, and debating societies. Moreover, in 1896, fraternities were providing housing for 122 students.[29] That fact alone mitigated much of the censure that fell upon fraternities because of occasional reprehensible conduct.

DEFENDERS OF CLASS HONOR

The reputation fraternities acquired for rowdiness was practically never earned as the result of organized activity of the brotherhoods. Instead, it was earned by individual members, or small groups of them, participating too zealously in the general rituals of college life. Long after they had graduated, the exploits of a fraternity's most daring members were recounted around the chapter house fireplace. With the telling, the rituals of student life at the University were perpetuated. None of the legends were so certain to make timid boys brave and brave boys foolish as those that told of some fraternity hero's exploits in the rivalry between the classes.

From 1869 to 1905, every class in the University enjoyed well-defined status and customs of its own. The Seniors were considered guardians of University spirit and tradition. They were seldom participants in adolescent foolishness, but they were always around to instruct the members of the lower classes in the manners—good or bad—of University life, and to settle quarrels among them. As befitted their dignity, they wore black top hats —a headgear often battered and dirty, but exclusively theirs. Also exclusively theirs was the privilege of sitting on the "Senior Bench" they built in the shape of a large "C" in 1898, but rebuilt in 1899 in more conventional form, near the door to the student store in North Hall.

The Juniors also wore top hats, called "plugs." Theirs were gray, and though they were battered as conscientiously as those of the Seniors, they were elegantly decorated with University, class, and fraternity emblems. The principal contribution of the Juniors to University life between 1874 and 1925 was publication of the *Blue and Gold,* the campus yearbook. In the hands of the Junior class, this popular annual not only recorded events of historical significance, but also provided a diversified sampling of collegiate humor. Another activity of the Juniors was the Junior Exhibition, begun in 1875. It began in the morning and continued until evening, featuring music, essays, debates, and athletic contests calculated to demonstrate the superior talents of the members of the class.

The role and conduct of the Sophomores, if it can be understood at all, is understood best after one becomes familiar with the lot that had been theirs as Freshmen.

The Freshmen at the University were presumed innocent of any subtlety of life and gullible in everything having to do with the University. They were hazed by the Sophomores and ignored by everyone else. Their annual extravaganza was a funeral for Bourdon and Minto at the end of the year. This custom was adapted from a practice at Yale. Its name came from two textbooks: Bourdon's *Elements of Algebra* and Minto's *Manual of English Prose*. Its classic form involved a mournful procession at nightfall when white-robed Freshmen carrying Chinese lanterns followed a casket containing the hated books through the Berkeley streets and onto the campus, where it was burned and buried. When the solemnities were over, according to a report in 1877, ". . . the ghostly garbs are doffed, and now begin the orgies." [30] These orgies came to involve considerable drinking and rough-housing that attracted a "great number of 'small boys,' tramps, and other outsiders," and to counter their pernicious effects the Berkeley Temperance Society gave a social in the Congregational Church after the burial of 1878.[31] By 1882 the event had been charged with another exhilarating ingredient, violent confrontation of the Freshmen with their tormentors—the Sophomores. That year, a student editorial scolded the Freshmen for their conduct: "Of course they did not mean to seriously injure any one, but they should have known that their excitement would not permit them to use clubs with delicate moderation." [32] By 1903, the burials were so dangerous to life, limb, and private property that they were abolished by edict of President Wheeler.

Sophomores were Freshmen grown a year older. The collegiate code gave them the role of hell-raisers and they seemed perfectly willing to play it even though upperclassmen smugly chided them for their transgressions. Thus, when members of the Sophomore class went to a San Francisco theater in their traditional campus garb—mortar boards and robes—the *Occident* berated them for "desiring merely to draw the attention of the audience from the stage to the queer 'things' in the boxes." [33]

Sophomores considered it their duty to harass the Juniors in return for torments suffered at their hands the year before. Their principal weapon was a "bogus" program written and printed by Sophomores to parody the Junior Exhibition. By 1968 standards, these programs were as offensive as nursery rhymes. By standards of the 1870s, however, they were "hardly the thing to bring into polite society." [34] The "bogus" program of 1879 was considered particularly offensive. A graduate of the University wrote to the *Alta Californian* that, "at the first glance, it appeared obscene and vulgar, and the impression that it is so grows with every subsequent reading." [35] The faculty was so upset that it expelled seven Sophomores believed most responsible for the publication.[36] To protect their classmates, twenty-seven more men of the class signed letters to the faculty claiming complicity. That left only nine of the forty-three men of the Sophomore class (1881) who were in no way involved in the incident. Despite the fact that a son of Regent McKee was one of the signators of the letter, the faculty obliged all of them with suspension. When a delegation of the offenders' parents arrived to ask for leniency, the faculty allowed them twenty minutes to make a presentation and then promptly resolved to hold to their original course until the suspended students volunteered to clear themselves and answer any questions the faculty might ask about the affair.[37] Twenty of the expelled or suspended students had been reinstated on the faculty's terms by the opening of the new term, but the morale of the class was so shattered by the harsh discipline imposed on its members that they forfeited their privilege as Juniors to edit the *Blue and Gold*. The members of Zeta Psi produced that year's annual in their stead.

The Junior Exhibition was again the target of Sophomore attack in 1884. According to the *Berkeleyan,* the Sophomores hid the gymnasium platform, defaced the walls of the building with bomb explosions, broke windows, and issued a "disgraceful bogus program." [38] For this infraction, the members of the offending class received the surprisingly mild punishment of being denied the privilege of holding a Junior Exhibition of their own in 1885.

THE RUSH

The Sophomores harassed the Juniors out of habit and revenge. They tormented the Freshmen out of a sense of duty imposed by collegiate tradition. They were prevented from subjecting individual Freshmen to pain and indignity by the Academic Senate's decree in 1881 that "hazing" would thereafter be punishable by dismissal.[39] That time-honored test of the manliness of University newcomers was soon replaced by the "rush." This sport had its variants, but the basic rules were simple. On a given day agreed upon by the two classes, or upon any insult to the honor of either class, the Sophomores and Freshmen would engage in hand-to-hand combat until one side had all of the members of the other thrown to the ground and tied up.

It was a dangerous pastime. In order to stop it, the faculty lectured their Freshmen students throughout 1891 to impress them with the tradition's evils. They tried to convince their young students that activities like the rush were "entirely out of date . . . discountenanced by the largest universities of the land," and that it was not nice "to get out and tear each other's clothes." [40] As a distraction, the faculty organized a football game between the Sophomores and Freshmen that year. They spoiled it, however, when "they first had a number of the fiercest of both classes declared physically incapacitated. . . ." [41] The editors of the *Blue and Gold* denounced the experiment, asserting that it did not satisfy the function of the rush at all. In the rush, they said, the Freshmen "of necessity organized and became acquainted before the contest, were well rubbed together in the course of it, and came out united and with the best of good feeling." [42] The contrasting result of the football game was that "one side won and the other side was beaten; and No. 2 laid it up against No. 1 as an injury which must be recompensed at the first opportunity." [43] The rush was brought back in 1893. In 1897, despite the fact that members of the football squad were forbidden to participate, the event resulted in two broken legs and a broken jaw.[44] Condemnation of the rush became stronger and was voiced by many responsible students, as well as by the faculty and outside observers. Castigated and outlawed, it died hard. In fact, the rush persisted until 1905 when President Wheeler was finally able to convince the lowerclassmen that the University had outgrown it. It is commemorated by a huge concrete "C" built on Charter Hill above the Greek Theatre.

CALIFORNIA TAKES TO THE FIELD—BUT SLOWLY

The rowdiness exemplified by the class rush and the "orgies" following the Bourdon–Minto burials might have had their roots in the unrestrained individualism commonly found in young societies. The fact that neither Oakland nor Berkeley offered students many places to go for amusement after class hours certainly contributed to their behavior. Moreover, the University did not have the resources to provide much more than academic instruction, and the faculty tended to let the students find their own interests and enthusiasms rather than guide them into organized extracurricular activities.

One notable result of the students' preferences for unregulated spare-time activity was that athletics played a minor role in their lives for many years. At Oakland there was class competition in baseball and football. Occasionally, one of the class teams would challenge a nearby high school to a game. But that was the extent of it, and from this unimpressive state of affairs, according to accounts in the *Berkeleyan* in 1873, athletics declined. In

1875, because the University teams had "a rather nondescript style of playing," [45] the editors of the *Berkeleyan* published the rules of the game of football as used at Eastern colleges, in hopes that it would stimulate more interest in the sport.

A rifle team and boat club were organized in 1876, and, in 1878, foot racing was taken up. Other sports would not develop until adequate facilities were available for them.

One of the first major clashes between students and the University administration occurred in 1875 when the University Base-Ball Convention, a student council governing conduct of inter-class baseball competition, was joined by the *Berkeleyan* in a campaign to force Secretary of the Regents R. E. C. Stearns to have a pile of rocks and rubble removed from the area used as a drill and sports field. [46]

When the playing field was finally cleared, the University still lacked indoor facilities for physical training and exercise. These were supplied in 1879, when A. K. P. Harmon, who made his fortune in Nevada mining investments, had a gymnasium designed and constructed at the University. The building was completed in January, 1879, and the University's first Field Day took place about four months later. The *Berkeleyan*'s description of this event was as follows: "The attendance was small, and a large part of those present were students. The exercises were opened with music, after which came the first round of a boxing match. After this, more music and another round, then more music and the first round of a Roman wrestling match. In this round Burke threw Rothchild to slow music. Then came the remaining round of the boxing match, Janes, '81 being declared the winner. Rothchild, '79 won the next two rounds of the wrestling match, and was declared the winner. More music, which was apparently played against time, was followed by a 100 yard dash. . . ." [47] Other events of the day were the standing wide jump, mile walk, mile run, quarter-mile run, high kick, standing high jump, running high jump, and hop, skip, and jump.

Another inducement to the development of athletics was the introduction of a cinder track on the western portion of the grounds in 1883. This was called the "campus," a term that was intended to distinguish it from the academic section of the University.

Competition with other schools picked up in 1886, and by 1893 the *Blue and Gold* was able to report: "In athletics the University has far excelled her record in any previous year. We have beaten our old rivals, the Olympic Club, in football, and have tied Stanford, and in field athletics we have beaten both. Beside a number of Coast records we now hold the world's hurdle record for 120 yards." [48]

That 120-yard hurdle record time of 15¾ seconds was made by Walter Henry. It was not recognized by officials of the American Athletic Union, however, because they believed it beyond human capacity. In 1895, some of them began to admit that they might have been wrong. That year, a small track team from the University went East and astonished sports fans by winning decisively against Princeton, Pennsylvania, and Illinois. Their triumphs ignited a latent University spirit at Berkeley. Class loyalties became subordinated to a greater loyalty to Alma Mater. Songs and cheers were composed in her honor, and the golden bear, whose silhouette had been sewn onto an improvised flag for the traveling track team, became her totem.

This new spirit was at its height during a championship baseball game between the University and Stanford in San Francisco on April 15, 1899. At the game, Stanford's rooters showed off a huge red axe they had used the night before to decapitate a blue-and-gold-clad dummy at a rally. Accompanied by cheers of "Give 'em the Axe," they used it during the game to taunt the Californians by chopping blue and gold ribbons into bits. After the game, nine sons of the Blue and Gold rushed the custodians of the Stanford Axe and stole it. A wild chase through San Francisco's streets ensued, but after sawing off the handle to facilitate concealment of the blade, the trophy was smuggled to Berkeley, where it was proudly exhibited the next day. Thirty-five years later it became a trophy awarded to the winner of the annual "Big Game" (football) between Stanford and Berkeley.[49]

THE GENTLE PASTIMES

Athletics could not fill all of the students' spare time, and general hell-raising and mayhem in connection with inter-class warfare occurred only a few times a year. There were many idle hours to be filled by exploiting what limited recreational opportunities were afforded by the University and its environs. Hiking and hunting in the Oakland hills were popular diversions, and everyone liked to sing. These three activities were sometimes combined when a group of students spent the day hunting in the hills and then, as night fell, roasted quail or even venison and finished the evening with a keg of beer, singing, dancing, and marching around the campfire. This was the basic form of the "bust" that was considered an appropriate way to celebrate anything from a baseball victory to the appearance of the full moon. One night in 1873 such a song-and-drinking fest was under way in the Berkeley foothills when the Regents were showing the campus off to a committee of legislators.[50] Two days later, a law was passed in Sacramento to prohibit the sale of spirituous liquor within two miles of the University's grounds. The bust continued to be a part of University life, however, and so did the singing.

Until the 1890s the University songs were such standards as "Bull Frog on the Bank," "Solomon Levi," and "Seeing Nellie Home." Early in that decade, the first University song was written. Sung, incredible as it sounds, to the tune of "Music in the Air," its main words were those of the college yell: "Ha Ha Ha, California, U.C. Berkeley, Zip, Boom Ah." It was easily improved on later in the decade with "Palms of Victory" and the "Golden Bear." "All Hail, Hail to California," "Fight for California," and the "Stanford Jonah," which are still popular, did not appear until after the turn of the century.[51]

At one time, all University classes had their own glee clubs, and during the 1890s and 1900s the Seniors gathered on the steps of North Hall for their "Senior Sing" once a week.[52] A University of California Glee Club that drew membership from the entire student body was formed in 1888.[53]

The first instrumental aggregation of the University was a brass band, student inspired, student organized, and virtually self-instructed. To provide the band with instruments, several Regents, President Gilman, ex-President Durant, and prominent Bay Area citizens donated enough money by early 1874 to pay for "a set of fourteen brass, German-silver-trimmed instruments." [54] A drum had been donated, too. All the band needed, one of its representatives told Gilman, was a large room for practice that should be "situated at a sufficient distance from recitation rooms to avoid disturbance." [55] It was anticipated for a while that the new band might be ready to make an appearance in June, 1874. Unhappily it was not. The next year, the *Berkeleyan* complained that the whole band project had failed and suggested that, in its place, a fife-and-drum corps be organized to enliven the drill of the University battalion.[56] A full-fledged marching band was not organized before 1891.[57] Until that date, instrumental music on the campus was imported from Bay Area military installations or was hired in San Francisco.

Mandolin and banjo clubs were organized in about 1895 under the direction of C. R. (Brick) Morse, '96. Morse later became director of the Glee Club, gave it a professional polish, and made it internationally famous as he led it on tours throughout the state, to Europe, and to the Orient.

Somewhat more cerebral than the musical organizations during the University's first three decades were the literary and debating societies. The Durant Rhetorical Society was the first one, and dated back to the old College of California days. Other societies with intellectual orientations were the Longfellow Memorial Association, German Club, Greek Club, Homer Club, Science Association, and three groups with interests in art.[58] All of them were in existence in 1900. The most notable organization of this type, however, was the Philosophical Union, formed in 1889, under the leadership of Professor George H. Howison, who came to the University five years before as the first Mills Professor of Intellectual and Moral Philosophy and Civil Polity.[59] The common practice of this society, which was open to the faculty, students, and interested members of the public, was to study the works of one contemporary philosopher for a full year. A highlight of the year was an address at the University by the philosopher himself. John Dewey presented the Philosophical Union address in 1899 and William James presented his theory of pragmatism for the first time at a meeting of the Union in 1898.[60]

In 1892, the old Durant and Neolaean Societies were consolidated into a single debating society called the Students' Congress,[61] which conducted its meetings in the manner of a legislative assembly. Debating in the familiar style also remained popular. In 1898, an audience "overcrowded Metropolitan Temple" [62] to hear a University of California team debate with Stanford on: "Resolved, that the system of unrestricted production of prison-made goods, for sale in the open market on the public account, is preferable as a system of prison management, to that which is in operation in the State of New York." [63] A special train carried supporters of the University of California to Stanford the same year to participate in the annual Carnot Debate. This debate was established in 1894, when Baron de Coubertin gave the University and Stanford money to buy each year a medal named for the assassinated French president. The medal was awarded to "the best extemporaneous speaker of the two universities, each being permitted to enter three men in the contest. The question of discussion must always be some phase of French history or politics." [64]

Off the campus, the social life of the students centered on evenings at the theater, opera, and other attractions of San Francisco, and parties at the homes of students living in the Bay Area. When Mills Seminary came to Oakland in 1871, the girls there began to invite the men of the University's Junior and Senior classes to musicals that featured chamber music and dancing. The University's own gala was a grand ball held each December in one of the finer hotels or meeting halls in Oakland or San Francisco.

STUDENT DISCIPLINE AND GOVERNMENT

When Clarence J. Wetmore, the first student to register in the University in 1869, wrote his name in the register, it appeared under this wording: "We, severally enter this University, with a full understanding and acknowledgement of these truths, vis: It is the duty of every Student to submit to the rules and government of the University. No combination, pledge, promise or vow can create an obligation to violate duty." [65] Beyond that pledge, few rules were imposed. The statutes of the University concerning student behavior were brief and vague:

> It is presumed that every student will deport himself, while at the University, with the same propriety which he would feel bound to observe elsewhere in society. Students are assumed to be gentlemen, and they will be treated as such.
> 1. During the hours set apart for University exercises, it will not be in order for students to linger about the grounds, the passages or the vacant rooms.
> 2. It will not be in order, at any time, to throw any kind of missiles upon the University premises, except such as are used in games of recreation permitted by the President.
> 3. At the end of each hour, the bell will ring, and the classes and sections will be dimissed.
> 4. It is not in order to leave a class room during the progress of any scholastic exercise. If extraordinary circumstances compel a student to withdraw, he will obtain the assent of the officer presiding, and will return as soon as possible.[66]

The four specific rules were no longer published after 1874, but the paragraph that introduced them was paraphrased in the University *Register* until 1879 in this form:

> The rules of the University are few; the exactions are strict. Good behavior, under all circumstances, regularity and punctual attendance at all appointed exercises, diligence in study, and the maintenance of thorough scholarship, are expected from all the students. Failures or negligence in any of these respects will render the student liable to private and public admonitions, to dismissal, and, in cases of heinous misdemeanors, to expulsion. Formal reports are not regularly transmitted to the parents, but the Professors will be ready to give information respecting the standing of a student, to his parent or guardian, whenever it is requested.[67]

President Reid, of course, relied upon the students' "better inclinations" [68] rather than rules to insure acceptable behavior. In support of his position, one could argue that the rules had not prevented the Bourdon–Minto burials from declining into a massive student free-for-all. They had not discouraged hazing. And they had not prevented the publication of the "bogus" that brought suspensions and expulsions to Sophomores in 1879. Far more influential than printed rules or official warnings published in the University *Register* was the leadership of members of the Senior class, who had, after all, been through all but one undergraduate year at Berkeley.

President Gilman attempted to communicate directly with students when he called meetings of the entire student body every Friday afternoon. Here, announcements of interest and value to the students were made, and distinguished visitors or members of the faculty spoke. Quite popular with the students when they first began, the meetings were later resented. On September 30, 1876, a writer in the *Berkeleyan* said: "It must be admitted by all of the students, that our Friday afternoon lectures are not popular. . . . How many would be present if Assembly did not immediately follow drill? The officers know that watchfulness is necessary, as the companies enter the room, to prevent desertion." [69] The weekly lectures were abandoned not long thereafter.

One of the reasons for the failure of both the lecture meetings started by President Gilman and the rules published in the University *Register* during the 1870s was that the University itself was too new and too unformed to command a loyalty capable of overriding that which any young man would have for his pals. The University, as such, was not really solving the students' day-to-day problems of finding places to live or devising entertainments for their free hours. Students were doing those things for themselves. Sometimes their solutions were embarrassing to the University. But in an entirely uncoordinated way they somehow managed to form clubs, find housing, make eating arrangements, locate students who shared special interests, and create a constellation of diverse student activities peculiarly appropriate to the needs and conditions of the University of California.

The first attempt to bring several of these activities together under a single authority was made in 1887, when the Associated Students of the Colleges of Letters and Sciences was created. Its announced purpose was to "effect a more perfect union of the student body, and provide an efficient government for the settlement of all matters of general student concern." [70] Its main functions were to control athletics and field days and to assume responsibilities for student welfare.[71] Two years after its establishment, it was renamed "Associated Students of the University of California."

Until the students could acquire a clearer idea of what their University really was and where they fit into its work, it would be impossible for the new student organization to realize its full potential. Until that time the students would continue to be governed according to unwritten articles of individual conscience and self-discipline reinforced occasionally by the brotherly advice of upperclassmen. They could have done much worse.

Chapter 12

MARTIN KELLOGG

REGENT BARTLETT and his committee were determined to find a man of prestige and experience to fill the presidency in 1892. To that end they had persuaded the Regents to enlarge the authority of the office. To find outstanding nominees, they consulted men like Charles Eliot of Harvard, James B. Angell of Michigan, Nicholas Murray Butler of Columbia, Jacob Gould Schurman of Cornell, and H. B. Adams of Johns Hopkins.[1] At least one of these, Schurman, was, himself, offered the presidency.[2]

A surprising result of their canvas was that Bernard Moses, a man already on the Berkeley campus, was as highly recommended to them as most available candidates from the top-flight institutions in the East. Then forty-six years old, Moses was a handsome man whose polished manner attested to his years of undergraduate study at the University of Michigan followed by graduate work at Leipzig, Berlin, Lund, Upsala, and Heidelberg, where he earned his Ph.D. degree. He joined the University of California faculty in 1875 as a professor of history with instructions also to teach either philosophy or political economy.[3]

Professor Moses was as respected at home as a teacher as he was respected elsewhere as a potentially important university administrator. Therefore, when Regent Bartlett asked for the opinion of the faculty on Moses' acceptability as president of the institution, he regarded the move as a formality. To his dismay, the faculty's response came in the form of a petition signed by twenty-two of the most respected members of the Academic Council, and concluded with the advice: "We do hereby respectfully submit as our profound conviction, based on an intimate knowledge of all the facts, that if a President is to be selected from the [Academic] Council, the choice should fall on Professor Martin Kellogg." [4]

Bartlett probably was not too surprised. In 1881, 1885, and 1888—each time, after LeConte, that the University needed a president—the name of Martin Kellogg inevitably found its way among the nominations. His association with the University from the days when it was no more than an alluring idea cherished by men like Henry Durant and Samuel Willey made him a sentimental favorite. His calm leadership of the faculty in the politically turbulent 1870s was credited in some quarters with having prevented wholesale faculty resignations when the University could least afford them. His years in the acting presidency had been constructive ones. Enrollment was on an upward trend. The University's popularity within and outside California was greater than ever. In 1892, although the University was only twenty-four years old, it stood sixth, after Harvard, Columbia, Yale, Michigan, and Cornell, in annual income; seventh in enrollment; fifth in the size of its faculty; and in a four-way tie for eighth position in the percentage of its students engaged in graduate studies.[5] Kellogg, as faculty leader since 1885 and acting president since 1890, could not, although he never sought it, be denied a large share of the credit for this impressive record.

Professor Moses wanted the presidency, and, within the severely inhibiting rules of propriety observed in an academic society, he openly sought it. Because of his relative youth and his talk of reforms and changes he would like to institute, he became known as a "radical" candidate for the presidency. For this reason, he appealed to Regent Bartlett's sense of what the University needed. After all, Bartlett was, himself, a formidable opponent of Stebbins and other "conservative" elements on the Board. Ironically, Professor Kellogg had been passed over for the presidency several times when Regent Stebbins played the kingmaker. In 1892, Kellogg was suddenly the champion of the conservatives on the Board of Regents. Even more surprising, the faculty that was usually characterized as being under tyrannization by Stebbins and his "ring" were now backing the conservative candidate by an overwhelming majority.

The Regents were supposed to choose a president in September, 1892, but postponed their decision, as a result of the faculty's attitude toward the Bartlett committee's candidate. While the matter was thus pending, alumni (who seemed to be completely divided between the candidates), students (who favored Moses without criticism of Kellogg), and newspaper editors (who were as divided as the alumni and the Regents) set forth their views, circulated petitions on behalf of their favorites, and turned the whole matter into a contest with all of the trappings of political electioneering.

The Regents who favored Moses were not, at first, put off by the faculty's opposition. It made no difference, one of them said, "whether the hired men of the institution at present working at Berkeley liked or disliked the actions of the Board of Regents or a President selected by the Board." [6] This faction also asserted that Kellogg was not entirely responsible for the University's success. Instead, they believed, the high standing of the University was only the natural result of a momentum provided by the growth of a prospering state. On this point, with more seriousness than was probably intended, one Regent wondered aloud if Bartlett's committee had "observed the success of the Board in 'running' the University without a president, and had the stupendous difficulty of finding any man who would combine so many excellences as were manifest in the board been exhaustively considered." [7]

The Regents met to decide the matter on January 24, 1893. Finally resigned to the folly of supporting a man who would not enjoy the confidence of the faculty, Regent Bartlett nominated Kellogg. Moses was also nominated. A lengthy debate ensued and several votes were taken in an effort to amass at least two-thirds of the votes of the Regents present for one candidate or another. This plan failed and Kellogg was eventually declared elected by a vote of nine to five.[8]

QUIET, CONSTRUCTIVE YEARS

Martin Kellogg was sixty-five years old when he assumed the presidency of the University of California. He was unimpressive in appearance and unpretentious in manner. To his wife, he was "that long-suffering m-a-n," [9] and his twenty-two years of unpublicized service to the University and its antecedent made the description apt.

Reporters in San Francisco were dismayed by his low-key responses to their burning questions soon after his election. One reporter asked if he planned any sweeping changes. The new president said he had a few in mind but that he had already put his main ideas into practice during the two years of his acting presidency. The reporter asked if the opening of Stanford University a little over a year before did not mean that the University of California would have to pursue a more vigorous policy to retain its prominence. Kellogg answered, "Why, that implies we are doing very little here, and that is not true. We are working effectively, even though with somewhat of quietude." [10] The reporter mentioned Stanford's President David Starr Jordan as a man who was making his institution popular by "bringing to bear his commanding personality in almost constant intercourse with society at large." Kellogg simply responded, "We are not quite so dull here as we appear." [11] He then enumerated the success of the University in accrediting high schools and offering extension lectures (inaugurated in 1892) in San Francisco, Oakland, and Los Angeles. He might also have mentioned a revitalization in the research and instruction going on in agriculture under Professor Hilgard. He did have a few ideas for the future, it turned out, and he shared them with the interviewing reporter. First, he mentioned his desire to institute a college of "pure" science to meet the needs of students not interested in technology. He also suggested that the University might exert its influence to alter high school courses so that secondary students who did not plan to go to college would have an alternate program of useful instruction.[12]

The accomplishments of Kellogg's presidency during the ensuing six years were significant without being spectacular. Colleges of Natural Science and Social Science which granted degrees without requiring students to take courses in Latin and Greek were organized. A College of Commerce and a new department of pedagogy were created. Summer sessions began for the benefit of California's school teachers who wanted to keep up with the latest knowledge. Administration of the University was modestly decentralized with the appointment of deans for each college to replace the single dean of the College of Letters and of the Colleges of Science. A Graduate Council was appointed to guide the studies of increasing numbers of postgraduate students. Finally, to encourage research, Kellogg persuaded the Regents to appropriate funds to publish faculty writings by the University Press.

After President Reid left the Unversity in 1885, the faculty carried on the work of visiting communities throughout the state, advising school boards about the University's admissions requirements and courses of instruction, and encouraging establishment of local high schools. During Kellogg's years in the presidency, this policy brought new benefits to the youth of the state, and to the University itself.

An inevitable consequence of the pressure exerted upon community school boards to offer high school level instruction was grass-roots pressure in Sacramento to make the financing of such offerings easier on local taxpayers. The legislature responded in 1891 with laws that authorized the establishment of county and union high school districts.

One provision of the new law required that the high school course of study be such "as will, when it is completed by the student, fit him for admission to the University of California." [13] This provision gave explicit legislative sanction to the role the University had already assumed as a pace setter for the state's secondary schools. The University accredited twenty-five new high schools in 1889–1891; thirty-one in 1891–1892; and forty in 1892–1893. When the Regents failed to appropriate funds to finance high school visitations in 1895, they were besieged by so many complaints that the examination of schools was resumed in 1896, even though only half of the usual appropriation was made for it.

The University's role in high school development was so completely recognized in Sacramento that, in 1897, a law was passed to require high schools to select their textbooks from a list prepared and approved by the "Accrediting Board of the State University." [14] The faculty greeted this vote of confidence with dismay, however. By action of the Academic Council they declared the new law "highly undesirable and contrary to sound public policy," [15] and refused to accept the responsibility it would thrust upon them.

Kellogg also succeeded in attracting philanthropy to the University. It was during his presidency, for instance, that Cora Jane Flood donated the Menlo Park estate developed by her father and a controlling interest in the Bear Gulch Water Company as an endowment for a foundation for the study of economics at the University. Also during his presidency, Phoebe Apperson Hearst's philanthropies began . . . including sponsorship of the dramatic, world-wide competition for the development of an architectural plan for the Berkeley campus.

In 1897, after a banquet celebrating the decision of the legislature to provide more amply for the University's permanent financial support, a newspaper remarked that it was strange when all of the congratulations were handed out "there was little said of the person who was aptly described by one of the alumni as 'our quiet, self-obliterating president,' who really stands in closer relations to the new prosperity of the University than anyone else." [16]

The Regents were so impressed with Kellogg's leadership that in 1897, Regent William T. Wallace, chairman of the committee to select committees, reported to the Board: "Your committee believes that the Executive Administration of the Colleges at Berkeley should be vested wholly in the President and that he should be held strictly accountable for the standing and efficiency of the colleges, the qualifications and abilities of the Professors and Instructors, and the conduct of the University generally." [17] To that end, his committee recommended that the Regents' Committee on Internal Administration be abolished. Regent Stebbins, after twenty-six years of continuous service, had completed his second term as a Regent in 1894 and was not on hand to protest. His old friend Regent Hallidie was, however, and succeeded in delaying the action for one month. But the Regents' desire to grant greater authority to the president was too strong and, although Hallidie was joined by a few other Regents and President Kellogg himself in resistance to the action, the committee was finally abolished in September, 1897.[18]

Just a year after Kellogg's hands were "unbound," as the newspapers liked to tell it, he submitted his resignation, effective March 23, 1899.[19] By that date he was seventy years old and ready to pass the presidency to a younger man.

Martin Kellogg, after three years as acting president and six as permanent president, broke the University's presidential jinx and lasted longer in office than any of his predecessors. The basic reasons for his success were his long, deeply involved association with the University and his cool, sensible approach to its administration. He saw the mistakes and achievements of his predecessors as a part of the entire history of the place and was able to use that perspective to good advantage. He could walk comfortably on both sides of the street—where Regents strode or where the faculty walked. He began, of course, as the faculty's man. He understood them and lived up to their standards of what an academic leader ought to be. For his time, he was also the perfect Regents' president—content to stay in the background, accurate in his interpretation of the concerns and attitudes within the campus, and sympathetic to the fears and ambitions of the Regents themselves. Excesses of student sport and recreation did not perturb Kellogg as deeply as they did his predecessors. That made him more poised in handling discipline cases. He was also a loyal rooter, not above tossing his derby high into the air when California triumphed on the field or diamond. That made him kindred to the spirit the students shared. He was also, and above all, dedicated to the upbuilding of the University and worked for that cause untiringly. That won him the respect and affection of everyone.

Under Martin Kellogg, the presidency had been only slightly strengthened. But it was no longer an office that could be ignored. And it was strong enough that a younger man, Benjamin Ide Wheeler, could take it and work wonders in the next quarter of a century.

Chapter 13

BENJAMIN IDE WHEELER

MARTIN KELLOGG's administration gave the faculty and students of the University a taste of institutional stability. During his presidency the legislature provided more adequate financial support. The students behaved well, and caused no scandals to arouse the indignation of the citizenry. The President's relationships with the Regents and the faculty were characterized by mutual respect. No University constituency made a bid for power to provide the public a spectacle of internal conflict. Never anxious for the limelight, the President avoided giving public speeches and stuck close to his desk in South Hall. Fortunately, he didn't have to do more to assure that the University was fairly treated in the state capital. As long as James Budd, a loyal alumnus, was governor of the state (1895–1899), the University's interests in Sacramento were adequately protected.

Kellogg's presidency and Budd's term as governor terminated within a few months of each other. Henry T. Gage, Budd's successor, came into office with an allegiance to no alma mater and a pledge to economize in every branch of government. This change in attitude at Sacramento worried Regent Reinstein, who wrote to Hallidie on February 27, 1899, to suggest "that something should be done to make the University's position more clear to the people of the State, or to their representatives in the Legislature, and to His Excellency, the Governor of the State, and perhaps all three of these sources." [1] One of the first things that had to be done, of course, was to find a new, vigorous, and personally appealing president to replace the seventy-year-old Martin Kellogg, who was scheduled to retire the following month. Reinstein's concern was properly directed to Hallidie, because Hallidie was chairman and Reinstein was a member of the Regents' committee to nominate a new chief executive.

The University's reputation for using up presidents rapidly made the committee's task difficult. To complicate matters further, Kellogg had not exercised the new powers given him in 1897 and the tradition of Regental rule remained strong. Furthermore, despite rules against the practice, members of the faculty were increasingly accustomed to take complaints and requests directly to members of the Board. A presidency that could be circumvented by both the Regents and the faculty was not easy to sell to a strong candidate.

Phoebe Apperson Hearst, another member of the committee to nominate a new president, wrote in October, 1898, ". . . the men we most desire to have will not leave other fields of work or opportunity unless they are practically guaranteed a long term and very full powers. This latter, it is difficult for the Regents to grant without abdicating their office. . . ." [2]

THE CANDIDATE AT CORNELL

Harvard's Charles W. Eliot recommended several men for the California presidency. The last one on his list was Benjamin Ide Wheeler, a professor of philology and Greek at Cornell. Eliot expressed bewilderment because Wheeler "still sticks to his Professorship, although I know he has been offered at least six presidencies, two of which were very good ones." [3] C. K. Adams, president of the University of Wisconsin, had also recommended Wheeler to Reinstein. [4] In February, 1899, Regent Arthur Rodgers, another member of the nominating committee, corresponded with Adolph C. Miller, an alumnus of the class of 1887, who was then a professor at the University of Chicago. The topic of their letters was Benjamin Ide Wheeler, whom Miller met while he, too, was on the faculty at Cornell. [5]

On September 7, 1871, about two weeks before the University of California began its third year in Oakland, seventeen-year-old Benjamin Ide Wheeler and three equally young companions entered the city of Providence, Rhode Island. "Fear of the wicked city filled our hearts," [6] he wrote later, and he and his friends, all classmates the previous year at the New London Academy in New Hampshire, spent a restless night in a downtown hotel awaiting the hour for taking entrance examinations for Brown University the next day.

Wheeler was a good student at Brown, where he earned membership in Phi Beta Kappa, became captain and first baseman of the baseball team, and was a member of the class crew. After receiving his bachelor's degree in 1875 and his master's in 1878, he remained at Brown as an instructor for a few years. In 1881 he married Amey Webb, of Providence, and, with his new bride, went to Germany for four years of study of classical philology at Berlin, Leipzig, Jena, and Heidelberg. Upon his return, with a Ph.D. degree, he taught for a year at Harvard and then went to Cornell, first as a professor of comparative philology and later as a professor of Greek and comparative philology.[7]

Wheeler's first personal encounter with a Regent of the University of California came in February, 1899. To prepare for it, he asked Adolph Miller for advice: "I know about the Univ. of Cal. in a general way," he wrote, "and have a very high respect for it. It has seemed to me the best and soundest institution west of Chicago. I have heard however that it is a hard berth for a president,—between Regents and Barons. Please tell me quick and tell me true all there is about the situation there." [8] Armed with whatever Miller saw fit to tell him, Wheeler met with Regent Rodgers in New York. Shortly thereafter, the Regents were invited to a secret dinner at San Francisco's University Club.[9] There, many of them met Wheeler for the first time.

Wheeler was not the only candidate. When the Regents met in June to make the final decision, four men were considered. One was James E. Stubbs, then president of the State University of Nevada. Another was Edward N. Vallandigham, a professor of English at the University of Delaware. The third was William Carey Jones, professor of jurisprudence at the University. Wheeler got eleven votes on the first ballot and the other candidates received one vote each.[10]

Before coming to the University, Wheeler wrote to the Regents to request that four conditions be met:

(1) That the President should be in *fact,* as in theory, the sole organ of communication between Faculty and Regents;
(2) That the President should have sole initiative in appointments and removals of professors and other teachers and in matters affecting salary;
(3) That the Board, however divided in opinion during discussion, should in all things the President is called upon to do regarding the Faculty, support him as a unit;
(4) That the President should be charged with the direction, subject to the Board, of all officers and employes of the University.[11]

Wheeler returned to California in July, 1899, to acquaint himself more fully with the University and to confer with some of the Regents. He did not leave until after the Regents met on July 18 and agreed to the conditions he had imposed for accepting the presidency. When he left, he did so with the announcement that he would leave Cornell in October to come to California permanently and assume his new duties.[12] With Wheeler's selection, Kellogg's presidency was formally concluded and Regent Hallidie was authorized to exercise the functions of the presidency until Wheeler returned.[13]

IT HAS BEEN GOOD TO BE HERE

In considerable detail Bay Area newspapers reported the preparations of the new president, his wife, and his young son to come to California. Not since Edward Holden had the University of California imported a president from the East. Not since Daniel Coit Gilman had it imported a president with so much favorable advance publicity.

As the day of President Wheeler's arrival approached, "a simple meeting on the campus between the President and the students" [14] was planned. It took place on October 3, the day after Wheeler arrived. Bareheaded, but impressively tailored and erect, he spoke to the students from a small platform near the campus flagpole. His message was a curious blend of erudition and pep-rally camaraderie. The style left no question as to who was the commanding presence, but its openness also suggested that any gulfs one might imagine to exist between a University president and his student body could, after all, be bridged by mutual candor and confidence. He spoke of the University as "a family's glorious old mother." [15] As such, she was entitled to affection and honor: "Love her. It does a man good to love noble things, to attach his life to noble allegiances. It is a good thing to love the church, it is a good thing to love the state, it is a good thing to love one's home, it is a good thing to be loyal to one's father and mother, and after the same sort it is good to be loyal to the University, which stands in life for the purest things and the cleanest, loftiest ideals." [16] He dismissed the students saying, "Now it has been good to be here and we will go unto our homes in peace." A man who could speak with such feelings and not seem pretentious was a new experience for the students at Berkeley. They went to the welcoming ceremony prepared to admire and respect him on the basis of his reputation as a teacher and scholar. After October 3, they were also prepared to follow him as a child follows a father.

SETTING A NEW TONE

The students at the University soon learned that their new president had no admiration for young men who brawled and damaged University property in the name of class honor. The student larks that involved heavy, organized drinking, challenges of civil or University authority, affronts to normally accepted standards of decency, and disrespect for persons and property of others incurred his displeasure and for virtually no other reason became less acceptable to the students themselves.

The change took a few years, but it came without formal regulations or intensified enforcement. It was achieved almost entirely by increasing the exposure of the students to the ideas and expectations of the President of their University.

The main device used to improve exposure was the University meeting, held every other Friday morning when the President was in town. University meetings featured talks by the President, members of the faculty, and visiting dignitaries. Wheeler himself usually presided and frequently took a few moments to give words of advice or to make important announcements. Time was sometimes allowed for student discussion, and, after the tradition became well established, students were invited to help arrange the meetings. When he learned that some students were staying away because they felt too restrained by the lecture-room atmosphere, Wheeler announced that students should feel free to sing, yell, and enjoy themselves within the bounds of good order.[17]

The first University meeting of the year always starred the President. It gave him a chance to welcome new students and tell them what he expected to be to them. "You are called to be the children of the University," he said, "and I am called to preach the Gospel." [18] His Gospel might have been labeled platitudinous were it not for his obvious sincerity in preaching it and his unmistakable expectation that his advice would be followed:

No college man has any right to believe in that damnable thing called a "pull." [19]

Beware of the men who advise you to be a little practical when they mean for you to be a little bad.[20]

An educated man will not be swayed by clamour or cowed by gossip and rumor. Human herds sometimes stampede like cattle, but one chief reason why we are taking pains to educate men is to eliminate the stampede.[21]

The man who lives by himself and hoards himself I am sorry for. The man who lives with other men gets more out of his college life.[22]

The University will regard as the highest type of student the man who can attain the distinction of being enrolled as a candidate for honors without becoming a "dig," who can share naturally and wholesomely in the activities of the campus, athletic or otherwise, and yet hold to the essential truth that good scholarship is the all-important college activity.[23]

Of such sentiments Wheeler composed his advice to Freshmen. But on these occasions he was always talking to the entire student body as well, reminding upperclassmen why, in his opinion, they were at the University, and encouraging them toward an honorable completion of their collegiate careers.

By thus giving his personal endorsement to precepts of honor, justice, truth, and other traditional virtues, he assured students that the guiding principles that they had relied upon when they were at home in Auburn, San Jose, or Redding were valid in Berkeley, too.

He repeated two themes over and over again because they were particularly relevant to the University community. The first was the democratic principle that every man should be judged for what he is and does and not by his heritage or associations. "Do not tolerate in yourself, do not recognize in others," he admonished, "an arbitrary self-rating according to unreal tests such as family connections, membership in particular bodies, and worldly possessions. There is a place where 'handsome is as handsome does'." [24] Conflict between the "Greeks" and independents, between the sons of wealthy parents and poor ones, between students of engineering and letters had no place in Wheeler's University. The second theme of President Wheeler's messages to students was that loyalty to the University was paramount. This applied to boosterism, which he unabashedly condoned. "Cheer for her," he said, "it will do your lungs good." [25] And he cheered for the University himself, explaining: "It is a very noisy thing, and a very undignified thing to do to join the great *concentus virtutum* which rises from the rooter's section on the great field day, but it is our way. . . ." [26] There was a deeper loyalty involved, too. It was a loyalty that put the good of the University above one's self, or one's affiliations. In accordance with this theme, he let the students know that he considered class rivalry and particularly the class rush an "obnoxious and a baleful thing, a thing which this University has outgrown." [27] Despite Wheeler's opposition, the rushes continued, usually under strict faculty surveillance, but not without injuries, until 1905. But on March 20 of that year, the members of the classes of 1907 and 1908 joined forces to build a huge concrete "C" on Charter Hill above the University grounds. The work was finished on Charter Day when the Sophomores and Freshmen, finally subordinating their traditional rivalry to their loyalty to the whole University, affixed a plaque to their handiwork. It read: "In

Memory of the Rush buried by the Classes of 1907 and 1908, March 23, 1905. *Requiescat in Pace.*"

Whether the student body consisted of 2,229 young men and women, as it did when he arrived, or almost 7,000 as it did in the last year of his administration, the principles President Wheeler espoused at University meetings and other student gatherings became an almost tangible force for cohesion and order in the University community.

STRENGTHENING STUDENT GOVERNMENT

Within a month after his first greetings to the students of the University around the campus flagpole, Wheeler was given an opportunity to test their sense of responsibility. James Whipple, the captain of the University of California football team, figured prominently in the defeat of Stanford in the 1899 Big Game. The next day, he was given all of the honors of a hero. He also faced faculty discipline for playing in the game with an academic deficiency and in defiance of explicit orders. Instead of allowing the faculty to handle the case in its usual manner, Wheeler turned it over to a committee of Seniors. After hearing the facts, this student committee recommended that Whipple be suspended for half a year. Their recommendation was subsequently accepted by the President.

Wheeler's conviction that students were capable of responsible judgment in matters of student conduct (particularly as long as he continued to preach the gospel of righteous collegiate behavior) led to the development of an "honor spirit" in examinations and the creation of an Honor Spirit Committee that later became the Undergraduate Student Affairs Committee. Dominated by Seniors, this committee could only recommend discipline for rules violations, but it relieved the faculty of an enormous amount of time-consuming investigation and deliberation on student conduct. It also promoted a campus-wide feeling that the rules were not just dictated by the administration or faculty, but actually indicated the students' own concepts of what was right and wrong. Violations became regarded as offenses against fellow students, and not just tests of administrative authority.

While the students' judiciary role was being strengthened, many of the activities and services developed by students on an *ad hoc* basis through the years began to be incorporated into a larger system of organization. In 1900, the constitution of the Associated Students of the University of California was revised. Membership was limited to dues-paying members, and a salaried manager was elected. In this new form, the ASUC absorbed many hitherto independent student activities, including athletic programs and a cooperative book store that had been operating since 1883. Even the Honor Spirit Committee that was created to exercise judiciary functions eventually became an ASUC agency.

In 1919, President Wheeler was able to report, "Gradually and imperceptibly the usages of student self-government have come to be accepted by the students without question; they know that student affairs have been turned over wholly and honestly to the students, and they therefore take the institution at full-face. There is practically no disorder among the students. Better than that, however, is the fact that the sturdy men are conscious of the power to govern themselves, and to have and to hold the latter as resident within them and not imposed upon them from without." [28]

WINNING PUBLIC SUPPORT

By taming the students and giving them a share of responsibility for the orderly function of the University, President Wheeler scored a double achievement. He made the University more stable internally and, at the same time, improved the view in which it was held by the general public. He further enhanced the public impression of the University by giving much of his time to representing it on speakers' platforms all over the state and by identifying it always with noble, popular men and causes. He spoke at county fairs, meetings of teachers' associations, and on lecture tours to remote California communities.

As the University became widely known outside of the state, partly through Wheeler's growing fame, it began to attract celebrated visitors. President Theodore Roosevelt was the Commencement speaker in 1903. In April, 1905, the Wheelers entertained William Howard Taft, Elihu Root, and Alice Roosevelt in their Berkeley home.

Californians were greatly relieved when Wheeler did not accept the presidency of the University of Illinois in 1904, of Massachusetts Institute of Technology in 1907, or of the University of Michigan in 1908. The Regents were so grateful he did not go to Michigan that they raised his salary from $10,000 to $12,000 a year.

When Edward Slosson published his book *Great American Universities* in 1910, he devoted one of its fifteen chapters to the University of California. The rating had been earned by genuine achievement in instruction and research. But it also derived in large measure from the celebrity and personal appeal of the ubiquitous President Wheeler.

HOST TO THE LEGISLATORS

When President Wheeler came to California, the state's population and wealth were increasing and more of its young people were attending the University. Property tax assessments, on the other hand, had actually declined during the previous seven years and, because they provided the base for the "two-penny" tax revenue relied upon for University support, gave President Wheeler and his financial advisers at Berkeley deep concern.

In 1901, Wheeler appeared twice before members of the legislature in Sacramento to explain why it would be impossible for the University to accommodate steady growth in enrollment and services out of a fixed and slightly declining income. The legislature responded by giving the University $100,000 to be used in addition to penny-tax revenues in 1901–1902. It also guaranteed the same amount annually for University support during the ten-year period beginning in 1905.

With the new income received from the legislature in 1901, the University began to relieve overloaded classrooms, replace outworn equipment in the laboratories and workshops, add several new departments, improve the library, obtain equipment for a modern dairy laboratory, and hire additional professors, instructors, and readers.

Though elected on an economy-in-government platform, Governor Gage approved of the supplementary appropriations, expressing the hope that "it is perhaps possible that the needs of the University will be fully met, and that the sad spectacle observed under previous administrations of officers of the University lobbying to secure the passage of needed appropriations will not again be witnessed." [29] That turned out to be a vain expectation, but, even so, the appropriations were of great assistance to the University. They were recorded as a part of the University's income until at least 1915. In addition, the legislature resumed pre-penny-tax practices of making special appropriations for special capital improvements, for agricultural research, and for other special projects initiated at its own request. Of course, the penny-tax income was also still provided for the University.

In 1903, President Wheeler invited the members of the legislature to Berkeley. Those who came were honored guests at the University meeting on January 15, were urged to visit classes and roam about on their own, and were entertained at the President's home for lunch. Ex-Governor Gage would have blanched to hear one of the senators, as he boarded a special train taking the delegation back to Sacramento, say, "This is the best lobbying that has ever been done." [30] They returned the hospitality by appropriating $25,000 towards construction of an administration and classroom building (California Hall).

The good relationship thus cultivated between the University and the legislature was threatened briefly in 1904, when the secretary of the Regents was caught paying a racetrack gambling debt with a check drawn on the Hearst estate and subsequent investigation revealed that he had passed some $75,000 through the betting windows over a period of several months. Because of his defalcation, a legislative inquiry sought to prove the Regents negligent in their management of the University's resources, but this move found no sympathy at all in the senate and the matter was allowed to rest.

The University's popularity was so great at this same time (1905) that the speaker of the assembly was quoted in advance of budget considerations as saying that the advice of President Wheeler would be sought to determine the University's needs "and definite steps will then be taken to supply those needs." [31] His word proved to be good on all counts. The University received not only its usual support, but also money to complete the unfinished President's House at Berkeley, continue Farmers' Institutes, and start a department of music.

DISASTER IN 1906

In the great earthquake and fire of 1906, only a "few tumbled chimney-tops" gave physical evidence of the April 18 disaster on the University's Berkeley campus. The University's financial losses, however, were calamitous.[32]

Overnight, the usual penny-tax revenues were reduced by $30,000 as a result of the destruction of taxable property in San Francisco.

The University-owned Johnson and Sacramento Buildings in San Francisco were completely destroyed, resulting in loss of $45,000 rental income in 1906 and $60,000 in 1907.

Even the principal of the University's endowment was impaired. The loss of the Johnson and Sacramento Buildings exceeded salvage and insurance collected on them by over $30,000. Another $58,400 was lost in stock depreciation caused by the fire. Buildings in which the University had acquired share ownership over the years were lost, causing further diminution of the value of the endowment.

The old Mark Hopkins mansion, said to have been built at a cost of $2,000,000 and worth immeasurably more with its valuable contents, was lost completely. The University also lost $8,840 when its dental clinic burned; $3,475 with the loss of its downtown dispensary; $3,275 in books and plans in the supervising architect's office in San Francisco; $3,854 as the estimated value of a model of the Berkeley campus and its future buildings; $2,100 in books that were in San Francisco waiting for binding; and $8,600 in damage to the buildings of the medical, dental, and pharmacy colleges.

The legislature came to the University's relief with a special appropriation of $83,800 to cover losses in current operating income caused by the disaster and, in 1909, granted further assistance to the University with passage of a new law increasing the ad valorem tax revenue of the University by a third penny.[33]

THE END OF THE PENNY TAXES

In his inaugural address in 1903, Governor George C. Pardee proposed to give the cities and counties exclusive authority to impose and collect real estate and property taxes. A constitutional amendment to carry out that proposal passed in 1910 and, instantly, the source of the University's revenues from the penny tax was eliminated. To provide continuing support for the University, the legislature passed a bill on April 25, 1911, which created an annual "State University Fund." In the first year of its establishment, 1911–1912, the fund consisted of an appropriation 7 per cent greater than the University received from the three-penny tax in its last year, 1910–1911. The total amount appropriated in 1911 under this formula was $760,527.70.[34] Thereafter until 1915, the legislature committed itself to augment the annual appropriation by 7 per cent each year. Three-fourths of the fund could be used by the Regents without restriction, but the rest was to be used only for permanent improvements.

Theoretically, the new "State University Fund" answered the familiar question of how the University could be made to operate automatically and perpetually without annual requests for financial support. As long as the University's rate of growth remained constant, and as long as that rate was about the same as the rate of economic growth of the state, the automatic augmentations should have been adequate. But neither condition prevailed very long. Almost as soon as the bill passed it became evident that the enrollment of the University was increasing by approximately 13 per cent a year—not by 7 per cent.[35] Costs of instruction were rising even faster than enrollment. These new costs might still have been met if endowment income had continued to rise, but it did not. In 1911 and 1912 it actually decreased and it fluctuated erratically for four years thereafter.

With a deficit in prospect for 1911–1912, Wheeler considered the possibility of charging a tuition, reporting in 1912, ". . . if it becomes finally evident that the maintenance of the university as it should be maintained represents too heavy a burden for the state, this [tuition] may be our only way of relief." [36] With the public opposition to a tuition in 1898 still in mind, the Regents did not push the idea again. Instead, the University had a deficit of $24,000 in 1911–1912 and $46,000 the following year.

In 1911, hoping that a specialist in business matters might solve their problems, the Regents created the office of comptroller of the University.[37] This new officer was to take charge of all business operations not specifically assigned to the secretary of the Regents by the Organic Act. He reported to the Regents on matters involving investments, endowment, and loans, and to the president of the University on matters involving the business affairs of the various University departments. In 1913, the comptroller was directed "to meet with State officers and the Legislature to present the University's financial needs and to carry through the Legislature the budget finally adopted jointly by the Board of Regents and the State Board of Control." [38] For this work, the first comptroller, Ralph P. Merritt, a graduate of the class of 1907, proved well suited. Convivial and direct in his relationships with legislators, he won the confidence they found it difficult to give to the somewhat imperious and aloof Wheeler. In the first year that Merritt represented the University in Sacramento, state appropriations for operating support were increased by more than 25 per cent. The total appropriation exceeded $1,000,000 for the first time in the University's history.

The automatic appropriations provided by the "State University Fund" Act in 1911 continued to be made throughout the Wheeler administration, but after 1913 they were by no means restricted to 7 per cent annual augmentation. The illusion that the University could be cranked up with automatic appropriations and left to operate perpetually without further legislative attention finally was abandoned and the University's officers willingly accepted the challenge of proving the merit of each year's request for support on the basis of demonstrable needs.

The normal channel for such requests, of course, was the legislature. In 1914, however, the University's need for money to complete the major buildings in the Hearst architectural plan was so great that the request was taken directly to the people of the state. Alumni obtained more than 300,000 signatures to place a bond issue on the ballot.[39] That November, the people endorsed the issue by a vote of about two to one. Their approval of the bond issue made $1,800,000 available for construction of new buildings for agriculture and chemistry and for completion of the library. A new classroom building built with bond-issue funds was completed in January, 1917, and named Benjamin Ide Wheeler Hall.[40]

NEW PHILANTHROPY

The stability that characterized Kellogg's administration gave way to an era of fast-paced progress under Wheeler. Both periods favored philanthropy. Mrs. Hearst's philanthropy of the 1890s continued.[41] Included among her later gifts were the Hearst Memorial Mining Building, the "old" Hearst Gymnasium for Women (destroyed by fire in 1922), an extension for Harmon Gymnasium, equipment for a department of pathology, histology, and psychology, financing for archaeological expeditions, and provision of University scholarships and professorships.

After the completion of the comprehensive development plan for the campus, new donors came forward to contribute to its fulfillment. Charles Franklin Doe, San Francisco businessman and bibliophile, who died in 1904, left 25 per cent of his estate to the University for the building of a library.[42] Another donor, Mrs. Peder Sather, widow of a pioneer California banker, provided money for a chair of classical literature in 1910, created a Sather Law Library Fund, and gave the money to build two of the most famous landmarks on the Berkeley campus, Sather Gate and Sather Tower (the Campanile). In 1901, Elizabeth Joselyn Boalt, widow of an early California lawyer who was interested in the University, donated $100,000 to the University for establishment of a law school and the erection of a law building. Later she gave $365,000 more to endow two law professorships. When he died in 1911, Ernest V. Cowell, a member of the class of 1880, created a trust that eventually yielded $260,000 towards construction of a hospital on the Berkeley campus.

BUILDING UP THE FACULTY

Some of President Wheeler's frequent trips to the East combined speaking engagements with opportunities to meet candidates for membership in the Berkeley faculty. By 1900, many of the strong, pioneering teachers of the University had died or had retired. Until Wheeler came, these senior men were often replaced by young instructors or assistants. Wheeler reversed this trend by seeking out strong, well-known teachers to fill the senior positions as they became open. It was a task that gave him considerable pleasure. He brought Henry Morse Stephens from Cornell to teach history, and Jacques Loeb from Chicago to teach physiology. Adolph C. Miller, another former colleague at Cornell who had moved on to the University of Chicago, was named Flood Professor of Economics at Berkeley. In anatomy, Wheeler brought in Herbert M. Evans. In zoology, he recruited Charles Atwood Kofoid, Samuel Jackson Holmes, and Joseph Grinnell. Charles Derleth, in civil engineering, and Frank H. Probert, in mining, joined the faculty. Griffith Evans and Florian Cajori were recruited for the mathematics department. Gilbert N. Lewis came to teach chemistry and brought Joel Hildebrand and many others into the college with him. Herbert E. Bolton in history, George R. Noyes in Slavic languages, Rudolph Schevill in Spanish, and C. G. Chinard in French came to the University during Wheeler's presidency. So did Alfred Louis Kroeber in anthropology. There were, of course, many, many others. But among those listed here are the men who made the Wheeler years the golden era of undergraduate instruction at the University of California. The memories of several of them have been perpetuated in the names of buildings and other memorials at Berkeley.

Although he recognized good teaching and recruited good teachers, President Wheeler did not have the knack of getting along well with his faculty. Unlike students, faculty members tended to be independent, skeptical, individualistic, specialized in their academic disciplines, and basically ungovernable by the broad, homely precepts Wheeler relied upon to keep students in line. As a result, Wheeler's approach to faculty relationships was almost precisely the opposite of his approach to students. With students, he enjoyed an open, brothers-in-arms relationship. With the faculty he was aloof and authoritarian. To students he gave considerable responsibility for their own affairs. To the faculty he gave nothing more than he found them with when he came, and assumed sole authority for appointing all department chairmen, all deans, and all members of Academic Senate committees. He determined all salaries and made all promotions with little or no consultation.[43] And he insisted that all faculty communications intended for the Regents go through him.

The faculty were not unaware of the difference between Wheeler's attitudes toward them and toward the students. Some of them resented it. In 1916, a new version of the *By Laws and Standing Rules of the Academic Senate and other Academic Bodies* was proposed.[44] It would have concentrated senate authority in an "Administrative Board" of forty-four members that included the president, dean of the faculties, recorder of the faculties, deans of schools and colleges, chairmen of certain faculty committees, and several other key faculty members. Because of its smaller size, this board could meet frequently and could not be as easily circumvented as the more cumbersome senate. Another proposal in 1916 was to appoint a standing committee to "suggest to the President of the University appointments of members of standing or special committees of the Academic Senate whose membership is not otherwise provided for." This proposal was an obvious bid for some of the authority being exercised by Wheeler unilaterally, or only after conference with a few close advisers. These proposals were not approved, but the fact that they were introduced at all indicated a restiveness in 1916 that would be perceived again, in a stronger form, four years later, when another man was president.

THE UNIVERSITY AND WORLD WAR I

In the summer of 1913, weary of University upbuilding and an especially difficult fight for legislative appropriations the previous spring, President Wheeler went to Germany and Bavaria for a month-long vacation. While he was in Germany, he renewed his acquaintance with Kaiser Wilhelm, whom he met for the first time as a Theodore Roosevelt Professor at the University of Berlin in 1909. At the end of a month, Wheeler still felt physically exhausted and was given six months more leave by the Regents. He spent the additional time in travels to Switzerland, Greece, Italy, and Egypt.[45] During Wheeler's absence, David Prescott Barrows, dean of the Academic Faculties, was acting president.

In January, 1914, Wheeler returned to the University. At first, Wheeler was inclined to regard the war that broke out in Europe after his return as nothing more than the failure of England and Germany to work together for peaceful settlement of quarrels among the emerging Balkan nations. Then, he became inclined to regard the whole affair as an object lesson in the folly of England's entangling alliances. An ardent neutralist, he was one of the main speakers at a peace rally held in the Greek Theatre on September 14. Three years later, however, when German hostility at sea increased the certainty of America's eventual involvement, Wheeler asked the Regents for authority, in the event of the outbreak of war, "to offer to the War Department such use of the grounds, buildings, and equipment at Berkeley and Davis as may accord with the plans and needs of the department in the training of troops." [46] His request was granted.

The day after the United States declared war against Germany, Wheeler appointed a faculty committee to process the requests of students for leaves in order to enlist in the armed services. A week later he spoke to the University cadets telling them that now, in 1917, "The chance for which the University has been waiting since its founding has arrived." [47] He ordered the cadets not to enlist in other organizations until the Army advised that they were needed and said he hoped that they could enter the national service as a unit.

Within the first few weeks of the war, 591 "emergency withdrawals" were made by men entering the armed forces.[48] Within the first year, one out of every three men registered for instruction had volunteered. In all, nearly a thousand students volunteered or were drafted. More than eighty lost their lives in the conflict.[49] One hundred and thirteen faculty members served as experts in the service of the nation's military forces—and many of them were commissioned officers.[50] Others served in high-level consulting positions for industry and food-production companies at home. Ralph Merritt, the University comptroller, served for the duration as Federal Food Administrator for California.

In order to marshal all of the University's resources for national service, a Military Bureau was established on the initiative of the Alumni Association. It kept a record of the names, locations, and skills of 3,070 men of the University—including faculty, alumni, and undergraduates.[51] From this roster, the government recruited experts to screen candidates for important technical positions and to recruit specialists. The bureau recruited an entire ambulance unit consisting of a first sergeant, second sergeant, corporal, two orderlies, two clerks, twenty-four drivers, three mechanics, and two cooks. It served with the French Army. The bureau also signed up women to serve as nurses and telephone operators in France.[52] Members of the Medical School faculty gave special short courses in the treatment of fractures, wounds, and shock for the benefit of Army medical officers, and the Department of Surgery organized Base Hospital Unit No. 30 for war service and instructed a considerable number of enlisted personnel.[53]

One of the largest University wartime training programs at Berkeley was the School of Military Aeronautics conducted under contract with the United States Army. The University provided instructors, barracks, and equipment, except for airplane engines and parts. An Army officer was commandant, but the courses and professors were organized under Baldwin M. Woods, a member of the University faculty. The school provided preflight training for almost 3000 cadet pilots before the end of the war.[54]

In May, 1918, the Army announced plans to form units of the Students' Army Training Corps at colleges and universities across the country. The plan made it possible for college-age men to enroll at a university or college and then enlist in the Army or Navy with the understanding that they would be assigned to a SATC unit on their campus. About 1,900 students took advantage of this opportunity at Berkeley.[55]

In the spring of 1918, anti-German sentiment reached near-hysteria levels in the Bay Area and the faculty and Regents were not immune to it. President Wheeler was advised by the Regents to dismiss any "disloyal" faculty member, "anything in the budget to the contrary notwithstanding." [56] The degree of I. W. D. Hackh was rescinded by the Regents after he had been dismissed from the University faculty for unexplained actions "inimical to the United States." [57] Alfred Forke, one of the world's leading Sinologists and holder of the Agassiz Professorship of Oriental Languages and Literature, was dismissed from the faculty for the same mysterious reason.[58] Two months later, the same fate befell Herman J. Weber, an associate professor of German.[59] There was agitation to drop the teaching of German from the curriculum, and all candidates for degrees were required to sign a pledge of loyalty, which came in three forms to accommodate the special circumstances of American citizens, citizens of neutral or enemy countries, and citizens of allied countries.[60]

Even President Wheeler became the target of abuse. In September, 1914, when war had broken out in Europe, the *Daily Californian* quoted Wheeler as saying, "The one faint hope is that England, when she sees how her action favors the policy of Russia and leads Russia inevitably down through the Dardanelles, may turn toward peace." [61] For the next year or so he joined many other leading Americans who advocated the strictest sort of neutrality for the United States and was quoted as saying that the war in Europe had come against the interests and desires of the Kaiser and that "it seems terrible to go to war with a nation which does not want to go to war with us, even if some of our ships have become victims of submarines." [62]

Despite these comments and actions, Wheeler's loyalty should never have been questioned. He initiated the move to place the full array of the University of California's services and facilities at the disposal of the nation for the war effort. He campaigned for Liberty Bonds and the National Service Committee. He spoke many times of his prayers and blessings for his sons who had been called to arms off the University campus. Such plainly patriotic activity was of no avail, however, in counteracting the mischief of an article appearing in an April, 1918, issue of *Town Talk,* a Bay Area magazine. This article dredged up many of Wheeler's pre-war sentiments, added them to a reminder that Wheeler had been a guest of the Kaiser during his visits in Germany, and let the implications lie.

It is doubtful that any of the Regents ever suspected Wheeler of anything but genuine loyalty to the United States, but he was by this time sixty-four years old, the demands of the war upon the University had become increasingly burdensome, and public restlessness over the current gossip had to be calmed. In May, 1918, therefore (the same time that Weber was dismissed), the Regents created an Advisory Committee of Deans to "assist" Wheeler in the exercise of his presidential functions. It was composed of the dean of the faculties, Charles Mills Gayley; the dean of the Graduate Division, William Carey Jones; and the dean of the College of Letters and Science, Henry Morse Stephens.[63] All were well known for their pro-British sympathies. The committee had considerable authority, though it usually acted in the name of the President and, apparently, with his consent.

The University recovered from its anti-German hysteria only a few months before it was hit by another wartime malady. On October 6, 1918, two students reported to the infirmary for treatment of influenza. Two days later there were three more cases, and the number increased every day thereafter until October 18, when seventy-four new cases were reported.[64] The dreaded Spanish flu, which had already hit the Eastern states, had arrived in California.

To combat the disease, women students were required to make gauze masks both for themselves and for the men.[65] Failure to wear these masks to class and in the library exposed students to a $500 fine.[66] All social functions were canceled and students were advised to avoid riding the streetcars.[67] A fraternity house taken over as a temporary hospital was filled within forty-eight hours. Three barracks buildings on campus were also filled up with patients. When the University physician, Robert T. Legge, contracted the disease, the fight against the epidemic was turned over to doctors from the Army Medical Corps. Between 600 and 700 military trainees came down with the disease and a slightly larger number of non-military students were afflicted. Pneumonia turned up in the second week of the epidemic and claimed the lives of twenty students and one faculty member.[68]

CONSOLIDATION AND EXPANSION

When President Wheeler arrived there were almost 200 students at Berkeley, and more than 600 in the departments and affiliated units in San Francisco. There were colleges of letters, social sciences, natural sciences, commerce, agriculture, mechanics, mining, civil engineering, and chemistry at Berkeley. All of them offered the bachelor's degree for four years of study.

Graduate instruction was given in a score of departments. At Mount Hamilton, there was the already famous Lick Observatory, which also provided opportunities for graduate study in astronomy. In San Francisco, there was an assortment of departments and affiliated units that included the Mark Hopkins Institute of Art, the Hastings College of the Law, the Medical Department, the Post Graduate Medical Department, the Dental Department, the California College of Pharmacy, and the California Veterinary College.[69] The Farmers' Institutes started in the last decade of the nineteenth century were immensely popular. During the same period, high school teachers began coming to Berkeley for summer courses in chemistry, physics, mathematics, and education. A University Extension program, consisting mainly of lectures by University faculty members, began in 1892 and was ready for expansion.

This growth was neither planned nor anticipated. To Wheeler fell the job of consolidating the gains that had been made, integrating loosely associated programs into the main framework of University endeavor, and filling obvious gaps in the educational offerings.

In his first report to the governor, Wheeler was particularly concerned with the relationship of the University to "a number of more or less closely connected professional schools located in San Francisco." [70] Unless they could be completely merged into the University on the same basis as the departments in Berkeley, he argued that their connections should terminate. Here, he was up against two long-standing University policies. One involved the process of affiliation that permitted an educational institution to become associated with the University while retaining considerable autonomy in its own management. Hastings College of the Law, the Mark Hopkins Institute of Art, the Post Graduate Medical Department, the California College of Pharmacy, and the California Veterinary College all had that status and were not inclined to give it up. The other policy involved money. Until Wheeler arrived, the Regents expected the professional schools in San Francisco to pay their own way and to make as few demands on the University's budget and personnel as possible.

The financial failure of the Veterinary Department and the loss of the hospital facilities of the Post Graduate Medical Department in the great fire of 1906 freed the University from some of its professional entanglements. The fire also destroyed the downtown infirmary, so the first two years of medical instruction were transferred to Berkeley to make room for a hospital in the Affiliated College buildings. By introducing courses in physiology, anatomy, pathology, and physiological chemistry on the home campus, academic ties to the Medical Department were strengthened as a matter of course. Wheeler hoped that eventually the clinical instruction of the last two years of medical school would also move to Berkeley, but, by 1911, he was reconciled to the necessity of leaving the University's Medical Department where clinical material was easily available. By conceding that point, however, he did not compromise in any way another desire that the standards of the Medical Department would be raised to equal or surpass those of other such institutions in the country. With this aim in mind, he joined the medical faculty in urging the Regents to consolidate medical instruction in San Francisco again. He also persuaded the Regents to stop treating the Medical Department as an affiliated unit and administer it as an integral part of the University. In doing so, the Regents accepted responsibilities for meeting the department's academic payroll and maintaining its facilities. Student fees were rechanneled into equipment and noninstructional services. Because it was, technically, a part of the Medical Department, the Department of Dentistry immediately achieved the same status.

At about the same time that the Regents were strengthening medical education in San Francisco, they received as a gift another medical department in Los Angeles. The new department, which was called the Los Angeles Medical Department, was fully organized and had been the medical department of the University of Southern California until it encountered financial difficulties and was offered to the Regents in 1909. After donations were made to clear the school of $20,000 in outstanding debts, the Regents accepted it. Until 1914 it provided both undergraduate and postgraduate instruction. Thereafter, it offered only postgraduate work. It was managed autonomously by its faculty and dean.[71]

Although he was unsure of the wisdom of removing any portion of the University's work from Berkeley, Wheeler accepted establishment of the University Farm at Davis in 1906 as unavoidable. After all, the legislature demanded it. He was more comfortable with the creation of specialized agricultural research stations at Whittier and Riverside, because they offered little instruction and could not duplicate the full range of instruction and research pursued by the College of Agriculture at Berkeley. In 1912, his attitude toward agricultural education conducted away from Berkeley had become more relaxed and he suggested that the day would eventually come when students of agriculture would engage in two years of basic, theoretical study at Berkeley and then move to Davis, Riverside, Whittier (subtropical horticulture), or the recently acquired Kearney Ranch in Fresno for specialized education.[72]

The geographical reach of the University was extended almost to the Mexican border in 1903, when the Marine Biological Association of San

Diego developed an institution to support scientific studies under the direction of William E. Ritter, professor of zoology on the Berkeley campus. In 1912, that work was integrated into the University under the aegis of the Scripps Institution for Biological Research. Ultimately, it became the Scripps Institution of Oceanography.[73]

During Wheeler's administration, the University's presence abroad was achieved with the establishment of an observatory on the summit of Cerro San Cristóbal in Chile in 1903, and with the explorations of archaeologists in Egypt, South America, Mexico, Greece, and Etruria under the sponsorship of Regent Hearst.

In 1902, a Department of University Extension was created, and under the direction of Henry Morse Stephens nineteen University Extension Centers were established throughout California. By 1911, however, the number was reduced to four—in Bakersfield, Sonoma, Sacramento, and Watsonville—because it became too difficult for the Berkeley faculty to travel to the other locations. Stephens' successor, Ira W. Howerth, expanded Extension efforts by developing programs geared to the special needs of California communities whether the courses were of University level or not. He also initiated correspondence instruction and developed the first Extension short course (in dentistry) in 1914. In 1917, when Professor Leon J. Richardson of the Department of Classics became director, the faculty was again given a strong voice in University Extension's development.[74]

Wheeler also encouraged summer sessions. In 1900 course offerings, previously limited to physics, chemistry, mathematics, history, and education, were extended, and instruction was given for the first time by a faculty hired and paid by the University specifically to teach summer courses. In the first year under this policy, 37 courses were offered in 11 departments and 433 students (compared to 161 the year before) were enrolled.[75]

Ralph Merritt once said that Wheeler "had the capacity and power to build the expandable foundations of the University of California today." [76] Actually, the University's flexibility seemed increasingly limited in the closing years of Wheeler's administration by detailed, outmoded provisions of the Organic Act, which were frozen into the state constitution in essentially the same form it passed in the legislature in 1868. On the initiative of the Regents, this obstacle was overcome in 1917, when Senator Arthur Breed introduced a resolution amending Article IX, Section 9 of the state constitution.

Breed's proposed amendment placed the University under the administration of the Regents, "subject only to such legislative control as may be necessary to insure compliance within the terms of the endowments of the university and the security of its funds." [77] Mention of the Organic Act or its amendments was omitted, thus discontinuing their constitutional status, and the president of the Alumni Association was added to the Board of Regents as an ex-officio member (according to Merritt, this was done to insure alumni support for the amendment when it was placed before the people of the state for ratification).[78] The new amendment also restricted use of endowments derived from the Morrill Land Grant Act to the purposes for which they were originally intended and declared that "the university shall be entirely independent of all political or sectarian influence and kept free therefrom in the appointment of its regents and in the administration of its affairs, and no person shall be debarred admission to any department of the university on account of sex." [79] By omission, it also removed the requirement that the governor's appointees to the Board of Regents be confirmed by the senate.

The new amendment was approved by the people of the state on November 5, 1918. Its effect was to move the University a little further in the direction of complete political independence and to free the faculty and the administration from outmoded restraints on the growth and reorganization of the University.

Another limitation on the development of the University was its historic orientation to the Bay Area and the farms and mountains of the northern part of the state. Until 1913, not one Regent was appointed from south of the Tehachapis, yet that area was assuming increasing importance in the economic and political complexion of the state.

In Los Angeles, local pride and a growing number of young people seeking collegiate education combined to create a demand for either a branch of the University or a duplicate of the one at Berkeley. The Regents, who did not feel they had enough money to operate the campuses at Berkeley and Davis, were reluctant to colonize in the southland, but they found the prospect of a second independent university anywhere in the state unappealing. Thus, when the president of the Los Angeles Normal School proposed that the University take over his institution and offer junior-college-level instruction in connection with a four-year course in education there, Wheeler saw an opportunity to forestall creation of a duplicate university and gave reluctant support to the merger that was accomplished by the legislature in 1919.

The University of California spirit and traditions that Benjamin Ide Wheeler cherished were those involving the sights, sounds, and seasons at Berkeley. To enhance the University's prestige and value, Wheeler was one of its most loving builders. In some ways, he built too well, for during his two decades in the presidency the University outgrew its natal campus and extended its activities to new places and into new services to the people of the state. In the process, it also outgrew the benevolent, paternalistic, autocratic style of the builder, and, in July, 1919, at the age of sixty-five, and tired after a score of eventful years in the University's service, Benjamin Ide Wheeler was persuaded to retire.

Chapter 14

PATRONS OF RESEARCH

NEITHER EQUIPMENT, building space, libraries, time, nor money were sufficient during the University's settling-in period to give much tangible support to research as an administrative policy. But the scholars were there and the role of research as the characterizing feature of a university was appreciated.

In his report to the governor in 1882, President Reid said that "the University that does not encourage in her professors the spirit of original work —that does not feel honored in being the means, through her professors, of enlarging the field of human knowledge . . .—deserves to have in her chairs only the men who have neither the ambition nor the capacity to do original work. For the present, perhaps we must leave to older and better endowed institutions the honor of supporting distinguished men, whose entire time may be devoted to investigation, but we cannot afford not to offer inducements to men with powers of original research to remain." [1]

On March 12, 1886, two months after he became president of the University, Edward Holden sent to each member of the Academic Senate, and to those ex-members whose addresses were known, a circular requesting a bibliography of all their published works, "with a view to publication in the future." [2]

The first faculty bibliography appeared in the president's report of 1886 and reflected prolific private research. Ever-expanding faculty bibliographies appeared regularly in subsequent presidents' reports.

In 1893, the Regents created a University of California Press, appropriating $1,000 in the annual budget for the printing of faculty monographs and authorizing a faculty committee on publications, which later became the Editorial Committee of the Academic Senate, to pass upon papers submitted for publication.[3] Beginning with the publication of the *Bulletin of the Department of Geology* in 1893, the press also instituted separate scientific series "whenever the results of the researches of . . . [University] workers in any given field seemed to be sufficiently numerous to keep a series alive. . . ." [4] By 1916, there were twenty-five series of publications devoted to the results of research, and the University Press reported: "The result of this policy has been, not only the accumulation of a most creditable collection of scholarly contributions in the completed volumes of our series, in widely diversified fields of investigation, but also a distinct stimulus to such investigation." [5]

Tangible support for the research efforts of faculty members has always come predominantly in the form of funds and materials from outside the University. In agriculture, state and federal government was the most important source. Private gifts supported research in several other fields. Some were very modest donations of money or scientific specimens. But research had great benefactors as well, and they accomplished for such fields as astronomy, marine biology, anthropology, paleontology, zoology, and medicine what state and federal subsidies accomplished in agriculture.

RESPONSIBILITY TO THE SOIL

The Organic Act of 1868 specifically made the University responsible for agricultural experimentation.[6] Fulfillment of that responsibility eventually led to the establishment of experimental laboratories in Berkeley in the 1870s and, after the passage of the Hatch Act in 1887,[7] to establishment of agricultural experiment sub-stations in the four main climatic regions of the state.[8] Other legislative support established a poultry experiment station at Petaluma (1903); an agricultural pathology laboratory in Whittier, with a branch at Riverside that evolved into the Citrus Experiment Station (1905); agricultural experiment stations in the Sacramento and San Joaquin Valleys for wheat-growing (1905); the University Farm at Davis (1905); [9] and the rice experiment station in the Sacramento Valley (1912). Hundreds of projects, including studies in soil technology, plant nutrition, plant pathology, agricultural chemistry, viticulture, pomology, landscape design, irrigation, and genetics, were carried out at these outposts of agricultural research.

KNOWLEDGE IN THE HEAVENS

When he provided funds for the observatory at Mount Hamilton, James Lick's intent was to provide for "a telescope superior to and more powerful than any telescope yet made, with all the machinery appertaining thereto, and appropriately connected therewith. . . ." [10] The largest telescope in existence at the time the one at Lick Observatory was finally ordered was a 30-inch refractor at the Imperial Observatory at Pulkowa, Russia.[11] Because the lens-makers refused to make a refractor bigger than 36 inches, the Lick Observatory trustees ordered one that size.[12]

In 1888, thirteen years after the observatory had been provided for, it was formally turned over to the University and became known as the Lick Astronomical Department of the University of California. Despite its departmental status, it had few students and usually only graduate students. Its small faculty of five or six professors and astronomers under the direction of Edward Holden devoted all of their time to research and began to flood the scientific literature with reports on their observations almost immediately after the observatory opened.

S. W. Burnham, a self-trained astronomer, specialized in observing double stars, and more than a third of the time available for using the 36-inch telescope was allotted to this work.[13] Another self-trained astronomer on the staff was E. E. Barnard, whose most dramatic discovery at Lick Observatory was the fifth satellite of Jupiter in 1892.[14] Two others were discovered by Lick astronomers within the next decade. Barnard's greatest reputation, however, was as a comet-finder. In one ten-year period he discovered nineteen comets, and in 1891 he discovered all five of the known comets of the year.[15] Max Schaeberle was another of the pioneers on Mount Hamilton, noted for the discovery of two comets, observations of the meridian circle, and extensive calculations of the orbits of comets and asteroids.[16] James E. Keeler, who became director for three years beginning in 1898, is credited with brilliant work in photographing stars and nebulae with the 36-inch reflector-type telescope presented to the observatory by Edward Crossley of Halifax, England, in 1895.[17] Keeler's work had considerable influence in turning the attention of astronomers to reflector-type instruments as the telescopes of the future.

Almost all of the work at Lick Observatory was financed from private contributions. Regent Charles F. Crocker subsidized the expedition of Burnham and Schaeberle to South America in December of 1889 to photograph a solar eclipse.[18] These photographs became famous because they demonstrated the "extension" of the outer corona of the sun. Crocker's interest in Lick Observatory was shared by his brother William H. Crocker and his brother's wife, and over a period of some forty years these three people contributed more than $80,000 for the support of the observatory and for astronomical expeditions to Japan, India, Georgia (United States), Sumatra, Egypt, Labrador, Russia, and Spain.

Another former Regent, Darius O. Mills, became the principal donor supporting the work of Lick astronomers in Chile between 1900 and 1928. Planned under the guidance of William Wallace Campbell, director of Lick Observatory from 1901 to 1930, the object of the Chilean observations was to secure measures of the radial velocities of the far southern stars, to supplement the measure of the more northerly stars being made at Mount Hamilton. After three years of preparation, including the manufacture and testing of the needed instruments, a University of California outpost was erected on the top of the middle peak of Cerro San Cristóbal behind the city of Santiago.[19] Originally, the astronomers expected to complete their work within three years, but international demands for more information from the Southern Hemisphere location kept it open until 1928. Almost $200,000 was spent in establishing and maintaining the D. O. Mills Observatory, all of which was subscribed by private gifts. The results of twenty-five years of observation at the observatory appeared in February, 1928, in the book *Stellar Radial Velocities,* by William Wallace Campbell and Joseph Haine Moore.

The *Encyclopedia Americana* reported in 1918: "The success of the Lick Observatory . . . must be regarded as one of the most extraordinary developments of our time. . . . The observations of Burnham and Barnard excited universal interest, both among astronomers and the public. . . . Its most epoch-making work is due . . . to Campbell, by measurements of the motions of stars in the line of sight with the spectroscope, who, armed with the best spectograph that human art could make . . . has . . . brought into these measures a degree of precision never before reached."[20]

THE MARINE BIOLOGY LABORATORY

As early as 1877, interest in establishing a marine biology station as part of the University was expressed by President LeConte, who said, ". . . It is

quite essential to have a 'Zoological Station' and an Aquarium at some convenient place on the coast." [21] In 1886, President Holden urged the Regents
to accept a 6-acre site overlooking the ocean in San Francisco and offered as
a gift by Adolph Sutro, later mayor of that city, saying, "This site is an ideal
one for a seaside biological laboratory. . . ." [22]

Beginning in 1892, William E. Ritter, chairman of the Department of
Zoology at Berkeley, began to make summer field trips along the California
coast to investigate animal life of the Pacific shores. In 1903, this work was
done at Coronado, and in September of that year the Marine Biological Association of San Diego, a private organization supported generously by
Ellen Browning Scripps and her half-brother E. W. Scripps, the famous
newspaper publisher, was formed to develop a permanent research facility
for the work of Ritter and other marine biologists.[23]

The association built a temporary laboratory in 1904 on property in La
Jolla that was made available by the city of San Diego. Four years later, the
association purchased another tract of some 160 acres near La Jolla and
announced plans to build a permanent facility consisting of a laboratory and
cottages for scientists and their families.[24] Only a laboratory had been completed in 1912 [25] when the station was rechristened the "Scripps Institution
for Biological Research of the University of California" and transferred to
the Regents.[26] In discussing the new name, Ritter stressed the importance of
the word "research," which he said was included "from the mature conviction that whatever work may now or hereafter be taken up, should be based
upon, and so subordinate, to research." [27] Instruction was available at the
graduate level only.

For collecting specimens from the ocean, E. W. Scripps contributed a
converted pilot boat, the *Loma*, to the laboratory in 1904.[28] When the *Loma*
was wrecked in 1906, a new vessel equipped for dredging and other collection of materials was built with funds from an endowment given to the laboratory by Miss Ellen B. Scripps.[29] Named the *Alexander Agassiz*, this 85-
foot craft served the institution until it proved too uneconomical to operate
and was sold in 1917.[30] In 1926, a smaller, more inexpensive boat, the
Scripps, was acquired and served the cause of science for a decade.[31] The
University fleet grew thereafter, and in 1966 consisted of eight ships, ranging in size from the 65-foot inshore cargo and passenger vessel *T-441*, to the
213-foot rescue and salvage vessel *Argo*.[32]

The first research at the La Jolla laboratory emphasized marine biology
almost exclusively, but gradually, characteristics of the ocean that affected
marine life came under study. In 1915, the institution built a 1,000-foot
concrete pier for the dual purpose of accommodating apparatus for near-

shore scientific observations and reaching unpolluted salt water that could be pumped ashore for laboratory use. Daily sea-temperature and salinity observations began from the pier in 1916.[33]

During World War I, Scripps Institution scientists advised the State Game and Fish Commission as to when kelp should be harvested; undertook experimental fishing to determine the full extent of the area from which tuna could be obtained by commercial fishermen; reported on the relation of fishing done in Mexican-controlled waters to that done in American-controlled waters; investigated alternatives to canning for the preserving of fish; and brought the institution's research on the food supply and environment of commercial fishes into the service of the fishing industry.[34]

After the war, research at the institution became increasingly diversified, touching on more and more aspects of the sea not strictly related to biology. This work was encouraged by Ritter, the first director, and his successor, Thomas Wayland Vaughan. On October 13, 1925, the Regents recognized the broadened concerns of the institution by renaming it the "Scripps Institution of Oceanography." [35]

MAN, NATURE, AND ANTIQUITY

Anthropological research had its benefactress in Phoebe Apperson Hearst, one of the University's most generous patrons. Mrs. Hearst was an avid collector of art and antiquities, which she proposed to give to the University. To augment her collections, in 1899 she provided funds for expeditions headed by competent archaeologists to places rich in deposits of the relics of ancient man. The distinguished Egyptologist George A. Reisner was commissioned to make a five-year expedition to Egypt. For work in Peru, she hired and outfitted a German archaeologist, Max Uhle. A classical scholar, Alfred Emerson, was sent to Europe to buy materials of Greek, Roman, and Etruscan antiquity. A doctor of medicine, Philip Mills Jones, was placed in charge of collecting archaeological materials from California.[36]

The materials acquired through these far-flung expeditions carried out in the name of the University began to arrive in Berkeley in 1901, outgrew space made available in a large, vacated house on College Avenue, and two years later could not even be contained in a 60-by-80-foot galvanized-iron warehouse built on campus at Mrs. Hearst's expense. In 1903, most of the growing collection was moved to a building of the Affiliated Colleges on Parnassus Heights in San Francisco originally constructed for Hastings College of the Law but never occupied. There, what became known as the Museum of Anthropology of the University had its headquarters for twenty-eight years. In 1911, exhibitions were opened to the public with a reception given by Mrs. Hearst, and during the next two decades 334,000 visitors saw the museum's collections.[37]

An inevitable by-product of the Hearst archaeological expeditions was the development of a staff at the University to catalogue and describe the collections. Such a staff was organized in 1901 as the Department of Anthropology under F. W. Putnam of the Peabody Museum at Harvard and was financed almost entirely by Mrs. Hearst until 1906.[38] Because Professor Putnam could spend only three months of the year at Berkeley, most of the department's affairs were under the practical management of a twenty-five-year-old Ph.D. from Columbia, Alfred L. Kroeber. In addition to serving as curator of the anthropology museum in Putnam's absence, Kroeber taught the first course in anthropology offered by the University. He was the guiding spirit in the department from about 1905 until his retirement in 1946.

In addition to assuming responsibilities for the Hearst archaeological collections, the University's Department of Anthropology made extensive investigations of California shell mounds, caves, and gravel deposits and conducted meticulous research on the twenty-one languages and eighty dialects found among California Indians. By 1912, President Wheeler was able to report to the governor that "there are now, indeed, few parts of the world concerning whose aboriginal inhabitants and prehistory there is as much information extant and on record as about California. To date 11 volumes have been issued in the University of California publications in American Archaeology and Ethnology. The curator reports that 'the department now possesses more than 200 manuscript books of notes, nearly 6000 negatives, over 1700 phonograph records, more than 10,000 phonetic tracings, and anthropometric sets of measurements of about 500 individuals.' " [39]

Research in paleontology and zoology was aided through the interest of another University benefactress, Miss Annie M. Alexander. The daughter of a pioneer Hawaiian sugar cane grower, Miss Alexander had an unbounded love of the out-of-doors and was a strong and skilled hiker, swimmer, and huntress. In the fall of 1900, she began attending the lectures of John C. Merriam, assistant professor of paleontology and historic geology at Berkeley. From that time until her death, she became an avid collector of fossils, financing and participating in University field trips in northern California and Oregon in the summers of 1901, 1902, and 1903,[40] and subsequently collecting on her own in California and Nevada.

Miss Alexander's interest stimulated the development of a new Department of Paleontology in 1909,[41] and in 1912, President Wheeler reported that paleontological research of the University was concentrated on Cenozoic deposits of the Great Basin region, "ranging from an investigation of the Mohave Desert region north through Nevada and into southeast Oregon," on studies of deposits in the famous Pleistocene asphalt at Rancho La Brea in southern California, and on Cenozoic formations of the Coast Range region of California.[42] He reported the discovery of two new fossil-bearing areas containing mammalian remains near the summit of the Sierra at Tehachapi in 1915,[43] and noted that eight different field investigations were under way in 1920.[44] In 1921, financial contributions from Miss Alexander made possible the creation of a Museum of Paleontology at the University.[45]

The rapidity with which the native game birds and mammals of the West were disappearing and the need for skeletons of present-day vertebrates for use in tracing fossil relationships led Miss Alexander to begin corresponding with President Wheeler in October of 1907 about establishing a Museum of Vertebrate Zoology at the University. The Regents accepted her plan in March of 1908, and Joseph Grinnell, a young naturalist whose private research museum in Pasadena had impressed Miss Alexander on a visit in 1906, was appointed the museum's first director.[46] Until 1919, Miss Alexander provided generous monthly payments for the museum's support. Thereafter, her principal support of the museum's work was a $200,000 perpetual endowment given to the Regents in 1919 and a $250,000 endowment donated in 1936.[47]

Miss Alexander's gifts to the University included more than money, however. More than 20,500 specimens in the Museum of Vertebrate Zoology at the University are available because of her purchases or personal collecting along the coast from Alaska to Baja California. Thousands of specimens in the Museum of Paleontology came from her own personal collecting in California and Nevada. She also collected 17,851 plant specimens which she donated to the University's herbarium.[48]

THE MEDICAL SCIENCES

For several decades, the Medical Department of the University produced new doctors with a teaching staff composed almost entirely of practicing physicians and surgeons. This fact distressed Dean A. A. D'Ancona in 1900 to the extent that he reported, "It is impossible for a physician actively engaged in the practice of medicine to teach the fundamental subjects in a medical course satisfactorily. Efficient instruction and original investigation in these subjects are possible only when the instructors devote their entire time to their College work." [49]

President Wheeler and the Regents obviously agreed, because, in 1902, a new plan for medical education at the University was announced. Thereafter, professors at Berkeley taught premedical students, with physics, chemistry, and biology forming the core of a two-year program. At the same time, three purely academic (as opposed to "professional") departments were created for medical students.[50] They were the Departments of Physiology, Anatomy, and Pathology, and their establishment made possible genuine beginnings in medical research at the University.

To assume responsibility for the physiology department, the University was fortunate to acquire the distinguished services of Dr. Jacques Loeb,[51] then professor of physiology at the University of Chicago.[52] Before accepting the position, Loeb secured a promise that he be headquartered in a research laboratory at Berkeley as a member of the College of Letters and Sciences with a joint appointment in the Medical Department in San Francisco.[53] To make this possible, Regent Rudolph Spreckels provided funds for construction of "Physiology Hall, a temporary building on the Berkeley campus where Dr. Loeb's work is to find shelter," and Dr. Max Herzstein donated funds for the building's scientific equipment.[54] Two years later, President Wheeler reported to the governor that "it was understood by those who furnished the means for the department and its equipment that, in addition to the instruction given to Medical and College students, scientific research should be given a prominent place in the aim of the department." [55] Such research began almost immediately, and establishment of a physiological bulletin at the University was also announced in 1904.

Another University of Chicago man, Dr. Joseph Marshall Flint, came to California to assume direction of the new Department of Anatomy. This department was established in August, 1901, with Mrs. Hearst providing funds for its equipment and library. The research point of view was stressed even in the routine work of the department, and students helped collect statistics on the variations found in the body "in order to improve the norm." [56] The rise of the department to real distinction did not begin until 1915, however, when Dr. Herbert M. Evans, an alumnus who had studied and taught at Johns Hopkins University, arrived to become one of its professors.[57] Very soon after his arrival, Dr. Evans began his famous research in endocrinology and hormone production and studies that led to the discovery of Vitamin E.

The Department of Pathology, which also benefited from Mrs. Hearst's generosity, had as its first chairman Dr. Alonzo Englebert Taylor, whom Dean D'Ancona considered wasted in teaching and administrative chores.

210   THE UNIVERSITY OF CALIFORNIA 1868–1968

"It is a misfortune," he said, ". . . that one of his natural ability and training for research should be compelled to devote too much of his time to the routine work of his department. His contributions to the sum total of human knowledge have been so many that it would be a distinct gain to science and to the fame of the University to leave him far more time for original investigation." [58]

During the first decade of the twentieth century, medical research at the University flourished in the three new departments of physiology, anatomy, and pathology. It found a new focus in 1913 when Sophronia T. Hooper, widow of a wealthy San Francisco businessman, transferred to the University a deed of trust to properties valued at more than a million dollars. In accordance with her husband's wishes, it was to be used as an endowment for medical research. With these funds, the Regents established the George Williams Hooper Foundation for Medical Research and named Dr. George H. Whipple of Johns Hopkins University its first director.[59] By 1915, the foundation reported research in progress on metabolism of bile pigments and hemoglobin, chemistry of cancer growth, drugs to combat sleeping sickness, the prevalence and transmission of malaria in California, filterable viruses—"especially the virus of rabies"—hemorrhage or abnormal blood coagulation, and "the rhythm of various portions of the gastro-intestinal tract in health and disease." [60] Dr. Karl F. Meyer, professor of tropical medicine, began his thirty-nine-year association with the new foundation in 1915, becoming its acting director in 1921 and its director in 1924.[61] By the time of his retirement in 1954, Dr. Meyer was credited with research leading to a better understanding of the control of plague, Malta fever, psittacosis, encephalitis, tick fever, and mussel poisoning. He began his famous research into the causes of botulism in 1919 with a $48,000 grant from the National Canners' Association. This work led to the formulation of food-canning regulations that are now internationally recognized.[62]

Research was also done in the College of Dentistry. In the 1920s, the California Stomatological Research Group made studies of the mouth and its disorders, including research on mouth protozoa under Dr. C. A. Kofoid. The Dental Research Group, under Dr. Meyer, investigated the basic problem of pyorrhea, or inflammation of the gums.

SOCIAL SCIENCES AND THE HUMANITIES

Because it required expensive equipment and large travel budgets, research in the fields of astronomy, oceanography, anthropology, paleontology, zoology, and medicine required and obtained major philanthropic support during the University's first half-century. In other subjects, the basic equipment was usually inexpensive, and professors scrounged financial support from national foundations interested in research, from friends, or from their own bank accounts. In fields such as engineering, where results of research were quickly applicable to problems faced by industry, grants were often available from private firms. The social sciences and humanities were modestly supported because they lacked the glamour of medicine or astronomy, for example; because they were of less obvious utility than engineering; and because their needs for research funds were not great. What scholars in these fields needed most was books.

That Wheeler recognized their need is clear from his report to the governor in 1900: "As our library facilities are to-day, a Californian who undertakes a work of first-rate value in the field of humanistic scholarship, and generally too in the field of natural science, will find it necessary to remove for some considerable period to the seat of an eastern or European library. This represents an obstacle and handicap which we should not impose upon our scholars—which we indeed cannot impose if we aspire to obtain and hold for our professional chairs the best men the profession affords. Here, more than at any university of the country, a great library is needed and deserved." [63] When he wrote that report, the University possessed 80,224 catalogued books, a little more than half as many as the University of Michigan, little more than a third as many as Cornell, little more than a quarter as many as Columbia, and only about one-seventh as many as Harvard.[64] Through the work of Wheeler and Librarian Joseph C. Rowell, the University's collection grew to 400,000 by 1919.[65] To accommodate the growing collection, a new library was completed in 1911 and named for Charles Franklin Doe, who had provided more than half of the money for its construction.

In November, 1905, the University acquired its most famous special library collection with the purchase of the Bancroft library, consisting of books, manuscripts, maps, pictures, and other materials dealing with the history of the western United States, including Alaska and Hawaii, as well as Mexico and Central America.[66] The collection was started in 1859 by Hubert Howe Bancroft, a San Francisco bookseller who used it as the source for his own thirty-nine-volume history of western North America.[67] Herbert E. Bolton was appointed curator of the library in 1916 and chairman of the Department of History and director of the Bancroft Library in 1919, and he made the collection an almost dominating influence over historical research at the University for two decades.

Evidence of other research in social sciences and humanities at the close of the University's first half-century is provided by some of the works described in the list of semicentennial publications that appeared in 1918. Among them was a study of "the relation between certain moving forces and ideals in modern life, such as democracy, science, the modern industrial order, and certain aspects of philosophical idealism" by George Plimpton Adams, associate professor of philosophy; a book on the Greek theater of the fifth century by James Turney Allen, associate professor of Greek; *Shakespeare and the Founders of Liberty in America* by Charles Mills Gayley; *Methods and Materials of Literary Criticism,* which Gayley wrote with another member of the University English department, Benjamin Putnam Kurtz; Bernard Moses' 300-page *The Breakdown of Spanish Rule in South America;* and biographies of Cervantes (by Rudolph Schevill, professor of Spanish), Cicero (by Torsten Petersson, instructor in Latin), and Tolstoy (by George Rapall Noyes, associate professor of Slavic languages).[68]

THE BOARD OF RESEARCH

For many years, most University of California scholars neither expected nor required large financial grants to support their research. What they needed most was time, and, occasionally, travel expenses and clerical help. In 1915, the Regents created a special faculty committee, the Board of Research, whose function was to help cover the *incidental* expenses, and leaves of absence. After the first year of its operation, with a budget of $2,000, President Wheeler reported, ". . . Even with so small a sum as we had available very great aid could be furnished. . . . A definite extra grant of two or three hundred dollars just at the right time is likely to prove of positive benefit to some work of relatively large range. I shall recommend to the Regents a large increase of this budget for next year." [69]

The board not only advised the President where seed money might best be spent for research, but also regarding the delegation of faculty members to attend meetings of scholarly and professional associations.[70] Eventually, it became the principal advisory group on the University's research policy. The Regents increased the funds available for the board to $3,000 in 1916–1917 and $4,000 in 1917–1918. In that year, some typical grants were: $150 to provide Professor Bolton with editorial assistance on two books; $105 for Edward C. Tolman, who was engaged in a study "of inheritance of unusual ability in learning as exhibited in lower animals"; and $40 for astronomer Armin O. Leuschner for travel expenses in connection with his attendance at meetings of the National Academy of Sciences. The largest grant, $1,000, was to Gilbert N. Lewis of the Department of Chemistry for apparatus and assistance in investigations of the problems of low temperature.[71] Out of this project came the work in low-temperature research that earned a Nobel Prize in 1949 for one of Lewis's students, William F. Giauque.

The establishment of the Board of Research in 1915 most clearly marks the time when research was officially removed from its auxiliary-enterprise status and recognized as integral to the function of the University. Although respectable, even brilliant research was done by such men as the LeConte brothers and Hilgard in the 1870s and by others before 1915, scholarly investigation remained extracurricular. Only after the Regents gave scholarly investigation direct financial encouragement, and after administrative machinery was created to channel the University's limited research funds to the most promising projects, did research begin to mature at the University. Thereafter, the University seemed to expand in function even faster than it increased in physical size.

Chapter 15

EXPANSION IN THE SOUTHLAND

IN HIS INAUGURAL address, President Daniel Coit Gilman had declared the institution he was to lead to be the "University of this State," implicitly claiming every corner of the commonwealth as the University's domain. For almost half a century thereafter, the University was the state's only public, four-year, degree-granting institution of learning, and its leaders fought hard to keep it that way.

The existence of University-affiliated professional schools in San Francisco was tolerable, because such affiliations had been anticipated in the Organic Act. But bitter battles had been fought in the 1870s to keep the College of Agriculture and the College of Mechanical Arts located at Berkeley as integral parts of the University, and the establishment of a University Farm at Davis as late as 1906 had been regarded by Eugene Hilgard, retired dean of the College of Agriculture, as again a threat to the University's unity.

Harry S. Pritchett, president of the Carnegie Institution for the Advancement of Teaching and former president of the Massachusetts Institute of Technology, warned Californians in 1909 against dividing their University. In a Charter Day address at the University, he noted that the Organic Act "wisely made the school of agriculture and the school of mines parts of a single institution. It may be that California virtue is so high that it might have dealt successfully with a divided university; but if the history of other states points any moral, one may suspect, at least, had the wise lawmakers of that period established a State university at Berkeley and a college of agriculture and mechanic arts at Los Angeles, the State would by this time have had upon its hands two weak competing institutions instead of a single strong university which stands today in the front rank of American institutions of the higher learning." [1]

Two years later, President Wheeler clarified his own conception of California's undivided University in a statement that clearly sought a compromise between the ideal of indivisibility and the realities of California geography and the University's history. He said, "The University of California is a phase of the state. It is not localized at one place. It conducts endeavors in higher learning and in research at Davis, in the City of San Francisco, on the top of Mount Hamilton, at Whittier in Southern California, and at Los Angeles in the form of a medical school . . . it is the state when the state addresses itself to a certain line of action." [2]

A NEW TERRITORY ATTRACTS ATTENTION

A fact that University leaders tended to neglect at this time was the rapid rate of population growth evident in the southern part of the state. When the University of California was established in 1868, less than 45,000 people— only about 8 per cent of the whole population of the state—lived south of the Tehachapi Mountains. San Francisco and Alameda counties alone provided residence for nearly a third of the state's people, and the University's location in that population center was considered reasonably convenient to young people in other central and northern California counties as well. For four decades, there was little concern for the hardship of students who traveled 500 miles from Los Angeles or 600 miles from San Diego to attend the

University. Their determination was applauded, but they were too few in number to make successful demands for university facilities closer to their homes.

By 1910, there were nearly five times as many people in California as there were in 1868;[3] the state's population in the south was enjoying rapid growth in response to a diversification of the economy there and to improvements in transportation and shipping that linked Los Angeles to the rest of the country. For the first time, the population of Los Angeles was greater than that of San Francisco.[4]

To serve the growing population in the south, a dozen or so private colleges and universities were established in southern California by 1910,[5] but students from that region still came to Berkeley in increasing numbers. In fact, in 1912, Los Angeles sent more Freshmen to the University than did San Francisco.[6] This not only inconvenienced students coming from 500 miles away, but also taxed the physical capacity of the Berkeley campus.

PASADENA'S BID

Aware of these new circumstances, southern California boosters began to insist upon the development of a four-year, state-supported institution of higher learning in their area. This objective received the special attention of Senator Lee C. Gates of Los Angeles, who introduced a bill in the 1911 session of the state legislature that would have created a "technical school" in southern California offering instruction in "agricultural, commercial, industrial, scientific and technical work."[7] Senator Gates carefully avoided calling his proposed institution a university, but by giving it an independent board of regents, and by leaving the character of its instruction so vague, he aroused the anxieties of all who supported the "undivided University" doctrine.

Senator Gates allowed the bill to die without a fight, however, when the trustees of Throop Polytechnic Institute in Pasadena offered their campus and buildings for a new state institution. But he wrote a new bill to create a "California institute of technology,"[8] with instruction strictly limited to the various fields of engineering, located in "the premises and buildings in the city of Pasadena . . . conveyed to the Throop Polytechnic Institute by Arthur H. Fleming [a trustee of that institution]. . . ."[9] This school would offer academic degrees and be controlled by an independent governing board. Because the work of the proposed institution seemed so restricted, some alumni and friends of the University living in southern California regarded it as no genuine threat to the University and supported its establishment. But most alumni and many informed observers considered the measure the first step toward duplicating the University of California in Pasadena. J. A. B. Scherer, the president of Throop Polytechnic Institute, disassociated himself from the California Institute of Technology scheme by declaring it "a provincialism on the part of its instigators." [10] An editorialist in the San Francisco *Call* brought the fears of all University of California supporters into the open by saying: "By concentrating its resources on the Berkeley colleges [the state] is just about able to keep them going on a fairly adequate basis and no more. . . . To split up the University would make these conditions much worse instead of better." [11]

The three features of the Gates bills that most alarmed the Regents of the University were (1) autonomous operation of the new institute by an independent board of trustees, (2) lack of assurance that the institute's curriculum would not someday duplicate that of the University, and (3) infringement of the University's exclusive privilege, among public institutions, to grant degrees. They also lacked confidence in the state's ability to provide adequate financial support for two university-level programs.

The students of the University called a mass meeting on February 20, 1911, to discuss the proposed institute. They subsequently prepared a circular containing brief arguments against the Gates bill for students to send home to their relatives. Under the leadership of James K. Moffitt, later a Regent, the alumni also took up arms, and Milton Farmer, secretary of the Alumni Association, wrote strong anti-"second university" editorials for the *California Alumni Weekly*.

As the time for a decision on the matter approached, President Wheeler released a score of telegrams from the nation's top leaders in higher education. All of them opposed Senator Gates's proposed action. The United States Commissioner of Education said that all attempts to operate two universities in other states had proved to be "demoralizing" and urged California to keep its system of higher education unified.[12] Columbia's President Butler advised, "Local pride and zeal should not be permitted to override plain interest of whole state." [13] President Mezes of Texas (who was also a University of California alumnus) warned that having more than one state institution of higher learning "divides the support of the people and confuses their minds." [14] And Stanford's President Jordan said it would be "a blunder which would deepen into a crime." [15] Several of the messages alluded to the University's national stature and the possibility that other states would follow California's lead in dealing with the technical-institute proposal. For this reason, Nebraska's President Avery called the proposed action "almost a national calamity." [16] All of these remarks were read into debate on the matter in Sacramento by Senator Stetson of Oakland, and on March 10, 1911, the senate voted twenty-one to fourteen against the measure.[17] Almost nine years later, Throop College of Technology became California Institute of Technology after all, but under private auspices.

TWO CAUTIOUS STEPS SOUTH

Defeat of the Gates bills in 1911 made it clear that all attempts to create new California public university systems would be thwarted in the state senate, for there, members from the rural counties knew the University through its service to agriculture in their districts, were in the majority, and were inclined to support the University when it considered itself threatened.

Rather than waste time in direct confrontation with the University, the southern California strategists rechanneled their efforts into getting the University itself to make its presence felt in their area. The man best able to lead the University on that course was Edward A. Dickson, a young Los Angeles journalist who had helped Hiram Johnson win the California governorship in 1910 and who, in 1913, at the age of thirty-four, was appointed the first Regent of the University from south of the Tehachapis. As political editor of the Los Angeles *Express,* Dickson was closely in touch with the sentiments of southern Californians and knew that they were determined, one way or another, to have a state college or university. A graduate of the University's class of 1901, Dickson had a profound affection for his alma mater and understood the "undivided University" concept and the anxieties of President Wheeler and most of the Regents about sharing the University's functions with new state institutions.

In 1915, Dickson persuaded President Wheeler that one way to calm down agitation for a second university in the south—at least temporarily —was to establish a University outpost of some kind in Los Angeles. The most obvious step would be to open a University Extension office in that city. Wheeler later obtained the Regents' endorsement of this proposal and Regent Dickson opened an office for the University in the old Union League Building at Hill and Second Streets.

The first Extension Division offering in Los Angeles was a series of lectures on the services of the University during the war then in progress. President Wheeler faced a packed auditorium for the first lecture and was followed by such popular and eminent Berkeley scholars and teachers as Charles Mills Gayley, Henry Morse Stephens, A. O. Leuschner, Carl C. Plehn, Bernard Moses, and Herbert E. Bolton.[18]

A year later, in 1916, the Teachers' Association of Southern California asked Dickson if a University summer session could be held in the Los Angeles area. They came to him because he was southern California's only Regent and was on the advisory committee for University Extension in that part of the state. They also sent a petition to the Board of Regents, who took no immediate action, but asked President Wheeler to investigate. On February 16, 1916, Wheeler wrote to Dickson indicating his ambivalent feelings on the matter: It involved "more mechanisms and more complications," but maybe southern California had a reasonable claim.[19] The University could not provide in Los Angeles the library, equipment, and atmosphere available at Berkeley, but the summer session would provide an opportunity "to bring our teachers to the attention and acquaintance of the south."[20]

Subsequent investigations were inconclusive. The first investigator, Leon J. Richardson, associate professor of Latin, reported, in effect, that there was no demand for a University summer session in Los Angeles after all. Dickson and the other Regents did not trust this report, however, and demanded another investigation. This time, Walter Morris Hart, professor of English and dean of the summer session, met with leading southern California educators and civic leaders gathered together by Dickson and was thoroughly impressed by the intense desire for a University summer session there. To reconcile the conflicting reports of Richardson and Hart, a faculty committee investigated and rendered a report substantially negative to the proposal. Still dissatisfied, President Wheeler, Dean Hart, and Regents Arthur Foster and John A. Britton went to Los Angeles to study the situation for themselves and returned to Berkeley convinced that the plan had merit and that Dean Hart had been right. The Regents quickly approved their recommendation that summer sessions be instituted in southern California.

In the summer of 1918, twenty-two courses were offered in the facilities of a new high school building in Los Angeles. They were attended by 630 people. Dean Hart later reported that because of the national emergency, many of the courses emphasized "war work of one sort or another," and also that the Los Angeles experiment "must be regarded as a success."[21]

On November 6, 1918, Albert Shiels, superintendent of schools in Los Angeles, was quoted as saying, "The University had introduced extension courses here, and last summer established a summer school in city premises; these are admirable moves and seem to be pioneering for the idea of a permanent establishment." [22] Local pride and a genuine demand for more higher education facilities in the southland was not satisfied with just a summer school, and talk of a new college or university financed by the state and located in Los Angeles became incessant among southern educators.

In 1915, a petition to the legislature from a Los Angeles commercial association had requested study on the "matter of the establishment of a coordinate State University in Southern California." [23] Nothing constructive came of that request, but other schemes, including one to ask the University to take over an old high school campus and offer instruction at the Freshman and Sophomore levels, reached considerable maturity. The backers of this plan, including Regent Dickson, who by this time was increasingly active in the movement to locate a branch of the University in Los Angeles, threatened to ask the legislature for authority to create a municipal college with an independent board of directors if the Regents turned down their proposal.[24] This would have been that ominous "second university" that haunted the Regents whenever needs for new centers of higher education anywhere in the state were discussed. To banish the spectre, the Regents were going to have to make some accommodation soon to the claims of the growing southland.

THE LOS ANGELES NORMAL SCHOOL

For many years, the most advanced *public* institution of higher learning in southern California was the Los Angeles State Normal School. Created in 1881 as a branch of the state normal school at San Jose, it first offered instruction in buildings erected in an orange grove less than a mile from the Los Angeles business district.[25] Though still restricted—as were all normal schools originally—to a two-year teacher training curriculum and optional four-year, non-degree courses in the arts, it was made a separate institution with its own board of trustees in 1887.[26] Between 1881 and 1907 the city of Los Angeles grew in population from 11,000 to 350,000.[27] Its business district closed in on the crowded campus of the normal school and a move to larger quarters became clearly necessary. In 1914, the Los Angeles State Normal School resettled its staff and less than 700 students in a new Vermont Avenue plant built to accommodate an enrollment of 3,000.[28]

The excess capacity of the new campus reflected the ambitions of the school's president, Jesse F. Millspaugh. Quite apart from efforts to bring more higher education to the south, there was already an agreement among heads of the state's normal schools that they would offer a third year of instruction in 1920, but Millspaugh wanted to do even more and planned to offer an optional fourth year of work. Still more radical, however, was his intention to offer a bachelor's degree to students who completed the full four years of training.[29] In this intention, of course, he challenged the generally accepted understanding that the University of California was the state's only public degree-granting institution.

When Millspaugh resigned from the presidency because of ill health in 1917, his successor, Ernest C. Moore, carried forward his plan. Moore had been a professor of philosophy and education at Berkeley from 1898 to 1906, superintendent of public schools in Los Angeles from 1906 to 1910, and, subsequently, a professor at Yale and Harvard.[30] He was on very friendly terms with President Wheeler, and Dickson had been one of his students at the University. He was also a loyal advocate of the "undivided University" principle, though he believed it would accommodate the ambitions he and Millspaugh shared for offering degrees at the Los Angeles State Normal School. He made this position clear to Wheeler in a letter written on February 20, 1918:

It seems to me that you are absolutely right when in your annual Report you say that "thus far the degree-granting power as exercised on behalf of the State has been limited to the Board of Regents and it would seem wisely so limited." . . . We of the Los Angeles State Normal School are disposed to do all in our power to keep the degree-granting power of the State in the hands of a single corporation, provided that corporation is disposed to consider and provide for the real and pressing educational needs of the several parts of the State. If it is not, we intend to do our utmost to develop our work independently.[31]

In the same letter, Moore asked Wheeler to request the Regents to study the possibility of some kind of affiliation of the University and the Los Angeles State Normal School. Involved was the possible transfer of the normal school's staff and new campus to the University. There, the Regents would operate the teachers college and such other colleges as it might want to establish. If the Regents agreed to the plan, they would incur heavy financial and administrative responsibilities for an educational operation frighteningly distant from Berkeley. They would also expose themselves to inevitable future demands for complete University offerings at Los Angeles, and, conceivably, in other population centers as well. The alternative, though, was that southern California interests would make good explicit threats to create a competing public university if the Regents persisted in ignoring their calls for service.

Moore's suggestion of a possible affiliation of the Los Angeles State Normal School with the University was discussed informally by the Regents throughout the spring of 1918. On June 11, the Regents authorized the appointment of a special conference committee to discuss the matter with a similar committee of the Los Angeles State Normal School trustees.[32] The chairman of the Regents' committee was Chester H. Rowell, a new Regent who, like Dickson, was a newspaper editor (Fresno *Republican*) and a prominent supporter of Hiram Johnson in 1910. The other members were Dickson, still the only Regent from southern California, and Rudolph Taussig, a San Francisco merchant who was also, for many years, a trustee of the Mechanics' Institute. Rowell was cool to the merger proposal on the grounds that the University had a hard enough time financing operations at Berkeley without additional burdens in Los Angeles. He also did not believe that training elementary teachers was a proper university function. Taussig at first tended to follow his chairman's lead while Dickson backed the Los Angeles State Normal School proposal and worked hard to arouse sentiment for it in the southern part of the state.

After conferring with some of the Los Angeles State Normal School trustees, and with other people in southern California, Rowell concluded that although the public clamor in the area seemed to be for a "university," further inquiry revealed a desire only for the instruction offered in the first two years of the University at Berkeley. He conceded that this much of the University's instruction was, indeed, "distributable," while the more specialized Junior, Senior, and graduate offerings were not. His quandary after conceding that much was whether the University should, in effect, assume responsibility for a "junior college" system in California, and whether there was any way to keep a junior college operation linked to a four-year teachers college from expanding into the "undistributable" areas of University work.[33]

At the suggestion of Rowell's committee, President Moore and Richard Melrose, president of the Los Angeles Normal School trustees, met with the Regents' Executive Committee on November 19, 1918. The Regents stated that although they were unalterably opposed to any arrangement which would make possible a second state university in southern California, they might be "in a receptive mood" toward a plan to operate a junior college in connection with Moore's proposed four-year teachers college, contingent upon the substantial agreement of all education groups in Los Angeles.[34]

The Regents were stalling for time. They did not expect that Moore and Melrose could negotiate agreements with all of the people interested in higher education developments in Los Angeles in very short order, and

during the time such activity would require, they planned to give more lei-
surely study to the proposition the Los Angeles State Normal School had put
before them. President Wheeler was understandably amazed when, less
than four weeks later, he received a copy of a letter that began: "The Regents of the University have approved a plan to integrate this School with
the University. . . ." [35]

The same statement, attributed to Moore, turned up in Dickson's Los
Angeles *Express* and subsequently in newspapers throughout the country.[36]
Moreover, the Los Angeles City Council and Board of Education were already on record by November 19 as formally endorsing the affiliation
scheme Moore and Melrose had discussed with the Regents' Executive
Committee just a month before.[37] Regent Rowell wrote to Moore on December 26 to insist that only the Executive Committee, and not the full Board of
Regents, so far discussed the affiliation proposal, that they did not in any
case agree to anything more than further consideration in a "receptive attitude," and that they had never gone so far as to agree to offer a four-year
course leading to a bachelor's degree and a two-year course for general
work, as Moore was quoted in various newspapers as saying.[38]

Moore responded that he and Melrose "distinctly understood that we
came to a clear and definite agreement with the Regents that, if we united
the various factors in the situation, the Regents would approve and would
assist in putting this measure through." And it became evident that he and
Melrose had substantially completed the assignment the Executive Committee had given them: "Every single principal of a Los Angeles Junior College," the Chamber of Commerce, county supervisors, Municipal League,
alumni of the University, and the City Teachers' Club had given endorsements. They also had the backing of the legislators of southern California.
The only opposition left, according to Moore, consisted of "three or four
real estate dealers . . . who clamor and will continue to clamor for 'an independent State University in Elysian Park.' " [39]

THE OTHER NORMAL SCHOOLS PROTEST

The newspaper stories that so aroused Regent Rowell also brought to the
surface a current of opposition to the merger plan that had been developing
among principals of the various state normal schools. In general, their complaint was simply that what was good enough for the Los Angeles State Normal School was good enough for them. They, too, should be allowed to offer
baccalaureate programs in their teacher-training departments, to call them-

selves "teachers colleges," and to offer instruction in courses other than education.

At a meeting on January 21, 1919, the normal school principals officially refused to endorse a merger of the Los Angeles State Normal School with the University of California.[40] Had they done no more, they might have at least delayed the affiliation. The Regents were not enthusiastic about the merger either and would have welcomed a reason to give it further study. But the normal school principals went a step further and proposed legislation that would rename all normal schools "teachers colleges" and authorize them to initiate college work that would further teacher training.[41] The threat of that measure—college-level endeavor that might someday compete with the undergraduate work of the University—attracted a delegation of Regents, including Chester Rowell, to a State Board of Education meeting in Sacramento two days later. There, they found themselves in the position of helping Moore, Dickson, and others oppose the normal school principals' proposals and defending the negotiations between the Regents and the trustees of the Los Angeles State Normal School during the preceding year. Moore later regarded this as a pivotal meeting, bringing him and the Regents finally into accord on merger plans.[42]

A bill reflecting Moore's understanding of the accord reached in Sacramento was introduced on January 23, 1919, by Los Angeles Assemblyman Alexander Fleming. It abolished the State Normal School at Los Angeles and transferred its property to the Regents. It also required the Regents to operate a teachers college with a four-year program leading to a bachelor's degree.[43]

It became evident in the next few weeks that the Regents were still not as unanimously in favor of the merger as Moore believed. On March 23, 1919, speaking ostensibly in tribute to retiring President Benjamin Ide Wheeler, the eloquent Regent and alumnus Charles Stetson Wheeler asserted that:

> This institution [the University] is the completest expression that we have of the spirituality of the sovereign people of California. It in a larger sense is truly the soul of the sovereign state . . . . That soul cannot be divided and continue a soul fit to occupy the body of the sovereign state of California. I say these things because there have been, there are, and there will continue to be, men within the confines of our borders,—principally newcomers to our commonwealth—who fail utterly to comprehend the spirit that animated our fathers when they put this great soul into the sovereign state. These newcomers make the absurd mistake of conceiving this to be the University of San Francisco or of Oakland; and they would, if they could, invade the sacred precincts of the Ark of the Covenant; they would lay rude hands upon it

and would rend it asunder; they would seize the sacred scroll, would tear it in two, and would leave one-half of it here in our midst and would set the other half at some center convenient to a real estate market south of the Tehachapi.[44]

Regent Rowell wanted to defer action for at least two years, during which time more study could be made of California's whole education structure.[45] To this end, he and other Regents, working through the Executive Committee of the Board in February and March, 1919, sought to so amend the pending legislation on the matter that Moore could no longer accept it. The most significant of these efforts was one to remove all mention of bachelor's degrees for the proposed teachers college. Because the degree-granting privilege for the teachers college was the main object of the merger from Moore's point of view, no one anticipated that he would ever consent to its omission from the bill. The Regents supported their position by telling Moore that their right to grant degrees came from the state constitution and that they neither wanted nor needed to have the legislature tell them which degrees to grant in Los Angeles.[46]

Moore, as expected, remained insistent upon including a reference to degrees in the bill, until representatives of the other normal schools appeared in Sacramento to object that the proposed degree-granting privilege was an unfair advantage that should be granted to all teachers colleges or none.[47] To avoid a deadlock in the legislature on the issue, Moore changed his mind suddenly, and agreed to have the reference left out of the final version of the bill.[48] The Los Angeles State Normal School bill, effective July 24, 1919, was passed on April 22, and signed into law on May 23, 1919.[49]

Between June 11, 1918, when Rowell's committee was appointed, and June 10, 1919, the full Board of Regents took no action on the Los Angeles Normal School matter. All discussion took place within its Executive Committee. Thus, no mention of final accord on the merger is made in the minutes of the Board until after the enabling legislation passed. Then, on June 10, 1919, there is this entry: "In view of the signing of Assembly Bill No. 626 by the Governor of California and the creation thereby of a branch of the University of California at the site of the Los Angeles Normal School . . ." the Regents voted to call their new campus the "Southern California Branch" of the University, to name E. C. Moore as its director, and to name Professor Monroe Deutsch; Professor Baldwin Woods, University examiner for the junior colleges; and Robert G. Sproul, the comptroller, members of an advisory administrative board to aid Director Moore in setting up the academic program for the coming year.[50]

TIGHT CONTROL FROM BERKELEY

With the transfer of the Los Angeles State Normal School to the Regents in January, 1919, Ernest Moore had won an incomplete victory. The status of teachers' courses in the University's Southern Branch was not much improved over what it had been in the normal school. No baccalaureate degrees were offered, and there was no instruction authorized beyond the second year. President Wheeler, who had been reticent but resigned to the creation of the Southern Branch, retired in June, 1919. His successor, David Prescott Barrows, was openly skeptical about the venture and advocated a lead-footed evolutionary development of the University's new facility.

Barrows was influenced by two considerations. First, there was his solid conviction that the University would remain, insofar as possible, a one-campus institution. "I view centrifugal tendencies within the University with great concern," [51] he said in 1920, and went on to suggest that "no graver responsibility faces the Regents at the present time than to provide those great resources and facilities which the advancing departments of our institution require, and at the same time keep the University in the embrace of a single bond and a single fellowship." [52] Second, he was concerned with new efforts of certain agricultural interests to separate the College of Agriculture from Berkeley. The success of the Southern Branch would tend to prove the feasibility of their scheme. Until that matter was put to rest, President Barrows tended to restrain Southern Branch developments.

Director Moore had little autonomy. The Advisory Administrative Board, with no membership from the old normal school or from the Southern Branch itself, worked out the details of the new curriculum. To make sure that all of the normal school faculty members brought over to the University system met standards comparable to those applied at Berkeley, Professors Deutsch and Woods, the advisory board's academic members, visited the classes of every faculty member. In two years, about fifty Southern Branch faculty members were let go as a result of these investigations, "with practically no repercussions." [53]

The business affairs of the Southern Branch were the responsibility of the University comptroller at Berkeley, but in 1921, Robert Underhill, assistant to the comptroller, was sent to Los Angeles to assume responsibility for the purchasing, accounting, grounds and buildings, and the publication division there. At first, every requisition for supplies and equipment had to be sent to Berkeley for approval by Comptroller Sproul or a deputy—a process that required, on the average, fourteen days. Only after Underhill submitted a study of the inefficiency of such delays was the Southern Branch authorized to make purchases on its own.[54]

"For me," Moore later wrote, "the first years of the Southern Branch of the University are not the pleasantest of memories. We felt we had been harshly dealt with. . . . Folks passing along Vermont Avenue not seldom pointed the finger of scorn at us and said, 'There is the Normal School that thought it could be a university.' . . ." [55]

THE INEVITABLE ENLARGEMENT

When the Southern Branch opened in its new University status in 1919, it enrolled 2,300 students. About 1,000 of these were in the teachers' courses, and President Barrows noted that they constituted about 40 per cent of the teacher candidates in the state.[56] The importance of the teachers' "courses" (they were not referred to as a "college" until 1922) was emphasized by Director Moore in 1921, when he called the Training School, with 525 children, "our largest laboratory." [57] The city of Los Angeles cooperated in this work by permitting the use of its Grand Avenue and Thirty-sixth Street schools as supplemental training centers.[58]

The support of southern California school systems made it difficult for President Barrows to hold down the development of the Southern Branch. Another constructive influence was the Regents' new committee on the Southern Branch of the University and Scripps Institution for Biological Research. In 1920, Edward A. Dickson became chairman of this committee and continued to serve in that capacity until 1948, when he became chairman of the Board. Other committee members were the second and third southern California Regents, Mrs. Margaret Sartori and George Ira Cochran; Regents Rowell and Taussig; and State Superintendent of Public Instruction Will C. Wood.[59] Director Moore was often in contact with the members of this committee who resided in Los Angeles to discuss his problems and progress. Though conspicuously loyal to his alma mater at Berkeley, Regent Dickson soon made the development of the Southern Branch a personal crusade. He was frequently on the Southern Branch campus for personal inspections and conferences with officers and was a scrappy champion for it at Regents' meetings.

Many Regents accepted the Southern Branch into the University with the understanding that it would never offer more than junior-college-level work. But circumstances changed considerably in 1921, when the legislature changed the name of normal schools to "teachers colleges" and authorized them, as they became ready, to expand their offerings to four years and to grant bachelor's degrees.[60] As a result, teaching courses within the Southern Branch were suddenly more restricted than they would have been if they had not become a part of the University in 1919.

On February 14, 1922, the Regents remedied that disadvantage by creating a teachers college in the Southern Branch and authorizing it to develop four-year courses leading to the bachelor's degree.[61] Planning of the new courses was accomplished with the assistance of a committee of the Academic Senate at Berkeley.

These new developments whetted the appetite of Los Angeles civic leaders for more instruction in the junior college in the Southern Branch. Sensitive to this desire, on January 9, 1923, Regent Dickson proposed to the Southern Branch Committee that a third year be instituted. His committee agreed, but only on the condition that the need for a third year be proven and that money to pay for it be obtained without jeopardizing adequate financial support for the Berkeley campus.[62] Dickson believed that these provisions were intended to frustrate (at least for several years) the third-year plan in Los Angeles.[63] President Barrows would surely declare the program unnecessary, and no one knew at the time where any money not previously authorized for Berkeley's expenditure would come from.

But there was a way around these conditions, and the Los Angeles civic and education leaders found it immediately. They persuaded their state senator, Charles W. Lyon, to introduce a bill that read: "Section 1. The regents of the University of California are hereby authorized to provide and shall provide during the year commencing July 1, 1923, and thereafter, such junior (third year) courses of university grade in a college of letters and sciences at the University of California, southern branch, in Los Angeles, as they may deem proper, and during the year beginning July 1, 1924, and thereafter, such senior (fourth year) courses of university grade in a college of letters and sciences at the University of California, southern branch in Los Angeles, as they may deem proper, which junior and senior courses shall lead to the degree of bachelor of arts." [64] The same bill appropriated $400,000 to carry out its provisions.

Once the Lyon bill was introduced, the Regents could not refuse to authorize the third-year plan without, in effect, saying "no" to the citizens of Los Angeles. If President Barrows, in accordance with the January 9 action of the Southern Branch Committee, dared to deny the need for a third year in the face of the Lyon bill, he would have to accept an abnormally heavy burden of proof. Despite the fact that the Lyon bill intruded shamefully on the constitutional authority of the Regents, the Board paid it heed. By a one-vote majority, they voted on February 13 to introduce a third year of instruction at Los Angeles in the coming year. The only proviso they made in this action was that adequate financial support for Berkeley not be jeopardized.[65]

President Barrows never gave up his opposition to hasty expansion in the south, and in the last annual report of his presidency he expressed concern that the University's "branches, grown heavy with their own weight, may, by pressure from external agencies, be forced apart from the parent institution. . . .

"There are those in the state who seek to establish in other centers, newer state universities which would duplicate in every respect the parent institution at Berkeley. But the period of establishment of new state universities has ended. No more will arise except by duplication within a state." [66]

President Campbell drew the line on Southern Branch development as firmly as Barrows did, but at a different level. In August, 1923, he asked the Regents to appoint a committee to study the question of starting a fourth year of instruction there. A committee was accordingly appointed, and its recommendation that the University offer Senior-year instruction in Los Angeles beginning on July 1, 1924, was approved by the Board in December, 1923,[67] with the stipulation, however, ". . . that it is not the intention of the Regents and is, in fact contrary to their policy to look forward to making provisions for graduate instruction at the Southern Branch." [68] President Campbell could not be moved from that stipulation throughout the years of his administration.

THE MOVE TO WESTWOOD

The continuing growth of population in southern California and the extension of the Southern Branch's curriculum into the fourth collegiate year brought more students than its Vermont Avenue campus could hold. For expansion, the Regents started to buy 15 acres near the campus. Purchases were nearly complete in 1924 when the Regents realized that, even with their new land, they had only 40 acres hemmed in by the surrounding community. The University campus emerging in the southland deserved something more spacious and inspiring, and Regent Dickson had just such a spot in mind.

Sometime in the spring of 1923, Dickson and a fellow alumnus, Irwin J. Muma, were walking in the vicinity of Bel-Air on land that had been part of the famous Wolfskill Rancho. From an elevated point on the rancho they could see the ocean, while behind them were hills of a size and character that reminded them of Berkeley.[69] When it was apparent that the Southern Branch needed new land, an entirely new site, for expansion, Dickson remembered this place. He learned that it had been owned most recently by Arthur Letts, a prominent Los Angeles merchant, but was then controlled by two brothers, Dr. Edwin Janss and Harold Janss, who were also Letts's sons-in-law. When Dickson talked to them about the site as a possible University location, they seemed to appreciate immediately the potential for their property if the campus actually was put on part of it. They agreed to make available 200 acres for a campus and to plan a college town to adjoin it. Dickson later showed the site to President Campbell, Comptroller Sproul, and Professor Baldwin Woods. Regent Guy C. Earl came down to look at it too and agreed with Dickson that it was an eminently desirable location. But, before moving to acquire it, Earl felt that it would be wise to find out if there were not other sites in southern California that might equal or surpass it.[70]

Acting on Earl's suggestion, the Regents authorized an announcement that they would consider offers in several southern California counties of sites for a new University campus, provided the land was offered free of cost. The Regents also invited a group of seventeen southern Californians, nominated by Dickson, to form a Citizens' Committee on Sites to cooperate with the southern Regents in securing a new campus.

Seventeen pieces of property were offered, four of which were promising enough to warrant serious consideration, but Campbell, as well as Dickson, preferred the Wolfskill Rancho, which, the President felt, "seems to possess superior advantages and to offer an ideal site." [71] Even while other sites were being investigated, the Citizens' Committee was acquiring options on neighboring land to enlarge the 200 acres promised by the Janss brothers to 383 acres.[72]

On March 21, 1925, the Regents heard reports from their Southern Branch Committee and the Citizens' Committee, both of which favored the Westwood site (as the Wolfskill property's location was becoming known). They liked its beauty, climate, and accessibility. They also appreciated the encouragement that the citizens of Los Angeles and the immediately neighboring cities had given the Southern Branch since 1919 and did not want to move the campus out of range of their support. Since the property had to be free, the Citizens' Committee suggested that friends of the University be allowed to buy it and present it as a gift to the Regents. The judgment of the Regents' Southern Branch Committee and the Citizens' Committee was accepted, and the Regents shortly announced that the Wolfskill Rancho property had been selected as the permanent site of the University's Southern Branch.

The best friends of the University's Southern Branch were the communities that would benefit by having it located close at hand. These were Los Angeles, Beverly Hills, Santa Monica, and Venice. Comptroller Sproul suggested that these cities be asked to buy the desired site and turn it over to the University. The total price was more than $1,000,000. To help cover it, Los Angeles placed a $700,000 bond issue on the ballot in the spring of 1925. The other cities followed this lead, with issues of $100,000 in Beverly Hills, $120,000 in Santa Monica, and $50,000 in Venice. After these issues were passed, the Los Angeles County Supervisors approved expenditure of another $100,000 to cover the deficit.[73]

James R. Martin, secretary of the Citizens' Committee, became executive secretary for the whole bond campaign effort. Since most of the money was to come from Los Angeles, the biggest campaign was made there. Hundreds of thousands of blue-and-gold posters, car-cards, stickers, and bumper strips were printed and distributed. School children in every school in the city were supplied with four-page brochures to take home to their parents. Another million pamphlets were distributed by hand and by mail to southern California voters. Student speakers from the Southern Branch attended all important public gatherings to put in a word for the bond issue. Radio messages were delivered into the voters' homes, and a ten-minute movie depicting the sorrow of a family separated from their college-bound son carried the message that they could be spared their grief if they kept the University close to home. On the eve of the election, the students of the Southern Branch staged a "Mammoth Bonfire" on the Westwood site and paraded in their pajamas hoping to leave an impression that would stick with Los Angeles citizens at least through election day. Then, on election day itself, the students were present at the polls, decked out in blue and gold, loaded with literature for the voters, and prepared to transport people to the polls in their cars. All of these efforts proved worthwhile, and the bond issue passed in Los Angeles by an overwhelming margin.[74] Bond issues in other cities also passed easily, although their campaigns were somewhat more modest.

On February 9, 1926, James R. Martin had the historic privilege of giving to the Regents of the University of California separate deeds from Los Angeles, Beverly Hills, Santa Monica, and Venice for their parts of the 383-acre Westwood site. Resolutions of gratitude were passed, and plans for dedication of the site were put into motion.

THE ACADEMIC FUTURE

In 1924, the Southern Branch of the University of California was a degree-granting, two-college, four-year University campus planning to move to bigger quarters. What kind of program would be accommodated at the new location? President Campbell and the Academic Senate gave that question careful consideration.

Farmers and farm organizations in southern California urged the University to open a second college of agriculture in connection with the new campus and suggested that no less than 600 acres would be required for it. After discussing this matter with the Regents' Agricultural Committee on November 21, 1924, however, President Campbell recommended against the proposal.[75] In part, his arguments echoed the by-now-familiar refrain that one good college of agriculture would be better than two weak ones. More specific, however, was his contention that agricultural college enrollments were dropping at institutions all over the country and barely holding their own at the University of California, although the state's population was increasing steadily. Moreover, the area in which the Southern Branch was located was essentially urban in character, and an agricultural college would be out of place there. Finally, agricultural instruction was fantastically expensive, and the University could not afford the cost of offering it in two widely separated places. Campbell's recommendation was that instead of opening a second agricultural college in Los Angeles, advanced instruction in citriculture and subtropical horticulture be offered at the Citrus Experiment Station in Riverside in the form of inter-session and summer session courses. The Board of Regents later concurred in Campbell's proposition that the College of Agriculture should remain undivided at Berkeley, but refused to permit the transferal of any instruction from Berkeley to Riverside at that time.[76]

A more prolonged controversy involved the role of the Teachers College on the Westwood campus. President Campbell and members of the Academic Senate at Berkeley were solidly of the opinion that the training of elementary school teachers was not a proper function of the University. The members of the Senate's Educational Policy Committee considered this question at a meeting on October 23, 1923, and concluded to ask that the President consider separating the Teachers College from the University. Their recommendation was timely, coming in the midst of discussions about physical expansion at Los Angeles. The committee members asserted that the coexistence of the Teachers College and a partial or complete letters and science course was "illogical," and asked why one of the state's teachers colleges should be under the University while the others were under the State Board of Education. They considered the aims of the two colleges so distinct that it was "unwholesome" to mix the two kinds of students in the same courses—an eventuality quite likely with the establishment of a full college course at the Southern Branch. They said the Vermont Avenue campus was too small for both activities and suggested that the Teachers College be allowed to keep it while the University sought a new site for the College of Letters and Science. Then they asked for early action: "No better opportunity is likely to arise than the present for outlining a broad policy that will include the growth of the real University and the elimination of an illogical and undesirable 'side line.' " [77]

President Campbell was in sympathy with the faculty committee, but did not press the matter with the Regents for over a year. In the meantime, he discussed the subject with Dickson. At first, the President suggested turning the Teachers College back to the state, but in the face of Dickson's strong objections to that idea, later offered a compromise that would retain the Teachers College as a part of the University but remaining at Vermont Avenue when the rest of the Southern Branch moved to Westwood. Dickson also opposed this plan, but there were other Regents who favored the separation. One of them, of course, was Chester Rowell, who had not been anxious to make the teachers course of the Los Angeles State Normal School a part of the University in the first place. Another was Garrett McEnerny, who, on March 10, 1925, while the search for a new Southern Branch site was coming to an end, introduced a resolution that the "College of Letters and Science . . . be conducted on the new [Westwood] site and that the Teachers' College be conducted at the present location." [78] Dickson was absent from the meeting, and McEnerny's resolution was passed unanimously, with even southern California Regents voting for it. Dickson was shocked when he learned what happened, and announced that he would work to rescind the action.

The battleground for the contest between Dickson and President Campbell over the separation of the Teachers College was the building plan for the new campus. Dickson insisted on basing his building cost estimates on enrollment figures that included students in the Teachers College. President Campbell was equally insistent that the estimates should be based upon the separation that, to his mind, had already become a matter of policy. On December 14, 1926, in an effort to avoid responsibility for the inevitable, Campbell insisted that the minutes of a Regents meeting held that day include the statement: "Regent Dickson's proposal [for buildings] is one which concerns the public policy of the University, and not its academic policy. This is a subject, therefore, upon which the President is not called upon to make a presidential recommendation. Each Regent should cast his vote in accordance with his own judgement of Regent Dickson's proposal in its relationship to good public policy." [79]

While awaiting an opportunity for a new showdown on the basic issue of separation, Dickson entered into informal discussions with the southern California Regents, his friend Regent Earl, and others who might be swayed to his view. He reminded them that unless the Vermont campus was sold, the University would not have all the money it needed for construction at Westwood. Moreover, he pointed out that the University owed some consideration to Director Moore, who had been so instrumental in making the Southern Branch possible, but would be certainly frozen out of the University if the separation were to take place. At a Board meeting on August 14, 1928, Dickson brought the question of separation up for review, and this time, by a narrow majority, he won.[80]

THE WESTWOOD CAMPUS

Regent Dickson had talked a great deal about the Berkeley campus, and so had other alumni of the University who lived in southern California after their graduation. During his years of activity on behalf of the Southern Branch, James R. Martin was thoroughly indoctrinated by these Old Blues in the Berkeley traditions and landmarks. One that particularly appealed to him was Founders' Rock, where the College of California pioneers were said to have gathered back in 1860 to dedicate the college site at Berkeley. Regrettably, there were no large rocks in Westwood, so Martin had one weighing 75 tons hauled in from Hemet in Riverside County and unloaded at approximately the spot where Dickson and his friend had stood in 1923 to reflect upon the similarity of the view to that they had known at Berkeley as students. At this place, on October 25, 1926, Governor Friend W. Richardson, students of the Southern Branch, and University officers gathered to dedicate the Westwood site. A month later, California citizens approved a $6,000,000 bond issue, half of which was to provide new buildings at Los Angeles. The other half was for replacing old wooden buildings in Berkeley. On September 12, 1927, ground was broken for the new campus.

Four buildings of Romanesque architecture were ready for occupancy by May, 1929: the library, Royce Hall with its auditorium and classrooms, the

Physics–Biology Building, and the Chemistry Building. Located around a central quadrangle, they were designed by architect George W. Kelham [81] and built of brick and stone, with tiled roofs.

"Official" moving day was May 31, 1929. On that day, a University-owned truck, loaded with furniture and equipment, led a parade of students' automobiles out to the new campus. The ROTC band played on the steps of Royce Hall and subsequently at the library, and visitors roamed the campus, attempting to imagine it in operation the following fall.

The big move took place after summer sessions were over in August. Under the strategic command of Assistant Comptroller Robert Underhill, moving vans made ninety-six trips the first day, a Friday, and thirty-eight the following Monday. Nearly three hundred students were hired to load and unload the vans and place the furniture where it belonged in the new buildings. In less than a week, the University was settling comfortably into new quarters.[82]

On February 1, 1927, the Regents officially changed the name of the Southern Branch to "The University of California at Los Angeles." [83] But more than a name had changed. The confining concept of a university as a locale was replaced with the notion that it was an idea, or an endeavor, that need not be staked down to one spot, but could be encountered in more than one location at the same time.

Had this concept of the University of California been grasped in the beginning, some of the Regents, the faculty, alumni of the Berkeley campus, and the University presidents during the 1920s might have accepted UCLA's inevitable emergence with better grace. The University might have given its services to southern California because they were needed and wanted there. Instead, it gave them out of fear of competition from other institutions. The University might have initiated an enlargement of curriculum because the campus was maturing under the guidance of a faculty using Berkeley standards as a model and enriching itself with well-qualified men and women. Instead, the curriculum was extended because political pressure was applied from Sacramento.

The southern Californians who worked so hard for UCLA's establishment also were short-sighted. Ernest Moore wanted his normal school to become a part of the University because he wanted to be able to grant bachelor's degrees. Citizens of Los Angeles wanted the University to offer junior-college instruction so that they would not have to provide it themselves with local taxes. Civic pride and vanity were at least as instrumental in UCLA's creation as was local aspiration for educational opportunities.

It is now clear that the University of California could not have served the state well without accepting its responsibilities in any area where its services and influence were needed. The success of the venture at Los Angeles proved for all time that, with adequate legislative and public assistance, the University could serve young men and women in centers distant from Berkeley without sacrifice of integrity, and marked the beginning of a multi-campus development destined to become the University of California's most innovative and distinctive characteristic.

III

Branching Out

CRANCEONED

EVEN before Benjamin Ide Wheeler's twenty years of leadership as president of the University of California ended, his concept of the University as a close-knit family of students, faculty members, administrators, and alumni bound by common loyalties began to be eroded by new forces inside and outside of the University. The family concept was plausible when "home" was a single campus with nearby affiliates devoted to special functions, but when a new addition was acquired 500 miles away, the analogy became strained. It lost force, too, when its benevolent but authoritarian father was no longer around to give his little lectures on the character of the good Californian and to say what had to be done. In his absence, many of the family traditions that had bound the University together began to give way. Students turned student self-government and self-restraint into a massive structure of activities which required increasingly detailed regulation. The faculty, meanwhile, turned their energies to acquiring larger governing powers for themselves and became immersed in increasingly sophisticated research.

Presidents David Prescott Barrows and William Wallace Campbell took their turns at leading the University during the period when the faculty was most actively asserting its rights to greater authority; when the partisans of the Southern Branch were prematurely demanding that their functions and support be expanded; when youth was losing its prewar inhibitions and embarrassing its elders; and when enrollment-growth continued to outdistance financial support. Under the stress of these developments, Barrows' un-

237

happy tenancy of the president's office lasted only three and a half years. Campbell's less difficult presidency endured for seven.

Robert Gordon Sproul came to the presidency in 1930 with a broad personal knowledge of the University acquired first as a student when Wheeler still reigned and later as a popular young administrator during a period that spanned Wheeler's last five years in the presidency and the administrations of both Barrows and Campbell. Although he was not an academic man, Sproul enjoyed the confidence of many faculty members and popularity among his fellow alumni and influential sectors of the general public. His administration was to last twenty-eight years, surviving the great depression, World War II, the explosive enrollment growth of the postwar period, and the loyalty-oath controversy that threatened to bring the University to ruin.

Sproul could not restore the sense of "family" that Wheeler had created. The University had become too big for that. But he was able to build a new kind of loyalty based upon the University's achievements and its contributions to the people of the state. On this basis, he was able to argue effectively for support not only from within the University, but also from the legislature and the people of the state. The University's size, in this context, was not necessarily a fault, and, in fact, Sproul made it a virtue, first emphasizing the diversity of its work at Berkeley, Los Angeles, and several research stations, and then speaking of the eight "campuses" of "One Great University," with Sproul himself the personification of its unity.

The "One University" idea frightened some educators and legislators because they believed it meant the University wanted to have jurisdiction over all public higher education in the state. As a result, Sproul's administration encountered many of the same pressures from the public and college officials that befell administrations of the University during the early years of UCLA's development. Sproul was able to work out voluntary coordination systems so that the University and other colleges and universities would not be in direct competition, but he could not steer the University away from conflict permanently.

Internally, the "One University" idea succeeded extremely well in keeping the various elements of the University together through a great depression, war, and nearly catastrophic loyalty-oath dispute.

Chapter 16

THE FACULTY ASSERTS ITSELF

THE FOUNDERS OF the University failed to discern clearly that the government and structure of the faculty would have to adjust to expansion and growth. They were not, after all, academicians and they were loath to incorporate into the Organic Act their imperfect knowledge of course development, degree requirements, and other educational mysteries of professorship. They met whatever responsibilities they felt they had in these areas by making the president of the University the president of all the faculties and responsible to the all-powerful Regents. For these reasons, the history of faculty government during the first half-century of the University was one of continual adjustment to new policies and projects voted by the Regents and to the ebb and flow of presidential authority.

With the development of professional schools and affiliates in San Francisco, for instance, it became increasingly difficult for the faculties of the several colleges of the University to deliberate jointly on curricular changes, degree requirements, student discipline, and other internal matters exclusively involving a college at Berkeley. Moreover, the faculty at Berkeley had little interest or competence in making judgments on similar matters for the professional schools in San Francisco. In 1885, therefore, the faculties at Berkeley organized, as a committee of the Academic Senate, what they called the Academic Council. This committee was made up solely of members of the Berkeley faculty. Between meetings of the senate, held only twice a year, the council was empowered with provisional authority on all questions that required senate action.[1] In 1887, a Professional Council was created by the senate. Consisting of the president and two representatives of each of the colleges of law, medicine, dentistry, and pharmacy, this council was charged with regulating, subject to Academic Senate approval, matters in which the several professional schools shared concern.

With the enlargement of the University, both at Berkeley and at other

239

locations in the state, the Academic Senate authorized a special committee to propose "a method by which greater unity in plans for the development of the University may be brought about between the academic and professional faculties." [2] The committee's recommendation, read and adopted at a meeting of the senate of November 17, 1909, was that a University Council be created.[3] It would be composed of the president of the University; five members of the joint faculties of letters, social sciences, and natural sciences; one member from each of the faculties of commerce, agriculture, chemistry, mining, civil engineering, and mechanics; one member of the Lick Astronomical Department; two members from each of the faculties of law, medicine, dentistry, pharmacy, and art; the dean of the faculties; and the dean of the graduate school.[4] Thus, the faculties, which had been divided by the creation of the Academic Council and the Professional Council in the 1880s, were reunited.

The University Council's authority was, in practice, quite weak. It was concerned only with a very few matters common to all of the colleges and faculties represented and was specifically prohibited from deliberations on matters previously entrusted to the Academic and Professional Councils.

This constant reorganization of the structure of faculty government in the 1890s and 1900s produced a certain amount of wheel-spinning. Some of the new councils and committees seemed to mitigate or even cancel out the effectiveness of the old ones. Moreover, throughout the first fifty years of the University's life, the Regents and president tended to accept the judgment of the Academic Senate mainly on the questions of curriculum planning, degree and entrance requirements, and student discipline. On other matters of educational policy they turned to Regental committees, deans of the colleges, and chairmen of departments.

Particularly after Kellogg became president, the deans were relied upon to advise the president on which faculty members should be hired or promoted, how much money their departments needed each fiscal year, and whether certain courses should be retained or dropped. President Wheeler relied on department chairmen for the same kind of advice. The practice was expedient, free of parliamentary folderol, and none too restrictive of presidential initiative. But it was dangerous. It deprived many faculty members of an opportunity to suggest alternative courses of action and invited charges that the deans, department chairmen, and even the president were guilty of preferential treatment of certain members of the faculty.

President Wheeler not only circumvented the Academic Senate in seeking advice, but dominated the faculty in other ways. He hired and fired professors personally, appointed all deans and department chairmen, and named the members of all Academic Senate committees. He devised the University budget himself, and, in the process, was able to encourage or discourage the work of the various departments as he chose. He personally presided over meetings of the Academic Council and Senate and on at least one occasion was suspected of giving the floor only to those who would agree with his own position.[5]

The members of the Academic Senate took one important step toward regaining influence when they voted in 1915 to dissolve the Academic Council.[6] That committee had always had an ambiguous existence and, because it preempted the most significant academic concerns for its exclusive supervision, it tended to weaken that part of the University charged by law with faculty government—the Academic Senate.

Further reform was proposed in 1916 when a new set of By Laws and Standing Rules of the Academic Senate was submitted for adoption. One of the new rules created a standing committee that would nominate members for the various senate committees, thus ending the President's unilateral action in such appointments.[7] Another created four new councils (for letters and science, engineering, agriculture, and the Graduate Division), in which the work of the senate could be broken down for greater efficiency.[8] Yet another, obviously intended to replace the administration's reliance upon advice of deans and department chairmen with a procedure reflecting the broader interests of the faculty, created a General Administrative Board of forty-four members to act "in behalf of the Academic Senate in all purely administrative matters." [9] The proposed board included most of the deans, many University officers, and the chairmen of most Academic Senate committees. None of these new proposals were adopted by the senate in 1916, but the fact that such reforms were contemplated indicated that there was a new mood among members of the faculty. After World War I, that mood again prevailed and led the faculty to a larger role in determining University policies.

THE TIMING OF CHANGE

The faculty was not ready to make a bid for additional power before World War I. The old tradition of Regental and presidential dominance was widely accepted as a fact of University life up to that time and the University itself was eminent, riding a crest of public goodwill. Its chief executive was an internationally famous educator, beloved by students and alumni. The need for change did not appear pressing.

The war disarranged all of these conditions. The Regents placed the entire University at the disposal of the federal government, and the campus at Berkeley took on many aspects of a military encampment. President Wheeler's authority was weakened by the creation of the Advisory Committee of Deans in April, 1918, and the normal pattern of faculty government was changed by the creation of an Emergency Council with all of the powers of the senate "in order that important war work on the academic side of the University might be carried forward without delay."

A survey made in 1915–1916 of twenty-one leading American institutions, including the University of California, reported "a growing tendency all over the country to increase the administrative powers of the faculty." [10] In 1918, the American Association of University Professors reported that a study of 110 leading colleges and universities revealed greater faculty participation in appointments, nominations, drafting budgets, and general consultation on important matters.[11] The University of California would inevitably be caught up in these national trends.

Change in the University was facilitated when the whole basis of its structure and governance was shifted from the detailed and outmoded provisions of the 1868 Organic Act to an amended Section 9, Article IX, of the state constitution in 1918. The amendment gave the Regents full authority in the administration of the University and made it possible for the faculty to change their own role in the institution simply by convincing the Regents that a change was needed.

The decline of Wheeler's personal influence in 1918 and 1919 also favored a move toward a greater faculty role in University operations. The faculty wanted authority to nominate deans, department chairmen, and members of the Academic Senate committees. They also wanted an established direct channel of communication to the Regents. The appointment of the Advisory Committee of Deans to share the President's wartime burdens in May, 1918, strengthened the faculty's hand in making such demands because it stood as a Regental acknowledgment that academic people might, after all, be competent in the administration of University policies.

PROPOSALS FOR REORGANIZATION

In June, 1919, the Board of Regents decided not to appoint a successor immediately upon Wheeler's retirement in July, but, instead, to place the executive authority of the University in the hands of an "Administrative

Board" to consist of Professors William Carey Jones and Charles Mills Gayley, carry-overs from the old Advisory Committee of Deans, and University Comptroller Ralph Merritt.[12]

The Administrative Board assumed full control in July, 1919. After twenty years of experience, the faculty had learned to live with Wheeler's benevolent autocracy, but they found the new board intolerable. Its members often acted precipitously and at cross-purposes. The permanence of its decisions could not be relied upon. It could not solve the most urgent pending problem: faculty salaries virtually stood still while the cost of living rose steeply. The board was also suspected of misrepresenting faculty opinion to the Regents.

In early September, faculty members were already attending informal meetings to discuss ways in which the lot of the professor could be improved. A step considered basic was to determine how the Academic Senate might be "reorganized on more democratic lines." [13] Leaders of the group were not unknown firebrands. They included some of the University's most celebrated professors and several college deans. At an open meeting of the faculty on September 24, the basic ideas of these "rebels" were discussed. Subsequently, resolutions were prepared and presented at a special meeting of the Academic Senate on October 1 and 2.

The intent of the resolutions, the faculty was informed, was (1) to place more definitely upon the faculty the responsibility in matters within its jurisdiction; (2) to insure adequate expression of faculty opinion on University matters; (3) to provide that actions and opinions ascribed to the faculty of the University should in fact be the actions and opinions of the faculty or its authorized representatives; and (4) to provide for a more active participation of the faculty in matters pertaining to the well-being and the working conditions of the teaching force at the University.[14]

Approximately 260 faculty members were convened for the October 1 meeting. They were asked to approve a proposed memorial to the Regents which made several specific demands. After prolonged debate that was conducted in two separate meetings the memorial, with only minor alterations calculated to soften its tone, was approved by a rising vote of 132 to 13.[15]

Sent to the Regents on October 3, the memorial was a respectful document, indicating a desire for cooperation with the Regents and the University's administrative officers, noting that the time seemed opportune for considering the organization of the senate and its relations with the Regents, and notifying the Board of its readiness to appoint a committee to confer on five specific propositions:

(1) a. The Dean of the Faculties should be elected by the Academic Senate and should be its presiding officer.
b. The Dean of the Graduate Division should be elected by the Academic Senate on nomination of the Graduate Council.
c. The deans of the several colleges should be elected by their respective college faculties, and should be the presiding officers of the faculties of these colleges.
d. The title Dean should be restricted to the elected presiding officer of the Academic Senate, or of a college or other designated faculty group.
(2) The privilege of a vote in the Academic Senate should be extended to all instructors after two years' service.
(3) One or more representatives of the faculty, elected by the Academic Senate, should be authorized to sit in an advisory capacity with the Board of Regents.
(4) Departmental chairmen should be elected by the members of their respective departments, such members to include instructors who have a vote in the Academic Senate.
(5) Whenever the occasion arises for the selection of a new President, the Academic Senate should be consulted in reference thereto.[16]

At that same meeting, the faculty approved a new by-law: "A standing Committee on Committees shall be elected each year by the Academic Senate, to nominate to the Senate the members to be elected to all other standing committees of the Senate, except the University Council." [17] This new committee proved to be the very heart of the reorganization that the faculty devised, for it insured faculty control of Academic Senate affairs. The committee was considered so important that, in subsequent action, special provisions were made for the election of its members (who were to consist of the dean of the University ex officio and six members elected by the senate).[18]

THE REGENTS' REACTION

The Academic Senate's memorial did not take the Regents by surprise. They had known for some time that there were members of the faculty intent on strengthening the senate's authority. Although some of the Regents resisted the faculty proposals because they believed that the authority of the Regents legally could not be shared, their resistance was overcome by a genuine fear that the faculty, already restive over low salaries, might leave if frustrated in efforts to gain better control over academic affairs. The Regents also realized that whatever concessions the Board might make could easily be taken away later if they proved dangerous or unfeasible.

On November 3, 1919, William Carey Jones advised the Academic Senate that the Regents had authorized their Executive Committee to arrange for a conference with a committee of faculty members selected by the senate.[19] The proposed meeting took place on November 24, with Professors George P. Adams, Andrew C. Lawson, Gilbert N. Lewis, George D. Louderback, and Orrin K. McMurray representing the faculty. At that meeting, the Regents announced that a subcommittee of the Board would be appointed to consult further with the faculty. They also asked the faculty conference committee for recommendations on nominations for a new president of the University. This request was declined by the faculty committee on the grounds that it was unauthorized to represent the faculty in that matter.[20]

The Regents' subcommittee on conferences with the faculty was composed of James K. Moffitt, as chairman; John A. Britton, vice-president of Pacific Gas and Electric Company; Wigginton Creed, the first president of the California Alumni Association to serve as an ex-officio Regent under provisions of the constitutional amendment of 1918; Chester H. Rowell; and Rudolph Taussig. Monsignor Charles A. Ramm, an alumnus of the class of 1884 and a Regent since 1912, took Rowell's place on the committee when illness forced the Fresno editor to forego the assignment.[21]

No decisions came from faculty–Regent consultations for many months after the November 24 meeting. In the meantime, the Regents selected a new president.

THE COMPTROLLER AND THE COLONEL

"The old University of California is as entirely dead as the old Yale or the old Harvard and it is quite time that the new University should be organized." [22] That was the judgment of Henry Morse Stephens, member of the Advisory Committee of Deans, in a letter to Regent Rudolph Taussig on April 14, 1919.

Professor Stephens' letter was prompted, in part, by the knowledge that the Regents were thinking about a successor to Wheeler. "No living human man can possibly know enough of all the departments of activity in the University," he wrote, ". . . to know how wisely to select new members of his faculty or to promote or to encourage old members." [23] He recommended that the next president "not be a specialist in any line of scholarly activity," but "be a man who will understand the State of California, who will realise the future demands on the University and who will be broad enough to be interested in every line of work." [24] To assist a president of this type, Stephens suggested that the Regents appoint independent advisers "of wisdom, experience and personality," [25] who could not be fired by the president and who could exercise veto power on academic questions—particularly those involving professorial appointments. The president would get additional assistance from the chief executives (deans) of the major departments of the University, such as agriculture, education, and the social sciences. Chosen, like the president, for administrative ability, these executives would be granted considerable autonomy in making appointments and devising their budgets. Although Stephens was concerned primarily with the nature of the presidency, he also noted that "the faculty feel that they should have more share in the responsibilities of running the University." [26]

The candidate of the dominant Regents was Ralph P. Merritt, University comptroller and secretary of the Regents, who neatly fit Henry Morse Stephens' recommendations as to the qualifications of the next president. Merritt had been Stephens' good friend and had spent many evenings in philosophical discussion and fellowship with a group of men, including Regents Taussig and Earl, that met regularly in Stephens' rooms at the Faculty Club.[27] At commencement in 1919, the Regents bestowed upon him an LL.D. degree. Officially, the degree honored Merritt for his service in the Federal Food Administration during World War I, but skeptics regarded it as an attempt to endow him with academic respectability. In July, the Regents made him a member of the Administrative Board. In doing so, they balanced the academic point of view of Professors Jones and Gayley with a man fully acquainted with the University's business affairs, but again, skeptics regarded his appointment as a move to prepare the faculty for his exercise of full administrative authority as president.

The faculty—or at least its new "rebel" leadership—opposed Merritt's election to the presidency. So did Regent Rowell, who said he admired Merritt, but did not consider him the right man to be president of an academic institution.[28] On Rowell's insistence, the Merritt sponsors agreed to delay a final vote on the presidency until a search had been made in the East. But they were confident that they had enough votes to elect Merritt to the post unless the Eastern search turned up an impressive alternative.[29]

Merritt was somewhat embarrassed by the support given him for the presidency. He had not thought of himself as a candidate for that job at any time and worried about being unable to win the full support of the faculty at a time when their mood toward the administration was already belligerent. In October, 1919, he asked that his name be withdrawn from consideration.[30]

In his place, Merritt recalled years later, he suggested that the Regents nominate David P. Barrows,[31] former dean of the faculties, who had recently returned to the University after about eight months' leave as a lieutenant colonel and intelligence officer for the American Expeditionary Forces in Siberia.[32] Those Regents who objected to Merritt's becoming president gave their backing to James Rowland Angell of the University of Chicago. On December 2, 1919, the Regents chose Barrows over Angell [33] by a six-to-four vote. For the public record, they adopted a motion to make the election unanimous.

The new president had the credentials of an academician, including an M.A. degree from the University of California and a Ph.D. from the University of Chicago. But his life did not follow the normal mode of the professor, combining as it did alternate periods of research and teaching and active service to the government. He began teaching at San Diego State College in 1897 but was in Manila about two years later, serving as superintendent of schools under Governor-General William H. Taft. Later, he was chief of the Bureau of Non-Christian Tribes of the Philippine Islands and, in 1903, was director of education there. He visited the University in 1907 as a lecturer in anthropology and then returned in 1910 with an appointment as professor of education. A year later he was named professor of political science, and in 1913 was appointed dean of the faculties. In the fall of that year, he acted as president while Wheeler was on leave.[34]

Barrows' University service was interrupted again by World War I. He served with Herbert Hoover on the American Commission for Relief in Belgium from December, 1915, to June, 1916, and in 1917 he was commissioned a major in the United States Army and stationed in the Philippines. Then came the Siberian assignment in 1918 and 1919. After the war he remained in the National Guard, eventually assuming command of the Fortieth Division with the rank of major general.[35]

Before he became president of the University, Barrows had visited in many foreign countries and had seen much of his own. He was a perceptive observer wherever he went and, upon his return, proved always to be an engaging and enlightening reporter, a talent that gave him access to the pages of well-known periodicals and to the rostrums of lecture halls and made him immensely popular with his students and alumni. His faculty colleagues considered him a better choice than Merritt would have been for the presidency, but they were not so enthusiastic about his election that they forgot their campaign to acquire more authority for the Academic Senate.

THE NEW ORDERS

Throughout the first six months of 1920, the faculty and the Regents discussed what the senate's conference committee referred to as "the constitution and government of the University." [36] During this time, a new set of proposed Standing Orders of the Board of Regents was drawn up.

The new orders made the president of the University "the executive head of the university in all its departments," charging him with the responsibility of recommending to the Regents "appointments, promotions, demotions and dismissals of members of the academic senate." [37] He could take such actions, however, when they affected professorial positions, only after consultation with the "properly constituted advisory bodies of the academic senate." [38] Appointment of deans and directors was left in the hands of the Regents on recommendation of the president, who in turn was required to consult proper committees of the Academic Senate.

The new orders required the president to report to the senate concerning changes in educational policy, to transmit to the Regents any communication addressed to them by the senate, and to advise the faculty of all acts by the Regents and state government "which affect the conduct of education and research within the university." [39]

The Regents empowered the Academic Senate to determine its own membership, choose its own chairman, and select its committees. Membership was extended to instructors, though only those with two years of service would be allowed to vote.[40] The responsibilities of the senate remained those assigned to it by the Organic Act, but, in addition, the Regents authorized it to select a committee to advise the president on budget matters.[41]

The new orders also gave members of departments the authority to organize their own administration and required that the appointment of department chairmen be made annually upon nomination from each department.[42]

Finally, in order to keep the channels of communication between the faculty and the Regents open, the new Standing Orders required creation of a conference committee of the Regents and the senate made up of five members from each body. The president and comptroller of the University were made ex-officio members of this committee.[43]

Although Barrows assumed the presidency immediately after his election, he took no active part in the deliberations between the Regents and the Academic Senate's conference committee. He indicated his intentions when he attended his first Academic Senate meeting as president on December 19,

1919, and announced that he understood the faculty's desire to appoint its own presiding officer and offered: "If you will for this meeting, or permanently, choose a presiding officer, I will be pleased to give him the chair." [44] But although he indicated his intention to retain the appointive function of the presidency as it had been defined at the beginning of Wheeler's administration, he invited the senate to nominate a slate of candidates from which he could choose a dean of the faculties and dean of the Graduate Division to replace the recently resigned Gayley and Jones.

The Academic Senate approved the new Standing Orders of March 29, 1920, but for some reason, the Regents did not approve them until June 24. In doing so, the word "academic" was inserted in a key sentence to make it read: "The president of the University shall be the executive head of the university in all its *academic* departments." [45]

When President Barrows first saw the statement—after his return from summer travels—he asked the Regents to delete it.[46] His objections were met, however, by assurances that the amendment was not intended to diminish the authority of the president.[47] With this assurance, he told the faculty on October 1, 1920, that "it is not the intention of the Regents to alter in any manner the present position and responsibilities of the President." [48]

THE FACULTY AND THE BUDGET

The new Standing Orders authorized a committee of the Academic Senate to advise the president on budget matters, but, to the chagrin of the faculty, President Barrows did not fully rely on their new committee for advice. Professor George D. Louderback, a member of the first senate Committee on Budget and Inter-Departmental Relations who served as its chairman from 1923–1931, estimated that the President accepted only about 85 per cent of the faculty's recommendations on the first budget prepared under the new orders.[49] Barrows explained to Louderback at the time that it had not been possible to check back with the committee when his changes were made, saying, "This is not due to any desire on the part of the Regents or myself to fail to take the Senate fully into confidence, but due to the delicate nature of this business. . . ." [50]

When J. Frank Daniel, chairman of the committee in 1921–1922, asked why changes were made in the budget without consulting his committee in advance, Barrows responded abruptly: ". . . The President of the University is not responsible to the Budget Committee for the budget. He is responsible to the Regents for the budget." [51] He refused to explain his changes because he felt that to do so might establish a precedent in the president's relationship to the committee.

The faculty was dissatisfied with Barrows' response and appointed a committee of fifteen members to investigate his failure to comply with the Standing Orders of the Regents.[52] In a written response to this committee, President Barrows revealed his regret that the president no longer had the decisive voice in appointing members of Academic Senate committees having to do with administrative matters.[53] In this view he was encouraged by his secretary, Morse Cartwright, who, earlier in the year, submitted a memorandum listing thirteen committees whose "responsibilities are in every case ones which the President is accountable to the Regents for. It is undoubtedly true that the President needs faculty advice in these matters, but the committees giving such advice should be appointed by the President and not by the Senate." [54] Cartwright recommended that the Committee on Budget and Inter-Departmental Relations be abolished.[55]

In his memorandum to the faculty committee of fifteen, Barrows also indicated that he felt no constraint in seeking advice outside of the senate committees when he needed it, though he acknowledged that if this occurred too often because the president did not have confidence in the senate committees, the "working understanding" necessary to the system would be prejudiced.

His fundamental point, however, was that although the senate had certain rights in determining academic standards, "there must be 'twilight zones' in the respective spheres of authority and a wise restraint that prevents anyone constantly seeking to define the full limits of his legal authority and to act up to them." [56]

The committee of fifteen, formally known as the "Special Committee on Administrative Methods," reported in May, 1922, that there was no reason for any major change in the Standing Orders of the Regents, "which has become known as the Constitution." [57] It did, however, caution faculty members against rendering advice to the President on matters not relevant to their own committee service and urged appointment of a new Committee on Administrative Personnel "to advise with the President regarding administrative appointments of an academic type [department chairmen, for instance]." [58]

Three days after the committee's report was made, President Barrows asked the Regents to relieve him of the presidency in respect for "my preference for the activities and freedom of a university teacher rather than for the responsibilities of an executive head of a university." They asked that he remain in office another year, his resignation becoming effective on June 30, 1923.[59]

TROUBLESOME YEARS

In response to an inquiry from the assistant superintendent of schools in Oakland, Barrows wrote on May 20, 1922, to assure him that "difficulties with the Academic Senate have had nothing to do with determining my resignation. While our system of conduct of affairs is not wholly satisfactory, it is somewhat awkward, and imposes a good deal of extra expense of time upon the President than a more autocratic system, I do not think it impossible of discharge." [60] Barrows was realistic enough to see that the frictions that had developed did not necessarily have a personal basis. His difficulty lay simply in the fact that he was the first president required to operate under the new orders, and until the new system was shaken down, the presidency could not be easy for anyone.

It could not have been easy in any case between 1919 and 1921. In addition to the development of a new scheme of University governance, the University had a new, ambitious Southern Branch in Los Angeles. Barrows opposed too rapid expansion and development there and was consequently at odds with much of the public in Los Angeles and with a few key Regents, though in harmony with the Berkeley faculty as a whole.

Barrows' concerns for the Southern Branch were intensified when a legislative study-committee proposed to allow for the creation of junior college districts in the state and to provide them with state financial support.[61] He unsuccessfully opposed the legislation in 1921 that enacted these proposals, advocating that for several years, at least, the University should have exclusive responsibility for providing lower-division education for California's college students.

President Barrows also had financial difficulties to contend with. Budgets were tight and faculty salaries were low. The University of California had spent beyond its means before he came to office, but he was the first president to present a deficit budget, explaining that the University had outgrown its basis of support. He was referring to the old 1910 arrangement whereby the University appropriation was to be increased by 7 per cent each year. This automatic-increase formula was apparently still honored, and by 1920 the annual legislative appropriation had needed to be augmented by special appropriations.

In 1920, University students and alumni campaigned vigorously for an amendment to the state constitution which would levy an ad valorem tax of 1.2 mills on each dollar of assessed property valuation for the support of the University. The so-called University Tax Amendment was, in effect, a new version of the old penny taxes. It did not win approval of the people, but in 1921 Barrows succeeded in getting the legislature to raise the base of its annual appropriation to $9,000,000, and prepared to make the University live with the 7-per-cent-increase formula from this new level.[62] To avoid further deficits, he got the Regents to approve an incidental fee of $25 every half-year.[63] The new fee incorporated the laboratory and diploma charges that had been collected for several years.

Despite the inadequacy of University resources, faculty salaries began to improve under Barrows' administration. In March, 1920, he secured approval of a plan for regular salary advancement after satisfactory service for a prescribed period.[64] The new plan began to solve some of the academic salary problems that had boggled both President Wheeler and the Administrative Board, and gave professors a salary range of $4,000 to $8,000 a year, with the highest grades "reserved for men of especial eminence and value." [65]

In 1920, Comptroller Merritt resigned from the University to work for the nomination of Herbert Hoover to the Presidency of the United States. His successor was a vigorous, thoroughly popular young assistant, Robert Gordon Sproul, who soon inherited Merritt's influential sponsors on the Board of Regents. Inclined to interpret his responsibilities broadly, Sproul did not fear to take the initiative when a course seemed prudent and to the University's best interests. As a result he soon acquired some of the administrative functions that had traditionally belonged to the president—at the same time that the president's authority in other matters was being assumed by committees of the Academic Senate. The unresolved character of the relationship with Sproul undoubtedly complicated Barrows' presidency.

The University also was involved in agricultural problems at this time. Disillusioned by the collapse of wartime prosperity, farm interests were again agitating for changes in agricultural education. One of the most alarming proposals to come out of the resulting unrest was that the College of Agriculture be separated from the University of California and that the financial support received through the Morrill Land Grant Act be withdrawn at the same time. Legislative hearings were held on the complaints and proposals of the farmers. It was Comptroller Sproul who led the University out of this situation by suggesting appointment of a Special Commission of Agricultural Education to head off precipitous action and to give detailed study to the subject under legislative inquiry. His idea was accepted, and later he, along with Elwood Mead, Professor of Rural Institutions, was appointed to the commission by Governor William D. Stephens.[66]

A second agricultural problem involved Academic Senate membership and was related to the "faculty revolt." By asking that the senate be allowed to establish its own membership rules, the faculty committee conferring with the Regents had not been acting solely out of concern for theoretical principle. In 1919, farm advisers and other agriculturists in University employ, on campus for a conference, attended an Academic Senate meeting. Under broad interpretations of the Regents' policies, they were entitled to vote, and they did so, over the objections of the majority of the non-agriculture membership.[67] To prevent a repeat of such an occurrence, the Academic Senate's Committee on Rules recommended that only staff members engaged in "strictly academic work" [68] be allowed membership in the senate. The ruling barred teachers at Davis from the senate because their instruction was not then at the University level. It also barred membership to others employed by the College of Agriculture who did no formal teaching at all. To solve the problem, a department of agriculture, offering academic instruction, was formed within the college. In matters of internal concern, all members of the college had a voice and a vote. But only those who were also in the Department of Agriculture were entitled to membership in the senate.

In addition to all of these greater concerns, Barrows dealt, unpopularly, with many less important ones. In February, 1920, he prevented Raymond Robins, a former Red Cross official who had performed the office of intermediary between the American ambassador and Lenin's government, from speaking on campus because of his reputed Bolshevik actions.[69] The incident brought considerable public notice, which displeased Regent Rowell, who later said, "What Barrows forgot was that it was the President of the University and not Colonel David P. Barrows, late chief of the American Secret Service in Siberia, who was acting." [70] The Regents overruled Barrows on other matters: on moving the Medical School to Berkeley; on the location of the football stadium in Strawberry Canyon (he wanted it in the city of Berkeley); and in refusing to appoint his personal aide as an assistant to the president.

The accumulation of all these problems, big and small, may have created too much presidency to be handled in a short period of time. To cope with them, Barrows felt the need for greater initiative and authority than he had been allowed, by the Regents on the one hand and the faculty on the other. His misfortune had been to step into the presidency when the University was too fluid in its state of development to be managed authoritatively by anyone.

FACULTY DISILLUSIONMENT

The success of the "faculty revolt" was not complete. For one thing, the provision for a "Committee on Conference" that was supposed to give the faculty direct communication with the Regents turned out to be a one-sided arrangement; the faculty members talked, and the Regents listened. All efforts to get the Regents to discuss matters upon which Board decisions were imminent failed. The senate's representatives on the conference committee were turned down in their requests to get a second hearing for Professor Weber, who had been dismissed from the faculty during the war, and to acquire copies of the minutes of the Regents' meetings. Their request to play a role in the deliberations on a new president to succeed Barrows that would be more than "the privilege of merely suggesting names" [71] was also denied.

The Academic Senate's Committee on Conference was also concerned about the waning power of the presidency. In a letter to Regent James K. Moffitt, chairman of the combined committees on conference, the faculty's chairman, Gilbert N. Lewis, asserted that "contrary to an opinion that has sometimes been expressed the Faculty of the University of California desire and have desired an increase in the presidential authority." [72] He continued by pointing out that in June, 1920, the Regents had appeared to curtail the influence of the president by making him executive head of the University not in all departments but only in all academic departments. Insisting that the division between academic and nonacademic matters in the University was not as clear as originally supposed by the Regents, and expressing concern over the "extension of the Comptroller's Office far beyond the plan contemplated when the office was first established," he offered several suggestions.

First, he suggested that except for the investment and care of University funds, all problems of the University should be regarded as academic problems. Second, the president and his delegates should alone be authorized to represent the Regents and the University before the legislature in Sacramento. (That representation had been made by the comptroller since 1913.) Third, branches of the University should report to the Regents through the president instead of through a committee of the Board. Fourth, the duties of the comptroller of the University and secretary of the Board of Regents should be divided. And, finally, the office of the comptroller should be located in San Francisco, rather than Berkeley. At this point there seemed to be no personal animosity against Robert Gordon Sproul, the incumbent comptroller. But there was obvious concern that his office had become so powerful that the academic concerns of the University might easily be overshadowed by considerations of financial and political expediency.[73]

By this time, word was out that the Regents had decided to name William Wallace Campbell, director of the Lick Observatory, as Barrows' successor in the presidency. Then sixty years old, Campbell had spent half his life associated with the University of California, as student, astronomer, and for twenty-three years as director of the Lick Observatory. Although many Regents were not enthusiastic about Campbell's election to the presidency, he appealed to the majority of the Board for several reasons. He was respected by, if not popular with, the members of the faculty; he was available; and he had a good record as a scholar and an administrator at the Observatory. Moreover, his relatively advanced age made him an "interim" president who would serve until someone else could be groomed or found for the job permanently.

When he found out that Campbell was under consideration, Barrows encouraged him to take the position.[74] He and Gilbert Lewis warned Campbell, however, first to get in writing from the Regents a clarification of his role as president.

On December 27, 1922, Campbell wrote to the Regents, saying that he could not accept the presidency unless certain conditions were met: (1) that the word *academic* be removed from the Standing Orders adopted June 24, 1920, defining the powers of the president; (2) that standing orders giving the faculty access to the Regents be amended or repealed so that the president would again be, as Wheeler had been, the only channel of communication between the two bodies; (3) that the conference committee be abolished.[75]

Not only were these conditions met, but the Regents also revised the definition of the authority of the comptroller so that it could not be construed to confer upon him any of the duties of the president. In the same regard, the comptroller was required to report all business matters affecting academic departments of the University to the president, who would in turn report them to the Regents.[76]

By demanding that the presidency be strengthened after inroads had been made on it by the gains of the faculty revolt, Campbell made the position of the chief executive of the University tenable. But, by exercising his presidential powers with restraint and by relying heavily upon the advice of the faculty, Campbell also gave the "new constitution" of the University a chance to work.

During the seven years of Campbell's presidency, the University enjoyed the same kind of quiet growth it had experienced under Kellogg in the late 1890s. The University's Southern Branch, by then a four-year institution called the University of California at Los Angeles, or UCLA, was moved to a new campus. The people passed a state bond issued to construct buildings on that new campus and to replace temporary wooden structures on the Berkeley campus. Private philanthropy made Bowles Hall, the University's first residence hall, possible and provided funds to create the Giannini Foundation of Agricultural Economics. To make the campus more hospitable to students from abroad, John D. Rockefeller, Jr., contributed funds to build an International House at Berkeley.

Because Campbell spent much of his time at Mount Hamilton and because the burdens of the presidency had become too much for one man in any case, on May 12, 1925, the Regents created two vice-presidencies. One, with responsibilities for academic matters, was filled by former Dean of the Faculties Walter Morris Hart. The other, with responsibilities for business affairs of the University, was given to Robert Gordon Sproul.[77]

In 1930, mainly because of his advancing age, President Campbell was retired by the Regents and given a year's leave with full compensation.

The faculty revolt and the tandem administrations of Barrows and Campbell, each in its own way, prepared the University for expansion. At the end of Wheeler's administration, the University was already too big for one man to administer by benevolent autocracy. It also had too little internal discipline to prosper under the inconsistent administration of a junta. When the faculty came forward in 1919 and 1929 to demand a larger share of the burden of University government, their interest was in acquiring rights and privileges they deemed essential if they were to be effective academicians. But, after their success, they soon learned the validity of the advice given to Louderback by Arthur L. Wheeler of the department of Latin at Bryn Mawr, who wrote in November, 1919: ". . . Liberty means work for the liberated. If a faculty secures a share in the administration it must not expect to shirk its increased expenditure of time." [78] The "liberated" faculty at Berkeley took to its administrative chores conscientiously and in the process relieved the Regents and other administrative officers of tasks that would have been unbearably demanding as the University continued to grow.

During Barrows' administration the new organization was thoroughly tested—by friction between the president and the strengthened faculty, and by tension between the University and the special interests of outsiders. Flaws revealed during this brief period of tribulation were corrected before Campbell came to the presidency. During the tranquil, prosperous, and comfortable years of his administration, precedents were set for orderly conference between the president and the faculty, and between the president and the Regents. With the appointment of vice-presidents, the administrative capability of the University was still further extended. But the most important achievement of the whole period between 1919 and 1925 was to put the academic activity of the University on a self-governing basis. As soon as that was achieved in a way acceptable to both the Regents and the administration, it was possible to consider selecting a new kind of University president.

Chapter 17

ROBERT GORDON SPROUL'S ONE UNIVERSITY

IN 1919, Guy C. Earl was a leader among those Regents who favored electing University Comptroller Ralph Merritt as Benjamin Ide Wheeler's successor to the presidency. He was thwarted by Regents who feared that a president without an academic background would not succeed in winning the full support of the faculty. Ten years later, when Regents Earl and Dickson advanced the candidacy of another comptroller, Robert Gordon Sproul, as a successor to Campbell, new conditions prevailed. The authority of the Academic Senate was better defined than in 1919, and the faculty therefore had less to fear from a president drawn from administrative ranks. Barrows and Campbell had not proved that University presidents recruited from the faculty were infallible. And, finally, Robert Gordon Sproul was a man with uncommon ability and personality, respected by many members of the faculty and by virtually all of the Regents.

In June, 1929, the Regents decided to make Sproul, the thirty-eight-year-old comptroller, the University's eleventh president and he assumed the presidency in July, 1930, after Campbell retired.

When Sproul's election was announced, some newspapers emphasized that he was a native son of California and the first alumnus of the University to become its president. Others stressed the Horatio Alger quality of his rise to eminence. He is the son of an accountant for the Southern Pacific railroad and made his own way through childhood and youth as a newspaper boy, messenger, railroad timekeeper, and salesman. As a student, he enrolled in engineering, earned a letter in track, and became president of the University YMCA. He was also an officer in the cadet corps and a drum major in the band. After graduating in 1913, he worked for the city of Oakland for a year and then returned to the University as cashier. Sproul became Ralph Merritt's assistant during World War I and succeeded him as comptroller, secretary of the Regents, and land agent when Merritt left the University in 1920.

Two of Sproul's most remarkable personal characteristics, a reverberating voice and a phenomenal memory, helped him win the awe of legislators when he went to Sacramento during the presidencies of Barrows and Campbell to defend the University's requests for financial support. His quick recall of facts and statistics made him virtually unchallengeable in debate. His knowledge, love, and mastery of the sounds of spoken English made him one of the nation's finest orators. These talents alone would have made him awesome, perhaps even unapproachable, had he not also been blessed with a cordial nature and easy humor that revealed his appreciation of the hopes and anxieties of common men.

Although he spoke frequently and articulately on the functions of a university and the purposes of an education, Sproul's ideas on these subjects were not shaped by esoteric educationalism. Instead, they were the products of his personal experience, the examples of his predecessors (particularly Wheeler), the political stance of progressive Republicanism, the morality of the Presbyterian church, and the ethics of his fellow Rotarians. Generalized for application to the nonpartisan, nondenominational University, his ideas meshed so completely with the central themes of the American creed that people in all walks of life accepted them readily. Newspaper editors praised him for his horse sense and cited him as a proof that opportunities for advancement to high places on the strength of character and persistence still existed. One editor was so impressed by the new president in 1930 that he suggested Governor Rolph ask Sproul to reform the whole educational system of California. Without enumerating the evils that needed correction, he further suggested that the governor appoint no member of the Board of Regents or the State Board of Education who did not agree to follow Sproul's advice until the reform was complete.[1]

Sproul had no desire for such responsibility and claimed no expertise in the field of education. On the contrary, he was aware that he had no comprehensive knowledge of the development of higher education in the country and, in his letter accepting the presidency, requested a six-month leave of absence to give concentrated study to that subject. He then picked out twenty institutions that seemed to offer lessons relevant to his impending responsibilities and read the inaugural addresses of their presidents.[2] He also toured many colleges and universities to interview administrators in person.

In the business affairs of the University, of course, Sproul had knowledge and authority equaled by no one. During Barrows' administration, he took the initiative in any matter he found unattended in the management of the University's business affairs and carried responsibilities thus assumed into Campbell's administration. He was also the first president to have represented the University in Sacramento before taking office. From this experience came his tendency to gauge the legislature's receptivity as well as the University's needs in making requests for appropriations. It was also evident in his approach to University expansion. New facilities were developed not only in accordance with need, but also within the limits of what the president and his representatives in Sacramento believed the state could reasonably afford.

THE STRINGENCIES OF THE DEPRESSION

California could afford very little in the 1930s and state appropriations for the operation of the University dropped from $9,972,000 in 1929–1930 to $8,632,000 by 1932–1933.[3] Anticipating further cutbacks in the 1933–1934 University appropriation, President Sproul memorialized all department chairmen on August 3, 1932, to exercise "most exigent economy during the year," and in December proposed the creation of a faculty Committee on Educational Policy to help keep departmental budgets at a level which could be met by the state in its current financial position.[4]

Throughout the spring of 1933 Sproul campaigned against further reduction of the University budget. In his Charter Day banquet address to alumni at the Hotel Oakland on March 23, he claimed that the ratio of the University's appropriations to state expenditures in the decade just past had been decreased by 15 per cent, while that of other agencies had increased from 44 to 912 per cent. He also pointed out that University faculty salaries were far lower than the average of those in the seven leading Universities of the United States—Chicago, Cornell, Illinois, Michigan, Princeton, Stanford, and Columbia.[5]

On April 5, he went on the radio to state the University's case against cutbacks. For 1931–1933, he said, the state's appropriation to the University was $17,035,891, and that, despite an 8 per cent enrollment increase, the University had already acceded to a request from the governor to make do with $3,000,000 less for 1933–1935 because of the financial condition of the state. Moreover, the University had agreed to cut nonacademic salaries so that they would be in line with those of employees of other state government departments. Despite these University concessions, Sproul said, the Assembly Ways and Means Committee sought further reduction by over $2,000,000. If such cuts were made, Sproul warned, there would have to be drastic curtailment of programs in the College of Agriculture, practically all indigent patients would have to be turned away from clinical treatment at the School of Medicine, and such programs as the Institute of Child Welfare and the Bureau of Public Administration would also suffer. Worst of all, students would be penalized. "Youth comes but once in a lifetime," Sproul said, "and must be given its opportunity for higher education today or not at all." [6]

Following Sproul's broadcast, students at Berkeley and UCLA wrote home to their parents, asking them to tell their legislators to refuse to pass further budget cuts.[7] The California Alumni Association and the Berkeley Chamber of Commerce voted resolutions condemning further budget reductions.[8] Farmers sent telegrams to legislators and farm organizations, protesting the threatened curtailment of agricultural services rendered by the University.[9] One assemblyman reportedly received two hundred telegrams in two days on the subject.[10]

The showdown came on April 29, 1933, after two days and nights of consideration of the bill, when appropriations greater than those recommended by both the Assembly Ways and Means Committee and the Senate Finance Committee were passed on the floor.[11] With this appropriation and other funds, the Regents put together a final budget of $9,421,465 for 1933–1934 [12]—about a third less than the one for the previous year. To meet the limitations of this budget, the Regents considered raising student fees but soon abandoned that idea, curtailing University activities and reducing academic salaries instead.[13]

President Sproul hoped to obtain appropriations for 1935–1937 that were sufficiently large to restore the salary cuts that had been made as a result of the 1933 economies. But, although the University's enrollment was increasing, the state's financial circumstances were still desperate, and Frank Merriam, who had succeeded Governor Rolph in 1934, insisted that the appropriations for 1935–1937 not exceed those of the previous biennium. Taking the University's case directly to the legislature, President

Sproul received a special appropriation of $1,455,000 in addition to the general allotment, but Governor Merriam chopped off $455,000 of that amount before he signed the measure.

By 1939, the imposition of rigid economies upon the University was reaching a critical point. The 1937–1939 appropriation was about $2,000,000 greater than the biennium before, but student enrollments had also increased, and the University had not yet regained the loss suffered in 1933–1935. The ratio of faculty members to students was steadily falling, and the replacement of key men of the faculty who resigned, retired, or died was often postponed. In one small department, all five members resigned to accept better-paying offers elsewhere.[14] The miracle was that despite the fact that faculty salaries were held below the 1931–1932 level, "a sound nucleus of outstanding men had been maintained in virtually every field." [15]

After the United States entered World War II, the state legislature continued to vote somewhat modest appropriations for the University in view of declining enrollments and the curtailment of many programs. The University's total operating income increased sharply, however, as a result of research funds made available by the federal government.

MOUNTING COMPETITION

A general economic depression was only one cause of the University's financial difficulties during the early years of Sproul's presidency. The Southern Branch experiment was watched carefully, not only by the Regents, the faculty at Berkeley, and the legislature, but also by other California institutions of higher learning. To meet enrollment growth naturally attending a 66 per cent population increase in the state between 1920 and 1930, the state's thirty-four junior colleges and seven teachers' colleges demanded increasing portions of available tax dollars. The legislature could not fully accede to such demands as long as the intentions of the University were not clear. When President Sproul was rounding up student, alumni, and public support for the University appropriation bills in 1935, the Sacramento *Bee* asserted that "an increasing number of citizens strongly are convinced the time has arrived to put a check on the omnivorous appetite of the Berkeley institution for more and more millions as well as to curb its apparent determination to throttle any educational progress in the state outside the reach of its own domineering influence." [16]

Claims that the University opposed the development of other public institutions of higher learning were overdrawn, but had some foundation. President Barrows had opposed the 1921 legislation that gave state financial support to local junior college districts. Eight years later, the University also opposed a bill introduced by State Senator J. M. Inman which proposed to expand Sacramento Junior College into a four-year college and to appropriate $300,000 for its support.[17] Fresno, Redding, and San Diego were reported to be interested in similar projects. On October 6, 1930, President Sproul commented upon the proposal at a meeting of the Academic Senate. He said that California did not need more four-year colleges admitting anyone, but rather more junior colleges for those who wanted more education than high schools could provide but "whose talents do not lie along the line of a university career." [18]

On Charter Day, 1931, Sproul called for organized alumni effort to stop the "regional college" movement represented by the Fresno and Sacramento proposals. "Let us see that it [the University] meets the cultural demands of all," he said, "or at any rate of all the important groups in the commonwealth. But let us not exchange it for a collection of little replicas, responding to purely local needs." [19] Regional college proponents replied that Sproul was "selfish and short-sighted" for "attempting to shut out all other institutions from benefits of state appropriations except the University of California and its little brother in Los Angeles. . . ." [20]

At the height of the controversy, President Sproul sent Monroe E. Deutsch, then vice-president and provost of the University, to New York to ask Henry Suzzallo, president of the Carnegie Foundation for the Advancement of Teaching, to conduct a study of the California educational system. On condition that proper financial arrangements could be made, Suzzallo agreed to a study jointly supported by the Carnegie Corporation of New York and the State of California. Advised of this development, friends of the University in the legislature introduced a bill authorizing Governor Rolph to appoint "an educational research foundation of nation-wide scope" [21] to make the study proposed. The Carnegie Foundation for the Advancement of Teaching was, of course, selected to do the survey and began its work in mid-October, 1931.

Throughout the ensuing months, while the consultants investigated and deliberated, the antagonists in the fight over the regional colleges slugged it out verbally on speaking platforms, in the newspapers, and over the radio. One extremely important alliance made during this period was that between the University and the junior colleges. Throughout the dispute, Sproul spoke warmly of these institutions and was gratified when the California Association of Junior Colleges voted unanimously to oppose upward extension of any of their number.[22] Two years later, Sproul predicted that "eventually all college training will stop at the junior college level and universities will begin with the present junior year." [23]

But the value of junior colleges was not an issue in the regional college fight. Neither were the state's teachers' colleges, although Sproul officially opposed any suggestions that they might extend their instruction beyond that for training elementary-school teachers. The central issue was whether four-year colleges of unrestricted function could be located about the state almost at the will of local legislators. While Sproul, on behalf of the University, insisted they should not, others maintained that the University was two crowded, too choosy in the selection of its students, and too remote from some parts of the state to serve all students desiring higher education.

The Carnegie Foundation for the Advancement of Teaching completed its report, usually called the Suzzallo Report, in June, 1932. One of its most astonishing recommendations was that the University's Board of Regents assume jurisdiction over all institutions of higher education in California above the junior college level.[24] Sproul told the Regents that he thought they had enough to do without this extra responsibility but the "logic of this proposal is so great that I am convinced it will not be possible permanently to resist it." [25] The report recommended that the legislature not authorize any further expansion of senior colleges apart from Berkeley and Los Angeles until those campuses have "reached the saturation point" and the finances of the state are "sufficiently prosperous," [26] and further that the offerings of the teachers' colleges be studied with a view toward eliminating from the curriculum courses that were inappropriate to their function,[27] that those institutions not admit any students beyond the junior college level for training as secondary-school teachers,[28] and that the Berkeley campus drop its elementary teacher-training courses.[29]

In order that California might enjoy a more orderly development of its higher education, the Suzzallo Report recommended establishment of a State Council for Educational Planning and Coordination.[30] The legislature created such an agency in 1933, and its members included President Sproul, the state superintendent of public instruction, a Regent, a member of the State Board of Education, and five citizens-at-large.[31] The council thus created was without genuine authority, however, and failed to stop the flood of proposals to establish new four-year colleges or alter the functions of existing institutions of higher education.

With the backing of State Superintendent of Instruction Vierling Kersey, some of the presidents of California's teachers' colleges proposed to convert their institutions into liberal arts colleges simply by eliminating their requirement that twelve units of work in education courses were essential to the curriculum leading to an A.B. degree.[32] Several communities continued to work for the conversion of their junior colleges into four-year institutions. President Sproul did not like any of these new proposals, and warned that if four-year colleges were started wherever there is a center of population, California's educational system "will face the certainty of mediocrity and the possibility of bankruptcy." [33] As will be seen subsequently, however, the problem of competition and duplicated effort in higher education continued to plague the University throughout Sproul's administration.

COOPERATION WITH THE HIGH SCHOOLS

While the University sought to improve its relationship with other California institutions of higher learning, it also had to cope with a tenuous relationship with the high schools. The University's system of accreditation that had been inaugurated in the 1890s to encourage the development of good-quality high schools in the state had evolved by 1919 into a system where graduates of accredited high schools were admitted to the University entirely upon the basis of their principals' recommendation. The push in this direction came from the principals themselves, who came to resent the University's unilateral role in passing judgment upon the ability of their schools to graduate students capable of University work. By 1927, however, the high school principals had changed their mind. For one thing, the State Board of Education's definition of "minimum core" subjects for high school graduation omitted some that were essential as preparation for University studies. For another, the principals' privilege of recommending their graduates for University admissions was a prize of doubtful value. Along with that power came pressures from University alumni, members of local boards of education, parents, and even college officials to recommend marginal students. At the same time, every high school's standing, as determined by the scholastic success of its graduates during their first semester at the University, was published annually. Giving in to local pressures could seriously jeopardize the high school's reputation in the community. Some principals became so fearful of sullying their record that they recommended only their most scholastically elite graduates for University admission. In the process, good or average students at excellent high schools were sometimes denied access to a University education. To remedy the situation, the principals initiated action returning responsibility for determining who should enter the University to the University faculty. Negotiations to this end were completed in 1931 after Sproul assumed office.

To guide the University's admissions officer, an academic standard involving a specified pattern of University preparatory subjects was adopted. Fifteen units were required for admission. These were distributed as follows: (a) history, one unit; (b) English, three units; (c) mathematics (elementary algebra and plane geometry), two units; (d) science (chemistry, physics, biology, botany, or zoology), one unit; (e) foreign language, two units; (f) advanced mathematics, or chemistry or physics, or foreign language, one or two units; (g) electives from history, English, mathematics, natural science, foreign language, drawing, one or two units; (h) unrestricted electives, three units. To be eligible for admission, high school graduates had to receive an A or B in at least ten of the twelve units specified in categories (a) to (g) inclusive, and have no grade lower than a C in any of the fifteen units.[34]

The policy was modified in 1933 to eliminate consideration of junior high school grades in determining admissions eligibility although junior high school work continued to be accepted in satisfaction of course requirements. Grade requirements were changed from a minimum of eight Bs out of ten units to a B average in the required subjects (a) to (f) taken in the last three years of high school. These requirements were supplemented in 1936 by the adoption of four alternative admission plans. All of the alternatives required substantial preparation in academic subjects and high grades. But they permitted slight, specific deviations in certain details of the normal admissions pattern.

President Sproul helped ease the relationships between the University and California's high schools still more in May, 1936, when he said:

> Whatever criticism may be leveled for its having played martinet, over arbitrary regulations that have since been quietly abandoned, the University is willing to accept because the result has justified the means. . . .
>
> There is no longer any need for laying down the law about standards of training. With few exceptions, the secondary schools are watching this aspect of their work more carefully and guarding it more successfully than any outside authority could hope to do. Consequently, the University can lay aside its gavel, take off its powdered wig, and step down from the bench to become just one of the members of civilization's family, discussing with the others, plans for the family's future.[35]

The following fall, President Sproul announced establishment of an Office of Relations with Schools, with representatives in Los Angeles and Berkeley. The responsibility of the office was to cooperate with the secondary schools and "to aid them in whatever ways may be found desirable." [36]

At the same time, significant changes were made in admissions and accrediting procedures. Once placed on the accredited lists, secondary schools would remain there without applying for reaccrediting. A new system of advising high schools of their standing in code was adopted so that public embarrassment for schools low on the list could be avoided.

The new practices, along with sensitive and considerate administration of the University's admissions requirements, helped immensely to improve the relationship of the University with California's high schools.

THE TWO-LEGGED UNIVERSITY

When Sproul became president of the University, UCLA had just moved to its new site at Westwood. With 6391 students, it was a complete undergraduate campus serving the increasingly populous and wealthy southland. In contrast to both Barrows and Campbell, who had resisted the rapid development of UCLA because they feared that it would lead to a division of the University, Sproul accepted it as a natural and unavoidable solution to the problem of rendering adequate University services to a long state with population centers 500 miles apart. He had been a member of President Wheeler's commission to study the feasibility of the southern branch operations and reminded UCLA's students of that fact when he spoke to them for the first time as president in 1930, saying, "I am no 'carpet-bagger' from the north. I have been a part of this institution [UCLA] since the time it was a dream." [37]

But UCLA was still unfinished University business in many ways. It offered no graduate instruction, and its faculty government was subject to many policies decided upon by the Academic Senate in Berkeley.

In July, 1930, President Sproul appointed a nine-man committee to investigate the feasibility of offering graduate work at UCLA. This committee studied the question during the summer and then recommended that graduate degrees should be offered in biology, English, geography, history, mathematics, physics, psychology, and political science. Soon, thereafter, economics, education, and philosophy were added to the list. [38]

In preliminary budgets prepared for 1931, President Sproul included a request for $120,000 for UCLA graduate work but the governor cut it out. It was included again in an early version of the budget for 1933–1935, but the Regents withdrew the item when they learned that Governor Rolph insisted upon drastic economies in state operations. [39] Despite the enormity of the general cut (at least 17½ per cent) in the University's appropriations expected in 1933, a group called the Citizen's University Council of Organizations, enjoying the support of UCLA alumni and individual faculty members, sent a lobbyist to Sacramento to seek $120,000 for a UCLA graduate school.[40] The legislature sympathized with their cause even though the Regents actively opposed the expenditure and recommended $75,000 for introduction of graduate work at UCLA.[41]

President Sproul and the Regents criticized this action on two counts. First, they believed it was unreasonable for the state to demand that the University cut its budget for ongoing projects and then appropriate funds for new work the Regents had already decided could be postponed. Second, they considered the legislature's action an unconstitutional interference in the internal management of the University. Southern California pressure was too hard to resist, however, and after once refusing to accept the $75,000 appropriation or to introduce graduate work at UCLA, the Regents yielded on August 8, 1933, authorizing the introduction of graduate work leading to the master's degree in twelve fields. In fear that acceptance of the $75,000 appropriation would set a bad precedent for future Regental-legislative relations, use of the money was left to Sproul's discretion. It eventually reverted to the state treasury in disuse.[42]

Once graduate work began at UCLA, President Sproul knew that it would be only a matter of time before the Regents were asked to extend it to the Ph.D. level. In anticipation of those requests, he sounded out faculty opinion at Berkeley in the fall of 1935. The response, surprisingly, favored the introduction of doctoral programs at UCLA for reasons that varied from an admission that such programs need not detract from the financial support given to research at Berkeley, and were needed to serve students living in the populous Los Angeles area, to more important considerations that Ph.D. programs would have a beneficent effect upon the morale and caliber of the UCLA faculty and that the pressure for such programs could not, in any case, be withstood very long. On the basis of this advice and subsequent reports of a special committee of Berkeley faculty members appointed to investigate the matter in detail, the Regents established Ph.D. programs at UCLA in 1936.[43] In 1938, Kenneth P. Bailey was the first UCLA recipient of the degree, earning it in the department of history.[44]

To give UCLA's faculty a more influential voice in the determination of the University's academic policies, the Academic Senate was reorganized in 1933 to provide for separate sections in the northern and southern parts of the state. The Northern Section consisted of faculty members at Berkeley, the medical complex in San Francisco, Davis, and the Lick Observatory. The Southern Section consisted of faculty members at UCLA, the Citrus

Experiment Station at Riverside, and the Scripps Institution of Oceanography at La Jolla. To be effective, all legislation of the Academic Senate binding on members of the faculty on all campuses required the concurrence of both sections. Previously, UCLA's faculty had only advisory powers through an Academic Council of the University of California at Los Angeles, which had status only as a standing committee of the Senate.[45]

ONE UNIVERSITY

Because UCLA dominated the University's activities in southern California and Berkeley dominated them in the north, a writer discussing President Sproul's appointment in 1930 called his article "Two-Legged University." [46] UCLA's Provost Moore used the same phrase in welcoming Sproul to a student assembly in September of 1931.[47] Sproul, however, preferred to emphasize the unity of the entire University, rather than the development of its two major divisions.

In an address to students at UCLA on September 27, 1932, Sproul said, "We are building one great university in California. Let no small mind direct you along the paths of suspicion, distrust or jealousy." [48] The following January, the editor of UCLA's *Daily Bruin* picked up the phrase "One Great University" as a title for an editorial protesting introduction of a bill in Sacramento that would divide the University into two parts. The bill in question was introduced by Assemblyman Charles W. Dempster of Los Angeles. His object was to create a second university in southern California composed of UCLA, the Scripps Institution at La Jolla, the Citrus Experiment Station at Riverside, the Kellogg Institute of Animal Husbandry at Pomona, and the teachers' colleges at Santa Barbara and San Diego.[49] Opposition came not only from the University but also from some of the other institutions the new university was supposed to annex, and failure of the bill to win passage was inevitable. But the proposal was symptomatic of a turn of mind encountered in California every once in a while, and President Sproul had to stay on guard to prevent unrestrained sectionalism from pulling the University apart.

The danger of ill-feeling between the two campuses increased in 1933 when UCLA and Berkeley began to compete against each other in intercollegiate athletics, although neither Sproul nor Provost Moore conceded that the rivalry need be anything more than what might be sporting. Speaking to a group of UCLA boosters in 1934, Moore tried to dispel new rumors that efforts would be made to split the two campuses. He said, "The paternal attitude [at Berkeley] has given way with grace and ease to one of deep brotherhood. Equality between the two branches has been effected in every line of University activity, not the least of which is athletics." [50]

In February, 1936, Moore resigned the provostship, and President Sproul announced that he would move his family to UCLA in September to take personal charge of the campus. There were three reasons for his decision: Provost Moore's retirement came suddenly and the President had no one in mind for his replacement; he wanted to take advantage of the opportunity to acquire firsthand knowledge of UCLA and its relationships with the southern part of the state; and his presence on the campus would dramatize the unity of the University. During his absence, Vice-President and Provost Monroe E. Deutsch was in charge at Berkeley.

One of Sproul's jobs in Los Angeles was to bolster morale at UCLA, where the fact that the campus at Berkeley was referred to as "California," according to long-standing tradition, was considered a slight to the southern campus,[51] and where hard work and rapid growth that would have been proclaimed a miracle in an independent institution seemed to go unnoticed. Sproul provided balm for these feelings of inferiority in October, 1936, when he said, "Because of the greater population and wealth in southern California I expect some day to see the UCLA campus outstrip the Berkeley campus." [52] With 7252 undergraduates, 598 graduate students, and 259 faculty members on a new campus, UCLA was well on its way to such distinction. That same year, in fact, UCLA beat Berkeley in football for the first time.

Divisive sounds were suddenly heard in the northern section of the University. On September 29, the president of the Berkeley alumni in Fresno, Al E. Marsella, wrote to Robert Sibley, executive manager of the California Alumni Association, protesting the continuance of UCLA as a part of the University. "When it was a lower division branch of the University there was no conflict," he said,

> . . . but now that it has become a big college of its own, it should stand on its own feet.
> Our great state university, at Berkeley, is losing its entity. The Los Angeles branch has stolen our name, colors, traditions and reputation, and now even has taken our president.[53]

The *Daily Bruin*'s answer to such talk was embodied in a reprint of Sproul's remarks to the UCLA student body earlier in the year, when he urged:

May I count upon you to raise your eyes beyond the narrow boundaries of provincialism and support me in a program built not alone for Los Angeles but for California?

If not, we shall all go down together, for the dark clouds of unregulated educational expansion, now gathering on the horizon, presage a storm that no single part of the University can hope alone to ride to permanent safety.[54]

Marsella's call for a division of the University in 1936 was more impertinent than it was dangerous, but it added an illustration to others that might have been cited to demonstrate the difficulties of building support for the "One University" idea.

A subtle shift in the One University concept occurred at about this time. Sproul and other administrators began to speak not of just UCLA and Berkeley, but of "two great major campuses, and five others to be conducted as a single institution." The "five others"—Mount Hamilton, Scripps Institution of Oceanography, San Francisco, the Citrus Experiment Station at Riverside, and Davis—had been around before UCLA was established, but they were generally regarded as auxiliary facilities of the Berkeley campus and not as separate entities. By 1939, this new concept of the University was sufficiently strong to lead the Associated Students at Davis to suggest that Sproul reside on that campus for one or two weeks out of the year. The editor of the *Davis Enterprise* endorsed the idea, contributing his own facetious suggestion that all of the problems of the campus be saved up so that the President could settle them during his annual term of residency.[55]

The "All California" spirit was also fostered by the California Club, an expansion of the organization developed by students in 1934 to "develop and maintain the highest possible standard of sportsmanship, friendship, and cooperation of students" at UCLA and Berkeley. In 1940 the club had chapters at Davis and San Francisco and held its first annual convention. Eight years later, all students on all campuses of the University began to have an opportunity to participate in the fellowship of the entire University family when the first "All-University Weekend" was held at Berkeley. On that occasion Sproul said, "This reunion, if enjoyed in the right spirit, can give strength and meaning to the ideal of One University, for it is by personal meetings and the sharing of common experiences that understanding is achieved and friendships are formed."[56]

But building a One University spirit was only part of President Sproul's problem. A much more fundamental part was keeping the University functioning administratively as an efficient and productive institution.

ADMINISTERING FAR-FLUNG CAMPUSES

The administration of the multiunit institution Sproul was called to lead in 1930 was, to a considerable extent, improvised. For over fifty years new units had been created as opportunity, demand, or necessity arose, and had been fitted into the structure wherever it seemed most appropriate at the time. The professional colleges in San Francisco and the California School of Fine Arts (formerly the Mark Hopkins Institute of Art) operated under the direction of deans who reported to the president. The Lick Observatory at Mount Hamilton, the Scripps Institution of Oceanography at La Jolla, and UCLA were under the authority of directors who reported to the president. The Davis campus and the Citrus Experiment Station at Riverside were under the authority of directors who reported to the dean of the College of Agriculture.

Business management on all units of the University was exercised by the comptroller, who reported jointly to the Regents and the president. At some of the larger units, such as San Francisco, Davis, and UCLA, assistant comptrollers handled these matters in cooperation—but not subordinately—with the directors and deans. The assistant comptroller at UCLA handled business matters for all University establishments in southern California for many years.

When Sproul became president, he vacated four offices—those of vice-president, comptroller, secretary of the Regents, and land agent. The authority represented by those titles was too general for one man and Sproul decided to divide it up in 1930.[57] Those functions relating to the internal business affairs of the University—accounting, purchasing, maintenance of facilities, and personnel—were assigned to Luther Nichols, who had been assistant comptroller under Sproul. Nichols also retained the title of comptroller and reported to both the President and the Regents. The external affairs of the University, those having to do with business transactions of the Regents, were assigned to another former assistant comptroller, Robert Underhill. Underhill, who had served the University in southern California operations from 1922 to 1930, became secretary of the Regents and land agent of the University. Three years later, he also became treasurer of the University. In all of those capacities, Underhill reported directly to the Regents.[58]

The vice-presidency that Sproul had occupied was not immediately filled, but in July, 1930, the vice-presidency formerly held by dean of the University Walter Morris Hart, regarded generally as Sproul's closest competition to succeed Campbell as president,[59] was given to Monroe E. Deutsch. A graduate of the University, Deutsch joined the faculty at Berkeley in 1906, became professor of Latin in 1922, dean of the College of Letters and Sciences in 1927, and vice-president and dean of the University in 1930. In this capacity, Deutsch was the principal academic administrator of the University, second in command to Sproul in many matters, with particular responsibility for the Berkeley campus. In 1931, Ernest C. Moore's position at UCLA was recognized as being parallel to that of Deutsch, and he also received the title of vice-president. At the same time, both Moore and Deutsch were named provosts with a subtle distinction between them found in the fact that Deutsch was officially "Provost of the University," while Moore was "Provost of the University of California at Los Angeles." [60]

In practice, the power enjoyed by Deutsch and Moore on their respective campuses was limited. Sproul retained authority in all budget matters and in the appointment of tenure faculty members, department chairmen, and deans. Neither could easily contravene the directives of the comptroller on business matters affecting their campuses.

President Sproul was aware of the inadequacies of the University's administrative organization. In the first six years of his presidency, University enrollment grew from 19,773 to 25,145; [61] the book value of University land, buildings, and improvements increased from $32,000,000 to almost $38,000,000,[62] and endowment grew from almost $16,700,000 to nearly $24,000,000.[63] By 1936, 1331 faculty members were employed by the University,[64] and annual expenditures exceeded $11,900,000.[65] In addition to these conditions, Sproul had to consider persistent suggestions that the University absorb some or all of California's state colleges (as the teachers' colleges were known after 1935).[66] Fitting such institutions into the University comfortably would require that the limits of central and local administrative authority be well defined in advance. One reason Sproul did not immediately nominate a successor for Ernest C. Moore when he retired from the UCLA provostship in 1936 was his feeling that the authority of the position in the context of possible future developments should be fully considered first. Early in 1937, after spending a few months at UCLA himself, Sproul began to draft a statement of policy on University organization. The University had three choices, he said:

I. A single University of California with a centralized administration, such as we have this year for the first time, with one president and such vice-presidents as are necessary. Such a system requires that the president spend a considerable part of his time in Los Angeles so that he may be fully conversant with the problems of that large, important, and growing division of the University and recognized as its leader by students, faculty, alumni and the general public. . . .

II. A single University of California with a decentralized administration such as we have had in the past (actually, though not on paper) with one president and such vice-presidents as are needed. Under this system the president maintained his permanent headquarters on one campus and occasionally visited the others. . . .

For comparatively small and slow-growing divisions of the University this is a practical arrangement. For Berkeley and Los Angeles it will mean that the local vice-president will be generally regarded as the real leader of the institution under his immediate direction and the president simply as a coordinating officer. . . . The logical end product of the system will be a president for each part of the institution and a chancellor connected with no part but maintaining general oversight over all parts. . . .

III. Separation of the University of California into two independent universities, one comprising the departments, colleges, schools, etc. in Berkeley, Davis, San Francisco, Fresno and Mt. Hamilton, the other the similar activities in Los Angeles, Riverside, Pomona and San Diego.[67]

Sproul probably had no fear that the Regents would entertain the third choice. Opposition to dividing the University was tightly fixed to the foundations of long-standing policy. He criticized decentralization as cumbersome and expensive and said that under it "the president or chancellor would have little or no authority and not enough coordinating functions to keep him reasonably busy. Moreover, he would be so divorced from the actual work of the University that he would inevitably become a politician rather than an educator." [68]

The Regents approved Sproul's first "choice" as official policy in February, 1937.[69] On March 9, Earle R. Hedrick, chairman of the mathematics department of UCLA, was named vice-president and provost for the Los Angeles campus.[70] On the surface, the new centralized pattern of organization seemed to work well, but after Hedrick's retirement in 1942, the possibility of further administrative policy revision arose, and the faculty at both Berkeley and Los Angeles began to express grievances.

Much of the faculty's restiveness came from conditions imposed by World

War II. They were teaching on an accelerated schedule of three terms a year without the usual three-month summer break, and had little time for research and the campus politics that was a concomitant of faculty self-government. Whenever they dropped the initiative in their governmental role, various administrative departments, notably that of the comptroller, picked it up to keep the University moving—sometimes stepping on academic toes in the process.[71]

Aware of the faculty unrest, and sensing a continued weakness in the University's administrative machinery, Sproul again delayed filling the provostship at UCLA and placed the campus under the direction of a three-man Interim Administrative Committee consisting of professors Gordon S. Watkins, Bennet M. Allen, and J. Harold Williams.[72]

Sproul's failure to appoint a provost at UCLA immediately after Hedrick's retirement was regarded by many faculty members as a symptom of his unwillingness to share the power and authority of the presidency with anyone. They feared that he might be postponing as long as possible the time when he had to come to terms with the fact that the University had become too big for day-to-day management by one man. In the ensuing months, therefore, they attempted to persuade him to appoint strong administrators at Berkeley and UCLA and delegate as much responsibility to those officers as he could. Sproul's own concept of his problem was that it was the faculty, and not the administration, that had become too big for him to deal with effectively. The solution he looked for was one that would preserve the powers of the faculty while reducing the number of faculty members the president of the University would have to deal with directly. To this end, he proposed in the fall of 1942 that the Academic Senate's Committee on Educational Policy be replaced by what he called an Executive Committee. It would have seventeen members, including the chairman of the senate (i.e., the president of the University); the vice-chairmen of the Northern and Southern Sections; five members of each section selected by their respective committees on committees; and four members of the senate who were administrators (e.g., provosts and deans) chosen by the president. The new committee would screen all legislation proposed for senate action, determine which measures needed action of only one section and which needed action of both, and develop procedures for breaking deadlocks when the two sections failed to agree.[73]

This suggestion received no endorsement from Sproul's advisers on the faculty and was dropped. But it gave evidence that the President was entertaining ideas for improving his relationships with the faculty and for making the administration of the University more efficient. With this in mind, Dean

Joel Hildebrand made a speech to the Academic Senate on April 5, 1943, in which he outlined some of the problems:

> The fact is that the President divides his attention between seven campuses and numerous public affairs. He has but limited time, therefore, to devote to any one of the scores of departments directly responsible to him. His contacts with members of the faculty are rare. Even a department chairman may have to wait days for an interview and weeks for a decision. The administration seems to be trailing its business rather than steering it. There is little leisure for long-range planning. There is little delegation of authority, even when the President is absent. The government is then carried on by mail. There is no administrative officer whose business it is to sit down and discuss with a department chairman the work, welfare, and future of his department.[74]

These were strong words from a man who liked Sproul immensely and was one of the President's most trusted advisers. Sproul later denied some of Hildebrand's charges but gave his full cooperation to a Committee on the Organization of the University that was created at the same meeting "to consider the present organization of the University, particularly as it affects the units under the jurisdiction of the Northern Section of the Academic Senate. . . ." [75] A similar committee was organized by the Southern Section.

After the committees were appointed, Sproul shared another proposal with them. It involved organizing the University along divisional lines, with semiautonomous administrative units for such disciplines as the agricultural sciences, humanities, natural sciences, medical sciences, and social sciences. The administrators of these units would have direct authority over the departments related to their division on all campuses and would be delegated some of the powers traditionally exercised by the president, but none of those exercised by the Academic Senate.[76] In practice, this would have been a highly centralized system and would have taken the administration deeply into academic affairs.

Sproul's idea was apparently ignored by the Committees on Organization. Instead they favored a decentralized scheme that gave considerable authority to the principal officers of the major University campuses. President Sproul took an important step in that direction in October, 1943, when he recommended to the Regents that the chief local administrator at UCLA be a provost, appointed by the Regents on recommendation of the president, and that he have "full authority under the president, to administer the departments of the Los Angeles and La Jolla campuses, with the exception of Agriculture, for which special organizational arrangements are necessary on all campuses because of its relation with the Federal Government." [77] The

President told the Regents that the intent of his recommendation was to centralize policy-making in the office of the president, while decentralizing execution of policy as it affected the Los Angeles and La Jolla campuses.[78]

Beyond that action Sproul was not anxious to go. When he received a draft report of the Southern Section's Committee of Organization, he commented on it at considerable length, with the effect of neutralizing most suggestions made for increasing the delegation of power to the UCLA provost.[79] After Sproul's suggestions were incorporated in the committee's proposals, the duties of the provost remained largely those delegated since 1930, namely "to advise and assist the President in educational policies, faculty relations, coordination of the work of departments, colleges and schools, problems of personnel in the teaching staff, preparation of educational budgets, and such other matters as may be delegated to them by the President." [80]

Paradoxically, one of Sproul's difficulties in filling the provostship at UCLA in 1943 and 1944 was that he found it hard to invite a man of stature to fill what he considered a number-two position. It was with considerable difficulty, therefore, that a group of UCLA professors and alumni persuaded him to offer the provostship to Clarence Dykstra in 1944. Dykstra was well known as an educator and governmental administrator, having served as teacher and professor of political science at UCLA, commissioner of the Los Angeles Department of Water and Power, city manager of Cincinnati, president of the University of Wisconsin, national director of Selective Service, and chairman of the National Defense Mediation Board.[81]

For reasons difficult now to understand, Dykstra was not immediately appointed vice-president of the University and provost of the University of California at Los Angeles—the titles of his predecessors. Instead, he was provost of the University. Three years later, however, he did receive the additional title of vice-president and his powers were basically parallel to those that had evolved for Deutsch, who, as was made explicit in January, 1945, could make decisions affecting all departments of the Berkeley campus that were not "statewide" in character. Those decisions were final as long as they were made "in accordance with the policies laid down by the Regents and the President of the University, and within the limits of the annual budgets established for the departments by the Regents." [82] Dykstra believed this power was intended to make him equivalent to the President in UCLA's administration, but he soon learned that Sproul reserved to himself considerable authority for UCLA matters.

Administrative authority was not much more generously delegated at Berkeley, where Vice-President Deutsch's responsibilities were determined pretty much by the chores Sproul specifically assigned to him. In point of fact, most of the control of the Berkeley campus remained in the President's hands and the burden of that responsibility was enormous. Until 1947, for instance, Sproul dealt directly with department chairmen on budgetary matters. This was not particularly difficult in the professional schools, where the dean and the department chairman were usually the same person. But in the College of Letters and Science at Berkeley alone, with its more than fifty departments, the dean had no budgetary role at all and the President worked with the chairmen directly. When Alva R. Davis, one of the most respected men on the faculty, became dean of the College of Letters and Science in 1947, the faculty, led by John D. Hicks, then just retiring as dean of the Graduate Division, and Ira B. Cross, of the Department of Economics, decided to seek a change. After discussing the matter with the President, they won the official recommendation of the Academic Senate that the new dean of the College of Letters and Science be granted budgetary authority for the departments under his jurisdiction. Partly because of his admiration for Dean Davis as a loyal faculty member and a proven administrator, Sproul accepted that recommendation.

It would be unfair to suggest that such administrative problems were of no concern to Sproul. They were. But his conception of his responsibilities to the Regents, and his unique experience with so many management concerns of the University even before he became president, made it difficult for him to share his burdens very widely. Moreover, administration in his view was not the important thing about the University: "Methods and organizations are valuable only as they help to bring the student and teacher together in a favorable atmosphere, where flint may strike steel and spark find tinder, or, at least, moss find new boulders on which to cling and lend beauty to an otherwise desolate landscape. The only thing that really counts, if my observation is worth anything, is the relation between a student with an observing eye and eager mind, on the one hand, and a teacher with an overflowing mind, library and laboratory on the other." [83] In accordance with that precept, Sproul devoted enormous amounts of time to enhancing the quality of the University's faculty. In reviewing the dossiers on men recommended for appointment or promotion, he was extremely sensitive to subtle omissions or overguarded endorsements. Recommendations containing such defects were promptly returned to their authors for elaboration, and sometimes Sproul went still farther than that, enlisting the aid of faculty confidants in obtaining more objective evidence.

Because Sproul's most persistently held tenet of educational philosophy was that "the prime purpose of a State university is the development of intelligent leadership in the body politic," [84] he judged faculty members not only on the basis of their research, but also upon their ability to stimulate a life-long quest for truth. "The student who goes to a university where there are no great teachers gets a gold brick," [85] he said, and he gave teaching ability special attention in making appointments and promotions of University faculty members.

The faculty welcomed Sproul's imposition of rigorous standards on their performance. Most of them would undoubtedly agree with Sproul's successor, Clark Kerr, who spoke of this role as one of the most important ones a president can exercise: "If that is done badly and you do everything else well, you don't have a great university, but if that is done well and everything else is done badly you can still have a great university. . . . He [Sproul] was very conscientious about it and he was also very perceptive, and this was one of his real contributions." [86]

Once a great faculty is recruited, it is important to retain it, and Sproul would often find administrative funds to buy research equipment or to provide other encouragement for outstanding scholars.

The most dramatic example of Sproul's willingness to support faculty research is found in the assistance and encouragement he gave to Ernest O. Lawrence, who, in 1929, invented the cyclotron that could be used to unlock the heart of the atom. Sproul not only helped Lawrence to find outside assistance for his research, but permitted the bending of rules and tradition to keep him on the faculty. In 1930, the twenty-nine-year-old physicist received an attractive offer from Northwestern University. To keep him in Berkeley, a hastily formed committee under the chairmanship of S. J. Holmes recommended to Sproul that Lawrence be elevated to the rank of full professor and be given a $1200 increase in salary. Sproul approved the recommendation, and Lawrence not only received the appointment but the munificent salary of $4500 a year as well.

It was at Berkeley, then, that Lawrence continued the development of new and bigger machines for the investigation of the atom. In 1931, with a grant from the National Research Council, he made an 11-inch unit using a 1-ton magnet. In 1931 and 1932, a 74-ton magnet was used in building a 27-inch cyclotron (later developed into a 37-inch). In 1936, the Radiation Laboratory was established, with Lawrence as its director, and in 1937, with a grant from William H. Crocker in memory of his son and with another grant from the Rockefeller Foundation, the Crocker Laboratory was built to provide the first building for the cyclotron. The cyclotron built there was a 60-inch unit using a 220-ton magnet. In the fall of 1940, construction began on a 184-inch synchrotron with a 4000-ton magnet. It was financed jointly by the Rockefeller Foundation and the University and completed in 1946.

Although Sproul's encouragement of Lawrence's work was particularly dramatic and portentous, it was by no means an isolated example of his interest in supporting research. Examples are available in other fields as well.

As government, industry, and foundations called more frequently upon University faculty members for consultation and research activities, Sproul recognized the legitimacy of their assistance in furthering the accumulation of knowledge and was the first president to refer to public service outside the field of agriculture as equal to teaching and research as a function of the University of California.

For these and numerous other contributions to the academic life of the University, Sproul soon overcame any doubts that might have resided in the hearts of professors who regarded a "nonacademic" president as a potential hazard. On the occasion of his twenty-fifth year as president, the sentiments of the faculty toward Sproul were probably accurately stated by Professor Joel Hildebrand, who said:

> Professors are hard to please, as they should be because timid uncritical men cannot train youth for courage and adventure, and the president who retains his intellectual and moral stature under their cold scrutiny is indeed a good one. Many a president has had to take refuge in aloofness and the authority of his position. Not so President Sproul. He is the kind of president who can be called by his first name without loss of dignity. His government by cooperation rather than ukase has fostered a fine sense of loyalty and responsibility. We respect his wisdom as we like his friendly humanity.[87]

THE LURE OF BUSINESS AND POLITICS

The admiration of the faculty was shared by the students and the general public. They admired Sproul's courage in accepting the guardianship of the gangling, irrepressible, and exuberant institution the University of California had become in its first sixty-two years. They liked his good humor and confidence in the University's future. They were grateful for his persuasiveness in making the University's case before the legislature. And they were proud of the fact that he was an alumnus with a love for the University's traditions and heritage. In 1939, when he was offered $50,000 a year to become president of the Anglo California National Bank, several thousand students [88] massed in front of the President's House at Berkeley to urge him to stay. When he turned the job down, the state legislature introduced a resolution praising him for his courage and foresight, and scores of newspapers editorialized on his selflessness and dedication to the young people of the state. The Regents subsequently voted to assure the President of a lifetime retirement income of $12,000 a year. Board Chairman Garrett W. McEnerney said that Sproul turned down salary increases offered at the same time and would continue to receive $15,000 a year.[89]

After Sproul turned down the bank job (and actually there were two rival offers made at about the same time),[90] there were rumors that he might become a candidate for United States senator, governor of the state, or even President of the United States. Actually, such ideas were not new. Sproul had also been suggested as a gubernatorial candidate in 1932 and 1933, and in 1937 he was reportedly under consideration for an executive position with the Republican National Committee.[91] In 1940 he was touted as a possible recall candidate against Governor Olson,[92] and in 1946 was nominated for Secretary of the Interior by Florida's Senator Claude Pepper.[93] Sproul consistently discouraged public speculation on his possible elevation to high political office, however, and assumed his most prominent political role in 1948, when he nominated his good friend and fellow alumnus Earl Warren for the United States presidency. That honor was marred, however, by the fact that the convention chairman, Joe Martin, introduced him as Gordon P. Sproul of the University of Southern California.[94]

In 1947, Columbia University tried to woo Sproul away. But at this time he was at the height of his popularity. He had seen the University through the depression years and had strengthened the faculty despite national economic disaster and a world war. He had helped accelerate the development of a general University campus of impressive magnitude. And he had succeeded to a remarkable degree in his goal of making himself the symbol of the "One University" idea. Again students demonstrated to keep him in California, and their requests were echoed by the faculty and the Regents. When he announced his decision to stay, the Regents showed their gratitude by raising his salary to $20,000 a year.[95]

Chapter 18

THE STUDENTS BETWEEN
TWO WARS

PRESIDENT WHEELER emphasized the style of student life and preached the values of self-reliance, personal integrity, wholesome and stimulating associations, and dedication to the University's aspirations and welfare. While he was around to provide the guiding inspiration, students took great pride in conducting themselves and their organized activities in ways that demonstrated the wisdom of their president's teaching. Wheeler responded by delegating to students increasing responsibility for the management of their own affairs, and by encouraging the formulation of new student clubs and activities.

Wheeler's retirement in 1919 caused no important changes in the academic life of students. This continued to consist of the familiar cycle of lectures, recitations, laboratory experiments, library study periods, term papers, seminars, and examinations that theoretically claimed at least twenty-four hours of a student's time every week and sometimes demanded more.

In contrast, the style of extracurricular student life changed markedly when Wheeler retired. But the change was only partly attributable to Wheeler's leaving. It was also attributable to youth's exuberant release from the somber restraints of the war years, symbolized by the flapper, with her short skirt, bobbed hair, and painted face, who, according to the popular notion of the times, shared the male collegian's fabled (but probably exaggerated) tastes for tobacco, gin, and free love.

Student activities, conducted without the subtle moral overtones of the Wheeler era, fitted the new mood. They provided opportunities for students to cultivate personal interests and talents. They gave students a way to contribute to what was vaguely called "the good of the University." They created situations in which students could expand their personal acquaintances. Moreover, they sometimes offered financial rewards; when the average salary of an associate professor was $3284 a year, the student editor of the *Blue and Gold* received $3000 out of the yearbook's profits.[1] The Big Man on Campus was likely to be the one with the longest list of activities under his name in the class roster, and, accordingly, the glee clubs, bands, debate teams, athletic squads, class committees, spirit organizations, and publications flourished.

The rise of activities forced the classes into secondary importance. By 1922, the constitutions of the student associations at both Berkeley and UCLA gave the majority of student seats on their legislative councils to activity representatives. These associations were themselves activities at that time, in the sense that one voluntarily joined them by paying membership dues. But they controlled the machinery of student discipline, the bookstores, athletics, almost all special-interest activities, and many student services. They were, therefore, the *de facto* student government for members and nonmembers alike.

In 1923, the expanded role of extracurricular activities was made physically evident with the completion of a new $310,000 student union at Berkeley, built with funds from the ASUC and gifts from alumni and private citizens. It provided rooms for student officers, facilities for activities, and new space for a bookstore, barber shop, restaurant, and other student services. In 1930 a student union with similar features was built at UCLA with funds donated by Mrs. William G. Kerckhoff. A building for student publications at Berkeley was completed in 1931.

The concentration of control of student activities under large associations made calendar planning, bookkeeping, and financial management easier. On the less positive side, the central student government became too big (controlling over a million and a quarter dollars of assets at Berkeley in 1930) and too formal. Burdened with rule-making, it lost its ability to extend the California spirit into the academic, moral, and ethical life of the whole University on an informal basis—the function Wheeler originally assigned to it.

Almost precisely to the degree that the student associations became more involved in activity control and less concerned with the moral and ethical standards appropriate for a young person claiming University of California affiliation, the faculty lost interest in the so-called California spirit. Some of this disenchantment was caused by envy, evidenced by a professor's remark that students enjoyed more self-government under Wheeler than the professors did. A perceptible tendency of the student tribunal that heard cases of student misconduct to be increasingly lenient in the discipline of students charged with cheating and other academic infractions further weakened the student-faculty relationship. Gradually, the faculty began to dissociate itself from student affairs. In 1921, they took the first and most important step in that direction when they transferred all responsibility for student discipline to the administration,[2] where it was subsequently handled by deans. The transfer was particularly remarkable because student discipline was among the specific functions of the faculty cited in the Organic Act.

By the middle of the 1920s, therefore, student activities were no longer regarded as essential to the health of the University. Student activity, including the frivolity of dances and rallies and the hoopla attendant on athletics, were conceived as grit in the educational tumbler that produced well-rounded, socially accomplished, and polished individuals. By the time Robert Gordon Sproul became president in 1930, this concept was so well established that he encouraged students to take part in extracurricular activities as a "profitable investment in the assets from which men and women must expect their dividends of personal happiness and public leadership in later life." [3] In the middle of the Depression, when there was genuine anxiety among students who would soon be seeking jobs, Everett Van Every of the Bureau of Occupations at Berkeley was more pointed than that, reporting that "campus activity people have always held a favored position in the employment market." [4] Thus enjoying official sanction from the administration and endowed with a value believed negotiable in the labor market, the most prestigious activities had difficulty keeping membership to a manageable size. They did it by adopting recruiting and promotion systems that ruthlessly "cut" students who were not promoted from one rank to another at the end of the semester. This "up or out" system enhanced the prestige of active students on campus, made room for fresh talent at Freshman ranks, and concentrated control in the hands of a relatively few Seniors.

Almost all of the fraternities and sororities that now exist on the Berkeley, Los Angeles, and San Francisco campuses were established before 1930 [5] and they played a significant role in sustaining the activity orientation of student life. Their leaders stressed the importance of service to the University and encouraged their members to participate in extracurricular pursuits. Moreover, because they were easily organized *en masse* for student projects and had a built-in source of man- and womanpower at their disposal, their members fared well in student-body elections. It is not surprising, therefore, that fraternities gave UCLA all of its student-body presidents until Dean McHenry won the post in 1931, and did the same thing at Berkeley until John A. Reynolds, a member of the University's first residence hall (Bowles Hall), won the election in 1929.

The expansion of student government and student activities in the decades between the wars was a source of considerable pride for the University and Presidents Barrows, Campbell, and Sproul frequently gave it public praise. But the University could not afford to offend the public press, prospective donors, or legislators and the presidents occasionally had to place limits on student enthusiasm. One such limit was drawn in 1920, when President Barrows suspended the Skull and Keys Honors Society for performance of a skit of dubious taste during its public initiation. More interesting limitations were drawn in a series of administrative actions involving the student press.

ERRANT EDITORS

Student publications were extremely difficult to control. Censorship prior to publication was unfeasible, and offensive to the spirit of an academic community. Moreover, some of the publications, though published by student organizations, were for many years legal corporations beyond direct control by either the administration or the ASUC.

The *Occident,* a literary journal, enjoyed such status even after its publisher, the English Club, was absorbed by the ASUC in 1922. The quality of this periodical was high. It enjoyed the support of many faculty members and such well-known literary figures as the radical novelist and reformer Upton Sinclair.[6] In the early 1920s the magazine, from its off-campus position, assumed the role of loyal opposition to the University administration and its articles and stories frequently had controversial themes.

In 1925, the editor of the *Occident,* a daring young man named Lewis Russell, published a story called "Immanuel" for the magazine's November issue. Written by Donald Cary Williams, a graduate student in philosophy, it described a visit of God to Joseph at the birth of Christ, during which they briefly discussed the baby's parenthood.[7] President Campbell found the story offensive, not for its theology or literary quality but rather for ". . . its irreverence, flippancy, and obscenity,—the obscenity exemplified especially by the statement concerning the possible or probable assignation at which God was present." [8] Charges against Russell were taken before the Student Affairs Committee, which demanded that Russell resign his editorship.[9] Russell refused, and, in his defense, the entire English Club moved off-campus on the initiative and under the leadership of its faculty associates.[10] Despite pleas of Williams' former professors, including the president of Occidental College, that he not be penalized for writing the story, President Campbell withdrew the scholarship that provided his financial support.

Russell survived the "Immanuel" incident unscathed, but he was undone a few months later when he published a story written by Tom Tomson. Called "Green," this story contrasted the cheap, crude attitudes of an experienced fraternity Romeo with those of a young man whose ideas on sex came from experiences in the farming country from which he came.[11] The story was considered offensive to the campus community on two counts. It treated sex too explicitly and cast aspersions on the morality of fraternity men. On the recommendation of the Student Affairs Committee, Campbell promptly expelled Russell from the University. One more issue of *Occident* appeared after Russell's expulsion, and then the magazine folded, though it was later revived under ASUC auspices.

A hit-and-run student press, issuing newspapers or magazines that appeared only once or twice a year and offered their readers heavy-handed satire and broad humor, was especially lively in the twenties and thirties.

President Barrows encountered difficulty with such a publication called the *Laughing Horse,* which appeared for the first time in 1922 and claimed as its mission a "healthful reaction to the whole timid, vacillating conservative spirit which now prevails over this land." [12] Barrows expelled its editor for printing a letter from D. H. Lawrence which satirically discussed castrating a bad author. More notorious was the *Raspberry Press,* edited by members of the men's journalism society. In November, 1927, this paper published a story alleging that a University vice-president had made unusually high profits on his sale of Berkeley property upon which the International House was built. Three members of the fraternity, including the editor of the *Daily Californian* and the student-body president, were immediately placed on probation for seven and a half months. The fact that this penalty had been summarily invoked by President Campbell aroused student leaders to demand an explanation for the abandonment of regular student-government channels in discipline cases. If the Student Affairs Committee could handle the Russell cases in 1925, why could it not handle the *Raspberry Press* editors in 1927? Was Campbell afraid that the students would find that the allegations against Vice-President Hart were true? Campbell responded with this statement of the boundaries of student authority as he then conceived it:

It is not a question of what the findings of the Undergraduate Student Affairs Committee would be in the present case: to that point I

have given no consideration whatever. The real question is, shall similar cases be referred to the Undergraduate Student Affairs Committee
for all time?

A decision to that effect would be equivalent to saying that a student
on any campus of the University of California may publicly and in
print attack the good name and the motives of a member of the Faculty, ... of a President of the University, of a Regent, ... and be
amenable only to the Undergraduate Student Affairs Committee. ...
The University of California is not administrable on that principle.

... The student government is administered upon the basis of the
Constitution granted to it or approved by the President.[13]

Later in 1928, when both the *Dill Pickle,* a women's counterpart of the
Raspberry Press, and the *Raspberry Press* itself published several off-color
items, Campbell, without consulting anyone,[14] suspended both publications
for six months and placed them on probation for another six.

When publication of the *Raspberry Press* resumed in 1929, Campbell
warned the editors that each writer would be held personally responsible for
whatever he wrote. The editors accepted that condition, but asserted that
the Student Affairs Committee should decide the guilt or innocence of any
offender. On that point Campbell demurred, writing:

The Presidents of the University of California have regrettably come
to the conclusion that offenses of an obscene character ... must be
dealt with by the Presidents or by their selected representatives ... the
people of the State of California and the Regents ... have not gone to
the editors of the Raspberry Presses and asked why such offenses have
been committed; they have gone to the President of the University to
ask why are such acts ... permitted either on the campus or off the
campus. In my opinion, the people of the State and the Regents of the
University were absolutely right in their belief that the President was
responsible.[15]

The counterpart of the *Raspberry Press* at UCLA was called *Hells Bells.*
In January, 1926, Director Moore suspended the editors of this paper for
publication of "highly reprehensible items" and "indecent statements that
affront the good name of the women of the University." [16] Three years later,
he suspended thirteen members of the journalism society after appearance
of an issue of *Hells Bells* considered offensive by the faculty and declared
detrimental to the reputation and character of certain University personali-
ties.[17]

Unlike Campbell, President Sproul preferred to work through student
government in handling discipline of editors who overstepped the bounds of

what he considered good taste. Precedent for this was set in 1932 when the ASUC president at Berkeley rushed an advance copy of the *Raspberry Press* to Dean Thomas Putnam because it contained questionable material, including items allegedly critical of current ASUC policies.[18] After consultation with the Student Affairs Committee, the entire issue was confiscated and secretly burned.[19] In 1934, the *Raspberry Press* was banned permanently by Sproul on recommendation of the ASUC Executive Committee. This time, its downfall was caused by an article about faculty members going to a nude party.[20]

The *ad hoc* student press was not particularly important, but in its excesses it tested the limits of administrative tolerance of student behavior and morality and helped define the authority assumed to reside with student governments. Far more influential in the day-to-day affairs of the students were the *Daily Californian* at Berkeley, the *Daily Bruin* at Los Angeles, and the *Cal Aggie* at Davis. Though they were never hesitant to voice opinions, these publications tended to adhere conservatively to the "good of the University" guidelines that still had influence over the majority of the students. With few exceptions, editors were inclined to battle more against the student government on questions of control and jurisdiction than against the administration over matters of taste or suppression. They were too busy reporting day-to-day news to indulge in the experimentation so attractive to the editors of the hit-and-run student press, and they catered to an audience swept up in the activity whirl of student life. The models of the hit-and-run editors were writers like Fitzgerald and Hemingway, satirists like Mencken, and radicals like Sinclair, while the models of the principal student newspapers were the editors of the metropolitan dailies. All in all, the idols of the student newspapers were easier to emulate, and seldom led their disciples into genuine difficulty.

SOMETHING TO SHOUT ABOUT

The student newspapers helped sustain student activities by giving them publicity. Fraternities and sororities contributed by providing participants in wholesale numbers. Intercollegiate athletics helped by providing a focus for the whole complex of student enthusiasms that participation in activities fostered.

At no time in the history of the University did California athletes give students as much to shout about as they did after World War I. Between September, 1920, and October, 1925, Berkeley's football teams, coached by a miracle-worker named Andrew Latham Smith, were undefeated in fifty outings, though they were tied four times. Called the "Wonder Teams," these great aggregations of gridiron talent scored 1649 to their opponents' 139 points and defeated Stanford in five consecutive games. They played in the Rose Bowl twice, defeating Ohio State by 28–0 in 1921 and playing Washington and Jefferson to a 0–0 tie in 1922.[21]

In 1921, football was important enough at the University to command a new stadium, and the Associated Students and the alumni conducted a subscription program to build one. With more than a million dollars subscribed for the project, construction commenced in 1922, and the new stadium, dedicated to World War I casualties from the University and seating some 75,000 people, was completed in time for the Big Game with Stanford in 1923.

But Berkeley was not a one-sport campus. Able students could participate in intercollegiate baseball, basketball, crew, cross-country running, football, soccer, swimming, tennis, track and field, and water polo teams in 1920, and boxing, golf, gymnastics, and wrestling were introduced in the 1930s. Berkeley won the Pacific Coast Conference championships in basketball in 1925, 1926, 1927, and 1928 and in track and field in 1919, 1920, and 1923. It won the California Intercollegiate Baseball Association championships in 1916, 1917, 1920, 1921, 1928, and 1929. The crew won the Intercollegiate Regatta Association championships at Poughkeepsie in both 1928 and 1932 and went on to place first in Olympic Crew races in the same years at Amsterdam and Long Beach, California.

Los Angeles and Davis also developed strong athletic programs in the decades between world wars. UCLA won the Southern California Intercollegiate championship in football in 1927 and in golf in 1934. It began its great successes in tennis by winning the Pacific Coast Conference title in 1932. Davis was also strong in tennis, winning the Far Western Intercollegiate Athletic championships in that sport in 1933, 1934, 1941, and 1942. In the same conference, Davis won titles in basketball in 1939 and 1940, and in golf in 1940 and 1942.

In the 1930s, the Golden Bears at Berkeley found baseball to be their strongest major sport, and won California Intercollegiate Baseball championships in six of the decade's seasons. In wrestling the team did still better, winning in nine out of ten years. Berkeley also won Southern Division PCC championships in basketball in 1931, 1932, and 1939, and in tennis in 1930, 1933, 1937, and 1938. But football remained the most popular sport, despite a series of disappointing seasons in the early 1930s. One important football game in that period was the first one played between the Berkeley and Los Angeles campuses of the University in 1933. It ended in a 0–0 tie.

From the beginning of his long administration, Robert Gordon Sproul made it clear that he did not believe that the University of California should resort to high-pressure recruiting, subsistence scholarships, and other extravagances to attract outstanding athletes. "No matter what others may do," he said, "I believe that California teams should continue to be made up of genuine students who have been attracted to our campus in a normal way and not by subsidies, scholarships, and special inducements. . . . I want the teams for which I cheer—win, lose, or draw—to be a natural outgrowth of the University which I love, and not a group of gladiators who have gathered where the pay is best." [22] In keeping with that philosophy, he took the lead in efforts of the Pacific Coast Conference to curb excesses in recruiting and to restrain tendencies toward the commercialization of intercollegiate sports.

In 1935, under a new football coach, Leonard (Stub) Allison, the Golden Bears began another famous era, with only Stanford spoiling their undefeated season's record.[23]

The way students became excited over football was both impressive and frightful. In 1936, 2500 students, out of a total enrollment of fewer than 8000, made the trip from Los Angeles to Berkeley to watch the Bruins play against the Bears; [24] Stanford raiders intent on painting the "Big C" red beat two student guards unconscious; [25] and students were so exuberant after Big Game rallies in Berkeley that twenty of them had to be arrested for breaking store windows, rioting, and destruction to streetcars.[26] The 1937 season was even bigger. Allison's "Thunder Team" went undefeated (with one tie) in conference play and welcomed 1938 by beating Alabama in the Rose Bowl on New Year's Day. More students were jailed that year for Big Game rioting [27] and some of the rioters were also penalized by the University.[28] In 1940 a homecoming parade was introduced as a part of Big Game week celebrations to replace the nighttime rallies and reduce vandalism. This plan almost worked. Berkeley police said that the 1940 Big Game week was the quietest in years, and they jailed only thirty students for building bonfires in the city streets on the night before the game.[29]

THE HARDER FACTS OF LIFE

The Big Game riots exhibited collegiate irresponsibility at its worst, and the participants were always liable to receive stern punishment. But they were also viewed with a degree of indulgence. Much of the collegiate experience in the United States was still regarded in the 1930s as an unpleasant but probably inevitable concomitant of society's determination to protect its most able youth from the heavy responsibilities of adult life until, miraculously, on Commencement Day, they were ready for them.

With the onset of the Depression, some students assumed such responsibilities despite society's intent. They became aware by observation if not from personal experience of the existence of poverty and the agonies of chilled spines and empty stomachs. Out of their awareness came a resolve to improve the human condition wherever and as best they could. They found places to start among classmates who were at the mercy of greedy landlords and exploitive employers, or were denied good living accommodations because of their race.

The ASUC Welfare Committee, originally created to teach underclassmen "our student self-government and honor spirit and to instill in them the true California traditions and ideals," [30] became increasingly concerned during the Depression with the dignity of students as human beings and with making the conditions of everyday living suitable to that estate.

The need of students for low-cost housing that met reasonable standards of cleanliness, roominess, and convenience was high on the list of the new concerns. It was tackled first by fourteen young men who, encouraged by Harry Kingman, secretary of Stiles Hall, the University YMCA at Berkeley, started the first cooperative boarding house in Berkeley in 1933.[31] Each student contributed three hours of work a day to help maintain the house and paid ten dollars a month for room and board. Their modest enterprise grew into the impressive Students Cooperative Association which, after six years, housed over five hundred students in five dormitories—including one for women.[32] By 1939, rates at the cooperatives were $22.50 to $25.00 per month, plus four hours of required work a week.[33] Cooperatives also began at Los Angeles in 1935 and were consolidated into a single hall for four hundred students in 1938.[34] All cooperatives followed a policy of renting to students of all races and religions and usually had a waiting list of prospective members.

But cooperative dormitories did not satisfy all student-housing needs. At Berkeley, in 1938, an ASUC Welfare Council study revealed that exorbitant rents were charged by landlords in the community and that abominable conditions frequently prevailed in rooming and boarding houses.[35] That year, all five candidates for the student body presidency agreed that housing was the most serious student issue,[36] and in April, the Alumni Association offered to raise two million dollars for dormitory construction on all campuses.[37]

Satisfied that more housing would actually be provided, the *Daily Californian* and many student leaders advocated that the proposed dormitories be cooperatives, emulating the success of those started five years earlier. But President Sproul opposed this idea, indicating that he preferred that cooperatives remain marginal rather than primary competition for other (i.e., private) housing systems.[38] That his views on the subject were settled University policy became evident on November 1, 1938, when Comptroller Luther Nichols was quoted in the student newspaper to the effect that the administration's housing committee would not even consider a student petition asking that the proposed dormitory at Berkeley be a cooperative.[39] A year later, the University released findings of an administrative study which showed that the greatest demand for dormitories was for those in the medium, not the lowest, price range.[40]

The cost and caliber of housing were not the only issue interesting students. In 1937, student criticism against local boarding houses for refusing accommodations to non-Caucasians and foreign students became increasingly strong.[41] A race-relations group affiliated with the YWCA at Berkeley circulated petitions against discrimination in boarding houses,[42] and an editor of the *Daily Californian* suggested that the University's "approved lists" of student housing be limited to those that did not discriminate on the basis of race.[43] University officials resisted that idea and also opposed—without success—motions of the ASUC executive committee "to endorse and approve" houses on its own, using discrimination as a criterion.[44] The dean of the undergraduates at Berkeley also opposed another ASUC motion to support a petition calling for students to boycott discriminatory boarding houses.[45]

In January, 1940, to relieve the housing problem, the California Alumni Association agreed on plans to build a women's dormitory on the Berkeley hillside across Piedmont Avenue from Founders' Rock.[46] For this purpose the association would loan $200,000 from its endowment, and the rest would come from donations. The plan was altered later that year, however, when Rosalie Meyer Stern decided to give a residence hall to the University in memory of her husband, Sigmund Stern, and selected the site favored by the alumni. Because she was ready to proceed immediately with construction, the association deferred to her wishes and decided to build a men's dormitory elsewhere on the campus.[47] This decision was rescinded in March, 1941, however, when the association decided not to proceed with dormitory fund-raising because of "world conditions." [48]

Second only to housing as a practical matter of everyday student concern were jobs and fair practices of student employment. To give concentrated attention to this matter, the ASUC Executive Committee created a Labor Board in April, 1937. Functioning as a subsidiary of the Welfare Council, its purpose included "the investigation of working conditions . . . ; hearing student grievances; . . . compiling surveys . . . ; assisting in the making of new standards, and in the criticism and maintenance of the old." [49] Its most ingenious contribution was the initiation of a "Fair Bear" sticker to be displayed in the windows of Berkeley employers who complied with ASUC Labor Board standards, including a forty-cent minimum hourly wage for students. This program was approved by the ASUC Executive Committee in November, 1937, and the first stickers were put up in January, 1938. More teeth were put into the "Fair Bear" program in 1940, when strikes and boycotts were initiated against employers who failed to comply with the ASUC's standards.

The "Fair Bear" stickers were so successful that "Clean Bear" cards were later devised by the Welfare Council for display in Berkeley restaurants that met the council's standards for cleanliness and sanitation. This official student seal of approval was respected not only by students but also by the other citizens of the Berkeley community.

In tackling labor, housing, health, and racial discrimination problems in the 1930s the University's student government made an important departure from its activity orientation of the twenties. But there were limits to what students could do in these fields without the cooperation of the University administration and the community. In some cases, such as housing, the University eventually took over the students' program completely, making its own statistical studies, investigating living conditions, and preparing lists of approved accommodations. The city's health department eventually exercised such thorough control of sanitary conditions in restaurants that there was little left a student committee to do in that matter. There is still a "Fair Bear" wage, and there is still official student body action on housing matters, but these concerns are not as visible as they were in the late 1930s.

President Sproul would have been happier if the new interests of the students in welfare programs had never developed. While he was devoted to students, he also seemed to accept the old-world university tradition that students should be pretty much on their own in matters of housing, employment, and choices of places to eat. Moreover, student agencies that became concerned with these matters often created friction between the University and the landlords, employers, and merchants of the outside community. Obviously uncomfortable in that state of affairs, President Sproul criticized the work of the Welfare Council in 1941, and suggested that it turn its attention away from housing, employment, and racial discrimination and concentrate

on controlling intercampus raids, bolstering college spirit, increasing turn-
outs in student-body elections, and preventing students participating in
picket lines from wearing clothing or symbols identifying them with the
University of California.[50]

But by 1941 the students had ventured too far into new ground to be easily turned back. The activities of the 1920s and 1930s may have satisfied a
generation liberating itself from the stuffy morality and ethics of the pre-
World War I period. But the Depression gave that same generation a crisis
of its own to live with, and many students felt an obligation to face up to it
whether they were expected to or not. The extent of that determination is
indicated by the fact that the Welfare Council and its subsidiary boards continued to watchdog student working and living conditions despite the administration's reservations. Moreover, student government itself was over-
hauled again in 1941, and the old activity council representatives to the
ASUC's executive committee were replaced by representatives elected by
students at large.[51]

THE RADICALS

In May, 1920, Genevieve Taggard, editor of the *Occident* for 1917–1919,
wrote a touching vignette for the magazine about the "shabby young man"
who came to Sather Gate every Monday morning to sell *The World Tomor-
row, The Nation,* and *The Liberator.* She said, "They put him in jail several
times, black-listed him, insulted him continually, and gradually bore down
upon him that he was 'queer.' " One day, some Sophomores took his papers
and burned them in the street while a crowd gathered to laugh.[52] The shabby
young man was Herman Meyling, and his presence was one of the few visible signs that anyone around the University of California entertained unconventional political thoughts. Few people ever bought his literature, but
radicals did exist on the campus and were well known to their professors
and fellow students. They did not organize, however, until after the Depression.

On the whole, the students in the 1930s were politically conservative, giving Republican candidates substantial majorities in every straw vote taken
at important election seasons. But these polls also revealed a visible segment
of student opinion favoring Socialist and even Communist candidates. In a
1932 straw vote, for instance, Norman Thomas outpolled Franklin Roosevelt by about 130 votes a few weeks before the election.[53] By 1940, Roosevelt was running a very strong second to Wendell Willkie at the straw vote

polls, but both Thomas and Communist Earl Browder were getting the support of between a hundred and two hundred students apiece.[54]

The emergence of openly radical student organizations in the University coincided with national developments in 1931. The Depression had made educational opportunities for many students less certain. Graduates of the nation's colleges and universities were sending word back to the campuses that jobs were not plentiful and that a degree was not the key to good positions it once had been. With the American economy in a wreck, alternative systems were no longer unthinkable. Some student liberals became interested in the programs of the Student League for Industrial Democracy (SLID) that had evolved out of the old Intercollegiate Socialist Society formed by Jack London, Upton Sinclair, and others in 1905, while more revolutionary socialists were attracted to the Young People's Socialist League (YPSL), the youth section of the Socialist Party. Students attracted by communism joined either the Young Communist League (YCL), which was most faithful to the party program, or the more broadly oriented National Student League (NSL), where students and intellectuals were regarded with less suspicion.[55]

At Berkeley, the NSL had an informal association with an organization called the Social Problems Club, formed on January 16, 1931. The aim of the founders of this club was the development of a society "that believed that the extracurricular activities of university students should not be restricted to football, fraternities, sororities, and teas," and "viewed with regret the puerile and ignominious role played in domestic and international affairs by American students as contrasted with the mature, significant political potency of students in practically all other countries." [56] In March, 1932, a Social Problems Club was formed at UCLA.[57]

In contrast to such organizations as YPSL, YCL, and SLID, the Social Problems Clubs obscured or de-emphasized political ideology and concerned themselves with a broad range of problems specifically appealing to students. They became champions of maximum independence for student government and for the freedom of students to speak and hear speakers on any subject anywhere on campus. They favored intramural athletics as, in their view, a more democratic alternative to intercollegiate sports. They supported ASUC efforts to improve student housing, to end the exploitation of working students, and to stop racial discrimination. The Social Problems Clubs also provided some of the leadership for the student peace movement. Beginning in 1935, they promoted annual "strikes" for peace, during which several thousand students gathered at Sather Gate for an hour or so to hear pacifist speakers. They were also active in pamphleteering, in sponsoring discussion sessions, and continuous opposition to compulsory ROTC at the University. This was in part a generational reaction, and was encountered among college youth of the 1930s throughout the world. Thus, while the peace movement was inspired and programmed originally by the more radical elements on the campus, it gradually drew support from many students who were not normally active in political affairs. By 1937, student concern for peace was so general that an ASUC Peace Committee was created as an agency of the student government.

Student radicals frightened much of the public, and their disdain for University procedures and traditions angered the Regents, the President, many faculty members, and the majority of students. But they had their defenders. In March, 1931, the editor of the *Daily Bruin* wrote:

> It has been the fashion, among off-campus busybodies and collegiate cynics, to droop the mouth in a deprecating manner when speaking of our small band of campus communists and radicals of other varieties. The conventional attitude has been that these benighted individuals are mildly crazy and hence not accountable for their actions, yet simultaneously, singularly and dangerously perverted, and therefore to be punished for their economic and social heresies.
>
> Contrary to the general viewpoint, we believe that we have too few radicals, and not too many. Our collegiate dissenters display a genuine interest in contemporary problems, and for the most part they are well-informed concerning them.[58]

Few succeeding editors of the prewar period were as tolerant. Radical students engaged in too much disruptive and graceless conduct to appeal to conventional students. In the fall of 1932, radical students picketed the Army-Navy game being held in California Memorial Stadium as a gesture of protest against war. Six of the students were arrested but later released with a warning that repeated behavior of the same kind would result in jail sentences.[59] In April, 1933, members of the Social Problems Club presented handbills protesting Japanese imperialism in Manchuria to a group of young campus visitors—Japanese naval cadets paying their respects to President Sproul.[60] In September, 1933, a disgruntled founder of the Social Problems Club and several companions used tear-gas bombs to rout two students who were selling copies of the club's mimeographed paper, *The Student Outpost,* from a table at Sather Gate.[61] Captured by police, the principal bomber claimed that he had helped found the club as a study group only to learn that it had become subverted by Communists.[62] In October, 1933, a group of students joined a cotton-pickers' strike.[63] The editor of the *Daily*

Californian attempted to dissociate the majority of the students at the University from such behavior when he wrote:

> Most of us here look with disfavor upon students, who by radical action, bring unfavorable comment upon the University. The radical group in the University is denied recognition by the Associated Students. Radical students are exceptions on the campus and their actions should be considered in this respect.[64]

The University's administration began to take steps in 1933 to make the disaffiliation of such groups even more pronounced than the *Daily Californian* implied. In August, 1933, Louis O'Brien, assistant dean of the undergraduates, and Thomas M. Putnam, dean of the undergraduates, prepared a "Memorandum to the President concerning Social Problems Club." It suggested five courses of action:

1. All requests for meetings on the campus should be denied;
2. Permission to display notices on bulletin boards should be denied;
3. The ASUC should be requested to ignore the existence of the Club;
4. The *Californian* should be requested to withhold publicity;
5. Organizations unofficially connected with the University such as International House, YMCA, YWCA, Hillel, Newman Club should be requested to deny hospitality to the Club.[65]

The first two steps were codified into regulations of the University which allowed only groups "approved by the chairman of any one of our University departments of instruction as being an important adjunct to the work of that department" to use rooms on the campus, and denied use of bulletin boards "to all notices . . . save those which are purely official." [66]

President Sproul's decision not to invoke the fifth recommendation of his deans—i.e., asking organizations like the YMCA and Hillel to deny hospitality to the Social Problems Club—proved to be very useful. As long as they remained open to groups and speakers with all shades of opinion, such organizations could offer students the essential elements of a free forum without involving the University in any politically vulnerable way. Under the leadership of its secretary, Harry Kingman, Stiles Hall, the University YMCA, became especially well known as a sanctuary for free speech and assembly.

The 1933 rules were not adequate. For one thing, their strict interpretation would deny use of University facilities to groups recognized by the Associated Students. In 1934, a committee composed of Professor Joel Hilde-brand, Professor Paul Cadman, and Harry Kingman proposed that organizations that might use the University buildings be divided into three classifications: those directly under ASUC control, honor societies, and other professional groups sponsored by the faculty, and "all other student organizations." When this division was made, "notice should then be given that groups in the third category shall not employ the name of the University on any publication, meeting notice, membership card, or on any printed matter having to do with the affairs of the group without specific approval of the President or his representative." From these beginnings there began to emerge rules on the use of University facilities that came to be known as Regulation 17. Since it succeeded in keeping the University free of complic-ity in any political expression on the campus, the regulation was reasonably successful. But it also came to be regarded as repressive of free speech on campus and was constantly subject to attack, not only by radical political groups but also by members of the faculty and student body who deemed it incompatible with freedoms appropriate to an academic community.

SPROUL STUMPS AGAINST COMMUNISM

With a Socialist-recently-turned-Democrat running for governor on a radi-cal program to End Poverty in California (EPIC), with labor unrest tying up shipping from San Diego to Seattle, and with University students teasing the public with debate topics like "Communism is fit for America," Califor-nians were jittery in 1934.[67] To calm their fears as far as the University was concerned, President Sproul gave a series of speeches and wrote several articles that year making his position toward communism clear. He began moderately, assuring members of thirty Rotary Clubs meeting jointly in Los Angeles that although the "self-advertised group of radicals" at the Univer-sity were a public nuisance, they were only a minute minority of all of the students and had no influence on University policy.[68] On August 21, 1934, he welcomed new students at Berkeley by saying, "I am no flag-waving jingo. But I have grown infinitely weary with the deprecation of America and of American institutions by pseudo-intellectuals hanging on the fringe of a student body or faculty." [69] At UCLA a month later he told students, "If you do not believe in America and American institutions, you have no place in a university of the state." [70]

Sproul's campaign against communism was a campaign to reassure the public its University was in safe hands. At Los Angeles, Provost Ernest C.

Moore also opposed communism, and nursed great fears of its dangers to the University. In a letter to President Sproul on May 10, 1934, he said, "I think we must give our thought to finding a way by which we can stop everything that has the appearance even of communist activity on any campus of the University and, for that matter, on any public school grounds in the state. We will have to have drastic legislation perhaps. If they are making 'class war' it will not be enough for us merely to 'turn the other cheek.' " [71]

INSURGENCE AT LOS ANGELES

A superficial impression of UCLA in 1934 was that it was unlikely ground for student political uprising. Provost Moore's worries about communism were well known to student leaders, and they were careful not to stir them up needlessly. [72] Student-body president Porter Hendricks' open letter to his successor John Burnside in 1934 said little about radicals and, instead, emphasized the importance of campus unity, the fun he had working with members of the University administration, UCLA's need to develop friendship with other schools, and the necessity of continuing good Freshman orientation programs. [73] Six months later, Burnside was suspended by Provost Moore for using his position to "further the revolutionary activities of the National Students League, a communistic organization which has bedeviled the University . . . " and for using his office "to destroy the University by handing it over to communists." [74]

The incident that led to this drastic action had a two-year history. As early as 1932, UCLA had what was called an "open forum," a series of meetings, controlled by the administration, at which faculty and students could discuss current affairs. In March, 1934, a new format for these meetings was instituted. It provided time for an opening speech by a faculty member, lasting ten minutes, followed by open discussion for fifty minutes. The editor of the *Daily Bruin* regarded the first meeting under the new format as a test of the University's ability to cope with free discussion. The topic for this meeting was "The Russo-Japanese Crisis," but the editor timidly predicted, "If the participants demonstrate that they can stick to the subject under discussion, and that they can appropriately follow accepted rules of order, the scope of topics will be enlarged." [75] He then added ominously, "This is the wish of Provost Moore who has led with a deft hand the path of students through controversial subjects for many years." [76] The meeting came off without untoward incident.

In October of that year, with the election approaching, Celeste Strack, "a

21-year-old blondish, blue-eyed young lady who is more trouble to university officials than a bumblebee at a nudist clambake," [77] on behalf of the National Student League, requested permission to hold a student forum to discuss the issues of the gubernatorial contest. Provost Moore turned down her request and she approached Burnside and other ASUC officers to see if there was a way for the forum to be held under student-body auspices. Moore warned Burnside not to have the ASUC discuss the matter, but negotiations on the forum proceeded until Moore announced the suspensions of Miss Strack, Burnside, and three other student leaders for one year.

The Los Angeles *Times* reported that more than 80 per cent of the student body at UCLA supported Moore's action,[78] but, the next day, two thousand students went on "strike" in protest against the suspensions, and one policeman received a cut on his face while attempting to prevent students from speaking at the rally.[79] To add to mounting tension in Los Angeles, 150 athletes met to form a vigilante group calling themselves "UCLA Americans" and pledged to "purge the campus of radicals." [80] They hinted that they had Moore's support and a spokesman revealed that the provost had some twenty to thirty students at UCLA under observation for "radical tendencies." [81]

A mass meeting to protest the UCLA suspensions was held at Berkeley at 10 A.M. November 5. In the radical lexicon of this period, the meeting was called a "strike," although its two thousand participants missed only an hour or so of studies and there was no attempt to stop the University operation. Most students followed their usual ten-o'clock routine on November 5, but a large crowd gathered at Sather Gate for a mass meeting, where the speakers were given a shower of tomatoes and eggs and were booed.[82] The campus community was more shocked by the behavior of the egg- and tomato-throwers than it was by the strike itself, and the Student Affairs Committee was asked to investigate the incident. When it reported, the committee criticized the strike-disrupters for disorderly conduct and the strike-organizers for misrepresenting the student body, but recommended that no one be punished.

A few days before the Berkeley strike, President Sproul went to Los Angeles on what was announced as his regular monthly visit to UCLA. On November 13, after interviews with Moore, the suspended students, and members of the faculty, Sproul reinstated the four student officers. They escaped with a reprimand for insubordination in refusing to stop discussing the student-controlled forum proposal when Provost Moore asked them to, but they were cleared of any charges that they were helping to destroy the University or were working for the National Students League. Miss Strack remained on suspension pending further investigation, but was finally reinstated on December 10 after pledging that she would not hold any unauthorized meetings on the campus.

President Sproul was widely acclaimed by moderates and liberals throughout the state for his fair handling of the suspensions. The Los Angeles *Daily Illustrated News* said the President handled the problem at UCLA "like a practical, fact-concerned American instead of like a dictator mainly interested in lurid gossip," [83] and the Los Angeles *Evening Post* said it was fortunate that Sproul "happens to be a man who refuses to believe that anyone with an independent idea is a Communist." [84] Moore, of course, continued to have the applause of conservative and patriotic groups for his crusade against encroaching communism. The net effect of the whole episode, however, was to convince many Californians that the University was, in fact, a haven for subversives and it would take all of the best statesmanship that President Sproul, members of the faculty, student leaders, and other University partisans could put together to offset that impression.

TRENDS OF TWO DECADES

Participation in the radical student movement of the 1930s was quite small, involving perhaps a hundred individuals in the entire University. But peace and the issues of student housing and labor were sufficiently general to permit radicals and nonradicals to work together and gave student life a new character.

Almost more remarkable than the influence of the student radicals, however, was the stamina of "California spirit" as enunciated during the Wheeler years. Even though it was scorned by most radicals, eroded to some extent by preemptive administrative disciplinary procedures, and abandoned almost entirely by the faculty, it had a strong hold on students throughout the 1920s and 1930s. Indeed, the hold was so strong that most of the students of the University during this period gave little encouragement to patterns of thinking and behavior that taunted authority, offended prevailing morality and custom, and developed pretensions of responsibility for the imperfections of a world controlled by older generations.

Student life when Barrows assumed the presidency was almost entirely true to the Wheeler model, and its principal characteristic was that students were so busy in activities that their transgressions were inevitably those of excessive fervor as opposed to alien political behavior. The same held true during Campbell's administration.

President Sproul's administration spanned the time when students first departed from the activity-oriented life to become concerned with such bread-and-butter problems as housing, employment opportunities, and racial discrimination. Pursuing that new direction without interruption, the students might have arrived earlier than they actually did at a point where they demanded more responsibility for ordering their lives at the University and more freedom of operation at the outer boundaries of traditional student life. This tendency was contained by the administration when it pre-empted some of the more useful welfare programs the students devised. It was also restrained by a rejuvenated California spirit of Wheeler genre. Sproul, after all, was an undergraduate at Berkeley while Wheeler was still president, and he later served on Wheeler's administrative staff. The California spirit blended well with Sproul's personal convictions, and his easy manner with students, his form of public address, and his immense love of the University made him almost as effective as the high priest of the California spirit as Wheeler was. Under his leadership, therefore, that spirit remained alive and made the University fundamentally inhospitable to the style and tactics of the student radicals.

While the radical student organizations made little progress in their work on behalf of national economic reforms and political revolution, they found many sympathetic ears in the student body for their advocacy of world disarmament and peace. But even as they urged an end to the Reserve Officers Training Corps in colleges and universities, asked that the country remain free from entangling alliances, and demonstrated annually against militarism of all kinds, the world was fused for explosion and their efforts came to nothing.

Chapter 19

DURING WORLD WAR II

AS ADOLF HITLER gained power in Germany and the pattern of his bid for world domination became perceptible, America pursued the difficult policy of official neutrality on the one hand, and assistance—short of troop commitments—to the victims of Axis aggression on the other. The ambiguity of this policy was uncomfortable. Students and faculty members could be found on both sides of the intervention issue, but the majority shared the dominant American isolationism and held fast to the ideal of an uninterrupted peace. They advocated strict American neutrality and often stood opposed to loans and assistance to European belligerents, to compulsory military training through ROTC programs, and to profit-making in war-equipment industries.

Compulsory ROTC, an immediate and highly visible manifestation of militarism, was an especially prominent target of the pacifists. In 1934 Provost Moore, with approval of the President, suspended two UCLA students, Albert Hamilton and W. Alonzo Reynolds, for refusing to participate in ROTC drill.[1] As sons of Methodist ministers, they explained their refusal to drill as an exercise of religious conscience. They appealed their suspensions to the United States Supreme Court, contending that compulsory military training in state universities was repugnant to the fourteenth amendment of the federal Constitution and in violation of the Kellogg–Briand Pact. Their appeal lost in a decision rendered on December 3, 1934,[2] but their cause remained quite alive for three more decades.

Student antiwar activities at the University of California were actually part of an international movement. In February, 1933, students at Oxford University had pledged that under no circumstances would they "fight for king and country." [3] American students soon took up the "Oxford Pledge" by stating their refusal "to support the United States government in any war it may conduct." [4]

In the spring of 1935, a Berkeley group called the Anti-War Committee published a series of "Bulletins," the first issue of which rallied participation in a national student antiwar "strike" scheduled for 11 A.M. on April 12, 1935.[5] Two weeks later, police arrested eighteen students for passing out the bulletins in violation of a 1913 Berkeley ordinance prohibiting distribution of leaflets except house-to-house.[6] The bulletins continued to appear, still urging the students to participate in the strike and charging that the arrested students had been denied constitutional rights.[7] They also charged that the student arrests had been made at the request of University officials as a means of discouraging demonstrations that might be an embarrassing distraction to legislators who were, at that very time, considering the University's budget.[8] Student-government officers at Berkeley gave the Anti-War Committee no encouragement. When the arrested students asked for ASUC assistance in meeting their bail, ASUC president Alden Smith refused, saying that he was not in sympathy with "the revolutionary activities of these students." [9] The *Daily Californian* charged that the arrests had been arranged by some of the students arrested in order to provide a test case, and its editor suggested that the Berkeley police had therefore been "framed." [10]

The arrested leaflet-distributors never came to trial. On April 9, the Berkeley city council began to revise the law the distributors were alleged to have broken, and the cases against the students were dismissed.[11]

The "strike" took place throughout the country on April 12, 1935, as scheduled. In Berkeley, President Robert Gordon Sproul refused to allow the strikers to rally in the Hearst Greek Theatre, so they held their meeting on city property just outside Sather Gate. The Berkeley *Daily Gazette,* often critical of the student peace movement, estimated that 2000 students attended the rally and that of these "250 were in sincere protest." [12] The rest were spectators. The strikers passed resolutions condemning compulsory military training and the arrest of students participating in antiwar demonstrations, but their meeting was calm and orderly. At UCLA, where 1500 [13] students demonstrated against any United States involvement in the war, the meeting was also peaceful. One of its organizers was Celeste Strack, reinstated after her suspension the previous fall for alleged "subversive activities." At colleges and universities throughout the country, students held demonstrations.[14] In some places the faculty and administration helped arrange the meetings. In others outraged officials attempted to break them up, causing riot and, occasionally, injury on some campuses.

Antiwar agitation among students did not end with the strike of 1935. In a February, 1936, ballot Berkeley students opposed compulsory ROTC by a vote of 1281 to 537,[15] but the Regents reaffirmed existing policy on the matter in March, asserting that maintenance of ROTC on a compulsory basis was not only required of them by the Organic Act of 1868 but was also academically sound. By 1937, a permanent Peace Committee was created as an official agency of the ASUC. Its function was to sponsor large-scale peace meetings each semester and promote discussion on peace and war. In 1938, this new committee issued a report that challenged the Regents' rationale for continuing compulsory ROTC. The committee claimed that students so intensely disliked the course that they had been known to give the Fascist salute when marching before the University's president and military officers during a review, to hum Fascist anthems in the ranks, and deliberately to violate regulations concerning the wearing of their uniforms. The report also insisted that the Regents overestimated the extent of their legal obligations to make the military training compulsory. The Morrill Land Grant Act mentioned training in military science and tactics among subjects to be included in the curriculum of a land-grant college, but did not make such courses mandatory for all students. Besides, the Organic Act had a tenuous hold on the Regents in 1938, because in most respects it was an amendment to the state constitution of 1918 that stood moot on the ROTC question. Finally, the Peace Committee produced correspondence which indicated that the War Department itself preferred to leave the question of whether military training should be compulsory or elective to the colleges.[16] Turning to a list of advantages of military training cited by the Regents and other proponents of the *status quo,* the report tried to show that compulsory ROTC was not necessarily sound academically and was not particularly useful in maintaining a student's physical well-being or in preparing him for military leadership.

Sproul asked Bruce Allen, a second-year law student at Boalt Hall, to prepare a rebuttal to the report. Allen's response contended that the legal conclusions offered by the ASUC Peace Committee were still subject to interpretation and stressed the importance of the ROTC program for national defense. As a response to the argument that students disliked the course, he offered results of a survey of sixteen thousand men from fifty-four institutions who had gone to school between 1920 and 1930. Of these men, 81 per cent favored military training as a required two-year course. More than 90 per cent asserted they derived something of value from their military courses.[17]

The issue of compulsory ROTC was still very much alive in August, 1939, when the Nazi-Soviet pact was signed, and in September, when Poland fell, but thereafter it was an issue far too small to consume the full measure of the students' anxiety for peace. Their attention turned, in some confusion, to the policies of the national government. A straw vote conducted in mid-September revealed the students to be lining up with America's isolationists. They opposed Franklin D. Roosevelt's attempts to revise American neutrality laws so that aid to Europe's democratic powers could be more direct and more substantial before it was too late. They took the position that the United States should not fight in a European war unless Germany were winning. Then it should only offer military aid. They also said they would not enter into war unless they were drafted.[18]

The following month, the ASUC Peace Committee prepared an antiwar petition that was circulated among faculty, students, and administrators. President Sproul refused to sign when he read the last sentence: "We wish to inform our government that we will volunteer for prison rather than volunteer for service if the United States enters this war." [19] In Sproul's view, if

Congress declared war, all citizens were obligated to accept the declaration as a mandate to serve. In no other way could a democratic government succeed.[20]

Student pacifists held "The Yanks Are Not Coming" rallies in April of both 1940 and 1941 with about the same-sized crowds that had been attending the so-called strikes since 1935. Kept off-campus, the rallies interfered little, if at all, with University operations.

THE VOICE OF LEADERSHIP

President Sproul repeatedly told student pacifists that he shared their aversion to war. But Hitler's ruthless government of the German people, the persecution of the Jews, and schemes for extending the shadow of Fascism across the face of the earth shocked him. He regarded the fall of each democratic nation in Europe as a warning and considered both the American isolationist and the American advocate of disarmament to be dangerously ignorant of the realities of the Axis drive for power. In his Commencement address in May, 1940, he described "the only practical course" as one of American preparedness accompanied by a policy of extending "moral and material support to the rule of equity and law elsewhere, and to those peoples whose ideals we share. If we are then attacked by dictators, by the priests of political witchcraft, we shall be able to strike back, and not strike softly." [21] This course was not then an obvious part of American foreign policy. In fact, it ran counter to strong conservative, isolationist sentiment that prevailed in many parts of the country.

With the defeat of France a few weeks after Sproul's remarks were uttered and with Roosevelt's election to his third term the following fall, national policy became more openly the one long favored by Sproul. In August, 1940, speaking to the student body at Berkeley, President Sproul gave that policy more complete endorsement. He pledged assistance "without reservation" to the national defense program and proposed that the University be named as an agency of the government to help in defense endeavors. He said that he was counting upon the immediate cooperation and overwhelming support of students and faculty in the matter and warned, "Those who prefer to fiddle while Rome burns, or accelerate the pace of destruction by building private bonfires, shall get little sympathy from me. . . . It may be necessary to have some of them defer their enjoyment of an education at the state's expense." [22]

Early in the fall, President Roosevelt called the National Guard to active duty, and it took many members of the faculty, student body, and administrative staff of the University. Other qualified men volunteered. Passage of the Selective Service Act in September resulted in further reduction of student and teaching ranks. In the ensuing academic year, the total male University enrollment dropped by more than two thousand, although Roosevelt's advice to young people was to consider it their "patriotic duty to continue the normal course of their education unless and until they are called, so that they will be well-prepared for greatest usefulness to their country." [23]

President Sproul gave the same advice during a University meeting in September, 1940, where again he pledged the full resources of the University to the service of the President and Congress of the United States in the national emergency. That pledge could involve, he said, shifts in curricula to give more emphasis to vocational and professional subjects. It could also mean (and eventually did) an acceleration of the instruction program so that trained men could be available for national service more rapidly and students would have a better opportunity to complete their education before being called to service. Not content with enlisting only the University of California in the cause of national defense, Sproul called educators and civil leaders from all over the state to Berkeley in October, 1940, for discussions on the relation of education to the national emergency.

During most of 1941, the United States was officially neutral, although the lend-lease program, enacted in the spring of the year, made it possible to send defense materials to Great Britain and, later, Russia. In August, Sproul assumed leadership of a committee organizing Fight for Freedom, Inc., a group that supported American foreign policy to the limit and beyond—advocating direct military intervention to defeat the Axis in Europe. Under the auspices of Fight for Freedom, Sproul was heard on the radio near the end of the month, urging Californians to form or join local chapters of the organization and asking how "some among us" can "advocate that we stand idle while the catastrophe we can prevent occurs before our eyes? How can they ignore . . . a lesson written in the epitaphs of twelve nations?" [24] Pacifists and neutralists protested that Sproul's radio addresses were an abuse of his University office, even though he had carefully indicated that he spoke for himself and not for the institution. Newspapers throughout the state supported his views and Governor Culbert Olson not only endorsed Sproul's views but also suggested in a barb to the pacifists that freedom of speech should not be limited to the isolationists.[25]

AN ARSENAL OF KNOWLEDGE

Response to President Sproul's pledge to support the national defense effort with the full resources of the University was almost imperceptible at first. Through informal, largely personal contacts with scientific colleagues working on military problems in the East, a few professors at the University became involved in defense research in the summer or early fall of 1940. There was enough of this activity by October for President Sproul to close some laboratories at Berkeley and Los Angeles to foreign visitors.[26] He also authorized the locking of laboratory doors for "either secrecy or safety." [27] At UCLA, the National Academy of Sciences asked Professor Vern O. Knudsen to make a study of the adequacy of the United States Navy's anti-submarine detection systems. Following preliminary research in the fall and winter of 1940, intensive research under Knudsen's direction at a special laboratory in San Diego began in the spring of the following year. In November, 1940, two young assistant professors of physics at Berkeley, Luis Alvarez and Edwin M. McMillan, were granted leave to do "war defense work" on radar at the Massachusetts Institute of Technology.[28]

Another visitor to MIT that fall was Robert M. Underhill, secretary and treasurer of the Board of Regents. During his visit he inspected the radar laboratory, where he saw perhaps a hundred people engaged in what he was told was important secret defense research. Underhill was not equipped by education or inclination to grasp the scientific significance of what he saw, but he understood immediately the business and administrative implications for a university that operated such large-scale research programs. He was easily impressed, therefore, when his host, the treasurer of MIT, warned him that the University of California would surely be involved in such research in the future and that he had better get ready to manage the business end of it.[29] On his return to Berkeley, he conferred immediately with President Sproul and, at Sproul's suggestion, with the Finance Committee of the Regents.[30]

President Sproul announced one result of these discussions to the public on January 24, 1941. At a press conference, he said that the University was entering into the national defense program in many ways. The University was placing the cyclotron and its products at the disposal of the federal government and was cooperating with the aircraft industry in training skilled workmen and providing teachers of skilled labor. It was offering short courses for engineers and conducting research on methods of lessening bleeding and shock from wounds, on respiratory illnesses, and on mosquito control. The University was training weathermen for the Army, Navy, and United States Weather Bureau, and helping to mobilize people who spoke Russian, Chinese, and Japanese.

To coordinate all of this defense activity, the University formed a Defense Council,[31] with President Sproul as its chairman, Underhill as executive vice-chairman, and eight members: Amos U. Christie, Frederick W. Cozens, Stanley B. Freeborn, Ivan M. Linforth, Harry M. Showman, Edwin C. Voorhies, Roscoe A. Weaver, and George D. Louderback. The leadership of the committee was significant. By virtue of his office and his ability to speak clearly upon the great issues at stake, the President was able to mobilize the students and the faculty to the service of whatever course national preparedness would require the University to take. To the treasurer of the Regents fell the job of working behind the scenes to negotiate contracts for top-secret research as demanded by the military services, the National Defense Research Committee, and other agencies.

On the day before Pearl Harbor, Ernest O. Lawrence, the University's famous atomic scientist, met in Washington, D.C., with James B. Conant, president of Harvard and chairman of the National Defense Research Committee; Lyman Briggs, director of the United States Bureau of Standards; and Arthur H. Compton, chairman of the Department of Physics at the University of Chicago,[32] and learned that the President of the United States had decided to proceed with the development of an atomic bomb.[33] Lawrence had warmly encouraged such effort for several months. Vital to the endeavor would be continuation of work at Berkeley on the separation of the highly fissionable isotope uranium 235, but plutonium, discovered in the spring of 1941 by Glenn T. Seaborg and other scientists using the sixty-inch cyclotron at Berkeley, also had a fissionable isotope and thus suggested itself as an alternate fuel to uranium 235 for an atomic weapon. Lawrence convinced Conant and Compton that research should proceed on both isotopes simultaneously.[34] Production of plutonium in the quantities needed posed difficulties that Seaborg and another group of scientists would try to solve at the University of Chicago. These activities would have top priority and would command a desperate kind of diligence among the scientists involved, for Germany was already on the track of answers to the problems associated with the production of atomic weapons. If such weapons had to be created, they were convinced, it was in the interests of the free world that the United States make them first.

The big government contracts Underhill had been told to expect soon were flooding in. The first one, effective just twenty-four days after the Japanese attack on Pearl Harbor, was for $340,000 to support work that Lawrence had promised to pursue at Berkeley on the separation of uranium 235. That work was so promising that the government allocated $3,000,000 to it six months later. By May 1, 1943, the entire operation of the Radiation Laboratory at Berkeley was supported by the Manhattan Engineering District of the United States Army.[35] On the hills above the campus, a vast compound of laboratories was built. At its wartime peak the Radiation Laboratory employed 1250 workers and expenditure ran to $500,000 a month.[36]

In the summer of 1942, a group of scientists met regularly in a seminar room of the physics building, LeConte Hall, at Berkeley. Among them were Robert Server, Edward Teller, Hans Bethe, Emil Konopinski, and Felix Bloch. Their leader was J. Robert Oppenheimer, a tall string of-a-man known throughout the world of science for a mighty intellect and gentle humaneness. Working with a chalk on a blackboard, this small scientific task force prepared a preliminary blueprint for an atomic bomb.[37] By fall all they needed was a place to test their ideas. In November, 1942, Oppenheimer and McMillan from the University, and General Leslie R. Groves and Lieutenant Colonel W. H. Dudley of the Manhattan District investigated and rejected a site in a deep valley at Jamez Springs, New Mexico. Oppenheimer then suggested that they look at a boy's school located thirty miles from a ranch he owned in the same state. The four men immediately drove to this spot and agreed that it had the features they were looking for.[38] It was isolated and spacious with, it seemed at the time, sufficient buildings to house the staff and equipment contemplated for the project. On December 7, 1942, the owners of the Los Alamos Ranch School received notices that their property was being taken over by the War Department.[39]

Immediately after the site was secured, Oppenheimer and his colleagues began the difficult task of recruiting scientists and technicians for jobs that could not be described, at a place that could not be named, for a period of time that could not be predicted. Those who accepted lived for several years in a weird world of fictitious names, secrecy, and isolation. They could not travel beyond Santa Fe, New Mexico, without special permission. They could tell no one what they were doing. Their automobile licenses were issued to code numbers instead of names. Their address was just P.O. Box 1663, Santa Fe, New Mexico. If children were born, the same box number appeared as the place of birth on birth certificates. To that address came a cyclotron from Harvard University, Van de Graff generators from the University of Wisconsin, a Cockcroft-Walton accelerator from the University of Illinois, and carloads of technical equipment.[40]

In the spring of 1943, General Groves began negotiating with Treasurer

Underhill for a nonprofit contract to place control of the new laboratory in the hands of the University of California, with Oppenheimer as its director. These negotiations faltered from time to time because Groves' determination to keep the function of the laboratory a secret was matched exactly by Underhill's determination to know where it was and to have satisfaction that it was under proper business management.[41] By April 20, Underhill was given enough information to assure him of the importance of the project, and with his signature he at last placed the University in control of the laboratory retroactive to the preceding January.[42]

The remote laboratory on the mesas above Santa Fe was soon the center of massive scientific effort. Instead of thirty scientists, as initially expected, more than three thousand people eventually came. Among them, for varying periods, were Enrico Fermi, Neils Bohr, Hans Bethe, Edward Teller, Bruno Rossi, Sir James Chadwick, Edwin McMillan, Emilio Segrè, Joseph Kennedy, Luis Alvarez, and other famous pioneers of the nuclear age. Crude temporary housing was built for technicians and their families. Larger buildings were erected to house the gigantic machinery that was essential to atomic research.[43]

At the Coral Sea, Corregidor, North Africa, the Solomon Islands, Anzio, and Normandy, the war took its frightful course while the inhabitants of Los Alamos led their strange, remote lives in service to science and the instrument that might bring an early Allied victory. To similar ends, under less dramatic circumstances, the University directed other research efforts.

The development of sonar at the laboratories in San Diego started by Vern Knudsen gave American sailors a distinct edge in antisubmarine warfare in both the Atlantic and the Pacific. Thousands of lives and thousands of tons of combat and relief supplies escaped destruction because of its effectiveness. During the deadly first minutes of invasions from the sea, American soldiers gained an advantage from University scientists' suggestions concerning the most efficient hull shape and propulsion methods to be used for the landing craft that brought them ashore. They also benefited from research at Scripps Institution of Oceanography that made it possible to estimate, in advance and from considerable distance, the depth of water and ferocity of breakers along a coastline. University engineers conducted studies to improve antennas for naval communication equipment and to determine why some of the early mass-produced Liberty and Victory ships that carried supplies all over the world would sometimes crack in two while at sea. Allied pilots were helped by UCLA research on heating military aircraft cabins to keep crews and equipment in top efficiency condition and on ways to keep ice off of leading edges of airplane wings, tail surfaces, and antennas.

At Berkeley, metallurgists worked to make magnesium alloys, important to the aircraft industry, stronger and more malleable. At Hamilton Field, north of San Francisco, Berkeley engineers worked to strengthen runways for use by the giant airplanes that were developed during the war period.[44] In the field of medicine, research was conducted on epidemic diseases. A. P. Krueger, of the department of bacteriology, worked for seven years to train scientists as a traveling field unit to combat epidemic diseases only to find himself and his entire staff drafted in August, 1940, to continue their work for the Navy.[45] Engineers, anthropologists, and doctors worked together to improve artificial limbs for the more than seventeen thousand military amputees who would return from the war.[46] The San Francisco Medical Center also conducted research on the high-altitude bends, fatigue, dietary regimes, and applications of sulphonamide compounds for treating burns and wounds.

Agriculture's scientists improved food supplies with the development of the sugarbeet harvester and the improvement of processes for drying meats, vegetables, fruits, eggs, and milk. For civilians at home, they published how-to booklets on production of food for a family by growing victory gardens. One of the most spectacular contributions of the agriculturists was the demonstration that guayule, or native rubber, could be grown in California with sufficient success to relieve the rubber shortage caused by the loss of Malaya and the Netherlands East Indies to the Japanese.[47] Only the subsequent development of cheaper synthetic rubber forestalled an all-out effort at native rubber production.

The University's income from government contracts for the year ending June 30, 1942, was $1,560,000. It jumped to almost $8,250,000 the next year, to almost $23,000,000 in 1944, and to $25,952,483 by June 30, 1945. For the whole period 1940–1945, the University expended more than $57,000,000 on work authorized by 165 government contracts.[48]

ADJUSTMENTS ON THE CAMPUSES

On October 27, 1942, President Sproul wrote a letter to one of his principal advisers, Joel H. Hildebrand, professor of chemistry and dean of the College of Letters and Science at Berkeley. Sproul had read an article in an official publication of the United States Office of Education which urged that "college entrance requirements, as well as requirements for graduation from high school, need adjustment in wartime. The substitution of war service, war production, and other forms of participating work experience in critically needed occupations for class attendance may be encouraged, at least during the period of the war emergency. . . ." The same article called for a campaign by professional educators to "break down the existing prejudices in favor of the strictly academic college preparatory course," and asserted that state and regional accrediting systems "must adjust their requirements." [49] Sproul denounced the article as dictatorial and "very much like a declaration of war." [50] His reaction, shared completely by Hildebrand, revealed that there was, after all, a limit to the extent to which the University of California was prepared to render wartime service. That limit was reached when the desired service adulterated standards, or led the University upon a course incompatible with its basic function, hostile to scholarship, or repressive of freedom. Sproul regarded the government's advice on admissions policy for universities to be a step in the direction taken by the Nazis in the ruin of Germany's institutions of higher learning. Sproul wanted nothing of that sort to happen in America. To insure that it would not, he took prompt initiative to place the control of any wartime adjustments that had to be made by the University in the hands of its own faculty and administration.

On December 29, 1941, newspapers in California were reporting that a University War Council, composed of thirty administrators and faculty members on the Berkeley, Los Angeles, Davis, and San Francisco campuses, had already recommended major changes. Among them was the speeding up of instruction by substituting three sixteen-week semesters per year for the usual two longer ones; substituting "pass-fail" grading for the old As, Bs, Cs, Ds, and Fs to simplify record-keeping for students whose education could be interrupted at any time for military service; eliminating nonessential courses and instituting some that were specifically related to wartime needs; simplifying administration in every way possible so that less manpower would be required; and giving more emphasis to physical education.[51] Most of these recommendations were put into effect. The three-term calendar went into operation in June, 1942, and was not terminated until 1945. Courses like "Wartime Problems of the Food Industry," "Nutrition in Peace Time and War," and "Spherical Trigonometry and Navigational Astronomy" appeared in the catalogues.[52] Students were required to take at least one National Service Course from a list of offerings designed to train them for some form of emergency service.[53] Teaching staffs were placed on a six-day working week, and retired faculty members were brought back to the classrooms to replace men and women who left for military service or war research.[54]

The recommendation for "pass or fail" grading was not instituted. Instead, Emergency Executive Committees of the Northern and Southern Sections of the Academic Senate agreed upon policies that permitted partial credits under traditional grades for courses interrupted for military service.

To save administrative expense, no vice-president was named to replace UCLA's chief executive, Earle R. Hedrick, when he resigned in 1942. Between 1942 and 1945 UCLA was administered by an interim committee of faculty members that included Gordon S. Watkins, Bennet M. Allen, and J. Harold Williams.

The most obvious change on the campuses, of course, was a sudden decline in male population. Berkeley's prewar enrollment of 11,180 men dropped to 4274 in 1944–1945.[55] In the same period, UCLA's male enrollment dropped from 5107 to 2407.[56] In San Francisco, the schools of dentistry and medicine had an uninterrupted increase in enrollment because the military services, anticipating a need for trained doctors and dentists if the war was prolonged, placed many students in those schools on reserve status. But in the College of Pharmacy, male enrollment dropped from 117 to 26, and in Hastings College of the Law, the enrollment plummeted from 254 to 34.[57]

Some of the male enrollment consisted of men in service reserve units. Both the Army and the Navy in 1943 launched training programs for young men with officer potential. These men were selected from within the services and as the result of testing high school seniors. Characteristically, Army Service Trainees underwent an education that was developed and taught by the Army itself, using the University's facilities. The work was divided into three cycles that in no way coincided with the regular schedules of the University.[58] Emphasis in the curriculum was on personnel psychology, languages (Far Eastern and European at Berkeley; Chinese, German, and Italian at UCLA), basic engineering, advanced Reserve Officer Training Corps studies, and physical education.[59] The so-called Area and Language studies developed by the Army were so successful in giving students oral proficiency in short periods of time that they were adopted by colleges and universities after the war.[60]

Headquarters for the Army training program at Berkeley was Bowles Hall, whose civilian residents were redirected to housing in fraternity and rooming houses. In Los Angeles, the Army took over fraternities and nearby apartments to house trainees.[61]

The Navy's program for training reservists was geared to the normal operations of the University. Members of the regular faculty taught the courses, which were attended by civilian students as well as reservists.[62] The curriculum was drawn essentially from the University catalog and included basic pre-medicine, ROTC engineering, electrical engineering, and aeronautical engineering.[63] At Berkeley, the Naval reserve enrollment was as high as one thousand.[64] At UCLA, it was about six hundred at its peak.[65] Fraternity and boarding houses furnished lodging for the students enrolled in the Navy program at UCLA.[66] At Berkeley, the Navy took over International House and, for the duration of the war, rechristened it Callaghan Hall,[67] in memory of a former exective officer of the Naval Reserve Officers Training Corps who lost his life on the bridge of the USS *San Francisco* off Savo Island in the South Pacific in November, 1942.

While the Army reservists marched to class, the Navy reservists joined the regular student throngs. Because their schedules were not synchronized with the rest of the University, the Army reservists had few opportunities to participate in many student activities. Naval trainees, on the other hand, participated as actively as their studies would permit, and found their way into student-government posts and varsity athletic teams.

While the Army Service Training Program and the Navy programs represented the major military instruction efforts, the University engaged in others as well. As early as September, 1940, UCLA became one of five centers in the United States used to train servicemen in meteorology; as many as 1187 men were enrolled.[68] An Army Air Forces Pre-Meteorology Program began at Berkeley in March, 1943.[69] Between September, 1941, and September, 1943, 294 students selected by the Navy studied in the United States Navy Diesel Power Plants Training Course and were commissioned reserve officers of the Navy on active duty. Professor Carl Vogt of the Department of Mechanical Engineering at Berkeley was put on active duty by the Navy and made supervisor of the program.[70]

The most dramatic military invasion of a University campus occurred at Davis, where instruction was discontinued and the entire facility, including dormitories and fraternity houses, was converted into a training school for the Army Signal Corps beginning in February, 1943.[71]

The University's training facilities were not utilized for military instruction alone. Through University of California Extension, a special Engineering, Science and Management War Training Program was developed. For taking such courses as "Aircraft Drafting, Tool Engineering and Physical Testing of Petroleum Products," on a full-time basis, students were paid $100 a month. Other courses were offered to help men and women train for higher positions.[72]

University officials tried to keep the University atmosphere as normal as possible. Insofar as the war imposed responsibilities on all loyal citizens, it was not allowed to be forgotten or put in the background. On the other hand, nothing was to be gained by allowing tensions to increase needlessly. Almost all activities of student life were sustained in one form or another. When male leadership was unavailable, women students bravely took over. Student-body presidencies, editorships, and even the supermasculine position of sports editor fell into the hands of coeds. To their surprise and disappointment, men returning to the campus found things operating very well, thank you, and coeds have not at any time since the war relinquished their right to hold any job for which they are qualified.

Fraternities and sororities encountered special problems. The sororities and some fraternities lost their houses to military-service training units between 1943 and 1944. For fraternities it was a blessing in disguise. With their own members off to war, the lease of their facilities to the government kept them solvent during the war years. When the government didn't want their houses, they either boarded nonmembers or leased their facilities to sororities or some other dispossessed group of students. One fraternity in Los Angeles maintained clubrooms in downtown Westwood for meetings and fellowship. But by May, 1944, only about fifteen fraternity houses were still active, rushing, pledging, and initiating.[73]

Athletic programs continued but were curtailed. Berkeley traveled to southern California twice a year and UCLA traveled north once, but there were no rooters' trains, and only daytime travel was permitted. Squads were limited to twenty-eight players to cut down team traveling expenses. Another economy move was the abandonment of the training table, but the coaches were not too sad to see it go since many of their players were in the military service training programs and eating well enough in any case. One of the most appreciated blessings to athletes was the declaration of the government in September, 1943, that except for those used in basketball, sports shoes would not be rationed.[74]

Stanford discontinued fielding a football team during the war, and to make up for the loss of the Big Game, Stanford and Berkeley challenged each other to a war-bond contest. Their goal was to raise $175,000 between them to buy one B-25 bomber. California raised $195,042.75 and Stanford raised $185,861.10—winning on the basis of a ratio of population to sales.[75]

There are no reliable records on how many California students, faculty, and alumni served or lost their lives during World War II, although some hint is given by the fact that a flag honoring 17,007 in the services from the

Berkeley campus alone was dedicated in September, 1943, when the war was only about half over.[76]

A TASTE OF VICTORY

In the spring of 1945, the nations united in war against the Axis looked optimistically to victory and to the peace that would follow. To plan for that peace and its possible preservation through international organization, the United Nations conferred in San Francisco in April, 1945. Students and faculty on the Berkeley campus had a grand bay-window view of the international history that occurred in the ensuing weeks. Some of the faculty members were called upon to render assistance as translators and technical experts. Students obtained jobs as messengers and in performing other tasks for delegates. The United Nations Charter, in several languages, was designed and printed by the University of California Press. A special library was established at Berkeley to be used as a reference source for conference delegates.

On May 4, in the Greek Theatre, a United Nations convocation was assembled, and honorary degrees were presented to Edward R. Stettinius, United States secretary of state; Anthony Eden, prime minister of the United Kingdom; T. V. Soong, acting prime minister of the Republic of China: Jan Christian Smuts, prime minister of the Union of South Africa; Ezequiel Padilla, foreign minister of Mexico; and George Bidault, minister of foreign affairs of the Provisional Government of France.

The conference was still in session when, on May 8, Germany surrendered. The news was greeted solemnly at both UCLA and Berkeley. At UCLA, someone announced the dismissal of classes over the Royce Hall address system, but Provost Clarence A. Dykstra urged the students to temper their joy with the realization "that neither total victory, nor the peace have been won yet." [77] At Berkeley, classes were held as usual, and leading faculty members expressed sentiments similar to those of Provost Dykstra.

THE FEARFUL LOAD

Late in the night of July 15, 1945, Edward Teller had just finished some last calculations in his laboratory at Los Alamos. On his way home he met a fellow scientist and asked, "Are you coming out to the explosion?" His friend said he was. There were snakes at the explosion site, and the scientists had been warned to watch for them. Teller asked his colleague what he was going to do about snakes. "I'll take a bottle of bourbon along," he announced. Teller then mentioned some concern he had as a result of the work he had been doing earlier in the evening. There was a possibility something important might have been overlooked, and the explosion could be adversely affected. "What," he asked, "do you think should be done?" His friend said, "I'll take another bottle." [78]

Early the next morning, Teller and other scientists and technicians were gathered in the desert of Jornada del Muerto, 250 miles south of Los Alamos.[79] In the center of the explosion site stood a tall tower. At the top of it hung a fat bomb, poised for explosion initiated by a device that used plutonium 239 as the detonating element.[80] Teller's group was some twenty miles away.[81] Much closer, in a control shelter, J. Robert Oppenheimer and a few others nervously awaited the clearing of a light rainfall that had already postponed the test for more than an hour. The test-announcer finally shouted "now," and there was a growling roar and an incredibly brilliant light that was seen up to 180 miles away.[82] A cloud rose to the stratosphere. The scientists watched it for a while and contemplated the size of the enormous crater that had been made in the desert by the explosion. After about an hour they got onto buses and, en route back to Los Alamos, regarded what they had done with a sober sense of achievement. They had created and successfully tested the world's first atomic bomb—the job they had come to Los Alamos to do.

On August 7, another version of the bomb, detonated by a uranium-235 device, was dropped over Hiroshima, Japan, and the world, for the first time, knew of the horror and devastation that nuclear weapons could cause. President Truman called upon Japan to surrender or suffer a "rain of ruin" from the air. On August 9, when no surrender had been received, an atomic bomb of the type first exploded in the New Mexican desert was dropped on Nagasaki. Five days later Japan surrendered.

The final victory was announced at 4 P.M., August 14.[83] The staff of the *Daily Californian* had awaited the news for three days and only one Bay Area newspaper beat it to the streets with a peace "extra." Patriotic songs rang from the Campanile, and a serpentine formed behind the marching band and wound its way down Shattuck Avenue, waving to Berkeley residents, throwing firecrackers, honking horns, and singing songs. At Oxford Hall, students proclaimed the news with a sign hung from their windows, threw water and confetti onto the street below, and then came down to build a large bonfire on the streetcar tracks that ran in front of their building.[84]

At UCLA, things were relatively quiet because the news came in the late afternoon when many students had gone home, but those who were there packed cars "far beyond the point of overflow" and streamed toward Westwood, honking horns and making as much noise as they could. Routed from a rehearsal, the University band gave a spontaneous concert of patriotic and University songs in front of the men's gym.[85]

President Sproul was abroad when the surrender came—acting as adviser to Edwin W. Pauley, United States member of the Reparations Commission of the United Nations. In his place, Vice-President Monroe Deutsch spoke simply for the University when he greeted the peace. He said, "How can we have other than hearts full of joy at the good news . . . ?" [86] The next day was declared an official holiday.

For the University of California, World War II was not just an episode to be endured and forgotten. It brought about permanent changes in the way the University was regarded by the public and the way it regarded itself. Requirements of the war efforts gave the University a part in one of the most dramatic demonstrations in the history of the world that research is more than a professorial hobby. With the Radiation Laboratory and Los Alamos examples as precedents, the sights of those seeking and granting money for research were raised to levels that were inconceivable in the 1930s. The pattern of research shifted from that of a professor assisted by his graduate students to that of teams of scholars, assisted not only by graduate students but also by large staffs of nonacademic personnel. This scale of research activity helped the University absorb large numbers of new graduate students after the war, particularly in engineering and the natural sciences. But the scale could not be sustained out of old prewar sources of financial support. The federal government and industry had, whether they intended to or not, become permanent partners of the University.

The wartime efforts to preserve normalcy in "student life" on the campuses of the University were not entirely successful. Traditions that depended upon the continuity of male leadership faltered. Activities that required large numbers of dedicated participants to be successful had to abandon the "up and out" recruiting and promotion systems of the prewar years and make do with the people at hand. Then too, the war itself was so overwhelming in its character and implications that student activities fell into a fairly low position on the scale of student values. By the end of the war, the way was clear for a new generation to reshape student life without regard for tradition.

Finally, because wartime is always a period of retrenchment for civilian activities, the University's efforts to solve problems of continuing growth, administrative efficiency, and relations with other higher-education institutions could not be as vigorous as they should have been. Catching up and meeting unanticipated new demands required extraordinary efforts in the postwar period.

Chapter 20

A TEST OF LOYALTY

TO PROSPER IN the decade immediately following World War II, the University of California needed friends. Its facilities, neglected to some extent during the Depression and the war, had to be repaired. It had to accommodate the shockwave of veterans who would come as students under the GI Bill. Its work in every field of knowledge was becoming more specialized, more profound, and more expensive. To catch up and keep pace with the demands of the age, the University's expenditures would go up threefold between 1944–1945 and 1954–1955.[1] To obtain the sufficient appropriations, the University needed the maximum confidence of the public and the legislature.

But those were not confident times. Many Americans were preoccupied with the possibility that undercover agents of hostile powers might assume control of the country's assembly lines, professions, and centers of education and research. A few espionage agents of the Soviet Union were, in fact, found in the United States and exposed with unsettling publicity. How many more were there? Where would they be found next? To find out, special committees were formed in trade and professional associations, in veterans' organizations, and in federal, state, and local governments. Their exemplars were Joseph McCarthy, United States Senator from Wisconsin, and the Un-American Activities Committee of California under State Senator Jack B. Tenney.

The search involved almost all American institutions, including the University of California. There, investigators pointed out, professors were entrusted with the soft putty of young minds. At the University, large numbers of scientists once collaborated on the super-secret atomic bomb and were still at work on mysterious instruments vital to the nation's defense. To make sure the University was free of subversive taint, the dead embers of the student radical movements of the Depression years were raked over, as were the activities of student pacifists in the years immediately preceding World War II. The case of Kenneth May, a young mathematics teaching assistant who was fired in 1940 because the Regents believed his commitments as a member of the Communist party were "incompatible with membership in the faculty of a State University," [2] was reentered in the record.

Memories of those prewar occurrences influenced the attitude with which Californians appraised the actions of a small group of UCLA students who joined a picket line in front of Warner Brothers Studio in Hollywood in October, 1945. Some of them carried banners that read: UCLA STUDENTS PROTEST PRODUCER VIOLENCE,[3] and some of the students involved were members of the UCLA's chapter of American Youth for Democracy, an organization considered a Communist front. Throughout November a legislative committee investigated the strike. Among the witnesses were several UCLA faculty members and the provost on that campus, Clarence Dykstra. This attention acutely embarrassed the Regents, and at their meeting in December, 1945, Lieutenant Governor Houser said that the students' action had "done great harm to the University in the Legislature" and that if the matter went unexplained and the Regents did not take action he was very doubtful if the University would receive "one-half of the funds requested for postwar buildings and perhaps would get nothing." [4]

On behalf of Regent Dickson, who was absent from the meeting, Houser then introduced the following resolutions:

> The basis of education and instruction at the University of California shall be loyalty to American institutions and to the American system of government. Any member of the faculty violating this principle shall be subject to dismissal.
>
> No student shall engage in any off-campus activity in which he shall do anything intended to or which does convey the impression that he represents the University or the student body, without first securing the written permission of the duly constituted University authority. Violation of this rule shall be cause for dismissal.[5]

The proposed resolutions were referred to a special Regents' committee that reported on January 4, 1946. The committee's version was less strident, but no less clear in its intent:

FIRMLY BELIEVING that the purpose for which universities exist is the search for truth in all fields of knowledge and its dissemination as widely as possible,

AND BELIEVING FURTHER that this purpose is best attained under a democratic form of government, which at the same time gives greater freedom and opportunity to men than any other,

THEREFORE, BE IT RESOLVED that any member of the faculty or student body seeking to alter our American government by other than constitutional means or to induce others to do so, shall, on proof of such charge, be subject to dismissal.[6]

No one was fired, but the Regents were on record once more with a policy unreservedly hostile to subversion.

UN-AMERICAN ACTIVITIES COMMITTEE REVELATIONS

Despite the Regents' firm action following the film strike incident, the University's supposed vulnerability to subversive influence continued to be a lively issue. A portion of Senator Tenney's Committee on Un-American Activities report issued in 1947 dealt with the way schools sponsored by the Communist party were "able to secure a certain degree of collaboration from faculty members of the University of California at Berkeley and at Los Angeles." [7] Among the witnesses it had called were "a number of the professors who had lectured at the People's Educational Center in Los Angeles." [8] Although one of these professors, Dean McHenry, the future first chancellor at Santa Cruz, was lauded by Tenney's committee for his "bold, frank and clear-cut stand" [9] in condemning communism, newspapers throughout the state tended to conclude that the mere attendance of the professors at the committee's hearings gave indication that there were, indeed, radicals on the University faculty.

The YMCAs and YWCAs associated with University of California were also targets of the committee. As a matter of policy, these organizations, with no University affiliation, allowed their facilities to be used by speakers and student groups of all political complexions. The Un-American Activities Committee objected that, because of their names, the organizations tended to mislead the public to the belief that the University itself endorsed or sponsored political programs that took place on their premises. A direct legislative attack on this problem was made in April, 1947, when the Education Code of California was amended to make it a misdemeanor for any person to use the name of the University or any abbreviation of it without the permission of the Regents.

The 1948 report of California's Senate Un-American Activities Committee was devoted to Communist-front organizations. It named a score or more University professors, students, or former students who had been involved, however remotely or innocently, with the groups under study. The most sensational portion of the report, however, was an excerpt from the testimony of Haakon M. Chevalier, a former assistant professor of French at Berkeley, who was alleged in the press and other reports to be active in the Communist movement, which indicated that he was not only acquainted with the University's J. Robert Oppenheimer, the man who directed the construction of the first atomic bomb, but also had once intended to enlist that distinguished physicist in the service of communism.[10]

Whatever their intent, the 1947 and 1948 reports of the Tenney committee helped to erode public confidence in the University of California. They did so just by giving the University and people associated with it scrupulous attention. Their revelations were not, in and of themselves, particularly damaging.

Near the opening of the 1949 session of the legislature, Tenney introduced thirteen bills, all designed to "isolate, expose and remove from positions of power and influence persons who are a dangerous menace to our freedom and security." [11] Among them was a bill making the teaching of communism, nazism, and fascism in the schools a misdemeanor. Another required all state employees to sign a disclaimer of membership in the Communist party. But the one most disconcerting to the University at the time was a proposed constitutional amendment (Senate Constitutional Amendment 13) that would give the legislature power to insure the loyalty of officers and employees of the University of California. The Regents resisted this measure out of a determination that their own constitutional prerogatives in the management of the University not be eroded. James H. Corley, comptroller of the University and its representative in Sacramento, believed that passage of the amendment could be forestalled if the Regents clearly preempted jurisdiction over loyalty matters on the campuses. In January, 1949, he suggested to President Sproul that one way to make this preemption would be to require the faculty and all other employees of the University to sign statements of their loyalty and disclaimers of commitments to any organization that would illegally overthrow the United States government.

DYKSTRA'S THORNY PROBLEMS

On February 1, 1949, the Regents of the University of Washington dismissed two of its faculty members, Herbert J. Phillips and Joseph Butterworth. Both men had previously admitted to a faculty committee that they were currently members of the Communist party. Their case was nationally significant because it was a challenge to the well-known position then held by the American Association of University Professors that "there is . . . nothing in the nature of the teaching profession which requires the automatic exclusion of Communists, and the attempt to exclude them would threaten our educational system." [12]

A few weeks after his dismissal from the University of Washington, Professor Phillips appeared in a debate at UCLA on the subject of whether a member of the Communist party could also be an objective teacher and impartial scholar. The debate was sponsored by the Graduate Student Association, with the permission of Provost Dykstra, on condition that only graduate students and faculty members be allowed to attend.

Undergraduates and some faculty members at UCLA immediately protested this restriction, and their protests gradually became amplified into the larger issue of the validity of the University's regulations, formulated by the President as early as 1933 to govern use of University facilities. Many students regarded the regulations as improperly and unnecessarily restrictive of discussion of political and religious issues on campus. As a result of these protests, the debate made the Los Angeles papers and came prominently to the attention of some of the Regents. Regent Edward Dickson, chairman of the Board, "father of UCLA," and a political conservative of long standing, took a keen interest in the situation and joined other Regents, at their meeting on February 25, in criticism of Dykstra for allowing Phillips to appear on campus. Dykstra's defense came from the first president of the UCLA Alumni Association to serve as a Regent—Paul Hutchinson. Regent Hutchinson contended that the problem was not one of the provost's judgment as much as it was one of ambiguous rules. Instead of taking any action against Dykstra in February, therefore, the Regents asked him to appear in April to explain his decision. They also named Hutchinson as chairman of a special committee to study regulation of political activities on the campus and the use of University facilities.[13]

During these same weeks, Provost Dykstra was troubled by another potentially explosive problem. On January 26, 1949, UCLA's Institute of Industrial Relations and the political science department had asked for authorization to invite British economist and political scientist Harold J. Laski, a prominent and articulate member of the British Labour party, to deliver two lectures on the campus. Dykstra agreed to Laski's appearance under the impression that he would be speaking at Berkeley as well. When he learned several weeks later that his understanding was wrong, he tried to find out if Laski's appearance would have had Sproul's blessings if the visitor's schedule had permitted a Berkeley engagement. President Sproul did not give a direct answer until March 21, when he told Dykstra that "the appearance of Laski on our campus would not be pleasing to the Board of Regents because some have charged Laski with being ultra-left and the Regents have a very firm policy as to Communists and alleged Communists." [14] On the strength of that opinion, Dykstra withdrew the permission to use University facilities for Laski's lecture and it was rescheduled in the Embassy Auditorium off-campus.

THE SANTA BARBARA SOLUTION

On March 25, 1949, the Regents gathered for a regular meeting in Santa Barbara. The big question was what could be done to bolster the University's loyalty stock, which seemed to be depreciating rapidly. President Sproul, whose patriotism roared through every public utterance and whose love for the University was that of an alumnus as well as its chief executive, found any suspicion of taint, however ill-founded, intolerable. He suggested that a positive demonstration of the University's loyalty to the nation was needed. Since 1942, the Regents had required all University employees to sign an oath of allegiance to the constitutions of the United States and California. The wording of the oath was identical to that prescribed for all public officers of the state under Article XX, Section 3, of the state constitution. Sproul now proposed that, in addition to affirming this constitutional oath, University employees be required to disclaim membership or commitments to any cause advocating unlawful overthrow of the government of the United States. The Regents thought well enough of this suggestion to have their attorney, John U. Calkins, with the help of Comptroller Corley, draft a proper declaration during the lunch hour. That afternoon, the Regents voted unanimously to adopt an oath for University employees, to take the following form:

> I do solemnly swear (or affirm) that I will support the Constitution of the United States and the Constitution of the State of California, and

that I will faithfully discharge the duties of my office according to the best of my ability; that I do not believe in, and I am not a member of, nor do I support any party or organization that believes in, advocates, or teaches the overthrow of the United States Government, by force or by any illegal or unconstitutional methods.[15]

If all, or almost all, members of the faculty and other employees promptly signed the new oath, President Sproul would have a pat and potent rejoinder for those who might continue to feed public hysteria with charges that the University was riddled with Communists. He was so sure that the new oath was uncontroversial that he made no special announcement of its adoption, and the faculty first learned officially of its existence in a fairly routine message from Robert M. Underhill, secretary of the Regents, printed in the May issue of the *Faculty Bulletin*. His message said only that signature of the new oath would be required as a part of the procedure for accepting appointments for 1949–1950 and that "salary checks cannot be released until acceptance letters have been returned to this office properly signed before a Notary Public." [16] The wording of the oath was not quoted. It was not known by most members of the faculty until just before the last Academic Senate meeting of the year in early June—ten weeks after the Regents' action at Santa Barbara.

RESISTANCE

There was no prolonged discussion of the oath on June 7, 1949, when the Northern Section of the Academic Senate held its regular meeting. There was only an announcement that a special meeting was to be held a week later to consider a resolution on the subject. The resolution thus advertised was formally heard by four hundred members of the senate on June 14 and was offered by Edward Chace Tolman, one of the nation's best-known psychologists, then in his thirty-first year as a member of the Berkeley faculty. His resolution assured the Regents that the members of the senate were loyal to the state and nation but that they objected to the sudden imposition of a further test of loyalty that might threaten academic freedom and tenure. The ultimate thrust of the resolution, though, was a request that the Regents delete from the traditional oath the amendments they had adopted at Santa Barbara on March 25.[17]

In the debate on Tolman's resolution, the arguments that would be heard again and again in the months ahead were given form: The wording of the Regents' oath was imprecise and ambiguous; the amendment was a redundancy, its intent having been already embraced by the broader constitu-

tional oath; signatures were being obtained under threat of loss of employment and were, therefore, not valid; the oath was ineffective. Anyone determined to destroy the nation would not hesitate to sign the Regents'
disclaimer. The oath also treated the wrong patient; while the country was
sick with hysteria, it was prescribed to purge the University of an infection
that could not be proved to exist and, if it actually did exist, was probably
innocuous. The oath was discriminatory; it singled out University employees for a test of loyalty that was applied to no one else.[18] The abrogation of
democratic faculty self-government implicit in the Regents' imposition of
the oath engendered further opposition among the faculty, and led some
men to charge that the oath itself was a first step toward nazism. Those with
a pragmatic turn of mind objected that the oath introduced a criterion of
professional competence hitherto considered incompatible with the University's tradition of faculty tenure.

Some faculty members supported the Regents' course and urged their colleagues to realize that the University faced problems with the legislature
and a misinformed public. Their signatures on an oath might be an important gesture in quashing criticism from superpatriots and witch-hunters.

At the end of the debate, the Tolman resolution was finally passed—
with important amendments. Originally, it requested deletion of the Regents' March 25 amendment to the constitutional oath. As passed, it requested deletion *or revision* of that amendment. Another change in the
original Tolman resolution directed the Senate's Advisory Committee to
work with the president of the University to find a solution to the oath problem.[19]

THE FACULTY TAKES THE INITIATIVE

The Advisory Committees were standing units of the two divisions of the
Academic Senate. In the north, the members were Joel Hildebrand, dean of
the College of Chemistry at Berkeley; Benjamin H. Lehman, professor of
English at Berkeley; and H. B. Walker, professor of agricultural engineering at Davis. In the south, all members were from UCLA. They were Martin
R. Huberty, professor of irrigation; Hugh Miller, professor of philosophy;
and John W. Olmsted, professor of history. In 1949–1950 Hildebrand was
succeeded by William R. Dennes, professor of philosophy, and Miller was
replaced by Gordon S. Watkins, professor of economics.[20] The Berkeley
Advisory Committee, under Hildebrand's leadership, moved first. On June
18, 1949, Professors Hildebrand and Lehman (Walker was in the East) met

with President Sproul. They asked for assurance that the normal procedures governing faculty privilege and tenure would be followed in any case that might arise from the oath issue, and they recommended that the oath be separated from letters of contract in order to remove the element of duress.

Hildebrand and Lehman then stated the possible effects of the oath:

> There are loyal, respected and distinguished members of the faculty who have announced that they will not swear to the second part of the oath as it now stands. Others have stated that they would sign but would immediately look for other positions. These are no idle threats. To lose able, loyal and conscientious men for such a cause would constitute a terrible blow to the distinction of the University.
>
> We believe it will not be difficult to make plain to the people of California the fundamental loyalty of the members of the faculty without recourse to devices which are probably illegal and certainly destructive of morale and injurious to the University.[21]

The Berkeley Advisory Committee offered two alternatives. The first would be a return to the oath required before March 25, supplemented by a statement of University policy to the effect that:

> It is the policy of the University not to employ nor to retain in its service any person whose commitments or obligations conflict with the free pursuit of knowledge or with the American system of free representative government. *Any person who is or who shall become a member of the Communist party, or who otherwise advocates doctrines or undertakes obligations inconsistent with this policy shall,* after the facts have been established by the University Administration and upon advice of the Committee on Privilege and Tenure of the Academic Senate, be deemed to have severed his connections with the University.[22]

The second alternative, to be invoked only "should the public relations of the University make an amplification of the [constitutional] oath . . . indispensable," would be a new clause to state " 'that I am not under any oath, nor a party to any agreement, nor as a member of any party or organization am I under any commitment, that is in conflict with my obligations under this oath.' "[23]

Hildebrand reviewed these deliberations with the Southern Section of the Academic Senate at a meeting on June 20. Then, on the motion of Carl Epling, vice-chairman-elect of the southern division, a resolution precisely parallel to that presented by Professor Tolman at Berkeley on June 14 was passed unanimously. The next day, members of the Southern Section's Advisory Committee wrote to President Sproul to express unanimous concurrence in the Hildebrand-Lehman-Walker memorandum of June 18.[24] If Sproul realized that only the Southern Section had heard the full content of the memorandum, that fact did not bother him. His complete faith in the northern Advisory Committee and his own estimate of the attitudes of the faculty suggested that the June 18 memorandum was a sound guide to an early solution of the oath dispute.

THE REGENTS TRY AGAIN

When the Regents gathered in Los Angeles for their June meeting, their primary concern was the problem of revising University regulations on the use of facilities and determining a new policy toward communism. At least two of the Regents, John Francis Neylan, an influential San Francisco attorney, and Farnham Griffiths, an outstanding attorney who was once President Wheeler's secretary, were not convinced at this point that a special oath was needed at the University. On June 23, these two drafted a statement of the University's policy toward communism which was considered that afternoon by a special committee under the chairmanship of Regent Hutchinson. This draft omitted reference to an oath, but Sproul urged that such a statement be included.

At the regular meeting of the Regents the next day, the Hutchinson committee's report was given. It declared the University to be dedicated to the "search for truth and its full exposition," and committed the Regents to the protection of the freedom of the University. It took note that freedom was menaced by the Communist party and reaffirmed the Regents' policy of 1940 that "no member of the Communist Party shall be employed by the University." Should any case arise on the faculty where this policy had to be enforced, procedures were outlined for the adequate safeguard of privilege and tenure as recommended by the Advisory Committee in its June 18 memorandum. Then, almost as an afterthought, the report resolved:

> And to implement the above stated policy, that the following oath be subscribed to by all members of the faculty, employees and administration of the University:
> "I do solemnly swear (or affirm) that I will support the Constitution of the United States and the Constitution of the State of California, and that I will faithfully discharge the duties of my office according to the best of my ability; that I am not a member of the Communist Party or under any oath, or a party to any agreement, or

under any commitment that is in conflict with my obligation under oath." [25]

The new policy was adopted *in toto* by a unanimous vote.

THE NON-SIGNERS ORGANIZE

The Regents' Communist Policy Statement on June 24, 1949, contained much of the language that first appeared in the memorandum to President Sproul from the Advisory Committee of the Northern Section on June 18. Even the new oath was—but for the words "I am not a member of the Communist Party"—this Advisory Committee's composition. But all that mattered to many professors was that the faculty resolutions calling for deletion of the March 25 oath had been disregarded, and that instead of working toward a solution of the oath controversy, the Berkeley Advisory Committee had inadvertently shown the way for the Regents to intensify it.

Faculty opposition to the new oath became known almost immediately. As early as June 27, about sixty professors met at the Faculty Club in Berkeley, where they protested the failure of the Advisory Committee to secure ratification of its own June 18 recommendations and declared themselves under no obligation to support its actions. Members of the Academic Senate in both the north and the south were urged not to sign the oath until the senate could meet to review the matter.

By September 6, signed oaths had been returned from only 50 per cent of those who had received them at Berkeley; 70 per cent at Davis; 40 per cent at Los Angeles; 100 per cent at Mount Hamilton; none at La Jolla; 100 per cent at Riverside; and an unspecified number at San Francisco.[26] Even when it was known that faculty members who did not sign the oath were not receiving letters of appointment, the rate of signatures was low.

The faculty's resistance utterly ruined the oath's value as a device to demonstrate to the public that University professors were above suspicion in loyalty matters. Many outsiders, however, were convinced that the oath was an undeserved assault on the freedom and dignity of the University's professors. People of this persuasion were found in large numbers among the faculties of the country's colleges and universities—an element of the population the University of California could alienate only with great risk.

At the urging of Professor Lehman, who had succeeded Hildebrand as chairman of the Northern Section's Advisory Committee, Sproul began to consider ways to withdraw the oath in September, 1949. But by that time it was too late. Regents and a large segment of the faculty were already adversaries. Neither side was willing to give in without concessions.

Resolutions passed by the Academic Senate in November gave new issues to the controversy. One of them suggested that the faculty had reservations about the Regents' policy against employing members of the Communist party. The other suggested that the Regents should give more adequate recognition to the role of faculty self-government and should exercise "a high degree of deference to faculty judgment in matters, such as qualifications for membership, which are peculiarly within the competence of the faculty." [27]

Particularly angered by the faculty's attitude was John Francis Neylan, who held a pivotal assignment in the oath controversy, having succeeded Regent Maurice E. Harrison as chairman of the Regents' special committee on conference with the faculty on the issue. Neylan's principal objective in the ensuing months was to convince the faculty that it should unequivocally approve the Regents' policy against the employment of members of the Communist party. His chief obstacle in that effort was the faculty's conference committee, under the chairmanship of Professor J. A. C. Grant of UCLA's Department of Political Science and Professor Malcolm Davisson of the Department of Economics at Berkeley. This committee was unwilling to discuss the oath itself until the Regents' policy against hiring Communists as members of the faculty was altered. With the regrettable experiences of the faculty Advisory Committee in mind, the Grant-Davisson committee also made progress difficult by refusing to negotiate on terms not clearly endorsed by the Academic Senate. The Regents' and faculty conference committees were still so far from agreement in January, 1950, that a motion by Neylan that his committee be dissolved was unanimously approved by the Board.

During the ensuing month, President Sproul sought a moderate position toward the oath that would be acceptable to the Regents and the faculty. He did not succeed, and, on February 24, 1950, the Board adopted a lengthy resolution containing the following paragraphs:

The Regents . . . give notice that a condition precedent to employment or renewal of employment in the University shall be execution of an oath in the form prescribed on June 24, 1949, or the equivalent affirmation that the appointee is not a member of the Communist Party, or under any oath or commitment, or a party to any agreement that is in conflict with the policy of the Regents excluding Communists from membership in the faculty of the University. Such oath or affirmation shall accompany the letter of acceptance of appointment and shall be a part thereof.

Each appointee will be notified that if an acceptance of appointment on the terms stated is not received by the Secretary of the Regents on or before April 30, 1950, he will be deemed to have severed his connection with the University as of June 30, 1950.[28]

The Regents' action of February 24, by a twelve-to-six vote, came to be known as "the sign-or-get-out ultimatum." The resolution's effect on the faculty was to unify it, for the ultimatum, for the first time, indicated that faculty members would be fired not for disloyalty to their country, or incompetence in their professions, but for insubordination to the will of the Regents. While many faculty members personally endorsed the Regents' policy on the hiring of Communist party members, very few accepted the ultimatum as a proper way to deal with the faculty on the matter. To coordinate their opposition with that of the Grant-Davisson committee, committees of seven were organized by the deans and department chairmen at Berkeley and Los Angeles.

Faculty opposition to the oath received potent support from the immensely popular Governor Earl Warren, who criticized the oath as an oath "any Communist would take . . . and laugh." [29] On March 4, 1950, President Sproul first made public his own reversal of opinion with respect to the oath, saying that "the welfare of the University would not be served by insisting upon a special form of oath as the single method of implementing, through the faculty, the Regents' policy of excluding Communists from University employment." [30] In the same statement he said ". . . this method [the oath] is regarded as a violation of both privilege and principle by many members of the faculty in whose loyalty I have complete confidence and for whom I hold the deepest respect and affection." [31] Another champion of the faculty cause was Monroe E. Deutsch, vice-president emeritus of the University, who enjoyed considerable popularity among the faculty, students, and alumni.

Given the impression by some statements of the Regents that the Board might be persuaded to rescind the oath if the faculty would endorse the Regents' 1940 policy on the employment of Communists, John D. Hicks, head of the Berkeley committee of seven, and other faculty leaders worked hard to obtain such endorsement. They achieved it in the Northern Section by a mail ballot vote of 724 to 203 in favor of a resolution that contained these words: "No person whose commitments or obligations to any organization, Communist or other, prejudice impartial scholarship and the free pursuit of truth will be employed by the University. Proved members of the Communist Party, by reason of such commitments to that Party, are not acceptable as members of the Faculty." [32]

At the Regents' meeting of March 31, however, the faculty members found Regent Neylan as unrelenting as ever. He denied that he had ever offered to have the oath rescinded in return for the faculty's compromise effort. After several hours of bitter argument, a motion to rescind the oath was put before the Board. Regents Brodie Ahlport, Samuel Collins, Edward Dickson, L. M. Giannini, Fred M. Jordan, Goodwin Knight, Arthur McFadden, William G. Merchant, Neylan, and Norman V. Sprague voted no. Regents Sidney Ehrman, Earl Fenston, Farnham Griffiths, Cornelius Haggerty, Victor Hansen, Edward Heller, Roy Simpson, Sproul, Jesse Steinhart, and Governor Warren voted aye. The motion thus failed on a ten-to-ten vote.

As the deadline for signing the oath came nearer, Sproul sought new alternatives to the "sign-or-get-out ultimatum." Faculty committees in both the north and the south worked toward the same ends. Their progress was frustratingly insignificant.

THE ALUMNI COMPROMISE

Early in 1950, the California Alumni Association's governing board authorized its president, Regent William Hale, to appoint a committee to study the oath dispute and recommend action to the council. Appointed on March 7, the committee included Stephen D. Bechtel, president and director of the Bechtel Construction Corporation, San Francisco, as chairman; Paul Davies, president of Food Machinery and Chemical Corporation, San Jose; Dr. William Deamer, professor at Berkeley (later succeeded by Donald H. McLaughlin, president of Homestake Mining Corporation); Milton H. Esberg, Jr., partner in a San Francisco public relations firm; and Mrs. Kathryn Fletcher, Berkeley civic leader.[33] Stanley E. McCaffrey, executive manager of the association, attended the meetings and frequently participated.

The committee's work was welcomed by the leaders of all factions in the dispute, and Professor Hicks, Regent Neylan, and others conferred with Bechtel on all of the issues. On April 13, President Sproul invited the committee to attempt to bring about some solution. The committee intensified its study on the basis of that request, reported to the Alumni Council on April 19, and forwarded its report to the President immediately thereafter.

After reviewing the Bechtel committee report with a committee of the faculty, Sproul incorporated it into a resolution that he offered to the Regents on April 21. This rather lengthy resolution reaffirmed the stand of the Regents against employment of Communist party members. It required employees to sign (1) the constitutional oath required of all California public officials and (2) acceptance of appointment by a letter including the following:

> Having taken the constitutional oath of office required of public officials of the State of California, I hereby formally acknowledge my acceptance of the position and salary named, and also state that I am not a member of the Communist Party or any other organization which advocates the overthrow of the Government by force or violence, and that I have no commitments in conflict with my responsibilities with respect to impartial scholarship and free pursuit of truth. I understand that the foregoing is a condition of my employment and a consideration of payment of my salary.[34]

The resolution then provided that faculty members who failed to comply would be permitted to petition the President for a review of their cases by the Academic Senate's Committee on Privilege and Tenure. The Regents would not be permitted to act on such cases until hearing the senate committee's findings and recommendations. May 15, 1950, was fixed as the deadline for signing the new contracts.

The main gains of the faculty through the compromise were an alternative to the "sign-or-get-out" ultimatum with its April 30 deadline, the right of a hearing if they failed to sign, and Regental recognition of a role for the senate's Committee on Privilege and Tenure in executing the new policies. The passage of the resolution gave them little to celebrate.

THE DISMISSALS

When Professor Hicks returned to Berkeley from the Regents' meeting on April 21, 1950, he announced that "there is a guarantee that no man or woman shall be dismissed provided the Committee, the President, and the Regents can find assurance that his inability to sign the contract required arises solely out of good conscience. Unless such individuals are proved to be members of the Communist Party, a condition we believe cannot be shown in any instance to exist, they will not be dismissed from the University, in spite of their unwillingness to sign the suggested contract." [35]

On May 13, the Committees on Privilege and Tenure in both the north and the south met with President Sproul to work out guidelines for their procedures in the coming weeks. They agreed to find out from each petitioner why he had not signed the contract, to determine if failure to sign stemmed from conscientious objections to an oath or from disloyalty, and to ascertain what relationship, if any, the petitioner had or might have had in the past with the Communist party.

In the ensuing weeks, the Southern Section's committee heard twenty-seven petitioners. All but one were recommended as having fulfilled all conditions of employment at the University except signing the new contract. The northern committee heard fifty-two people. It reported favorably on forty-seven cases. In five cases, the petitioners refused to discuss their position vis-à-vis communism and were recommended unfavorably to the President, but only for "lack of cooperation." [36]

In addition to the cases involving members of the Academic Senate, there were eighty-one other cases. Of these, fifty-eight resulted in favorable recommendations and eight resulted in unfavorable recommendations. No action was taken in another fifteen cases where it was known that the petitioners, for reasons in no way associated with the oath, would not be reappointed for the ensuing year.[37]

President Sproul gave his own report and recommendations to the Regents on June 23. He recommended that 157 nonacademic and non-senate employees be dismissed as of June 30, 1950. His recommendations in the case of senate-member petitioners paralleled those of the Committees on Privilege and Tenure. Even some of the more temperate Regents were concerned about the number of favorable recommendations. For them, the problem was that if this large number were allowed to escape the requirement of signing an oath or contract in 1950, it would encourage still larger numbers not to sign in the next year, and soon the oath would be largely disregarded. Debate was inconclusive, however, and the only action taken was to allow contracts to expire for nonacademic and non-senate employees who had not signed the oath but whose reemployment was not contemplated in any case.

In the ensuing days, several of the non-signers of senate rank whose fate still rested with the Regents signed their contracts. But thirty-one non-signers, under the leadership of Edward C. Tolman, formed what they called the Group for Academic Freedom. Its purpose was to obtain financial assistance for persons dismissed for failure to sign, to seek public understanding of their position, and to formulate plans for their legal defense in case they were dismissed. This group worked under serious handicaps, without access to University facilities for their headquarters and with only such funds as they could raise from friends and colleagues. *The Year of the Oath,* by Professor George Stewart and other faculty members, was prepared at about this time as a tract on the faculty's position and an antidote to discouragement within the ranks of those fighting against the oath.

By July 21, the makeup of the cases before the Regents had changed by reason of resignation, late signature, late hearing reports, and administrative errors. The number of non-senate academic and nonacademic employees recommended for retention had dropped to 84. Of the 62 senate members recommended favorably on June 23, 22 had eventually signed and 1 had resigned. Sproul's report to the Regents that day requested that 73 names be stricken from the list of 157 non-senate academic and nonacademic employees dismissed in June, that 6 senate non-signers be dismissed, and that 39 senate non-signers be reappointed for the coming year on the basis of favorable endorsement by the Committees on Privilege and Tenure.[38]

The President's recommendations touched off another long and bitter debate in the Regents' meeting, during which several persons spoke on behalf of the President's request, including Clark Kerr, then director of the Institute of Industrial Relations at Berkeley. The burden of their remarks was that dismissal of the 39 senate non-signers would actually be the dismissal of otherwise loyal men, some of them the more "spirited" and able members of the faculty. It would destroy faculty confidence in the sincerity of the Regents in accepting the alumni compromise (as its terms were understood by the faculty), and would undermine faith of the faculty in its own Committees on Privilege and Tenure. The President's recommendations were finally accepted by a vote of ten to nine, although Regent Neylan served notice that he would bring the matter up for reconsideration at the August meeting, thus suspending the Regents' action until August.

The interim was an anxious one for the non-signers, who found themselves more alienated than they had expected. Within the faculty, disputes over policies, tactics, and strategy in fighting the oath had ruptured lifetime friendships. Teachers and scholars who had wrestled with their consciences and signed either the oath of June 24, 1949, or the contract of April 21, 1950, had put the issue behind them and returned to scholarly pursuits and teaching. Up to the very eye of the Regents' final decision, the non-signers were under intense pressure to do the same.

On August 25, 1950, the Regents resumed consideration of President Sproul's recommendations on retention of the non-signers. As the debate took its course, the issue became strangely redefined. It was no longer whether there were Communists on the faculty who should be dismissed (no Regent could prove that there were), but whether or not the Regents would expel members of the faculty to demonstrate the penalty for disobeying their orders. By a vote of twelve to ten, the Regents decided in the affirmative.[39] Thirty-one faculty members were dismissed. Among them were several senior and very respected professors, some of whom had given more than thirty years in service to the University. Professor Tolman, a leader of the non-signers from the beginning, was one of them. In the psychology department at Berkeley, two full professors, an assistant professor, and a lecturer joined Tolman in the non-signers' ranks. Berkeley almost lost a professor of physics, a professor of philosophy, two professors of mathematics, a professor of economics, a professor of Greek, and a professor of history. Almost all of them were people of considerable professional reputation.

By the fall of 1950 some of the oath's consequences were evident in other ways. Fifty-five courses of instruction were no longer offered because their teachers had been fired. Other faculty members had resigned. There was almost universal agreement on the faculty that those who had been fired had lost their jobs needlessly.

At this time, Governor Earl Warren supported legislation requiring all state employees to sign an oath of loyalty. Unlike the Regents' oath, it did not single out University employees as subject to its requirements. Named for its author, Assemblyman Harold Levering, the act was signed on October 3, 1950.[40] The new oath affirmed the signer's support of the constitutions of the United States and California. It also disclaimed advocacy of or membership in any party or organization advocating overthrow of the government by force or violence or unlawful means.

At least one Regent was willing at this point to remove the Regents' loyalty test in favor of the Levering oath. He might have had wider support if the case of the non-signers against the Regents had not by this time already reached the courts. In December, the Regents voted to require University employees to sign the Levering oath as well as the allegiance to the California constitution and the Regents' declaration imposed on August 25, 1950.

LEGAL ACTION

The non-signers filed briefs seeking a writ of mandate for reinstatement in the District Court of Appeals on August 31 and November 10, 1950. They contended that the state constitution expressly forbade any oath, declaration, or test of loyalty as a condition of appointment to any public office or trust beyond the allegiance specified in the constitution itself (Article XX, Section 3). They also contended that the constitution required the University to "be entirely independent of all political or sectarian influence and kept free therefrom in the appointment of its regents and in the administration of its affairs . . . ," and that academic freedom at the University could be preserved only if those guarantees were maintained. Finally, they asserted that the action to dismiss them was illegal because in the August action the principle of faculty tenure during good behavior and efficient service had been abused.

The Regents filed briefs in October and December, 1950, asserting that the petitioners were not public officers within the meaning of that phrase as contained in the constitution; that the Regents had full constitutional authority in matters of faculty appointment, promotion, and dismissal; that since the Communist party was a conspiracy and not a political party, the allegation that the Regents' oath was a political test was not valid; and that the "good behavior" understood to underlie a professor's right to tenure implied adherence to regulations legally applied to the governance of the University by the Regents.

The court decided favorably for Tolman and the non-signers on the grounds that the University was to be independent of all political and sectarian influence and that the faculty, as officers of a public trust, could not be subjected to any narrower test of loyalty than the constitution of California prescribed.[41]

The Regents decided not to appeal the decision, but the Supreme Court of California took the case under advisement on its own motion. While a decision from that body was awaited, the composition of the Board of Regents shifted so that its majority succeeded, by November, 1951, in enacting a new statement of policy that discontinued use of the Regents' special loyalty declaration as a condition of employment, but reaffirmed the Regents' intention to bar members of the Communist party from employment.

The Supreme Court made its decision on October 17, 1952. Surprisingly, its judgment was not based on any of the issues raised by the parties in their pleadings. Rather, the case was decided on a question which the Supreme Court itself posed and on which it had sought and obtained supplemental briefs from the contending forces. The court held that state laws, one of which dated back to 1872, occupied the entire field of loyalty legislation and that "university personnel cannot properly be required to execute any other oath or declaration relating to loyalty than that prescribed for all state employees." [42] It concluded: "No question is raised as to petitioners' loyalty or as to their qualifications to teach, and they are entitled to a writ directing respondents to issue to each of petitioners a letter of appointment to his post on the faculty of the university upon his taking the oath now required of all public employees by the Levering Act." [43]

As a result of this judgment, most of the non-signers eventually returned to their teaching duties, although some had reached retirement age and others had found employment elsewhere more to their liking. In March,

1956, while the non-signers' suit for back pay and other benefits was still pending in the Superior Court of Sacramento, a settlement was reached whereby they received credit toward sabbatical leave and pension rights as though their employment had been continuous. They also received financial settlements equal to the difference between what they would have earned in uninterrupted service and what they had, in fact, received from other sources during the period July 1, 1950, to December 31, 1952.

On December 21, 1967, in the wake of new United States Supreme Court decisions on loyalty-oath cases across the country, the California Supreme Court held invalid provisions of the oath required under the Levering Act that related to membership in subversive organizations and advocacy of the violent overthrow of the government.[44] This action restored the University's status on loyalty oaths to essentially what it was when the dispute began in 1949.

THE MEANING OF THE OATH DISPUTE

Virtually none of the objectives sought by the parties to the oath conflict were completely met as a result of the dispute itself. Instead of quieting public suspicion of the loyalty of University employees, the conflict amplified the accusing whispers. The faculty won no new freedoms and earned no new responsibilities in University government. Individuals paid a heavy price for their principles. Some lost their jobs. Some who had earned the affection of the whole University family suddenly found themselves with depreciated prestige and influence. There was a loss of talent—represented by the men who were dismissed, those who permanently resigned to avoid turmoil and a compromise with principle, and those who refused invitations to join the University faculty for the same reasons. The *esprit de corps,* the shared sense of what the University was, as cultivated by Wheeler and Sproul, was shattered. And at a meeting of educational leaders, the provost at one of the nation's leading universities invited speculation on which institution would rise to fill the vacancy caused by Berkeley's inevitable fall from the ranks of what he called the big six—Harvard, Yale, Columbia, Chicago, Michigan, and Berkeley.[45]

The spectacle of a great University suffering self-induced anguish demands explanations of causes and effects. During the four decades that preceded the dispute, the character of the University had become fixed in the mold fashioned for it by Wheeler. Its traditions were essentially collegiate. Its governance was essentially autocratic. Within rather narrow margins of freedom given to him by the Regents, Sproul had initiated policies affording consultation with trusted faculty advisers on key issues. But the University was getting big beyond the comprehension and control of any one man. The young faculty members recruited by Sproul and department chairmen during the 1930s and 1940s were bringing with them new ideas about the role of the professor in research and teaching. Integrating those ideas into the University of Caifornia required a broader faculty participation and interest in the institution than existed in 1949. The oath dispute, for all of its trauma, activated such interest. It forced each faculty member to decide, as an individual matter, the price he was willing to pay for academic freedom. Except in vaguely remote and theoretical terms, that question had not arisen at the University before. So while the faculty did not gain any new freedom (and probably lost some) during the oath dispute, it gained a renewed respect for the importance of faculty self-government and a sense of what academic freedom was in practice and what its reasonable limitations might be at the University of California. The creation of standing senate Committees on Academic Freedom can be viewed as evidence of that new awareness and of a determination to protect legitimate faculty freedom from unreasonable abrogation. The dispute also raised questions about how new faculty colleagues should be selected and the extent of the rights of a faculty member in good standing to hold his job as long as he was competent and of unsullied moral character. Out of the new awareness of these considerations of academic life would come gradually improved processes of faculty appointment and, in 1958, a clear and formal policy on tenure, which the faculty hitherto presumed to exist but which had force only as a matter of custom.

Chapter 21

POSTWAR EXPANSION

WHEN THE United States declared war against the Axis powers in 1941, the University catalogue listed seven "campuses": Berkeley; UCLA; the professional schools in San Francisco; the College of Agriculture at Davis; the College of Agriculture (Citrus Experiment Station) at Riverside; Lick Astronomical Department at Mount Hamilton; and Scripps Institution of Oceanography at La Jolla.[1] Only two of the campuses—Berkeley and UCLA—offered a complete undergraduate curriculum. Three—Riverside, Scripps Institution of Oceanography, and Lick Observatory—were primarily research installations [2] having only a few graduate students.[3] The professional schools in San Francisco specialized in the medical sciences and law.

Although it still specialized in agriculture, the Davis campus had gradually expanded its instructional program. Its first students in 1909 had been young boys just out of high school who sought nondegree vocational training in agriculture. Their course lasted two years, and they were not regarded by the faculty at Berkeley as comparable to regular lower-division students at the University. Although agriculture students from Berkeley often enrolled in courses at Davis for a spring semester (animal husbandry students had to spend two semesters there) to gain familiarity with practical farming and the experimental work conducted there, the campus offered no degrees.

Because the level and character of agriculture instruction was for so long distinct from other University work, some farming interests resumed efforts to separate the College of Agriculture and the Davis campus from the University of California and make it a separate institution.[4] Partly to silence such talk, the Regents voted on January 16, 1922, to institute University courses for Freshmen and Sophomores at Davis,[5] and in 1922–1923, the first year under this policy, 253 of the 388 students enrolled there were in the new "degree program." [6] The remainder were in the long-established two-year vocational course or were taking graduate work. Several new faculty members were hired to broaden the course offerings,[7] and, by sharing faculty members with Berkeley departments, the Davis campus was soon able to offer courses in all but a few of the general fields normally included in a complete undergraduate program. Further evolution in this direction was interrupted in 1943, when the entire Davis campus was taken over by the Signal Corps of the United States Army for the duration of the war.

SANTA BARBARA STATE COLLEGE

In 1944, the University was forced to assume responsibility for undergraduate instruction at a new location—Santa Barbara.

The pressure for this action had been building for nearly a decade. In

1935, the legislature dropped the word *teachers* from the names of the California state teachers' colleges and authorized those institutions to award bachelor's degrees in fields other than education.[8] With their new flexibility, the best of the state colleges attracted students from all over the country, boasted faculties that were well leavened with Ph.D.s, and announced new fields of instruction with alarming frequency. They were directly competitive with the University in many undergraduate courses.

Santa Barbara State College was small, but it also ranked among the best in the state college system. It was founded in 1891 by Miss Anna S. C. Blake as a manual training school specializing in the teaching of cooking, sewing, and sloyd (manual training). Miss Blake hired a young local high school graduate, Miss Ednah A. Rich, as the only teacher and supported the school financially until 1899, when she donated it to the Santa Barbara school system. The city added teacher training in manual arts to the program and continued to operate the school until 1909, when the state took it over and renamed it the Santa Barbara State Normal School of Manual Arts and Home Economics. The first male student enrolled in 1911, and two years later the school moved to a new site near the Santa Barbara Mission later called the "Riviera Campus." The pioneering Miss Rich remained the administrative head of the institution until 1916. Her successor, Frank H. Ball, was forced by ill health to retire from the presidency after two years, and Stanford-educated Clarence L. Phelps assumed leadership of the college in 1918.

Because the school's emphasis on manual arts proved too narrow to attract a large student body, the state threatened to abandon the school in 1919. Phelps saved it by convincing the state that instead of giving the school up, funds should be provided to broaden its program. "Manual Arts and Home Economics" was dropped from the college's name that year, and two years later Phelps successfully led efforts of the state normal school presidents to change the names of their institutions to state teachers' colleges and to increase their offerings from two to four years.[9]

Santa Barbara State Teachers College enjoyed the distinction of being one of the country's few institutions to specialize in the preparation of manual-arts teachers while offering the enlarged work of all California state teachers' colleges at the same time. It grew steadily and, in 1935, became a state college.[10] Meanwhile, in 1932, a new site had been obtained on the mesa overlooking the Pacific. By 1940, President Phelps was able to report the beginning of construction on the mesa, student enrollment "twice that of 1936," and the introduction of "five new lines of work . . . two in science and three in the social sciences." [11] He proudly noted that "the year has been marked by the addition of a number of faculty members who have been prepared in the best colleges and universities; internal activities have been co-ordinated for a larger student group, and the student body with an excellent organization has carried on a superior type of college government." [12] By 1941, there were 1918 students at the college.[13]

LOCAL PRESSURES

While President Phelps was building Santa Barbara State College into a strong and distinctive institution in its own right, powerful men in Santa Barbara promoted the idea of endowing it with the prestige of the University's name as well. The Santa Barbara County Chamber of Commerce became interested in such a plan as early as 1935.[14] A powerful force in the movement to make Santa Barbara State College part of the University was Thomas M. Storke, publisher of the Santa Barbara *News-Press,* who was convinced that the establishment of a University of California campus would enrich the educational and cultural development of the city and contribute to its economic progress. He placed the full influence of his person and his newspaper behind the idea and received the support of Santa Barbara's assemblyman, Alfred W. "Bobby" Robertson, and State Senator Clarence Ward.[15] To rally local civic interest and generate enthusiasm for the project among University alumni, they enlisted Miss Pearl Chase, a community leader and alumna of both Santa Barbara State College and the Berkeley campus.[16]

Legislative efforts to make Santa Barbara State College into a unit of the University began in 1939, with the introduction of Assembly Bill No. 861, which authorized branches of the University at both Santa Barbara and Fresno. This measure was amended to require that the State Council for Educational Planning and Coordination "make a comprehensive survey of the entire higher educational system of the State, with particular reference to the need and possibility of the establishment of a branch of the University of California in Santa Barbara County or some central point in the San Joaquin Valley. . . ." [17] This study yielded only a report that the council found the State Department of Education (which controlled state colleges) and the University "forced into conflict by the lack of provision for integration, and for authority to sponsor some publicly acceptable policy." [18] In the absence of a "mutually agreed upon philosophy or joint program," the council recommended that the status of all public institutions of education in California remain unchanged pending further studies.[19] When the report was released in 1941, that recommendation was enough to defeat another bill that would have made Santa Barbara State College a part of the University.[20]

In April, 1943, legislation to transfer the college to the University was approved by the Senate Education Committee, but President Phelps sought to head it off with public protest before it reached the floor. He predicted that the transfer would "bring utter ruin" to his college because its course of instruction would be changed and its drawing power would suffer.[21]

A STEP TOWARD UNIFICATION

The welfare of the college was only one consideration. The proposed transfer of Santa Barbara State College to the University was also part of the larger problem of unification and control of California's systems of higher education. President Sproul and the Regents regarded the matter in that light, as did State Superintendent of Public Instruction Walter F. Dexter and the State Board of Education. Between August, 1942, and March, 1943, this problem was studied by a special committee appointed by Sproul and Dexter. Ernest J. Jaqua, president of Scripps College, was the committee chairman, and membership was drawn from all sectors of California higher education.

The committee considered four alternatives: (1) the *status quo;* (2) a dual administration of higher education, with reduction of the number of Regents, change of the Board's title, and a special committee of the Board charged with responsibility for the state colleges. Under this plan, the State Board of Education would relinquish all direct administration of the state colleges in favor of the new "board of higher education" and confine itself to the administration of the public schools, including the junior colleges; (3) abolishment of the State Board of Education, leaving the Regents in charge of higher education and an elected state superintendent of education in charge of general public education; and (4) a board of overseers responsible for "oversight and direction of all public education in the state from kindergarten to the University." [22] Despite some opposition from representatives of the state colleges on the committee, the second alternative was finally endorsed and placed before the Regents' Committee on Educational Policies and Relations in the form of a proposed amendment to Article IX, Section 9, of the state constitution.[23]

Three other propositions were considered by the Regents' Committee on Educational Policies and Relations at the same time. One was that all state colleges as a bloc be accepted into the University under the existing Board of Regents. Another was that the state colleges be accepted one at a time under the existing Board. The third was that the Regents not accept any state colleges at all. Under the chairmanship of Regent Chester H. Rowell, who was prominently involved in the transfer of the Los Angeles Normal School to the University in 1919, the committee rejected the proposed constitutional amendment and accepted, instead, the proposal that the Regents accept all of the state colleges as a bloc.[24] Rowell's argument for this position was that although the University's status without the state colleges was ideal, the Regents' refusal to take part in an amalgamation would not prevent the state colleges from continuing "their encroachment as a separate system. . . ." [25] He considered that possibility a "greater evil" than burdening the University with additional units.[26] The Regents rejected the recommendation of Rowell's committee and resolved instead "that in light of the existing situation and based on our view of what is best for the University of California at the present time, the Board of Regents expresses itself as opposed to making any of the State colleges a part of the University of California." [27]

Despite this action, efforts to pass a new bill to transfer Santa Barbara State College to the Regents went on unabated in the 1943 session, and it was passed in the assembly on April 9. Clarence Ward had the bill amended in the senate to protect the jobs of members of the college faculty, and, on May 5, the assembly concurred in that amendment, and the bill was ordered enrolled.[28]

When Governor Warren asked Sproul whether or not he should sign the measure, Sproul wrote a letter reviewing the history of the bill and its predecessors and the problems of coordinating University and state college efforts. As arguments against the bill, Sproul cited the administrative burden already borne by the University, the fear that new regional centers would lead the University into political situations, and the difficulties in faculty recruitment that might be created. On the positive side, he pointed out the success of UCLA under the Regents' management, that the transfer might be a step toward coordinating higher education, that the transfer would not interfere with the constitutional safeguards of the University, and that Santa Barbara would provide a third center to "balance, as it were, Berkeley and Los Angeles." [29] He concluded, "If there is to be unification of higher education in California, it will apparently come, as in the case of the Los Angeles Normal School, by the transfer of single institutions to the University." [30]

Governor Warren signed the bill on June 8, 1943. It abolished the Santa Barbara State College, created a Santa Barbara branch of the University of California, transferred the college's property to the Regents, and guaranteed college employees continued employment under the new management.

The Regents were given two years to decide whether or not to accept the transfer.[31]

Before deciding, the Regents consulted the University faculty and a group of Santa Barbara citizens that included several professors from the college. The University's faculty committee reported on September 2, supporting the transfer on the condition that it was regarded as part of a general University policy of creating regional colleges to provide sound general collegiate education, teacher training, and courses of local interest. But, the faculty advised, such institutions should not be "miniature or embryo universities," and should not be developed to conduct extensive research or to offer graduate instruction.[32] The consultation with Santa Barbara citizens and educators took place on September 23. President Phelps, Assemblyman Robertson, Miss Chase, and leaders of Santa Barbara civic and cultural organizations attended. President Phelps showed continued concern that his college might become second-rate under the University's management, but President Sproul reassured him that the University would not permit this to happen. The Regents wanted to know about the Santa Barbarans' expectations of the college under University control and were told "Everything about Santa Barbara is small but excellent. That is what we believe in. If the Branch is comparatively small, it must be of the highest possible type and that is the reason we have come to the University of California and asked them to take cver." [33]

In his final report to the Regents on the question of transferring Santa Barbara State College to the University, Sproul took the viewpoint of the faculty and the citizens of Santa Barbara into consideration. "Santa Barbara State College should not be taken over . . . ," he said, "unless [the Regents] regard it as the first step in a policy of unification of higher education." [34] He stressed that he was not advocating that the Regents campaign to take over state colleges, but saying only that the Regents "should be ready to receive them whenever circumstances make it suitable to do so." [35] If the Regents accepted the transfer, Sproul urged that their resolution to do so "should make clear that they do not propose to establish another complete university comparable to those now at Berkeley and Los Angeles, and that they are not planning a graduate school. . . . The institution should be primarily an undergraduate institution, emphasizing, as it now does, the industrial arts, home economics, art, music, and teacher training, but at the same time giving substantial general education." [36] The Committee on Educational Policies and Relations recommended that the Santa Barbara State College become a part of the University under the conditions Sproul had set forth. The Regents accepted that recommendation on October 22, 1943, and the transfer took place on July 1 of the following year. The newly acquired campus was called Santa Barbara College of the University of California.

The Regents' acceptance of Santa Barbara State College delighted the Santa Barbara residents who had worked hard to see that merger come about, but it upset many alumni of the college who were proud of it as it was. It also upset the presidents, alumni, and community friends of several other state colleges who liked the independence and character of their institutions and did not wish to see them become parts of a giant system. They speculated that the Regents intended to snatch up all state colleges eventually, and, in the corridors of the state capitol, the University was frequently called an "octopus." [37] The epithet was not entirely inappropriate, because the transfer of Santa Barbara State College did give the University an eighth campus and a presence in a new part of the state. On November 5, 1946, however, the people of California made certain that the University would not acquire other existing state colleges without almost insuperable difficulty. They did so by approving an initiative constitutional amendment, backed by the State Board of Education,[38] the primary purpose of which was to guarantee adequate appropriations for education in California, including minimum teachers' salaries of $2400 a year. The measure had considerable appeal, but one of its little-discussed provisions defined the public schools of California so as to include the state colleges and directed that "no school or college or any other part of the Public School System shall be, directly or indirectly, transferred from the Public School System or placed under the jurisdiction of any authority other than one included within the Public School System." [39] More tersely, there could never be another Santa Barbara.

THE EIGHTH CAMPUS

Santa Barbara State College did not mesh easily with the University. The average salaries of its professors were about six hundred dollars lower than the minimum paid to professors at Berkeley and Los Angeles.[40] Admissions requirements were less rigorous than those of the University, and degrees were granted on the basis of lower academic achievement.[41] The industrial-arts program that made the college unique and accounted for much of its national reputation was an enterprise outside the University's previous experience. The college library, though modestly famous as the depository for the Wyles Collection of Lincolniana, contained only thirty thousand volumes, far too few for a University campus.[42]

In December, 1943, following the precedent set at Los Angeles twenty-four years earlier, President Sproul appointed a special committee to help ease Santa Barbara State College into the University and named President Phelps as chairman. Other members were University Vice-President Deutsch; William H. Ellison, professor of history at Santa Barbara; Claude B. Hutchison, dean of the College of Agriculture; Gordon S. Watkins, dean of the College of Letters and Science at UCLA; George D. Louderback, former dean of the College of Letters and Science at Berkeley; and William G. Young, chairman of the Department of Chemistry at UCLA.[43] This committee recommended that Santa Barbara College be classified into two divisions: the Academic Division, including candidates for general teaching credentials; and the Applied Arts Division, including students in industrial arts, home economics, art, music, and physical education. The committee advised that, provisionally, admissions requirements at Santa Barbara be set somewhat lower than those for the Berkeley and Los Angeles campuses and that only the bachelor of arts and the bachelor of applied arts degrees be offered.[44] They regarded the faculty of the new campus as comparable to one of the colleges at Berkeley (e.g. the College of Letters and Science). On their recommendation, the Santa Barbara Coordinating Academic Council was created, consisting of three members each from the Northern and Southern Sections of the Academic Senate and three from the new college. The function of this council was to make certain that actions taken by the college faculty were in accord with general Academic Senate policy. If so, the actions of the college faculty were declared immediately effective. If not, they were subject to further deliberation by the senate itself.[45] To advise on administrative matters, President Sproul named three UCLA faculty members and two Berkeley faculty members to an Administrative Board. Three members of the board—Dean Watkins and Professors Louderback and Young—were members of the original advisory committee. The two new men were J. Harold Williams, professor of education and dean of the summer sessions at UCLA, and George P. Adams, professor of philosophy at Berkeley.[46] President Phelps continued to be the chief administrative officer at Santa Barbara, with the title of provost.

Provost Phelps had little opportunity to continue the expansion of his college as a part of the University. He was hampered by all the uncertainties that attended the change of management, and by the continuation of World War II and the related restrictions on construction. Moreover, the Regents clearly intended that the new campus remain small and exerted no pressure to increase its enrollment beyond the 1660 students the college brought to the University in 1944. In 1946, at the age of sixty-three and after twenty-six years as head of the college, Phelps retired.

To succeed Phelps, the Regents selected J. Harold Williams, a member of the Administrative Board, as acting provost. Because he did not expect to remain in that position very long, Williams left his main household in Los Angeles and resided in an apartment in Santa Barbara, rejoining his wife on weekends and special occasions. His "acting" provostship lasted four years, however, and in 1950, he was appointed provost without qualification and served in that capacity for five more years. Provost Williams was often at odds with some of Santa Barbara's civic leaders who wanted the campus to grow large like UCLA or Berkeley. He also had a remote personal style that newspaper reporters could not treat enthusiastically. To the public, therefore, he lacked color. But to his colleagues on the campus he showed a relaxed, informal personality. His close advisers frequently met with him in his apartment, often adjourning to the kitchen to continue their discussion over cold cuts and beer. Provost Williams understood the byways of academic government at Berkeley and UCLA and knew the important administrative channels in the University. With this knowledge and understanding, he was effective in his relationships with the other campuses and was able to prepare his own faculty at Santa Barbara for the larger role it would play in the academic government of the University in the future.

Williams first intended to make Phelps' dream of a new campus for the entire college come true on the mesa site, but University engineers and planners saw that there were only about one hundred acres there and that much of the land was not suitable for buildings and other campus facilities. Negotiations to add land to the site were also snarled and unpromising, so in 1948 President Sproul asked Secretary Underhill to try to find about two hundred acres that might be more suitable elsewhere in the Santa Barbara vicinity. Before Underhill could make that search, however, Comptroller James H. Corley advised Sproul that the Marine Corps Air Station at Goleta, about eight miles north of Santa Barbara, was being abandoned and might be obtained from the United States War Assets Administration.[47] The station was located on another seaside mesa with long stretches of sandy beach on one side. There were about four hundred acres there and improvements that included miles of paved road, a water system, a sewage disposal plant, and seventy-five other buildings, some of which could be used as temporary classrooms, dormitories, dining halls, and recreation facilities.[48] Government regulations provided that if it were used for educational purposes, the property could be obtained free.[49] The Regents took the site late in 1949, and Provost Williams and the faculty began planning its use for a small liberal arts college of superior quality, anticipating an eventual enrollment of between 3000 and 3500 students.[50]

POSTWAR BUILDING

After World War II, the University's enrollment jumped tremendously. By 1948–1949, Berkeley's student body had grown from a prewar 17,013 to 25,852 members.[51] In the same period, the number of students at UCLA increased from 10,112 to 16,879.[52] One factor in this immediate postwar growth was the University's share of the hundred of thousands of war veterans who used their government educational benefits at California colleges and universities. To accommodate them, on some campuses surplus army barracks were hauled in to provide classroom and study space. Living accommodations for veterans and their families were arranged in abandoned war housing units or temporary structures built in communities near University campuses.

The veterans complicated matters because they came in such large numbers within a brief period of time (roughly 1945–1951).[53] But the University was already short of facilities before they came. There had been little building activity during the Depression and war years, yet the University's enrollment under peacetime conditions had increased by 10,000 students between 1930 and 1941.[54] A considerable amount of building was necessary at the first opportunity after the war just to catch up to this prewar demand. By resorting to emergency measures the University accommodated the immediate postwar enrollment increase in commendable fashion. But it could not sustain indefinitely an educational program involving that many students without larger, permanent facilities. With the help of federal loans and money drawn from state reserves, the Regents began to authorize construction of new projects on almost every campus, beginning in 1946.

In 1946, construction began on a $1,132,000 chemistry building at Berkeley.[55] A new building for the School of Forestry was begun at about the same time. By 1949, the total postwar construction expenditures of the University had reached $109,000,000.[56] By December of that year, ten postwar projects had been completed or were under construction at Berkeley, and five more were projected. The latter included new classroom, law, home economics, and public health buildings and a student union.[57] At Los Angeles that winter, three major projects were completed. They included a new library wing, a $1,500,000 business administration and economics building, and a service building. Two projects were under construction and four were scheduled to begin the following spring. Among them was a $15,500,000 medical center. In the planning stage were buildings for a new law school; a home economics and an education and art building; and additions to the administration building and the men's and women's gymnasiums.[58] At Davis, a large hall for a new school of veterinary medicine and a building for the plant sciences were completed in 1949, and appropriations were made for food technology, home economics, poultry husbandry, and soils and irrigation buildings, student health services, and several other projects.[59]

At San Francisco, the list of approved projects included a new building for Hastings College of the Law, a medical science building, and a teaching hospital.[60] At La Jolla, a new library, museum, and aquarium building was listed among the projects completed or in progress.[61]

PREPARING FOR THE SECOND WAVE

Although the postwar building program was intended primarily to provide facilities the University had long needed and gone without, it also helped provide for the veterans' enrollment. A great deal of it also satisfied southern California demands for nearby professional education in medicine, law, and engineering. But as time passed the objective of the University's building program shifted from catching up with current demand to preparing for a new wave of increasing enrollment. Almost immediately after the war, statistics released by the State Office of Planning and Research, the United States Bureau of the Census, and the United States Office of Education portended a future demand for higher education so enormous that it challenged belief. The evidence suggested that veteran enrollment would begin to subside in the early 1950s (and it did), but that a new and still bigger wave of students would begin to arrive at the nation's colleges and universities during the second half of that decade. In California, the places vacated by graduating veterans would be taken by the large number of young people migrating to the state with their parents.[62] Unlike the enrollment wave swollen by veterans during 1945–1951, the second wave would not subside in the predictable future.

The impending enrollments were a challenge and opportunity for all institutions of higher education in California, and there was considerable danger that the enrollments might be used as a rationale for unreasonable and unrestrained expansion of public colleges and University campuses. The danger was all the greater because the Council for the Planning and Coordination of Higher Education created in 1933 had proved ineffective. To take its place, Regents and members of the State Board of Education meeting in Sproul's home in 1945 devised, as a new coordinating agency, a Liaison Committee of the two groups. Financed by a $50,000 state appropriation in 1947, this committee commissioned a full-scale study of California's needs in higher education. Immediate direction of the study was entrusted to a three-man team led by George D. Strayer, professor emeritus of Teachers College, Columbia University. The other members were Monroe E. Deutsch, who retired as vice-president and provost of the University on August 17, 1947, and Aubrey A. Douglass, associate state superintendent of public instruction. They were assisted by an eight-member staff. Their report was issued on March 1, 1948, under the official title *A Report of a Survey of the Needs of California in Higher Education.*

Informally known as the Strayer Report, its pages contained careful descriptions of the size and functions of existing systems of public higher education in the state and a detailed analysis of the needs of ten geographic sections of California for college or University facilities. The report recommended that new state colleges be established in Sacramento, the Los Angeles metropolitan area, and southeast Los Angeles and Orange Counties.[63] These and all existing state colleges, the report said, should be authorized to grant master's degrees,[64] but the University should continue to have "exclusive responsibility among the public higher institutions, for training the professions, for graduate work on the doctors' level, and for research and scholarly endeavor of the highest type." [65] In order that the University might fulfill that responsibility properly, the report urged the legislature to give generous support to the University's existing medical center at San Francisco and the one proposed for UCLA.[66] It also recommended that engineering facilities be increased on both campuses.[67]

The Strayer Report favored the idea that the University should, without abandoning lower-division instruction, emphasize work at the upper-division and graduate levels.[68] In doing so, it would make room for students interested in the work the University was best suited for, while at the same time promoting a natural diversion of lower-division students to the junior colleges and state colleges. Hopefully, that diversion would enable Berkeley and UCLA to plan on enrollments no larger than 20,000 each (although Berkeley was substantially beyond that level when the report was issued).

The report accepted the fact that the Santa Barbara campus was "apparently planned" for only 3000 to 3500 students and suggested no greater enrollment there.[69] At Davis, on the other hand, the survey committee believed that the program should be expanded to provide for "1,550 to 1,800 additional undergraduate students in the humanities, the social sciences, and the natural sciences. . . ." [70]

As presented in preliminary form to President Sproul's Advisory Conference in Los Angeles on January 30, 1948, the report also recommended development of a four-year college in the Riverside–San Bernardino area. Whether the new college should be a state college or a campus of the University was not, at that time, specified.[71] A month later, however, when the report was published, it said that the Riverside–San Bernardino area "shows a need for a public four-year institution with a student capacity of 1,500 students. The Survey Committee recommends that a branch of the University be developed on [the Citrus Experiment Station] campus as a liberal arts college providing education appropriate to the unique functions of the University." [72]

When the Strayer Report was issued, the total University enrollment was 48,340, including 25,325 at Berkeley, 16,412 at Los Angeles, 2134 at Davis, and 3052 at Santa Barbara.[73] If all of the report's recommendations were followed, the University would have a capacity of 48,500 students, redistributed to include 20,000 each at Berkeley and Los Angeles, 3500 at Davis, 3500 at Santa Barbara, and 1500 at Riverside,[74] accommodating about 21 per cent of California's estimated student population in 1960.[75]

The report was approved by both the Board of Regents and the State Board of Education and thus acquired status as a compact guiding the efforts of both bodies as they planned to meet their respective responsibilities in the face of the rising enrollments.

The findings of the Strayer Report were not surprising to the Regents or to members of the University faculty. In February, 1947, a full year before the report was issued, President Sproul had stated views that were remarkably consonant with the report's conclusions. He said:

The goal of our great nation should be not a university education for all, but rather equal opportunity for all to get a good education of the kind for which they are qualified by natural endowments and industrious application, for as many years, more or less than four beyond high school, as may be necessary.

Translating this ideal into the terms of the California situation [, it] seems to me . . . that the University should restrict its lower division to students of exceptional academic attainments, in numbers equated to its facilities and the size of faculty required for its advanced work, while it continues to emphasize professional and graduate education, which are the peculiar fields of the University, fields which it should cultivate as its own, and to the exclusion of other State educational institutions. From this statement concerning the University, I would leave out Santa Barbara College, which it seems to me should be operated by the University as a model state college, with an enriched offering in the area of the liberal arts. I should be disposed also to treat [the] Davis campus as *sui generis,* but broadening the scope of its offerings so that students might receive a more rounded education, without detracting from its accent on agriculture.[76]

PLANNING EXPANSION AT DAVIS AND RIVERSIDE

On June 18, 1948, at the suggestion of Dean Hutchison, President Sproul appointed a thirteen-man committee to study and advise "in respect to the organization and development" of the new programs at Davis and Riverside. The chairman of the committee was Harry B. Walker, professor of agricultural engineering at Davis.[77] The membership was drawn from several campuses and from the University's administration, but six of the members were in agricultural fields and indicated the concern of both Dean Hutchison and the President that the new developments should not in any way jeopardize agricultural endeavors already in progress at the two locations.[78] There was a degree of urgency in the committee's work because the legislature had appropriated $2,000,000 in 1948 to initiate planning of the two new colleges of liberal arts and was expecting a progress report in the spring of 1949.

To perform its assignment most efficiently, the committee was divided into five subcommittees, each of which was responsible for some phase of the general study. One subcommittee developed plans for curriculum and academic staffing, another worked out a scheme of administrative relationships between the new units and the rest of the University, a third concentrated on physical needs, a fourth on student and faculty housing, and the fifth on agricultural expansion at Riverside.

The most important recommendations for Riverside were that the campus be established in the general vicinity of the Citrus Experiment Station buildings, that it anticipate an initial enrollment of 1000 students, but build immediately for a capacity of 1500; that the College of Liberal Arts provide instruction "ordinarily associated with the best private colleges of liberal arts"; and that the campus be placed under the direction of a provost reporting directly to the president. Instruction should first be offered, the committee agreed, in four basic areas: humanities, social sciences, life sciences, and physical sciences, with the usual provisions for physical education, hygiene, and military science. There would be no major offerings in agriculture, but upper-division work in plant sciences, soil sciences, entomology, and agricultural economics should be offered, and the lower-division program should include courses that would qualify students for transfer in agricultural majors elsewhere in the University. The committee estimated that an initial staff of forty-six academic members and sixty-eight nonacademic employees would be required at the outset. Because the committee believed that facilities already existed in Riverside to absorb the small student body contemplated, it recommended that housing for either students or faculty members not be built immediately, although facilities for four hundred students should be included in an over-all construction program for the campus.[79]

In the language of the committee's reports, the recommendations for Davis were almost identical to those for Riverside. The principal difference, of course, was that there were already more faculty members and physical facilities at Davis than there were at Riverside. Only thirty-one new faculty members were needed at Davis, for example, and a classroom and office building was all that was requested by way of new physical facilities to get its program started. Administratively, there was another difference. The entire campus would be under a provost, but the new liberal arts college would be under a dean. The provost would report to the president "through the Vice-President in charge of agriculture." Moreover, the committee recommended that the liberal arts college at Davis "be closely integrated with the activities of the College of Agriculture in order to promote the emphasis to be placed on instruction and research in agriculture." [80]

The committee's final report was available in September, 1948, and the Regents first acted on its recommendations in February of the following year, when they approved an administrative plan that made the new general education curriculum at Riverside a part of the statewide College of Agriculture. The principal administrative officer at Riverside was to be a provost, but he would report to the president through the vice-president in charge of agriculture—the procedure the committee had recommended for Davis, but not for Riverside.[81]

In September, 1949, President Sproul announced that Gordon S. Watkins would be the first provost at Riverside. A native of Wales, Watkins had come to the United States at the age of seventeen. He had studied at the University of Montana, where he received his A.B., the University of Illinois, where he received his M.A., and at the University of Pennsylvania, where he received his Ph.D. in economics in 1918. After spending eight years as a member of the faculty at the University of Illinois, he was appointed professor of economics at UCLA. There he was not only an outstanding professor but also an able administrator. For ten years he was dean of UCLA's College of Letters and Science and for six years dean of the summer session.[82] He had served on committees to advise the president or the Academic Senate on many matters, including the development of the campus at Santa Barbara. A member of the committee of thirteen to advise on Davis and Riverside, he was chairman of its subcommittee to study the expanded curriculum at Riverside.

Provost Watkins undertook the skeletal organization of the new college at Riverside virtually on his own. He drew up the rough specifications to guide architects in planning buildings, named the key administrators—including a librarian and registrar, and appointed men to head the five main academic divisions. This work was interrupted by the Korean War. Later, while construction was still in progress on the first five buildings for the campus, Watkins and his staff began to fill in the details of the academic plan for the campus.

The development of a College of Letters and Science at Davis was less dramatic. The campus was already a part of the College of Agriculture and was under the direction of an assistant dean, Knowles Ryerson, who had been a student at Davis in 1916 and had later served as an official of the United States Department of Agriculture. He became the chief administrative officer at Davis in 1937 and served in that capacity until 1952, when he became dean of the College of Agriculture at Berkeley.[83]

Many of the "liberal arts" courses planned for the new College of Letters and Science were already offered in existing departments at Davis. Thus, in 1951, few people were upset when Dean Hutchison announced to the Academic Senate that because of a temporary drop in enrollment, "it now seems advisable to open the new college at Davis on a scale limited to courses already being given there by the College of Agriculture, or which can be inaugurated in 1951–52 without additional appointments to the faculty. Accordingly, the [Regents' agricultural] committee recommends that a College of Letters and Science be organized at Davis immediately, and opened in September, 1951, with majors leading to the A.B. degree in botany, chemistry, English, history, and zoology. The committee also finds that courses in the first three years of majors in mathematics and physics are available." [84] In the same announcement, Dean Hutchison announced that the Korean War would require postponement of the opening of the College of Letters and Science at Riverside until 1953.[85]

NEW PROBLEMS OF MANAGEMENT

The Korean War was not the only disruptive element in the University's expansion to accommodate growing enrollment. The loyalty-oath controversy was a major distraction from the summer of 1949 to the end of 1950. More-over, the new physical arrangement of the University on campuses scattered all over the state invalidated existing administrative policies and organiza-tion. The University was no longer one major campus with several special-ized branches, as it was when Sproul first came to it as a student in 1909. Nor was it the "two-legged" University he was chosen to lead in 1930. In 1951, the number of campuses was eight, instead of seven, and two of the older "special" campuses, Davis and Riverside, were in the process of alter-ation to serve more general functions.

Despite these changes, the University's administration remained highly centralized. The Regents considered and adapted an incredibly detailed budget, and all changes in that document required their approval. They also approved all contracts, regardless of their size. President Sproul, Comp-troller Corley (who became vice-president—business affairs in 1949), and other statewide University officers had jurisdiction over business manage-ment, accounting, nonacademic personnel, admissions, public information, and many other activities at all University levels. Agriculture, public health, the Graduate Divisions, and several research institutes were regarded as "statewide" departments that reported directly to the president. President Sproul's burdens became still heavier in 1947 when Vice-President and Provost Deutsch retired.[86] Partly because he did not want to select a new man when the administrative structure of the University was under review, and partly because he thoroughly enjoyed personal contact with students and faculty members, Sproul personally assumed, in addition to his normal duties, the work of Berkeley's chief administrative officer and did not relin-quish it until 1952.

In 1948, the Regents employed the Public Administration Service, a management consulting firm, to review their administrative structure and procedures. This firm's investigators recommended that the unity of the University should be preserved, but that "there must be decentralization in the University to the maximum extent compatible with unity." They sug-gested, for example, that provosts with considerable autonomy be appointed on six of the University's campuses—Riverside, Santa Barbara, Los Angeles, Berkeley, San Francisco, and Davis. Scripps Institution of Ocean-ography was to be under the supervision of the provost at UCLA rather than reporting to the president. Similarly, Lick Observatory was to be under the jurisdiction of the provost at Berkeley. The report suggested that the new provosts' authority include administration of campus business and fi-nancial affairs and the hiring of nonacademic personnel. The president, the report recommended, should be given more authority for day-to-day decisions formerly reserved to the Regents and, at the same time, should delegate detailed matters so that he would have more time to formulate general University policies and programs for the Regents to consider.[87]

The Public Administration Service's recommendations were not implemented—at least not in the form in which they were presented—but a few changes did come during the next three years, and they met some of the general objectives recommended by the Public Administration Service.

In March, 1951, the Regents gave final approval to a new plan of organization. As announced by President Sproul, in the April issue of the *Faculty Bulletin,* the new organization was designed to "streamline the administrative machinery of an enlarged University . . . ," to define the duties of its officers, and to give the various campuses "the maximum degree of autonomy consistent with unity." The top officers of the University under the new plan were the president, the chancellor of the University of California at Berkeley, the chancellor of the University of California at Los Angeles, the vice-president of the University, the vice-president—agricultural science, the vice-president—business affairs, the vice-president—medical and health sciences, and the vice-president—University Extension. At the time of the announcement, only three of the vice-presidencies were filled: The vice-president of the University was Claude B. Hutchison, who also served as dean of the College of Agriculture; James H. Corley was vice-president —business affairs; and Baldwin M. Woods was vice-president—University Extension. There were no chief administrators at either Los Angeles or Berkeley. Clarence Dykstra had died in office as provost at UCLA in 1950, and no one had yet been appointed to succeed Deutsch at Berkeley. At Santa Barbara, Davis, and Riverside, the chief administrators were still called provosts. The incumbents at these campuses when the new organization was announced were J. Harold Williams, Knowles Ryerson, and Gordon S. Watkins, respectively.

The first chancellorship to be filled was the one at Los Angeles. There, Dr. Raymond B. Allen, a graduate of the University of Minnesota who received his M.D. from that institution in 1928, assumed the position. Dr. Allen practiced medicine briefly in the 1930s and then, after studies at the Mayo Foundation Division of the University of Minnesota's Graduate Division, began a career in medical administration, serving at the College of Physicians and Surgeons of Columbia University, Wayne University's College of Medicine, the Chicago Colleges of the University of Illinois, and Illinois' College of Medicine. He became president of the University of Washington in 1946, a year after schools of dentistry and medicine were started there. As president of the University of Washington, Dr. Allen had received considerable national attention when he recommended dismissal of several faculty members who failed to cooperate in his investigation of charges that they were either past or present members of the Communist party.

At Berkeley, the first chancellor was Clark Kerr, who had come to the University in 1945 as an associate professor of industrial relations with responsibility for organizing an Institute of Industrial Relations. Kerr was generally regarded as the choice of the Berkeley faculty for the chancellorship, having become widely respected as a member of several key faculty committees during the loyalty-oath controversy.

The Regents' decision to establish colleges of letters and science at Riverside and Davis prompted Vice-President Hutchison and some of his associates to review the general organization of the College of Agriculture. In a letter to President Sproul, Hutchison proposed that a Division of Agriculture be established and that it consist of: (1) the statewide College of Agriculture (Berkeley-Davis-Riverside-Los Angeles), with its Agricultural Experiment Station and Agricultural Experiment Service; (2) the School of Forestry at Berkeley; (3) the School of Veterinary Medicine at Davis; (4) the College of Letters and Science at Davis; and (5) the College of Letters and Science at Riverside.[88] The division would be placed under the direction of a vice-president of the University, functioning, as Hutchison did, as dean of the College of Agriculture. The men serving as "assistant deans" in charge of agriculture at Berkeley, Davis, and Los Angeles would become "deans" and would also become "assistant directors" of the Agricultural Experiment Station to indicate their authority over agricultural research conducted at their units.[89] Although Hutchison's plan was given consideration by the Regents, their decision was not announced until his retirement was near. On May 1, 1952, President Sproul announced that Harry R. Wellman, then chairman of the Division of Agricultural Economics and director of the Giannini Foundation of Agricultural Economics, had been appointed as the University's first vice-president—agricultural sciences. Wellman succeeded Hutchison as the "chief statewide administrative officer for the agricultural activities of the University," and in that capacity he had over-all supervision of "the teaching, research, and extension of the College of Agriculture on the Berkeley, Davis, Los Angeles, and Riverside campuses, the eight outlying field stations upon which the College conducts research, and of the 49 University of California Farm Advisor Offices offering assistance to farmers at county level." [90] Under the new plan of organization, as suggested by Hutchison, the provosts at Riverside and Davis reported to the president through the new vice-president.

CHANGES IN FACULTY GOVERNMENT

The same expansion that made administrative reorganization imperative after the war compelled the faculty to consider changes in its own procedures of government. By 1950, there were more than 3200 faculty members in the University system—about twice the number in 1941.[91] Even though the faculty were organized into two sections of the Academic Senate—northern and southern—they could no longer function effectively in their traditional town-hall fashion. When issues before the senate were provocative, as was the loyalty-oath question in 1949–1951, the senate required the largest halls on campus for its assembly. In such large gatherings, debate was either prolonged and confusing or skillfully dominated by articulate minorities. These weaknesses became the subject of extended deliberation by special faculty committees in both the Northern and Southern Sections. The Northern Section's committee acted first on April 14, 1952,[92] when its chairman, Frank L. Kidner, professor of economics at Berkeley, reported on a plan for the reorganization of the section that delegated virtually all faculty authority to a Representative Assembly. Technically a standing committee of the Northern Section, the Representative Assembly was elected so that groups of academic departments in the Berkeley, Davis, and San Francisco divisions were all represented. Its officers were identical to those of the senate, and it was empowered to act for the Northern Section in all matters except memorials and petitions addressed to the Regents. Except for the provisions that the senate could, within a reasonable time, or upon the initiative of twenty-five or more voting members, reconsider assembly decisions or direct it to deliberate on certain subjects, the decisions of the assembly were considered final. This plan was enacted by the Northern Section on June 3, 1952.[93]

A similar body, called the Legislative Assembly, was created by the Southern Section on December 17, 1952.[94]

By this time, the Northern Section had already delegated considerable authority over local matters to *divisions* at Davis and San Francisco. These divisions elected their own officers and appointed subcommittees that were counterparts of the major committees of the section. In the spring of 1955, the Special Committee on Reorganization for the Southern Section proposed to establish Los Angeles, Riverside, and Santa Barbara divisions in that section. For Santa Barbara's faculty, the suggestion meant more than local autonomy. It also meant that they would be, for the first time since the

University acquired their college, members of the Academic Senate. This required action of both sections and a change in the Standing Orders of the Regents. The Southern Section approved the plan in October, 1955,[95] the Northern Section approved the membership of Santa Barbara's faculty the following March.[96] The Standing Orders were amended accordingly on July 20, 1956.[97]

The reorganization and decentralization of the Academic Senate in the 1950s effectively protected the faculty from domination by unrepresentative minorities. It also made possible an enormous amount of delegation of authority to the faculties of individual campuses. Without that delegation it is doubtful that faculty government at a multicampus institution could have worked at all. The reforms also made the members of all faculties of the University equals insofar as their rights to a voice in academic affairs were concerned. Only their greater numbers and longer experience with faculty self-government gave UCLA and Berkeley continuing dominant positions in their respective sections of the senate.

At the Eighth All-University Faculty Conference in 1953, a study committee on Faculty Participating in Education Policy noted that "the faculty has played little, if any, part in the determination of policies affecting the growth of the University." [98] In a later passage, the committee said, ". . . Even the establishment of new campuses [has] usually come about as a result of requests or direct action of extra-University agencies, without consultation with any large segment of the faculty." [99]

The Regents and the administration might well have uttered the same complaint. They, after all, were forced by political considerations to accept Santa Barbara State College as a part of the University system, and by the realities of California's growing demand for educational opportunities, to expand existing facilities.

Precisely because the growth of the University was this far forced from without, rather than planned from within, President Sproul and the Regents had considerable difficulty in organizing it effectively. Part of the problem was that they did not believe that the state of California had enough money to support a system of several major, first-rate University centers. To avoid having to seek that kind of support, they sought to assign differentiated functions to the various campuses. For Berkeley and UCLA they reserved the broadest responsibilities for instruction and research. Expansion at Davis was held reasonably in line with development and needs for agricultural research and instruction.

At Santa Barbara and Riverside, emphasis was placed on excellence, smallness, and undergraduate programs. To further distinguish the major centers from the smaller units, UCLA and Berkeley were placed under the direction of chancellors, while the other campuses were directed by provosts. These distinctions could not be sustained very long. Continuing pressure of growing enrollment, the continuing threat of competition from other systems of higher education in the state, the need for expansion of graduate work and research to attract able teachers and scholars, and the natural tendency of the faculties and administrators on the several campuses to seek recognition through significant achievement in teaching and research all conspired to demand further expansion and elaboration of the scheme. Berkeley and UCLA, whether they wanted to or not, would have to share the University's resources with the newer campuses, as well as with each other. Concepts of the University changed profoundly. The stereotype of the American university with its one campus and assorted satellites was no longer appropriate to California's state university. It could remain neither small nor highly centralized. Between 1948 and 1956, this reality was recognized by the Regents, President Sproul, and the faculty when they worked out new administrative structures and academic government procedures appropriate to the University's multicampus system. The adjustments were incomplete only because both the Regents and President Sproul found it difficult to delegate powers and authority that had been associated with their offices for more than ninety years.

By the end of Sproul's administration as president, the University's policies toward expansion had altered. The preference of the President and the Regents for keeping the University as it was from 1919 to 1944 was obsolete by virtue of enrollment demands, and was also politically untenable. After the state constitution was amended in 1946 to prevent transfer of state or junior colleges to the University system, the acquisition of new campuses by independent legislative action was impossible. But future expansion as a public responsibility was shown to be imperative by the Strayer Report and subsequent studies that predicted enormous college and University enrollments in the coming decades. Thereafter, expansion was accepted as a fact of University life. Until 1957, it was met by expanding existing campuses. Later it would be met by building campuses from the ground up, and the multicampus University of California would no longer seem an accident of geography or an expedient of politics. Instead, the University's expansion to serve the coming generations without sacrifice of quality would become a deliberate policy of the Regents and the administration.

IV

Dynamics of the
Modern University

𝕮𝕺𝕮𝕺𝕮𝕺

IN THE eighth and ninth decades of its history, the University of California had all of the essential components of a mature and modern American university. It had good students who were carefully selected from among the top 15 per cent of the state's high school graduates. At the graduate level, its students were among the best products of colleges all over the world. There was a faculty of great eminence. An administration led by two outstanding presidents served it during these years. Its governing board was hard-working and deeply concerned about the University's welfare.

The University's research endeavors matured to an undisputed excellence in the decades after World War II. Enriched by the professorial talents of famous men and women in virtually every conceivable intellectual and artistic endeavor, the quality of teaching appeared manifestly to be of the highest level. Public service in agriculture, University Extension, and the contributions of organized research agencies and faculty experts were in evidence in every part of the life of the state. California's rapidly growing demand for men and women trained for the professions was being met by the University's professional and postgraduate schools.

The University's Regents and administration had discovered a way to provide services for large numbers of people in widely separated parts of the state. The University had five general campuses at Berkeley, Los Angeles,

Santa Barbara, Davis, and Riverside. Extension centers operated in both the north and south. Research stations dotted the California map wherever topography or climate best favored them or where they were relevant to specialized local conditions. There appeared to be no limit to the number of units that might eventually be established to perform the University's work.

Itself an intricate system of delicately balanced functions and authority, the University was also a part of a larger, still more complicated state system of higher education that included California's private colleges and universities and increasing numbers of public junior and state colleges. The University's future security required that all of these institutions work coordinately in educating the estimated hundreds of thousands who would eventually seek admission to their campuses. To avoid chaotic development that would inevitably result from a panic response to increasing enrollment demand, President Kerr and the Regents led efforts to write a new master plan for California higher education.

Students were profoundly affected by the University's expansion and adjustments to change. In the original structure of the University they were given little voice in the institution's policy-making. Throughout the ensuing years they were regarded as too young, too inexperienced, and too irresponsible to contribute seriously to planning and decisions affecting the general circumstances of student life. In 1964, members of a remarkably sophisticated student generation at Berkeley rebelled. They demanded privileges for on-campus political and social action and, more generally, recognition of their legitimate membership and interest in University affairs. The rebellion, which resulted in hundreds of arrests at its climax, forced a reexamination of some of the administrative and faculty attitudes toward students and prompted an acceleration of educational and administrative reforms that had long been under consideration but were forced into low priority by the continued urgencies of growth and expansion.

Creation of three new, somewhat experimental campuses at San Diego, Irvine, and Santa Cruz in the 1960s answered some of the problems of accommodating ever more students. But they helped to complicate the questions about the feasibility of a unified University with diversified components, the relative power and authority of the faculty, the Regents, the president, and the general public, and the most desirable and productive methods of higher education. Many of these questions remain undecided as the University ends its first century.

Chapter 22

ORGANIZED RESEARCH

AS LATE AS 1920, Professor John C. Merriam, chairman of the University's Research Board (subsequently president of Carnegie Institution), charged that the American university is "often financed almost exclusively for teaching and administration without reference to research, and it is assumed that the constructive work so necessary to the development of the faculty and students will be cared for in other ways." [1] The University of California was not exempt from his charge. In 1920, it had only $9000 available for research programs. The next year, with funds provided by Edward F. Searles and with increased Regental support, the research budget was enlarged to $32,317,[2] but that amount was still less than half of 1 per cent of the University's total expenditures for the year.

Despite meager financial encouragement of research endeavor, many members of the faculty insisted that research was the most characteristic feature of a university, as opposed to a college, and protected its status. In the 1920s, faculty members became accustomed to the formula that required that they spend six hours a week in the classroom; whatever time was needed for course preparation, for departmental and committee meetings, and for student conferences; and the remainder of their time in research. By the time Robert Gordon Sproul became president, research ability was a prime factor in faculty promotions and appointments. In his inaugural address he said that this was an "anomalous situation" in which "men who might be good teachers if they were encouraged by the hope of future advancement are drifting about in laboratories with a couple of test tubes in their hands making themselves useless in a most arduous and time-consuming way, while men who might be good investigators are wearing out their patience and the students in a vain effort to expound and to inspire large classes. . . ." [3] Ahead of his times, Sproul argued for a faculty consisting of some men who were primarily scholars and others who were primarily

366   THE UNIVERSITY OF CALIFORNIA 1868–1968

teachers. But the limitations of the budget and academic tradition favored the scholar-teacher. President Sproul sustained that tradition by championing the cause of teaching when nominations for faculty promotions came to his desk with perfunctory evidence of the candidates' classroom effectiveness, and on the other hand by improving the facilities and atmosphere in which research could be conducted.

THE UNIVERSITY'S SUPPORT

The University's basic support of research from the beginning has consisted of a portion of the scholar's salary, and such space, time, and supplies as are allocated to him for research by his department. The availability of good libraries and central University services also constitute a part of the University's contribution to research effort. In the humanities, the arts, and some of the social sciences, faculty members are able to accomplish significant research with little more support than this basic financing provides. But in other disciplines, scholars have been forced to seek extradepartmental money in order to complete their research and writing.

If a scholar needed only clerical assistance, travel funds, and special equipment that was not too expensive, the research grants set up by the Regents with an initial grant of $1000 in 1915, and administered since that time by campus committees on research, were available. By 1928, the total amount awarded by the Berkeley committee reached $93,877. During the Depression, funds for research support were severely limited. Then, during World War II, nondefense research was further curtailed because manpower shortages, accelerated teaching schedules, and travel restrictions kept professors in the classrooms. The scarcity of certain types of equipment also impaired wartime research. As a result of the Depression and wartime curtailments, the first postwar budgets for grants to be administered by the Berkeley campus Committee on Research were $98,000, only about $6000 more than they were in 1928.[4]

OUTSIDE SUPPORT

If scholars needed more funds and assistance than the University's departments or committees on research could provide, they turned to outside sources of financing. Precedent for such support was ample. Among other instances, it was observed in the establishment and support of the Lick Observatory, in the work of the Hooper Foundation in San Francisco, in the creation of the Heller Committee for Social Economics, and the Giannini Foundation for Agricultural Economics, and in the prewar development of Berkeley's Radiation Laboratory. Outside the field of agriculture, the major contributors to these endeavors were private individuals or companies. It was not until after World War II that federal support in nonagricultural disciplines became available. When it came, it was fantastically generous.

The exciting news accounts of the scientific endeavors that culminated in the frightening and spectacular conclusion of World War II at Hiroshima and Nagasaki not only melted some of the hostilities Americans previously held toward intellectuals of all sorts, but whetted the public appetite for new scientific miracles. The willingness of the people to have their government invest huge sums of money in research endeavors at American universities was a part of the new mood.

Science itself expanded as a result of the war experiences. Using techniques of team research that were characteristic of large wartime laboratories, they enlisted many able minds for a coordinated assault on research problems once set aside because they were too big for one man to handle. Originating in the physical sciences, such cooperative effort soon became common in the behavioral and social sciences as well. Ernest O. Lawrence's example of using expensive large-scale technical facilities as legitimate laboratory tools freed scholars of the notion that respectable scholarship was accomplished only with the paraphernalia a scientist could built with his own hands and finance out of departmental budgets. The scholar's sights were therefore raised beyond goals appropriate to pedestrian technology, and beyond the confines of severely restricted budgets. Almost overnight the scale of University research endeavor became enormous. And a big share of the bill was being paid by the federal government.

QUESTIONS OF INDEPENDENCE AND BALANCE

The bright new horizons of University research in the postwar world were viewed with uneven enthusiasm by members of the faculty. It was soon clear that all disciplines of learning would not have an equal share of the largesse forthcoming from government, industry, and foundations. The physical and health sciences, and most of the natural and social sciences, would attract the new research funds. But in the humanities, the arts, and some of the social sciences no hopes for increased financing were realistic.

The factor that determined allocation of the new research financing was the need for solutions to questions which, if unanswered, blocked the nation's technological progress or prevented rational approaches to social, economic, and political planning. Research that did not satisfy such needs could not attract outside support easily. This practical consideration intensified academic controversies over the merits of "applied" research. Several leaders of the faculty maintained that the bulk of the University's research should be what they called "pure" and "uncommitted," pursued only to satisfy the curiosity of the scholar without foreknowledge or concern for its ultimate usefulness. They considered the new financing provided by outside agencies, and particularly by the federal government, to be a potential threat to that principle. Some scholars, they believed, might be tempted to select research problems for which financial support was known to be available, instead of those that simply satisfied their urge to explore the "truth." Once engaged in a research project subsidized with extramural sums, a scholar might, in order to meet his scheduled commitments, be forced to shun the temptation to follow interesting byways of research that might yield unexpected knowledge.

Another fear raised by the sudden availability of outside research funds was that the University might lose effective control over scholarly endeavor on its campuses. The scholar, once responsible only to his department, often assumed additional obligations to extradepartmental research groups within the University, and to funding agencies outside the University. Maintaining a balance of research effort among the various disciplines became increasingly difficult for the University because it simply could not command enough funds to counterbalance massive efforts in one enterprise or another financed by government or industry.

Despite the difficulties and controversy implicit in accepting large extramural contracts and grants for research, these funds were welcomed by the less conservative faculty members. One very practical consideration was that if the University of California turned such grants down as a matter of principle, they would be given to other institutions or, in the form of subsidies, to private research and development firms. Distinguished scholars would follow support wherever it was found and the University might lose faculty strength, graduate students, and equipment and facilities as a result. Moreover, it was believed that well-established academic traditions of the University would protect the integrity of its research effort and discourage opportunism among scholars. Defenders of the new style of research and the massive outside contributions that made it possible also asserted that applied or developmental research was as valuable and respectable as so-called pure research. In fact, they considered the line between pure and applied research to be less sharply defined than many people supposed. Finally, the point that usually ended argument was the fact that the University could not, with its own funds or with appropriations from the state, support the costly, sophisticated research of the modern age.

President Sproul was among those who clearly favored the new approach to research. He not only found nothing unethical about the scholar who could anticipate the probable results of his research, but also expected faculty members to describe such expectations when applying for research assistance.[5] In various paraphrases, this requirement was reiterated every year beginning in 1946. One articulate critic of this policy—emphasizing research *projects* and welcoming research contracts—was Raymond Birge, chairman of the Department of Physics and chairman of the Berkeley campus Committee on Research from 1945 to 1953. In November, 1948, he wrote:

> Projects are, fundamentally, related to *development,* rather than to research. If a person has a carefully formulated *project,* and especially if he has a definite and detailed *budget,* the chances are 100 to 1 that the project is concerned with development. . . .[6]

Later in the same letter he says:

> Contract research may be welcomed as an *addition* to the usual University research, but *not* as a *substitute* for it. When the money volume of such contract research becomes 50 to 100 times as great as that of research supported directly by the University there is reason to fear the eventual extinction of the latter.[7]

Despite Professor Birge's arguments, President Sproul's policy prevailed. Birge was informed on May 2, 1949, for instance, that during the All-University Faculty Conference at Davis a few days earlier, Sproul had restated the need for project outlines and "implied that such projects as laymen might be able partly to understand, and as promised rather striking results, would supply him with the most effective 'sales talk.' "[8]

The argument did not end when Birge retired as chairman of the research committee at Berkeley. In 1955, his successor, Alden H. Miller, wrote to Chancellor Kerr to express "persistent concern of both faculty and regents that university research may be dictated as to type and quality by contract and donation money. The urge to seek contracts and special grants from outside is directly proportional to the amount of cutting which the research committee is forced to make in internal grants." [9] Miller's successor was a humanist, Henry Nash Smith of the English department, who wrote ". . . We have in mind this vast and increasing disproportion between intra-mural and extra-mural research funds. The problem of extra-mural funds is seen to be even more serious when we realize that these funds come preponderantly from one agency or another of the Federal government. . . ." [10]

THE EXAMPLE ON THE HILL

The Radiation Laboratory at Berkeley, although atypical in both size and function, is often cited as a "case in point" in discussions of the modern approach to University research. Supported almost entirely by the United States Atomic Energy Commission since 1947, its accelerators became increasingly larger and more sophisticated. New ones built after the war included the electron synchrotron and proton linear accelerator, built in 1948; the bevatron, 1954; the heavy ion linear accelerator, 1957; and the 88-inch spiral ridge cyclotron, 1962.[11] With these and the prewar machines, hundreds of artificial radioisotopes were discovered. To the four synthetic elements discovered by Radiation Laboratory scientists before World War II, nine more were added by the laboratory's scientists after the war and before 1961. In 1948, using the 184-inch cyclotron, scientists produced man-made mesons for the first time. With the bevatron, the antiproton and antineutron were discovered. By the spring of 1965, the talent and facilities available at the laboratory had made possible the discovery of about one-third of the approximately eighty known atomic particles and had revolutionized man's concepts of matter.[12]

The laboratory, renamed the Lawrence Radiation Laboratory in 1958 in memory of its founder, was also responsible for pioneering the use of cyclotron beams and radioisotopes in biology, medicine, agriculture, and industry. One of the leaders in the biological applications of nuclear science was Ernest Lawrence's brother John, a physician who came to Berkeley in 1937 from New Haven, Connecticut. He conducted experiments that led to the development of safety measures for working with nuclear materials and initiated experimentation with the now highly refined techniques for using heavy-particle, high-energy beams in biological research and in the diagnosis and treatment of disease.

In the spring of 1966, more than 120 faculty members had some affiliation with the laboratory, and 330 graduate-student research assistants were employed there.[13] Three years earlier, 54 Ph.D. theses were completed at the laboratory—14 per cent of all the Ph.D.s granted at Berkeley that year.[14]

The Lawrence Radiation Laboratory functioned more as a physical facility than it did as an academic or administrative unit, and it was so immense and so well supported financially that scholars who worked there enjoyed as much independence as (and, perhaps, even more than) some of their counterparts on the main campus. In these important respects it differed from many less well-endowed research groups in the University. But it was nevertheless regarded as a model for partnership between academia and government that could be fabulously productive and was worthy of emulation.

ORGANIZED RESEARCH

The virtues of organized research, sometimes involving scholars of several disciplines, was appreciated long before World War II. By that time there were about eighteen bureaus, centers, institutes, laboratories, museums, and research stations within the University.[15] Among the oldest were the Lick Observatory, the Scripps Institution of Oceanography, and the Hooper Foundation.

In 1927, the financial benefactions of the Laura Spelman Rockefeller Foundation of New York made possible the establishment and maintenance of an Institute for Child Welfare that later became a part of Berkeley's Institute of Human Development. This unit has studied physical and mental development and personality change in one group of people from birth through age thirty, and in another group from age ten to age forty. Its work has subsequently been supported by the Carnegie, Ford, and Rockefeller foundations and the National Institute of Mental Health. In 1932, the Rockefeller Foundation provided $182,000 [16] to support the eleven-year-old Bureau of Public Administration, whose staff built up a library and expertise in governmental affairs that became invaluable to legislators and public administrators.

Anticipating postwar difficulties between labor and management in California, Governor Warren asked the legislature to create Institutes of Industrial Relations at both the Berkeley and Los Angeles campuses. Two years later, in 1947, the state legislature created an Institute of Transportation and Traffic Engineering to "carry on research and education related to the design, operation, maintenance, and safety of highways, airports, and other facilities for public transportation." [17] Its facilities are located in Richmond, Berkeley, and Los Angeles.

In 1941, the early work in biology and medicine carried out in the Radiation Laboratory was placed under the direction of Dr. John H. Lawrence in a new Donner Laboratory. Funds for its first building were donated by William H. Donner, president of the Donner Foundation, in memory of his son, who died from cancer.[18]

With the exception of agricultural research projects and a few units supported by the legislature, it is evident that most of the organized research at the University before 1945 was financed by private philanthropy. With the end of the war and the availability of federal funds, organized research units proliferated rapidly. The University of California's *Centennial Record,* published in 1966, lists 131, and the roster does not include several that had been established and disbanded in the years after the war and one or two that were in the planning stages when the book was compiled. By 1968, the whole universe occupied their interest, as represented in such postwar units as the Division of Oceanic Research at San Diego; the Philip L. Boyd Desert Research Center; the White Mountain Research Station for high altitude studies; Space Sciences Laboratories at San Diego and Berkeley; a Space Sciences Center at UCLA; and a Universitywide Institute of Geophysics and Planetary Physics. Medical problems were the province of Cancer Research Institutes at UCLA and San Francisco; Cardiovascular Research units at UCLA and San Francisco; the Physiological Research Laboratory at San Diego; the Francis I. Proctor Foundation for Research in Ophthalmology at San Francisco; and the Jules Stein Eye Institute at UCLA. In Berkeley's Hormone Research Laboratory, established in 1950 as a successor to the endeavors of Dr. Herbert M. Evans' Institute of Experimental Biology in the 1920s, a staff under the direction of Dr. C. H. Li achieved the first isolation of five of the known pituitary hormones, including the growth hormone, somatotropin, and ACTH, the adrenal-stimulating hormone.[19] In the Virus Laboratory created at Berkeley in 1948, Nobel Laureate Wendell Stanley led research that resulted in new techniques in electron microscopy; new developments in ultracentrifugation, including new and powerful optical systems; the first crystallization of a polio virus; and the establishment of the exact sequence of the 158 amino acids in the subunit tobacco mosaic virus protein.[20] In the Chemical Biodynamics Laboratory, another unit that was originated at the Lawrence Radiation Laboratory, scientists under the direction of Nobel Laureate Melvin Calvin conducted studies using organic compounds that incorporate carbon-14, the radioisotope used as a tracer in chemistry and biology. The best-known work of the laboratory was undertaken in the study of photosynthesis.[21] Giant disc antennae of the Radio Astronomy Laboratory at Hat Creek monitored the heavens for new information on the structure and dynamics of the galaxy and on lunar and planetary astronomy.[22] The humanities were represented by such units as the Russian and East European Studies Center, The Center for the Study of Comparative Folklore and Mythology Studies, and the African Studies Center, all located at UCLA. (Comparable units in some of these fields were also established on other campuses.)

Some of the proliferation of organized research units after the war was caused by nothing more than the recognition by many faculty members that cooperative scholarly endeavor is a logical approach to some of their searches for new knowledge. But there were other advantages, too. Because organized research units are semiautonomous components of the University, their members often enjoy more freedom and independence than faculty members whose research is supported and controlled entirely by their departments. Research units are also attractive objects of extramural financial support, which means that they are often well-equipped, well-supplied, and well-staffed. In 1966–1967 more than 3269 people employed by the University engaged only in research and public service without teaching responsibilities.[23] Most of them were affiliated with the University's bureaus, centers, institutes, and laboratories. In the very nature of group effort, where there is a division of labor with shared credit, some scholars were able to appear frequently—along with their colleagues—as authors of scientific publications. Finally, only units supported by contracts—which provide research supplies, secretarial help, equipment, and graduate assistance—could hire graduate research assistants. This gave members of contract-supported research units a decided advantage since research assistants received substantially larger compensation than the teaching assistants who could be hired out of departmental funds.

Because a relatively small percentage of the University faculty is affiliated with research units, there was in 1968 understandable internal questioning of the role they play in the University's work and the advantages they provide for their members. The principle of organized research is too sound, however, to be set aside as a result of the debate. It is also a good investment. In 1963–1964, 28.8 per cent of the organized-research expenditures at Berkeley came from general funds; 3.3 per cent came from state agreements and appropriations; 58 per cent came from federal grants, contracts, and appropriations; 7.0 per cent came from gifts and private grants; 2.3 per cent came from endowments; and .6 per cent came from other sources.[24] And the dividends in new knowledge are enormous.

The fact remains that organized research is changing the character of the University in important ways unfamiliar to the general public. It is completely outside the daily experience of most undergraduate students and to date involves a minority of the faculty. Once considered incidental or auxiliary appendages to the University, increasingly such research agencies are becoming significant components of its organic structure. Achieving a more thorough assimilation of their activities than has thus far been possible may well be one of the major challenges of the University's second century.

THE OVERHEAD FACTOR

In March, 1940, Professor Birge wrote to President Sproul to warn him that Professor Lawrence would soon receive "a very large grant from an outside source," [25] and that the consequent enlargement of the atomic scientist's work would inevitably draw heavily upon overhead items provided by the physics department. In 1941, Birge reported that Lawrence had personally repaid the department several hundred dollars to offset hidden costs entailed in the operations of the Radiation Laboratory.[26] These incidents mark the beginning of University concern with protecting itself against loss of funds through expenditures incurred as a result of accepting grants or contracts of departmental administration, increased use of the library, maintenance of physical plants, use of office and laboratory space, and other items that would be difficult to track down individually for each project, but which in aggregate entail considerable expenditure.

During the war the federal government accepted a responsibility to provide funds to cover such indirect costs and, although the practices of government agencies has varied in the amount of overhead payments allowed, that precedent has been observed in all contract and grant negotiations since. Recently some government agencies have asserted that research projects under their sponsorship frequently involve instructional value for graduate students.[27] On that basis they have agreed to share rather than cover overhead costs incurred in research for which they have contracted.

In the early years of contract research, the Regents decided to use income from contract research overhead payments as a special fund. In the 1940s, occasional appropriations from the fund were made to the campuses or departments from which the payments originated, but the bulk of the fund was retained to finance self-liquidating projects like residence halls, dormitories, parking lots, and other such investments. Handled this way, the fund not only made campus improvements possible but also served as a hedge against the time when contracts and grants might not be as plentiful.[28]

In the winter of 1953–1954, a time when the state was beginning to dip into its reserves to meet expenses, the legislative analyst began to question the University's use of the overhead funds on contract research. In his report of the 1954–1955 budget, he noted that $13,580,000 had been accumulated by the Regents in two large reserve funds. Arguing that the overhead funds were actually reimbursement of expenses already incurred out of the state's general fund, he suggested that half of the overhead funds be applied to the University's operating budget that year and proposed that the legislature cut the budget accordingly. This was done, and negotiations between the state director of finance and the University's vice-president for business affairs resulted in an agreement that in future years half of the overhead payments on federal contracts would be used for educational purposes and self-liquidating projects selected by the Regents and the other half would be applied to the operating budget of the University. Ten years later, when federal-grant income began to produce sizable reserves in overhead payments, these, too, were divided.[29]

By 1966, half of all federal-grant payments were put into the University's general fund, state appropriations were reduced by an equal amount, and the other half was deposited in the Regents' Opportunity Fund, which is used for student aid and special programs for which state appropriations are not available. A particularly appropriate use of the funds was the creation of an Institute for Creative Arts in 1963 and a Humanities Institute in 1966.[30]

The development of large-scale research and the related dependence of the University on outside agencies for research support still troubles many faculty members. Some scientists who rely on massive, complex laboratory facilities are impatient with the time it takes to build them, and, later, with the internal regulations devised to govern use of the equipment. They are also restless with delays inevitably involved in cooperation with other scientists. They miss the independence and spontaneity enjoyed by scientists in simpler days. Outside of the sciences, many faculty members still express belief that the development of large, semiautonomous research units tends to break down the academic organization of the University and divide the loyalty of the scholar between the University and the source of his research support. Although their individual needs for research funds are relatively small, the social scientists and humanists still like to talk about how much they could accomplish with sums of money comparable to those available to their colleagues in the physical and health sciences. Students allege that the research complex of the University cheats them of the time and attention of their scholar-teachers.

Most of these concerns are endemic to all of American higher education. They cannot be settled or arbitrated easily because they are influenced by diverse points of view within the academic community and governed by the special laws of supply and demand at work in research economy. The academic world is also anxious that problems and imbalances be not so radically treated that the momentum of modern scholarship is impaired. For the growth of the research enterprise, and the enlargement of its outside support, has yielded impressive benefits. It has encouraged scholars to plan more boldly and ambitiously in devising research problems. It has assured them that financing and interdisciplinary cooperation is available to support valid and promising work. It has directed the scholar's attention beyond the boundaries of the University to the larger universe beyond it. And, for better or for worse, it has tended to break down the caste system within research itself so that "pure," "applied," and "developmental" research all enjoy academic respectability as long as they are conducted under strict observation and control according to the University's high standards of scholarship. This new flexibility helps to advance civilization. It also keeps the University relevant to the time and society it serves.

Chapter 23

CLARK KERR AND THE ERA OF PLANNING

CLARK KERR, the son of a Pennsylvania farmer-schoolteacher who became Berkeley's first chancellor in 1952 and the University's twelfth president in 1958, personifies in many ways the "educated man" of commencement-address fame. By what one guesses to be a conscious, continuous effort to develop his powers of observation, cultivate his personal tastes, seek out enriching experiences, and sharpen his intellectual acuity, he made himself into a man who commands international respect in two fields—higher education and industrial relations. Behind rimless glasses, his deep blue eyes are alert and incisive. Quick, firm movements of his body suggest an athletic bent once satisfied on the soccer field as a student at Swarthmore, and, later, with his children on the lot behind his El Cerrito home. His business attire, usually on the somber side, is impeccably neat, revealing a taste for order and precision. A similar clue was found in his offices, both as president and chancellor. There one found comfort in furnishings and decor that were unmistakably of top quality and a remarkable absence of mementos, gadgets, or even large piles of working documents to distract the occupant or his guests from conversation or deliberation.

As a University administrator, Clark Kerr's approach was pragmatic and deliberative. He gave study and planning high priority. Once long-range objectives were agreed upon, he worked toward their achievement by choosing from among carefully evaluated tactical alternatives. His research-and-planning approach put him in command of voluminous information which he used, with the scholar's facility for almost total recall, to explain or defend his policies. Some of his most impressive moments were those in which he appeared before committees of the Regents, small groups, or press conferences to talk informally, without notes, about the current problems and future needs of the University. His disarming candor and superior knowledge of relevant facts and figures were not easily challenged by adversaries.

On the platform, Kerr's oratorical style is derived from the lecture hall and the debate manual. His vocabulary is that of the social scientist, and he has often been misrepresented by critics who interpret too literally the analogies to higher education that he occasionally draws from concepts in industrial relations. He seldom tells a broad joke, but is deft at good-natured wit of the caliber that once led him to assert that his biggest problems as the chancellor at Berkeley were to find enough parking for the faculty, athletes for the alumni, and sex for the students.

Actually, parking was not as important to the faculty in 1952 as was reassurance that the loyalty-oath dispute and the continuing restraints of the McCarthy era had not destroyed academic freedom at the University. Chancellor Kerr made restoration of faculty confidence a major objective of his administration. When worried faculty members asked him if they should accept speaking engagements before off-campus organizations, he assured them that they need not have his permission one way or another, but should rely on their own judgment. He further demonstrated his intent to support faculty members against unreasonable infringements of their rights early in December, 1953, when Regent Neylan read to the full Board a quotation from a *Daily Californian* report of an off-campus address by Harold Winkler, an assistant professor of political science. According to the newspapers, Winkler said, ". . . There is something wrong with a young person today, especially in our rich and affluent United States, who is not idealistically inspired to the point of belonging to a communist, socialist, anarchist or other similarly inspired group." [1] Winkler protested that he had been misquoted in the *Daily Californian* and that his remark had been reported out of context. Even so, Kerr was under considerable pressure from several Regents to recommend Winkler's immediate dismissal. Chairman of the Board Edward A. Dickson even implied that Kerr's future at the University was at stake in the matter.[2]

Kerr insisted that Winkler not be dismissed. Such a dismissal would seriously damage the faculty's confidence that the University was committed to a policy of maximum personal freedoms. At a meeting memorable for its emotionalism and acrimony, a majority of the Board finally accepted Kerr's recommendation. A month or so later, Regent Dickson made a point of telling Kerr that, after thinking the matter over, he believed that Kerr had been right all along and that the correct action had been taken.[3]

Another move that restored faculty confidence in the University's concern for freedom was a modest revision that liberalized the long-controversial Rule 17. First pronounced in 1936 (as Regulation Number 11) and revised several times in the intervening years, the rule in its 1956 form stipulated that only faculty and employee organizations and student organizations recognized by the Associated Students or the dean of students could use University facilities for meetings of general student interest without special permission or an invitation from the president of the University. It was this rule that forced candidates for state and national office to address University students from trailers or platforms erected over the gutters of public streets on the periphery of the campuses. It also restricted the activities of student chapters of national professional organizations. Late in 1956, an ASUC committee proposed that student organizations that were not recognized by the ASUC or University and some organizations not associated in any way with the University be allowed to use the University facilities in conformity with specified procedures. These procedures fixed responsibility for expenses and conduct of the meetings and protected the University from involvement in religious or partisan political recruitment activities. Clark Kerr joined the student committee in making a presentation of the proposal to President Sproul. Subsequently, the proposal was referred to the Academic Freedom Committee of the Academic Senate for study and recommendation. On January 8, 1957, the Representative Assembly endorsed the proposal and, after further discussion at a conference of the University's vice-president, chief campus administrative officers, and Academic Senate representatives, Sproul announced the final revision.[4]

As revised in 1957, the rule permitted organizations of students who had a faculty adviser to use University facilities for special meetings even though they were not officially "recognized" by the ASUC or the University. It rescinded the requirement that controversial issues be discussed by a panel and replaced it with a statement that the University "recognizes a responsibility to encourage student groups to present two or more representative views of controversial issues whenever possible, within a reasonable period of time and under comparable circumstances." [5] It continued to prohibit use of University facilities for "the purpose of soliciting political party membership or religious conversion" and to prohibit the conduct and promotion of meetings so as to "involve the University in political or sectarian religious activities in a partisan way." [6]

Kerr's efforts to re-establish an atmosphere of freedom on the campus were seriously jeopardized in 1952 when Senator Hugh Burns, chairman of California's Senate Fact-Finding Sub-Committee on Un-American Activities, announced that every major California university and college had joined "to create a solid academic front . . . against the highly developed technique of the Communist Party to insinuate its members into our college campuses." [7] The *modus operandi* of the new effort required the appointment of "contact men" on every college and University campus. Only one of the University's contact men was identified publicly—Clark Kerr, at Berkeley. Kerr himself issued a statement saying that there had been no contact between him and Senator Burns' committee and that there would be none except after consultation with members of the faculty and with students.[8] Kerr's refusal to initiate contact so irritated Senator Burns and his principal investigator, Richard E. Combs, that Kerr became a frequent target of criticism in the committee's reports in subsequent years. Ironically, Kerr learned years later that another administrator, not he, performed the "contact man" responsibilities at Berkeley.[9]

Restoring an atmosphere of freedom was only one of the challenges of Berkeley's first chancellor. Even more difficult was the challenge to overcome the lethargy that had started to settle in about a campus that was weary after an exhausting loyalty-oath dispute, had no leadership exclusively its own in statewide councils, and seemed destined to mark time or even decline in stature as the building of new campuses continued. The new chancellor counteracted this deterioration in campus morale by his own public expressions of pride and optimism concerning Berkeley's future. He also directly involved members of the faculty in restoring campus momentum by naming them part-time assistants and, later, vice-chancellors in his office. He demonstrated his seriousness about working to enhance Berkeley's greatness by involving faculty members and students in long-range physical and academic planning for the campus.

In 1956, Berkeley's long-range development plan was reported to the

Regents. It called for the development of the central campus area for academic purposes, with clusters of buildings devoted to related subject matter. Several new buildings were plotted, each to be as large as its site would allow. But the over-all density of buildings to land area on the central campus would be limited to 25 per cent. This ratio would make possible the development of glades, plazas, and terraces to preserve the open feeling of the campus. Many old or temporary structures that had become inefficient, dangerous, or unsightly were marked for demolition to make way for new construction. Natural groves and woodlands along Strawberry Creek were retained, as were historic landmarks like South Hall, President's House, and Sather Gate. Nonacademic facilities were plotted on the campus periphery or on outlying properties.[10]

The needs of students for recreational, cultural, and living accommodations were given due attention, and provision was made for residence halls to accommodate 4800 students, for a new student center, and for new intramural playing fields.[11]

In the summer of 1957, Kerr submitted Berkeley's academic plan to the Regents. Consisting of more than 120 typewritten pages, this plan made thirteen major recommendations concerning optimum enrollment (25,000), the proper "mix" of undergraduates and graduates, admissions policies, student-faculty ratios, faculty recruitment, research expansion, and land acquisition. Each recommendation was backed up by careful documentation and statistics. The whole project had been initiated by the Chancellor himself in 1954, when he discovered that the committee appointed to advise him on physical development of the campus did not have enough information about academic goals to guide its work. In November, 1956, President Sproul requested that statements of academic policy for both Berkeley and Los Angeles be prepared for submission to the Regents as a guide for the development of major campuses. The administrative staff at Berkeley had a comfortable head start on this assignment, and Chancellor Kerr was able to make an impressive report to the Regents in July, 1957.

Implementation of these long-range plans provided reassurance to students and faculty members that the Berkeley campus would not be allowed to slide. Further evidence came from sources outside the University in 1957. On April 21, the Chicago *Tribune* published the results of a survey it had made among about fifty educators and administrative officers across the country who were asked to rate the departments of the top ten American universities. They rated twenty-four of Berkeley's twenty-eight departments outstanding and ranked the Berkeley campus third, immediately after Harvard and Yale, among the top ten universities in the country.[12] In December, the same year, the *Association of American Colleges Bulletin* reported that the University of California on all campuses ranked second to Columbia in the total number of doctoral degrees granted in all fields; third, behind Harvard and Columbia, in the number of departments in which more doctorates were awarded than at any other institution; and tied with Chicago in the number of fields in which it was ranked among the top five institutions in the country in doctorates awarded.[13]

In 1957 the Regents were seeking a successor to the retiring President Sproul, and Chancellor Kerr's record at Berkeley was by then impressive.

In June, Edwin Pauley, chairman of the Board of Regents, spoke to Kerr after the Berkeley commencement and suggested that there was a lot of planning required for the University in years ahead and that he hoped someone within the University and familiar with its work would be president when the work was undertaken. The Chancellor interpreted the remark as a hint that he might be under consideration as Robert Gordon Sproul's successor. Two months later another Regent, Edward Carter, congratulated Kerr on his academic plan for Berkeley and said, in effect, that he hoped that other members of the Board would share his estimate of what Kerr could do for the total University.

Until these two conversations in the summer of 1957, Chancellor Kerr and many other people in the University believed that the Regents had long before been committed to the election of UCLA's Chancellor Raymond B. Allen to the presidency when Sproul retired. Conclusive proof that this assumption was a mistake came about a week before the Regents' meeting at Davis in October, 1957, when Kerr was summoned to President Sproul's office and told that the Regents were about to ask him to become the next president of the University of California. When Kerr asked Sproul if he had any advice on what his response should be, the President said that if he could choose between being president of the University and serving on the Berkeley faculty, he would elect the latter. With that thought laid atop his own estimate of the toil and perils associated with the University's presidency, Kerr left to think the matter over for a few days. Then, just after the Regents' meeting, where he was unanimously elected president on October 18, 1957, he told the committee of Regents that called upon him that he realized that being president of the University was a tough job and that any president "would always have his head above the parapet with everybody shooting arrows at him." But if they wanted him, he would accept.

Clark Kerr assumed the duties of the presidency in July, 1958. The following September he was inaugurated in a seventeen-day series of ceremonies that were indicative of the change that had taken place in the University during the twenty-eight years of Sproul's leadership. In 1930, Sproul was invested with his office in what was essentially a Berkeley event—the seat of the University being allowed to represent the sum of its parts. In 1958, the University was regarded as having seven centers large enough for an inaugural observance and Clark Kerr traveled 2000 miles by air and 1500 miles by automobile to attend them. Students, faculty members, administrators, alumni, and public officials arranged in his honor thirteen receptions, four full-scale academic processions, five inaugural convocations, seven luncheons, four formal banquets, a review of the University's research fleet at La Jolla, production of a Greek trilogy, an opera, a concert of chamber music, and several press conferences.[14]

The University he was to lead included Berkeley, the "mother" campus, with general University offerings for 19,344 students; UCLA, with 16,488 students, distinguished and growing though only forty years old in the University system; Davis, still predominantly concerned with agriculture, although its seven-year-old College of Letters and Science was thriving; Santa Barbara, a "quality" liberal arts college with 2941 students; Riverside, where an "Amherst of the West" type of college of letters and science was in its fifth year, accommodating 1087 students; the San Francisco Medical Center, with 1569 students in medicine, dentistry, pharmacy, and nursing; La Jolla, with 51 graduate students enrolled in the Scripps Institution of Oceanography; and Hastings College of the Law, with 259 students.[15] In all, the University had almost 47,000 [16] students. To accommodate another 20,000 [17] students within the next seven years, the Regents had already agreed in principle to build new campuses in the Santa Clara County region, in the vicinity of San Diego, and in the rapidly growing Orange County.[18] Development of still another campus in the San Joaquin Valley was under serious discussion.[19]

One of Clark Kerr's tasks as president would be to coordinate this growth without sacrificing the University's quality, prestige, or public support. A corollary to this task was the need to rearrange administrative responsibility within the University so that the president had more time for executing broad policies, and so that chancellors or other chief executives had sufficient authority for the exercise of their responsibilities.

The Regents had anticipated this problem and beginning in 1951 increased the president's discretion in budget matters. The chancellors and provosts on the various campuses were given increased authority over business affairs beginning in 1953. In 1958 the president was authorized to solicit and accept gifts and negotiate research contracts involving sums up to $15,000.[20] During this period the Regents also relinquished their prerogatives to act on appointments and promotions of faculty members below tenure rank.

As a change in the presidency became more imminent, the Regents went even further. On April 18, 1958, they approved the employment of a new management consulting firm—Cresap, McCormick and Paget—"to review the organization and procedures of the over-all management of the University." This firm's report was delivered four months after Clark Kerr became president. It proposed two major changes. The first was that the president be the only University officer reporting directly to the Board of Regents. The second was that "to the maximum extent possible" the chief campus officer (chancellor or provost) be given administrative authority over all aspects of campus affairs and that direct-line administrative relationships between Universitywide officers and campus staff be eliminated.[21]

In August, 1959, about nine months after the consultants submitted their general recommendations, President Kerr reported on the progress that had been made in administrative reorganization since he became president.

For the first time since the position was created in 1949, the office of vice-president of the University, conceived as one truly second in command, was filled on July 18, 1958.[22] Its first occupant was Harry R. Wellman, who had been vice-president—agricultural sciences since 1952. A conservative, practical administrator, Wellman was highly regarded not only for his direction of the largest of the University's teaching and research divisions—agriculture—but also as an effective representative on committees concerned with University expansion and relations with other institutions. In time, he assumed major responsibility for academic matters and budget preparation.

At the same time that Wellman was named vice-president of the University, Glenn T. Seaborg, who shared a Nobel Prize in chemistry with Professor Edwin M. McMillan, was chosen to fill Kerr's position as chancellor at Berkeley.[23] Holding degrees from both UCLA and Berkeley, Seaborg had directed plutonium research for the Manhattan Project during World War II, and later became an associate director of the Lawrence Radiation Laboratory at Berkeley, a position he retained throughout his chancellorship.

Another important appointment was that of Dr. John B. de C. M. Saunders, professor of anatomy and dean of the College of Medicine, as provost at San Francisco.[24]

In the face of continually rising enrollments, it appeared foolish to hold Davis, Santa Barbara, and Riverside to specialized educational missions, and they were redesignated general campuses. Their provosts became chancellors in recognition of their new status.[25]

The roles of agriculture and University Extension were placed in a different perspective when the chief officers of these programs were designated deans instead of vice-presidents.[26]

To indicate their responsibilities to the University as well as to the Board of Regents, the general counsel and the secretary and treasurer of the Regents were given the added title of vice-president. The offices of vice-president–business affairs and controller were made reportable to the president instead of to the Regents.[27]

Seventeen statewide administrative committees were eliminated and three were transferred to campus jurisdiction.[28]

The size of the centralized administrative staff of the University was reduced as accounting, nonacademic personnel, and other activities were placed under the authority of chancellors and provosts. Budgets for such statewide activities as the School of Public Health, Institutes of Geophysics, Industrial Relations, Marine Resources, and Transportation and Traffic Engineering were transferred to appropriate campuses.[29]

By March, 1959, chancellors and the provost at San Francisco had greater latitude in making transfers of funds within approved budgets. Until that time, all such transfers required processing by a central office. Thereafter, 80 per cent could be made at the campus level.[30]

Through these and many other subtle but important administrative changes, President Kerr and the Regents achieved most of the things they could do unilaterally to prepare for University growth in the 1960s. But their ability to move faster and farther was limited by some brand-new facts of life. By 1958, the University of California was no longer the most-attended public institution of higher education in the state. The junior colleges and state colleges were becoming more numerous and their enrollments were soaring. In Clark Kerr's last year as chancellor at Berkeley, the state colleges enrolled only 146 fewer students than the University did on all of its campuses.[31] The year he became president, the state colleges had 1200 more students than the University had and were ahead to stay.[32] In the same year, the junior colleges enrolled more students than the University and the state colleges combined.[33] What is more, there were institutions within both the junior-college and state-college systems that had distinguished histories and deserved their reputations for quality programs. With loyal constituencies of alumni, students' parents, and proud citizens of the communities in which they were located, they also had considerable political muscle. In their newfound strength and significance, many of them began to consider entering new educational territory—some of which historically belonged to the University of California. In August, 1958, just a month after he assumed the presidency, Clark Kerr told Regents attending a meeting of their Educational Policy Committee of his concern for the University's future in the absence of reliable information about the unfolding pattern of higher education in the state.

COLLEGES IN THE PORK BARREL

Legislative leaders were also concerned about the lack of planning for the future of California's higher education. With an eye on the limited financial resources of the state and with their consciences nagging them to resist efforts to squander appropriations for colleges and campuses where they were not needed or upon programs that were costly duplicates of existing adequate efforts, they required more convincing guidance. Without it they had no way to refute unreasonable requests of either their lawmaking colleagues or the voters back home.

The Strayer Report of 1948 lost its effectiveness as a guide for planning; the legislature authorized a new, more comprehensive study in 1953. It was conducted by the staff of the Liaison Committee of the Regents and the State Board of Education with T. R. McConnell, former chancellor of the University of Buffalo, as chief consultant. Called *A Restudy of the Needs of California in Higher Education,* the "McConnell Report," or simply the "Restudy," predicted that by 1965 the state's colleges and universities, both public and private, would have to accommodate up to 254,000 students, more than twice the number projected for 1955.[34] Despite this predicted increase, and because its authors rejected the assumptions of the Strayer Report that there is some optimum limitation on the size of an institution of higher learning, the McConnell Report recommended that enrollment ceilings on the University and state colleges be lifted and that no new state colleges or University campuses be built until after further review in 1965.[35]

The McConnell Report's recommendation that no new four-year campuses be built was ignored by many legislators. Almost as soon as the 1955 session opened, five Alameda County assemblymen and another from San Joaquin County introduced a bill to establish a state college in the southern portion of Alameda County.[36] Nine days later, Assemblyman Ralph M. Brown introduced a bill to establish a state college in his own Stanislaus County.[37] In the senate, where a bill to establish a state college in Sonoma County was already in the hopper, Hugh P. Donnelly of Stanislaus County introduced a bill for the establishment of eight new state colleges in Stanislaus, Imperial, Santa Cruz, Alameda, Kern, Sonoma, Amador, and Napa-

Solano counties.[38] Donnelly's bill ignored the 1953 recommendation of the joint staff of the Regents and the State Board of Education that no state college be established in the Modesto area (Stanislaus County) until it was clear that it could succeed without injury to the long-established Modesto Junior College.[39]

Although the bill was certain to have the support of senators whose counties would benefit by receiving new state colleges if it passed, many senators were alarmed by the incredible ease with which they could bring eight new state colleges into being, with all the expense for construction, maintenance, and operation, and with virtually no knowledge of whether any of the colleges was actually needed. When the Donnelly bill reached the floor, Senator George Miller, Jr., of Contra Costa County led the action to amend it to death by offering a proposal to establish a college in his own home district and inviting other senators to do the same. In all, eleven amendments, each adding another state college to the eight in the original bill, were offered.[40] One of them, called "Frog U.," was to be located in Angels Camp, made famous by Mark Twain's story "The Celebrated Jumping Frog of Calaveras County." The bill failed by a final vote of fourteen to twenty.[41] At the same session, a bill by Senator Nathan Coombs calling for establishment of a state college to serve Napa and Solano counties passed both houses.[42] Governor Goodwin Knight did not approve it, however, and it died by pocket veto on July 13. All other bills introduced in that session for the establishment of state colleges died without final action.

Before the 1955 session adjourned, however, several bills and resolutions requesting studies of the need for additional state colleges or University campuses were passed. Though responsibility for making the studies was at first shared by a variety of legislative committees, the State Department of Education, and the Board of Regents, the work was actually performed by the joint staff of the Liaison Committee of the Regents and of the State Board of Education.[43] The joint staff members were Thomas C. Holy, special consultant to the president of the University, and H. H. Semans, specialist in higher education for the State Department of Education.

The Semans-Holy study, called officially *A Study of the Need for Additional Centers of Public Higher Education in California* and more commonly the "Additional Centers" Report, accepted as inevitable, and perhaps even desirable, moves by legislators to establish new centers of higher learning, and it recommended that the 1955 Restudy moratorium on such action be abandoned.[44] It then provided relevant technical data and enrollment projections to guide the legislators and the Regents in determining where new centers should be located. On the basis of the report's recommended priorities, the Regents authorized, in 1957, establishment of new general campuses to serve population centers in San Diego, the South Central Coast, and southeast Los Angeles County and Orange County. On the strength of the same recommendations, they authorized study of the San Joaquin Valley as a fourth possible campus location.[45]

In the 1957 session of the legislature, twenty-two bills to establish state colleges, to change their functions or government, or to acquire land for college expansion were introduced. Assemblyman Brown and Senator Donnelly made a new effort to establish a state college in Stanislaus County although the Additional Centers Report gave that location relatively low priority.[46] In the assembly, twenty authors joined to introduce a bill to establish a state college in Alameda County. It passed after amendment to authorize establishment of a state college in Orange County and site acquisition for state colleges in Stanislaus County and one of the North Bay counties.[47] Since Alameda County was the first-priority location for a state college on the Additional Centers list, it would appear that the report's recommendations had been followed. However, the report had also specified that such a college should not be built until two new junior colleges were built in the same area.[48] It acknowledged that there was some evidence of need for a new state college in the Los Angeles and Orange County area, but pointed out that there were many junior colleges, state colleges, private institutions, and campuses of the University nearby and that "further intensive study of this area at a later date is necessary before additional state colleges are contemplated." [49] Stanislaus County stood fifth and the North Bay counties stood eighth on the report's priority list. Obviously, the bill establishing state colleges in Alameda and Orange counties and authorizing site acquisition for colleges in Stanislaus and one of the North Bay counties violated both the spirit and letter of the Additional Centers report.

There was another mild flurry of resolutions regarding studies for new colleges in the sessions of the legislature in 1958. There were also signs that more attempts to create new state colleges or modify the functions or government of existing ones would be made when the legislature convened in January, 1959. In an effort to return some of the initiative for higher-education development to the universities and colleges, President Kerr and Superintendent of Public Instruction Roy Simpson went to their respective boards in 1958 with a proposal for a new instrument of coordination to supplement the existing Liaison Committee.[50] To be called the Joint Advisory Committee, it would report directly to the president of the University and the superintendent of public instruction. Unlike the Liaison Committee, which drew its members from the Board of Regents and the State Board of

Education and represented the junior colleges and independent colleges and universities only indirectly, the new committee, created in December, 1958, drew its members from the staff leadership of all four segments of higher education in the state. The University's representatives were Vice-President Harry Wellman and three chancellors.[51] The state colleges were represented by the head of the State College Division of the State Department of Education and three state college presidents. The junior colleges were represented by the State Department of Education's consultant on junior colleges and three junior college officials. The presidents of four independent colleges and universities, including the University of Southern California and Stanford University, completed the committee roster.

Before the committee could become effective, no less than twenty-three bills, three resolutions, and two constitutional amendments were introduced with intent to establish or study the need for new centers of higher education, change the function of existing institutions, or change the present structure for the organization, control, and administration of public colleges and universities in California.[52] The state had obviously outgrown the informal, voluntary coordinating machinery developed by the Regents and the State Board of Education when the Liaison Committee was established in 1945, and the legislators lacked proper guidance in higher-education affairs. Several enlightened lawmakers, most notably Senator George Miller of Contra Costa County and Assemblywoman Dorothy Donohoe of Bakersfield, began to have doubts that they could hold back reckless pork-barrel legislation in higher education without help from the colleges and universities themselves. Miss Donohoe became chairman of the Assembly Education Committee in 1959, and, as one tool to restore some order in the situation, she submitted Assembly Concurrent Resolution No. 88 on March 4, 1959. This resolution requested the Liaison Committee to develop a new master plan "for the development, expansion, and integration of the facilities, curriculum, and standards of higher education, in junior colleges, state colleges, the University of California, and other institutions of higher education of the State, to meet the needs of the State during the next 10 years and thereafter. . . ." [53]

FURTHER ATTEMPTS AT BILATERAL COORDINATION

While action was still pending on Miss Donohoe's resolution, the Regents of the University and the State Board of Education held an unprecedented joint meeting on March 14, 1959, at the Alumni House on the Berkeley campus, where Miss Donohoe announced that both the senate and assembly had agreed to defer action on all bills having to do with the establishment of new state colleges or creation of new patterns of education until the two boards could work out formulas that would assist the legislature in following a coordinated plan. Unless some solution to the problems of mass education were found soon, she told them, the state would find itself with "fifteen or eighteen state-supported universities all competing for the tax dollar." [54] To put aside any "it can't happen here" attitudes, she reminded the two boards that the legislature had already granted "prerogatives . . . to meet special needs, such as the offering of graduate instruction in engineering at San Jose State College." [55] She also warned that "if the practice of adopting special legislation to meet specific problems is continued without a well-defined plan, education in California will 'grow like Topsy.' " [56]

At the same meeting a report of the Liaison Committee gave recommendations for improving the coordinating procedures among California's public higher-education systems. The Liaison Committee urged that it should study ways in which its functions might be augmented in the interests of coordination and it suggested that the Joint Advisory Committee also study ways of improving coordination. Both committees were to report at another meeting of the two boards on April 15.[57]

The Liaison Committee also sought agreement from the joint boards on propositions that the new campuses already authorized must be placed in operation "as soon as the fiscal condition of the State will permit"; [58] that the boards should continue to reassess priorities for establishing new campuses with the highest priorities; and that adequate junior colleges should be provided in an area before the establishment of additional state colleges and University campuses.[59] The two boards were ready for agreement on all of these points in March. Tempers flared, however, over another Liaison Committee recommendation that no new campuses for the state colleges or the University be established for two years without prior approval by both boards. Raymond J. Daba of the State Board of Education protested that this policy would make it possible for one board to, in effect, veto the decision of the other.[60] Clark Kerr defended the recommendation and criticized a report made earlier in the meeting by Superintendent Simpson because it presented a list of priorities for new state colleges that differed significantly from the Semans-Holy list and had not been shown to the Regents before its release.[61] The ensuing arguments became so heated that, three weeks later, a San Francisco newspaper declared the state colleges and the University "Locked in Perilous Battle." [62]

Assemblywoman Donohoe was extremely disappointed by her glimpse at the joint meeting of the existing coordination of higher education in California. On April 3, after a meeting of the Liaison Committee with several legislators, she was so angered by hearing her colleagues talk about their obligations to take state colleges home to their constituents that she protested, "I keep hearing, 'Mine, mine, mine.' But we need to say 'our State.' " [63]

To insure that the joint boards would make more progress at their April 15 meeting in Los Angeles than they had in Berkeley in March, Governor Brown attended the session. In a blunt speech on the eve of the meeting, he warned that if the Regents and the State Board of Education could not voluntarily cooperate to solve the state's higher-education problems, or "if pseudo-cooperations should lead to mutual log-rolling by which each approves the projects of the other in order to have license for its own—then we may be compelled to consider other structural possibilities." [64] As though to reinforce that threat, an influential group of legislators came to the meeting in the private planes of Regents Edwin Pauley and Samuel Mosher.

By this time, it was generally understood that a thorough review of higher-education policy in California was overdue. The old idea that the Regents and the State Board of Education between them could call the tune for all institutions of higher learning in the state had lost validity. The sixty-three locally controlled junior colleges were so numerous and so significant in the number of young people they served that what happened to them influenced the future of all other colleges and universities in the state. And, of course, the four-year institutions could not plan well for the future without knowing the direction of junior college developments. The state could no longer afford the inefficiency of supporting state colleges as individual, virtually autonomous institutions subject to rather loose control by a subdivision of the State Department of Education. They needed a governing board of their own.

Because of the very rapid increase in enrollments, it was necessary in 1959–1960 to predict more accurately than ever before how many students would be attending which kinds of colleges and campuses in California. To do so would require new, firm agreements on the admissions requirements to be established for each segment of higher education. To avoid costly duplication of effort, it would be necessary to redefine the functions of the junior colleges, state colleges, and the University. Finally, to protect the whole scheme of higher education from undue political interference and the wasteful log-rolling that was so prevalent in the 1950s, some new, politically independent agency was needed to provide coordination. The question before the joint boards in April, 1959, was really whether the outline of these needed developments would be worked out by the colleges and universities themselves or by the legislature. The legislators at the meeting decided to force the colleges and universities to work it out themselves and endorsed Miss Donohoe's assembly concurrent resolution calling for a new master plan that would be developed under the direction of the Liaison Committee. They also accepted, for the time being, all of the guidelines for the establishment of new centers that were proposed at the March meeting in Berkeley—including the provision that "no new campus for the state colleges or for the University of California, other than those already approved, shall be established without prior approval of both boards." [65]

Indications that a new plan, backed by both boards, would soon be available to guide higher-education development gave key legislators the ammunition they needed to hold off all pending legislation on the subject. But they warned that they could not do so for more than a year and requested that the study be completed in time for the budget session of the legislature on February 1, 1960.[66]

ORGANIZING THE STUDY

The Liaison Committee met in Sacramento on June 3, 1959, to work out procedures. Its members agreed that a "Master Plan Survey Team" would do the actual work. The team's membership would include the joint staff of the Liaison Committee—Thomas Holy and Arthur D. Browne [67]—and representatives of the University, the state colleges, and the junior colleges. Later Howard A. Campion joined the joint staff as a representative of the junior colleges, and a representative of the private colleges and universities was added to the survey team.

After it was readily agreed that the chairman of the team should be some strong figure from one of the state's independent colleges, President Kerr and Superintendent Simpson placed a call to Arthur G. Coons, president of Occidental College, while the meeting in Sacramento was still in progress, and he accepted the job on the spot. The selection of President Coons as the survey-team chairman was a master stroke. Tall, white-haired, shrewdly practical, widely respected, and excitingly vital, President Coons proved to be an unrelenting taskmaster.

The state colleges' representative on the team was forty-two-year-old Glenn Dumke, president of San Francisco State College since 1957. A graduate of Occidental College, he had taught history there after receiving his doctorate at UCLA and had been dean of the faculty at Occidental for seven years before accepting the state college presidency.

The University's representative was Dean E. McHenry, academic assistant to President Kerr and professor of political science at UCLA. A close friend of Kerr since they were graduate students together at Stanford in the 1930s, McHenry had once been student-body president at UCLA, had been an active alumnus of that campus, and had served it as a faculty member and administrator from 1939 on. His background was enriched with a thorough knowledge of California politics gained through a lifetime of scholarly inquiry as well as experience as a candidate for public office in the early 1950s.

The junior colleges were represented by Henry T. Tyler, a counselor at Modesto Junior College and executive secretary of the California Junior College Association. Robert J. Wert, vice-provost of Stanford University, was the independent-college member of the team.

What amounted to ex-officio status was informally granted to a young, bright consultant to the Assembly Education Committee, Keith Sexton. He served the invaluable function of providing liaison between the survey team and the Assembly Education Committee, under Miss Donohoe.

The Master Plan Survey Team, backed up by special study committees on finances, admissions, institutional capacities and area needs, enrollment projections, adult education, and costs, prepared monthly reports. These were reviewed by the Joint Advisory Committee representing the University, the state colleges, the junior colleges, and the independent colleges and universities, whose recommendations and comments were then relayed to the Liaison Committee by President Kerr and Superintendent Simpson.

It was in their vital role as the bridge between the two committees that Kerr and Simpson came to be regarded as the architects of the Master Plan. Throughout the deliberations of the survey team, Dean McHenry and Glenn Dumke regarded themselves as staff representatives of the President and the superintendent, respectively. Thus, when any new approach or solution to a problem pending before the team was under consideration, one or the other would sometimes ask to be excused, as they often said, to "check with Moscow." President Kerr made direct contacts with several state college presidents to suggest solutions to some of the more stubborn disagreements over the relationship between the state colleges and the University.

One particularly difficult issue involved the desire of some state college presidents to further expand the work of their institutions. The functions of the state colleges had been expanding since 1923, when (as state teachers' colleges) they were first authorized to offer the A.B. degree: in 1935, they were permitted to provide instruction in fields other than teacher education; and in 1948, they were authorized to grant the M.A. degree. Some state colleges served these expanded functions so completely by 1959 that their presidents and faculties felt competent to embark on Ph.D.-level education. The state college representatives on the Master Plan Survey Team argued that their institutions not only had the competence for such work but an obligation to undertake it so that a national shortage of Ph.D.s could be quickly overcome. They also wanted the Ph.D. program so that they could attract top faculty prospects with the lure of challenging students and research opportunities. At this point, the Ph.D. issue merged with the equally sensitive issue of extending to state colleges authority for conducting original research. President Kerr and the Regents opposed authorizing Ph.D. research programs for the state colleges. After forty years of expanding state-college functions, Ph.D. programs, research, and professional schools of medicine, law, veterinary medicine, and dentistry remained the prime distinguishing feature of the University. If these endeavors were also undertaken at the state colleges, California would, in fact, have two duplicate, competitive university systems—a prospect that the Regents had resisted since the turn of the century. The University representatives on the survey team also argued that graduate instruction and research were both expensive activities, supported to a considerable extent by nonstate grants, contracts, and gifts. If two state systems began to call upon these resources, there was a danger that instead of having one good University, California would have two or more mediocre ones. Finally, there was evidence that the great demand for Ph.D.s in 1959 was not permanent and that the University and private institutions in California could meet that demand with increasing ease as it began to level off.

On the question of expanding graduate work in the state colleges, a key meeting, later referred to as "the Little Summit," was held in Kerr's office in University Hall at Berkeley. It was attended by Arthur Coons, Glenn Dumke, Robert Wert, and Dean McHenry from the survey team; William Blair, president of the State Board of Education; Donald McLaughlin, chairman of the Board of Regents; and Edward Carter, chairman of the Regents Committee on Educational Policy. At an earlier date, Dean McHenry had sounded out the state colleges on their willingness to settle for the doctorate in education—this in line with their heritage as teacher-training institutions—but this feeler was declined. At the meeting in Berkeley, President Kerr proposed that arrangements be made for the award of joint doctorates by the University and the state colleges. This proposal was accepted, and, to the degree that the development of a master plan depended upon this crucial agreement, such a plan was very likely saved at this meeting.

THE MASTER PLAN

On December 7, 1959, the survey team began formulating the conclusions of its studies, and presented most of them to the Liaison Committee on December 9.[68] Recommendations concerning the much-discussed issues of the differentiation of function and the way in which California's higher education would be structured and coordinated in the future were finally drafted on December 17. The next day the whole plan was presented to a joint meeting of the Regents and the State Board of Education.[69]

The final report was completed on schedule and dealt boldly with long-standing problems of California higher education. There was evidence of compromise, of course, but it was overshadowed, in the main, by evidence of an effort to treat California higher education, public and private, as a combination of interdependent, complementing subsystems, each of which had a role in providing for every California youth an opportunity to pursue education, public and private, to the highest level of his interests and capabilities.

At the heart of the plan was a constitutional amendment which declared that California's public higher education "shall consist of the junior colleges, the State College System, and the University of California. Each shall strive for excellence in its sphere. . . ." [70]

To the junior colleges, the amendment gave the function of giving instruction up to and including the fourteenth grade, including college courses for transfer to higher institutions, vocational and technical education leading to employment, and general or liberal arts courses. They could grant the associate in arts and the associate in science degrees.[71]

The amendment removed the state colleges from the supervision of the State Board of Education and gave them their own board of trustees. These trustees would have sixteen-year terms and would enjoy protection from political interference comparable to that allowed the University. In addition to their long-standing functions of teacher education, instruction in the liberal arts and sciences, and instruction in professions and applied fields requiring more than two years of collegiate education, the state colleges were authorized to conduct research "consistent with the primary function of the state colleges" (instruction and teacher education), and to award doctorate degrees jointly with the University.[72]

The University's governmental structure was left unchanged, but its functions were redefined:

1. To "provide instruction in the liberal arts and sciences and in the professions, including teacher education. . . ."
2. To "have exclusive jurisdiction over training for the professions," with specific—though not restrictive—mention of dentistry, law, medicine, veterinary medicine, and graduate architecture.
3. To "have the sole authority in public higher education to award the doctor's degree in all fields of learning, *except that* it may agree with the state colleges to award joint doctor's degrees in selected fields."
4. To "be the primary state-supported academic agency for research. . . ." [73]

The constitutional amendment also created a Coordinating Council for Higher Education composed of three members from each of the four systems of higher education in the state. It would have a staff and a director and would have the following functions:

1. Review of budgets and capital outlay requests of the University and the state college system, and presentation of its comments on the general level of support sought to the governor.
2. Interpretation of the functional differentiation among the publicly supported institutions—and advisory functions to the Regents and trustees of the state college system on programs appropriate to each.
3. Development of plans for the orderly growth of higher education and recommendations to the governing boards on need for and location of new facilities and programs.[74]

The constitutional definition of the coordinating machinery, of the government of the state colleges, and of the functions of the four segments of higher education was considered vital by President Kerr and members of the survey team. In no other form could these points of the Master Plan be secured against circumvention by the college or university system or the legislature.

Constitutional protection of other provisions of the Master Plan was not regarded as so necessary, although the agreements themselves were of great importance. Among them were:

1. That junior colleges would continue to admit all high school graduates, but that the state colleges should tighten their admission

requirements so that only 33⅓ per cent of high-school graduates were eligible, and that the University should tighten its requirements to admit only the top 12½ per cent of high-school graduates. In this way, all high-school graduates would have some opportunity to pursue college-level education, but only those most likely to succeed would be admitted to the senior institutions.[75]

2. That no state colleges or University campus would be established in areas where local citizens had not provided adequate junior colleges and that the legislature, by increasing financial support, would encourage junior college development to accommodate 250,000 students by 1975.[76]

3. That new state colleges would be built first in the vicinity of the Los Angeles International Airport and in the San Bernardino–Riverside County area by 1965, and that studies would be made in 1965 and again in 1970 of the need for state colleges in Los Angeles–Orange County, Redwood City, Contra Costa County, and the south coastal area near Ventura.[77]

4. That the Los Angeles and Berkeley campuses of the University would be planned for a maximum enrollment of 27,500 students each and that the new campuses approved by the Regents in 1957 would be completed without delay.[78]

5. That more efficient use of existing facilities would be realized through more intensive scheduling of rooms and laboratories for instruction and by providing funds so that the state colleges and the University could study the possible adoption of a year-round instruction calendar.[79]

6. That tuition at the state colleges and the University would remain free, that incidental fees would be high enough to cover the true costs of such items as student health services, counseling, and other services, but that operation of parking lots, residence halls, and other such facilities would be mainly self-supporting.[80]

7. That the legislature would provide new scholarships and loans for students.[81]

The Board of Regents and the State Board of Education unanimously approved the Master Plan at their meeting on December 18, 1959.[82] President Kerr promptly released a statement in which he called the plan "a milestone in the history of California higher education."

To some, the significant achievement was not the plan but the reestablishment of harmony between two of the state's systems of higher education, the state colleges and the University. Still others found most important the fact that, for the first time, the junior colleges and the independent colleges had been given due recognition in the contemplated coordinating machinery. Most educators, newspapers, and other observers hailed it as a

masterful accomplishment. The most important judgment, however, had yet
to be rendered. It would come in Sacramento the following spring.

Governor Brown was impressed with the Master Plan and made it the
subject of a special call of the legislature in 1960. President Kerr, members
of the Board of Regents, representatives of the State Board of Education,
and stalwarts of the survey team soon found themselves on the speakers'
circuit or in the hearing rooms in Sacramento testifying to their belief in the
soundness of the plan. The Academic Senate endorsed it. So did the University's student bodies. Alumni of the University met in small groups to study
its provisions—all the better to speak authoritatively about it in their own
communities.

All of this effort was exerted to secure passage of the Master Plan with as
little change as possible, for while its authors considered it sound in its total-
ity, they fretted about the delicate balance of compromise that was involved
in some of its components. People unfamiliar with the tenuousness of such
accords might bring the whole plan into collapse by inadvertently moving a
keystone out of place.

President Kerr, in particular, was dismayed to learn in late March or
early April that the legislature would enact the plan by statute, including
those portions proposed by the survey team as constitutional amendments.
There was also a question of whether or not Regental acceptance of statutory regulation of the University's functions, policies, and relationships with
other institutions of higher education might start to erode its historic independence. More immediately, the President doubted that statutes, which
could be easily changed, were firm enough foundations for the massive
higher-education complex the Master Plan envisioned.

Senator Miller and many of his colleagues believed, on the other hand,
that it was folly to freeze an untried scheme into the constitution and that
doing so would place the future development of public higher education, in
most important respects, beyond the reach of the people's representatives in
the legislature. Rather than risk defeat of the whole Master Plan by insisting
upon the proposed constitutional amendment, President Kerr was eventually persuaded to accept enactment of the Master Plan by statute with the
understanding that efforts to incorporate important provisions into the constitution could be made later if such action proved desirable and feasible.[83]

George Miller's Senate Bill 33, which embodies all of the major features
of the Master Plan, was passed by a vote of thirty-six to one in the senate and
unanimously by the assembly.[84] On April 26, 1960, it was signed by Governor Brown, who called it "the most significant step California has ever taken

in planning for the education of our youth." [85] Tragically, on April 4, 1960, with the Master Plan in the final stages of legislative consideration, Dorothy Donohoe died suddenly. She had given the Master Plan far more than her usual dedication and effort, and her colleagues in the legislature showed their gratitude by officially renaming the Master Plan legislation the Donohoe Higher Education Act. The printed Master Plan report was dedicated to her memory.

THE PLAN IN ACTION

In line with Master Plan recommendations, the University lost no time in developing new campuses at Irvine, Santa Cruz, and San Diego. It tightened its admissions requirements; de-emphasized lower-division instruction (thus diverting large numbers of students to junior colleges and state colleges); improved room scheduling to an extent that weekly classhour use per room rose from 18.9 to 31.1 and percentage of occupancy rose from 46 to 55; built the Master Plan's enrollment ranges for campuses into long-range academic plans for the University; raised student fees to cover the real cost of services rendered; and made library facilities available to the faculties of other institutions of higher learning on a basis "essentially equal to those of the University faculty members." [86] In 1967, the University joined San Diego State College in conferring the Ph.D. degree in chemistry upon Robert P. Metzger, the first recipient of the joint degree authorized by the Master Plan.[87]

Within the University, one of the most controversial provisions of the Master Plan was that the University and state colleges go into year-round operations to make more efficient use of their facilities during the summer months. The proposal was not really new, and had been suggested by economy-minded legislators for many years. But it was difficult to achieve in the face of considerable faculty opposition. In 1962, after a series of detailed studies and a favorable faculty vote that revealed the Berkeley Division of the Academic Senate to be more resistant to the idea than the other divisions, the Regents approved establishment of a full three-term (quarter system) University calendar. Three new campuses opened on the three-term system in the fall of 1965. The older ones began operating under the system in the fall of 1966.

The effectiveness of the coordinating council created by the Donohoe Act was vital to the Master Plan's success. The new council consisted of three representatives each from the junior colleges, state colleges, independent institutions, and the University, and three "public" representatives appointed by the governor.[88] The council's beginnings were unsteady: meetings were poorly attended; it was unsure about the extent of its authority; and its staff was not properly organized for useful service. By 1963, however, the council began to perform with more confidence. In that year and in 1964, it was able to restrain legislators from creating several new state colleges without its advice.[89] It forestalled what may have been a premature investigation of the effectiveness of the Donohoe Act and other legislation on Master Plan recommendations by preparing a report of its own that indicated that, by 1966, no less than sixty of the sixty-seven recommendations of the Master Plan had been implemented either in full or in part.[90] The council developed programs reviewing academic plans of the state colleges and the University to discover potential areas of needless duplication.[91] It also devised an approach to reviewing budgets of the public higher-education system that complemented rather than duplicated the reviews of the State Department of Finance and the legislative analyst.[92] With the passage of federal-aid-to-education bills by Congress in 1963, the coordinating council assumed a new role as the administrator of federal funds for institutions of higher education in the state.[93]

In 1965, an amendment to the Donohoe Act placed three more "public" representatives on the council and required that all representatives had to be present in person if their votes were to be counted. These changes improved attendance and minimized the possibility of education representatives dominating decisions of the council by bloc voting. They also made the council less an internal instrument of the colleges and universities of the state and more an agency serving the state government. This shift in character was further emphasized in 1966 when the offices of the council were moved from San Francisco to Sacramento.[94]

It is still too early to tell whether the Master Plan of 1960 was an expedient or a long-range solution to the need for orderly development of California's higher education. But its service to date has been immense. It has forced the University of California and the other segments of public higher education in the state to view themselves as parts of California's massive effort to provide higher education for all of its young people up to such levels as they are able to reach with success. It has imposed reasonable discipline upon the physical and academic program-planning of the colleges and universities of the state. And it restrained, for a few years at least, external pressures that threatened to wreak chaos out of the carefully planned efforts of California's public colleges and the University to build new campuses, improve operating efficiency, and make thoughtful reappraisal of their future goals as they prepared to make room for the coming thousands of students.

Chapter 24

NEW AND EMERGING CAMPUSES

THE UNIVERSITY OF California grew for almost ninety years before it was big enough to accommodate the 64,194 students on its campuses in 1957.[1] At a conference at Lake Arrowhead in the summer of that year, the Regents heard reports that promised they would either have to double the University's total capacity within a single decade or abandon their historic policy of admitting all qualified students who applied to enter. They decided on a policy of growth and, in so doing, accepted a formidable challenge. The scope and functions of existing campuses had to be re-evaluated, and more new buildings had to be constructed. New campuses had to be built. The first of these would be those recommended by the Liaison Committee of the Regents and the State Board of Education in its 1957 report, *The Need for Additional Centers of Public Higher Education in California,* and would be located in Southeast Los Angeles and Orange County, Santa Clara Valley and South Central Coast, San Diego–La Jolla, and the San Joaquin Valley. Before they left Lake Arrowhead, the Regents committed themselves to a policy of growth.

At their regular June meeting in Davis, the Regents requested funds from the legislature to finance studies of specific campus sites [2] and named Regent Philip L. Boyd, well-known southern California rancher and Riverside civic leader, chairman [3] of a special site-selection committee.

GUIDELINES FOR BERKELEY AND UCLA

About a year later, the Regents approved an educational policy for Berkeley and UCLA. Both campuses, they said, would be comprehensive in nature and would have research, instruction, professional training, and public service as their controlling purposes. The two campuses would seek to recruit and hold "a distinguished faculty of scholars," [4] and maintain libraries and laboratories commensurate with outstanding teaching and research. Their enrollments would be limited (originally to 25,000 students), and more of their students would be in graduate and upper-division work than in lower-division. In budgeting, the Regents planned to observe the principle that both campuses "should be comparable in size and have equal opportunities for developing programs which, although not identical but rather complementary, are of equivalent quality." [5]

The formulation of the general policies of Berkeley and UCLA was made when Dr. Raymond B. Allen was in his sixth year as chancellor at UCLA. The following year, 1959, he resigned and was succeeded by sixty-five-year-old Vern O. Knudsen, a distinguished physicist and acoustics expert who had been a member of the UCLA faculty since 1922 and had served in several important administrative positions on the campus before assuming the chancellorship. Because Knudsen was nearing retirement, President Kerr began looking for a permanent chancellor in late 1959 and early 1960. A leading candidate was Dr. Franklin D. Murphy, who, as chancellor of the University of Kansas since 1951, was nationally respected as a young and aggressive leader in American higher education. After speaking to Dr. Murphy by telephone and more extensively at a meeting they both attended in Santiago, Chile, Kerr persuaded him to visit the campus and meet members of the faculty and the Board of Regents. After two such visits, Dr. Murphy agreed to become UCLA's chancellor and assumed his duties in that capacity in the fall of 1960.[6]

A NEW ROLE FOR SANTA BARBARA

When Kerr became the president in July, 1958, Santa Barbara had been without a permanent chief campus officer for several years. In 1955, Clark Kuebler, then president of Ripon College, was chosen to succeed J. Harold Williams as provost. He served for only ten months, however, before he was arrested in New York for alleged "felonious assault and improper proposal." Kuebler denied the allegation and seven prominent churchmen and business executives appeared at the court hearing as character witnesses. Because of lack of evidence against him, he was cleared, but he resigned as provost at Santa Barbara "out of respect and affection" for the University. After Kuebler's departure from Santa Barbara, John C. Snidecor, dean of the Division of Applied Arts, served as acting provost for five months. In July, 1956, that position was assumed by Elmer R. Noble, dean of the College of Letters and Science. Under his administration three of the first permanent buildings were completed on the Goleta campus, and several others were under construction or in the planning stage. Noble also supervised preparation of an Academic Master Plan for Santa Barbara and submitted it to the Regents in June, 1958.

On September 19, 1958, the role of the Santa Barbara campus was completely recast by the Regents. They declared it a general campus and raised its enrollment target from 3500 to 10,000 students.[7] The undergraduate work stressing liberal education (formerly the primary mission of the campus) would be maintained, the Regents decided, but it would be supplemented by a strong graduate program emphasizing research and professional training. A new name, "University of California, Santa Barbara," was authorized to replace "Santa Barbara College." The chief campus officer would now be chancellor instead of a provost.

In view of the Regents' decision to expand the University as rapidly as possible to accommodate more students, the decision to make Santa Barbara College a general campus of the University was a logical one. It had plenty of room for growth on its new Goleta site and had proven ability to draw students from all over the state. Even so, some faculty members were disappointed that the original plans to develop the campus into a small, first-rate liberal and applied arts institution were abandoned. Others were chagrined because Santa Barbara's famous industrial arts program, the oldest part of its academic heritage, was under attack. Educators within and outside the University charged that this program encroached upon the domain of state and junior colleges and was incompatible with University functions. In December, 1958, President Kerr announced that the program would be discontinued.[8]

The first chancellor at Santa Barbara was Samuel B. Gould, who came to the campus from Antioch College, Ohio, where he had been president since 1954. Famous for his cogent and eloquent addresses concerning education, Gould used his talents in statesmanship effectively after he assumed the chancellorship in June, 1959.[9] With them he did more, perhaps, than any other man to convince the President and the Regents that small campuses were full-fledged components of the University system and should be so regarded in planning and budgeting. The same talents helped him convince the Santa Barbara faculty that they could develop a truly distinguished University campus at Santa Barbara and persuade the students and alumni that the campus offered even more excitement as a university than it did as a college. During Gould's chancellorship, Santa Barbara's first two professional schools—Education and Engineering—were authorized by the Regents. A new College of Letters and Science was established in July, 1961.

One of Chancellor Gould's impressive achievements was the initiation of the University's "Education Abroad" program, which enables qualified upper-division students of any campus to attend cooperating institutions abroad and receive credit on their home campus for one year of academic work. The first Education Abroad center was established at the University of Bordeaux, France, for the academic year 1962–1963. Before this center was opened, however, Chancellor Gould resigned to accept the presidency of the Educational Broadcasting Corporation in New York, which operated Station WNDT. He later became Chancellor of the State University of New York.

Gould's successor, in July, 1962, was Vernon I. Cheadle, a botanist who was also serving as acting vice-chancellor at Davis. Under Cheadle's administration, Education Abroad centers were started at the Chinese University of Hong Kong; Delphi, Greece; George August University in Goettingen; International Christian University in Mitaka-Tokyo; The University of Edinburgh; The University of Lund; The University of Madrid; the University of Padua; The University of Sussex; the University of St. Andrews; Trinity College of Dublin University; The Hebrew University of Jerusalem; the American University of Beirut, Lebanon; and Mexico City. In 1967–1968 there were 380 students in these centers.[10]

Chancellor Cheadle began his stewardship when the Santa Barbara campus entered a period of explosive growth. During his first three years in office, enrollment grew from 4515 to 8589 students. In 1965, despite the fact that existing facilities and teaching staff were strained beyond normal capacity, all qualified students who wished to attend the campus, including some who were redirected from campuses that had reached capacity, were accepted. To accommodate the resulting enrollment increase, an accelerated building and development program was undertaken. By the fall of 1967, the campus accommodated 12,200 students.[11]

Graduate offerings increased from 18 masters and 5 doctoral programs in 1962 to 32 masters and 23 doctoral programs by 1967–1968.[12] Graduate-student enrollment during that period increased from 249 to 1500.[13] Santa Barbara's first organized research unit, the Institute of Environmental Stress, opened in 1965. Six other centers were created and proposals for three more were under consideration by 1968.

In 1967, a unique undergraduate college was established. Called the College of Creative Studies, it offers a special curriculum to selected students who have shown the capacity for independent, concentrated, and sustained work. Beginning with only 50 students, the college hopes to enroll 750 students, two-thirds of whom will be housed in their own residential community.

DEVELOPMENTS AT SAN FRANCISCO

At the same time the Regents made Santa Barbara a general campus, they provided new administrative organization for the San Francisco Medical Center. Until 1954, the deans of the Schools of Medicine, Dentistry, Pharmacy and Nursing all reported directly to the president of the University. After 1954, the deans served as members of an administrative committee with the dean of the School of Medicine as their chairman and chief executive of the Medical Center.[14] To that post in 1956 came Dr. John B. de C. M. Saunders, a native of South Africa who received his medical degrees at the University of Edinburgh in 1925 and joined the Berkeley faculty as assistant professor of anatomy in 1931. He became chairman of the Department of Anatomy at both Berkeley and San Francisco, serving in that capacity for eighteen years before he became dean of the School of Medicine.[15] In September, 1958, the Regents named Saunders the first provost for the San Francisco campus.[16] He was named chancellor in 1964.

Dr. Saunders' appointment recognized not only the new trends toward administrative unity but also other unifying factors at the Medical Center. Among them was the completion of the new five-hundred-bed Herbert C. Moffitt teaching hospital in 1955 and a new student union and a new Medical Sciences Building in 1958. The Medical Sciences Building provided classrooms for all four schools.[17] It also provided space so that the first two years of medical instruction that had been carried on at Berkeley since the San Francisco fire and earthquake in 1906 could at last be returned to San Francisco.

On July 1, 1966, Dr. Saunders left the chancellorship to return to teaching and research. He was succeeded by Dr. Willard C. Fleming, who had previously served as dean of the College of Dentistry 1939–1965,[18] vice-chancellor 1964–1965, and dean of students 1965–1966.

RIVERSIDE AND DAVIS BECOME GENERAL CAMPUSES

The College of Letters and Science at Riverside was built initially for a student body of 1500, and academic planning reflected the underlying assumption that the college would remain small. There were no separate upper- or lower-division requirements, only requirements for graduation. These included basic courses in general subjects like Western civilization and biology, comprehensive examinations, and a senior thesis.[19]

Enrollment had just passed the 1000 mark in April 1959, when the Regents decided to declare the Riverside campus "a general campus . . . , continuing its undergraduate and Citrus Experiment Station functions, and expanding when appropriate into other areas that are within the sphere of the University, including graduate, professional, and organized research work." [20] Even more explicitly than they did for Santa Barbara, the Regents declared that "distinction in undergraduate instruction shall be retained and graduate, research, and professional programs introduced only in a manner compatible with distinguished undergraduate instruction and consistent with the standards of the University." [21] They also decided upon a new maximum enrollment—5000 students.

The decision was not altogether unexpected. With enrollments dangerously near optimum at Berkeley and Los Angeles already, the Regents would seem derelict indeed if they permitted Riverside, with all of its spaciousness, to remain small and specialized. The decision was nevertheless resented by a considerable number of Riverside faculty members who doubted that the location of their campus could attract large numbers of students or who, like some faculty members at Santa Barbara, had found the idea of building a small liberal arts college of national, perhaps international, distinction a stimulating challenge.

Responsibility for directing the conversion of the campus to its new mission fell upon Herman T. Spieth, who had been brought to Riverside in 1953 as professor of zoology and chairman of the life sciences division. He was named provost at Riverside in 1956 when Gordon Watkins retired and received the title of chancellor in 1959 when Riverside was designated a general campus. Under Spieth's administration, the divisional system of academic organization with which the campus began was modified. Departments, which reported directly to the dean of the College of Letters and Science, were established. Capitalizing on the strong initial thrust of the College of Letters and Science, an emphasis on the liberal arts was retained, and a College of Agriculture was established in 1960. The first full-fledged graduate programs were offered the same year.

Spieth resigned the chancellorship to return to teaching and research at Davis in 1964. His successor was Ivan Hinderaker, a former chairman of the political science department at UCLA who also served as vice-chancellor for academic affairs at the University's new campus at Irvine before assuming his duties at Riverside. Under his leadership there has been active planning for new schools of administration and engineering and initiation of discussions on a new academic administration that would replace the large College of Letters and Science with smaller divisions.

The campus at Davis was designated a general campus in October, 1959, although the Regents specifically declared that its "College of Agriculture . . . will continue to be the University's major center for research and teaching in agriculture, which will remain a dominant emphasis. . . ." [22] Davis was also assigned another unique function. Because of its proximity to the State Capitol, the Regents suggested that it might give special attention "to the opportunities . . . to be a direct service to the State Government." [23] The new enrollment target would be 6000 students by 1970.

On the same day the new status of the Davis campus was announced, Emil M. Mrak, former chairman of the Department of Food Science and Technology, was inaugurated as chancellor. A native of San Francisco, Mrak received B.S., M.S., and Ph.D. degrees at Berkeley and was a member of the faculty there from 1936 to 1951, when his department was moved to Davis.

Since its designation as a general campus, a College of Engineering (1962) and a School of Law (1966) have been opened. The School of Medicine, which had been supervising interns and residents at the Sacramento County Hospital since fall, 1966, admitted its first class of M.D. students in fall, 1968. Schools of Dentistry, Nursing, Allied Health Sciences, and a graduate school of administration are contemplated.

A NEW PLAN FOR GROWTH

By the end of 1959, the University was planning for a student capacity of about 76,000 on its existing general campuses—Berkeley, UCLA, Davis, Riverside, and Santa Barbara. This figure accepted the recommendations of the Master Plan for California Higher Education that there be no more than 27,500 students on any University campus.[24] It also accepted the target enrollments announced when Davis, Riverside, and Santa Barbara were made general campuses. By 1975, the University would have to accommodate another 43,000 students to stay on schedule in meeting demands projected in the Master Plan.[25]

The President and Regents of the University had contemplated since 1957 that this extra capacity would be provided in new campuses. Financial officers in Sacramento, however, believed that more of it could be provided by still further expansion of existing facilities. To test this theory, President Kerr asked his assistants Earl Bolton and Robert S. Johnson to project the University's growth not only to 1975 but also to the year 2000. The findings of their report were astonishing. By the year 2000, if the University accepted about the same portion of California's total student population as it did in 1960, it would have 215,000 students, more than four times as many as were actually enrolled in 1961, and more than three times as many as could be accommodated on the five general campuses as then planned. Even more alarming than the size of the projected enrollment was the rate of its growth. Between 1965 and 1970, the report indicated, all of the currently planned capacity of the general campuses would be filled. Just to accommodate the overflow from Berkeley and UCLA, planned capacity at Davis, Riverside, and Santa Barbara would have to be increased immediately. Davis would have to accommodate 15,000 instead of 10,000 students; Santa Barbara would have 15,000 instead of 6000; and Riverside must plan for 10,000 instead of 5000. Because these new enrollment levels would be reached by 1970, new campuses would have to be ready to absorb the overflow by that time.[26]

Work on new campuses had to begin immediately. The Growth Report's authors estimated that fifteen years would be required from the time a site was selected to build a new campus to the point where it could accommodate 7500 students. Ultimately, the new growth plan projected enrollments of 27,500 for each of three proposed campuses already authorized by the Regents.[27]

The Regents approved the new growth report as general policy on June 17, 1960. Several days later they met in an all-day session with Governor Brown to impress upon him the urgency of proceeding with new campus development. The legislature supported the plan by appropriating $3,000,000 for new campus-site studies.

EXPANSION IN THE FAR SOUTH

At least five years before the Regents finally authorized development of new campuses in accordance with the 1960 growth plans, faculty members at the Scripps Institution of Oceanography were already thinking in terms of expansion. Under the leadership of their imaginative and energetic director, Roger Revelle, they talked about supplementing the instruction they gave to a relatively small number of graduate and postdoctoral students with a school of science and engineering.[28]

When the Regents authorized the new campus, it was at first envisioned that the new school would begin with a graduate curriculum in science and engineering comparable to that of the California Institute of Technology. This concept was strongly supported by leading citizens of San Diego, who appreciated the value of nearby technological expertise as an attraction to industry and the contributions that a larger University facility could make to the community. President Sproul favored the idea of expansion and presented it to the Regents on August 24, 1956, indicating that "already, on the basis of newspaper reports and preliminary discussions concerning the possible expansion, interest in joining the La Jolla staff has been shown by distinguished scientists from Europe and other parts of the United States." [29] Acting on his recommendation, the Regents voted to "expand, over a period of years, the faculty and facilities of the La Jolla Campus to provide a graduate program in sciences and technology, with such undergraduate instruction as is essential to support the graduate program." [30]

Community support for the idea was made evident in the fall of 1956 when citizens of San Diego voted to transfer about fifty-nine acres of mesa land near the Scripps Institution of Oceanography to the University as a site for the proposed school. Industrial support came quickly—notably from the General Dynamics Corporation, which contributed a large sum of money used, beginning in July, 1957, for the recruitment of faculty members.

The original plan for the school was modified in August, 1957. Confronted by the need to grow rapidly at all levels to satisfy enrollment demand, the Regents approved a proposal that "a large campus" of the University be developed in the San Diego–La Jolla areas, "fulfilling the functions of a major university including both undergraduate and graduate instruction. . . ." [31] At the same meeting, the Regents voted to extend the authorization for a school of science and engineering given the year before to "include undergraduate programs as well as graduate programs emphasizing science and technology, and sufficient instruction in other fields to insure the opportunity for a well-rounded education; and that this initial step be executed in a manner consistent with the development of a general University campus." [32] Roger Revelle was named, in addition to his positions as director of the campus and of Scripps Institution of Oceanography, dean of the new school.

The La Jolla faculty planned to work rather slowly in the development of a general campus "from the top." Good faculty members in any field would be recruited as soon as they were available, not when they were needed to complete a curriculum sequence or meet a campus development schedule.

Hopefully, these professors would bring their graduate- and postdoctoral-student following with them. Other graduate students would be recruited on the strength of the faculty's distinction. After the graduate program was operating smoothly, undergraduate students might be enrolled, slowly at first, perhaps in an honors curriculum.

Consistent with this plan, Roger Revelle announced in May, 1960, that the School of Science and Engineering at La Jolla would accept its first graduate students in the fall. Instruction would be offered in the fields of physics, chemistry, biology, and the earth sciences by a faculty of twenty. Temporarily, the classes would be conducted in buildings of the Scripps Institution of Oceanography.[33]

By this time, and after considering several possibilities, the Regents were concentrating their interest on mesa lands northeast of the Scripps Institution, contiguous to the property offered for the School of Science and Engineering, as the permanent site for a new general campus. Before making the selection final, however, they stipulated that the land in question, about 450 acres, as well as 500 acres in Camp Matthews, a Marine Corps rifle range adjoining the site, be obtained from the city of San Diego and the federal government as a gift. They also wanted to satisfy themselves that a community to provide housing and other conveniences for faculty members, students, and staff members would be developed adjacent to the site and that the routing of proposed freeways and the noise of aircraft based in the vicinity would not interfere with University use of the property.[34]

The first of these conditions was satisfied in November, 1958, when the citizens of San Diego, at the urging of local University of California alumni and civic leaders, overwhelmingly approved a local measure to transfer 450 acres of the desired site to the University. In acknowledgment of this generosity, Revelle said, "In financial terms alone, this is one of the most princely single gifts ever offered to the University. The land is relatively level and is situated on a beautiful mesa overlooking the ocean—prime subdivision land. No exact value can be set on it, but at present it is probably worth between three and five million dollars and its value can be expected to increase." [35]

In March, 1960, the Regents voted to accept the first parcel of land offered by the city of San Diego and approved preliminary plans for the construction of the first buildings of the new School of Science and Engineering. The full plan contemplated seven academic buildings, two residence halls, a dining commons, and a recreation building.[36]

In the summer of 1960, the Regents were satisfied that most of the conditions they had imposed for the acceptance of the La Jolla site would be met and voted to accept the 450 acres the city of San Diego had offered them there.[37] Later in the year, they officially named the new campus "University of California, San Diego." The first chancellor of the University of California, San Diego, was Herbert F. York, a thirty-nine-year-old University physicist who, in 1960, was on leave for national service as Director of Defense Research and Engineering in Washington, D.C. A graduate of the University of Rochester in 1942, York received his Ph.D. degree at Berkeley in 1949 and became a member of the University faculty in 1951. In 1954, he was named director of the Lawrence Radiation Laboratory at Livermore and was serving in that position when he was called into government service. York assumed the responsibilities of his chancellorship at San Diego in July, 1961,[38] and became almost immediately involved in working out long-range academic and physical-development plans for the campus, relying upon many of Revelle's ideas.

Revelle's original concept of the physical development of the San Diego campus had involved the creation of several "little universities." The supervising architects for the School of Science and Engineering (Risley and Gould) worked out a scheme based on that idea before planning the first buildings of the campus. An adaptation of this scheme that calls for the development of three semiautonomous universities, or clusters of colleges, "each having depth in the humanities, social sciences, natural sciences, and technology," [39] was later developed by Robert E. Alexander, FAIA, and Associates in drawing up a long-range physical plan for the campus. The first cluster, to be completed by 1975, would consist of four colleges, each of which would enroll about 2300 students. While there would be attempts to unify all elements of the campus, each cluster of colleges, and all colleges within them, would be distinctive in significant ways.

In the summer of 1963, the School of Science and Engineering was moved from its temporary quarters in Scripps Institution buildings to a seven-story graduate laboratory and office building up on the mesa. By the end of the year, a five-story laboratory building for physics and chemistry was completed there, and a four-story biology and chemistry laboratory and library, and a social sciences and humanities building were under construction. In October, this complex was officially designated by the Regents as the First College of the projected general campus,[40] and the School of Science and Engineering ceased to exist.

Under pressure of enrollment demands, the original plan of the faculty to begin undergraduate work at San Diego slowly had to be abandoned. The legacy of the original plan, however, was a stellar faculty recruited during the School of Science and Engineering phase of the campus' development.

The distinguished scholars who came to San Diego during that period included Nobel Laureate Harold Urey and Mrs. Maria Mayer, who received a Nobel Prize three years after joining the faculty.[41] In the summer of 1963, the science and engineering faculty was supplemented by ten staff members in the humanities and social science, and departments of philosophy and literature were created.

The First College accepted its first undergraduates, 181 Freshmen, in September, 1964. Its curriculum was radical. There were no electives for lower-division students and few in the undergraduate program as a whole. The first two years of study placed heavy emphasis on mathematics, sciences, and languages. Students could not declare a major until their junior year. The emphasis on science and mathematics was insisted upon not only by faculty members in scientific disciplines, but also by those in the humanities and social sciences who were concerned that graduates of the college in any discipline should not be "scientifically illiterate." [42] With experience, the program was slightly altered to permit several alternative curricula to meet the needs of students with different levels of preparation for scientific study. It was intended that the college would graduate historians, philosophers, and social scientists, but, as it turned out, its reputation became such that it attracted few students planning to make their careers in nonscience fields. This is beginning to change.

In January, 1965, the First College at San Diego was renamed Revelle College in honor of the man who had pioneered its development. Roger Revelle had remained at San Diego as dean and director until July, 1961, when Herbert York assumed the responsibilities of the chancellorship. At that time he took a leave of absence to serve as Science Adviser to the United States Secretary of the Interior, but returned to the University in 1963 as Dean of Research. He served in that position and as Director of Scripps Institution of Oceanography until he left, in 1964, to become the director of the new Center for Population Studies at Harvard.[43]

At the end of 1963, with much of the initial planning for the new general campus completed, York experienced premonitory symptoms of heart trouble and decided to resign as chancellor. For about a year, however, he remained in office while a successor was sought. To provide some relief from his administrative burdens, John S. Galbraith, a professor of history at UCLA, was asked to move to San Diego to become vice-chancellor. He arrived in July, 1964, and in November agreed to accept appointment as chancellor. Born in Glasgow, Scotland, on November 10, 1916, Galbraith received his A.B. degree at Miami University (Ohio) in 1938. He then attended the University of Iowa, where he earned his M.A. and Ph.D. degrees.

He joined the UCLA faculty in 1948 as an assistant professor of history and remained there until his move to San Diego.[44]

Organization of a second college at San Diego began in 1964. Named for John Muir, the famous California naturalist, it emphasizes direct student involvement in creativity and research and capitalizes on learning opportunities not only in the classrooms, but also in residence halls and other college facilities.[45] Its first students were accepted in 1967 in temporary quarters on a part of the campus that had once been Camp Matthews. As soon as its permanent buildings are completed, its students and faculty will move, and a third college will be started in the Camp Matthews facilities.

As chancellor at San Diego, Galbraith soon found that citizens in the neighboring community did not fully understand that the presence of a University brings more than technological know-how and cultural enrichment to a region. The protests of a group of students and several faculty members when the United States intervened in a crisis in the Dominican Republic in May, 1965, and similar activities protesting American involvements in Vietnam in October, 1965, drew heated criticism from some leaders of the San Diego community. Galbraith found that no small part of his job as chancellor was explaining that society's values and traditions are frequently challenged as a result of intellectual activity on a college campus, but that the community benefits in the long run by assuming a tolerant attitude.

Within the University, his most difficult problems derived from the unorthodox history of the San Diego campus. Started in the late 1950s as a graduate school with a large number of internationally known faculty members receiving over-scale salaries (generally supported by private philanthropy), it was soon regarded by other institutions of higher learning, including some of the University's own campuses, as the "spoiled child" of the University system.

After four years as San Diego's chief executive officer, Galbraith resigned in the fall of 1968 so that he could accept the Smuts Visiting Fellowship at Cambridge for the 1968–1969 academic year.

THE SOUTH CENTRAL COAST CAMPUS

In 1957, the California State Senate asked the Regents to study possible University sites in the Monterey Peninsula. During the same session an assembly concurrent resolution asked the Regents to consider the virtues of the Santa Clara Valley as a campus location.[46] In December, 1959, after some one hundred locations had been considered, the Regents voted to concentrate their attention on the Almaden Valley in Santa Clara County for the general location of a campus to serve the South Central Coast region.[47]

Unfortunately, public announcement of the Regents' decision caused land values to increase drastically in the Almaden Valley area and made it difficult for the Regents to acquire the site they needed from the several owners who would have been involved. After another year of study their interest shifted to a new site. It consisted of nearly two thousand acres of ranchland at Santa Cruz and was characterized by a varied topography and vegetation ranging from grasslands to forests of second-growth redwoods. To the south and southeast, there were magnificent views of Monterey Bay. Abandoned quarries and long-cold kilns on the site were reminders of a once-flourishing lime production that contributed to the fortunes of pioneer rancher Henry Cowell, his descendants, and the S. H. Cowell Foundation, from which the site was finally purchased by the Regents.

On the afternoon of June 23, 1961, Dean McHenry, who was then serving simultaneously as a professor at UCLA and a member of the president's staff as dean of academic planning, received a phone message at his Westwood home that President Kerr was planning to stop by for a visit. McHenry and the President were good friends. They had been graduate students together at Stanford and had worked closely together during the development of the Master Plan for California Higher Education in 1959 and 1960. When Kerr arrived he asked McHenry if he would be interested in the chancellorship of the new campus at Santa Cruz. Kerr did not know that only a few days before McHenry had presented a speech in that area and had already concluded that the position the President now offered was, of all of those in the University, the one he would most like to have. He quickly accepted and at the Regents meeting in July his appointment was made official.

When they were graduate students at Stanford, McHenry and Kerr had frequently exchanged notes on their undergraduate experiences. McHenry was an alumnus of UCLA, which was beginning to develop the rich resources of a major university. Kerr was a former honors student at Swarthmore, a distinguished liberal arts college. Somehow, they believed, it must be possible to offer the students the advantages of both kinds of institution. The opportunity to try was presented at Santa Cruz.

Other useful ideas were contained in two reports that had been prepared by members of the faculty while Kerr was still chancellor at Berkeley. One of them came from a group of faculty members who had Stephen Pepper, professor of philosophy, as their spokesman. Upon learning about plans to build several large residence halls at Berkeley, they proposed that these units be more than bedrooms and dining halls. Instead, each one could be the nucleus of a residential college conducted within the jurisdiction of the College of Letters and Science in a manner similar to that of the house system at Harvard or Oxford. Kerr had been so impressed by this report that he had tried to stimulate faculty interest in putting such a plan in action, but was unable to get enough support to pursue it formally. Another idea came from an *ad hoc* group of faculty members for whom Jacobus tenBroek, then professor of speech, and R. Nevitt Sanford, a professor of psychology who later abandoned Berkeley for Stanford, were spokesmen. This idea suggested that an experimental college be established within the College of Letters and Science at Berkeley. In addition to reviewing these proposals, Chancellor McHenry studied institutions where house systems or cluster colleges had been in operation. These included Yale, Harvard, the Claremont Colleges in Southern California, the University of the Pacific in Stockton, California, and, of course, Oxford and Cambridge.

In July, 1962, McHenry moved to Santa Cruz. After two years in rented space at Cabrillo College, he set up administrative offices in what was once the cookhouse of the old Cowell ranch. A temporary library and an office for campus architects and engineers were accommodated in the refurbished carriage house. On the scene, he was in a better position to cultivate the already strong support for the campus in the city of Santa Cruz and other nearby communities, to supervise campus planning, and personally to guard the natural beauties of the campus that was to be built there. He took this latter function very seriously, periodically checking personally to see that no more trees were cut than was absolutely necessary and that no unnecessary roadways were put in while the campus was under construction. On one occasion, he even joined firefighting crews when the campus forests were threatened by a potential holocaust.

With the advice of supervising architects John Carl Warnecke and Associates, aided by consulting architects Anshen and Allen, Theodore C. Bernardi, and Ernest J. Kump, and landscape architect Thomas D. Church,[48] physical attributes of the campus took shape. The basic unit would be a residential college with some unique approach to learning. The first one would have about 600 students. Subsequent ones would have as few as 250 and as many as 1000, depending upon their approach and function. In all, between 15 and 20 colleges were contemplated.

Each college would have resident accommodations for at least half of its students and would provide classrooms, lounges, small libraries containing recreational reading material and general reference collections, and such other facilities as could be economically provided to enhance its autonomy.

Facilities for intramural athletics and physical education instruction would be built in proximity to the colleges. At the core of the campus would be such major facilities as administration buildings, the main library, and central academic structures. Intruding into this area would be the principal science building with its laboratories and offices. Automobile traffic would be routed around the campus perimeter so that there would be little interference with pedestrian activity in the area of the college.

The first college, which emphasizes a humanistic approach to learning, is named Cowell College, in honor of the pioneers who had owned the Santa Cruz site and in grateful acknowledgment of more than $900,000 for the college's establishment that was given by the S. H. Cowell Foundation.

Faculty recruitment began with the appointment of a provost for the college. He was Page Smith, a distinguished UCLA historian who had graduated from Dartmouth in 1940 and had experienced close student-faculty relationships at Harvard, where he did graduate work leading to his doctorate in 1951.[49] He was subsequently joined by scores of faculty members who were intrigued by the Santa Cruz approach to higher education and were interested in participating in a pioneering venture. Among them were men in their fifties or older who already had distinguished reputations at other institutions. The first faculty also included young men in their twenties and early thirties who had been chosen from the top of the recent crop of Ph.D.s.

On September 27, 1965, Cowell College opened with 650 students. Some of the central service buildings were not complete, and those who resided on the campus lived in house trailers until residence halls were built. Campus paths were still dusty and there were long lines for meals served in the field house. But the students found the inconveniences tolerable and enjoyed pioneering. As one Freshman said, "I like the fact that there is no tradition here to bind us one way or another." [50]

According to the master plan for the campus, one new college was to be opened almost every year until its capacity was reached. To keep up with that schedule, Chancellor McHenry had to obtain annually between three and a half million and five million dollars in state appropriations and loans for basic construction. In addition to this basic amount, approximately half a million dollars were needed in private gifts. This money was to be used to provide houses for the college provosts, apartments for some of the faculty members, college libraries, and other facilities uniquely required by a campus organized on the college plan.

The second college, Adlai E. Stevenson College, named for the distinguished American ambassador to the United Nations, opened on schedule in 1966 with an academic perspective largely influenced by the social sciences.

Its special goals include "development of understanding of the modern social sciences and their actual and potential contributions to society and to the individual; development of some grasp of both the humanistic and scientific components of social science; development of knowledge of 'external,' as well as American, cultures and societies." [51] Crown College, named to acknowledge the generosity of the Crown-Zellerbach Foundation in contributing $500,000 toward its development as a liberal arts college with science and the scientific method providing the general orientation, opened in 1967. A fourth college was scheduled to open in the fall of 1968. It was supported by the Charles Merrill Trust, which gave $650,000 to launch it. Merrill College will organize its educational program around the problem of poverty at home and abroad.

Because students are not required to take all of their courses in their own college (inasmuch as many courses are not duplicated in all colleges, they could not do so if they wanted to), the addition of colleges expands and deepens the general curriculum of the Santa Cruz campus. Another feature of the campus that appeals to many students is that grading is normally on a pass or fail basis. In upper-division work, a few Boards of Studies have chosen to assign letter grades to students pursuing courses in their majors. Concern that this system would jeopardize the chances of Santa Cruz graduates for entering graduate schools was abated when many of the members of the first graduating class were admitted to graduate schools, including those at Harvard, Princeton, and Berkeley.

The "cluster college" concept in operation at Santa Cruz has attracted nationwide publicity as an answer to the challenge offered to the campus by Clark Kerr: ". . . to make the University seem smaller even as it grows larger. . . ." [52]

Thus far it is working well, with each college developing its own traditions and forms of student and faculty governance. Its greatest difficulty may be in holding to the schedule of its master plan, which calls for the creation of a new college almost every year in the coming decades.

THE IRVINE CAMPUS

In 1961, sixty-eight land-grant colleges, institutes, and universities across the country began to plan celebration of the Morrill Land Grant Act Centennial in 1962. A question that must have occurred to thoughtful men at many of these institutions was: What would a land grant university be like if we had the opportunity to start all over again in building it today? Certainly that question occurred to Daniel G. Aldrich, dean of agricultural sciences for the University of California and a leader in planning the national Land Grant Centennial. It also occurred to President Clark Kerr. An opportunity to build such an institution came with the Regents' decision to build a new campus in the Southeast Los Angeles–Orange County area, where an estimated 4,000,000 people would be living by the year 2000.[53]

William L. Pereira of Pereira & Luckman, the firm that had already helped to choose the San Diego site and was assigned the task of investigating the Southeast Los Angeles–Orange County sites as well, studied twenty-three sites in the area before settling upon three located within 90,000 acres of ranch lands owned by the Irvine Company. After several months of negotiations, 1000 acres of this property were given to the University by the owners. A few miles inland from Newport Beach, the site was described as being located "on gently rolling land with an inspiring outlook to the north and west over the Santa Ana Basin." [54] It was officially accepted by the Regents in July, 1960.[55] Later the Regents bought 510 acres of adjoining land for faculty housing and other University-related use.[56]

In the summer of 1961, several Regents spoke to Dean Aldrich informally about the possibility that he might leave agriculture and move to southern California to become chancellor of the new campus. In November, President Kerr was more definite. He told Aldrich that the Regents believed that he was the man for the job and wanted him to think carefully about accepting it. He did, most consciously and deliberately, on an airplane trip from Corvalis, Oregon, to San Francisco on December 6, 1961. He realized that he had been spending a lot of time visiting land-grant colleges all over the country and advising them on what they should be doing for the future. Now, he was being given the opportunity to build a campus and put some of his ideas into practice. He decided that if he could have a relatively free hand in building the kind of campus he believed was needed, he would accept the chancellorship.[57] Clark Kerr and the Regents agreed with his objectives and he was officially appointed on January 19, 1962,[58] but remained in his office as dean of agricultural sciences until November, when money became available for campus development at what was now officially designated "University of California, Irvine." [59]

The essence of Aldrich's goal at Irvine was to make every academic activity on the campus relevant to the needs of society. Put another way, the University campus he wanted to build would be as essential to all endeavors in the state as its college of agriculture was to rural California and to the agricultural business and industry. Irvine was a logical place to make such an effort because it was in the heart of an area that was rapidly urbanizing, and campus and community could grow together.

Almost as soon as Aldrich was appointed chancellor, he began to seek opportunities to make the presence of the University felt in the community. With the help of University of California Extension, a series of chancellor's lectures was presented in Garden Grove. Extension instruction was offered in mathematics and engineering at Buena Park High School, and by the time the Irvine campus enrolled its first students, Orange County extension offerings were the second largest of all areas in the state. When the campus opened, it assumed responsibility for extension programs throughout Orange County and in the Long Beach area as well. The University's library services were made available to the growing complex of research and development firms and to public schools in the area. In 1962, Chancellor Aldrich met with several leaders of Orange County's industrial community and formed an organization called Project 21, which concerns itself with planning for the twenty-first century. As the project developed, a third partner, the Orange County Planning Commission, was added. The University's role in the project was to make experts from the campus and elsewhere available to the community to analyze problems and submit alternative solutions. The private-industry and political components of the project would then translate the information offered by the University into action.

Interraction between the University and community is also provided by nearby companies that made their plants and laboratories available as teaching resources for Irvine's engineering students, that organized summer job programs for engineering students, and that made some of their expert staff members available as lecturers on the campus.

Aldrich made a personal link to the community by becoming a member of almost every civic organization that wanted him. He served on the board of the Orange County Philharmonic Society, the Orange Coast Association, the Orange Chamber of Commerce, the Newport Harbor Chamber of Commerce, the Opera Association, the Boy Scout Orange Empire Council, and many others. Moreover, although the University controls land that is eventually planned for development of faculty housing, Aldrich decided to defer such use, partly because he did not want the community around the campus to grow too fast and prematurely fix the character of the immediate neighborhood, and partly because the delay encouraged staff and faculty members to live in several nearby communities where they have been encouraged to become active in civic life and thereby make the University's presence constructively felt.

In the academic planning for the Irvine campus, Aldrich chose to follow the traditional patterns of Berkeley and UCLA, building a college of letters and science to provide the basic disciplines which, in Aldrich's terms, "undergird any university enterprise." [60] He also wanted professional schools at the outset, and the industrial character of the surrounding area suggested that the first ones should be schools of engineering and of administration. The School of Engineering was created by the Regents in June, 1965.[61] A Graduate School of Administration opened in September 1966.[62]

The College of Letters and Sciences was organized on a divisional basis, initially to include divisions of social science, humanities, biological sciences, physical sciences, and fine arts, and offer perhaps a dozen majors, including education. The principal author of this plan was Ivan Hinderaker, who served as vice-chancellor for academic affairs at Irvine before becoming chancellor at Riverside. Hinderaker's idea was to appoint deans with strong authority for each of the divisions and to give them as much freedom as possible in determining the internal organization of their divisions.[63] As a result, some divisions have departments, and others do not. In 1967, the Academic Senate at Irvine voted to redesignate these divisions as "schools," with all deans reporting to the vice-chancellor for academic affairs.

The physical plan for the campus was strongly influenced by President Clark Kerr, who sketched it out roughly on a piece of yellow paper still preserved in the Irvine campus archives. Kerr's idea was that the campus should be arranged with the most generally used facilities at its core and the most specialized facilities at the periphery. The rough plan is in the form of concentric circles, with the library and College of Letters and Sciences near the center, which later was designated as a campus park, and professional schools, residence halls, and other facilities located in other concentric rings around the Letters and Science core.

Another unique feature of the plan as finally worked out by the architect, Pereira, was that the buildings would be arranged like the spokes of a wheel. Between them there would be sites for faculty homes, educational foundations, and other quasi-educational facilities. Known as "inclusion areas," each of these developments would be bounded by the campus on at least two sides. Since there would be three of them (excluding one which would provide a mall leading to the campus core) the philosophical idea of creating a maximum contact between campus and community is ingeniously served by the plan.

The first buildings of the campus included a library, a campus hall housing a gymnasium-assembly room and student health and University extension facilities, a dining commons, student housing for five hundred students, a Natural Science and Science Lecture Hall, Fine Arts and Humanities-Social Sciences buildings, a central heating and air-conditioning plant, and a corporation yard. All of these facilities were completed in 1965.[64]

Although the campus was originally planned for a charter enrollment of five hundred, Aldrich insisted that it accept as many qualified students as wanted to come. He felt this was necessary in line with his promises to the people of the East Los Angeles–Orange County area that their support would be rewarded by a University-level education for their children. On the strength of the promise, many Orange County high school graduates in 1963 and 1964 attended local junior colleges until the Irvine campus was ready. When the doors were opened on September 26, 1965, 1589 students, including 140 graduate students, enrolled.[65] Waiting to teach them were 114 faculty members: 26 professors, 15 associate professors, and 56 assistant professors; 99 of them held doctorates.[66]

In keeping with Aldrich's philosophy of gearing his campus work to the needs of society and to the pace of technological development anticipated in the twenty-first century, the campus has been encouraged to develop practical and imaginative uses of television, computers, language laboratories, and other modern electronic and mechanical instruments in instruction and research.[67]

Now under construction is a new medical school to be occupied by the faculty of the California College of Medicine, a Los Angeles institution whose heritage can be traced back to 1896. The College was affiliated with the University in March, 1965, but was redesignated a department of the University in October of the same year and a part of the Irvine campus in 1967.

THE COST OF EXPANSION

With the enlargement of the enrollment capacity of the Berkeley, Los Angeles, Davis, Santa Barbara, and Riverside campuses and the opening of general campuses at San Diego, Santa Cruz, and Irvine, the University was able to accept 91,535 students for the quarter beginning January 2, 1968.[68] That was almost twice as many as had been enrolled in the University a decade before. Achieving such growth required enormous efforts on the part of the Regents and the University staff. It was also expensive.

Between June, 1957, when the Regents reaffirmed the University policy of refusing no qualified students admission, and the end of the 1967 fiscal year, annual operating expenditures of the University rose from $249,-

146,000 [69] to $365,356,000.[70] During the same decade, a total of $718,-149,000,[71] was spent for new buildings or improvements on existing and developing campuses.

The sources for funds for both operations and capital improvements were, as they had been from the University's beginning, somewhat diverse, including federal funds, gifts, loans, student fees, and state appropriations. The generosity of the legislature during this time of upbuilding was a vital factor. State appropriations for operations increased from $84,772,000 [72] in 1957–1958 to an estimated $240,675,000 in 1966–1967.[73] State support for building programs was substantial, totaling $69,021,328 in 1963–1964, when construction at the newer campuses was at its peak, dropping slightly in 1964–1965 and 1965–1966, and then increasing again to $67,394,000 in 1966–1967.[74]

Unable to pay for badly needed capital improvements out of current revenues, not only in education but also in other state institutions, the California legislature asked the people of the state to approve bond issues for $200,000,000 in 1956; $200,000,000 in 1958; $270,000,000 in 1962; and $380,000,000 in 1964.[75] Included in projects to be financed by each of the bond issues were buildings for the University of California. Before each election in which the bonds were presented to California citizens, alumni and friends of the University of California played a prominent role in organizing voter support. Every proposed bond issue passed. (In 1962, however, a proposed bond issue failed when first submitted in June and had to be reworded and resubmitted at a special election in November before California voters would give it the two-thirds margin of approval required for passage.)

In 1965, the University's administrative staff began to review the 1960 growth plan. The planners soon discovered that the estimate of 214,000 students in the year 2000 would be at least 60,000 students short of foreseeable enrollment. To meet this new demand, they recommended that the enrollment limits set for Davis, Santa Barbara, and Riverside be lifted and that all general campuses have enrollments of between 15,000 and 27,500 students, but that once targets are set, the University should commit itself to accommodate additional students on new campuses and no campus should endeavor to attain massive size. In the words of the report, "With a single university campus, as with the dinosaur, the body can become too large for the brain and the central nervous system." To accommodate a rapid enrollment increase anticipated in the late 1970s, the planners recommended that a new campus be built in the San Francisco Bay area in about 1972 and that another of two projected campuses be built in the Los Angeles area in 1975. A campus in the San Joaquin Valley, favorably considered by the Regents in

1957, was resubmitted as a fourth new campus to be considered. After thorough study by academic, administrative, and Regental committees, the planners' proposals were submitted to the Regents, approved in principle, and ordered submitted to the California Coordinating Council for Higher Education in June, 1966, as part of the University's master academic plan.[76]

Of special concern to the planners in drawing up the 1966 growth plan was the ability of the state to finance it. They concluded, "It is expected that the growth in the population of the state will almost match the growth in the undergraduate student body between now and the year 2000. It is expected that rising per capita income of about three per cent per annum will support increases in quality within the University and any differential increase in University costs over costs generally. . . ." [77] They also concluded, however, that the costs of graduate instruction, which would also increase as the percentage of graduate students increased, would require more of the state's per capita income than the University was then receiving and recommended continuing studies of the problem.

MORE DECENTRALIZATION

As important as the problem of financing was the problem of efficient administration, which became increasingly complicated with the development of new campuses. This, too, was studied during 1965. In March, the chancellors were asked to reply to detailed questions concerning campus-Universitywide relations. On the basis of their replies and subsequent conferences, an outline of proposals was prepared and presented to the Regents in May. In June, a more detailed version of the suggested administrative reorganization was completed, and President Kerr announced his intention to ask for amendments to the bylaws and standing orders of the Regents so that still greater authority could be delegated from the Board through the president to the chancellors.[78]

Kerr's reorganization plan was based on three familiar assumptions:

a. There will continue to be one University of California as provided in the Constitution of the State of California.
b. The Board of Regents will retain its historic position as the final governing authority of the University.
c. The University will continue to embrace the Master Plan for Higher Education, which is serving the state so effectively.[79]

Under the reorganization, chancellors were given more leeway in establishing departments, colleges, and other academic administrative units; in offering degrees; in appointing and promoting faculty members to the tenure level; in appointing and fixing salaries of most campus administrators; in administering gifts and fund-raising programs; in approaching research grants and contracts up to $1,000,000 per year (per individual grant or contract); in appointing executive architects; and in arranging public ceremonies. In order to extend this authority to the chancellors, much of it had to be first delegated to the president by the Regents. This delegation was achieved in December, through a series of amendments to the bylaws and standing orders of the Regents.[80] By approving these amendments, the Regents started to do what professional administrative consultants had been recommending that they do since the 1940s—withdraw from the detailed administration of the University and concentrate on general policy.

In 1963, President Clark Kerr presented the annual Godkin Lectures at Harvard, choosing as his subject *The Uses of the University*. In them, he attempted to describe the development of the modern American university, which at one point he said "is an imperative rather than a reasoned choice among elegant alternatives. . . ." [81] If smallness and simplicity had been a choice reasonably open to the Regents, administrators, and faculty members of the University of California in 1957, they undoubtedly would have preferred it. For better or worse, that choice was not in fact available to them. They already knew of the incessant and accelerating growth of California's population, and realized that one of its implications was inevitably that more young men and women would demand opportunities for a university education. In 1957, they had also concluded that it was to the ultimate benefit of the state and nation that those demands not be denied. They understood, because the University had become one of its most important sources, that new knowledge was also proliferating. Although knowledge has no visible bulk, it requires space as surely as students do—in libraries, in laboratories, and in the accommodation of new departments and disciplines. By accepting these realities, those who were charged with deciding the University's destiny committed themselves to an obligation to make it grow.

Beyond that commitment, which was indeed a response to imperatives, many choices seemed available to the University. There were choices of locations for new campuses. There were choices between sizes of campus units and the ways in which they were organized internally. There were choices of approach to the learning experience, and there were choices among relationships that might be established between disciplines on the campus and between the campus and its surrounding community. By starting to plan in the 1950s the President, the chancellors, and the faculty leaders protected the opportunities for making the choices that were available to them. They found themselves engaged in an exciting and creative endeavor that resulted in an entirely new kind of institution that was incredibly diverse in the character of its many parts, yet unmistakably unified under many of the same traditions and aspirations that had guided the University since 1868. Learning to administer this new institution economically and efficiently would become a time-consuming preoccupation of the Regents, the president, the chancellors, and the other administrative officers of the University. Maintaining its distinction among the world's universities was a task that fell most heavily upon the faculty, which pursued research and the recruitment of eminent or promising colleagues with unprecedented fervor. On the newer campuses, faculty members accepted their creative opportunities as a challenge. On the other campuses, faculty members regarded the development of the new campus as a competition for once unquestioned pre-eminence and worked hard to retain and enhance their distinction. But they also tended to regard growth as a trend toward fragmentation of University loyalty and patronage from the general public, and as a force for unwelcome change in familiar ways of doing things. Other challenges to tradition were made by the many young faculty members from all parts of the world who were brought in to help teach the growing student body and were unfamiliar with the University's heritage.

As President Kerr also pointed out in *The Uses of the University,* students, whose increasing number, more than any other factor, was forcing growth and change in American universities, were also restless. "There is an incipient revolt of undergraduate students against the faculty," he said; "the revolt that used to be against the faculty *in loco parentis* is now against the faculty *in absentia.* The students find themselves under a blanket of impersonal rules for admissions, for scholarships, for examinations, for degrees. The students also want to be treated as distinct individuals. . . . If the faculty looks on itself as a guild, the undergraduate students are coming to look upon themselves more as a 'class'; some may even feel like a 'lumpen proletariat.' Lack of faculty concern for teaching, endless rules and requirements, and impersonality are the inciting causes." [82]

The student revolt that Kerr anticipated occurred on the Berkeley campus of the University of California soon thereafter and very nearly overshadowed the unprecedented growth and achievement of the last decade of the University's century.

Chapter 25

THE LIBERATED STUDENTS

BETWEEN World War II and the fall of 1964, student life at the University of California went through a series of transformations.

At first there was a period of quiet conformity to the values and traditions of the Wheeler-Sproul era. This conformity was due in part to a conscious desire of students, faculty, and administrators to re-establish the atmosphere of the prewar years. It was reinforced by the ambivalent influence of large numbers of war veterans who, in carefree moments, often spurred their less worldly classmates to excessive observance of collegiate frivolities but, in pursuit of education, made competition in the classroom so grim that choice between indulging in curricular and extracurricular activity became difficult. Easily identified by the military-uniform remnants that they adapted into their civilian wardrobes, the veterans also kept wartime patriotic sentiment alive on University campuses and were, consequently, a factor in deterring an early revival of the militant student radicalism that had emerged in the 1930s. An even stronger deterrent was the aftershock of the war itself and the efforts of a victorious but frightened people to protect themselves from internal revolution by repression of speech, thought, and action. This curious spectacle bewildered the college generation for almost a decade. During the period, intercollegiate athletics and extracurricular activities flourished on all campuses. But there were already signs that among college-age youth there were students whose educational background, life experiences, and parental training emphasized values that were, if not antithetical to collegiate conformity, at least conducive to a search for alternatives.

Following the departure of the war veterans and the relaxation of political tensions after 1955, student concern for problems of mankind beyond the University campus became more evident. It was manifested for several years in efforts to translate those problems into projects that could be approached within existing structures and sanctions of the Associated Students and University policies.

In the 1960s there was a shift in both the nature and the setting of student activity. It was no longer oriented to the campus but rather was oriented to the world at large, and students were found participating in civil-rights demonstrations in the American South, in tutorial programs for underprivileged children, and in community-development projects abroad.

THE CONFORMING INFLUENCES

President Sproul had deliberately encouraged continuance of as many student activities as possible during World War II as a means of maintaining student morale and preserving traditions that might suffer if neglected. Students who came to the University when the war was over accepted student life as they found it. Class organizations, student government, and scores of committees all regained their prewar vigor. Musical organizations could recruit well-balanced ranges of voices and instrumentalists. Student publications enlisted enough reporters to cover the campus beats. Drama groups found casting easier. On the larger campuses there were enough students who shared such hobbies as hiking, skiing, flying airplanes, sailing, and photography to make possible the formation of clubs to serve them. Student-body officers enjoyed both power and prestige.

Intercollegiate athletics provided focus for school spirit and, in the postwar period, all of the University's existing campuses had reason at one time or another to be proud of their athletes.

In the 1948 Olympics, the Berkeley crew, a UCLA basketball player—Don Barksdale—and two Berkeley alumni—pole-vaulter Guinn Smith, '42, and swimmer Ann Curtis, '46—won gold medals for the United States. Four years later, UCLA's Cy Young won a gold medal throwing the javelin. In 1956, Berkeley's Leamon King was a member of the American 400-meter relay team that won a gold medal. In 1960, UCLA's Rafer Johnson won a gold medal in the decathlon. Berkeley's Jack Yerman and Darrall Imhoff won first-place Olympic honors the same year—Yerman as a member of the winning 1600-meter relay team and Imhoff as a member of the champion United States basketball team. Another UCLA athlete, Walt

Hazzard, won a gold medal as a member of the winning basketball team in 1964.[1]

Lynn O. (Pappy) Waldorf came to Berkeley in 1947 to arouse a sleeping giant. He succeeded in coaching victory-hungry football teams to three Pacific Coast Conference Championships in a row, beginning in 1948. UCLA's football team, coached by Henry R. (Red) Sanders, dominated the coast with three consecutive conference championships, beginning in 1953. Three years later, Berkeley enjoyed another sweet but brief reign as football champion.[2]

UCLA won PCC basketball championships in 1950, 1952, and 1956 and then yielded the victor's crown to Berkeley, where teams coached to precision by Pete Newell won three-in-a-row championships in 1957, 1958, and 1959. Berkeley's baseball team won the National Collegiate Athletic Association championship in 1947 and again in 1957. Its crew won the Intercollegiate Regatta Association races in 1949, 1960, 1961, and 1964.[3]

In the Far-Western Intercollegiate Athletic Conference, Davis won championships in baseball in 1950; in basketball (co-championship) in 1952; in football in 1947 (co-championship), 1949, 1951, and 1956; in swimming in 1949 and 1951; in tennis in 1952; and in track and field in 1948, 1949, 1951, and 1952. Santa Barbara won California Collegiate Athletic Association victories in basketball in 1961; in baseball in 1952; in tennis in 1953, 1954, 1955, 1956, and 1957; and in track and field in 1960.[4]

In the mid-1950s the luster of California athletics was dulled (though only slightly) when both the Berkeley and Los Angeles campuses were penalized by the Pacific Coast Conference for illegal recruiting of athletes, or for giving them unauthorized assistance. President Sproul attempted to work out more stringent rules for members of the conference, but did not succeed, and instead persuaded the Regents to withdraw Berkeley and UCLA from the PCC. His successor, Clark Kerr, subsequently helped organize a new conference consisting of schools that maintained athletic programs comparable in size and conduct to those of the University's major campuses. Called the Athletic Association of Western Universities,[5] the new conference originally included the University of Southern California and the University of Washington. Stanford and the University of Oregon joined later.

Another influence for the preservation of tradition was rendered by fraternities and sororities. Immediately after the war, those at Berkeley and Los Angeles repossessed their houses from wartime tenants and resumed operations. Many of them built new, enlarged houses. Six new fraternities were started at UCLA and two at Berkeley.[6] Ten new fraternities were started at Davis (there had been only one before the war), and all of Santa

Barbara's thirteen fraternities and nine sororities were established after the war.[7]

From these organizations, from the University residence halls built both before and after the war, and from cooperatives and other organized living groups came most of the man- and woman-power to organize parades and rallies and perform the tedious behind-the-scenes labor of student self-government and its subsidiary clubs and activities.

The collegiate tradition and the conforming influence of traditional student government, organized living groups, and intercollegiate athletes as a focus for student loyalty and enthusiasm remained visible well into the 1960s. In its most frivolous forms, the collegiate tradition was seen in UCLA's challenge to USC for a noodle-eating contest,[8] in pushcart races at Santa Barbara,[9] in the dropping of watermelons from a seven-story building at San Diego to celebrate the end of finals,[10] and in the 1964 record of a Berkeley student who took a shower that lasted thirty-three hours, thirty-three minutes, and thirty-three seconds.[11] But collegiate tradition was stronger on some campuses than on others. On smaller campuses, like Davis, Santa Barbara, and Riverside, where there were few graduate students and where circumstances favored either the collegiate ways of life or concentration on academic affairs, the Wheeler-Sproul tradition endured and was dominant. At UCLA, where more than a third of the students lived with their own families or relatives [12] and up to 40 per cent traveled from six to twenty miles a day to attend classes,[13] traditions were sparse though hardy. Extracurricular activities were sustained primarily by a relatively few students in fraternities, sororities, cooperatives, and nearby private rooms and apartments. Student activities remained, from the days of Provost Moore, under close administrative scrutiny. UCLA's neighbors, business and professional people residing in high-priced homes and apartments, also exerted a conservative influence. Ironically, at Berkeley, where the Wheeler-Sproul tradition was born, it was increasingly in competition with new student interests and altered by new conditions of student life.

THE SOPHISTICATED GENERATION

About a decade after World War II, college and university administrators throughout the country noticed something different about their students. Intellectually, they seemed much more liberated than their parents had been. Television, paperback books, more community tolerance for candor in literature and entertainment, increasing opportunity and ease of travel, new theories of child-raising that encouraged independent experience, and accelerated and more imaginative elementary and secondary school education made college-age youth more sophisticated than they had been in earlier generations. Products of an affluent society, they often had financial resources of their own to give them independence to indulge personal tastes and interests.

None of the characteristics of the new students was incompatible with traditional student life so long as the tradition was protected by the campus mores and was valid in the context of campus environment. Those conditions did not prevail on all campuses of the University.

Postwar enrollment growth, which peaked in 1948–1949 when the full force of veteran enrollments was felt, declined to a low of 38,032 on all campuses (still almost 10,000 greater than before the war) in 1953–1954,[14] and then began a steady and spectacular rise to 95,337 in 1967.[15] Simple concepts such as senior control, the honor spirit, and the close-knit University family were not easily grasped by students who were constituents of student bodies with ten to twenty thousand members.

As new campuses developed, Universitywide tradition lost some of its overriding influence at the student level, not only at young campuses, but at the older ones as well.

By 1955, almost 12 per cent of the students on all campuses of the University came from outside California. At Berkeley that year, almost 15 per cent came from out-of-state.[16] These students lacked not only an orientation toward campus customs and tradition but also an orientation toward the educational objectives of the state. There were also increasing numbers of transfers to the University from colleges and universities inside California, with the result that fewer students had a full four-year undergraduate experience at the University. And there were the increasing numbers of graduate students, most of whom were transfers from other institutions and almost all of whom were, until very recent years, considered academic apprentices to the faculty and believed to be uninterested in undergraduate pursuits outside the classroom. These factors had greater impact, of course, on the larger campuses.

Undergraduate student conduct became a secondary concern of many faculty members who were more interested in enhancing the University's eminence through research and public service. Accordingly, administrators and faculty members who continued to assert that constructive student activity outside the classroom was essential to the health and stature of the University came to be regarded by students as patronizing and hypocritical.

BERKELEY'S SECOND CULTURE

Influences that threatened the collegiate tradition were aggravated at Berkeley because that campus was bigger and because its way of life was changing under pressures of unique circumstances. A large portion of the student body was literally on its own. Its members attended classes on the campus and used its facilities for study and recreation. But they were beyond the reach of campus tradition and student government. Their life style, morals, and values were shaped by personal experience and the examples they found among their associates. They were, in a sense, alienated, but they were alienated by choice and resented the invasion of their private lives by University authorities.

Students who could not find accommodations in existing fraternities, sororities, boarding houses, and residence halls right after the war moved into rooms and apartments in low-rent areas adjacent to the campus. In these accommodations they discovered freedom from regulation and devised routines of daily living to suit their personal class, work, and study schedules. At first a necessity of crowded postwar conditions, this style of life eventually became preferred by many students. By 1956, almost as many single students lived in apartments as lived in fraternities or sororities.[17] Within the ensuing decade, student apartment-dwellers significantly outnumbered students in fraternities and sororities and were untouched by the influences favoring tradition and conformity those organizations tended to exert. By 1960, bohemian nonstudents, migrating from San Francisco and attracted by the parklike campus and intellectual and cultural atmosphere at Berkeley, moved into the same inexpensive housing areas where students had their rooms and apartments. Intriguing, adventurous, colorful, and unconventional, they brought with them a culture of their own that competed successfully with the collegiate tradition for student loyalties.

Chancellors Kerr, Seaborg, and Strong worked hard to make the campus the center of student interest. Not since the 1920s was so much done to provide physical accommodations for student activities. Residence halls, a new dining commons, a new student union, and new intramural sports fields were built. Through the generosity of Walter A. Haas, a Berkeley alumnus and wealthy San Francisco manufacturer, a recreational area for students and University personnel was built in Strawberry Canyon. It provided a large swimming pool (eventually two), tennis courts, playing fields, and a clubhouse. A special assistant was added to the chancellor's staff to handle student affairs. Counseling service, to guide students in career decisions and choices of academic goals, once available only to veterans, was made available to all students. As essential and valuable as these facilities and services were, they did not draw students closer to the University as had been hoped. The new residence halls were soon regarded as no less restrictive than fraternities and sororities, so they failed to attract the apartment-dwellers. The location of the new Student Center, at the boundary between campus and community, tended to emphasize rather than obscure the double role of students as scholars and citizens.

By the middle of the 1950s, students whose major concerns lay outside the campuses began to expose those interests. They did so at first by translating social, political, and economic problems into campus programs and issues. They worked against economic exploitation by continuing efforts to maintain minimum wages for student labor in surrounding communities and by working for fair-rent scales in student housing. They worked against racial segregation by exerting pressures on local landlords to open rooms and apartments to Negro and Oriental students, and by calling attention to the fact that some fraternities and sororities had clauses in their charters that discriminated against students who were members of racial or religious minorities. They sought world peace through new student government agencies that fostered international understanding.

THE UBIQUITOUS STUDENT NEWSPAPERS

Some of the earliest attempts to bridge the gap between campus and the outside world were made by the student press. Although not without precedent even in pre-World War II periods, these efforts in the 1950s occasionally earned campus newspaper editors the wrath of University officialdom and of the general public. In 1951, the *Daily Californian* published an eyewitness account of a youth festival held in East Berlin. Some readers considered the article sympathetic to international communism. John Francis Neylan, for one, brought the article to the attention of the Board of Regents, which resolved that President Sproul propose means of insuring "greater responsibility" in the newspaper.[18] At the next meeting of the Board, Sproul reported that although 90 per cent of the news in the paper concerned campus events and was drawn from wire-service reports, "evidence was shown, especially in feature articles and the Ice Box (letters to the editor), that communists and fellow travelers were given coverage and space disproportionate to their numbers."[19] To remedy the situation, and on recommendation of the ASUC Executive Committee, he appointed an advisory board for the paper, composed of students, members of the paper's editorial board, and representatives of the faculty, administration, and alumni. The committee's function was to "study policies and procedures . . . which control appointment of editors, policy formulation and coverage. . . ." [20] Another recommendation, later dropped, was that an adult "adviser" be engaged to give daily counsel to the editors.[21]

In 1955, after a series of episodes involving advertisements of meetings where Communists spoke and editorials that protested loyalty-oath requirements for ROTC candidates, UCLA's Dean of Students Milton E. Hahn, with the consent of Chancellor Raymond B. Allen, issued an administrative directive requiring that the editor of the *Daily Bruin* be elected by the student body, that the length of articles by contributors other than regular members of the paper's staff be limited to 150 words, and that articles of "highly controversial nature" be matched in the same issue by "materials with an opposing viewpoint." [22] The UCLA Student Legislative Council refused to co-sign the Chancellor's directive, but a new student-body constitution later in the year gave the Legislative Council more control over appointment of the newspaper's editor. In 1956, Dean Hahn called control of the *Daily Bruin* the key to the complete control of the University, which he pictured as the goal of subversives on campus.[23]

Despite these efforts at administrative control, the student newspapers, in their news columns and in their editorials, continued to prepare students for interest and participation in social and political causes both on and off the campus.

RELEASE FROM PRESSURE

Before students became truly active in social and political affairs, they had to shake off some of the repressions of the immediate postwar period. In Berkeley, they did it dramatically on an unusually hot May 16, 1956. It all began when members of several fraternities and sororities began engaging in water fights,[24] activities for which there was ample precedent in even cooler temperatures. By 7 P.M. about a thousand students jammed a one-block area south of campus, dousing each other with hoses and water thrown from cans, buckets, and wastebaskets.[25] After about two and a half hours of this sport, they began to return to their homes, wet, tired, and happy. But water fights had started on the north side of campus too, and at about 10 P.M. part of that crowd, inspired by newspaper accounts of spring "riots" at colleges and universities elsewhere in the country, set out for new adventures. Following a pattern first seen at the University of Michigan in 1952,[26] the male rioters at Berkeley decided to raid female living quarters to steal lingerie. Their ensuing "panty raids" were every bit as sensational as their prototypes in the East. Thousands of students joined or watched the mobs enter twenty-six sororities and residence halls.[27] When losses were added up in the following weeks, they amounted to nearly $12,000 and involved furnishings, property, and—of course—garments.[28]

Members of fraternities and men's residence halls and cooperatives collected money to make restitution, returned as many of the stolen items as they could, and fined or restricted their fellows who had participated in the affair. In addition, sixty-six individual cases were considered serious enough to refer to the campus Committee on Student Conduct, which recommended that two students be dismissed, two be suspended for the current semester, eighteen be barred from future registration for two semesters, fourteen be censured, and thirty-three be placed on probation.[29]

Obviously, the direct cause of the panty raids of 1956 is found in the fact that the day on which they occurred was ninety degrees and, once the students found a pleasant way to beat the heat, one thing led to another. More subtle explanations were offered by the administration. Among them were the lack of adequate student recreational facilities at Berkeley and the absence of a campus tradition strong enough to make such behavior unthinkable. These deficiencies were genuine. But the real significance of the panty raids at Berkeley might well be that they occurred precisely at the time when America was beginning to shake off the repressive fears of the McCarthy period and when all but a few veterans had left the campus. In that context, the raids may be seen as an explosive celebration of a release from restraint. It can also be viewed as one final fling at collegiate irresponsibility, for 1956 marks the end of the era of the "silent generation" that worried experts on student behavior throughout the first decade and a half after World War II. In 1957, at Berkeley, renewed student concern for the world beyond the campus would be intensified.

GADFLY POLITICS

Students whose major concerns lay outside the campuses began to reveal their interests immediately after the war by translating social, political, and economic problems into campus programs and issues. They resumed efforts of the 1930s to work against economic exploitation of student labor and student tenants of private rooming and boarding houses. They worked against racial segregation by exerting pressures on local landlords to open rooms to students of all races and by calling attention to the fact that some fraternities and sororities had discrimination clauses in their charters. They sought world peace through new student-government agencies that fostered international understanding, student travel abroad, and service projects and voluntary financial assistance for underdeveloped countries; scholarships for foreign students also were developed as part of these efforts.

These interests of socially aware and concerned students intensified after the veterans left and the McCarthy period ended. One instrument of the intensification was the formation of liberal student political parties, beginning in 1957. The first such party at Berkeley was called TASC—Toward an Active Student Community—and was an outgrowth of abortive efforts to elect student-body officers who would vote for a resolution demanding an end to racial discrimination in fraternities and sororities.

Unsuccessful in their first student-body election, TASC's leaders formed a new party called Slate, taking its name from the fact that it backed a full ticket of candidates for student offices in 1957. All of its candidates supported a program designed to attract the "dispirited, radical and liberal elements of the student body." [30] Stumping for an end to racial discrimination in Greek societies, for Fair Bear price programs for local merchants and landlords in the community, and for "academic freedom," Slate's candidates succeeded in increasing the participation in student-body elections at Berkeley from 2962 in the spring of 1957 to 5861 in the spring of 1958.[31] In 1959, Slate followers elected a student-body president and several members of the ASUC Executive Committee.[32] Between 1958 and 1961, it was a recognized student organization, privileged to use University facilities for its meetings.

One of Slate's most popular services was the publication of a "Supplement to the General Catalog" of the Berkeley campus, in which candid student opinions on courses and professors was printed. Though the published ratings were not scientifically derived, they were gratefully accepted by students of all political persuasions and filled a need that formal academic counseling procedures did not satisfy. With this service and with a platform addressing issues of concern to widely divergent constituencies in the student body, Slate was able to exert an influence out of proportion to its actual membership, which was variously estimated at between seventy-five and two hundred people.

Slate opposed compulsory ROTC at the University and claimed victory in that effort when, on May 18, 1962, the Regents voted to make the course voluntary.[33] Although the Academic Senate and the University administration played the most effective roles in achieving this action, Slate cannot be denied a fair share of credit inasmuch as its efforts helped to keep the issue alive.

Slate's success at Berkeley inspired the formation of similar organizations on other campuses, and parts of the Slate platform turned up as election issues in student-body races throughout the University. Three of the most popular objectives were elimination of faculty, alumni, and administrative representation on student legislative bodies; liberalization of rules governing use of University facilities for meetings; and the extension of student-government authority to permit student committees and councils to take stands on off-campus issues.

THE KERR DIRECTIVES

To guide chancellors and deans of students in dealing with the new student demands, President Clark Kerr issued revised regulations on October 23, 1959. To a considerable extent they were a restatement of long-understood policy. On campuses where the local administration traditionally had been strict, the new regulations extended student privileges. On others, they only made existing policy more explicit and eliminated conflicting provisions.

Introducing the rules, President Kerr pointed out that the authority of student government was derived from the Regents through the president and the chief campus officers. One of the new provisions required acknowledgement of that source of authority in the preambles to student-government constitutions. Kerr also pointed out that student governments frequently acted in ways that affected the interests of the administration, alumni, and faculty, and that "some participation" by these components of the University must exist on student governing boards. To assure that that participation would be preserved, chancellors were empowered, in effect, to veto efforts to remove it.[34]

The new rules, called (to the President's displeasure) the "Kerr Directives" by the student press, enjoined student governments from taking positions on off-campus political, religious, economic, international, or other issues of the time without permission of the chancellor. Student newspapers were permitted to take editorial positions on issues of the day provided that they made clear that their opinions "do not represent the view of the University or of the student government." [35]

The old Regulation 17 was superseded by the new directives with slight moderation. One of these removed restrictions on the campus appearances of candidates for public office. But the rules continued to prohibit use of University facilities for soliciting political party memberships, or for religious worship, exercise, or conversion; for raising money for projects not connected with an authorized University activity; for distributing literature without the permission of proper authorities; or for events that interfered with the academic program of the University.

The rules were not popular. Students at Riverside picketed the chancellor's office to denounce them. Student editors at Berkeley, Riverside, and Santa Barbara signed a joint editorial condemning them. The student government at UCLA passed a resolution in opposition. The editor of the UCR *Highlander* summed up the protest in a way that gives an interesting view of the character of the student bodies of several campuses:

> It appears that Riverside has been one of the leaders against the original directives, with Berkeley naturally taking a considerable role. . . . Santa Barbara's newspaper opposed the directive from the beginning also, although little more than that was done. The Los Angeles campus was exceptionally slow in deciding anything, which some cynics have suggested as being quite typical of anything there.[36]

In February, 1961, the directives were further amended by President Kerr to permit the exhibition or distribution of noncommercial literature in accordance with rules to be devised by the chancellors.[37] In August, a more equitable definition of student organizations entitled to use the University's facilities was incorporated in the regulations.[38]

There were several major tests of the directives. At Berkeley in May, 1961, the ASUC Executive Committee passed a resolution condemning the University of Chicago for dismissing one of its faculty members who wrote a letter to the student newspaper there asserting that premarital sex relations, in some cases, might justify the sanction of society. When student officers refused the administration's request that they rescind the motion, Chancellor Seaborg ruled the action "null and void" and wrote a letter to the president of the University of Illinois to advise him of that action. President Kerr threatened to make ASUC membership voluntary instead of compulsory (with attendant loss of revenue) if the Executive Committee continued to attempt to speak for all students on off-campus issues.[39] Five years later, the president of the Associated Students at the Riverside campus resigned, declaring, "What remains of student government is a hollow shell, a sham, a mockery of the democratic process it was intended to serve." His action followed an indication by Chancellor Ivan Hinderaker that the Legislative Council would be vacated for the remainder of the school year if it did not rescind a resolution calling on the President of the United States to intervene in racial unrest in Selma, Alabama.[40] The resolution was rescinded and, in all, six members of the council resigned. A subsequent poll of Riverside students revealed that they did not believe the Kerr directives should be modified but would have approved passage of the Selma Resolution if the Kerr directives had not prohibited it.[41]

THE OPEN FORUM

What students most frequently referred to as the Kerr directives was called the open forum policy by the President and other administrative officers of the University. The President repeatedly asserted that the rules, despite their unpopularity, were not all new, but altered old rules to make it easier for students to present and hear speakers on all sides of controversial issues.

Slate tested the tolerance of the new rules in March, 1961, by inviting Frank Wilkinson, a man twice called before the House Committee on Un-American Activities, to speak on the Berkeley campus. At the time of the invitation it was known that Wilkinson would soon begin to serve a one-year prison term for contempt of Congress. Thirty-five carloads of Bay Area citizens joined a caravan to Sacramento, where they protested Wilkinson's impending campus appearance. Governor Brown told them he would not intervene, saying, "This country has become great because we let everybody speak their piece . . . if they violate the law, if they urge revolution by force or violence, then we can put them in jail. But to ban them before we know what they're going to say, I think that is a very serious mistake." [42] University officials also refused to intervene.

President Kerr and Chancellor Strong both issued statements. President Kerr said: "The University is not engaged in making ideas safe for students. It is engaged in making students safe for ideas. Thus it permits the freest expression of views before students, trusting to their good sense in passing judgment on these views." [43] Chancellor Strong emphasized that "about 600 speakers a year appear on the Berkeley campus sponsored by various groups and speaking on a wide diversity of subjects.

"The University does not endorse in any way the views expressed at meetings of this nature," he said, "but holds that our facilities must remain available to provide an open forum for thought and expression." [44]

Open-discussion or "Hyde Park" areas were authorized on several campuses in 1962. Access to their use required only advance notification of the proper authorities. These areas served some of the functions Sather Gate did at Berkeley before construction of the Student Center placed it a block within the campus boundaries. The "Hyde Park" area set aside at Berkeley was in the Student Center Plaza, but this location did not satisfy students because it was a new and unfamiliar campus feature and was not readily visible from the most traveled cross-campus routes.

Under the new rules, the chancellors on the various campuses had considerable latitude in deciding who could appear as speakers. In 1962, Chancellor Herman Spieth at Riverside refused to permit Nobel Laureate Linus Pauling to speak on disarmament because that subject was outside the famous scientist's acknowledged competence. In the same year, both Chancellor Spieth at Riverside and Chancellor Murphy at Los Angeles refused to allow Dorothy Healey, former chairman of the Southern California Communist Party, to speak on campus. In this case they based their decision on the fact that the University had long-standing rules prohibiting the hiring of Communists as members of the faculty and denying use of University facilities to Communists. Three months later six students at Riverside, all members of Declare, a student organization similar to Slate at Berkeley, filed suit against the University contesting the ruling prohibiting Dorothy Healey from speaking on campus.[45]

The Riverside case was still pending in the courts on June 21, 1963, when the Regents by a vote of fifteen to two [46] removed the ban on Communist speakers. Justifying removal of the ban were the facts that students could and did hear Communist speakers at off-campus meetings and that the ideas of Communists were available to students in the daily press, over the radio, on television, and in books and periodicals in University libraries. Moreover, the ban usually gave the Communist speakers seeking use of University facilities publicity far out of proportion to their actual influence with students. President Kerr predicted that without the ban, "our students will be properly seen as the interrogators of Communists rather than appear as their 'defenders' through support of the 'right' of Communists to speak on campus." [47] Almost immediately after the Regents lifted the ban, Communist speakers were invited to several University campuses. In each instance they were greeted by large, attentive, polite but unimpressed student audiences.

A NEW OUTWARD DIRECTION FOR STUDENT ACTION

Ironically, as the restrictions on what students could do on campus were being lifted, students were attempting to expand the roles that they could play in improving society outside campus boundaries. Katherine Towle, a former commander of the Women's Marines who served as Berkeley's dean of students from 1961 to 1965, characterized students of that period as "articulate, eager, knowledgeable, independent and imbued with idealism." [48]

The idealism of students was nationwide in the 1960s, inspired to a considerable degree by President John F. Kennedy, who insisted that all citizens of the United States had a responsibility for direct participation in political and social action aimed at improving the way of life of mankind. By 1966, according to a University report, eight thousand students, roughly one out of ten on all campuses, "spend afternoons, weekends and vacations working in disadvantaged areas throughout California and the world." [49]

On almost every campus, students raised funds and enlisted as volunteer counselors for summer camps for underprivileged children. Volunteer student tutors and teachers' helpers were recruited on most campuses. Several student-organized tutorial projects helped children whose educational opportunities would be otherwise limited keep up with studies and develop motivation for learning. Those helped by such programs included children in urban ghettos and in farm-worker camps. Students from Berkeley and Davis volunteered to spend ten weeks of their summer in central Mexican towns and villages, building, teaching, and helping with community development in a program called Amigos Anonymous. A similar effort, Project Amigos, took students to Mexico to adapt surplus war-housing units for use as community centers, schools, and health clinics in underprivileged areas of the country. UCLA organized one of the first and largest collegiate blood drives in the country. In 1966, students there contributed 1127 pints of blood to the Red Cross. Five hundred students worked at making the drive successful. Project India at UCLA and Project Pakistan at Santa Barbara had the improvement of international understanding through direct people-to-people relationships as their goals. Students at Berkeley became "big brothers" to predelinquent boys. Students at Riverside volunteered as companions to mental patients in the state hospital at Patton and as volunteer assistants at the Peppermint Ridge School for the Mentally Retarded. The Medical Center at San Francisco outfitted a mobile clinic that took students and faculty members to areas in California where medical services were not readily available. Another mobile clinic provided dental and medical care for migrant farm workers. By 1966 some of these programs were more than five years old.[50]

The Peace Corps was immensely popular with University of California students. Berkeley alone supplied 791 Peace Corps volunteers, twice as many as any other institution in the country, in the first five years of the program's existence. UCLA ranked fifth in the nation with 357 volunteers. Every campus but Santa Cruz had been represented in the Peace Corps by 1966.[51]

Idealism also led students into controversial causes. In the spring of 1961 when Caryl Chessman, Los Angeles' "Red light bandit," who escaped the gas chamber for twelve years through legal delays, was executed, students at both Berkeley and Los Angeles joined protests against capital punishment. About 150 students at UCLA attended a noon rally on May 2 to hear speeches against capital punishment.[52] Berkeley students joined picket lines in Sacramento and participated in a march and vigil at San Quentin on the eve of the execution.

That same year, students at Berkeley were among the angry crowd that was denied admittance to the small room in the San Francisco City Hall where the House Un-American Activities Committee held hearings on the possible influence of Communists in the teaching profession. Singing or chanting in the corridor when they found they could not be admitted, the would-be spectators were quelled with fire hoses and many of them were dragged down water-slicked staircases to police vans. About sixty-eight people, some of them University students, were arrested, but charges against them were later dismissed by San Francisco's Municipal Judge Albert Axelrod, who said that most of those arrested had been punished enough already. Furthermore, in his opinion, they were "clean cut American College students" who wanted to "exercise their prerogatives of protesting what they believed to be an undemocratic hearing." [53] Regrettably, Judge Axelrod's decision did not settle the matter. A private company acquired newsreels of the incident and put together a pro-HUAC documentary called *Operation Abolition*. Shown to civic organizations, veterans' groups, and college and university gatherings all over the country, the films showed ugly scenes of angry, defiant witnesses, and drenched, indignant, sprawling young people in conflict with policemen. Although students from many colleges participated in the incident, the film emphasized the participation of students from the University of California to the point where most viewers forgot that while a few hundred students were at the hearings that unhappy day, more than eighteen thousand remained at their studies in Berkeley.

In the early 1960s, perhaps thirty or forty University students joined Freedom Riders from all over the country who spent their summers helping Negroes fight for their constitutional rights in the southern states. In those activities they learned the horrors of violence and intimidation. They also learned the techniques of civil disobedience. In 1961, more than three thousand students at UCLA signed a petition asking the ASUCLA to lend money from its general funds to provide bail for arrested Freedom Riders from the campus.[54] When the Legislative Council denied the request it was made the subject of a referendum and won by a vote of 2086 to 1435,[55] but the ASUCLA Board of Control, composed mainly of nonstudents, overruled the election and refused to make the loans. This action led Platform, a student political party at UCLA, to charge that student government had been taken out of student hands.[56] On March 4, 1962, an *ad hoc* committee of UCLA law students led a rally to protest the Board of Control's action. Several hundred students attended. The issue remained volatile until March 19, when Chancellor Murphy announced that students who required financial assistance could apply for loans through the University loan office. The usual $600 ceiling was raised to enable those who needed it to borrow the $1000 required for bail. Murphy himself reportedly made a contribution to the loan fund after the demonstration.[57]

The example of the Freedom Riders in the southern states inspired sympathy civil-rights demonstrations in California. Picketing of chain stores that had been the targets of sit-ins in the South was common, and students of several University campuses participated. By the spring of 1964, civil-rights activity had more immediate goals—more Negro employment. Students sat-in at restaurants, picketed stores, shopped-in at supermarkets, marched in front of automobile agencies, and sat-in at San Francisco's historic Sheraton-Palace Hotel in efforts to force those establishments to hire more Negroes.

At the Sheraton-Palace Hotel there were picket lines on March 1 and a massive sit-in, involving 1500 or more people, on March 6, 7, and 8. At San Francisco's Cadillac automobile agency, hundreds of civil-rights demonstrators sat-in on the showroom floor on March 14. In these demonstrations about 500 people, including many University students, were arrested.

Assemblyman Don Mulford and State Senator Hugh Burns both demanded that the University assume responsibility for student participation in these civil-rights disturbances. Mulford demanded a review of the records of University students with two or more arrests for penal-code violations to determine if they were suitable members of the student body. He also announced plans to introduce legislation to prevent the "misuse" of a state university or college name and advocated the creation of a joint legislative committee on civil rights and disorders.[58]

President Kerr responded to Mulford's proposals in a Charter Day address on the Davis campus in May. In that address he said that proposals to expel students arrested or convicted for participation in illegal kinds of civil-rights demonstrations were impractical and improper. They were impractical because the University, which "must and will maintain academic and campus discipline" among its 60,000 students, could not possibly maintain surveillance of them "in their home towns, in their home states, their home countries, or whatever parts of the state or world they may visit in their roles as individual citizens." [59] Moreover, what should the University do about arrests for a broad spectrum of other types of offenses, "ranging from felonies to traffic violations to overindulgence in Big Game fervor?" [60] Kerr insisted that "the activities of students acting as private citizens off-campus on non-University matters are outside the sphere of the University," [61] but he also said that "students, individually or collectively, should not and cannot take the name of the University with them as they move into religious or political or other non-University activities; nor should they or can they use University facilities in connection with such affairs." [62] At their May meeting, these statements were unanimously endorsed by the Regents.[63]

For development of the open-forum policy and lifting the ban on Communist speakers, President Kerr and the Regents received the seventh Alexander Meiklejohn award of the American Association of University Professors, for outstanding contributions to the cause of academic freedom.[64] The award was presented in April, 1964. Two months later, Kerr received the second Human Relations Award of the Regional Advisory Board of the Anti-Defamation League of B'nai B'rith for "constructive efforts on behalf of academic freedom, and for placing the University community in the forefront of those forces encouraging free discussion of all subjects." [65] These awards climaxed an almost fourteen-year effort of Kerr and the Regents to overcome the University's loss of prestige in academic-freedom matters in the wake of the loyalty-oath controversy.

People who had been associated with the University for the preceding two decades knew that what President Kerr and the Regents had done was an achievement of considerable substance. Much had been accomplished to give the students more opportunities to invite and hear speakers on diverse and even controversial topics.

Students, however, were aware only of what they found when they arrived. For some of them what they found was not enough to help them play the new, liberated roles they wanted to play in society. Students who transferred to the University of California from eastern colleges often reported that the new privileges worked into the Kerr directives between 1959 and 1964 were already old and taken for granted at the schools they came from. A few may have known that Stanford University and San Francisco State College had already gone farther in liberalizing their rules on student government and use of campus facilities than the University had. (Kerr did not know about this until late in 1964).[66] Because the University was distinguished and enlightened in other respects, students were inclined to regard its failure to conform to the more lenient practices elsewhere as deliberate policy. They could live with it, however, because the new rules left the Hyde Park areas as a safety valve for student expression, and they still had access to off-campus facilities and locations to pursue activities not allowed on the campus. One of these that was particularly well located was a strip of brick-paved property at the edge of the campus on Bancroft Way and the south entrance to the Berkeley campus. Part of that area belonged to the city, which frequently issued permits for recruiting tables and street meetings of a political or religious nature. This area was very narrow, only ten feet wide, but it abutted another strip, twenty-six feet wide and ninety feet long, that belonged to the Regents and was so marked by metal plates sunk in the sidewalk. In 1959, at President Kerr's request, the Regents voted to turn this strip over to the city of Berkeley. Student activities in the old Sather Gate tradition legally could be carried on there if the strip were no longer University property. President Kerr did not learn that the Regents' decision had not been carried out until the Bancroft strip became disputed territory in a rebellion that shook Berkeley campus to its foundations.

Chapter 26

THE BERKELEY REBELLION

IN THE SUMMER of 1964, students from all parts of the United States went to the South to register Negro voters and in other ways play an active role in breaking down barriers to racial equality. Their risks and their achievements were fully covered by television, magazine, and newspaper reporters. In the Bay Area, massive civil-rights demonstrations were in the planning stages. That same summer students were thinking about politics, for it was then that the Democrats nominated Lyndon Johnson at Atlantic City, and, in San Francisco, the Republicans chose conservative Barry Goldwater to be their candidate. The election campaign to follow was expected to be hard-fought and emotional; student involvement was expected to be intense.

On the Berkeley campus, several meetings were held during the summer to discuss certain rules and regulations. Among the participants at various times were Vice-Chancellor Alex Sherriffs, Dean of Students Katherine Towle, Associate Deans Arleigh Williams and Betty Neely, Forrest Tregea, executive director of the ASUC, Captain Frank Woodward of the campus police department, and Richard P. Hafner, public affairs officer. Control of bicycle riding on the campus was one item on the agenda. Another subject was the playing of bongo drums and other noise-making around the fountain in the Sproul Hall Plaza. Incidental to these discussions, someone made the observation that the area outside the posts in the entrance to the campus at Bancroft Way was being misused under terms of University policy.

It was true that during the summer, and particularly during the Republican convention in San Francisco, card tables had been set up in that area to recruit support for candidates, pass out literature, and collect funds for the benefit of the civil-rights movement and other causes. After deliberations on July 22, July 29, and September 4,[1] the Berkeley campus administration decided that ample opportunities existed on other parts of the campus for students to hear speakers, pass out handbills, and put up posters and that the University-owned portion of Bancroft strip should not be treated as exempt from existing regulations governing use of University facilities.

Dean of Students Katherine Towle [2] and Dean of Men Arleigh Williams opposed this decision. For several years political, social-action, and religious organizations had used the strip without University interference. Suddenly to ban such activity there would close an effective and useful safety valve at the beginning of a politically volatile term. Despite these arguments, Alex Sherriffs, vice-chancellor for student affairs, insisted that officers of student organizations be notified that the strip was University property and that, effective September 21, it could no longer be used "for the purpose of soliciting party membership, or supporting or opposing particular candidates for propositions in local, state or national elections." [3] Dean Towle's letters to this effect were dated September 14, the day before registration for the new term. Their contents were reported to the general student body in the *Daily Californian* on September 17.

President Kerr learned of the new orders on September 18, the day after his return to Berkeley from Asia, where he had opened University Abroad centers in Hong Kong and Tokyo. At first he was puzzled as to how the Berkeley campus could ban political activity from an area the Regents had ordered transferred to the city of Berkeley in 1959. To his chagrin, he learned that the property had not in fact been transferred.[4] Later in the day he met with Chancellor Strong, Vice-Chancellor Sherriffs, Dean Towle, and Public Affairs Officer Hafner. Notes on that meeting taken by the Chancellor's administrative assistant, Mrs. Kathlyn C. Malloy, took the form of policy guidelines. The first one says "The President said there is to be no distribution of action literature on the campus anywhere. This means no supporting one candidate or another, no literature on such things as a call for a meeting to organize a picket or stage a demonstration. Speakers can advocate causes and take stands on issues but cannot distribute literature such as bumper strips." [5] A subsequent entry says "The area at Bancroft and Telegraph between the posts and the plaques is University property and there are to be no speakers there—no literature distributed which can be claimed to be propaganda—no table except that the dean of students will permit a number of tables to be manned at all times. A poster may be affixed to the tables. Otherwise no posters." [6] While not directly attributed to Kerr, this entry was accepted as presidental policy, as was a subsequent entry that extended the Hyde Park area on campus to Sproul Hall steps on an experimental basis.[7] Kerr recalls that he was not pleased with the decision to restrict use of the Bancroft strip, but for several reasons decided to let the new orders stand. Control of student affairs had been decentralized to the campus administrators, and his interference might imply lack of confidence in both Chancellor Strong and the principle of local autonomy. Moreover, Kerr had been out of the country for six weeks and doubted that his estimate of the importance of the strip as a safety valve for student political activity was any better than that of the Berkeley administration.[8]

Between September 16, when the student organizations received Dean Towle's letter, and September 21, when the Chancellor's decision on the strip was to be enforced, the student groups affected by the order banded together in what they called the United Front. This composite organization represented a full political spectrum. Several religious organizations also participated. On the evening of September 20, this group voted to "picket, conduct vigils, rallies and touch off civil disobedience" [9] if the administration did not yield its position on the strip. At a meeting with Dean Towle on September 21, United Front representatives agreed to accept a few procedural changes in the University's policy, including the restriction of the number of tables that could be set up in the strip and Dean Towle's offer (in accordance with decisions at the September 18 meeting with President Kerr) to designate the entrance to Sproul Hall as a "Hyde Park area" on an experimental basis. But on the fundamental questions of on-campus freedom of advocacy for political and social action and the privilege to raise money for off-campus causes, Dean Towle was bound by Regental policy and the United Front representatives were bound by commitments voted the night before.[10] Negotiations failed, therefore, and that night seventy-five students held an all-night vigil on the Sproul Hall steps to show their displeasure.[11]

The next day, the ASUC Senate (as the legislative arm of student government had been designated since 1962) voted to ask the Regents to "allow free political and social action" on the strip and discussed the possibility of buying the disputed territory for a student free-speech area.[12]

On the same day, September 22, Chancellor Strong defended the decision on the strip and asserted in a public statement that "a full spectrum of political and social views can be heard on campus. . . ." [13] He also observed that the regulations concerning the strip were consistent with the University's policies on political action enunciated by President Kerr. This was a reference to Kerr's statements at Davis the preceding spring to the effect that students were entitled to freedom of political and social action off-campus as private citizens under the protection and regulation of civil law, but that they could not engage in such activities in the name of the University or use the University's facilities as a place to take political and social action.

The Regents' Committee on Educational Policy met two days later and discussed several possible liberalizations of campus rules and regulations governing student political activity. At the conclusion of the discussions, the committee voted to permit students to distribute materials presenting points of view for or against a proposition, a candidate, or with respect to a social or political issue. Recruitment of individuals for direct social or political action was expressly prohibited, however,[14] and all other existing regulations on the subject were reaffirmed.

On September 28, students deliberately defied University rules. Political groups set up recruiting tables at Sather Gate and held a rally in front of Wheeler Hall without obtaining prior permission. Later they marched *en masse* to the first University Meeting of the year, where Chancellor Strong was announcing the new Regents' policy which, he said, would permit the on-campus distribution of literature, campaign buttons, and bumper strips that advocated "yes" and "no" votes on propositions and candidates.[15] This concession gave some of the United Front's leaders a feeling of success. But instead of accepting the concession and abandoning further protests, they resolved to extend their objectives to include not only restoration of the Bancroft strip as an open political activity area but also to extend whatever freedom was gained there to the entire campus.[16]

A campaign of flagrant rule violation to achieve these goals began on September 29. Recruiting and information tables were set up on the Bancroft strip and in front of Sather Gate, and most of them were unauthorized. Dean Williams and police officers warned students at the illegal tables of their infractions. One of them, Arthur Goldberg, was asked to make an appointment with Williams, presumably to discuss disciplinary procedure.[17] Tables appeared again at noon the next day. Two of those tables, set up by the Student Non-Violent Coordinating Committee (SNCC, a civil-rights group) and the Campus Congress of Racial Equality (CORE), had been denied permits because the dean's office suspected they might be used to raise funds—as indeed they were.[18] Five students manning the two tables were asked to appear in Dean Williams' office for disciplinary hearings at 3 P.M. the same day.[19]

A NEW ISSUE TO BROADEN THE PROTEST

While Dean Williams was citing students at the illegal tables on September 30, Jack Weinberg, a member of CORE and a former mathematics student at the University, mounted a concrete railing outside Sather Gate and shouted at passing students to draw their attention to what was happening. Once a crowd gathered, he spoke at some length, drawing upon a speech he had heard at a meeting of the Independent Socialist Club the night before.[20] Called "Clark Kerr's View of the University as a Factory," the speech had been given by Hal Draper, a member of the library staff at Berkeley, who had been a student activist during the 1930s as a leader of the Young People's Socialist League. Draper's speech attempted to show that the President of the University of California was the nation's leading advocate of the American university as an inescapably mechanistic and inhuman institution captive to powerful outside interests. By drawing upon this speech, Weinberg introduced a new ingredient into the cauldron of student unrest and shifted the aim of student opposition from Chancellor Strong and his various advisers to the much-more-prominent President Kerr. In the rhetoric of student dissent thereafter, dehumanized education, of which Kerr was construed to be the personification, became a popular and prevalent theme. The call to rebellion, with this new issue, attracted more students than before because its object was no longer just political privileges but also freedom from an allegedly oppressive, impersonal system that transcended all immediate issues and made student life, when one thought about it that way, a misery.

THE FIRST SIT-IN

While Weinberg and others spoke to the crowd at Sather Gate, improvised petitions were circulated. Signed by five hundred students, they said: "We the undersigned have jointly manned tables at Sather Gate, realizing that we were in violation of University edicts to the contrary. We realize we may be subject to expulsion." [21]

Several hundred students showed up for the disciplinary hearings scheduled in Dean Williams' office at 3 P.M. They were led by Mario Savio, a wild-haired, intense Junior in philosophy who had only weeks before been in civil-rights work in Mississippi; Arthur Goldberg, a graduate student and former president of Slate; and Sandor Fuchs, then president of Slate. An hour later, Dean Williams asked the five students originally cited and Savio, Fuchs, and Goldberg to come into his office. They refused, with Savio saying to the crowd, "They can't take action against all these people who are here. They're scared. We're staying." [22] Money was collected to buy food and by 5 P.M. women students in the crowd were preparing sandwiches for dinner.

At about midnight Chancellor Strong issued a statement declaring that some students continued to violate campus regulations in efforts to secure privileges of raising funds and planning and organizing off-campus social and political action. Because he believed the limits of University policy had been set by the Regents' Educational Policy Committee on September 24, Strong said the students' demands could not be met and rule violators could not escape disciplinary action. He concluded by announcing that the eight students who had refused to meet with Williams earlier that day were indefinitely suspended.

Strong's announcement hardened resistance to the administration and Savio announced new objectives: "(1) a fight for the dropping of disciplinary action against the suspended students, (2) a continuation of the fight for the demands on the Free Speech areas, including a proposed meeting with Chancellor Strong, and (3) the stipulation that no disciplinary action be taken against any students participating in further demonstrations." [23]

At some point in the evening, leaders of the protest realized that their endeavor was no longer that of a coalition of organizations. It was now an organization of individuals and was rechristened the Free Speech Movement (FSM).[24] After voting to hold a rally on Sproul Hall steps the following noon, the students participating in the sit-in decided to go home. They left Sproul Hall just before 3 A.M. on October 1.

THE POLICE CAR ENTRAPMENT

Protests continued on October 1, and at about 10 A.M. more illegal tables appeared. Boldly sitting at one located at the foot of Sproul Hall steps was Jack Weinberg. When he refused to identify himself or to leave the table, he was arrested by campus police. Because he went limp in the style of civil-rights demonstrators, the arresting officers decided not to try to carry Weinberg into Sproul Hall, where the police department was, but to use a police car instead. Within the few moments it took for the police car to arrive, a sizable crowd had gathered. Once Weinberg was in the car, more than one hundred of his supporters sat or lay down to block all four of its wheels.

The car, with Weinberg still in it, remained under student siege for thirty-two hours. Chancellor Strong refused to negotiate on any of the issues in the FSM-administration dispute until the demonstration was broken up and the police car was freed. The FSM leadership refused to give up the car until there were negotiations. Attempts of ASUC President Charles Powell to mediate the stalemate failed, mainly because only a minority of the protestors were from that part of the student body that felt allegiance to recognized student government and many of them believed that the ASUC was vulnerable to administrative manipulation and could be neither impartial as a mediator nor effective as a spokesman for the FSM cause. At midafternoon on October 1, some of the demonstrators, led by Savio, again went into Sproul Hall for a sit-in. Determined to stay there, they jammed the doors of the building when campus and Berkeley policemen tried to lock them at 6:15 P.M. Later, however, they returned to the plaza so that the demonstration could exhibit a united front.

About 10 P.M. President Kerr, who had been in San Francisco most of the day attending a meeting of the American Council of Education, received a phone call from Vice-Chancellor Sherriffs, who outlined the situation on the campus and asked for suggestions on what might be done. On the basis of conversations with Earl C. Bolton, Vice-President–University Relations, earlier in the day, Kerr advised that nothing be done until about four o'clock the next morning, at which time there would be relatively few demonstrators, probably less than a hundred on the campus, and a relatively small number of policemen could recapture the car and make any arrests that might be necessary.[25]

This proposal was given serious consideration by Berkeley administrators but was rejected unanimously by law-enforcement agencies who were contacted. Their explanation was that 4 A.M. was a busy time for their departments and they could not afford to spare the men, and a nighttime operation of the type contemplated was hazardous. At about 11:15 P.M., students who opposed the FSM demonstration began drifting into the campus in small groups. They stood at the outskirts of the crowd and heckled speakers who were still using the roof of the police car as a dais.[26] A potentially ugly conflict between students was avoided when Father James Fisher of Newman Hall (Catholic student center) mounted the police car and issued a plea for peace,[27] and members of the dean's office staff moved through the crowd quietly to persuade antidemonstrators to go home.[28]

The police car was still trapped the following afternoon, when Chancellor Strong called Kerr and asked him to relay a request to Governor Brown that the National Guard be placed on twenty-five-minute alert. Kerr talked to Governor Brown by telephone twice late in the evening of October 1. In the first conversation, the Governor refused to send the National Guard because that tactic was too thoroughly identified with efforts to break up civil-rights demonstrations in places like Alabama and Mississippi.[29] The Governor's reservations were justified. Many students involved in the FSM were civil-rights activists and had asserted from the beginning that the University's ban on political and social action on the Bancroft strip was actually an attempt to prevent students from participating in sit-ins and pickets planned by the Bay Area civil-rights groups.[30] Use of the National Guard would have reinforced their arguments. On a second call, Governor Brown promised to make California State Highway Patrolmen available if their help was absolutely necessary and all efforts to settle the dispute without force failed. Kerr was pessimistic in his reply. The FSM and the Berkeley administration were deadlocked and no peaceful negotiations seemed likely.[31]

Later in the afternoon, Kerr was contacted by his office at a San Francisco television studio where he was participating in an interview program and asked if he would meet with a group of faculty members who believed they had a solution to the situation at Berkeley. This group had met with the Chancellor and Vice-Chancellor Lincoln Constance earlier in the afternoon. The FSM leaders also wanted to meet with the President. Kerr agreed to a meeting with the students provided that the editor of the *Daily Californian,* the president of the ASUC, and Chancellor Strong were also present.[32]

The President got back to Berkeley just as five hundred policemen and California State Highway Patrolmen were gathering at the north and south entrances to Sproul Hall and forming ranks in a roadway just behind the building.

The students and the faculty group arrived at Kerr's office at about the same time. When they sat down, the student to Kerr's left was president of the Young Republicans for Goldwater. Mario Savio, Sandor Fuchs, and Jackie Goldberg, sister of the suspended Arthur Goldberg, were there at the beginning and representatives of several student religious organizations came in later. Savio presented a student proposal that Kerr found unacceptable. Then the faculty group's proposal was presented and discussed.[33]

Chancellor Strong was restless and was called away to the phone several times to persuade police authorities to refrain from action until the negotiations were completed. He was not in favor of the discussions, incidentally, because they were contrary to his personal position—that there be no negotiations until the demonstration ended.

In the meeting room, some of the students worried that there would be violent confrontation between students and the police before an agreement was reached. Their fears drove them to seek an honorable accord early. Finally, about 7 P.M., agreement was reached on these points:

1. The student demonstrators shall desist from all forms of their illegal protest against University regulations.
2. The committee representing students (including leaders of the demonstration), faculty, and administration will immediately be set up to conduct discussions and hearing into all aspects of political behavior on campus and its control and to make recommendations to the administration.
3. The arrested man will be booked, released on his own recognizance, and the University (complainant) will not press charges.
4. The duration of the suspension of the suspended students will be submitted within one week to the Student Conduct Committee of the Academic Senate.
5. Activity may be continued by student organizations in accordance with existing University regulations.
6. The President of the University has already declared his willingness to support deeding certain University property at the end of Telegraph Avenue to the City of Berkeley or to the ASUC.[34]

About fifteen minutes later, Savio climbed to the top of the besieged police car and, with Kerr, Strong, and members of the faculty looking on from Sproul Hall steps, read the six points of agreement. Then he said, "Let us agree by acclamation to accept this document. I ask you to rise quietly and with dignity, and go home." It was about 7:40 P.M.[35]

At a press conference ten minutes later, President Kerr announced that law and order had been restored at Berkeley "without the use of force."

Regulations of the University remained unchanged. The arrested student had been booked. The eight suspended students were still suspended, but their cases were to be reviewed by a faculty committee.[36] The next day, Edward W. Carter, chairman of the Board of Regents, issued a statement commending Kerr and his administrative staff for the settlement and remarking that "it is regrettable that a relatively small number of students, together with certain off-campus agitators, should have precipitated so unfortunate an incident." [37]

THE UNTENABLE TREATY

The agreement that ended the police-car entrapment had the weaknesses of any document prepared under pressure. Some of its sections were ambiguous. Others were based on erroneous assumptions. There was not, for instance, any "Student Conduct Committee of the Academic Senate." The only existing committee on student conduct was an administrative one, appointed by the chancellor and advisory to him. No one caught this embarrassing error until Chancellor Strong assigned the eight suspensions to his administrative committee on October 5. On the same day, he appointed four faculty members, four administrators, and two students to the Study Committee on Campus Political Activity created by the agreement. Two student positions were left open, to be filled by persons chosen by FSM.[38]

Chancellor Strong's swift action in abiding by the terms of the agreement of October 2 was soon denounced by the FSM leaders. They claimed that they had been consulted on none of the appointments to the study committee and that referral of the suspension to an administrative, instead of a faculty, committee was a betrayal since the administrators and the suspended students were, in a sense, adversaries.[39] The complaints of the FSM were accommodated on October 15 after further negotiations that enlarged the study committee to add two more students, two faculty members to be selected by the Academic Senate, and two administrators to be selected by the President. The FSM steering committee would appoint students to fill not only the two new places on the committee but also the two left open for them. In addition to this change, President Kerr and Chancellor Strong asked the Academic Senate to appoint a new *ad hoc* committee to hear the cases of the eight suspended students.[40] The Academic Senate voted to appoint that committee with Ira M. Heyman, professor of law, as chairman.

The reconstituted Study Committee on Campus Political Activity, under its chairman, Robley Williams, professor of molecular biology, made considerable progress until it attempted to recommend policies governing on-campus advocacy of off-campus action. Who was to judge whether the actions advocated were legal or not? Would no decision be made until after the advocated action took place? If the advocated action resulted in arrest, trial, and punishment by civil authority, would the University also impose punishment? The students adopted the position that "in the area of first amendment rights and civil liberties, the University may impose no disciplinary action against members of the University community and organizations. In this area, members of the University community and organizations are subject only to the civil authorities." [41] The faculty and administrative members favored different answers. Irritated and impatient with the impasse, the FSM Steering Committee called for a protest rally and deliberate violation of University regulations for November 9.[42] The names of seventy-five students found allegedly breaking University rules that day were collected by representatives of the dean's office, and President Kerr and Chancellor Strong announced that because the FSM had "abrogated the agreement of October 2," the Study Committee on Campus Political Activity would be immediately dissolved.[43] They announced that "we shall now seek advice on rules governing political action on campus from students through the ASUC and from the faculty through the Academic Senate." [44]

This return to pre-FSM channels of campus communication was welcomed by many students, faculty members, and alumni, who, from the first, had regarded efforts to deal directly with the student rebels a mistake. These older channels of communication had several weaknesses, however: The machinery of student government was too slow-moving for the pace of the rebellion. ASUC leaders lacked the crude toughness of Mario Savio and other FSM standard-bearers. The ASUC, deliberately insulated from social and political activism for generations, lacked experience with the whole point of the rebellion. The ASUC did not command the allegiance of the rebels and the rebels' sympathizers among undergraduates. The ASUC also did not command the support of any of the graduate students (about 37 per cent of the student body in 1964), who had been voted out of the ASUC in a disputed election in 1959.

The FSM happened to emerge at a time when graduate assistants in some departments had nonpolitical grievances. They complained that they had too many students or too much responsibility without adequate guidance. They were concerned, too, about the effects of this situation on undergraduate education. These resentments augmented political motivations that drew graduate students to the rebels' cause. Although all graduate students did not participate in the rebellion, those who did played a key role. Steve

Weissman, chairman of the Graduate Coordinating Committee, was regarded as FSM's most articulate spokesman. After the failure of the Study
Committee on Campus Political Activity, the Graduate Coordinating Committee endorsed the massive violation of campus regulations that occurred on
November 9 and 10, and almost 150 graduate students manned tables and
collected funds without permits. Weissman also warned that teaching assistants and faculty members would strike if any students were arrested.[45]

While a strike of undergraduate students could produce embarrassing
headlines and considerable internal trauma, it could not debilitate the University. Loss of the teaching research assistants was another matter. They
were the ones who helped make it possible for professors to find time for
research and other functions of their positions. They were also essential to
the success of large lecture courses and instruction involving drill and recitation.

Weissman's assurances that the faculty would also strike were presump-
tuous, although many faculty members were known to sympathize with the
goals of the FSM. As with the graduate students, there were also dissatisfac-
tions within the faculty that were not immediately related to free speech and
advocacy issues. There was faculty resentment of several Universitywide
policies. One of these was that the UCLA library was to be expanded to the
point where it could render services in the southern part of the state that
were equal to those available from the library at Berkeley. During this expansion, acquisition of books at Berkeley would be somewhat curtailed.
Another was the refusal of the Universitywide administration to permit
Berkeley to raise its admissions requirements higher than those of other
campuses. This measure was attractive to many faculty members because it
would help preserve the quality of education at Berkeley while holding the
line on student enrollment. President Kerr and the Regents opposed the
idea because it would create a caste system of student bodies within the University and make it hard for other campuses to get their fair share of top
candidates for admission. The quarter system, scheduled to go into effect in
1966, was opposed by most faculty members although, as an alternative to
two other plans of year-round operation, it had received a plurality of the
votes of the Berkeley division of the Academic Senate,[46] and this, it was contended, was a grant of faculty approval. The Berkeley campus had also lost
power as a result of Academic Senate revision that removed its veto on Universitywide faculty decisions. Finally, an academic-freedom issue had recently arisen when Chancellor Strong notified Eli Katz, an acting assistant
professor of German, who refused to answer questions concerning alleged
Communist affiliations, that he would not be rehired for the coming term.

Chancellor Strong took the position that he had an administrative duty to decide, in this case, whether Katz was "employable" under the Regents' policies before his academic qualifications could be judged by the Academic Senate's budget committee. All of these grievances influenced those faculty members who were inclined to view the FSM dispute as a bid for student power that had to be granted, if at all, by the administration—the common enemy. From this group of dissatisfied faculty members, and from an overlapping number who were primarily motivated by political and philosophical liberality, sympathy for students, and concern for the success of the civil-rights movements, emerged the "Committee of Two Hundred." This *ad hoc* committee, without Academic Senate recognition and sympathetic to the student rebels, met frequently to seek solutions to the dispute that would answer legitimate student demands.

On November 12, the special Academic Senate committee that heard the cases of the suspended students issued its report.[47] Emphasizing that it was concerned only with events taking place through September 30 (before the police car entrapment), the committee recommended that the six students charged only with operating tables without a permit, raising money for unauthorized purposes, and failing to report to Dean Williams when requested to do so be reinstated as of the date of their suspensions and that their penalty be changed from suspension to "censure." The committee recommended that the suspensions of Goldberg and Savio be set for a period of only six weeks beginning September 30, 1964 (six weeks previously). It explained this leniency by pointing out that all of the people observed in violation of the rules with which the suspended students were charged were not cited, that the original penalties were more severe than they would have been for similar offenses under normal conditions, and that some of the regulations that were violated were vague and inapplicable to activities upon which charges were based. President Kerr and Chancellor Strong criticized the committee for making its report to the Academic Senate instead of to the chancellor, but issued no further comment on the penalties themselves until the Regents' meeting at Berkeley on November 20.

From November 9 to November 20, students continued to set up unauthorized tables on the campus, recruited partisans for off-campus causes, and collected money in defiance of regulations. On November 20, the day of the Regents' meeting, more than three thousand students attended a Sproul Hall steps rally. One of the attractions was Joan Baez, the popular folk singer who was already well identified with civil-rights and pacifist causes. From this rally, many of the students marched north through Sather Gate to Cross-Campus Road and then turned west to the lawn across Oxford Street from University Hall where the Regents were to meet. Five FSM members were permitted to attend the meeting.

The Regents, on recommendation of President Kerr and Chancellor Strong, strengthened the penalties recommended by the *ad hoc* faculty committee. All of the cited students were suspended from September 30 until November 20, 1964—the date of the Regents' meeting. In addition, Goldberg and Savio were placed on probation for the remainder of the semester. The Regents also directed that new disciplinary procedures be instituted for violations that took place after September 30, and that University rules and regulations be clarified and incorporate explicit penalties for specific violations.[48]

After disposing of the disciplinary cases, the Regents formulated some general policies. One restated an existing regulation that "all students and student organizations . . . obey the laws of the State and community. . . ." [49] The other was "that certain campus facilities, carefully selected and properly regulated, may be used by students and staff for planning, implementing or raising funds or recruiting participants for lawful off-campus action, not for unlawful off-campus action." [50] With that action, the Regents established official policy on the question that had deadlocked the Study Committee on Campus Political Activity earlier in the month.

The FSM was not pleased with the Regents' action but was divided in its response. Some, led by Mario Savio, favored immediate disruptive activity and staged a brief sit-in in Sproul Hall the following Monday afternoon. Others favored a response that would test the legality of basic FSM demands. The moderate course prevailed because many students who had supported the FSM accepted the finality of the Regents' action and were content that the University's regulations had, in fact, been considerably liberalized since September 14. The regulations were even more explicitly liberalized the next day when Chancellor Strong announced that authorized student organizations would be permitted to accept donations, recruit members, and distribute political and social-action material from tables at several announced campus locations, as long as such activity was confined to students, staff, and faculty members.[51] Many people believed the worst of the rebellion was over.

During the Thanksgiving holidays, letters prepared by the General Counsel's office and signed by Chancellor Strong arrived at the homes of several FSM leaders, including Mario Savio and Art Goldberg. The letters formally charged them with offenses committed during the police car entrapment. These charges included encouragement of the demonstrators, interference with officers closing the doors to Sproul Hall (which involved an allegation that Mario Savio bit one of the officers in the leg), and intimidation of police officers. The students were ordered to appear before the Faculty Committee on Student Conduct. These letters rekindled FSM fires. Although the Regents' resolution of November 20 explicitly demanded further disciplinary action against rules violators, the opinion was widely held among students that an amnesty for all violations prior to that action prevailed. This impression was reinforced by the fact that a considerable length of time had elapsed since the police car incident and no charges had yet been made. As Bettina Aptheker, daughter of the editor of the Communist theoretical journal *Political Affairs* and a member of the FSM steering committee, recalled later, "I knew that was it. That's what we were waiting for. For the final atrocity. . . ." [52] The FSM steering committee sent a letter to President Kerr demanding that the charges be dropped, but the President did not respond. On November 30, the Graduate Coordinating Council, in keeping with its promise of November 9, announced a meeting to plan a strike of teaching assistants.[53] The same day, UCLA students sympathetic with the FSM held a rally.

On December 1 the FSM warned that if the administration did not agree to drop action against the FSM leaders, change rules so that only the courts could regulate the content of political speech, and agree to invoke no further discipline against students or student organizations for political actions, the rebels would engage in "direct action." [54] A sit-in was scheduled for December 2.

YOU'VE GOT TO MAKE IT STOP

The rally on Sproul Hall steps on December 2 was one of the largest in the University's history. Folk singer Joan Baez was there again, as was Mario Savio. The FSM ultimatum was not met, and Savio prepared his followers for the ordeal ahead of them:

> There is a time when the operation of the machine becomes so odious, makes you so sick at heart, that you can't take part; you can't tacitly take part, and you've got to put your bodies upon the gears and upon the wheels, upon the levers, upon all the apparatus and you've got to make it stop. And you've got to indicate to the people who run it, to the people who own it, that unless you're free, the machines will be prevented from working at all.[55]

Then, as Joan Baez sang the civil-rights anthem "We Shall Overcome," one thousand people walked into Sproul Hall to fill its corridors on all four floors. During the afternoon, the demonstrators sang folk songs, studied, played cards, or just talked. At 6:45 P.M. University Police Lieutenant Merrill Chandler advised the students that the building would close at 7 P.M. Thereafter, anyone who wanted to leave was allowed to do so, but no one was admitted. Few left. Food was hauled in with ropes hanging from a second-floor balcony. Still later, movies were shown on the walls of the building, and "classes" in subjects of the students' own choosing were conducted by teaching assistants. There was a Hanukkah service on one floor and dancing on another. By 1 A.M., the lights were turned off and the demonstrators tried to sleep.

A STRATEGY MEETING AT THE AIRPORT

While students were taking over Sproul Hall, a small group of Regents that included Edward Carter, chairman of the Board, Donald McLaughlin, chairman of the Committee on Educational Policy, and Theodore Meyer, chairman of the Finance Committee, met at the San Francisco Airport with President Kerr and Vice-President Bolton. Chancellor Strong remained behind to execute a tentative plan to declare the sit-in illegal and have the building cleared. At the airport, Kerr argued that immediate forced eviction of the students would be a mistake. He said that the students would eventually realize that the major goals of their protest had been won on November 20 when the Regents not only extended freedom of advocacy to the Bancroft strip, but to other parts of the campus as well. He also advised that removing students from the top floors of Sproul Hall would be difficult and almost impossible without force and later charges of police violence and brutality.[56] The Regents agreed that further effort should be made to settle the matter peacefully.

When President Kerr reached his home in El Cerrito later that night, he contacted Governor Brown and reported on the discussion he had just had with the Regents. Kerr suggested that he and the Governor go to Sproul Hall together in the middle of the following morning and that they assess the situation and discuss the problem with the students. Although he was displeased to learn that there was another sit-in in Sproul Hall, Brown agreed with Kerr's proposal, only to change his mind later in the evening. He called Kerr back and said after talking to law-enforcement officers he had decided to have the students evicted (but not necessarily arrested) and wanted the University's cooperation.[57]

PLEASE GO

At about 3 A.M. on December 3, Chancellor Strong moved from floor to floor in Sproul Hall. Using a bullhorn, he told the students sitting and lying in the halls that they were engaged in an illegal assemblage and asked them to "please go."

When he had completed his announcement, more than six hundred officers, including California Highway Patrolmen, began to arrest the demonstrators who failed to leave. Some students went limp when arrested and had to be carried or dragged downstairs for booking and loading into vans and buses headed for the Santa Rita Rehabilitation Center and the Berkeley and Oakland city jails. It took more than twelve hours to clear the building.

Arrests were still being made when students and faculty members arrived on campus for classes that morning. Large crowds surrounded the building to watch and listen to the shouts and cries that came sporadically from within. In tears of anguish, some of the FSM supporters were moving around the plaza shouting, "They're beating them!" (There were no beatings, but some of the arrests required force.)

When the buildings on campus opened for the day, most of them were being picketed at all entrances. Faculty members, teaching assistants, and students were asked to stay away to protest the arrests. The strike had a noticeable but not incapacitating effect.

In a special meeting at 1 P.M. on December 3, about eight hundred faculty members passed a resolution calling for unity and an end to the "series of provocation and reprisal that has resulted in disaster." The same resolution asked:

> that the new liberalized rules for the campus be immediately implemented,
> that all disciplinary proceedings against students for acts committed prior to December 3 be dropped,
> that a faculty committee be created to hear student appeals in cases involving discipline for violations relating to political action, and
> that the Regents retract their decision to prosecute students for participating in such action.[58]

A much-publicized statement read at the faculty meeting carried the unanimous endorsement of the executive committee of the Berkeley chapter of the American Association of University Professors. It asserted that the crisis could not be resolved without amnesty for past offenses and a new chief campus officer at Berkeley "who will have the confidence of the University community." [59]

A wire signed by 361 faculty members was sent to Governor Brown. It protested the use of highway patrolmen on the campus and requested release of the arrested students.[60]

The strike continued on the next day (a Friday), and strike leaders planned further picketing and class boycotts for the following Monday.

On Saturday, December 5, the council of the California Alumni Association voted to "support firm disciplinary action including expulsion or dismissal where warranted," and urged students, faculty, and citizens "who have an ingrained respect for law and order" to defend the University administration's "maintenance of traditional democratic principles and processes." [61]

That evening, the ASUC Senate held an emergency meeting and passed a resolution urging faculty members and teaching assistants to resume instruction, asking that the new rules be immediately enforced, asking the courts to recognize extenuating circumstances in considering the cases of the arrested students, assuming responsibility for starting legal proceedings to resolve the question of jurisdiction of advocacy of illegal off-campus political action, and urging amnesty for students subject to pending disciplinary action.

That same night, Chancellor Strong was admitted to the University of California Hospital in San Francisco with what was later diagnosed as a gall bladder attack. Staff members there estimated he would be confined for about a week.

THE GREEK THEATRE INCIDENT

Chairmen of the academic departments at Berkeley, under the leadership of Robert A. Scalapino of the political science department, worked out a five-point proposal for ending the dispute. As discussed with Governor Brown, President Kerr, and several Regents on Sunday, December 6, the proposals were:

1. The University Community shall be governed by orderly and lawful procedures in the settlement of issues; and the full and free pursuit of educational activities on this campus shall be maintained.
2. The University Community shall abide by the new and liberalized political action rules [as announced by the Regents on November 20]

and await the report of the Senate Committee on Academic Freedom.

3. The Departmental Chairmen believe that the acts of civil disobedience on December 2 and 3 were unwarranted and that they obstruct rational and fair consideration of the grievances brought forward by the students.

4. The cases of all students arrested in connection with the sit-ins in Sproul Hall on December 2 and 3 are now before the Courts. The University will accept the Court's judgment in these cases as the full discipline for those offenses.

   In the light of cases now and prospectively before the Courts, the University will not prosecute charges against any students for actions prior to December 2 and 3; but the University will invoke disciplinary actions for any violations henceforth.

5. All classes shall be conducted as scheduled.[62]

With the blessings of the Regents, Kerr agreed to accept the proposals publicly at an extraordinary University meeting in the Greek Theatre on Monday, December 7. To keep the atmosphere of that meeting free of all semblance of authority or intimidation, the chairman decided that chores normally performed by campus policemen at such gatherings should be performed, instead, by student athletes. No uniformed policemen were to be nearer than one hundred yards of the theatre stage.[63]

On Sunday evening, December 6, the Committee of Two Hundred met in the Life Sciences Building to discuss proposals for ending campus strife. Fairly late in the evening, one of the department chairmen came to the meeting and outlined the points that President Kerr agreed to accept at the convocation the next day. Many members of the Committee of Two Hundred felt that the department chairmen's solution was inadequate. Its only concession was the one of amnesty, and the general tone of the five points was reproachful. Convinced that this approach would not settle the dispute, the committee authorized a steering committee under the chairmanship of Howard K. Schachman, professor of biochemistry and virology, to continue to work on an alternative set of proposals. The steering committee completed its work that same night, drawing ideas from the resolutions enacted at the general faculty meeting of December 3.

At the Greek Theatre the next morning, President Kerr called the proposals of the department chairmen "our maximum effort to attain peace and decency";[64] he declared them in force immediately and promised to ask the Regents to go "one additional mile" toward a liberalized code to govern political activity in the University.[65] The reaction to President Kerr's address was mixed. His audience contained many people who welcomed his leadership and gave him an ovation when he was introduced. Others in the audience, particularly those active in the FSM, were skeptical, and fearful that the President's proposals might carry the day and undercut their efforts to obtain more drastic concessions. Some observers believed that those fears were justified when Clark Kerr received another ovation at the end of his remarks. But that judgment was premature. Mario Savio had been making his way to the stage as the President concluded. During the final ovation, he started walking toward the microphone, only to be grabbed by several uniformed policemen who suddenly appeared, contrary to all plans,[66] through the stage entrances. As a shocked audience watched, the rebel leader was dragged off stage. Everything that Kerr had hoped to gain by the meeting was lost in those few seconds. After several confused minutes, Savio was finally permitted to speak [67] and went to the rostrum to announce a rally on Sproul Hall steps. "Please leave here," he said. "Clear this disastrous scene, and get down to discussing the issues." [68]

THE DECEMBER 8 RESOLUTIONS

Within the hour after the Greek Theatre meeting on December 7, FSM followers and thousands of student and faculty observers gathered in Sproul Plaza. There the FSM rejected by acclamation the department chairmen's proposals and endorsed a draft of a resolution that had been prepared on the night of December 6 by the Steering Committee of Two Hundred. Knowing that the resolution would be offered at a meeting of the Academic Senate the next day, the FSM leadership decided to suspend the strike to "give them [the faculty] . . . one day of real peace and quiet." [69] If the resolution was rejected, or if there was further grievance to the students between midnight, December 7, and the conclusion of the Academic Senate meeting the next day, the strike would resume.

On the afternoon of December 7, President Kerr accepted an invitation to meet with several faculty members in Barrows Hall. The meetings began in the office of Professor Scalapino and subsequently moved to a nearby seminar room. Kerr was accompanied by Vice-President Earl Bolton and, later, by representatives of the general counsel's office. During these meetings the proposals of the Committee of Two Hundred were discussed. The President commented upon the wording of some of them and indicated that several changes would be necessary to satisfy him or the Regents. When the proposals were, in fact, amended later in the day, several faculty members who had attended the afternoon discussions believed that the President's reservations had been satisfied and word soon spread that the resolutions had his endorsement. The resolutions gained still more appeal when faculty members learned that they had been revised and would be presented under the sponsorship of the Academic Freedom Committee of the Academic Senate.

On December 8, President Kerr denied the rumors that he had endorsed the resolutions that would be voted upon that afternoon, and warned that his name should not be used in their behalf. In a long series of telephone conversations with Professor Scalapino, he also refused to agree to support any further liberalization of the policy he had accepted publicly in the Greek Theatre the day before. By this time, however, his support for alternative proposals was largely academic. Faculty sentiment, including that of many of the department chairmen who had stood behind the proposals presented in the Greek Theatre the day before, had decided to support the resolutions that originated with the Committee of Two Hundred.

Several thousand students surrounded Wheeler auditorium on the afternoon of December 8, leaving only narrow corridors through the crowd for the convenience of professors entering the building. Over a loudspeaker system installed for their benefit, the students standing outside could hear the proceedings. These included introduction of amendments by faculty conservatives who believed that the Academic Freedom Committee's resolutions went too far. All of these amendments were defeated. Then, by a vote of 824 to 115, the senate finally passed this resolution:

> In order to end the present crisis, to establish the confidence and trust essential to the restoration of normal University life, and to create a campus environment that encourages students to exercise free and responsible citizenship in the University and in the community at large, the Committee on Academic Freedom of the Berkeley Division of the Academic Senate moves the following propositions:
>
> 1. That there shall be no University disciplinary measures against members or organizations of the University community for activities prior to December 8 connected with the current controversy over political speech and activity.
> 2. That the time, place, and manner of conducting political activity on the campus shall be subject to reasonable regulations to prevent interference with the normal functions of the University; that the regulations now in effect for this purpose shall remain in effect provisionally pending a future report of the Committee on Academic Freedom concerning the minimal regulations necessary.
> 3. That the content of speech or advocacy should not be restricted

by the University. Off-campus political activities shall not be subject to University regulation. On-campus advocacy or organization of such activities shall be subject only to such limitations as may be imposed under Section 2.

4. That future disciplinary measures in the area of political activity shall be determined by a committee appointed by and responsible to the Academic Senate.

5. That the Division pledge unremitting effort to secure the adoption of the foregoing policies and call on all members of the University community to join with the faculty in its efforts to restore the University to its normal functions.[70]

In a companion resolution, the senate created an emergency Executive Committee consisting of six elected members and the chairman of the Berkeley Division, "to represent the Division in dealing with problems arising out of the present academic year."

As they left Wheeler Hall, the members of the senate were cheered and applauded by the waiting crowds of students.

The FSM victory was evident in more than the faculty action. Something profound had happened to students at Berkeley, as was evidenced by another development on December 8. All seven Slate candidates who ran for office were victors in an ASUC election that attracted only 1800 voters. They promised "to immediately implement its [Slate's] program upon taking office, including full freedom of speech on campus, a co-op ASUC store, low cost student apartments, and the readmission of graduate students [to the ASUC]." [71] Charles Powell, ASUC President, re-evaluated the role that the ASUC and moderate students had played during the controversy: "Overall, we've missed the boat. We have in many ways been inadequate in dealing with the free speech problem." [72]

THE REGENTS REACT

Neither the administration nor the Regents replied directly to the December 8 resolutions. As chairman of the Board, Regent Carter simply issued a statement that reminded the general public that the Regents, not the faculty, held the final authority for University governance. His statement said:

The Constitution of the State of California clearly charges the Regents with full and ultimate authority for conducting the affairs of the University of California. This they exercise principally through their appointed administrative officers and by delegation of certain specific but revocable powers to properly constituted academic bodies.

It now appears that on the Berkeley campus these traditional methods have proved inadequate to deal effectively with the extraordinary problems created there by regrettable recent incidents. Hence, the Regents will consider this whole matter directly at their next meeting now scheduled to be held on December 18 in Los Angeles.[73]

President Kerr said that so many basic changes in University policy were involved in the resolutions that he could not comment until after the December Regents' meeting.

Chancellor Strong was released from the hospital in time to attend the December Regents' meeting at Los Angeles. There, after a dinner for Regents and Chancellors, December 16, he presented a report on the Berkeley campus in which he complained of "an undermining of the respect for those campus officers normally responsible for carrying out the policies of the University. Too often there has been the announcement that 'henceforth law and order will prevail,' followed by vacillation, concessions, compromises, and retreats." [74] He criticized the pact that President Kerr had signed with the students to end the police car entrapment on October 2 and the declaration of amnesty made by the President at the December 7 convocation. He concluded his report with six recommendations. These were that disciplinary actions against students with violations subsequent to September 30 proceed; that the authority of the campus (chancellor) be stabilized; that a statement of facts and principles be prepared to correct misrepresentations and misconceptions concerning the dispute; that the University remain steady against threats, pressures, and defiance employed to seek changes of policies and rules; that existing channels of administration be adhered to; and that the campus prepare itself to take prompt action to curb and control continued "agitations" and machinations from the FSM and its sympathizers. . . ." [75]

In making this report, Chancellor Strong had abundant support from the California Alumni Association and thousands of private citizens who had written to commend him for his firm stand against the FSM. He also enjoyed the support of several Regents, including William Forbes, former president of the UCLA Alumni Association; Mrs. Catherine C. Hearst, San Francisco civic leader and granddaughter-in-law of Phoebe Apperson Hearst; and John Canaday, another former president of the UCLA Alumni Association and a Los Angeles aircraft company vice-president. Other Regents, however, believed that Strong's statement, which could be interpreted as a challenge to the authority of President Kerr, was injudicious, possibly born of his fatigue and frustration after nearly three months of confrontation with the FSM and its apologists, and of his resentment of public criticism that the

Berkeley administration had not acted swiftly or severely enough against rule violators.

On December 18, after conferences with the emergency Executive Committee of the Berkeley Division of the Academic Senate and after hearing a report from the Academic Council, which represented the faculties of all the campuses, the Regents acted formally. They expressed gratitude to the Berkeley faculty for its proposals, stated their respect for the convictions "held by a large number of students concerning civil rights and individual liberties," and reaffirmed "devotion" to the first and fourteenth amendments to the Constitution, drawing attention to the recent liberalization of rules governing expression of opinion on the campus. They also adopted a four-point resolution that had been worked out the night before by President Kerr and several Regents, including Chairman Carter. It read:

1. The Regents direct the administration to preserve law and order on the campuses of the University of California, and to take the necessary steps to insure orderly pursuit of its educational functions.
2. The Regents reconfirm that ultimate authority for student discipline within the University is constitutionally vested in the Regents, and is a matter not subject to negotiation. Implementation of disciplinary policies will continue to be delegated, as provided in the by-laws and standing orders of the Regents, to the President and Chancellors, who will seek advice of the appropriate faculty committees in individual cases.
3. The Regents will undertake a comprehensive review of University policies with the intent of providing maximum freedom on campus consistent with individual and group responsibility. A committee of Regents will be appointed to consult with students, faculty and other interested persons and to make recommendations to the board.
4. Pending results of this study, existing rules will be enforced. The policies of the Regents do not contemplate that advocacy or content of speech shall be restricted beyond the purview of the First and Fourteenth Amendments to the Constitution.[76]

In an executive session immediately following the meeting, a motion was passed to appoint a committee to "investigate the basic causes of recent disturbances on the Berkeley campus and to recommend to the Regents what actions . . . may be indicated." [77] A revision of this motion the following month extended the scope of the committee's research to the entire University.

The emergency Executive Committee of the faculty released a statement on December 18 advising that although the Regents had not adopted the December 8 resolutions as University policy, "the base is being established for full political freedom within academic order," and called on all members of the University community to join in strengthening it.[78] FSM leaders were unhappy with the outcome of the meeting, however, and threatened renewed disturbances if the University administration committed any further "atrocity" such as suspending students involved in the sit-ins of December 2 and 3.

THE INTERIM LEADERSHIP OF MARTIN MEYERSON

After the December Regents' meeting, attempts were made by the Board to lighten the administrative burdens of Chancellor Strong. He was not only under attack from student demonstrators, but for some time had also been criticized by members of the faculty as being responsible for Berkeley's difficulty in retaining primacy among the University's campuses and for his position on the Katz case. (In November, 1964, the Berkeley Division of the Academic Senate condemned Strong's action in the case by a vote of 267 to 79). In the closing weeks of 1964, it was also clear that in his unyielding approach to the student rebellion, Strong was far out of step with the majority sentiment of the faculty.

To relieve the chancellor of some of these pressures, the Regents decided, just before Christmas, to appoint a vice-chancellor, who, in addition to other duties as the chancellor's surrogate, would have responsibilities for academic planning and in the area of student political activity. To provide added support, several deans at Berkeley were appointed to provide the chancellor's office a sounding board for policy decisions and to deliberate and prepare position papers on issues confronting the campus. The man selected for the position was Martin Meyerson, formerly director of the Joint Center for Urban Studies of MIT and Harvard, and former Williams Professor of City Planning and Urban Research at Harvard. He had come to Berkeley a year before to assume the deanship of Berkeley's new College of Environmental Design. He was articulate and well-respected by those members of the faculty who had the chance to know him during his first year on the campus.

Before Meyerson could assume the position of vice-chancellor, an incident occurred which altered his status significantly. During the last week of December, 1964, the Academic Freedom Committee of the Academic Senate issued a report containing recommendations for the regulation of student political activity. Similar recommendations had been under study by other faculty and administrative committees. On December 30, the various proposals were presented at a meeting at the University House attended by members of the Regents' committee appointed twelve days earlier to review University policies "with the intent of providing maximum freedom on campus consistent with individual and group responsibility." [79] The chairman was Theodore R. Meyer. Others present at the meeting were Meyerson, the chairman of the Academic Freedom Committee, a representative of the Chancellor's Student Affairs Committee, and the chairman of the Emergency Committee of the Academic Senate. It was Strong's understanding that the faculty representatives at the meeting were in substantial agreement with the Academic Freedom Committee proposals. Members of the Meyer committee objected, in Strong's opinion, on only one major provision. The next morning, as directed at the meeting, he began to prepare a statement for the student newspaper that would serve as an announcement to students when they returned to classes after the Christmas holidays. It said: "Beginning Monday, January 4, the new campus regulations proposed by the Academic Senate's Committee on Academic Freedom, will be in effect provisionally. These regulations will be reviewed by the Academic Senate at its meeting Tuesday, January 5. Student meetings will be permitted temporarily on the steps of Sproul Hall, pending completion of a new open discussion area nearby, recommended by the committee's report." [80]

When he read the Chancellor's statement on the evening of December 31, President Kerr was surprised and angry. He had attended meetings with the Regents earlier in the day at which it was made clear that members of the Meyer Committee objected to the Academic Freedom Committee's recommendation on several points and Chancellor Strong had been advised of these discussions by telephone. In the light of those meetings, the Chancellor's announcement seemed confused and to give inadequate explanation of the Regents' position. The President insisted upon a correction. The new statement appeared in the *Gazette* on January 1 and read:

> The recommendations of the Senate Committee on Academic Freedom contain minor points that require further study and clarification.
> The statement by me yesterday should not be taken as implying approval in full of the committee's recommendations.[81]

Despite Chancellor Strong's clarifying statement, several Regents, including, most notably, Chairman Carter, believed that the incident indicated the need for a change in Berkeley campus leadership. At a special meeting of the Board on January 2, the Regents decided to grant Strong a leave of absence "to recuperate from his recent illness," and Meyerson was appointed "acting Chancellor" for an indefinite period.[82]

Meyerson's basic liberality had a soothing effect on the Berkeley campus. Rallies on Sproul Hall steps were almost daily occurrences after he came into office, but most of them were so conducted as to avoid confrontation with the administration.[83] Subjects discussed included the American involvement in the war in Vietnam and civil rights. For a brief time, at least, the administration-baiting that was once the staple of FSM rallies became the spice but not the substance of the student activists' rhetoric. Reorganized as the Free Student Union later in the spring of 1965, the FSM lost much of its following to more specialized organizations involved in political and social action. The tension that remained on campus was tolerable as long as the faculty, administration, or Regents did not over-react to student dissent, advocacy, or expression with disciplinary actions that could be considered infringement of constitutionally protected rights.

FOUR-LETTER WORDS

A well-publicized test of Berkeley's tolerance came in March, 1965, when a delicate-featured, long-haired, barefooted young man (not a student) appeared on campus with a sign hung around his neck. On the sign was one offensive four-letter word. The youth was arrested by campus police on charges of outraging public decency. During the next two days, the boy's sympathizers introduced similar signs on the campus, held rallies at which the offending word was amplified all over the Sproul Plaza, and claimed that the administration had again deprived students of free speech. In all, three students and six nonstudents were arrested for participation in what were called the "filthy speech" rallies. These attracted small audiences, but were fully covered by the daily press and radio and television stations. Many Regents, Governor Brown, many alumni, and some legislators were indignant. Chancellor Meyerson's attempts swiftly to invoke orderly disciplinary procedures failed because two faculty committees refused to handle the distasteful matter. While Meyerson was trying to work out alternative procedures, Governor Brown called President Kerr to say that the talk in Sacramento was that the offending students should be expelled immediately, without trial.

Regent Carter called both Kerr and Meyerson several times during the next few days to inquire about disciplinary action against the filthy speech offenders. On the morning of March 9 he called the President and Acting

Chancellor again and, according to their understanding of the conversations, indicated that if disciplinary action was not initiated before 5 P.M. he would call a Regents' meeting on the matter. Such an action, Kerr and Meyerson agreed, would be an intrusion of the Regents into administrative affairs and it would amount to a declaration of no confidence in Meyerson. President Kerr decided to "call down a plague on everybody's house"—the students for behaving so disgustingly, the faculty for refusing to help, and the Regents for stepping into an administrative matter.[84] He told Meyerson he intended to resign and asked if Meyerson wanted to join him. Because he felt that he could not comply with Regent Carter's demands, which he interpreted as demanding expulsion without proper hearings, and because he felt the University could not function if the Regents intervened in administrative affairs, Meyerson agreed. Later that day, reporters were summoned to a conference room on the seventh floor of University Hall where Kerr and Meyerson distributed prepared statements saying they intended to resign. The "filthy speech" incidents of the previous week were only obliquely referred to in the statements of resignation. Meyerson said: "What might have been regarded earlier as childish bad taste has become to many the last straw of contempt." [85] Kerr said: "Responsibility is the other side of the coin on which freedom is written. It cannot be enforced by Regents and administrators alone, but only by the total University community. The necessity for responsibility has now been presented in a clear-cut manner to the Berkeley campus. It can only preserve freedom by avoiding license." [86] Neither Regent Carter nor Governor Brown heard about the resignations until the press had been called.

The Berkeley Division of the Academic Senate called a special meeting for Friday, March 12, to discuss the pending resignations. That morning the Oakland *Tribune* released copyrighted stories based on documents prepared by Chancellor Strong during his last days as an active chancellor. These stories reiterated Strong's charges before the Regents that his firm hand in the FSM crisis had been stayed by appeasements and capitulations of the President.

At the special Academic Senate meeting, resolutions asking Kerr and Meyerson to remain in their posts were approved by a vote of 891 to 23.[87] The Senate resolved that because of "his leadership, his tact, wisdom and vision" [88] Meyerson be named permanent chancellor at Berkeley. On the morning of March 13, the day of the Regents' meeting, verbatim accounts of the documents upon which the *Tribune* based its stories the previous day were published in the San Francisco *Examiner*. Publication of these documents distressed Chancellor Strong, who had previously made them available only to a few individuals on a confidential basis. As soon as they appeared, he decided that confidentiality had been so seriously breached he could no longer serve as chancellor of the University and prepared a letter of resignation that was subsequently hand-delivered to the Regents.

On March 13, several Regents, including Governor Brown, convinced President Kerr and Acting Chancellor Meyerson that they should abandon their intentions to resign. After a meeting with the Board that lasted for several hours during the afternoon, Kerr read a statement to the press that said in part:

> After discussion with the Board of Regents, Acting Chancellor Meyerson and I have decided to withdraw our resignations pending further discussions with the Board. These resignations were made without full opportunity for Board consideration, which we regret.[89]

At the same meeting, Regent Carter announced that effective immediately, Edward Strong had resigned as chancellor at Berkeley.

THE MEYER AND BYRNE REPORTS

In April, 1965, the Regents received the first of two major reports of committees created the previous December to study various parts of the FSM controversy. It came from the "Meyer Committee," which in addition to the chairman, Theodore Meyer, president of the Mechanics Institute of San Francisco and ex-officio Regent, consisted of Regents Canaday, Hearst, Heller, Laurence J. Kennedy, McLaughlin, Mosher, Carter, and President Kerr. The committee redrafted all existing University regulations on student government, use of University facilities, and political action. It also left all discipline, except expulsion, in the hands of the chancellor.[90] In this respect the Meyer Committee Report was specifically at variance with the December 8 regulations of the Academic Senate, which provided that discipline in matters affecting political action should be handled by a faculty committee.

While the report was still under consideration, a second report was issued. This one was commissioned by the special committee created in December to research basic factors contributing to the unrest of the University. The chairman of that committee was Regent Forbes. Members were Regents Boyd, William K. Coblentz, Pauley, Chandler, Tapp, and Simon. The investigator for the committee was Jerome C. Byrne, a young Beverly Hills attorney. His lengthy report emphasized the impotence of student governments, the confused lines of authority in University administration, and the immense and detailed burdens of the Regents. It absolved the Free Speech Movement of charges made in some quarters that it was controlled by Communists and chided the University for rules and regulations that were out of keeping with the liberated generation's desire to play an active part in political and social action. It recommended virtually complete autonomy for the campuses, which should, the report said, be "chartered" by the statewide system with their own goals and methods.

According to other recommendations, the Regents should remove themselves from the day-to-day decisions of University operations, concentrating only on broad policy; the president of the University should be the chairman of the Board, spokesman for the University system, and its chief budget officer; and student governments should be permitted to express themselves on off-campus issues as long as they did not identify their views as those of the University.[91]

Many of the Byrne Report's recommendations concerned matters that had been under consideration by President Kerr and the Regents for some time. Only the emergency of the rebellion had delayed their deliberations from coming to a constructive conclusion. For that, among other reasons,[92] on May 21, the Regents deferred action on the Byrne Report until after the President's plans for reorganization were considered. At the May meeting, the Meyer Committee's report was also turned over to President Kerr with instruction that it be used for reference in developing new regulations on student conduct, organizations, and the use of University facilities.

With the cooperation of the chancellors of all campuses, President Kerr prepared new rules that were reported to the Regents at their June meeting. Based to a considerable extent upon the Meyer Report, they were more flexible in such matters as the authority of student organizations to take stands on non-University issues and permitting fund-raising on the campus. They also required, rather than permitted, chancellors to establish "open discussion areas" and to develop standards of fairness for disciplinary procedures. Chancellors were given considerable latitude in adapting the rules to their own campuses. The new rules were declared effective on July 1, 1965.[93]

THE TRIALS AND SENTENCES

Of the 773 persons originally arrested in Sproul Hall December 3, 690 pleaded innocent, 75 pleaded no contest, and 8 were handled in juvenile court. Of those who pleaded innocent, 155 went on mass trial in the court of Municipal Judge Rupert Crittenden on April 1, 1965. The fate of the remainder was to be judged on the evidence presented in the first trial. On June 28, Judge Crittenden began to announce his decisions. Ultimately, 670 were found guilty of trespass, resisting arrest, or both. Fines ranging from $25 to $400 and jail sentences ranging from 25 days to 120 days were pronounced in accordance with the degree of participation in the Sproul Hall sit-ins. Those who just sat-in paid fines. Those who went limp or resisted arrest paid fines, received jail sentences, or both. Highest sentences were given to Mario Savio, Jack Weinberg, and Arthur Goldberg, each of whom was sentenced to 120 days in jail. Appeals on behalf of 565 of those convicted were carried all of the way to the United States Supreme Court, which, on June 13, 1967, refused to review the cases.

In April, 1965, Acting Chancellor Meyerson, guided by findings of an *ad hoc* faculty committee, dismissed Arthur Goldberg from the University and suspended three other students for taking part in the "filthy speech episode" the month before. In June, one of the students who was arrested in this incident was given a suspended ten-day sentence by Berkeley-Albany Municipal Judge Floyd Talbott. Goldberg was sentenced to two consecutive thirty-day terms and a third student was sentenced to twenty days in jail.

Because it was so spectacular and so diligently covered by Bay Area press, radio, and television, the Berkeley rebellion had national impact. Educators, sociologists, psychologists, and politicians all went to their typewriters to get their interpretations on paper and, ultimately, into print. *Berkeley* became synonymous with dissent, bohemianism, and organized confrontation of authority. The new image appealed to adventurous, intellectually active people and did not seriously impair faculty or student recruiting (although there was a short-lived dip in Freshman enrollments in 1965). But the image angered alumni, private citizens, and prospective philanthropists who regarded the rebellion as symptomatic of the University's decline from honored greatness or, worse, as an incipient movement that was potentially destructive of American society.

Internally, the rebellion forced the faculty and administration to consider the possibility that students were a more important constituency than previously had been assumed. Moreover, it became necessary to consider the possibility that student government and activities as customarily encouraged by the administration were not involvement in the University but diversion from involvement. Students who recognized the difference demanded responsibility commensurate with their interests and abilities. The events of 1964 and 1965 also emphasized inadequacies of the undergraduate teaching program at Berkeley and inspired reforms to improve it.

The rebellion made the University vulnerable to unrelenting public kibitzing, to the frustration of incessant confrontation between students and administration, and to the trauma of dissension within the faculty. All of this took its toll on the University's leadership. Chancellor Strong was forced to resign because his approach to the problems ended in deadlock. Acting Chancellor Meyerson could not take a firm grip on his job because he was too liberal for the comfort of some of the Regents to be confirmed unanimously. The Regents became as sharply divided along liberal-conservative lines as they had been during the loyalty-oath dispute more than a decade earlier. Because he was viewed from within and without the University as the engineer of Strong's fall from power, President Kerr lost both a personal friend and the backing of several influential Regents who supported the Chancellor throughout the dispute. This loss eventually contributed to the downfall of Kerr himself.

Chapter 27

AFTERMATH OF THE REBELLION

THE ANGRY PROTESTS of student rebels in 1964 were more than demands for political freedom. They were also desperate attempts to communicate dissatisfaction with the form and quality of undergraduate education at Berkeley. Their complaints, though unresolved, were not new. Among them were the assertions that preoccupation with graduate instruction and research had left faculty members little time or energy for undergraduate teaching; that the undergraduate curriculum was too rigid, had too little relation to the concerns of their generation, and geared to outmoded concepts of what educated men needed to be or to know; that emphasis on grades spoiled the natural excitement of discovery and learning; that too many of their classes were taught by teaching assistants; [1] that there was too much distance between students and teachers; and that counseling and advising systems were perfunctory and unsatisfactory.

The president and chancellors of the University were aware of these complaints, and efforts were made to improve undergraduate instruction long before the fall of 1964. Educational reform was deliberately and automatically built into the academic plans of the newer campuses of the University. Even on the older campuses, where faculties tended to be conservative and reluctant to accept change, special Regental support was given to studies of revised undergraduate curricula. Experiments with new and imaginative teaching methods on other campuses were promised similar assistance.[2]

The conversion to the quarter system, which had been so vigorously resisted by many faculty members, presented an opportunity for re-evaluation and adjustment of courses on all campuses. At Santa Barbara, of a total of 1170 quarter courses contemplated for 1966–1967, 201 were entirely new and 434 were revised "beyond the mechanical transition from semester to quarter status." [3] In the College of Agriculture at Davis, the number of curricula was reduced from 13 to 7 by combining some subjects to form new courses. For example, plant science, animal science, and entomology were combined into one curriculum in agricultural biosciences. The number of majors in the college was reduced from 47 to 17.[4] At Berkeley, 36 per cent of the courses were revised, 13 per cent were eliminated, and 26 per cent were new. Only about a fourth of the courses on the campus were converted to the quarter system with little or no change.[5]

On several campuses, faculties experimented with interdepartmental approaches to education. At UCLA, a three-quarter natural science course was devised for students in the humanities or social sciences. The first quarter, under the jurisdiction of the physics department, was built around the concept of the atom, while covering basic principles of science. The second, conducted by the chemistry department, was concerned with the molecule "from proton to protein." In the third quarter, students were offered three choices of relative specialization—astronomy, meteorology, or geology.[6] At Berkeley, a new three-quarter biology course replaced introductory courses in botany and zoology, and a new contemporary natural science course for nonscience majors was developed to replace courses for nonmajors in botany, zoology, physics, and genetics.[7] Also at Berkeley, an Experimental College, proposed to President Kerr as early as the summer of 1964, came into existence.

Authorized by the College of Letters and Science in the spring of 1965, the Experimental College was the brainchild of Joseph Tussman, a professor of philosophy. It involved a thematic approach to lower-division instruction. Small group discussions and heavy assignments of reading and writing were featured. Five professors from several disciplines (including speech, political science, philosophy, and aeronautical science) were given departmental leaves of absence to serve as faculty members for the new college. In an abandoned fraternity house north of campus, the college enrolled 150 students in September, 1965. The "house" was their headquarters. There they heard lectures twice a week and gathered for group discussions, recreational reading, and informal conversation. The first part of their two-year program was based upon selected readings concerning two periods— Greece during the Peloponnesian Wars and seventeenth-century England. The second year focused on America.[8] At the end of the first year of operations, Professor Tussman reported difficulties in getting other faculty members to serve the college, but assured the faculty of the College of Letters and Science that "our faith in the fundamental conception is strong and unshaken." [9]

THE MUSCATINE REPORT

Although educational innovation was underway within the University in 1964, the rebellion spurred it on. Neil Smelser, a professor of sociology who was later named the chancellor's assistant in charge of educational development, acknowledged the impact of the rebellion on educational policy in February, 1965, when he said: "To some degree the . . . recent crisis has caused people to think very profoundly about the total character of this institution. . . . A great many reforms are being talked about at all levels. . . ." [10]

On the first of March, 1965, Acting Chancellor Meyerson spoke to the Academic Senate at Berkeley and suggested that a select committee of the faculty be appointed to consider four questions:

1. How can we provide a general education commensurate with the excitement and fluidity of modern knowledge?
2. How shall we in this large diversified seat of learning provide communities or centers for intellectual identification?
3. Can we not reassess the way we evaluate the progress of learners, whether they be faculty or students?
4. What are the best ways in which we as a community of scholars may rededicate ourselves as a self-conscious community of teachers, both at the undergraduate level of instruction and the graduate? [11]

Meyerson's recommendation was acted upon by the Emergency Executive Committee of the Academic Senate on March 8. The committee called for establishment of a Select Committee on Education at Berkeley,

(a) to find the ways in which the traditions of human learning and scientific inquiry can be best advanced under the challenging conditions of size and scale that confront our university community;

(b) to examine the various changes in educational programs currently under consideration in the several schools and colleges; to seek by appropriate means to communicate information concerning these programs to the wider campus community; and to consider the implications of these programs in the light of (a) above.[12]

Education at Berkeley, the report of the Select Committee on Education, was released in March, 1966. More than two thousand copies were distributed by the office of the chancellor to members of the faculty, University officials, prominent educators, and friends of the campus. Because it concerned the Berkeley campus, whose fame in 1966 rested almost equally upon academic excellence and student rebellion, the report was eagerly sought by readers elsewhere, and more than five thousand copies were sold by the University of California Press within a year. A second edition carries "The Muscatine Report" on the cover of the paperback edition as an alternate title, acknowledging the nomenclature accepted on the campus itself, and recognizing the role of the select committee's chairman, Professor Charles Muscatine, in the report's preparation.

The authors of the report accepted the irreversible realities of higher education in the 1960s; the changing role of the university in modern society; the proliferation of knowledge; population growth and changes in our social expectations; the emergence of a new generation of students; and a future whose promise "is not stasis but accelerated change." [13] They acknowledged the desire of some students for "an adequate connection between their education and what they feel to be their primary concerns as human beings and as citizens," [14] something that they either lacked or found obscure in the University's offerings. The committee adopted a frankly pluralistic approach to education, but while its members could not agree on many subjects that every student should know, they suggested that some values and experiences that students might profitably share could include "the exposure to a noble stance, both scientific and humane, that will be exemplified in the conduct of every one of us." [15] The report asserted that "research (or creativity) is of the very character of this campus . . . ," [16] and that eminence in that endeavor should be maintained, although "we find no place on the faculty for researchers who are not teachers." [17] In discussing the students, the report emphasized that "in the end we must try to build bridges across the gulf between generations that separates students from their teachers and from their own past. Personal contact with professors will tend to dispel the legends that circulate about the achievement orientation of the faculty and will make the students more likely to develop respect for hard intellectual work." [18]

After making this analysis of prevailing conditions and expectations, the committee made forty-two specific recommendations. Broadly speaking, these were intended to improve the educational experience at Berkeley by raising the quality of teaching (by professors and teaching assistants alike); by breaking down traditional departmental barriers so that a more diversified and more adventurous curriculum could be provided; by making possible a tradition of continuing educational experiment and innovation; by giving students more representation in councils where academic policy is formulated; by removing the pressures of the grading system from students venturing into academic courses outside their major interests; and by altering entrance requirements in favor of students with maturity, judgment, and academic aptitude sufficient to cope with the responsibility, independence, and variety of new choices that would become available to them.

The Academic Senate at Berkeley acted on the committee's recommendations between March 31 and November 8, 1966. Sixteen of them were adopted, either as submitted or with revision; ten were received and placed on file; eight were referred to a college, or to the graduate council; four were "approved"; three were withdrawn (because they were incorporated in resolutions already passed); and one (to count units of credit but to disregard grade points in courses taken in an undergraduate's first quarter of residence) failed to pass.

One of the key recommendations, guaranteeing that concern with educational reform would not stop with the Muscatine Report, created a Board of Educational Development (BED) to stimulate and encourage educational experiments. One of its members would be a new administrative officer (later called an assistant chancellor) with responsibilities for educational development. This proposal had high priority, and was the first one considered and adopted by the Academic Senate.

Reception of the Muscatine Report and its handling by the Academic Senate was predominantly favorable. Although many of the proposals of the report were not really innovations in American higher education, they were new for Berkeley and were welcomed as refreshing and promising alternatives to tired, uninspired, and ineffective approaches too long familiar. Some students criticized the report because it did not give students representation on the Board of Educational Development.[19] Other critics claimed that this board was just another committee to which the major work of the

Select Committee would be delegated.[20] Finally, there was concern that the reforms suggested in the Muscatine Report altered structures and procedures instead of principles.[21] But these criticisms could not devalue the report's importance. A serious attempt had been made to improve the educational experience and meet student demands for a better academic life at Berkeley. By making that attempt, the University's oldest campus began to participate in the same spirit of modernization, innovation, and experimentation that was so challenging to the new and emerging campuses.

THE KNELLER REPORT

UCLA's faculty joined the same movement in the spring of 1966 when its Academic Senate created a Committee on Academic Innovation and Development under the chairmanship of Professor George F. Kneller. Much more modest in length and format than the Muscatine Report, the report of this committee considered many of the same problems discussed by the Select Committee at Berkeley. Three general subjects were emphasized: greater freedom that would make "the student a more active participant in the life of the University . . ."; [22] placing sharper focus on "the place and function of teaching . . ."; [23] and giving "curricular offerings a different dimension from that normally provided by departments." [24] The committee proposed fifty-two recommendations, many of which paralleled those found in the Muscatine Report. It sought creation of a Council on Educational Development, for instance, that would have functions similar to Berkeley's BED. But it was somewhat more forthright in its approach to fundamental principles. It recognized, for instance, that in the process of rapid growth, the basic purposes of the University might have been lost or forgotten, and recommended that UCLA's Academic Senate Committee on Educational Policy prepare a new document "clarifying and redefining the purposes of the University from the point of view of our own academic community." [25] A University College for lower-division students was recommended.[26] The committee also advised that a campus grievance officer or Ombudsman, with access to all campus offices and agencies, be created.[27] His job would be to help students find their way through campus bureaucracy when they encountered problems. This report was not enthusiastically received and most of its recommendations were entrusted to various departments and committees for further consideration or implementation.

A NEW CHANCELLOR AT BERKELEY

Before the Select Committee of the Berkeley faculty completed the Muscatine Report, the Berkeley campus had a new chancellor. During the search for a permanent chancellor to succeed Strong, many people regarded Martin Meyerson as the favorite. He was already acting chancellor and enjoyed considerable support from the Berkeley faculty. Initially, he had also enjoyed much student support, but as student radicals learned that his sympathy for their idealism did not condone unrelenting pressure to force the administration into absolute, unnegotiable positions, he lost some of their loyalty. He also failed to win the unanimous support of the Regents.

After considering many candidates for the chancellorship, committees of faculty members, students, and alumni ultimately agreed to support Roger W. Heyns, then vice-president for academic affairs at the University of Michigan. Forty-seven years old at the time of his selection, Heyns was a native of Michigan and a graduate of Calvin College in Grand Rapids. He received his master's and doctor's degrees at the University of Michigan and began his academic career there as an instructor in psychology in 1947. At the time of his appointment to the chancellorship at Berkeley, he was judged a likely successor to Michigan's President Harlan Hatcher, who was nearing retirement.

On September 22, 1965, in an appearance in the Greek Theatre that was in many ways reminiscent of Benjamin Ide Wheeler's appearance before the campus flagpole in 1899, Heyns shunned the stage and spoke from the floor. Speaking of his conversations with students, Regents, alumni, and faculty members since his arrival in Berkeley, he said: "I am convinced that it is the collective judgment of these thoughtful people, whose love and respect for this University is every bit as intense as that of any one of this audience, that this exciting University will apply intelligently the lessons of last year. They recognize that Berkeley's problems are those of the nation, that Berkeley needs time to solve them." [28]

MORE POLITICAL UNREST

Increasingly after Heyns' arrival, the attention of students was pulled off campus to the continuing national struggles for civil rights and to issues posed by the frustrating war in Vietnam.

These interests were not confined to Berkeley. In February, 1965,

SCRAP, a civil-rights organization, applied for campus recognition at Riverside.[29] In March, Santa Barbara Friends of SNCC planned a local sympathy and freedom march to protest violence in Selma, Alabama.[30] A vigil at UCLA protested the same situation and raised $700 for telegrams of protest to President Johnson and California's senators.[31] The student-body president and five members of the student council resigned when the chancellor suggested that the student executive council's motion to rescind a resolution asking President Johnson to intervene in Selma was illegal under existing regulations.[32] The ASUC at Berkeley passed a similar resolution by a vote of twelve to five on March 16,[33] and a week later Chancellor Meyerson announced his intention to ask the Regents to make ASUC membership voluntary, "for a variety of reasons." [34] In February, 1966, four UCLA students were sentenced to jail terms after conviction for disturbing the peace during a 1964 sit-in at the Westwood Bank of America to protest the bank's hiring practices.[35]

A marathon thirty-three-hour Vietnam teach-in was held on an athletic field (now covered by the Zellerbach Auditorium-Theater) in Berkeley in May, 1965. Crowds of up to five thousand people gathered there to hear such notables as Mario Savio and the famous pediatrician, Dr. Benjamin Spock, denounce American participation in the war.[36] The following October, students joined marches from downtown Berkeley to the Oakland Army base in an antiwar protest. In the same month, two thousand people participated at a UCLA rally [37] and as many as sixty people at one time joined a twenty-four-hour vigil at Riverside to protest the war.[38] A month later, from two hundred to two thousand students participated in a Vietnam teach-in at UCLA, and the *Daily Bruin* reported, "For 12 hours Friday, the University of California, Los Angeles, acquired the image of Berkeley." [39] The following March, an antiwar Peace Rights Organizing Committee picketed a United States Marine Corps recruiting table on the Berkeley campus.[40] On March 24, along the main library walk at the Santa Barbara campus, forty members of the Santa Barbara community held a noon-hour silent vigil to protest the war.[41] This form of protest was later copied at ninety-four other colleges and universities in the country, including UCLA.[42]

ATTEMPTS TO RESHAPE BERKELEY'S STUDENT GOVERNMENT

While faculty committees were re-evaluating academic programs at Berkeley and political activists were continuing to provide distractions from traditional student concerns, the ASUC Senate and other student leaders worked to regain for recognized student government some of the influence it lost during the rebellion. In the minds of many students, such influence was unattainable until graduate students, removed from membership in the ASUC on petition of 1300 [43] of their number (5565) in 1959, once again became members. Without them, the ASUC could claim to represent only about 60 per cent of the student body. It would also be deprived of the sophisticated brand of leadership graduate students provided during the rebellion. Opposition to readmitting graduate students to ASUC membership came from students whose interests were served by traditional student activities, and from those who assumed that Slate's support of the measure indicated that the graduate students would give student government at Berkeley an activist, radical inclination. Many administrators shared this view. The question was the subject of polls and elections throughout the spring of 1965, most of which clearly favored re-entry of graduate students into the ASUC.[44] But the victories at the poll were nullified, once by the Regents, on grounds that insufficient graduate-student votes had been cast to justify imposing compulsory student-body membership fees,[45] and once by the student judicial committee because it was proposed that graduate students who had not paid such fees have the same voting privileges as undergraduates who had paid them.[46] In an unofficial but impressive showing, the Graduate Student Coordinating Committee held a "freedom ballot" in early April that favored a re-entry amendment to the ASUC constitution by a vote of 7184 to 868.[47] On April 27, the ASUC Senate circumvented all existing bans on graduate student membership by making it available on a voluntary basis to any graduate student willing to pay the $3.25 membership fee.[48]

Students also made an attempt to restructure their government through a revised constitution. On March 30, 1966, a long-drawn-out, controversial constitutional convention ended. Its thirty-page achievement was, in many ways, an attempt to codify gains some students assumed were won during the rebellion. It de-emphasized traditional student activities and gave considerable attention to students' rights, students' relationships to the rest of the community, and students' powers in participating in making educational and regulative policies for the University. It declared student government to be completely independent of University authority—a direct challenge to the Kerr directives. Chancellor Meyerson warned that if the new constitution was approved, he would take over direct responsibility for existing ASUC programs and activities.[49] On April 29, after three days of balloting, the new constitution failed by a vote of 5068 to 6082.[50] Five days later, in a regular student body election, a "moderate" candidate defeated a Slate candidate for ASUC president by a nearly two-to-one margin in the heaviest voting in years.

THE PRESIDENT IN TROUBLE

Despite his formidable reputation as a statesman of American higher education, and despite his impressive achievements in building, planning, and reorganizing the University to provide quality education for unprecedented numbers of students, Kerr's hold on the presidency became more and more precarious after the fall of 1964. The rebellion at Berkeley and subsequent student activism offended much of the public and many legislators. Kerr, as the University's chief administrator, was held responsible for the disturbances. He was also vulnerable as a former chancellor at Berkeley and because he chose to play a direct role in trying to restore peace there after he became president. Outraged citizens and politicians called for Kerr's resignation fairly early in the postrebellion period.

Several Regents had become opponents of Kerr before the rebellion. Their disagreements stemmed from questions of Regental and administrative authority. The rebellion intensified some of this residual dissatisfaction and lost the President the full confidence of one or two other Regents as well. He lost favor with more of his former supporters when Strong was forced to resign, and lost still more when he and Meyerson resigned in March, 1965, and then withdrew their resignations. The Oakland *Tribune* bluntly claimed at about this time that the wrong man was allowed to leave when Chancellor Strong resigned.[51]

The few Regents who were most vigorous in their opposition to Kerr could not do much while the rebellion was in its most furious stages. There was a question as to whether the president of a nine-campus institution could fairly be held responsible for a disturbance that was obviously localized at Berkeley. Moreover, the responsibility for calming the rebellion was theoretically an administrative one, and the Regents needed the President for liaison. Then too, Kerr himself was under heavy fire from the rebels, and forsaking him might be interpreted as capitulation.

By the summer of 1965, most of the fury of the rebellion had been spent, the fate of the arrested demonstrators was in the hands of the courts, rules had been revised, and efforts to get a new chancellor at Berkeley were coming to a conclusion. From that time on, Clark Kerr's security in the presidency depended upon continuing peace at Berkeley, upon positive achievements to neutralize the negative criticism of the University generated by the

FSM demonstrations, and upon Kerr's ability to avoid supplying his opponents with the occasion or excuse to attack him. Those conditions, not entirely within his control, could not be met.

ANOTHER BURNS REPORT

The Berkeley rebellion was never allowed to die. Student activists used the Sproul Hall steps almost daily for rallies on almost every conceivable subject. Many of their convocations involved procedures and incidents planned to test the new regulations. Some of them were offensive to members of the faculty, student body, and general public. The rebellion was interpreted and reinterpreted by scholars and journalists, and each new explanation of what happened in the tense months of 1964 and 1965 rekindled antagonisms before they could cool.

Clark Kerr's political foes capitalized upon the sustained public interest. One of these was State Senator Hugh Burns, who, in June, 1965, released the thirteenth report of his State Senate fact-finding Subcommittee on Un-American Activities. Its content purported to be the results of investigations demonstrating that Communists had been instrumental in bringing about the rebellion of 1964. It put much of the blame, however, on the administration of Clark Kerr, which "welcomes Communist organizations, throws the portals open to Communist speakers, and exhibits an easy tolerance of Communist activities that defies all reason." [52]

At the June, 1965, meeting of the Regents, Edwin Pauley, who had become disenchanted with Kerr early in his administration, had some advance copies of the report, which was discussed during a session from which President Kerr excused himself. Kerr learned later that his dismissal had been discussed on the day of that meeting, but that no motion was ever introduced for that purpose.[53] Governor Brown, who later criticized the Burns Report, was Kerr's most prominent champion during the debates. While the Regents discussed the Burns Report, President Kerr, against the advice of several Regents and administrators, was formulating a reply to it that claimed thirty-one specific inaccuracies ranging "from serious errors, which do grave injustices to individuals and the University, to minor mistakes which do not greatly affect the substance of the report but which reveal an apparent lack of knowledge about, respect for, or even concern for the facts." [54] He challenged Senator Burns to either withdraw the report or remove it from legislative protection against libel suits. Burns did not do either.

STUDENT DISSENT AS A CAMPAIGN ISSUE

Student involvement in civil rights and antiwar movements intensified just in time to make an already spirited 1966 state election campaign still livelier. Governor Brown, proud of the fact that California's Master Plan for Higher Education was developed and implemented during his administration was opposed by Ronald Reagan, motion picture and television actor, who had achieved prominence in national politics in 1964 when he was an articulate supporter of Barry Goldwater's campaign for the United States presidency. Because newspapers continued in 1966 to give a great deal of attention to student unrest throughout the country, particularly at the University of California, the University became a campaign issue. Governor Brown defended it on the strength of its remarkable record of achievements in teaching, research, and public service. His challenger questioned the cost of its operations, the soundness of its general operations, and the adequacy of its administration—with particular reference to the control of student unrest.

In March, 1966, there was more national attention on Berkeley as a center of dissent. On Charter Day, a small group of students, nonstudents, and faculty members opposed to American participation in the war in Vietnam rose from their seats and walked out when an honorary degree was presented to America's ambassador to the United Nations, Arthur Goldberg.[55] Later in the day, a large audience applauded their antiwar champion, Professor Franz Schurman of the University's Center for the Chinese Studies, but accorded Goldberg only a silent response in a debate over United States policies in Vietnam.[56]

That night, six thousand people, many of them students, attended a fund-raising dance in Harmon Gymnasium at Berkeley, sponsored by the Vietnam Day Committee, an antiwar group. Newspaper reports of the meeting said that the odor of marijuana hung over the gymnasium when it was over, that there were beer cans left behind by the participants, that slides of nude male and female torsos had been projected on the walls, and that there had been sexual activity in the dark recesses of the bleachers. Regent Hearst called the event "a shambles that disgraced us all." [57] Chancellor Heyns said that the event had been overattended and underpoliced, but that steps were being taken to prevent anything like it from happening again.[58]

Later in the spring, critics of the University and of Clark Kerr got another assist from State Senator Hugh Burns, who issued a supplement to the thirteenth report of his Subcommittee on Un-American Activities. This report described all of the activities of the Vietnam Day Committee, pointing out that many of its leaders had also been leaders in the FSM. It mentioned the VDC dance on the night of March 25, 1966. Then, to demonstrate how far the University's standards of conduct had fallen, it reported that the San Francisco Mime Troupe, a group banned from San Francisco parks because of its allegedly lewd performances, had been allowed to appear at Berkeley. It also discussed a sensational series of articles in the *Daily Californian* that suggested homosexuality was not only present, but common, in a large segment of the student body and brazenly initiated its readers to a graphic but highly esoteric vocabulary. Finally, the report was critical of the University's handling of the Eli Katz case (Katz was eventually rehired as an acting assistant professor pending a hearing by the Academic Senate's Committee on Academic Privilege and Tenure.) [59]

Again Kerr criticized the Burns committee report and demanded that it be issued without legislative privilege. Chancellor Heyns objected that, although the report purported to be a factual one concerning the Berkeley campus, "no one from the subcommittee has even spoken to me about it." [60] The Regents appointed a special committee to investigate and reply to the Burns report charges. Regent Jesse W. Tapp, former chairman of the Bank of America and president of the State Agricultural Society, was its chairman. This committee pointed out that, although the problems at Berkeley were highly publicized, they "exist in varying degrees at other universities and colleges in California and throughout the nation." That some errors in judgment may have been made was acknowledged, but, the committee said, ". . . It would be unrealistic to expect otherwise in an institution of such size and complexity. . . ." [61] Regents Hearst, Haldeman, Rafferty, Pauley, Forbes, and Canaday all expressed their disagreement with the Tapp committee report at the regular Regents meeting on September 16.[62]

The following month, Regent Canady wrote a letter to President Kerr, with copies to the Regents, asking the attitude of the University administration toward future appearances of the San Francisco Mime Troupe on University campuses and stating that they should be barred from further use of University facilities.[63] In the same letter he stated that Mario Savio, "or any other student who advocates violence and disregard for University regulations and civil law," [64] should be considered ineligible for readmission to any campus of the University. President Kerr stated in response to the letter that both questions had been placed in the hands of the chancellors in accordance with the University's decentralization policy. He suggested that the Regents might wish to stipulate guidelines for deciding on the suitability of theatrical performances on campus, but that they should leave the actual decisions to the chancellors.[65] Most of the Regents accepted Kerr's response but he did not miss the warning that came in an earlier part of the meeting when a Regental vote of "pride and confidence" in the President, the chancellors, and the faculty was forced aside in favor of a substitute resolution that expressed "wholehearted support" of the Regents "for the whole University of California." [66]

During October, the contest between gubernatorial candidates Brown and Reagan began to peak. Reagan promised that there would be a full-scale investigation of the University if he were elected. He even had a chief investigator in mind: John A. McCone, former director of the CIA and Berkeley Alumnus of the Year in 1960.[67] Max Rafferty, a Reagan supporter and incumbent candidate for state superintendent of public instruction, helped impress upon the public the possibility that an investigation of the University was in order by alleging that the University offered "a four year course in sex, drugs and treason." [68]

Despite the fact that it was a hot political issue, the University did not lose the good will and support of the people of the state. In the November election, they overwhelmingly approved a $230,000,000 bond issue for higher-education construction, of which $114,825,325 was to be spent for new University buildings and improvements. President Kerr and other University officials devoted a considerable amount of time campaigning for it.[69]

Ronald Reagan defeated Governor Brown in the 1966 election by an impressive margin. His victory was followed almost immediately by speculation that Clark Kerr would soon resign from the presidency of the University and that UCLA's Chancellor Murphy, whose politics were believed to be more compatible with those of the governor-elect, would take Kerr's place.

WEEKS OF SPECULATION

President Kerr was aware, soon after the election, that his position had weakened. From a source that could not be discounted, he also knew that there was some substance to the speculation that Reagan's backers would like to see Chancellor Murphy become president of the University. But Kerr decided to continue as president as long as he could do so without injury to the University. He believed that his record as president had been a good one, and that once the new governor became involved in the day-to-day work of his office, he might come to understand the University and its president better.

At a reception at Regent Haldeman's house in Los Angeles on the night of the November Regents' meeting, Kerr met Reagan for the first time, but they had no chance to talk. During the evening, two different Regents came to him at different times and told him in a sympathetic and friendly way that he ought to be looking for another job because things were going to be difficult for him. In subsequent weeks he talked to other Regents who had been his good friends but who had also supported Reagan's candidacy for governor. They, along with at least one Regent who opposed Reagan's bid for the governorship, told Kerr he should resign, preferably before January 1. They liked him, knew what he had done for the University, and did not wish to see him hurt, but they were of the opinion that a change was inevitable and probably desirable.

On the strength of this advice, Kerr began to think in terms of submitting his resignation in June, 1967, to be effective the June following. This would give him six months to size up the situation and remove his decision from any political contexts. It would also allow him to complete ten years in the presidency, and to serve in that office during the University's centennial year.

THE STRIKE OF 1966

Before he could settle upon any course definitely, however, there was another distraction at Berkeley. On November 30, United States Marine Corps recruiters had set up a recruting table in the Student Union. A woman who was opposed to the war had set up her own table next to it and other people began to picket the Marine table. Because the woman was not a student and had no permission to preside at one in the building, she was asked to remove her table. A crowded demonstration of several hundred ensued. Late in the afternoon, nine persons were arrested—including Mario Savio, who came onto the campus as the disturbance started and assumed a role of leadership among the dissenters.

That evening a boycott of classes was called for at a mass student meeting, and on the following day the teaching-assistants local of the American Federation of Teachers and the ASUC Senate both sanctioned the "strike." On the following Monday, however, the Academic Senate declared that the student strike should end immediately and the ASUC Senate withdrew its support.

By Tuesday noon the strike had pretty well spent itself, but at a special meeting at the Oakland airport, the Regents declared "that it is its firm policy, effective as of today, that University personnel, including all levels of faculty and teaching assistants, who participate in any strike or otherwise fail to meet their assigned duties in an effort to disrupt University administration, teaching, or research, will thereby be subject to termination of their employment relationship with the University, denial of re-employment, or the imposition of other appropriate sanctions." [70]

At the special "strike" meeting of the Board of Regents in December, word was passed to Kerr that Regent Pauley intended to introduce a motion for his dismissal, but the motion was never made.

CONFRONTATION AND DISMISSAL

Late in December, President Kerr made a trip to the Orient, visiting Saigon and Hong Kong. While he was away, University officials participated in a conference in Sacramento where the new Governor's staff outlined tentative budget plans. The outlook for the University was gloomy. The Governor was determined to realize significant economies to balance his budget and institutions of higher education, along with other departments, were being asked to accept drastic cuts. The substance of some of these discussions was reported by William Trombley, education writer for the Los Angeles *Times,* in an article appearing on January 5, 1967. The article said that the University was being asked to make cuts amounting to about $35,000,000; that the Regents would be asked to relinquish to the state their special funds derived from federal research overhead (estimated at between $6,000,000 and $7,000,000 annually); that the University abandon plans to initiate a summer quarter at Berkeley in 1967–1968 (with resulting estimated savings of $5,000,000 for that year); and that tuition of $400 a year (in addition to the $275 incidental fees then in effect) be imposed. Trombley's article quoted one unidentified University official as saying that the combined budget cut and tuition proposal was "the worst setback for higher education in the state since the Depression." [71] Because of the magnitude of the requested cuts, and because premature publication of the Governor's plans in the press surprised many Regents, Theodore Meyer, chairman of the Board, on the recommendation of Vice-President Harry R. Wellman (as acting president), called a special Regents' meeting for January 9. At that meeting, Gordon Smith, the Governor's director of finance, would personally present the Governor's thinking concerning the University budget. Notified of the meeting by phone, President Kerr made arrangements to fly home immediately.

The meeting did not go well. Finance Director Smith outlined his proposals, asking the Regents to accept a reduction from the $278,000,000 contained in their original request to $192,000,000. He repeated his suggestions that the Regents delay year-round operations at Berkeley, that they give $22,000,000 of their special funds to the state to meet operation expenditures, and that they impose tuition. The audience, containing students, let its displeasure be known with hisses and boos. Several Regents and UCLA's Chancellor Murphy spoke in unmistakable opposition to Smith's proposals.[72]

Later in the week, Kerr and several Regents went to Sacramento to confer with the Governor in person. Kerr had planned to offer a compromise that would reduce the University's request for state appropriations from $278,000,000 to about $250,000,000 but neither the Governor nor the finance director was receptive to his proposals.

Shortly after the University delegation left the Governor's office, some of the Regents were called back in. President Kerr was not among them.

On the way back to Berkeley that same day, President Kerr stopped at the Davis campus for a late lunch and a conference with Chancellor Mrak. During that meeting, the possibility that the University might have to restrict its enrollment in the face of inadequate financing was discussed. Chancellor Mrak warned that if such a contingency were seriously contemplated, all of the chancellors should coordinate their admissions programs. Otherwise, some campuses might admit too many students too early. Both Mrak and Chancellor Cheadle had their acceptance letters virtually ready to mail.

When Kerr returned to Berkeley, he asked Vice-President Wellman to notify the chancellors that all letters accepting students for the coming term should be held up until after a meeting of chief campus officers planned for the following week. News of this action came to the attention of the public press in Riverside, and Governor Reagan and Gordon Smith could not be persuaded that the resulting publicity was not planted to generate public pressure for a more favorable University budget.

The following week, President Kerr became aware that his dismissal, increasingly the source of conjecture throughout the state, might be imminent if not already decided. The Governor canceled an appointment with him. Finance Director Smith declined to see him. At a Sacramento reception for legislators and top state officials, a Republican assemblyman who was friendly to the President told him that a campaign against him was soon to be launched throughout the state.

THE DECISION

As the regular January meeting of the Regents approached, Bay Area politicians, including Assemblyman Don Mulford and County Supervisor Kent Purcel, began demanding Kerr's dismissal. Speculation that he would be fired in February appeared in the Los Angeles *Times* and San Francisco *Examiner*.

On the morning of January 20, President Kerr decided that there would be no point in waiting until February to be fired. Although the Academic Council, aware of Kerr's difficulties, had already canvassed the nine divisions of the Academic Senate and learned that the President had overwhelming faculty support, he could not count on a majority of the Regents. Governor Reagan had used the University's alleged mismanagement as a campaign issue. Allan Grant, appointed by Reagan as the new president of the State Board of Agriculture, was expected to oppose the President if there was a showdown.[73] Several Regents had worked on behalf of Reagan's campaign and Kerr believed that he could not be certain of their support for him as president of the University. In addition, there were at least five Regents who consistently voted against Kerr's position on regulations for student government, use of University facilities, and freedom of expression on campuses. This group also contained four or five Regents who had been loyal to Chancellor Strong. This new division of the Board would be very difficult for Kerr to work with in the coming years.

On the morning of the Regents' meeting, President Kerr met with the chairman of the Board, Theodore Meyer, and Vice-Chairman Dorothy B. Chandler. At that meeting, he told them that since most of the Regents had apparently decided that he was going to be dismissed in the near future, it would be better for the University if they did it that day. He did not believe that he could represent the University in difficult negotiations over the budget if the people across the table from him knew that he was going to be fired, perhaps within thirty days.

The President's decision that action on his dismissal should be taken at the first meeting attended by the new Governor took most of the Regents by surprise. Some wanted to postpone consideration of the subject until another time, but others, including several who had sought Kerr's dismissal for many months, successfully prevented further delay. The President's situation was discussed between twelve-thirty and two in the afternoon, while Kerr remained in his office. Shortly after 2 P.M., Chairman Meyer and Regent Chandler went to Kerr's office and told him that he had been dismissed by a vote of fourteen to eight. (Every Regent was present for Governor Reagan's first Board meeting, but Superintendent of Public Instruction Rafferty left before the vote.) They asked him to resign rather than be fired, but he refused. He explained that his resignation, so soon after the election, might in future years be regarded as a precedent that would weaken the University's constitutional autonomy. When the Regents called the staff back into session, Kerr went down to the meeting, where he learned for the first time that his dismissal was to be effective immediately.

In a press conference later in the day, Chairman Meyer read the following statement:

> The Regents today voted to terminate the tenure of Clark Kerr as President of the University, effective immediately. The vote was 14 to 8. In taking this action the Board felt that the state of uncertainty which had prevailed for many months concerning the President's status should be resolved without further delay. The Board is deeply grateful to Dr. Kerr for his long and valuable services as Chancellor and President of the University. . . ." [74]

In a separate press conference, Clark Kerr expressed gratitude for the opportunity that had been given him to serve the University as chancellor and president and spoke of the progress that had been made during his administration. He concluded with a plea for continuing autonomy for the University and said that the responsibility of the Regents to exercise that autonomy, as served by their long terms, was "not to respond too quickly, and too completely, to the swirls of the political winds in the state." [75]

Asked by a reporter if he was surprised by his dismissal, Kerr said, ". . . It's hard to say 'surprise.' After all, the President of the University takes a final examination every month. And, I've taken a lot of final examinations and passed them; this time I didn't." [76]

The immediate successor to Kerr was Harry Wellman, who had served as second-in-command throughout Kerr's administration. Already serving the University on an extended basis after reaching retirement age, the sixty-eight-year-old vice-president was named acting president to serve until a permanent successor was found.

Four days after his dismissal, the Carnegie Foundation for the Advancement of Teaching announced that Kerr had accepted the chairmanship of a three- to six-year study on the future, structure, and financing of American higher education. Later, Kerr announced his decision also to remain at the

University of California as professor of industrial relations, a tenured position he had held throughout his presidency.

THE BUDGET AND TUITION BATTLES

Following the dismissal of Clark Kerr, the Regents and Acting President Wellman continued to seek adequate financing for 1967–1968 operations of the University. The Governor's proposed cuts in the Regents' request for a $278,000,000 operating budget and his related insistence upon charging tuition at the University and state colleges were controversial even before he took office. By February 2, 52 per cent of the people questioned in a California poll favored budget cuts (though not necessarily as heavy as those proposed by the Governor), and 51 per cent favored charging tuition.[77] To inform the public of the consequences of these policies, Universitywide officials, chancellors, and faculty members issued statements, made speeches before alumni and civic organizations, and testified before legislative committees. On February 9, between two thousand and three thousand students marched to Sacramento for a vigil to protest budget cuts and the threat of tuition. Two days later, five thousand students participated in a similar march. Governor Reagan greeted both groups but remained firm in his original decisions.[78]

In a move clearly intended to demonstrate cooperation with the new state administration, on February 15 the Regents voted to reduce their request from $278,000,000 to $264,000,000.[79] This cut eliminated almost all new programs proposed for 1967–1968, including huge portions of funds required for administrative expense, institutional services, library acquisitions, and maintenance and operations. In addition to these sacrifices, the Regents volunteered $19,000,000 from their special funds and from federal contract and grant overhead funds to offset part of the expense.[80] This contribution reduced the amount actually requested from the state general fund to $245,000,000. The most significant action of the Regents that day, taken on the recommendation of Regent Carter as chairman of finance, was to authorize the administration to proceed with student admissions and faculty recruitment on the basis of a still more conservative level of expenditures, $255,000,000, that they would guarantee.[81] Despite the Regents' insistence that they sought and needed the $264,000,000 budget, the lower figure remained the practical target throughout subsequent negotiations. To meet it, the legislature needed to appropriate only $236,000,000.

At the same February meeting, the Regents voted to "make no change in their long established non-tuition policy for California students through the Spring Quarter of 1968" and to postpone further consideration of student fees until April, 1967.[82]

On February 28, the Governor announced his intention of approving a $216,000,000 appropriation for the University, counting upon Regents' funds to make up the difference between what was given and what was needed.[83] Under the continued pressure of a Democrat-controlled state assembly and of Regental and public demand, he was forced to offer more state funds. In March, he proposed that $231,000,000 be provided by the state, that $21,000,000 be provided by the Regents, and that $2,000,000 from medicine and medical payments to University hospitals be substituted for general fund support. These sums totaled $254,000,000.[84] When the state budget was finally passed by the legislature in June, the appropriation to the University amounted to approximately $258,000,000.[85] Certain items were blue-penciled by the Governor, however, until, partly by inadvertence, the appropriation was actually reduced slightly below the amount he had proposed to approve in March. The final University budget as approved by the Governor and reported to the Regents' Finance Committee in July, 1967, totaled $251,500,000,[86] of which $230,700,000 was provided by the state and $20,800,000 by the Regents. The Regents later appropriated another $4,000,000 to alleviate the severity of cuts that had been made. The effect of this supplementary appropriation was to raise the budget to the $255,000,000 accepted as minimal by the Regents the preceding February.

In a separate request, the Regents asked for funds to provide a 7½ per cent increase in salaries and a little more than 3 per cent increase in fringe benefits for the faculty. The legislature approved the requests, but the Governor approved only a 5 per cent salary increase.[87]

The tuition question stayed alive throughout 1967. At a special meeting on the subject in August, Governor Reagan moved "that the Board of Regents adopt tuition as a policy of the University of California." [88] His motion was defeated, but later in the day the Regents agreed that a "charge" to be determined by a special committee be "paid by all resident students." It was not until the ensuing January that this committee presented a recommendation that additional student fees of $156 for three quarters be adopted. In April, however, this amount was substantially reduced, and the committee recommended an augmentation of only $81 a year.[89] The increase, together with the incidental fees already charged, were redesignated "registration fees" and totaled $300 for a three-quarter year. Most of the income from the new fees was earmarked for financial assistance for needy students and augmentation of student services.[90]

At the same time fees for California residents were increased, tuition for out-of-state students was increased from $327 to $400 a quarter.[91]

THE THIRTEENTH PRESIDENT

Throughout the debates and negotiations on budget and tuition that oc-curred during 1967, a key role was played by the University's vice-president for administration, Charles J. Hitch. He was the one called upon to explain the significance of the impending budget cuts to the chancellors in January, 1967, and to the Regents on many subsequent occasions. His budget staff provided the factual and analytical data used in determining final policy on the troublesome question of student fees. And when the budget was finally passed, Vice-President Hitch was the one who gave the Regents' Committee on Finance a detailed report on the University's ability to live with it.

The quiet-spoken vice-president was a graduate of the University of Ari-zona, a former graduate student at Harvard, and a former Rhodes Scholar and Fellow at Queens College, Oxford, where he taught economics for thir-teen years. He also served as visiting professor at the University of São Paulo, Brazil, in 1947, at UCLA in 1949–1950, and at Yale in 1957. Be-fore entering the Army during World War II, the young economist served with the United States Lend Lease mission in 1941–1942 and the War Production Board. In the Army, he was assigned to a unit analyzing the ef-fects of Allied air raids. In 1948, he became associated with the RAND Corporation, an elite nonprofit research and development organization. He was chairman of RAND's planning and research council when, in 1961, Robert McNamara called him to public service again as assistant secretary and comptroller of the United States Department of Defense.[92] Hitch's bril-liant record in making improvements in management procedures and mod-ernizing cost-accounting and budgeting processes for one of the govern-ment's largest and most complicated departments became well known among economists and management experts throughout the country. Through his writings and his contributions as a member of general scholarly committees and societies, he was also known and respected in academic cir-cles. Clark Kerr decided that Hitch was precisely the kind of person the University of California needed to insure that its continuing growth and ex-pansion were achieved economically and in accordance with sound finan-cial and business practices. He succeeded in convincing Hitch to leave the

Defense Department in 1965 to become vice-president—business and finance at the University.

In 1966, Hitch's title changed to that of vice-president of the University for administration, and he was made responsible for the coordination of the functions of vice-presidents for business and finance, physical planning and construction, and governmental relations and of the director of the budget.[93]

Because of his experience and position, Hitch was considered a logical candidate to succeed Clark Kerr in the presidency. But his public exposure in California had been limited, and, although he was very well known to the Regents and to many faculty leaders, the press considered him a "mystery man." More frequently mentioned candidates were the chancellors of the two largest campuses, Roger Heyns at Berkeley and Franklin Murphy at UCLA,[94] both of whom voluntarily withdrew their names from consideration. United States Secretary of Health, Education, and Welfare John W. Gardner was probably the most seriously considered nominee among several distinguished persons outside the University. All speculation ended in September, 1967, when the Regents approved the unanimous recommendation of their special committee on the selection of a president and named Hitch to the position effective January 1, 1968. The selection pleased Acting President Wellman, who called Hitch "probably the best qualified man in America to head this institution." [95] It also pleased a faculty advisory committee, which revealed that the new president's name had been on its "very small list of strongly favored candidates." [96] Former President Kerr was also enthusiastic, calling Hitch "an excellent scholar, an experienced administrator and a superb analyst." [97]

In accepting the presidency, Hitch issued a statement that indicated his concern that Californians understand and continue to support the University with the generosity demonstrated by previous generations. He realized that this was sometimes difficult, for, as he said, universities are "harbingers of change, . . . concerned with . . . the whole sweep of man's experience and with the scientific frontier. If you find a university that is not striking some sparks, you can assume that it is dead. . . ." [98] In a passage similar to one found in Daniel Coit Gilman's inaugural address ninety-six years earlier, he said, ". . . I count on the Regents to defend and protect the University's autonomy. The University measures its contribution to society and to individuals in years and decades, not in weeks or months; yet short-term strains and conflicts can be very dangerous to it. The Regents have the job of assuring that the University will endure for the long run, that it will not be overwhelmed by the public passions of the moment. I am confident of their capacity to fulfill this indispensable role. . . ." [99]

Specific major problems confronted by the new President were indicated by the trend of questions and answers at his first press conference after assuming office. One of them was the "financial squeeze," which he said was caused by "inelastic tax structures and burgeoning requirements on the states, particularly in the areas of medical aid, welfare and education." [100] Another was maintenance of quality as the University continues to grow. Student unrest, he said, was a "national fact of life . . ." for which "I've met nobody who thinks he has the answer." [101] Changes in the wording of the United States Selective Service laws which removed deferments for graduate students (except in the health sciences) beginning with the 1968–1969 academic year were also cited. These changes, Hitch said, would "gut graduate schools throughout the country." [102] On an earlier occasion, Hitch had mentioned the challenge of the University to "help all minority groups gain access to higher education." [103]

Perhaps the biggest job of all was to meet society's expectations. "A great deal is demanded of us," Hitch told the California School Board Association just before becoming president. "We carry the aspirations of a whole society as well as those of individual parents and students. We are expected to do many things that other social agencies, such as the home and the church, have failed to do. . . . We must make clear how many of 'our problems' are not generated by us but are reflections of society at large and what our role is . . . with respect to them." [104]

Chapter 28

CHANGE AND THE EVOLVING PURPOSE

THE ONE-HUNDRED-YEAR-OLD University of California is not a dream come true. Its founders envisioned something more modest, an institution for their own time. They wanted a place where California's youth could find as much book wisdom as their minds could hold and as much civility as they could learn from each other and from the examples of their teachers. They wanted a source of practical information about the crops they planted, the animals they raised, the mines they worked, and the roads, bridges, and buildings they constructed.

Fortunately, although the founders' vision of California's need for a University did not encompass the functions and potentials recognized today, their wisdom in giving the University of California flexible foundations, organizations, and government enabled it to change and grow. Because the founders imposed few restrictions, latter-day builders have been able to create one of the most imposing, influential, and complicated institutions of higher learning ever devised. Its nine general campuses, now in various stages of development and maturity, offer instruction to more than ninety thousand students. Large, sophisticated research stations explore the ocean depths, desert expanses, high mountain atmospheres, the nucleus of the atom and the outer reaches of the heavens. In more than 130 organized research units and more than 300 departments of instruction and research, scholars pose questions, seek answers, and pose new questions in a time-honored process that constantly enlarges the knowledge available to mankind.

This diversity of activity is, to a remarkable degree, the result of continuous interaction between ever-increasing amounts of new knowledge and the changing condition and values of the state and nation. Within the lifetime of the University of California, this interaction has occurred with increasing frequency and impact and has altered the University itself as much as it has altered the society it serves.

THE UNIVERSITY AND THE STATE

Californians are proud and practical citizens, fully aware of the importance of a good educational system to the welfare of their state. As the "crown jewel" of that system, the University has been treated by the budget-makers in Sacramento with a generosity that is particularly remarkable when one remembers that the founding legislators were naïvely under the impression that it would eventually become entirely self-sufficient.

Because such independence was not achieved, the legislature became not only the guarantor of operational funds but also an initiator of growth and expansion. Campuses at UCLA, Davis, and Santa Barbara were all established by legislative directive. UCLA's professional schools of law, medicine, and engineering were created in similar fashion. Several organized research units of the University were created by the legislature as part of its efforts to solve public problems. By 1966, 8.16 per cent of California's general-fund revenue was devoted to support of the University of California.[1] A long-range fiscal program delivered to the Regents in July, 1967, indicated that, in order to meet the University's needs, this would have to increase to nearly 10 per cent in 1971–1972 but could then decrease to 8.93 per cent in 1975–1976.[2] During the same period, the total operating expenditures of the University would reach at least one billion dollars. Because of increases in income from student fees, federal government grants and contracts, and other sources, however, the state's contribution to University support would decrease from 50 to 40 per cent of total expenditures.[3] During the same ten-year period, capital-outlay expenditures would average over $151,000,000 a year.[4] Of that amount, $80,000,000 in state funds would be needed.[5]

To support operations of the University in 1968–1969, the Regents asked the Governor and the legislature for $311,000,000.[6] It soon became clear, however, that this request would not be met. The Governor asked the legislature to approve only $280,000,000 for the University,[7] an amount President Hitch told the Regents was actually no more than the stripped-down budget of $264,000,000 the Regents finally requested (but did not get) in 1967–1968, with adjustments for normal salary increases and promotions.[8] If the University's quality was not to be impaired by financial inadequacies, the President advised, it might have to turn away as many as 7000 new students in 1968–1969.[9] In March, for the first time in the University's history, the Regents instructed the administration to hold back on admissions of students applying after March 1 until such time as it was certain that enough money would be available to accept larger enrollments without jeopardizing the quality of the University's instruction and research.[10] Made with great difficulty, and hopefully on a temporary basis, the Regents' choice of quality education over quantity education had far-reaching implications not only for the University but for other institutions of higher learning as well.

All of California's colleges and universities were confronted by the choice of quality versus quantity in one form or another in 1968. For public institutions, the choice was complicated by the state's financial difficulties— insufficient public revenues to pay for the services in demand. It was also complicated by continuing disagreement—only eight years after passage of California's Master Plan for Higher Education—over such questions as faculty salary differentials between systems of higher education, the independence of the University and state colleges from legislative management, the forms of college and university governance, and the nomenclature and functions of the various institutions. In 1968, an Orange County senator proposed a constitutional amendment that would place the Regents directly under the control of the legislature,[11] but his bill did not reach the floor. There was a campaign to rename California's state colleges so that they would be called state universities. There were proposals from legislators and independent students of higher education in the state that the terms of the Regents be reduced from sixteen to ten or eight years, and that some of the ex-officio Regents who held their positions on the Board by virtue of elective public office be removed. A preliminary proposal of a joint legislative committee on California Higher Education, created in the heat of the public reaction to Berkeley's rebellion in 1964, suggested the creation of a single system of public higher education, broken down into regional clusters, each of which would contain a university campus, state colleges, and one or more junior colleges.[12] Under this plan, the University of California would, in fact, cease to exist. Alteration of California's system of higher education was also subject to consideration by the state's Constitutional Revision Commission, which had been at work since 1964.

Historically, in times of crisis, the University has been able to depend upon the loyalty of its alumni, now numbering in excess of 250,000, and the majority of the legislature. An important factor in the University's legislative support has been the interest of the rural-dominated senate and of assemblymen from agricultural districts. The dividends of the state's investment in the University have been visible and impressive in the farming areas, and voters there have insisted that its efforts not be impaired. As recently as 1968, when organized research funds for the University were cut drastically, the budget bill passed with a provision that only 24.7 per cent of that cut could be taken in agricultural projects.[13]

The urbanization of California, which is expected to accelerate, creates new problems for the state and new opportunities for the University. Without diminishing services to the state's agricultural areas, the University must respond more visibly than in the past to the needs of the cities. In May, 1968, President Hitch recognized this responsibility by directing that the University on all of its campuses mobilize its resources to help deal with America's urban crisis. In a report to the Regents, he said that the effort would involve reorganization of University Extension "to carry thought and research from the campus to the heart of the city"; [14] would include an inventory of University research effort that might be helpful to cities; and would provide budgets for computer-aided studies of urban problems.[15] He announced that immediate steps were being taken to implement the program. These included provision of $1,000,000 for aid to disadvantaged students; strengthening teacher-training programs within the University; establishing a fair-employment coordinator in his own office to "push" the University's program for hiring members of minority groups; and attempting to recruit more minority-group students.[16] This effort, if fully pursued, will not only marshal the University's resources for service where they are desperately needed, but also promises to make the University a visible influence in parts of society that are seething with tension and controversy. It will therefore not only test the power of knowledge and intelligence as an answer to the urban crisis but will also test, more severely perhaps than ever before, the tolerance of Californians and their government for the direct involvement of the University in the sensitive issues that trouble the vital centers of their society.

THE REGENTS AS A SOURCE OF FLEXIBILITY

The University's ability to undertake new programs, such as a massive assault on urban problems, is ultimately derived from the broad powers entrusted to the Regents by the constitution of the state of California. That instrument gives the Regents full powers of organization and government, subject only to such legislative control "as may be necessary to insure compliance within the terms of the endowments of the university and the security of its funds." [17]

With this near-absolute power, the Regents can and do alter the size and mission of the University in response to the needs of the state and the growth of knowledge. None of the University's remarkable expansion, nor any of its distinction in diverse endeavors, could have been achieved without Regental consent. Much of it occurred through Regental initiative.

The flexibility of the Regents' policies has saved the University from obsolescence, and the Regents themselves have fought hard to preserve it. They have acceded, as in the legislature's establishment of the UCLA and Davis campuses, when failure to do so would clearly injure or restrict University endeavors. They have welcomed controlling legislation when it served to coordinate relationships between the University and other segments of California higher education, as did the Donohoe Act of 1960.[18] They also welcomed legislation controlling use of the University's name and facilities by people outside their jurisdiction. But during most of the University's first 100 years, they have zealously protected their independence.

Thus far in the University's history, the wisdom of granting the Regents independence and maximum authority over the institution's government has prevailed. In their relationships with the public and the government, the broad outline of the Regents' authority was essentially the same in 1968 as it was in 1868. Internally, Regental authority was still supreme, but it was delegated generously (if not always permanently) to the president and the chancellors as new campuses develop, as old ones grow, and as research and public service functions of the University become more elaborate and involved.

THE CHANGING PRESIDENCY

As conceived by the Organic Act, the president of the University was "President of the several Faculties and the executive head of the institution in all its departments, except as herein otherwise provided." [19] The exceptions involved business management, maintenance of buildings and grounds, and other such matters considered functions of the secretary of the Regents. Only with the arrival of Benjamin Ide Wheeler and the first substantial delegation of Regental authority to the president in budget matters, hiring and firing of employees, and in recommending appointment and promotion of faculty members did a strong administration begin to exist.

The position was vastly enlarged by President Sproul. When he became president in 1930, he vacated a position with four titles: comptroller, secretary of the Regents, land agent, and vice-president. One of his early presidential decisions was that these positions should be divided in such a way that more administrative functions came under either the direct supervision of the president or the joint supervision of the president and the Regents. By acknowledging, much more completely than did his predecessors, the validity of the concept of faculty self-government, Sproul not only enlarged the faculty's responsibilities, but drew a clearer line between academic and administrative affairs.

During Sproul's twenty-eight years in office the University first assumed its many-campus, many-function form. Although President Sproul was an instrument of that growth, he was uncomfortable with the loss of the personal involvement he once enjoyed in the management of its many parts and was slow to give up the close relationships that had historically existed between the president, the faculty, and student leaders, particularly at Berkeley. He strove to keep the University a relatively simple and centralized administrative system, even as it grew larger, and his policy of creating two large general campuses and several smaller liberal arts colleges was consistent with that approach.

When Clark Kerr became president in 1958, it was clear that the slow evolutionary growth of the University as envisaged by Sproul could not accommodate the enormous enrollments expected within the decade. All campuses of the University had to become bigger than originally planned by President Sproul and they would have to grow so rapidly that the president could not personally supervise all of the details of their development and operation. Many responsibilities once held by members of the president's staff were accordingly shifted to personnel on the several campuses.

Another, more subtle kind of decentralization of administrative authority took place in the course of the University's natural maturation. Certain administrators, faculty committees, departments of instruction and research, student governments, and other internal agencies acted with increasing independence in matters of routine. The president became involved only when radical innovation or a significant departure from accustomed procedure or policy was contemplated.

By 1968, the President of the University of California could find little in common with the daily life of the legendary Benjamin Ide Wheeler, who personally attended to many details of the University's administration, greeted students by name as he crossed the Berkeley campus on horseback, or offered paternal inspiration and advice at fortnightly University meetings.

In Clark Kerr's view, "the president in the multiversity is leader, educator, creator, initiator, wielder of power, pump; he is *also* officeholder, caretaker, inheritor, consensus-seeker, persuader, bottleneck. But he is mostly a mediator." [20] His principal tasks were to preserve peace among the many segments of the institution and to inspire and encourage progress.[21] In the public view, the president is also responsible for keeping the University at peace with the world. In a society where the public point of view is by no means homogeneous and is often inconsistent, that assignment is hopelessly impossible unless the president arbitrarily restricts the University's work and represses belief, expression, and action of students and faculty members both on and off the campuses. In lieu of peace, therefore, the president must offer interpretation and defense, and be prepared to act as a lightning rod for abuse and criticism when the public and its spokesmen are dissatisfied. Until the public understands his role and authority better than it does now, however, the president of the University must tolerate insecurity as bad but unavoidable company as he *accepts* the opportunity for leadership, exciting endeavor, and prestige that are the more rewarding benefits of his office.

THE ACADEMIC PRECINCTS

The University of California's faculty has enjoyed autonomy from the beginning. The concept of an Academic Senate for the "general administration" of the University was contained in the Organic Act, and, in 1883 (although minutes of the Senate attest to its prior existence for fourteen years) the Regents formally directed the faculty to organize such a body for the exercise of duties "enjoined upon it by law, and such other powers as may be conferred by the Board of Regents." [22]

Whatever its organic basis, the power of the faculty is immense. They are responsible for all of the University's work in teaching and research and most of it in public service. They are the only people genuinely knowledgeable about academic affairs, and their decisions concerning methods of teaching and content of courses of instruction are, for all practical purposes, decisive in the formulation of educational policy.

In the early decades of the University, the faculty had reasonably direct access to the Regents, and although they had no formal authority in personnel and budget actions, they exercised influence in such matters informally. During the Wheeler period, the presidency was strengthened, but, largely because of the dominating influence of Wheeler himself, faculty authority was weakened. After Wheeler resigned, the faculty sought to regain and enhance its earlier influence by demanding a stronger voice in the selection and promotion of their colleagues, opportunity to participate in the University's budget-making, and more authority for organizing their own government. This revolt marked the beginning of the strong faculty government that characterized the University for the remainder of its first century. Faculty government was further strengthened by President Robert Gordon Sproul, who drew a sharper line than his predecessors between decisions that required academic instead of administrative competence. During Clark Kerr's administration, faculty government was restructured so that the faculties of the larger campuses, and most particularly the one at Berkeley, lost what amounted to a veto power, and Universitywide academic policy became the province of an Academic Council composed of representatives of all of the campus divisions of the senate.

Although legally subordinate to both the Regents and the president of the University, the faculty functions virtually as a parallel institution. It has its own rules and regulations. It has its own code of ethics. It has external allegiances to professional and scholarly traditions and, increasingly, to outside sources of financial support.

Most of the educational policies that fell under student attack before, during, and after the Berkeley rebellion of 1964 were not instituted by the Regents or the administration. Instead, they were practices that had acquired sanction largely by tolerance over a long period of time. Emphasis upon graduate instruction and research to the detriment of undergraduate teaching; the remoteness of professors from their students; the impersonality of advising and counseling procedures; and the inflexibility of course and grade requirements were all rooted in academic practices only the faculty can control. Educational reform, though it could be requested and encouraged by the Regents and administration, was possible only if the faculty assumed responsibility for initiating it.

Through such studies as the Muscatine and Kneller reports, and through the work of new committees and boards of education innovation and development on several campuses, the faculty has clearly recognized the need for educational reforms. As educational innovation and experimentation have occurred, the campuses of the University have become more exciting academically. Students are able to find more courses that are relevant to the concerns of their own generation. They also find greater variety of learning situations—in lecture halls, recitation rooms, seminars, tutorials, group discussion, and self-instruction. Continuing innovation of this sort may well be an increasingly prominent activity of the University during the early decades of its second century.

THE QUESTION OF STUDENT POWER

One of the lessons of the student rebellion in 1964 was that the voice of students in University affairs—quite apart from "student" affairs—deserves a hearing. On some campuses of the University, there are students on several administrative and faculty committees and new channels through which students can express their concerns with education policy have been opened.

As expressed by chancellors and deans, the verdict on student participation in academic and administrative councils thus far is generally favorable. But no one pretends that it yet constitutes more than advisory power for the students. And only a few radicals advocate that it should be more except in nonacademic matters, including discipline, that exclusively or predominantly concern students.

It did not occur to the University's founders that students might have some role in the University other than that of customer for the institution's services. Student activities and student government were extemporized by the students themselves to fill the voids they found in University life. A latter-day extemporization of this sort is now found on the new campuses of the University, where the faculties and chancellors prefer that student life evolve naturally from student needs and interests, but on the older campuses, student activities and student government have been institutionalized for many years. At Berkeley, traditional student activities retained some vigor in 1968, but they have lost much of their prestige and their ability to influence attitudes and loyalties of the total student community. In the postrebellion years, student government at Berkeley was captured by that faction of students that sought deeper involvement of students in educational reforms and social and political action. Graduate students, particularly in the social sciences and humanities, could identify with these new programs, although they had in 1959 led the graduate-student movement that rejected involvement in the activity-oriented ASUC. On the grounds that no student government could be effective unless all students were a part of it, the ASUC has welcomed this interest and has persisted, against adminstrative advice and directives, in recognizing graduate students as members.

The dispute over graduate-student membership in the ASUC was lively throughout most of 1967. When the ASUC Senate persistently disregarded criteria and conditions of graduate-student membership imposed by Chancellor Heyns, he took action to curb its authority. On November 28, 1967, he transferred the ASUC Senate's power to collect and allocate ASUC funds to a new sixteen-member Union Program and Facilities Board (UPFB) composed of only eight students, the executive director of the ASUC, representatives of the chancellor, the dean of students, the dean of the graduate division, two faculty members, and representatives of the alumni association and nonacademic employees.[23] In resentment of the Chancellor's action, the ASUC Senate declared itself independent of his authority in January, 1968.

The postrebellion deterioration of student government at Berkeley was given detailed attention by a Study Commission on University Governance, composed of student and faculty members and reporting to both the Academic Senate and the ASUC. The majority members of the commission said that student government at Berkeley "is presently mired in a Serbonian Bog from which there can be no escape. Its legal standing is ambiguous; its political power is nonexistent; and the miasma of conflicting theories, incompatible functions, contrary procedures, and impossible rules which envelops the terrain makes it impossible for even the most earnest pilgrim to find his way to higher ground." [24] To remedy the situation, the commission proposed that an enlarged ASUC Senate assume responsibility for general student policy, while management of the student union and the conduct of student activities would be entrusted to a new Student Union Board of Directors.[25]

Although many students resented the Chancellor's creation of the Union Program and Facilities Board in the fall of 1967, they favored, in principle, the division of the ASUC's power and authority. Through negotiations with the Chancellor, an agreement was worked out by May 20, 1968, which would create three new agencies.[26] An enlarged ASUC Senate would continue to have concern for student programs in educational development, community projects, and student orientation. A second "Activities Board" with nine student members and one nonstudent member would supervise traditional activities. The third, a Facilities Board, would have seven student and five nonstudent representatives and would manage the physical assets and personnel of the ASUC.

For student activists, the shape of student government was important only to the extent that it might limit or enlarge their ability to engage in political and social action. Rarely sponsored by student governments, student rallies and protests were frequent throughout the fall of 1967. Some of them had civil-rights themes. Others protested the continuing war in Vietnam and the selective service system and weapons industries that sustained United States effort in that conflict.

At the end of the University's first hundred years, student militancy had become a national phenomenon. It had changed the style of extracurricular life not only at Berkeley, but also at other campuses and universities throughout the world. As it became more prevalent, it became increasingly difficult for the president and the chancellors to deal with. Attempts to develop orderly procedures for dissent and grievance were often rejected by students as attempts to cripple their effectiveness in seeking social reform and change. As students work and hope to make a better world, they are suspicious of all that has been done before, and are not yet certain whether their University is a friend or foe of their endeavor. This indecision is partly a symptom of the skepticism and mistrust typical of their generation. It is also a result of the fact that the University itself has changed and grown, shedding like outworn skin some of the concepts of its purposes enunciated by its past leaders.

THE EVOLVING PURPOSE

John W. Dwinelle and his fellow authors of the University's Organic Act wrote: "The University shall have for its design, to provide instruction and complete education in all the departments of science, literature, art, industrial and professional pursuits, and general education, and also special courses of instruction for the professions of agriculture, the mechanic arts, mining, military science, civil engineering, law, medicine, and commerce. . . ." [27] As a statement of purpose, the provision better suited a well-developed New England college (which is what most American universities were in those days) than they did a modern university. No mention was made of research. In other passages of the act, requiring the distribution of information, seeds, and plants to farmers, a public-service function is implied but not elaborated.

Later versions of a statement of purpose for the University of California were rhetorical, designed to inspire appreciation and enthusiasm for the University and to alert the public to the speaker's point of view. The important ones came from University presidents. Daniel Coit Gilman spoke of the University as a "group of agencies organized to advance the arts and sciences of every sort, and to train young men as scholars for all the intellectual callings of life. . . ." [28] He also urged upon Californians the examples of "the older institutions" which "are mostly complex, including a great variety of faculties, colleges, chairs, halls, scholarships, and collections, more or less closely bound together as an establishment, endowed with investments, privileges and immunities, and regarded as indispensable both to the moral and material progress of the community." [29]

Consistent with these views, Gilman was instrumental in the creation of the University's early professional schools and the establishment of the Lick Observatory as a part of the University. His attitude was hospitable to research, and his personal interest in the public lecture series conducted by University faculty members at the Mechanics Institute in San Francisco was antecedent to the development of a more sophisticated University of California Extension.

Although Gilman's concept of the University was "comprehensive," instruction remained its dominant function (in all fields but agriculture) well into the 1930s. The University was not richly endowed in the beginning, and instruction required most of the money available to it. Benjamin Ide Wheeler not only accepted this reality, he regarded it as almost a virtue. In his view, "The supreme purpose of the University is to provide living beings for the service of society—good citizens for the State." [30] Although he said "between research and instruction there can be no fixed boundary line," [31] the faculty of the University during most of his presidency was best known and remembered for its teaching ability. Wheeler himself accepted responsibility for making the University a proper moral influence upon its students. Like presidents of the older American colleges, who filled the imposing chairs of moral, ethical, and religious philosophy as a means of reaching the spirit and soul as well as the minds of students, Wheeler used the University meetings to talk of such virtues as honesty, loyalty, and generosity as essential equipment of the University of California man.

In March, 1932, President Robert Gordon Sproul pronounced the closest thing to a University of California creed that has ever been available. It was derived from the ideas of Gilman and Wheeler, but influenced by the nation's fears for the validity of its political and economic system.

> 1. We believe that the University should be the repository of the highest learning and best traditions of our democracy. This implies libraries and similar collections which represent the accumulated knowledge of the human race. It implies, also, the maintenance of the highest ideal of human behavior and human action to which the civilized world has attained, and a never ending effort to realize these or better ideals which the wisdom of man may from time to time dictate.
> 2. We believe that the University should be the training ground for the scholars needed in every generation to carry the light of learning forward into the darkness of the unknown, of the teachers in high schools and colleges and universities whose devoted lives must form the basis for the intellectual advancement of our country, of professional men in medicine, law, dentistry, pharmacy, engineering, agriculture, business, and public life upon whose integrity and proficiency depend much of the mental, physical, and material well-being of our people, and finally, of that large proportion of the state's population which is capable of studying and profiting by the various branches of knowledge beyond the realm of the secondary schools.[32]

At this point in Sproul's presidency, the University was still instruction-oriented to a great extent, although research was beginning to command more attention and financial support. Later in his administration, Sproul began to speak about teaching, research, and public service as the trinity of the University's purpose.

By stressing, far more than any of his predecessors, the importance of public service as a University function, Sproul helped to prepare the way for development of large-scale, subsidized research. Thereafter the University no longer had to rely upon the skill and intelligence of its graduates to make contributions to society. Its faculty and staff, using the University's research facilities, could make such contributions directly. The University's sources of support were diversified as industry and the federal government began to share some of the financial burdens of the state.

Talking about the modern American university in general, Clark Kerr said that "the ends are already given—the preservation of the eternal truths, the creation of new knowledge, the improvement of service wherever truth and knowledge of high order may serve the needs of man." [33] He thus succinctly validated the purposes expressed by his predecessor presidents at the University of California. What he added, however, was a philosophy that the University's purpose had to remain flexible. He spoke less frequently of purpose than he spoke of "uses" of the University, a concept that invites conjecture that the University might have as many purposes as it has users. The virtue of this view is that it does not restrain growth, experimentation, or innovation. The enormous growth achieved during Kerr's presidency might not have been if he had defined the University's function more rigidly or more narrowly.

In 1967, at the suggestion of Regent William E. Forbes, attempts were made to draw up a "white paper . . . that would not take more than 20 minutes to read, that would state in affirmative, unpolitical, noncontroversial terms the University point of view. . . ." [34] The effort failed because none of the drafts that were prepared could satisfy all of those whose approval was needed. This failure to commit the University's "point of view" to paper is, in a way, more eloquent than success might ever have been. It suggests that the University means many things to many people. It also testifies that the trinity of "teaching, research, and public service" may no longer be profound enough to explain the great size, the bewildering complexity, the remarkably variety, and the amazing flexibility of the University of California. Although there may be grave dangers in expanding an institution beyond a purpose readily comprehensible to all who perceive it and are touched by its endeavors, it may be advantageous to take that risk if the full impact of truth, learning, and wisdom is to be felt in all human endeavor. The University's commitment to that risk seems clear. It was reiterated by President Hitch in his inaugural address on May 23, 1968, when he said: "As we face the new century ahead, let us pledge our united efforts to build a University that is as large in spirit as the times demand." [35]

Notes

Chapter 1

1   Donald G. Tewksbury, *The Founding of American Colleges and Universities Before the Civil War* (New York, 1932), 1–28, 75–78.

2   *The Twenty Third Report of the American Home Missionary Society* (New York, 1849), 61.

3   Samuel H. Willey, "Diary, and Common-Place Book," entry for March 4, 1849 (University of California archives, Berkeley).

4   Letter from Samuel H. Willey to E. W. Gilman at Yale, May 1, 1869 (in "Letters of Samuel Hopkins Willey to Rev. E. W. Gilman and Sherman Day," University of California archives, Berkeley).

5   *Ibid.*

6   William Warren Ferrier, *Origin and Development of the University of California* (Berkeley, 1930), 93. This work quotes a letter to Larkin from his cousin, William M. Rogers, pastor of a Congregational church in Boston and overseer of Harvard College, who urged Larkin to become a patron of the Benicia university.

7   *Ibid.,* 102.

8   *Ibid.,* 112.

9   *Ibid.,* 98.

10   Original subscription list for college to be located at San Jose, May, 1850 (in "Documents of the College of California, 1849–1869," 7a, University of California archives, Berkeley).

11   Samuel H. Willey, "History of the College of California," *Papers of the California Historical Society* (San Francisco, 1887), I, ii, 6.

12   William Warren Ferrier, *Ninety Years of Education in California, 1846–1936* (Berkeley, 1937), 187, 199, 124; American Council on Education, *American Universities and Colleges* (9th ed.; Washington, D. C., 1964), 215.

13   Writers on the history of California education (Swett, Cloud, Ferrier) agree that there were few schools in the territory at the beginning of the American occupation. Counting the few they describe supplies a number considerably under twenty.

14   John Swett, *History of the Public School System of California* (San Francisco, 1876), 14–21.

15   Ferrier, *Ninety Years . . .* , 79.

16   *Ibid.,* 68–69.

17   Frederick Rudolph, *The American College and University* (New York, 1962), 48.

18   Ferrier, *Ninety Years . . .* , 152. Willey first learned of the project during a stopover in Sacramento on his first trip outside of Monterey after his arrival in California. There he met Rev. S. V. Blakeslee, who had come to California by an overland route, arriving in September, 1859, and had already obtained pledges for support of an institution of higher learning in California from men in San Jose. It was on the strength of these pledges that the whole College of California movement got underway.

19   Willey, "Diary, . . . ," entry for March 11, 1849.

20   William Warren Ferrier, *Henry Durant, First President, University of California* (Berkeley, 1942), 9–10.

21   As quoted in Ferrier, *Henry Durant . . .* , 17. Willey's remarks at convocation at Founders' Rock, 1896.

22   As quoted in Ferrier, *Ninety Years . . .* , 180.

23   As quoted in Ferrier, *Origin and Development . . .* , 128.

24   Edsen Adams, *Oakland's Early History* (Oakland, 1932), 9.

25   As quoted in Ferrier, *Origin and Development . . .* , 128.

26   *Ibid.*

27   As quoted in Ferrier, *Henry Durant . . .* , 15.

28   William Carey Jones, *Illustrated History of the University of California* (rev. ed.; San Francisco, 1901), 27. This building is colorfully described as a *"fandango* house." Both Jones and Ferrier agree on the location of the building. In Joseph E. Baker, *Past and Present of Alameda County, California* (Chicago, 1914), 356, there is mention of a Christmas dinner held by American settlers in Oakland in 1852: "The feast was held in an abandoned dance hall at *Fourth* and Broadway."

29   Letter from Henry Durant to Rev. E. B. Walsworth, May 27, 1853 (in "The Walsworth Correspondence," University of California archives, Berkeley).

30   As quoted in Ferrier, *Origin and Development . . .* , 131.

31   *Ibid.,* 128.

32   Henry Durant, "An Interview with President Durant on the Origin of the College and University of California," 2–4 (manuscript of transcribed interview, 1873, University of California archives, Berkeley).

33   *Ibid.,* 6–7.

34   *Ibid.,* 7–9.

35   Ferrier, *Origin and Development . . .* , 141.

36   *Ibid.*

37   Letter from Samuel Willey to Rev. E. B. Walsworth, September 26, 1853 (in "The Walsworth Correspondence," University of California archives, Berkeley).

38   "Samuel Bookstover Bell, D. C., and His Connection with Founding of State's First College, that Later Grew to be the University of California," *Grizzly Bear,* xxii (March, 1918), 11.

39   Josiah Royce, *California* ("American Commonwealths," ed. E. Scudder; Boston, New York, 1886), 424.

40   Ferrier, *Origin and Development . . .* , 143.

41   Horace Bushnell, *Movement for a University of California: A Statement to the Public, by the Trustees of the College of California, and An Appeal, By Dr. Bushnell,* 9–23 (in *Pamphlets on the College of California,* I, i, University of California archives, Berkeley).

42   *Ibid.,* 16.

43   Letter from Henry Durant to Rev. E. B. Walsworth, November 20, 1857 (in "The Walsworth Correspondence," University of California archives, Berkeley). The selection of the site was not officially approved until March, 1858. Durant's letter to Walsworth, however, speaks of the agreements for purchase as accomplished fact.

44   *Ibid.*

45   Willey, "History . . . ," 57.

46   *The Incorporation, Organic Basis, and Laws of the College of California* (San Francisco, 1862), 7 (in College of California, "Miscellany," iii, University of California archives, Berkeley).

47   *Ibid.*

48   *Ibid.*

49   Specifications relative to sale of college property in Oakland to Isaac M. Brayton (in College of California, "Letter Book," no. 70, University of California archives, Berkeley).

50   Letter from Sherman Day to Board of Trustees of the College of California, June 14, 1862 (in College of California, "Reports Made to the Board of Trustees," 9, University of California archives, Berkeley).

51   Letter from Rev. Milton Badger to Samuel H. Willey, February 19, 1853, as quoted in Ferrier, *Origin and Development . . . ,* 123.

52   As quoted in Ferrier, *Origin and Development . . . ,* 216.

53   *Ibid.,* 219.

54   Willey, "History . . . ," 84.

55   S. H. Willey, "Report on Finances and General Statement, 1862" (in College of California, "Reports Made to the Board of Trustees," 8, University of California archives, Berkeley).

Chapter 2

1   Cardinal Leonidas Goodwin, *The Establishment of State Government in California, 1846–1850* (New York, 1914), 230–32.

2   *Iowa Official Register* (1904), 65.

3   Donald G. Tewksbury, *The Founding of American Colleges and Universities Before the Civil War* (New York, 1932), 185–87.

4   This reference to branches of the University was probably borrowed from Article X, Section 5, of the Constitution of Michigan (1835), which undoubtedly was the original source of the Iowa provision (see: Wilfred B. Shaw [ed.], *The University of Michigan: An Encyclopedic Survey* [Ann Arbor, 1931], I, 137).

5   David Barrows Stewart, "The Development of Constitutional Provisions Pertaining to Education in California" (unpublished Ed.D. dissertation, School of Education, University of California), 80; Goodwin, 194.

6   California, Legislature, *Journal* (1851), 759.

7   *Ibid.*

8   Report of the California Senate Committee on Buildings and Grounds, 1850; correspondence of General Guadalupe Vallejo regarding the location of the state capital in Vallejo (California State Archives, Sacramento).

9   California, Legislature, *Journal* (1851), 78–81.

10   William Warren Ferrier, *Origin and Development of the University of California* (Berkeley, 1930), 25.

11   Shaw, II, 267. Michigan eventually received $548,744 for its seminary-of-learning lands.

12   California, Senate, *Bill 235* (California State Archives, Sacramento).

13   California, Superintendent of Public Instruction, *Seventh Annual Report,* 11 (California State Archives, Sacramento).

14   *Ibid.*

15   California, Assembly, *Bill 267,* 1860 (California State Archives, Sacramento).

16   *Ibid.*

17   *Ibid.*

18   California, Assembly, *Journal* (1862), 38.

19   *Ibid.,* 642.

20   Ferrier, 43.

21   U.S., *Statutes at Large* (1862), c. CXXX, sec. 4, p. 504.

22   Ferrier, 235–237.

23   *Report Relative to Establishing a State University, made in accordance with a concurrent resolution passed at the fourteenth session of the legislature* (in *Pamphlets on the College of California,* I, 12, University of California archives, Berkeley).

24   J. D. Whitney, *An Address Delivered at the Celebration of the Sixth Anniversary of the College of California, Held in Oakland, June 6, 1861* (San Francisco, 1861), 47 (in *Pamphlets on the College of California,* I, 7).

25   *Report Relative to Establishing a State University . . . ,* 25.

26   *Ibid.,* 23.

27   *Ibid.,* 24–25.

28   *Ibid.,* 28.

29   California, *Statutes* (1866), c. CCCCVIII, sec. 1, pp. 504–505.

30   *Ibid.,* sec. 13, p. 507.

31   *Ibid.,* sec. 27, p. 509.

32   Minutes of the Board of Directors of the Agricultural, Mining and Mechanical Arts College, June 20, 1866, 11 (California State Archives, Sacramento).

33 Minutes of the Board of Directors of the Agricultural, Mining and Mechanical Arts College, September 7, 1866, 13 (California State Archives, Sacramento).

34 *Ibid.*

35 *Deed Book H,* 111; *Deed Book I,* 61 (Alameda County Recorder's Office, Oakland).

36 Henry Durant, "An Interview with President Durant on the Origin of the College and University of California," 18–19 (manuscript of transcribed interview, 1873, University of California archives, Berkeley).

37 Mary Tennet Carleton, "The Byrnes of Berkeley," *California Historical Society Quarterly,* XVII (March, 1938), 41–42.

38 Durant, 19.

39 Benjamin Silliman, Jr., *The Truly Practical Man, Necessarily an Educated Man: Oration Delivered at the Commencement of the College of California, June 5, 1867* (in *Pamphlets on the College of California,* I).

40 Willey, 207.

41 Durant, 20–21.

42 Minutes of the Board of Trustees of the College of California, October 9, 1867, Vol. I, pp. 357–358 (Office of the Secretary of the Regents, Berkeley).

43 Report from the Office of the Board of Directors of the Agricultural, Mining and Mechanical Arts College, November 25, 1867 (California State Archives, Sacramento).

44 California, Assembly, *Journal* (1867), 45.

45 Ferrier, 272.

Chapter 3

1 Don A. Allen, Sr., *Legislative Sourcebook: The California Legislature and Reapportionment, 1849–1965* (Assembly of the State of California, 1965), 272.

2 Bill from the *Daily and Weekly Examiner* to the Regents (in Regents, "Correspondence and Papers," Box 1, Folder 4, University of California archives, Berkeley).

3 This procedure now appears contrived and complicated. The Organic Act originally provided for the election of honorary Regents by alumni of the University as soon as they numbered one hundred. Because of strong objections by one state senator, however, the provision was changed to require the procedure as described. The idea, apparently, was to balance the number of appointed Regents with the number of elected Regents, so that the governor could not control the full Board. The whole "honorary" classification was eliminated by the revision of the Political Code in 1872.

4 Leonard Ascher, "Lincoln's Administration and the New Almaden Scandal," *The Pacific Historical Review,* V, i (March, 1936), 42–43.

5 Ferrier says five of the eight appointees were Democrats (see: William

Warren Ferrier, *Origin and Development of the University of California* [Berkeley, 1930], 291).

6   Letter from Samuel H. Willey to Rev. Theron Baldwin, September 1, 1869 (in "Documents of the College of California, 1849–1869," 10, University of California archives, Berkeley).

7   California, *Statutes* (1867–1868), c. CCXLIV, sec. 18, p. 256.

8   *Ibid.*, sec. 13, p. 253.

9   Minutes of the Board of Regents, June 19, 1868, Vol. I, pp. 9–12 (Office of the Secretary of the Regents, University of California).

10   *University of California; Report and Resolutions of the Special Committee on the Organization of the Colleges of the University, Adopted by the Board of Regents, July 2, 1868, 5, 6, 10 (in Pamphlets on the University of California, 1861–1875,* I, ix, University of California archives, Berkeley).

11   Minutes of the Board of Regents, July 29, 1868, Vol. I, p. 28.

12   Julian Dana, *The Man Who Built San Francisco: A Study of Ralston's Journey with Banners* (New York, 1937).

13   Minutes of the Board of Regents, April 5, 1869, Vol. I, p. 77.

14   The presentation of the Supreme Court cases draws the burden of Willey's criticism in his memoranda of 1888 purported to show "that the transfer of the College of California to the State of California for the foundation of a University was not accomplished in such a spirit and manner as might have been looked for, on the part of the authorities and representatives of the state." ("Documents of the College of California, 1849–1869," 2, i, University of California archives, Berkeley.) The University president who won Willey's confidence in the University was Benjamin Ide Wheeler.

15   Minutes of the Board of Regents, October 22, 1869, Vol. I, p. 110; "Receipts and Disbursements of the University in Report of the Board of Regents of the University of California" March 23, 1868–December 1869, *Appendix to Journals of Senate and Assembly of the Eighteenth Session of the Legislature of the State of California* (Sacramento, 1870), II, 8.

16   *Report of the Regents of the University of California, Relative to the Operation and Progress of the Institution* (Sacramento, 1872), 14–15 (in President, *Report of the President of the University on Behalf of the Regents . . . 1869–79,* University of California archives, Berkeley).

17   *Ibid.*, 15.

18   Ralston's story is told in Julian Dana's *The Man Who Built San Francisco* and George D. Lyman's *Ralston's Ring: California Plunders the Comstock Lode* (New York, London, 1937).

19   Letter from Executive Committee of the Regents to Wright and Saunders, August 26, 1869 (in Regents, "Correspondence and Papers," Box 1, Folder 20).

20   Minutes of the Board of Regents, June 14, 1869; Vol. I, p. 91; Letter from Diaper and Saeltzer to the Regents, June 14, 1869 (in Regents, "Correspondence and Papers," Box 1, Folder 20).

21   Letter from Wright and Saunders to the Executive Committee of the Regents, August 27, 1869 (in Regents, "Correspondence and Papers," Box 1, Folder 20).

22   Memorandum of Agreement made August 31, 1869, between the Executive Committee of the Regents and Kenitzer and Farquharson, Architects (in Regents, "Correspondence and Papers," Box 1, Folder 20).

23   The fee for these services was $5,000, but only $2,500 was actually paid, because only one of the buildings was built under Farquharson's direction.

24   This was approximately where Sather Gate now stands.

25   Minutes of the Board of Regents, April 1, 1873, Vol. I, p. 305.

26   Minutes of the Board of Regents, September 6, 1873, Vol. I, pp. 328–329.

27   *University of California: Report . . . of the Special Committee on the Organization of the Colleges of the University . . .*, 3.

28   California, *Statutes* (1867–1868), c. CCCXIX, sec. 2, pp. 357–358.

29   "Report of the Board of Regents of the University of California," 8, *Appendix to Journals of Senate and Assembly of the Eighteenth Session of the Legislature of the State of California* (Sacramento, 1870), II, 8.

30   California, *Statutes* (1867–1868), c. CCCCXLVI, sec. 7, p. 588.

31   *University of California: Report . . . of the Special Committee on the Organization of the Colleges of the University . . .*, 8.

32   Paul W. Gates, "California's Agricultural Lands," *Pacific Historical Review*, XXX, ii (May, 1961), 109.

33   California, *Statutes* (1867–1868), c. CCXLIV, sec. 20, p. 257.

34   Minutes of the Board of Regents, June 25, 1868, Vol. I, p. 15.

35   Gates, 108.

36   U.S., *Statutes at Large* (1867–1869), c. LV, sec. 4, p. 68; U.S., *Statutes at Large* (1869–1871), c. CXXVI, p. 581.

37   Gates points out that similar privileges were enjoyed by Thomas B. Valentine, to whom 13,316 acres of public land scrip were granted in 1872 to satisfy his claim in a land-grant contest settled in his favor after the properties actually in dispute were in hands from which they could not be readily repossessed.

38   Letter from Isaac Friedlander to Henry Haight, February 8, 1869 (in Regents, "Correspondence and Papers," Box 1, Folder 12).

39   Gates, 112.

40   Gates, 120–121.

41   Frederick Rudolph, *The American College and University* (New York, 1862), 252.

42   Minutes of the Board of Regents, January 26, 1870, Vol. I, p. 124.

43   California, *Statutes* (1869–1870), c. CCCCLX, sec. 1, p. 668.

44   *Report of the Regents . . . , Relative to the Operation and Progress of the Institution*, 20.

45   California, *Statutes* (1871–1872), c. CCCXCIX, sec. 1, p. 554.

46   California, *Statutes* (1871–1872), c. DVIII, sec. 1, p. 747.

47   *University of California: Report . . . of the Special Committee on the Organization of the Colleges of the University . . .*, 2.

48   It was the difference between this amount and his professional salary of $300 a month that LeConte forfeited in the financial pinch of 1870.

49   This was possibly W. P. Trowbridge, a pioneer of Yale's Scientific School and thus a colleague of Daniel C. Gilman.

50   Ferrier, 327.

Chapter 4

1   As quoted in the introduction to Joseph LeConte, *Ware Sherman: A Journal of Three Months' Personal Experience in the Last Days of the Confederacy* (Berkeley, 1937), xix. This story of the LeContes' coming to the University of California is contained in an introduction to Joseph LeConte's memoir of Civil War experiences. The introduction was written by his daughter, Caroline.

2   Regents, "Correspondence and Papers," Box 1, Folder 15 (University of California archives, Berkeley).

3   After his election to the University faculty, Carr obligingly nominated McMynn for the professorship in mathematics. (See letter from Ezra S. Carr to the Executive Committee and Board of Regents of the University of California, July 15, 1869, in Regents, "Correspondence and Papers," Box 1, Folder 15.)

4   Ulysses S. Grant, *Personal Memoirs* (New York, 1885), II, 143–145.

5   Merle Curti and Vernon Carstensen, *The University of Wisconsin: A History, 1848–1925* (Madison, 1949), I, 180–181.

6   *Ibid.*, 180.

7   Letter from William T. Welcker to Andrew Moulder, April 28, 1869 (in Regents, "Correspondence and Papers," Box 1, Folder 15).

8   California, *Statutes* (1867–1869), c. CCXLIV, sec. 18, p. 256.

9   *Ibid.*

10   Minutes of the Academic Senate, in "Record of the Academic Senate," p. 1 (Office of the Academic Senate, University of California, Berkeley). At the meeting, the faculty decided that the final examination should have weight equal to the term's work in determining a student's class standing.

11   *Statutes of the University of California: Rules of Order and General Regulations Adopted by the Board of Regents of the University, December 13, 1869* (Sacramento, 1872), (in *Pamphlets on the University of California, 1861–1875* III, 5, University of California archives, Berkeley).

12   Regents, "Correspondence and Papers," Box 1, (1867–1871), Folder 34.

13   *Ibid.*

14   California, *Statutes* (1869–1870), c. V, p. 4.

15   Letter from John LeConte to Andrew Moulder, January 17, 1870 (in Regents, "Correspondence and Papers," Box 1, Folder 48).

16   Minutes of the Board of Regents, April 12, 1870, Vol. I, pp. 133–134, (Office of the Secretary of the Regents, University of California, Berkeley).

17   Minutes of the Board of Regents, May 25, 1870, Vol. I, 138.

18   *Ibid.*, p. 139.

19   U.S., *Statutes at Large* (1862), c. CXXX, sec. 4, p. 504.

20   Memorial from the Board of Trustees of the Mechanics' Institute to the legislature, January 25, 1870, as quoted in William Warren Ferrier, *Origin and Development of the University of California* (Berkeley, 1930), 309.

21   Minutes of the Board of Regents, July 19, 1870, Vol. I, p. 151.

22   Letter from John LeConte to Governor Henry Haight, July 30, 1870 (in Regents, "Correspondence and Papers," Box 1, Folder 46).

23   Minutes of the Academic Senate, August 29, 1870, in "Record of the Academic Senate," p. 16.

24   *Ibid.*

25   *Ibid.*, p. 17.

26   Emphasis added.

27   Report from Henry Durant to the Board of Regents, December 6, 1870 (in Regents, "Correspondence and Papers," Box 1, Folder 52). Emphasis added.

28   *Report of the Regents of the University of California Relative to the Operation and Progress of the Institution* (Sacramento, 1872), 10 (in President, *Report of the President of the University on Behalf of the Regents . . . 1869–79,* University of California archives, Berkeley).

29   Herman Adolph Spindt, "A History of the University of California and the Public High Schools of California, 1872–1945" (unpublished Ph.D. dissertation, Graduate Division, University of California, 1946), 9.

30   *Register of the University of California, Department of Letters and Science, 1872–73,* 26.

31   Minutes of the Academic Senate, February 25, 1873, in "Record of the Academic Senate," p. 147.

32   Minutes of the Academic Senate, April 2, 1873, in "Record of the Academic Senate," pp. 154–155.

33   Memorandum by Martin Kellogg, March 30, 1871, relative to duties of professors (in Regents, "Correspondence and Papers," Box 1, Folder 61).

34   *Ibid.*

35   *Ibid.*

36   University of California, *Centennial Record* (Berkeley, 1967), 264.

37   Letter from R. A. Fisher to Governor Henry Haight, November 1, 1870 (in Regents, "Correspondence and Papers," Box 1, Folder 33).

38   Minutes of the Board of Regents, November 2, 1870, Vol. I, p. 172.

39   San Francisco *Chronicle,* August 3, 1881 (in "Newspaper Clippings Relating to the University of California, 1874–1899," II, 75, University of California archives, Berkeley).

40   *Biennial Report of the Regents of the University of California, for the Years 1873–5* (Sacramento, 1875), 117 (in President, *Report of the President of the University on Behalf of the Regents . . . 1869–79*).

41   Letter from Charles F. Gompertz to R. E. C. Stearns, April 10, 1878 (in Regents, "Correspondence and Papers," Box 5, Folder F-G, 1878).

42   Letter from W. T. Welcker to R. E. C. Stearns, May 22, 1877 (in Regents, "Correspondence and Papers," Box 4, Folder T-Z).

43   Letter from W. T. Welcker to R. E. C. Stearns, June 4, 1877, *ibid.*

Chapter 5

1   Fabian Franklin, *The Life of Daniel Coit Gilman* (New York, 1910), 72–73.

2   Daniel C. Gilman, *The Building of the University: An Inaugural Address Delivered at Oakland, Nov. 7th, 1872* (San Francisco, 1872), 6 (in University of California, *Inaugurals, 1872–1899,* University of California archives, Berkeley).

3   *Ibid.,* 7.

4   *Ibid.,* 27.

5   *Ibid.,* 11.

6   *Ibid.*

7   *Ibid.*

8   California, *Political Code* (1874), Art. III, sec. 1425 (in *Register of the University of California, 1874* [Berkeley, 1874], 106 [University of California archives, Berkeley]).

9   Dr. H. M. Pond, "On Looking into an Album of Fifty Years Ago," *California Monthly,* XX (September, 1926), 38.

10   C. K. Bonestell, "Berkeley in the Seventies," *California Monthly,* XLIII (September, 1939), 5.

11   As quoted in Franklin, 130.

12   California, *Political Code* (1874), Art. I, sec. 1405 (in *Register of the University of California, 1874,* 105).

13   As quoted in Franklin, 130.

Chapter 6

1   Fabian Franklin, *The Life of Daniel Coit Gilman* (New York, 1910), 133.

2   San Francisco *Daily Evening Post,* January 12, 1874.

3   There were, in fact, several investigations: the original one, the one conducted by the senate, and a "reopened" assembly committee investigation. They lasted from about January 13 to March 2, 1874.

4   "Report of Assembly Committee on Public Buildings and Grounds in Relation to the Construction of the College of Letters," 8, in *Appendix to Journals of Senate and Assembly of the Twentieth Session of the Legislature of the State of California* (Sacramento, 1874) IV, ix.

5   Report of the Senate Committee on Public Buildings as found in the San Francisco *Daily Evening Post,* March 17, 1874.

6   "Report of Assembly Committee on Public Buildings . . . ," 9.

7   Minutes of the Board of Regents, October 28, 1874 Vol. II, p. 46, (in Office of the Secretary of the Regents, University of California, Berkeley).

8   *Memorial of the California State Grange and Mechanics' Deliberative Assembly on the State University* (Sacramento, 1874), 4 (in *Pamphlets on the University of California, 1861–1875,* I, xx, University of California archives, Berkeley).

9   *Ibid.,* 5. Carr asked for such a house as early as May 5, 1870 (Letter from Ezra Carr to the Regents, May 5, 1870, in Regents, "Correspondence and Papers," Box 3).

10   *Memorial of the California State Grange . . . ,* 5.

11   *Ibid.,* 9.

12   "Resolution of the Senate and Assembly Inquiring Into the Affairs of the University of California," *Statements of the Regents of the University of California, to the Joint Committee of the Legislature, March 3, 1874* (San Francisco, 1874), 5 (in *Pamphlets on the University of California, 1861–1875,* I, xxii).

13   *Ibid.,* 5.

14   "Response to the First Inquiry," *Statements of the Regents . . . to the Joint Committee of the Legislature . . . ,* 14–15.

15   *Ibid.,* 15.

16   *Ibid.,* 17.

17   "Response to the Fourth Inquiry," *Statements of the Regents . . . to the Joint Committee of the Legislature . . . ,* 67.

18   "Professor Swinton's Testimony Before the Legislature of California Given to the Joint Committee on University Affairs," March 11, 1874, in *The University of California and Its Relations to Industrial Education* (San Francisco, 1874), 55 (University of California archives, Berkeley).

19   *Ibid.*

20   "Report of the Joint Committee of the Senate and Assembly Appointed to Examine Into the Management of the University of California, Including the Administration of the Trusts Confided to the Regents Thereof," 4, in *Appendix to Journals of Senate and Assembly of the Twentieth Session of the Legislature of the State of California* (Sacramento, 1874), VI, i.

21   *Ibid.*

22   Franklin, 156.

23   *Ibid.,* 159–160.

24   *Ibid.,* 160.

25   *Ibid.,* 161.

26   Letter from P. A. Chadbourne to W. D. Whitney, February 26, 1875 (in "The Gilman Papers," II, 17, University of California archives, Berkeley).

27   "The Gilman Papers," II, 1–2.

28   *Preamble and Resolutions of the Joint Committee from the State Grange,*

Mechanics Deliberative Assembly, and Reply of the Board of Regents of the University of California, 2 (in *Pamphlets on the University of California, 1861–1875,* I, xxvi).

29   *Daily Evening Post,* August 3, 1874 (in Regents, "Correspondence and Papers," Box 3, envelope titled "Granger Resolutions and Comments of the Press on Action of Regents of State University").

30   As quoted in the *Chronicle,* August 17, 1874 (*ibid.*).

31   *Grass Valley Union,* clipping (*ibid.*).

32   *Ibid.*

33   *The University of California and Its Relations to Industrial Education* (San Francisco, 1874), 42 (in *Pamphlets, Historical and Critical . . . ,* II, University of California archives, Berkeley).

34   *Ibid.,* 29.

35   *Ibid.*

36   "The Gilman Papers," II, 89–90.

37   *Ibid.,* 172.

38   California, Assembly, *An Act to Reorganize and Simplify the School System and Public Education of the State of California,* Bill No. 374, Sec. 3, February 8, 1876 (in the California State Archives, Sacramento).

39   California, Senate, *An Act to Reorganize and Simplify the School System and Public Education of the State of California,* Bill No. 198, Secs. 3, 11, January 16, 1878 (in the California State Archives, Sacramento).

40   *Memorial from the Board of Regents: Disastrous Effects of the Passage of the Curtis Bill; Its Unconstitutionality* (February, 1878, No. 30), 9–10 (in *Bulletin, no. 1–37* [of the University of California], University of California archives, Berkeley).

41   The eight were Marion Biggs, Eugene Casserly, John S. Hager, Morris Estee, Hugh M. La Rue, J. West Martin, Charles F. Reed, and Joseph W. Winans. H. H. Haight was elected as a delegate, but died before the convention. Three future Regents were delegates: William H. L. Barnes, John Mansfield, and James M. Shafter.

42   California, *Debates and Proceedings of the Constitutional Convention of the State of California, Convened at the City of Sacramento, Saturday, September 28, 1878* (Sacramento, 1880), II, 1123.

43   California, *Debates and Proceedings of the Constitutional Convention . . . ,* II, 1110.

44   *Ibid.*

45   *Ibid.,* III, 1478.

46   *Ibid.*

47   *Ibid.,* 1516.

48   *Ibid.*

49   San Francisco *Bulletin,* March 13, 1879.

50   Regents, *Annual Report of the Secretary to the Board of Regents, 1887* (Sacramento, 1887), 7 (University of California archives, Berkeley).

Chapter 7

1   Untitled, undated, and unsigned document in the handwriting of J. Ham Harris. It is a series of extracts from minutes of Regents' meetings from April to October, 1874, dealing with the powers of the president. A penciled title labels the document "Appointments etc." (in Regents, "Correspondence and Papers," Box 2, Folder 34, University of California archives, Berkeley).

2   *Report of the Committee on Instruction and Visitation, to the Board of Regents, May 31, 1881,* 5 (in University of California, *Pamphlets on the University of California, 1868–1901,* no. 24, University of California archives, Berkeley).

3   *Ibid.*

4   Minutes of the Board of Regents, June 7, 1881, Vol. IV, p. 124 (Office of the Secretary of the Regents, University of California, Berkeley).

5   *The Wasp,* June 10, 1881, in "Newspaper Clippings Relating to the University of California, 1874–1899," II, 46 (University of California archives, Berkeley).

6   San Francisco *Examiner,* June 5, 1881, *Ibid.,* 32–33.

7   *Ibid.*

8   See particularly letter from Stearns to Davidson, June 3, 1879 (in George Davidson, "Correspondence and Papers," Box 22, folder of letters from Stearns, Bancroft Library, University of California, Berkeley). This letter bears out the aura of secrecy with which Stebbins operated and substantiates close relationships between Stearns, Davidson, and Stebbins, all principals in the uproar of 1881.

9   "The University War: Meeting of the Associated Alumni of California Last Evening," undated clipping from an unidentified newspaper in "Newspaper Clippings Relating to the University of California, 1874–1899," II, 53–54.

10   Oakland *Evening Tribune,* June 7, 1881, *Ibid.,* 35–36.

11   San Francisco *Examiner,* June 5, 1881, *Ibid.,* 32–33.

12   *Daily Examiner,* January 15, 1881, in "Newspaper Clippings Relating to the University of California, 1874–1899," III, 10.

13   The four Democrats were Regents Hager, Martin, Wallace, and McKee. McKee was not present at most of the meetings in the summer of 1881 during which the dispute over LeConte, Welcker, *et al.* raged.

14   Oakland *Evening Tribune,* June 4, 1881, in "Newspaper Clippings Relating to the University of California, 1874–1899," II, 30–31.

15   San Francisco *Chronicle,* June 7, 1881, *Ibid.,* 32–33.

16   *Alta Californian,* June 29, 1881; San Francisco *Examiner,* June 29, 1881, in "Newspaper Clippings Relating to the University of California, 1874–1899," II, 64a–64c, 64d–64f.

17   Minutes of the Board of Regents, June 28, 1881, Vol. IV, p. 140. The division of the Board was along "ring" and "anti-ring" lines.

18   Oakland *Times,* December 6, 1881, p. 3.

19   Entering students were examined to test their competence in higher arithmetic, including the extraction of square roots and cube roots and the metric system; algebra and quadratic equations; plane geometry; English grammar; geography; and history of the United States. Freshmen entering the College of Letters had to pass an additional examination in Latin grammar; four books of Caesar, six books of the *Aeneid,* six orations of Cicero; Greek grammar, and three books of the *Anabasis.*

20   President, *Report of the President for the Board of Regents: 1881–82* (Sacramento, 1882), 14 (University of California archives, Berkeley).

21   *Ibid.,* 5.

22   As quoted in May L. Cheney, "High School Legislation in California since 1879," *Pacific Educational Journal,* XI (March, 1895), 123.

23   Minutes of the Board of Regents, March 4, 1884, Vol. V., pp. 231–232.

24   Letter from William T. Reid to D. O. Mills, January 24, 1883, as quoted in Herman A. Spindt, "The University of California and William T. Reid," 20–22 (typescript, University of California archives, Berkeley).

25   The other Regent involved was Nathaniel Greene Curtis. Curtis and Stanford were appointed between sessions (biennial) of the legislature and, although their appointments were not confirmed, attended meetings and voted. Thus, historically, they are considered former Regents of the University between the dates of their appointments and resignations.

26   "Memorial of Dr. J. H. C. Bonté," in Regents, *Annual Report of the Secretary to the Board of Regents of the University of California, 1897* (Berkeley, 1898), 5–6 (University of California archives, Berkeley).

27   Minutes of the Board of Regents, February 3, 1882, Vol. IV, p. 275.

28   Other new Regents included Governor George Stoneman, Lieutenant Governor John Daggett, Speaker of the Assembly H. M. La Rue, P. A. Finigan, president of the State Agricultural Society, and three appointees named at the beginning of Stoneman's term as a result of the failure of the senate to confirm appointments made between sessions by his predecessor, Governor Perkins. The Stoneman appointees were Isaias Hellman, George T. Marye, and Arthur Rodgers.

29   William T. Reid, *Inaugural Address, Addresses at the Inauguration of W. T. Reid, August 23, 1881,* 43, *Inaugurals, 1872–1899* (University of California archives, Berkeley).

30   Lincoln Steffens, *The Autobiography of Lincoln Steffens* (New York, 1931), 117.

31   *Ibid.,* 117–118.

32   Oakland *Independent,* December 6, 1884, in "Newspaper Clippings Relating to the University of California, 1874–1899," IV, 53–54.

33   San Francisco *Daily Examiner,* December 28, 1884, *Ibid.,* 57.

34   Frank Soulé, "Scrapbooks of Newspaper Clippings Relating to the University of California 1879–1888," II, 2 (University of California archives, Berkeley).

35   John S. Hager, *Address . . . on the Occasion of the Inauguration of the President of the University of California . . . June 30, 1886,* 3, *Inaugurals, 1872–1899.*

36   Letter from Edward S. Holden to John S. Hager, July 1, 1885 (in Regents, "Correspondence and Papers," Box 9, Folder H, 1884–1886).

37   "The Class Rush," San Francisco *Report,* undated clipping from about September, 1886, in "University Scrapbook, 1864–1887" (University of California archives, Berkeley).

38   Letter from Edward S. Holden to the Academic Council, November 18, 1886 (in "Papers Relating to Lincoln Steffens as a Student at the University of California, 1886–1888," Manuscript Collection, Bancroft Library, University of California, Berkeley).

39   San Francisco *Chronicle,* June 29, 1887, in Soulé, "Scrapbooks of Newspaper Clippings Relating to the University of California 1879–1888," II, 76.

40   *Evening Tribune,* June 30, 1887, in Soulé, "Scrapbooks of Newspaper Clippings Relating to the University of California 1879–1888," II, 77; San Francisco *Chronicle,* June 29, 1887, in "Newspaper Clippings Relating to the University of California, 1874–1899," IV, 114.

41   Academic Council June–July, 1887 (in Academic Senate, "Correspondence and Papers," Box 2, Folder 41, University of California archives, Berkeley).

42   *Evening Post,* June 29, 1887, in Soulé, "Scrapbooks of Newspaper Clippings Relating to the University of California 1879–1888," II, 77.

43   Minutes of the Board of Regents, September 6, 1887, Vol. VII, p. 10.

44   Minutes of the Board of Regents, January 10, 1888, Vol. VII, p. 39.

45   *The Morning Times,* July 1, 1887; Berkeley *Advocate,* July 2, 1887, in Soulé, "Scrapbooks of Newspaper Clippings Relating to the University of California 1879–1888," II, 78.

46   San Francisco *Evening Post,* August 3, 1887. The appearance of Welcker and Campbell on this list is particularly interesting in light of the fact that Campbell was, as ex-officio Regent, also a member of Stebbins' Committee on Instruction and Visitation that recommended Welcker's dismissal in 1881.

47   For more biographical data see: Oakland *Evening Tribune,* January 23, 1888, February 8, 1888, in Soulé, "Scrapbooks of Newspaper clippings Relating to the University of California 1879–1888," II, 86, 88–89; Horace Davis, "How I Got into the Library Business," February, 1916 (Manuscript Collection, Bancroft Library); University of California, *Centennial Record* (Berkeley, 1967), 14.

48   Berkeley *Advocate,* January 25, 1888, in Soulé, "Scrapbooks of Newspaper Clippings Relating to the University of California 1879–1888," II, 86.

49   Minutes of the Board of Regents, February 7, 1888, Vol. VII, p. 59.

50   Letter from Horace Davis to Andrew Hallidie, March [?] 31, 1889 (in Regents, "Correspondence and Papers," Box 11, Folder D 1889).

51   Oakland *Tribune,* December 17, 1888, in "Newspaper Clippings Relating to the University of California, 1874–1899," V, 21.

52   *Ibid.* Regent Hallidie, in addition to Horace Davis, was a member of Stebbins' congregation.

53   When one of Stebbins' supporters heard this charge, he asked how the man who made it could possibly know. Professor Howison was known to have

lectured to some of Berkeley's most intellectually adept people without being understood. After one of his lectures, Joseph LeConte said that he believed he might be able to understand it if he could read it at least three times. There is ample evidence in Howison's writings that the charge of his atheism was untrue.

54   Minutes of the Board of Regents, executive session, June 25, 1889.

55   Petition of Faculty and Students (in Regents, "Correspondence and Papers," Box 12, Folder N–P 1889).

56   Regents, *Annual Report of the Secretary to the Board of Regents of the University of California, 1890* (Sacramento, 1890), 13.

57   *Ibid.,* 13.

58   Oakland *Daily Evening Tribune,* March 13, 1890, p. 5; San Francisco *Examiner,* March 14, 1890, p. 5.

59   Minutes of the Board of Regents, May 13, 1890, Vol. VIII, pp. 13–14.

60   Milicent Shinn, "University of California," *Overland Monthly,* XX (October, 1892), 359–360.

61   Letter from William T. Reid to D. O. Mills, March 12, 1885, as quoted in Spindt.

62   Fabian Franklin, *The Life of Daniel Coit Gilman* (New York, 1910), 123.

63   Oakland *Daily Tribune,* May 1, 1890, p. 1.

64   Minutes of the Board of Regents, November 11, 1890, Vol. VIII, p. 159.

65   Minutes of the Board of Regents, January 13, 1891, Vol. VIII, p. 191.

66   University of California, *Regents' Manual* (Berkeley, 1884), 223.

67   Minutes of the Board of Regents, January 13, 1891, Vol. VIII, p. 191.

68   Minutes of the Board of Regents, May 12, 1891, Vol. VIII, pp. 271–272.

69   *Ibid.,* p. 273.

70   Minutes of the Board of Regents, June 23, 1891, Vol. VIII, p. 332.

71   Actually, this was not a new policy. On March 2, 1886, the Regents voted that the president should be a member of all standing committees of the Regents. On October 26 of the same year, however, the order was amended and the President was given a voice without vote on committees of the Board. (Minutes of the Board of Regents, Vol. VI, pp. 125, 210.)

72   Minutes of the Board of Regents, April 12, 1892, executive session; Resolutions adopted April 12, 1892, under cover title, "Communication from Members of Academic Council: In Board, Sept. 6/92, Executive Session" (in Regents, "Correspondence and Papers," Box 16, Folder P–Q 1892).

Chapter 8

1   "Notes by A. J. M.," attached to "Financial Statement—Regents of the University, Aug. 25, 1870" (in Regents, "Correspondence and Papers," Box 1, Folder 36, University of California archives, Berkeley).

2   *The New York Times,* February 21, 1889.

3   "Notes by A. J. M."

4   *Biennial Report of the Regents of the University of California, for the Years 1872–73* (Sacramento, 1873), 45 (in President, *Report of the President of the University on Behalf of the Regents . . . 1869–79,* University of California archives, Berkeley).

5   Daniel C. Gilman, *The Building of the University: An Inaugural Address Delivered at Oakland, Nov. 7th, 1872* (San Francisco, 1872), 12, 13, *Inaugurals, 1872–1899* (University of California archives, Berkeley).

6   *Ibid.*

7   Milicent Shinn, "The University of California II. The Lick Astronomical Department," *Overland Monthly,* XX (November, 1892), 486.

8   Letter from Dean Thomas Bennett to the Regents, June 6, 1870 (in Regents, "Correspondence and Papers," Box 3).

9   Minutes of the Board of Regents, August 2, 1870, Vol. 1, pp. 153–154 (Office of the Secretary of the Regents, University of California, Berkeley).

10   Letter from Dean Thomas Bennett to Andrew J. Moulder, September 23, 1870; letter from Dr. J. D. B. Stillman to Andrew J. Moulder, October 8, 1870 (in Regents, "Correspondence and Papers," Box 3).

11   Minutes of the Board of Regents, December 6, 1870, Vol. 1, pp. 182–183.

12   William Warren Ferrier, *Origin and Development of the University of California* (Berkeley, 1930), 425.

13   *Ibid.,* 413.

14   *Ibid.*

15   *Ibid.,* 430.

16   *Ibid.,* 430–431.

17   J. G. Yager to R. E. C. Stearns, June 27, 1875 (in Regents, "Correspondence and Papers," Box 2, Folder 50).

18   Regents, *Annual Report to the Board of Regents of the University of California, . . . 1877* (San Francisco, 1877), 15 (University of California archives, Berkeley).

19   *Ibid.,* 16.

20   *Biennial Report of the Regents of the University of California, for the Years 1875–7* (Sacramento, 1877), 56 (in President, *Report of the President of the University on Behalf of the Regents . . . 1869–79*).

21   Regents, *Annual Report to the Board of Regents of the University of California, . . . 1878* (Berkeley, 1878), 23 (University of California archives, Berkeley).

22   *Ibid.,* 24.

23   *Biennial Report . . . 1875–7,* 56–57.

24   Regents, *Annual Report to the Board of Regents of the University of California, . . . 1879* (Berkeley, 1879), 18 (University of California archives, Berkeley).

25   University of California, *Centennial Record* (Berkeley, 1967), 59.

26   Minutes of the Board of Regents, December 13, 1869, Vol. I, p. 118.

27   Regents, *Annual Report of the Board of Regents of the University of California, . . . 1875* (Berkeley, 1875), 5 (University of California archives, Berkeley).

28   Regents, *Annual Report . . . 1878,* 29.

29   Regents, *Annual Report of the Secretary to the Board of Regents of the University of California, . . . 1882* (Sacramento, 1882), 9 (University of California archives, Berkeley).

30   California, *Statutes* (1877–1878), c. CCLXXVII, sec. 1, p. 337.

31   Regents, *Annual Report . . . 1878,* 13.

32   Sacramento *Daily Bee,* February 2, 1883, in "Newspaper Clippings Relating to the University of California, 1874–1899," IV, 32 (University of California archives, Berkeley).

33   California, *Statutes* (1877–1878), c. CCLXXVII, sec. 1, p. 337.

34   Regents, *Annual Report of the Secretary to the Board of Regents of the University of California, . . . 1883* (Sacramento, 1883), 16 (University of California archives, Berkeley).

35   "Quarterly Report of the President to the Hon. Board of Regents, December 2, 1884" (in Regents, "Correspondence and Papers," Box 7, Folder R).

36   Regents, *Annual Report of the Secretary to the Board of Regents of the University of California, . . . 1885* (Sacramento, 1885), 14, 15 (University of California archives, Berkeley).

37   President, *Biennial Report of the President of the University on Behalf of the Board of Regents, to . . . the Governor . . . , 1886* (Sacramento, 1886), 76, 77 (University of California archives, Berkeley).

38   E. W. Maslin to J. H. C. Bonté, January 5, 1886 [1887] (in Regents, "Correspondence and Papers," Box 7, folder labeled "California Legislature 1887").

39   Edward Holden to J. H. C. Bonté, February 10, 1887 (in Regents, "Correspondence and Papers," Box 11, Folder H 1887).

40   Regents, *Annual Report of the Secretary to the Board of Regents of the University of California, . . . 1889* (Sacramento, 1889), 25 (University of California archives, Berkeley).

41   Regents, *Annual Report of the Secretary to the Board of Regents of the University of California, . . . 1893* (Sacramento, 1893), 85 (University of California archives, Berkeley).

42   Morrill College Aid Act, as quoted in Regents, *Annual Report of the Secretary to the Board of Regents of the University of California, . . . 1891* (Sacramento, 1891), 31–33 (University of California archives, Berkeley).

43   Minutes of the Board of Regents, December 12, 1893, Vol. IX, pp. 390–391.

44   Martin Kellogg, *Needs of the State University* (Berkeley, December 20, 1894), printed leaflet in pamphlet box "Finance" (University of California archives, Berkeley).

45   Minutes of the Board of Regents, June 11, 1895, Vol. X, pp. 124, 125.

46   Regents, *Annual Report of the Secretary to the Board of Regents of the University of California, . . . 1896* (Sacramento, 1896), 46 (University of California archives, Berkeley).

47   Minutes of the Board of Regents, July 23, 1895, Vol. X, p. 139.

48   Mounted clipping from the San Francisco *News Letter,* March 7, 1897 (in pamphlet box "Finance," folder labeled "One Cent Stratton-Wright Act of 1897").

49   Regents, *Annual Report, . . . 1896,* 93.

50   *Ibid.,* 98.

51   *Ibid.,* 97.

52   *Ibid.,* 103.

53   "State University's New Income," clipping from San Francisco *Examiner,* February 20, 1897 (in pamphlet box "Finance," folder labeled "One Cent . . . Act of 1897").

54   Milicent Shinn, "University of California," *Overland Monthly,* XX (October, 1892), 362.

55   Minutes of the Board of Regents, April 28, 1896, Vol. X, p. 265.

56   Regents, *Annual Report of the Secretary to the Board of Regents of the University of California, . . . 1897* (Berkeley, 1898), 37 (University of California archives, Berkeley).

57   James H. Budd, *First Biennial Message of Governor James H. Budd, to the Legislature of the State of California* (Sacramento, 1897), 27.

58   Clipping, dated February 18, 1897, from San Francisco *Chronicle* (in pamphlet box "Finance," folder labeled "One Cent . . . Act of 1897").

59   "State University's New Income."

60   Minutes of the Board of Regents, May 9, 1899, Vol. XII, p. 277.

61   *Ibid.,* pp. 227, 229.

62   *Ibid.,* p. 228.

63   Minutes of the Board of Regents, May 12, 1899, Vol. XII, pp. 239–240.

64   Minutes of the Board of Regents, June 16, 1899, Vol. XII, pp. 277–288.

65   Clipping from San Francisco *Examiner,* June 27, 1899 (in pamphlet box "Finance").

66   Clipping from San Francisco *Examiner,* June 18, 1899, *ibid.*

67   Clippings from San Francisco *Bulletin,* June 25, 1899, and June 23, 1899, *ibid.*

68   San Francisco *Bulletin,* June 25, 1899, *ibid.*

69   Clipping from an unidentified paper, June 3, 1899, *ibid.*

70   Henry T. Gage, *First Biennial Message of Governor Henry T. Gage to the Legislature, of the State of California* (Sacramento, 1901), 23 (in *Appendix to the Journals of the Senate and Assembly of the Thirty-Fourth Session of the Legislature of the State of California* [Sacramento, 1901], Vol. I, no. 1).

71   *Ibid.,* 24–25.

Chapter 9

1   California, *Statutes* (1867–1868), c. CCXLIV, sec. 8, p. 250.

2   Letter from Samuel Willey to Sherman Day, November 16, 1863 (in "Letters from Samuel Willey to Rev. E. W. Gilman and Sherman Day," University of

California archives, Berkeley); William Warren Ferrier, *Origin and Development of the University of California* (Berkeley, 1930), 425–426.

3   Francis Tomlinson Gardner, "The Little Acorn: Hugh Huger Toland 1806–1880," read at the twenty-second annual meeting of the American Association of the History of Medicine, Lexington, Kentucky, May 23, 1949, 65–66.

4   Letter from Dr. Thos. Bennett to the Regents, June 6, 1870 (in Regents, "Correspondence and Papers," Box 3, University of California archives, Berkeley).

5   Memorial of the Faculty of the Medical Department of the University of the Pacific to the Regents (in Regents, "Correspondence and Papers," Box 3).

6   Report of Board of Medical Examiners to the Board of Regents, Nov. 10, 1870 (in Regents, "Correspondence and Papers," Box 1, Folder 47).

7   "Copy" of Toland's Proposition (in Regents, "Correspondence and Papers," Box 3).

8   W. E. Carter, brief history of the School of Medicine, 10–11 (untitled typescript, San Francisco Medical Center Library).

9   *Biennial Report of the Regents of the University of California, for the Years 1872–73* (Sacramento, 1873), 27 (in President, *Report of the President of the University on Behalf of the Regents . . . 1869–79,* University of California archives, Berkeley).

10   Henry Harris, *California's Medical Story* (San Francisco, 1932), 138.

11   *Biennial Report of the Regents of the University of California, for the Years 1873–5* (Sacramento, 1875), 96 (in President, *Report of the President of the University on Behalf of the Regents . . . 1869–79*).

12   *Annual Announcement of Lectures at Toland Hall Medical Department of the University of California . . . 1875* (San Francisco, 1875), 7 (in School of Medicine, San Francisco, *Announcement for the Academic Year,* University of California archives, Berkeley).

13   *Register of the University of California 1878–9* (Berkeley, 1878), 148 (University of California archives, Berkeley).

14   *Biennial Report of the Regents of the University of California, for the Years 1875–7* (Sacramento, 1877), 61 (in President, *Report of the President of the University on Behalf of the Regents . . . 1869–79*).

15   *Biennial Report of the Regents of the University of California, for the Years 1877–9* (Sacramento, 1879), 54, 59 (in President, *Report of the President of the University on Behalf of the Regents . . . 1869–79*).

16   *Register of the University of California 1883–84* (Berkeley, 1884), 94.

17   *Register of the University of California 1895–96* (Berkeley, 1896), 182.

18   *Register of the University of California 1893–94* (Berkeley, 1894), 114.

19   University of California, *Centennial Record* (Berkeley, 1967), 212–217.

20   Petition of a Committee of the Medical Faculty to the Regents, December 29, 1886 (in Regents, "Correspondence and Papers," Box 9, Folder F 1884–1886).

21   Minutes of the Board of Regents, February 10, 1887, Vol. VI, p. 242 (Office of the Secretary of the Regents, University of California, Berkeley).

22   Letter from A. A. D'Ancona to E. W. Davis, March 28, 1898 (in Regents, "Correspondence and Papers," Box 24, Folder D 1898).

23   Report of Committee on Status of the Medical Department (in Regents, "Correspondence and Papers," Box 24a, Folder titled "Medical Department, 1898").

24   Minutes of the Board of Regents, August 9, 1898, Vol. XII, p. 47.

25   William Carey Jones, *Illustrated History of the University of California* (Rev. ed.; San Francisco, 1901), 344–345.

26   *Ibid.*, 345.

27   Minutes of the Board of Regents, June 2, 1873, Vol. I, p. 318.

28   Jones, 345.

29   *Ibid.*

30   *Biennial Report ... 1873–5,* 100.

31   *Ibid.*

32   *Ibid.*

33   *Ibid.*

34   *Ibid.,* 102.

35   *Ibid.,* 100.

36   Jones, 347.

37   California, *Statutes* (1875–1876), c. CCCCXX, sec. 1–3, pp. 583–584.

38   *Centennial Record,* 212–215.

39   *Report of the Regents of the University of California, ... 1880* (Sacramento, 1880), 56 (in President, *Report of the President of the University on Behalf of the Regents ...*); President, *Biennial Report of the President of the University on Behalf of the Board of Regents to ... the Governor ... 1882–84* (Sacramento, 1884), 42 (University of California archives, Berkeley).

40   *Report of the Regents ... 1880,* 57.

41   President, *Biennial Report of the President of the University on Behalf of the Board of Regents to ... the Governor ... 1896–1898* (Berkeley, 1898), 43–44.

42   *Centennial Record,* 213–219.

43   *Register of the University of California 1870–71* (Oakland, 1870), 62.

44   Orrin Kip McMurray, "Serranus Clinton Hastings, Founder of Hastings College of the Law," in Hastings College of the Law, San Francisco, *Golden Jubilee Book, 1878–1928* (San Francisco, 1928), 7–9 (University of California archives, Berkeley).

45   William H. Waste, "The Founding of Hastings College of the Law," *Golden Jubilee Book, 1878–1928,* 13.

46   Serranus Clinton Hastings, *Address of S. C. Hastings, Founder of Hastings' Law Department of the University of California* (San Francisco, 1878), 6 (in Hastings College of the Law, San Francisco, *Addresses 1878–1881,* University of California archives, Berkeley).

47   California, *Statutes* (1877–1878), c. CCCLI, p. 533–534.

48   *Biennial Report ... 1877–9,* 69. There is some discrepancy in the dates

for the opening of Hastings College of the Law. Dean Pomeroy's printed address for that occasion is dated August 8, 1878. Jones and Ferrier both use the date of August 9, 1878. Reminiscences of alumni in the *Hastings College of the Law Golden Jubilee Book* give the date as August 12, 1878.

49   Waste, 14.

50   *Register of the University of California 1878–9* (Berkeley, 1878), 134.

51   Milicent Shinn, "University of California," *Overland Monthly*, XX (December, 1892), 585–*586*.

52   *Ibid.*

53   *Foltz v. Hoge* (1879), 54 Cal. 28.

54   Edward A. Hogan, "The First Seventy-Five Years," *California Monthly*, LXIII (May, 1953), 45.

55   *Ibid.*, 12–13.

56   A complete file of communications on this donation is published in the *Biennial Report . . . 1877–9*, 87–91.

57   Statement by the faculty of the Medical Department to the Regents, May 28, 1881 (in Regents, "Correspondence and Papers," Box 10, Folder titled "Organization of the Dental Dept., 1880s").

58   Minutes of the Board of Regents, September 7, 1881, Vol. IV, pp. 204–205.

59   Alonzo Phelps, *Contemporary Biography of California's Representative Men* (San Francisco, 1882), II, 124–127.

60   *Register of the University of California 1881–82* (Berkeley, 1882), 82–83.

61   President, *Biennial Report of the President of the University on Behalf of the Board of Regents to . . . the Governor . . . 1886* (Sacramento, 1886), 114–115; *Biennial Report . . . 1888*, 107.

62   Letter from C. L. Goddard to the Board of Regents, July 30, 1883 (in Regents, "Correspondence and Papers," Box 10, Folder titled "Organization of the Dental Dept., 1880s").

63   President, *Biennial Report . . . 1888*, 107.

64   President, *Biennial Report of the President of the University on Belief of the Board of Regents, to . . . the Governor . . . 1894* (Sacramento, 1895), 61.

65   Report of the Secretary to Board of Regents, 4 (in President, "Correspondence and Papers," Box 2a [1890s], Folder titled "Affiliation, Committee on," University of California archives, Berkeley).

66   Regents, *Annual Report of the Secretary to the Board of Regents of the University of California, . . . 1895* (Sacramento, 1895), 3–4.

67   J. H. Bonté to A. S. Hallidie, March 13, 1889 (in Regents, "Correspondence and Papers," Box 11, Folder H: 1889 to July).

68   Report of Minority Committee in Site for Affiliated College Building, In Board, September 10, 1895 (in Regents, "Correspondence and Papers," Box 18a, Folder 1895, Report 2413).

69   Joost and Woolley to A. S. Hallidie, August 12, 1895 (in Regents, "Correspondence and Papers," Box 21, Folder J 1895).

70   Adolph Sutro, "Letter to the Regents of the University of California and to the Committee of Affiliated Colleges on the Selection of a Site for the Affiliated Colleges," September 5, 1895, 3 (University of California archives, Berkeley).

71   Jones, 283–284.

72   Deed of Certain Property in San Francisco by Edward F. Searles to the Regents of the University of California, In Board, January 10, 1893 (in Regents, "Correspondence and Papers," Box 17).

73   Jones, 290.

74   Regents, *Annual Report of the Secretary to the Board of Regents of the University of California . . . 1894* (Sacramento, 1894), 119.

75   Martin Kellogg to A. S. Hallidie, February 14, 1896 (in Regents, "Correspondence and Papers," Box 2, Folder titled "Hallidie"); Regents, *Annual Report of the Secretary to the Board of Regents of the University of California, . . . 1899* (Sacramento, 1899), 48.

76   President, *Annual Report of the President of the University on Behalf of the Regents to . . . the Governor . . . 1914–1915* (Berkeley, 1915), 256 (University of California archives, Berkeley).

77   Regents, *Annual Report of the Secretary to the Board of Regents of the University of California . . . 1898* (Berkeley, 1898), 86 (University of California archives, Berkeley).

78   Minutes of the Board of Regents, September 14, 1897, Vol. XI, p. 171.

79   President, *Annual Report . . . 1914–1915,* 229–230.

Chapter 10

1   California, *Statutes* (1867–1868), c. CCXLIV, sec. 4, p. 249.

2   *Ibid.*

3   *Ibid.,* sec. 15, p. 254.

4   *Ibid.,* sec. 16, p. 255.

5   *Ibid.*

6   *Ibid.,* sec. 17, p. 255.

7   Minutes of the Board of Regents, June 15, 1871, Vol. I, p. 215 (Office of the Secretary of the Regents, University of California, Berkeley).

8   Minutes of the Board of Regents, April 8, 1872, Vol. I, p. 251.

9   *Report of the Regents of the University of California Relative to the Operations and Progress of the Institution* (Sacramento, 1872), 12 (in President, *Report of the President of the University on Behalf of the Regents . . . 1869–79,* University of California archives, Berkeley).

10   *Ibid.,* 12, 13.

11   *Biennial Report of the Regents of the University of California, for the Years 1873–5* (Sacramento, 1875), 61–63 (in President, *Report of the President of the University on Behalf of the Regents . . . 1869–79*).

12   Regents, *Annual Report of the Board of Regents of the University of California . . . 1875* (Berkeley, 1875), 10 (University of California archives, Berkeley).

13   *Biennial Report . . . 1873–5*, 61–63.

14   E. J. Wickson, "Beginnings of Agricultural Education and Research in California," *Report of the College of Agriculture and the Agricultural Experiment Station of the University of California, July 1, 1917–June 30, 1918* (Berkeley, 1918), 41–42 (University of California archives, Berkeley).

15   E. J. Wickson, "Address by E. J. Wickson," in "Addresses at Memorial Services in Honor of Dr. E. W. Hilgard, University of California, January 30, 1916," *University of California Chronicle*, XVIII (April, 1916), 163.

16   These matters are discussed in a slightly different context in Chapter 6.

17   *Biennial Report of the Regents of the University of California for the Years 1872–73* (Sacramento, 1873), 24 (in President, *Report of the President of the University on Behalf of the Regents . . . 1869–79*).

18   E. W. Hilgard, *Report on the Agricultural Experiment Stations of the University of California, with Descriptions of the Regions Represented: Being a Part of the Combined Reports for 1888 and 1889* (Sacramento, 1890), 38 (in *California Experiment Station Reports, 1886–1892*).

19   E. J. Wickson, "Beginnings . . . ," 61.

20   *Ibid.*, 95.

21   President, *Biennial Report of the President of the University on Behalf of the Board of Regents, to . . . the Governor . . . , 1890* (Sacramento, 1891), 89 (University of California archives, Berkeley).

22   E. W. Hilgard, *Report of Work of the Agricultural Experiment Station of the University of California from June 30, 1901, to June 30, 1903* (Sacramento, 1903), 9.

23   Wickson, "Address," 166–167.

24   E. J. Wickson, "Farmers' Institutes under the Auspices of the University," *Report of Work of the Agricultural Experiment Stations of the University of California for the Year 1892–93 and Part of 1894* (Sacramento, 1894), 23.

25   E. J. Wickson, "Farmers' Institutes," *Report of Work of the Agricultural Experiment Stations of the University of California for the Years 1898–1901* (Sacramento, 1902), 19.

26   E. W. Hilgard, "Letter of Transmittal," *Ibid.*, 15.

27   *Ibid.*

28   Wickson, "Beginnings . . . ," 58.

29   Letter from Ezra Carr to the Regents, May 5, 1870 (in Regents, "Correspondence and Papers," Box 3, University of California archives, Berkeley).

30   *Biennial Report of the Regents of the University of California for the Years 1875–7* (Sacramento, 1877), 81 (in President, *Report of the President of the University on Behalf of the Regents . . . 1869–79*).

31   *Ibid.*

32   *Ibid.*

33   *Ibid.*

34   "Peter J. Shields: Reminiscences: Tape recorded interviews for the Bancroft Library, December 30, 1953–July 1, 1954," 79 (Bancroft Library, University of California, Berkeley).

35   California, *Statutes* (1905), c. CXXIX, sec. 4, p. 133.

36   Robert Bynum, "Davis," in University of California, *Centennial Record* (Berkeley, 1967), 153.

37   Wickson, "Beginnings . . . ," 55.

38   *Ibid.*

39   "Peter J. Shields: Reminiscences," 84, 85.

40   Wickson, "Beginnings . . . ," 56.

41   U.S. Bureau of the Census, "Population, for States: 1790 to 1950," *Historical Statistics of the United States, Colonial Times to 1957* (Washington, D. C., 1960), 12–13.

42   The California farm population increased from 35,934 in 1880 to 72,542 in 1900. During the same period, the size of the average farm in California decreased from 462 to 397 acres. Warren Thompson, *Growth and Changes in California's Populations* (Los Angeles, 1955), 277.

43   Wickson, "Beginnings . . . ," 52.

44   Robert Glass Cleland, *From Wilderness to Empire* (New York, 1959), 200.

45   *Ibid.*

Chapter 11

1   The appointed Regents were George J. Ainsworth and Jacob Reinstein. The Governor was James H. Budd.

2   Josephine Lindley, of Sacramento, was the first woman to register, but Rose L. Scrivener, of Stockton, who registered in January, 1871, was the first woman to complete University work for the bachelor's degree.

3   *Report of the Regents of the University of California, Relative to the Operations and Progress of the Institution* (Sacramento, 1872), 7 (in President, *Report of the President of the University on Behalf of the Regents . . . 1869–79,* University of California archives, Berkeley).

4   *The Berkeleyan,* January, 1874, p. 10 (University of California archives, Berkeley).

5   *The Occident,* October 2, 1891, p. 4 (University of California archives, Berkeley).

6   *Biennial Report of the Regents of the University of California, for the Years 1873–5* (Sacramento, 1875), 114 (in President, *Report of the President of the University on Behalf of the Regents. . . 1869–79*).

7   *The Californian,* October 4, 1897, p. 1 (University of California archives, Berkeley). *The Californian,* founded in 1897, became the *Daily Californian* on October 25 of that year. Issues published from 1897 to the spring of 1899 are

located in the University archives. Issues from the fall of 1899 to the present are in the Newspaper Room of the University Library, Berkeley.

8   California, *Statutes* (1867–1868), c. CCXLIV, sec. 25, p. 258.

9   *University Echo,* July, 1873, p. 5 (University of California archives, Berkeley).

10   *Biennial Report of the Regents of the University of California, for the Years 1872–73* (Sacramento, 1873), 10 (in President, *Report of the President of the University on Behalf of the Regents . . . 1869–79*).

11   *The Berkeleyan,* May, 1874, p. 12.

12   *The Berkeleyan,* January, 1874, p. 6.

13   *The Berkeleyan,* August, 1874, p. 12.

14   *The Berkeleyan,* February 26, 1883.

15   William Warren Ferrier, *Berkeley, California* (Berkeley, 1933), 118.

16   *Ibid.*

17   President, *Biennial Report of the President of the University on Behalf of the Board of Regents to . . . the Governor . . . 1888* (Sacramento, 1889), 17 (University of California archives, Berkeley).

18   *Blue and Gold,* 1877, 65–69 (University of California Library, Berkeley).

19   Mary Bennett Ritter, *More Than Gold in California* (Berkeley, 1933), 207–208.

20   *Ibid.,* 210.

21   *Ibid.,* 213.

22   *Blue and Gold,* 1880, 48–53.

23   Information on the early years of Zeta Psi taken from Howard Bement, *The Story of Zeta Psi* (New York, 1928), 420–424.

24   *Blue and Gold,* 1880, 48–53.

25   *Ibid.*

26   Quoted in William Warren Ferrier, *Origin and Development of the University of California* (Berkeley, 1930), 653.

27   *Ibid.*

28   *The Occident,* April 26, 1889, pp. 114–117.

29   *The Californian,* October 4, 1897, p. 1.

30   *Blue and Gold,* 1877, 38, 39.

31   *The Berkeleyan,* May, 1878, p. 186.

32   *The Berkeleyan,* May 1, 1882, p. 4.

33   *The Occident,* January 11, 1889, p. 125.

34   *Alta Californian,* September 29, 1879, in Frank Soulé, "Scrapbooks of Newspaper Clippings Relating to the University of California 1879–1888," Vol. I, p. 2 (University of California archives, Berkeley).

35   *Ibid.*

36   Minutes of the Academic Senate, May 26, 1879, in "Record of the Academic Senate," Vol. II, pp. 186–187 (Office of the Academic Senate, University of California, Berkeley).

37   Minutes of the Academic Senate, August 25, 1879, in "Record of the Academic Senate," Vol. II, p. 209.

38   *The Berkeleyan*, October 27, 1884, p. 59.

39   Minutes of the Academic Senate, October 19, 1881, in "Record of the Academic Senate," Vol. II, p. 366. This was the fatal year for hazing. Fourteen members of the Sophomore class were suspended for hazing Freshmen. Among those suspended were a future president of the University of Texas, Sidney Mezes, and a future Monsignor and Regent, Charles Ramm.

40   *Blue and Gold*, 1892, 182–183.

41   *Ibid.*

42   *Ibid.*

43   *Ibid.*

44   *The Californian*, September 2, 1897, p. 1.

45   *The Berkeleyan*, February, 1875, p. 7.

46   *The Berkeleyan*, October 23, 1876, p. 4.

47   *The Berkeleyan*, May, 1879, p. 199.

48   *Blue and Gold*, 1894, 7–8.

49   There are many accounts of the "Rape of the Axe." The basic references for this particular passage are a reminiscence by C. E. Miller, a participant, in the *Daily Californian*, November 7, 1912, pp. 1–2; and the *Daily Californian*, April 18, 1899, pp. 1, 4. The Axe remained at Berkeley for thirty-one years before it was stolen from an armored car by Stanford students in 1931. In 1933 an agreement was reached whereby the Axe became the trophy for the winner of the annual "Big Game" (football), between California and Stanford.

50   H. M. Pond, "Reminiscences of '76," *California Monthly*, XX (October, 1926), 85.

51   Clinton R. "Brick" Morse, "The Songs of California," *California Monthly*, XLVII (October, 1941), 16, 17.

52   Farnham Griffiths, "Student Self Government at the University of California," *University of California Chronicle*, IX (April, 1907), 244.

53   *The Occident*, February 24, 1888, p. 22.

54   *The Berkeleyan*, February, 1874, p. 10.

55   *Ibid.*

56   *The Berkeleyan*, January, 1875, p. 8.

57   University of California, *Centennial Record* (Berkeley, 1967), 105.

58   *Blue and Gold*, 1900, 144–150.

59   President, *Biennial Report of the President of the University on Behalf of the Board of Regents to . . . the Governor . . . 1882–84* (Sacramento, 1884), 19.

60   *Blue and Gold*, 1900, 144; *Centennial Record*, 96.

61   *Blue and Gold*, 1897, 84.

62   *Blue and Gold*, 1900, 128.

63   *Ibid.*

64   *Daily Californian*, February 11, 1910, p. 1.

65   Register of Students September 24, 1869–April 21, 1871 (University of California archives, Berkeley).

66   University of California, *Statutes: Rules of Order and General Regulations Adopted by the Regents of the University, December 13, 1869* (Sacramento, 1869), 10–11 (University of California archives, Berkeley).

67   *Register of the University of California, 1879–80* (Berkeley, 1879), 33 (University of California archives, Berkeley).

68   William T. Reid, *Inaugural Address, Addresses at the Inauguration of W. T. Reid, August 23, 1881* (Sacramento, 1881), 43 (in University of California, *Inaugurals, 1872–1899,* University of California archives, Berkeley).

69   *The Berkeleyan,* September 30, 1876, p. 4.

70   *Blue and Gold,* 1889, 96.

71   *Ibid.*

Chapter 12

1   "The Undecided Regents," clipping dated September 9, 1892, from an unidentified San Francisco newspaper (in pamphlet box labeled "Newspaper Clippings," University of California archives, Berkeley).

2   Letter from J. G. Schurman to Columbus Bartlett, April 20, 1892 (in Regents, "Correspondence and Papers," Box 16, P–Q 1892).

3   William Carey Jones, *Illustrated History of the University of California* (Rev. ed.; San Francisco, 1901), 121.

4   Communication from Members of the Academic Council, August 29, 1892 (in Regents, "Correspondence and Papers," Box 16, Folder P–Q 1892).

5   Milicent Shinn, "University of California," *Overland Monthly,* XX (October, 1892), 339–340.

6   "Moses Not Acceptable," an undated clipping from an unidentified newspaper, dealing with the Regents' meeting of September 6, 1892 (in pamphlet box labeled "Newspaper Clippings," University of California archives, Berkeley).

7   *Ibid.*

8   Minutes of the Board of Regents, January 24, 1893, Vol. IX, p. 225 (Office of the Secretary of the Regents, University of California, Berkeley).

9   Annette J. Chamberlain, "Of the Home of President Kellogg" (Manuscript Collection, Bancroft Library, University of California, Berkeley).

10   San Francisco *Examiner,* January 27, 1893 (in "Newspaper Clippings Relating to the University of California, 1874–1899," VI, 13–14, University of California archives, Berkeley).

11   *Ibid.*

12   *Ibid.*

13   California, *Statutes* (1891), c. LXIII, sec. 6, p. 58.

14   University of California, Minutes of the Academic Council, August 14, 1892, as quoted in Herman Adolph Spindt, "A History of the Relations of the University of California and the Public Schools of California, 1872–1945" (unpublished Ph.D. dissertation, University of California, 1946), 57–58.

15   *Ibid.,* November 28, 1897, as quoted in Spindt, 58.

16   Oakland *Enquirer,* March 28, 1897 (in Milicent W. Shinn [compiler], "Martin Kellogg as President of the University of California: Opinions of Contemporaries," 1897, p. 1, University of California archives, Berkeley).

17   Minutes of the Board of Regents, July 13, 1897, Vol. XI, pp. 144–145.

18   Regents, *Annual Report of the Secretary to the Board of Regents of the University of California . . . 1898* (Berkeley, 1898), 91 (University of California archives, Berkeley).

19   Minutes of the Board of Regents, September 13, 1898, Vol. XII, p. 60.

Chapter 13

1   Letter from Jacob Reinstein to A. S. Hallidie, February 27, 1899 (in Regents, "Correspondence and Papers," Box 25, Folder R 1899, University of California archives, Berkeley).

2   Letter from Phoebe A. Hearst to Governor Budd, October 24, 1898 (in Regents, "Correspondence and Papers," Box 25, Folder on Presidency, 1899).

3   Letter from C. W. Eliot to Martin Kellogg, January 12, 1899 [copy] (*ibid.*).

4   Letter from C. K. Adams to J. B. Reinstein, November 16, 1898 [copy] (*ibid.*).

5   "Four Letters Relating to the Acceptancy by Benjamin Ide Wheeler of the Presidency of the University of California" (University of California archives, Berkeley).

6   *Daily Californian,* November 24, 1914, p. 4.

7   Benjamin Ide Wheeler, *The Abundant Life,* ed. Monroe E. Deutsch (Berkeley, 1926), 3–5.

8   Letter from Benjamin Ide Wheeler to A. C. Miller, postmarked February 4, 1899, in "Four Letters. . . ."

9   Letter from Arthur Rodgers to A. S. Hallidie, March 25, 1899 (in Regents, "Correspondence and Papers," Box 25, Folder R).

10   Minutes of the Board of Regents, June 16, 1899, Vol. XII, p. 292 (Office of the Secretary of the Regents, University of California, Berkeley).

11   Regents, *Annual Report of the Secretary to the Board of Regents of the University of California, . . . 1900* (Sacramento, 1901), 84–85 (University of California archives, Berkeley).

12   Minutes of the Board of Regents, July 18, 1899, Vol. XII, pp. 304–305.

13   *Ibid.,* p. 305.

14   *Daily Californian,* September 20, 1899, p. 1.

15   Wheeler, *The Abundant Life,* 27.

16   *Ibid.,* 27, 28.

17   *Daily Californian,* March 15, 1901, p. 2.

18   *Daily Californian,* August 21, 1900, p. 4.

19   *Ibid.*

20   *Daily Californian,* August 20, 1901, p. 3.

21   *Daily Californian,* August 23, 1910, p. 6.

22   *Daily Californian,* August 22, 1911, p. 1.

23   *Daily Californian,* August 21, 1916, p. 4.

24   *Daily Californian,* November 26, 1900, p. 4.

25   Wheeler, *The Abundant Life,* 27.

26   *Daily Californian,* November 26, 1900, p. 1.

27   *Daily Californian,* August 30, 1900, p. 1.

28   *Daily Californian,* April 7, 1919, p. 3.

29   Henry T. Gage, *Second Biennial Message of Governor Henry T. Gage to the Legislature of the State of California* (Sacramento, 1903), 55.

30   *Daily Californian,* January 19, 1903, p. 3.

31   *Daily Californian,* February 13, 1905, p. 1.

32   Regents, *The Report of the Secretary to the Regents of the University of California . . . 1906* (Sacramento, 1907), 3–6 (University of California archives, Berkeley).

33   California, *Statutes* (1909), c. 329, pp. 543–544.

34   President, *Biennial Report of the President of the University on Behalf of the Regents to . . . the Governor . . . 1910–1912* (Berkeley, 1912), 159 (University of California archives, Berkeley).

35   *Ibid.,* 7.

36   *Ibid.,* 10–11.

37   *Ibid.,* 192.

38   President, *Annual Report of the President of the University on Behalf of the Regents to . . . the Governor . . . 1914–1915* (Berkeley, 1915), 351 (University of California archives, Berkeley).

39   Ralph P. Merritt, " 'After Me Cometh a Builder,' " typescript completed under the auspices of the Regional Cultural History Project and the Oral History Program (University of California, Berkeley and Los Angeles, 1962), 33 (Bancroft Library, University of California, Berkeley).

40   William Warren Ferrier, *Origin and Development of the University of California* (Berkeley, 1930), 494–496.

41   President, *Biennial Report of the President of the University on Behalf of the Regents to . . . the Governor . . . 1898–1900* (Berkeley, 1900), 53–55 (University of California archives, Berkeley).

42   Regents, "Report of the Secretary to the Regents of the University of California, . . . 1904," 37 (typescript, University of California archives, Berkeley).

43   Arthur E. Hutson, "Faculty Government," in University of California, *Centennial Record* (Berkeley, 1967), 290.

44   *By Laws and Standing Rules of the Academic Senate and other Academic Bodies, Submitted to the Academic Senate by the Committee on Rules and Regulations* (Berkeley, April, 1916) (University of California archives, Berkeley).

45   *Daily Californian,* August 15, 1913, p. 1.

46   President, *Annual Report of the President of the University on Behalf of the Regents . . . to the Governor . . . 1916–1917* (Berkeley, 1917), 272 (University of California archives, Berkeley).

47   *Daily Californian,* April 10, 1917, p. 1.

48   President, *Annual Report . . . 1916–1917,* 6.

49   President, *Annual Report of the President of the University on Behalf of the Regents to . . . the Governor . . . 1917–1918* (Berkeley, 1918), 5 (University of California archives, Berkeley).

50   *Ibid.,* 10.

51   *Ibid.,* 25.

52   *Ibid.*

53   *University of California War Service Record for the Academic Year 1917–1918* (Berkeley, 1918), 119 (in President, *Annual Report . . . 1917–1918*).

54   *Ibid.,* 10–24; President, *Annual Report . . . 1917–1918,* 22.

55   President, *Annual Report . . . 1917–1918,* 6, 7.

56   *Ibid.,* 291.

57   *Ibid.,* 292.

58   *Ibid.,* 289.

59   *Ibid.,* 294.

60   *Ibid.,* 292.

61   *Daily Californian,* September 2, 1914, p. 1.

62   *Town Talk,* April 6, 1918, p. 9.

63   President, *Annual Report . . . 1917–1918,* 14.

64   *Ibid.,* 22–24.

65   *Daily Californian,* October 21, 1918, p. 1.

66   *Daily Californian,* October 30, 1918, p. 1.

67   *Daily Californian,* October 24, 1918, p. 1.

68   President, *Annual Report . . . 1919–1918,* 22–24.

69   University of California, *Register 1899–1900,* 45.

70   President, *Annual Report . . . 1898–1900,* 8.

71   *Centennial Record,* 371.

72   President, *Annual Report . . . 1910–1912,* 15–16.

73   Paul W. West, "Scripps Institution of Oceanography," *Centennial Record,* 507.

74   June Barth Dow, "University Extension," *Centennial Record,* 226–228.

75   President, *Annual Report . . . 1898–1900,* 26.

76   Merritt, 38.

77   California, Constitution, Article IX, Sec. 9.

78   Merritt, 62.

79   California, Constitution, Article IX, Sec. 9.

Chapter 14

1   President, *Report of the President for the Board of Regents, 1881–82* (Sacramento, 1882), 12 (University of California archives, Berkeley).

2   President, *Biennial Report of the President of the University on Behalf of the Board of Regents to the Governor . . . 1886* (Sacramento, 1886), 119 (University of California archives, Berkeley).

3   Regents, *Annual Report of the Secretary to the Board of Regents of the University of California . . . 1893* (Sacramento, 1893), 55 (University of California archives, Berkeley).

4   President, *Biennial Report of the President of the University on Behalf of the Regents to the Governor . . . 1902–1904* (Berkeley, 1904), 50 (University of California archives, Berkeley).

5   "University of California Press," in President, *Annual Report of the President of the University on Behalf of the Regents to . . . the Governor . . . 1915–1916* (Berkeley, 1916), 205 (University of California archives, Berkeley).

6   California, *Statutes* (1867–1868), c. CCXLIV, sec. 4, p. 249.

7   E. J. Wickson, "Beginnings of Agricultural Education and Research in California," *Report of the College of Agriculture and the Agricultural Experiment Station of the University of California, July 1, 1917–June 30, 1918* (Berkeley, 1918), 60 (University of California archives, Berkeley).

8   *Ibid.*, 61.

9   *Ibid.*, 55, 74, 88, 95.

10   Milicent W. Shinn, "The University of California II. The Lick Astronomical Department," *The Overland Monthly*, XX (November, 1892), 488.

11   *Ibid.*

12   *Ibid.*

13   *Ibid.*, 491–492.

14   *Ibid.*

15   *Ibid.*

16   *Ibid.*

17   A. E. Whitford, "Lick Observatory," in University of California, *Centennial Record* (Berkeley, 1967), 328.

18   Shinn, 498.

19   "Chile Station: an Outpost of the University," *California Monthly*, XIX (November, 1925), 139, 163.

20   Simon Newcomb, "Astronomy, History of," *Encyclopedia Americana* (1918) II, 460.

21   *Biennial Report of the Regents of the University of California for the Years 1875–7* (Sacramento, 1877), 57 (in President, *Report of the President of the University on Behalf of the Regents . . . 1869–79,* University of California archives, Berkeley).

22   President, *Biennial Report . . . 1886*, 29.

23   President, *Biennial Report . . . 1902–1904*, 46.

24   "The La Jolla Biological Station," *The University of California Chronicle*, X (January, 1908), 77.

25   President, *Biennial Report of the President of the University on Behalf of the Regents to the Governor . . . 1910–1912* (Berkeley, 1912), 149 (University of California archives, Berkeley).

26   *Ibid.*, 146.

27   *Ibid.*, 148.

28   Charles A. Kofoid, "The San Diego Marine Biological Laboratory," *The University of California Chronicle*, IX (January, 1907), 65; *Centennial Record*, 516.

29   President, *Biennial Report of the President of the University on Behalf of the Regents to . . . the Governor . . . 1906–1908* (Berkeley, 1908), 18 (University of California, Berkeley).

30   President, *Annual Report of the President of the University on Behalf of the Regents to the Governor . . . 1916–1917* (Berkeley, 1917), 153.

31   *Centennial Record*, 516.

32   *Ibid.*

33   Paul West, "Scripps Institution of Oceanography," *Centennial Record*, 507.

34   President, *Annual Report of the President of the University on Behalf of the Regents to the Governor . . . 1917–1918* (Berkeley, 1918).

35   West, 507.

36   "Workshop for the Study of Man," *California Monthly*, XLV (September, 1954), 17; "Man and His Works," *California Monthly*, XLV (September, 1954), 13.

37   "Workshop for the Study of Man," 17–18.

38   John H. Rowe, "Anthropology, Berkeley," *Centennial Record*, 78.

39   President, *Biennial Report . . . 1910–1912*, 31.

40   Hilda W. Grinnell, *Annie Montague Alexander* (Grinnell Naturalists Society, Museum of Vertebrate Zoology, Berkeley, 1958), 4.

41   C. L. Camp, "Paleontology, Berkeley," *Centennial Record*, 96.

42   President, *Biennial Report . . . 1910–1912*, 42.

43   President, *Annual Report of the President of the University on Behalf of the Regents to the Governor . . . 1914–1915* (Berkeley, 1915), 45 (University of California archives, Berkeley).

44   President, *Annual Report of the President of the University on Behalf of the Regents to the Governor . . . 1919–1920* (Berkeley, 1920), 44–45 (University of California archives, Berkeley).

45   Camp, 96.

46   Grinnell, 7.

47   *Ibid.*, 9.

48   *Ibid.*, 27.

49   President, *Biennial Report of the President of the University on Behalf of the Regents to the Governor . . . 1898–1900* (Berkeley, 1900), 79 (University of California archives, Berkeley).

50   President, *Biennial Report of the President of the University on Behalf of the Regents to the Governor . . . 1900–1902* (Berkeley, 1902), 48 (University of California archives, Berkeley).

51   Dr. Loeb was one of the models for the dedicated scientist Max Gottlieb in Sinclair Lewis's *Arrowsmith*.

52   President, *Biennial Report . . . 1900–1902,* 49.

53   Nello Pace, "Physiology—Anatomy, Berkeley," *Centennial Record,* 98.

54   President, *Biennial Report . . . 1900–1902,* 49.

55   President, *Biennial Report . . . 1902–1904,* 44.

56   President, *Biennial Report . . . 1900–1902,* 51.

57   Pace, 98.

58   President, *Biennial Report . . . 1900–1902,* 122.

59   President, *Annual Report of the President of the University on Behalf of the Regents to the Governor . . . 1912–1913* (Berkeley, 1913), 19 (University of California archives, Berkeley); President, *Annual Report of the President of the University on Behalf of the Regents to the Governor . . . 1913–1914* (Berkeley, 1914), 22 (University of California archives, Berkeley).

60   President, *Annual Report . . . 1914–1915,* 104–105.

61   *Centennial Record,* 248.

62   *California Monthly,* LXII (November, 1951), 4–5.

63   President, *Biennial Report . . . 1898–1900,* 28.

64   *Ibid.*

65   *Centennial Record,* 104.

66   James R. K. Kantor, Robert H. Becker, "Bancroft Library," *Centennial Record,* 45.

67   *Ibid.*

68   University of California, *The Semicentenary Celebration of the Founding of the University of California with an Account of the Conference on International Relations* (Berkeley, 1919), 549–563.

69   President, *Annual Report . . . 1915–1916,* 26.

70   President, *Annual Report . . . 1919–1920,* 156.

71   *Ibid.,* 159.

Chapter 15

1   *California Alumni Weekly,* November 19, 1910, p. 2.

2   Benjamin Ide Wheeler, "Charter Day Address," *University of California Chronicle,* XIII (April, 1911), 202.

3   "Population of California Counties," in Don A. Allen, Sr., *Legislative Sourcebook* (Sacramento, 1965), 154–155.

4   *Ibid.*

5   Security-First National Bank of Los Angeles, *Six Collegiate Decades: The Growth of Higher Education in Southern California* (Los Angeles, 1929). By 1910, the following institutions existed in southern California: Loyola University, University of Redlands, University of Southern California, La Verne College, Occidental College, Pasadena College, Pomona College, Whittier College, Throop Polytechnic Institute, and normal schools at Los Angeles and San Diego.

6   President, *Biennial Report of the President of the University on Behalf of the Regents to ... the Governor ... 1910–1912* (Berkeley, 1912), 8 (University of California archives, Berkeley).

7   Senate Bill 693, in California, Legislature, *Senate Bills* (1911), Vol. III.

8   Senate Bill 921, in California, Legislature, *Senate Bills* (1911), Vol. IV.

9   *Ibid.*

10   *Daily Californian,* February 20, 1911, p. 2.

11   San Francisco *Call,* January 24, 1911, as quoted in *California Alumni Weekly,* January 28, 1911, p. 2.

12   *Daily Californian,* March 8, 1911, p. 1.

13   *Ibid.*

14   *Ibid.*

15   *Daily Californian,* March 9, 1911, p. 1.

16   *Daily Californian,* March 8, 1911, p. 1.

17   *California Alumni Weekly,* March 11, 1911, p. 1.

18   Edward A. Dickson, *University of California at Los Angeles* (Los Angeles, 1955), 7, 8.

19   Letter from Benjamin Ide Wheeler to Edward A. Dickson, February 16, 1916, as reproduced in Dickson, 10–11.

20   *Ibid.*

21   President, *Annual Report of the President of the University 1918–1919* (Berkeley, 1920), 161 (University of California archives, Berkeley).

22   Los Angeles *Examiner,* November 6, 1918, as reproduced in Dickson, 14.

23   California, Legislature, *Journal of the Assembly During the Forty-First Session (1915)* (Sacramento, 1915), 443.

24   Dickson, 8–10.

25   James R. Martin, *The University of California (in Los Angeles)* (Los Angeles, 1925), 33. The site is now the location of the Los Angeles Public Library.

26   *Ibid.,* 36.

27   *Ibid.,* 38.

28   Report to the Board of Regents, from Conference Committee on Los Angeles State Normal School, September 10, 1918 (in Chester H. Rowell, "Correspondence and Papers," Box 11, folder on "California, University: University at Los Angeles," Bancroft Library of the University of California, Berkeley).

29 Martin, 41.

30 University of California, *Centennial Record* (Berkeley, 1967), 332.

31 University of California, *President's Report on the Relations of the Teachers College at Los Angeles to the University of California* (Berkeley, 1928), 2.

32 Minutes of the Board of Regents, June 11, 1918, Vol. XXI, p. 12 (Office of the Secretary to the Regents, University of California, Berkeley).

33 Report to the Board of Regents, from Conference Committee on Los Angeles State Normal School.

34 Minutes of the Executive Committee of the Board of Regents, November 19, 1918, as quoted in *President's Report on the Relations of the Teachers College . . . ,* 7.

35 Letter from Ernest C. Moore to Walter Morris Hart, December 12, 1918, as quoted in *President's Report on the Relations of the Teachers College . . . ,* 8.

36 Letter from Chester Rowell to Benjamin Ide Wheeler, December 21, 1918 (in Rowell, "Correspondence and Papers," Box 2, folder on "Nov.–Dec., 1918").

37 *President's Report on the Relations of the Teachers College . . . ,* 9.

38 Letter from Chester Rowell to Ernest C. Moore, December 26, 1918 (in Rowell, "Correspondence and Papers," Box 2, folder on "Nov.–Dec., 1918").

39 Letter from Ernest C. Moore to Chester Rowell, December 20, 1918 (in Rowell, "Correspondence and Papers," Box 11, folder on "California, University. University at Los Angeles").

40 Ernest C. Moore, *I Helped Make a University* (Los Angeles, 1952), 39.

41 *Ibid.*

42 *Ibid., 39–40.*

43 Assembly Bill 626, as introduced January 23, 1919, in California Legislature, *Assembly Bills* (1919), Vol. III.

44 Charles S. Wheeler, "Charter Day Address," *University of California Chronicle,* XXI (April, 1919), 168–169.

45 Letter from Chester Rowell to W. W. Campbell, May 31, 1928 (in Rowell, "Correspondence and Papers," Box 6, folder on 1928).

46 Moore, 43.

47 Letter from C. Rowell to W. W. Campbell, May 31, 1928.

48 Moore, 43.

49 *Assembly Final History* (1919), p. 198, in California, Legislature—Forty-Third Session, 1919, *Final Calendar* (Sacramento, 1919).

50 Minutes of the Board of Regents, June 10, 1919, Vol. XXI, p. 134–136.

51 "Memorandum from President," in President, *Annual Report of the President of the University 1920–1921* (Berkeley, 1922), 287–288 (University of California archives, Berkeley).

52 *Ibid.,* 288.

53 Interview with Baldwin Woods, June 29, 1956, p. 9 (Centennial Publications files).

54 Robert M. Underhill, interview with the author, June 27, 1966.

55   Moore, 63.

56   President, *Annual Report of the President of the University 1919–1920* (Berkeley, 1920), 6 (University of California archives, Berkeley).

57   Ernest C. Moore, "Southern Branch," in President, *Annual Report . . . 1920–1921,* 195.

58   *Ibid.*

59   *University of California Register,* 1920–1921—1947–1948.

60   California, *Statutes* (1921), c. 471, pp. 715–719.

61   Minutes of the Board of Regents, February 14, 1922, Vol. XXII, p. 449. The Academic Senate at Berkeley authorized the granting of the Bachelor of Science in Education (B.S.Ed.) degree provided the curriculum met certain standards insisted upon by the Academic Senate on March 27, 1922. Moore said he could not meet those standards so the senate recommended that the Regents authorize award of the Bachelor of Education (B.Ed.) degree. (Minutes of the Academic Senate, April 16, 1923, Vol. III, pp. 379–380; April 23, 1923, Vol. III, pp. 382–383, in Office of the Academic Senate, University of California, Berkeley.)

62   Minutes of the Regents' Committee on the Southern Branch of the University of California, January 9, 1923, as quoted in Dickson, 32–34.

63   Dickson, 33–36.

64   Senate Bill 10, in California, Legislature, *Senate Bills* (1923), Vol. I.

65   Minutes of the Board of Regents, executive session, February 13, 1923.

66   President, *Annual Report of the President of the University 1922–1923* (Berkeley, 1924), 3–4 (University of California archives, Berkeley).

67   Minutes of the Board of Regents, executive session, December 11, 1923.

68   *Ibid.*

69   Dickson, 41.

70   *Ibid.,* 43.

71   Martin, 73.

72   Dickson, 44–47.

73   Martin, 169–170. Martin says the total selling price of the property was $1,319,539.65, but the amount actually voted, according to his own recapitulation, was only $1,070,000. He does not explain the discrepancy.

74   Martin, 109–124.

75   Minutes of the Regents' Committee on Agriculture, November 21, 1924.

76   Martin, 54–69.

77   W. M. Hart, C. B. Lipman, G. D. Louderback (Sub-committee of Academic Senate Committee on Educational Policy), "Memorandum Concerning the Separation of the Teachers' College from the Southern Branch and from the University" (in George D. Louderback, "Correspondence and Papers," Carton 4, folder on "Committee on Educational Policy," section on "Reports, 1920–1952").

78   Minutes of the Board of Regents, executive session, March 10, 1925.

79   Minutes of the Board of Regents, December 14, 1926, Vol. XXIV, p. 458.

80   Minutes of the Board of Regents, executive session, August 14, 1928.

81   After Kelham's death, the building was supervised by the firm of Allison and Allison. That firm is credited as the actual architect of Royce Hall.

82   Robert M. Underhill, interview with the author, June 27, 1966.

83   Minutes of the Board of Regents, February 1, 1927, Vol. XXIV, p. 186.

Chapter 16

1   *By-Laws and Rules of Order of the Academic Senate of the University of California* (Berkeley, 1885), 4–5 (University of California archives, Berkeley).

2   Minutes of the Academic Senate, May 5, 1909, Vol. I, p. 285 (Office of the Academic Senate, University of California, Berkeley).

3   Minutes of the Academic Senate, November 17, 1909, Vol. I, p. 290.

4   *By-Laws, Rules of Order and Standing Rules of the Academic Senate: Standing Rules of the Academic and Graduate Councils: Joint Regulations of the Academic Faculties* (Berkeley, 1910), 6 (University of California archives, Berkeley).

5   Arthur E. Hutson, "Faculty Government," in University of California, *Centennial Record* (Berkeley, 1967), 290.

6   Minutes of the Academic Senate, May 5, 1915, Vol. I, p. 388.

7   *By-Laws and Standing Rules of the Academic Senate and Other Academic Bodies Submitted to the Academic Senate by the Committee on Rules and Regulations* (Berkeley, April, 1916), 8 (University of California archives, Berkeley).

8   *Ibid.*, 8, 9.

9   *Ibid.*, 6.

10   Harry Burton, *Aspects of College and University Administration: A Report to the Trustees of Dartmouth College* (Hanover, New Hampshire, 1916), 4.

11   "Report of Committee T on Place and Function of Faculties in University Government and Administration," *American Association of University Professors Bulletin,* VI (March, 1920), 17, 47.

12   Minutes of the Board of Regents, June 10, 1919, Vol. XXI, p. 135 (Office of the Secretary of the Regents, University of California, Berkeley). Merritt replaced Henry Morse Stephens, who collapsed and died on April 16, 1919, while riding on a San Francisco cable car and returning from Regent Phoebe Apperson Hearst's funeral.

13   Minutes of the Academic Senate, October 2, 1919, Vol. II, p. 358.

14   *Ibid.*

15   *Ibid.*, p. 357.

16   Memorial from the Academic Senate to the Regents of the University of California, in Minutes of the Academic Senate, October 2, 1919, Vol. II, p. 355.

17   *Manual of the Academic Senate* (Berkeley, November, 1925), 14.

18   *Ibid.*, 24.

19   Memorandum from William Carey Jones to Academic Senate, November 3, 1919, in Minutes of the Academic Senate, November 10, 1919, Vol. II, p. 365.

20   Minutes of the Academic Senate, November 10, 1919, Vol. II, p. 367; November 24, 1919, Vol. II, p. 376.

21   Conference Committee report to the Academic Senate [page titled in pencil: "Constitution and government of the University Adopted, March 29, 1920] (in Pamphlet Box, "Academic Senate, Special Reports, etc.," folder on "Academic Senate, Faculty Revolution," University of California archives, Berkeley); "Regents' Biographies," *Centennial Record,* 411, 412, 421.

22   Letter from Henry Morse Stephens to R. J. Taussig, April 14, 1919, p. 4 (in Henry Morse Stephens, "Correspondence and Papers," outgoing letters [arranged chronologically], Bancroft Library of the University of California).

23   *Ibid.,* pp. 4–5.

24   *Ibid.,* p. 5.

25   *Ibid.*

26   *Ibid.*

27   Ralph P. Merritt, " 'After Me Cometh a Builder,' " typescript completed under the auspices of the Regional Cultural History Project and the Oral History Program (University of California, Berkeley and Los Angeles, 1962), 70 (Bancroft Library).

28   Letter from Chester Rowell to Dr. John R. Haynes, April 23, 1919 (Chester H. Rowell, "Correspondence and Papers," Box 4, folder for 1919, Jan.–Apr., Bancroft Library).

29   *Ibid.*

30   Letter from Ralph P. Merritt to the Regents, March 16, 1920, in President, *Annual Report of the President of the University on Behalf of the Regents to ... the Governor ... 1919–1920* (Berkeley, 1920), 264–65 (University of California archives, Berkeley).

31   Merritt, " 'After Me Cometh a Builder,' " 41.

32   *Centennial Record,* 15, 16.

33   Minutes of the Board of Regents, December 2, 1919, Vol. XXI, p. 209.

34   *Centennial Record,* 15, 16.

35   *Ibid.*

36   Report to the Academic Senate of the University of California, submitted by G. P. Adams, A. C. Lawson, G. N. Lewis, G. D. Louderback, O. K. McMurray, in Minutes of the Academic Senate, March 29, 1920, Vol. II, p. 409.

37   *Ibid.*

38   *Ibid.*

39   *Ibid.*

40   *Ibid.,* p. 410.

41   *Ibid.*

42   *Ibid.*

43   *Ibid.,* p. 411.

44   Minutes of the Academic Senate, December 19, 1919, Vol. II, p. 377a.

45   Minutes of the Board of Regents, April 13, 1920, Vol. XXII, p. 11; June 24, 1920, Vol. XXII, p. 91. Italics added.

46   Letter from David P. Barrows to the Board of Regents, September 3, 1920 (in David P. Barrows, "Correspondence and Papers," outgoing letters [arranged chronologically], Bancroft Library).

47   Extract from Executive Committee Minutes of the Board of Regents, September 23, 1920 (appended to letter from Barrows to the Board of Regents, September 3, 1920).

48   "Standing Orders of the Board of Regents: Powers and Privileges of President and Faculties," communication from David P. Barrows to the Academic Senate, October 1, 1920, in Minutes of the Academic Senate, October 25, 1920, Vol. III, p. 18.

49   Letter from George D. Louderback to Harry B. Torrey, January 27, 1922 (in George D. Louderback, "Correspondence and Papers," Box 1, Bancroft Library).

50   Letter from David P. Barrows to George D. Louderback, December 15, 1920 (in Louderback, "Correspondence and Papers," Box 11, in folder on "California, University, Berkeley, President 1907–1922").

51   Letter from David P. Barrows to J. F. Daniel, April 10, 1922 (ibid.).

52   Letter from David P. Barrows to the Committee of Fifteen of the Academic Senate, April 17, 1922 (in Louderback, "Correspondence and Papers," Carton 3, folder on "Academic Senate; Committee of Fifteen, 1907–1922").

53   Ibid.

54   Memorandum to the President from Morse A. Cartwright, January 4, 1922 (Barrows, "Correspondence and Papers," Carton 18, folder on "University of California, Barrows—President: Memoranda, statements, etc.").

55   Ibid.

56   Letter from David P. Barrows to the Committee of Fifteen of the Academic Senate, April 17, 1922. Centennial publications files (University of California archives, Berkeley).

57   Report of the Special Committee on Administrative Methods, May 8, 1922 (in Pamphlet Box, "Academic Senate, Special Reports, etc.").

58   Ibid.

59   Letter from David P. Barrows to the Board of Regents, May 11, 1922 (in Barrows, "Correspondence and Papers," outgoing letters).

60   Letter from David P. Barrows to E. Morris Cox, May 20, 1922 (ibid.).

61   Hugh G. Price, "California Public Junior Colleges," Bulletin of the California State Department of Education, XXVII (February, 1958), 66–67.

62   President, Annual Report of the President of the University on Behalf of the Regents to . . . the Governor . . . 1920–1921 (Berkeley, 1922), 17 (University of California archives, Berkeley).

63   Ibid., 15.

64   Minutes of the Board of Regents, March 9, 1920, Vol. XXI, p. 247; President, Annual Report . . . 1920–1921, 7.

65   President, Annual Report . . . 1920–1921, 9.

66   George A. Pettitt, *Twenty-eight Years in the Life of a University President* (Berkeley, 1966), 11, 14–17.

67   "Preliminary ... Notes of a Conversation of Dean Emeritus G. D. Louderback with Walton Bean ... , October 12, 1953" (Regional Oral History Office, Bancroft Library).

68   President, *Annual Report ... 1920–1921*, 23.

69   *Daily Californian*, February 25, 1920, p. 1.

70   Letter from Chester Rowell to Arthur Arlett (Sr.), March 2, 1920 (in Rowell, "Correspondence and Papers," Box 5, folder on Mar.–May, 1920).

71   Minutes of Meeting of the Committee on Conference with the Faculty, October 9, 1922; November 12, 1922 (in Louderback, "Correspondence and Papers," Carton 3, folder on "Academic Senate, Committee on Committees: Misc.," section on "Elections, 1919–1954").

72   Letter from Gilbert N. Lewis to James K. Moffitt, December 13, 1922 (in Pamphlet Box, "Academic Senate, Special Reports, etc.," folder on "Academic Senate, Faculty Revolution").

73   *Ibid.*

74   Letter from Barrows to W. W. Campbell, December 1, 1922 (in Barrows, "Correspondence and Papers," outgoing letters).

75   Letter from W. W. Campbell to Executive Committee of the Board of Regents, December 27, 1922 (in Rowell, "Correspondence and Papers," Box 11, folder on "California, University, Regents").

76   Minutes of the Academic Senate, January 22, 1923, Vol. III, pp. 351–52.

77   President, *Annual Report of the President of the University on Behalf of the Regents to ... the Governor ... 1924–25 and 1925–26* (Berkeley, 1927), 148 (University of California archives, Berkeley).

78   Letter from Arthur L. Wheeler to G. D. Louderback, November 18, 1919 (in Louderback, "Correspondence and Papers," Box 8, folder on "Bryn Mawr College").

Chapter 17

1   "Hope for Educational Reform," editorial from unidentified newspaper around November, 1930, in Robert G. Sproul, "Clippings, 1916–1932" (University of California archives, Berkeley).

2   Robert G. Sproul, Inaugural Address, as quoted in George A. Pettitt, *Twenty-eight Years in the Life of a University President* (Berkeley, 1966).

3   Memorandum from President to Regents re *University Long Range Fiscal Program 1966/67–1975/76*, July 7, 1967, Appendix A-1.

4   Minutes of the Academic Senate, Northern Section, December 17, 1932, Vol. VII, p. 118 (Office of the Academic Senate, University of California, Berkeley).

5   Robert G. Sproul, "A Fair Deal for California's University" (address March 23, 1933), *California Monthly*, XXX (April, 1933), 8.

6   Robert G. Sproul, "Maintaining the Standards of California's University" (address over station KPO, April 5, 1933), in Robert G. Sproul, "Collected Papers," I (University of California archives, Berkeley).

7   *Daily Bruin,* April 5, 1933; April 6, 1933, in Sproul, "Clippings, 1933–1934."

8   Oakland *Post-Enquirer,* April 12 (or 13), 1933, in Sproul, "Clippings, 1933–1934."

9   Letter from Assemblyman E. H. Zion to Turlock *Daily Journal,* April, 1933, in Sproul, "Clippings, 1933–1934."

10   *Ibid.*

11   Sacramento *Bee,* April 29, 1933, in Sproul, "Clippings, 1933–1934."

12   Los Angeles *Times,* June 30, 1933, in Sproul, "Clippings, 1933–1934."

13   Richmond *Record Herald,* July 15, 1933, in Sproul, "Clippings, 1933–1934." Actually, incidental fees were increased by one dollar, but other miscellaneous fees of less than one dollar (i.e., gym suit fee) that had been collected separately were abandoned.

14   San Francisco *Commercial News,* editorial May 8, 1939, in Sproul, "Clippings, 1939–1941."

15   *Ibid.*

16   Sacramento *Bee,* March 8, 1935, in Sproul, "Clippings, 1935–1938."

17   Senate Bill 830, in California, Legislature, *Senate Bills* (1929), Vol. IV.

18   Minutes of the Academic Senate, October 6, 1930, Vol. VI, p. 195.

19   Clipping from unidentified newspaper, March 24, 1931, in Sproul, "Clippings, 1916–1932."

20   Clipping from unidentified newspaper, April, 1931, in Sproul, "Clippings, 1916–1932."

21   Senate Bill 895, in California, Legislature, *Senate Bills* (1931), Vol. V.

22   "Daniels Answers Sproul's College Opposition Talk," clipping from unidentified newspaper, March 23, 1932, in Sproul, "Clippings, 1916–1932."

23   Robert G. Sproul, Address to California Alumni Association, March 23, 1934, 7, in Sproul, "Collected Papers," I.

24   *State Higher Education in California: Report of the Carnegie Foundation for the Advancement of Teaching* (Sacramento, 1932), 22.

25   *University of California Clip Sheet,* September 20, 1932.

26   *State Higher Education in California,* 48.

27   *Ibid.,* 58.

28   *Ibid.,* 59.

29   *Ibid.,* 58.

30   *Ibid.,* 29.

31   University of California, *Centennial Record* (Berkeley, 1967), 305.

32   "Under the Capitol Dome," Riverside *Daily Press,* January 13, 1933, in Sproul, "Clippings, 1933–1934."

33   Robert G. Sproul, "Remarks . . . before California Alumni Association in Southern California," November 9, 1934, in Sproul, "Collected Papers," I.

34   Herman Adolph Spindt, "A History of the Relations of the University of California and the Public Schools of California, 1872–1945" (unpublished Ph.D. dissertation, University of California, 1946), 168–69.

35   Robert G. Sproul, "Relation of the University to the Secondary Schools," *Sierra Educational News,* XXXII (May, 1936), 14–16, as quoted in Spindt, 189–90.

36   Association of California Secondary School Principals, *Bulletin,* June, 1937, p. 12, as quoted in Spindt, 191.

37   "Dr. Sproul Speaks," *California Monthly,* XXV (November, 1930), 29–30.

38   G. Ross Robertson, "History of the Chemistry Department at UCLA" (unpublished typescript, 1959), p. 87 (University of California archives, Los Angeles).

39   Sacramento *Bee,* June 17, 1933, in Sproul, "Clippings, 1933–1934."

40   Westwood Hills *News,* January 6, 1933, in Sproul, "Clippings, 1933–1934."

41   *Daily Bruin,* April 6, 1933.

42   West Los Angeles *Independent,* August 11, 1933, in Sproul, "Clippings, 1933–1934"; Minutes of the Board of Regents, executive session, August 8, 1933.

43   Minutes of the Board of Regents, executive session, April 17, 1936.

44   *Centennial Record,* 365.

45   *Daily Bruin,* April 19, 1933, in Sproul, "Clippings, 1933–1934"; Minutes of the Academic Senate, March 27, 1933, Vol. VII, pp. 132–37; April 3, 1933, Vol. VII, pp. 138–44.

46   Freeman Tilden, "Two-Legged University," *World's Work,* LIX (July, 1930), 69.

47   *Daily Bruin,* September 21, 1931, in Sproul, "Clippings, 1916–1932."

48   Los Angeles *Examiner,* September 27, 1932, in Sproul, "Clippings, 1916–1932."

49   Riverside *Press,* editorial February 27, 1933, in Sproul, "Clippings, 1933–1934."

50   "One Great University," *Daily Bruin,* editorial January 31, 1933, in Sproul, "Clippings, 1933–1934."

51   "One University," *Daily Bruin,* editorial March 26, 1934, in Sproul, "Clippings, 1933–1934."

52   Andy Hamilton, "Sproul Takes Charge," *Los Angeles Times Magazine,* October 11, 1936, p. 11, in Sproul, "Clippings, 1935–1938."

53   Palo Alto *Times,* September 29, 1936, in Sproul, "Clippings, 1935–1938" (on the same page as clippings from October 30, 1936).

54   *Daily Bruin,* October 30, 1936, in Sproul, "Clippings, 1935–1938."

55   Davis *Enterprise,* November 24, 1939, in Sproul, "Clippings, 1939–1941."

56   *Daily Bruin,* November 5, 1948, p. 1.

57   Robert M. Underhill, interview with author, June 20, 1966.

58   *Ibid.*

59   *Ibid.*

60   *Catalogue of Officers and Students, 1931–32*, 5, 7, in *University of California Register 1931–32*, II.

61   *Centennial Record*, 220–21.

62   *Ibid.*, 295.

63   *Ibid.*

64   *Ibid.*, 275.

65   *Ibid.*, 295.

66   "A Tentative Program of Higher Education," August 20, 1935; Robert G. Sproul, first draft of a plan for University Organization (in Joel H. Hildebrand, "Papers" [unsorted material], folder on "University Organizations," University of California archives, Berkeley).

67   Robert G. Sproul to Regents Committee on Educational Policy (*ibid.*).

68   *Ibid.*

69   Robert G. Sproul to Joel H. Hildebrand, February 26, 1937 (in Hildebrand, "Papers," folder on "University Organization").

70   Minutes of the Board of Regents, March 9, 1937, Vol. XXIX, p. 340.

71   Report of the Special Committee on University Organization, presented June 2, 1943 to the Southern Section of the Academic Senate; Report of the Special Committee on University Organization to the members of the Academic Senate, Southern Section [undated, probably February, 1945] (in George D. Louderback, "Correspondence and Papers," Carton 6, folder on "Special Committee on Organization of the University: Reports [Northern and Southern Sections], section on "Southern, 1943–45," Bancroft Library of the University of California, Berkeley).

72   *Centennial Record*, 333.

73   Undated memorandum by Robert G. Sproul on faculty committees; letter from George D. Louderback to Sproul, November 12, 1942 (Louderback, "Correspondence and Papers," Box 6, folder on "Outgoing letters, 1942"); "Comments on Plan for an Executive Committee of the Academic Senate" by Joel H. Hildebrand, November 12, 1942 (in Louderback, "Correspondence and Papers," Carton 3, folder on "Emergency executive committee, misc." section on "Misc. Miscellany 1941–1944").

74   Minutes of the Academic Senate, Northern Section, April 5, 1943, Vol. V, series II, p. 202.

75   *Ibid.*, pp. 205–6.

76   Plan of Administrative Organization—University of California, by Robert G. Sproul, originally enclosed with his letter to George D. Louderback, April 21, 1943. In Louderback, "Correspondence and Papers": letter in Box 11, folder on "Presidents 1938–1943"; enclosed plan in Carton 6, folder on "Special Committee on Organization, Misc. (Drafts, Notes, etc.)."

77   Letter from Robert G. Sproul to R. W. Hodgson, Chairman of Special Committee on University Organization, Academic Senate, Southern Section, April 10, 1944 (in President, "Correspondence and Papers," 1944, folder 54).

78   *Ibid.*

79   *Ibid.*

80   *By-Laws and Standing Orders of the Regents of the University of California,* 1938, Ch. IX, sec. 2, p. 51.

81   "Clarence A. Dykstra Chosen UCLA Provost," *The UCLA Magazine,* XIX (November, 1944) 5, 6, 23.

82   *Faculty Bulletin,* XIV (January, 1945).

83   Robert G. Sproul, "After Twenty-five Years," The Ninety-third Commencement, 1956, in Pettitt, 250–51.

84   Los Angeles *Times,* November 5, 1930, Part II, p. 2.

85   *Ibid.*

86   Clark Kerr, interview with the author, June 13, 1967.

87   As quoted in Pettitt, 86.

88   Some papers said 10,000; others said 5000. The salary offered to Sproul was also variously reported as either $45,000 or $50,000, but the larger figure was used most frequently.

89   San Francisco *Chronicle,* undated, but probably August 30, 1940, in Sproul, "Clippings, 1939–1941."

90   *Ibid.,* March 10, 1939.

91   Los Angeles *Daily News,* December 18, 1937, in Sproul, "Clippings, 1935–1938."

92   San Francisco *News,* March 13, 1940, in Sproul, Clippings, 1939–1941."

93   Placentia *California Courier,* February 22, 1946, in Sproul, "Clippings, 1946–1947."

94   Los Angeles *Daily News,* June 24, 1948, in Sproul, "Clippings, 1948."

95   "Sproul Decides To Stay—," *California Monthly,* February, 1947, 7.

Chapter 18

1   Letter from W. W. Campbell to Joel Hildebrand, December 20, 1923 (in President, "Correspondence and Papers," Folder 32, University of California archives, Berkeley).

2   Minutes of the Academic Senate, April 26, 1921, Vol. III, p. 102 (Office of the Academic Senate, University of California, Berkeley).

3   *Daily Californian,* January 12, 1931, p. 1.

4   *Daily Californian,* February 4, 1936, p. 1.

5   University of California, *Centennial Record* (Berkeley, 1967), 300, 301, 509. Only two of the fraternities that existed in Berkeley in 1964 were established after 1930. All but one of UCLA's twenty-three sororities and all but two of Berkeley's twenty-four sororities were established by 1930.

6   Sinclair threatened public harassment of the University if a rumored expulsion of the *Occident*'s editor was carried out in 1925. Telegram from Upton

Sinclair to President Campbell, September 23, 1925 (in President, "Correspondence and Papers," 1925, Folder 1277).

7   *The Occident,* November, 1925, pp. 7–8.

8   Letter from W. W. Campbell to Brenton L. Metzler, November 25, 1925 (in President, "Correspondence and Papers," 1925, Folder 1277).

9   *Daily Californian,* November 25, 1925, p. 1.

10   San Francisco *Examiner,* February 6, 1926, pp. 1, 2.

11   Tom Tomson, "Green," *Occident,* March, 1926, pp. 15–16.

12   *Laughing Horse* [April, 1922] Vol. I, No. 1 (University of California archives, Berkeley).

13   Letter from W. W. Campbell to Wright Morton [ASUC President] , January 4, 1928 (in President, "Correspondence and Papers," Folder 1648).

14   Letter from W. W. Campbell to Robert Sibley, May 21, 1928 (in President, "Correspondence and Papers," 1928, Folder 122); "The Dill Pickle–Raspberry Embroglio," editorial, *California Monthly,* XXI (May, 1928).

15   Letter from W. W. Campbell to W. G. Foster, March 8, 1929 (in President, "Correspondence and Papers," 1929, Folder 205).

16   Los Angeles *Times,* January 24, 1926 (in UCLA Archives Ephemera file, folder on "California, University, Los Angeles, Hells Bells," University of California archives, Los Angeles).

17   *Daily Californian,* January 28, 1929, p. 1.

18   *Daily Californian,* December 1, 1932, p. 1.

19   *Daily Californian,* November 30, 1932, p. 1.

20   *Daily Californian,* April 5, 1934, p. 1.

21   Harry O. Bain, "Rare Moments in Bear Football," *California Monthly,* LXXVIII (October, 1967), 12.

22   Robert G. Sproul, "Big Game" *California Monthly,* XXV (November, 1930), 9.

23   *The Golden Book of California,* ed. Robert Sibley (Berkeley, 1937), 248.

24   *Daily Bruin,* October 15, 1936, p. 1.

25   *Daily Bruin,* November 20, 1936, p. 2.

26   *Daily Californian,* November 23, 1936, p. 1.

27   *Daily Californian,* November 22, 1937, p. 1.

28   *Daily Californian,* December 3, 1937, p. 1.

29   *Daily Californian,* November 29, 1940, p. 1.

30   *Blue and Gold,* 1921, p. 127.

31   Frank T. Lindgren, "Thirty Years of Co-operative Living," *California Monthly,* LXXIV (February, 1964), 12, 13.

32   William F. Calkins, "Cooperative Living," *California Monthly* XLIV (March, 1940), 21; *Daily Californian,* editorial November 1, 1940.

33   *Ibid.*

34   *Centennial Record,* 336.

35   *Daily Californian,* February 17, 1938, p. 1.

36   *Daily Californian,* April 4, 1938, p. 1.

37   *Daily Californian,* April 12, 1938, p. 1; Alumni Dormitory Committee, *A Discussion of the Needs at the University of California for Adequate Housing* (February, 1940) (University of California archives, Berkeley).

38   *Daily Californian,* October 20, 1938, pp. 1, 4.

39   *Daily Californian,* November 1, 1938, pp. 1, 6; November 4, 1938, p. 1.

40   *Daily Californian,* September 13, 1939, p. 4.

41   *Daily Californian,* August 30, 1937, p. 4.

42   *Daily Californian,* September 14, 1937, p. 4.

43   *Ibid.*

44   *Daily Californian,* September 16, 1937, p. 1.

45   *Ibid.*

46   Minutes of the Council of California Alumni Association, January 12, 1940.

47   Minutes of the Council of California Alumni Association, September 10, 1940.

48   Minutes of the Council of California Alumni Association, March 17, 1941.

49   Minutes of the ASUC Executive Committee, April 21, 1937; Report of Welfare Council, April 14, 1937 (in ASUC minutes book, following above-cited Executive Committee Minutes) (Eshleman Library, University of California, Berkeley).

50   *Daily Californian,* October 16, 1941, p. 1.

51   *Daily Californian,* March 27, 1941, p. 2.

52   *Occident,* May, 1920, pp. 481–84.

53   *Daily Californian,* October 20, 1932.

54   *Daily Californian,* November 5, 1940.

55   Hal Draper, "The Student Movement of the Thirties: A Political History," *As We Saw the Thirties,* ed. Rita J. Simon (Urbana, 1967), 157–58, 164–65.

56   *Student Outpost,* February 19, 1932 (University of California archives, Berkeley).

57   *Daily Bruin,* March 16, 1932.

58   *Daily Californian,* March 31, 1931, p. 4.

59   *Daily Californian,* November 14, 1932, p. 1.

60   *Daily Californian,* April 14, 1933, p. 8.

61   *Daily Californian,* September 22, 1933, pp. 1, 8.

62   *Daily Californian,* September 27, 1933, pp. 1, 2.

63   *Daily Californian,* October 30, 1933, p. 1.

64   *Ibid.,* p. 4.

65   "Memorandum to the President concerning Social Problems Club," from Louis O'Brien and Thomas Putnam August 18, 1933 (in President, "Correspondence and Papers," 1933, Folder 439, attached to a handwritten note signed O'B).

66   Letter from Monroe E. Deutsch to Colonel Charles Erskine Scott Wood, October 9, 1933 (in President, "Correspondence and Papers," 1933, Folder 439).

67   *Daily Californian,* March 2, 1934, p. 1; June 6, 1934, p. 1; September 24, 1934, p. 2.

68   San Francisco *Chronicle,* June 9, 1934, pp. 1, 2.

69   Pasadena *Star News,* August 21, 1934 (in Robert G. Sproul, "Clippings, 1933–1934," University of California archives, Berkeley).

70   Los Angeles *Examiner,* September 18, 1934 (in Sproul, "Clippings, 1933–1934").

71   Letter from Ernest C. Moore to Robert Gordon Sproul, May 10, 1934 (in President, "Correspondence and Papers," 1934, Folder 439).

72   Los Angeles debaters explained their refusal to debate communism by indicating that they did not want to offend the provost. The *Daily Bruin* presented little news of student political groups at UCLA, and most of the information we have about them today comes from the *Daily Californian* and political newsletters published at Berkeley.

73   *Daily Bruin,* May 25, 1934, pp. 1, 4.

74   *Daily Californian,* October 30, 1934, p. 1.

75   *Daily Bruin,* March 20, 1934, p. 4.

76   *Ibid.*

77   Long Beach *Sun,* March 11, 1935 (in Sproul, "Clippings, 1935–1938").

78   Los Angeles *Times,* October 31, 1934, pp. 1, 3.

79   *Daily Californian,* October 31, 1934, p. 1.

80   *Daily Californian,* November 1, 1934, p. 1.

81   *Ibid.*

82   Los Angeles *Times,* November 6, 1934, pp. 1, 2; *Daily Californian,* November 6, 1934, p. 1.

83   Los Angeles *Daily Illustrated News,* November 15, 1934, editorial (in Sproul, "Clippings, 1933–1934").

84   Los Angeles *Evening Post,* November 15, 1934, editorial (in Sproul, "Clippings, 1933–1934").

Chapter 19

1   *Daily Californian,* April 26, 1934, p. 5.

2   Hamilton v. The Regents of the University of California, *Cases Argued and Decided in the Supreme Court of the United States,* October Term, 1934, Case 245.

3   As quoted in Hal Draper, "The Student Movement of the Thirties: A Political History," *As We Saw the Thirties,* ed. Rita J. Simon (Urbana, 1967), 169.

4   *Ibid.*

5   Anti-War Bulletin No. 1, March 7, 1935, in "The Anti-War Movement of

the Students of the University of California, March–April, 1935" (University of California archives, Berkeley).

6   Anti-War Bulletin No. 4, March 22, 1935, in "The Anti-War Movement . . ."; Berkeley *Daily Gazette,* April 9, 1935, p. 1.

7   Anti-War Bulletin No. 5, March 25, 1935, in "The Anti-War Movement. . . ."

8   Anti-War Bulletin No. 4, March 22, 1935, in "The Anti-War Movement. . . ."

9   San Francisco *News,* March 23, 1935, in Robert G. Sproul, "Clippings, 1935–1938" (University of California archives, Berkeley).

10   *Daily Californian,* March 26, 1935, p. 1.

11   Berkeley *Daily Gazette,* April 9, 1935, p. 1.

12   Berkeley *Daily Gazette,* April 12, 1935, p. 1. The Anti-War Committee said there were 3500 on strike (Anti-War Bulletin No. 16, April 16, 1935, in "The Anti-War Movement . . .").

13   Berkeley *Daily Gazette,* April 12, 1935, p. 1.

14   San Francisco *Chronicle,* April 13, 1935, pp. 1, 3. The *Chronicle* estimated 50,000. The Anti-War Bulletin said there were 125,000.

15   *Daily Californian,* February 6, 1936, p. 1.

16   Associated Students University of California Peace Committee, "Survey of Compulsory ROTC" [1939] (University of California archives, Berkeley).

17   Bruce Allen, "ROTC Elective or Required?" [1940] (University of California archives, Berkeley).

18   *Daily Californian,* September 20, 1939, p. 1.

19   Los Angeles *Times,* October 17, 1939, p. 4; Berkeley *Gazette,* October 16, 1939, p. 3.

20   *Ibid.*

21   As quoted in George A. Pettitt, *Twenty-eight Years in the Life of a University President* (Berkeley, 1966), 224–25.

22   San Francisco *Call Bulletin,* August 30, 1940, in Sproul, "Clippings, 1939–1941."

23   University of California, *Faculty Bulletin,* X (September 15, 1940), 2.

24   Los Angeles *Times,* August 31, 1941, p. 6.

25   Los Angeles *News,* September 12, 1941, in Sproul, "Clippings, 1939–1941."

26   University of California, *Faculty Bulletin,* X (September 15, 1940), 1.

27   Los Angeles *Times,* October 6, 1940.

28   University of California, *Faculty Bulletin,* X (January 15, 1941), 2.

29   Robert M. Underhill, interview with the author, August 1, 1966.

30   *Ibid.*

31   Berkeley *Gazette,* January 24, 1941, pp. 1–2; University of California, *Faculty Bulletin,* X (March 15, 1941), pp. 1–2.

32   Kenneth S. Davis, *Experience of War: The United States in World War II* (New York, 1965), 79, 80.

33   *Ibid.,* 85.

34   *Ibid.,* 84, 86.

35   William S. Barton, "The University and the Atom," Los Angeles *Times,* January 2, 1955, as reprinted in *California Monthly,* LXV (March, 1955), 18.

36   *Ibid.*

37   Dan Wilkes, "The Story of the Los Alamos 'Campus,' " *California Monthly,* LX (June, 1950), 28.

38   Memorandum from D. M. Wilkes to Radiation Laboratory Files, December 12, 1967, prepared after consultation with E. M. McMillan.

39   Los Alamos Scientific Laboratory, *The First 20 Years at Los Alamos* (Albuquerque, 1963), 13 (University of California archives, Berkeley).

40   *Ibid.,* 18, 19; Wilkes, "The Story of the Los Alamos 'Campus,' " 29.

41   Robert M. Underhill, interview with the author, August 1, 1966.

42   "The First 20 Years at Los Alamos," 36–37.

43   Wilkes, "The Story of the Los Alamos 'Campus,' " 29.

44   "War Research Projects," typescript in file on "Wartime Contributions of the University," Office of Public Information, University of California, Berkeley.

45   George Pettitt, "The University and the War," typescript dated May 13 [1942], p. 5, in file on "Wartime Contributions of the University," Office of Public Information, Berkeley. Portions of this manuscript appeared in *California Monthly,* XLIX (September, 1942), 14–16.

46   "War Research Projects."

47   Jean Backus, "The Farmer Goes to War," *California Monthly,* L (April, 1943), 9.

48   University of California, *Financial Report, 1941–42,* 11; . . . , *1942–43,* 13; . . . , *1943–44,* 13; . . . , *1944–45,* 6, 13.

49   Letter from Robert Gordon Sproul to Professor J. H. Hildebrand, October 27, 1942 (in Joel Hildebrand, "Papers" [unsorted material], University of California archives, Berkeley).

50   *Ibid.*

51   *Lodi Sentinel,* December 29, 1941, in Sproul, "Clippings, 1939–1941"; Oakland *Tribune,* December 29, 1941.

52   Pettitt, "The University and the War," pp. 8–9, 10.

53   *Circular of Information, Berkeley, 1943–44,* 37; *Circular of Information, Los Angeles, 1943–44,* 39, in University of California, *Register, 1942–1943* (Berkeley, 1943).

54   *Seven Campuses,* April, 1942, 1, 2 (University of California archives, Berkeley).

55   University of California, *Centennial Record* (Berkeley, 1967), 222.

56   *Ibid.*

57   *Ibid.,* 223.

58   Leonard G. Frazier, "The Armed Forces Training Programs of the University of California; A Partial Survey of the Activities on Three of the Eight Campuses of the University of California in Training Members of the Armed

Forces During the War Years 1942 to 1945" (mimeographed report prepared in 1945 by the President's Office, University of California archives, Berkeley), 6.

59   *Ibid.,* 12–29.

60   *Ibid.,* 85.

61   *Ibid.,* 7

62   *Ibid.,* 44.

63   *Ibid.*

64   *Ibid.*

65   *Ibid.,* 51.

66   *Ibid.,* 52.

67   *Ibid.,* 45.

68   *Ibid.,* 68.

69   *Ibid.,* 74.

70   *Ibid.,* 79–80.

71   "University Goes to War," California Club Supplement, *Daily Californian,* March 25, 1943, p. 8.

72   Lucy Guild Quirk, "Our Campus Goes to War," *UCLA Magazine,* XVII (February, 1943), 6, 7.

73   Byron Atkinson, "Gayley Gulch Goes Military," *UCLA Magazine,* XVIII (May, 1944), 6.

74   "War and the Sports Scene," *California Monthly,* LI (September, 1943), 4.

75   *California Monthly,* LII (March, 1944), 20.

76   *California Monthly,* LII (January, 1944), 16, 17.

77   *California Bruin,* May 9, 1945, p. 1.

78   Edward Teller, "Our Nuclear Future," *California Monthly,* LXIX (September, 1958), 17–18.

79   "The First 20 Years at Los Alamos," 29.

80   Davis, 641.

81   Teller, 18.

82   Davis, 641, 642.

83   *Daily Californian,* August 16, 1945, pp. 1–2.

84   *Ibid.,* p. 1.

85   *California Bruin,* August 17, 1945, V-J Day Commemoration Edition, p. 5.

86   *Daily Californian,* August 14, 1945, V-J edition, p. 1.

Chapter 20

1   University of California, *Centennial Record* (Berkeley, 1967), 295.

2   Minutes of the Board of Regents, executive session, October 11, 1940 (Office of the Secretary of the Regents, University of California, Berkeley).

3   San Francisco *Examiner,* October 21, 1945, p. 4.

4   Minutes of the Board of Regents, December 14, 1945, Vol. XXXVI, p. 243.

5   *Ibid.*

6   Minutes of the Board of Regents, January 1, 1946, Vol. XXXVI, p. 249.

7   California, Legislature, *Report of the Joint Fact-Finding Committee to the Fifty-Seventh California Legislature* (Sacramento, 1947), 95.

8   *Ibid.*

9   *Ibid.*

10   California, Legislature, *Fourth Report of the Senate Fact-Finding Committee on Un-American Activities* (Sacramento, 1948), pp. 174–76.

11   California, Legislature, *Fifth Report of the Senate Fact-Finding Committee on Un-American Activities* (Sacramento, 1949), 591.

12   *American Association of University Professors Bulletin,* XXXIV (Spring, 1948), 127–28.

13   David P. Gardner, *The California Oath Controversy* (Berkeley, 1967), 14–21.

14   *Ibid.,* 18–20.

15   Minutes of the Board of Regents, March 25, 1949, Vol. XLI, p. 539.

16   University of California, *Faculty Bulletin,* XVIII (May, 1949), 2.

17   Minutes of the Academic Senate, Northern Section, June 14, 1949, Vol. VIII, part I, series II, p. 113 (Office of the Academic Senate, University of California, Berkeley).

18   The issues in the dispute are carefully stated in George R. Stewart, *The Year of the Oath* (New York, 1950), 20–26.

19   Minutes of the Academic Senate, Northern Section, June 14, 1949, Vol. VIII, part I, series II, p. 113.

20   Stewart, Appendix B, 152–53.

21   B. H. Lehman, J. H. Hildebrand, H.B. Walker to Robert G. Sproul, June 18, 1949, as contained in a memorandum from Lehman, Walker, and Hildebrand to Members of the Academic Senate, Northern Section, June 28, 1949 (in Academic Senate, Northern Section, Advisory Committee, Hildebrand file, University of California archives, Berkeley).

22   *Ibid.*

23   *Ibid.*

24   John W. Olmsted, Gordon S. Watkins, Martin R. Huberty to Robert G. Sproul, June 21, 1949, as contained in memorandum from Lehman, Walker, and Hildebrand . . . , June 28, 1949.

25   Minutes of the Board of Regents, June 24, 1949, Vol. XLII, p. 74.

26   Gardner, 55–68, 78–82.

27   Minutes of the Academic Senate, Northern Section, November 7, 1949, Vol. VIII, part II, series II, pp. 123–25.

28   Minutes of the Board of Regents, executive session, February 24, 1950, as quoted in Gardner, 264.

29   San Francisco *Chronicle,* March 1, 1950, p. 6.

30   San Francisco *Chronicle,* March 4, 1950, p. 2.

31   *Ibid.*

32   Minutes of the Academic Senate, Northern Section, March 7, 1950, Vol. VIII, part II, series II, p. 161.

33   Minutes of the Council of California Alumni Association, March 27, 1950, and April 19, 1950. Gardner indicates that McCaffrey was also a member of the committee (Gardner, 15).

34   Minutes of the Board of Regents, April 21, 1950, Vol. XLIV, p. 41.

35   Letter from John Hicks to Sproul, April 21, 1950, in Gardner, 160.

36   Gardner, 174–77.

37   *Ibid.,* 177.

38   *Ibid.,* 185–86.

39   Minutes of the Board of Regents, August 25, 1950, Vol. XLV, pp. 136–38.

40   California, *Statutes* (1951), c. 7, pp. 15–17.

41   "The University of California Loyalty Oath Situation: A Judicial Decision In the District Court of Appeal for the State of California In and for the Third Appellate District," *American Association of University Professors Bulletin,* XXXVII (Spring, 1951), 92–101.

42   Toman v. Underhill (1952) 39 Cal. 2d 709 at 710.

43   *Ibid.,* 713.

44   Vogel v. County of Los Angeles (1967) 68 Advance California Reports No. 1, p. 12.

45   Author's interview with Clark Kerr (who was in attendance at this meeting), June 13, 1967.

Chapter 21

1   University of California, *General Catalogue, 1941–42* (Berkeley, 1941), 13–15 (University of California archives, Berkeley).

2   See Chapter XVII.

3   University of California, *Centennial Record* (Berkeley, 1967), 222–23.

4   George A. Pettitt, *Twenty-eight Years in the Life of a University President* (Berkeley, 1966), 14.

5   President, *Annual Report of the President of the University on behalf of the Regents to . . . the Governor . . . 1921–1922* (Berkeley, 1922), 21 University of California archives, Berkeley).

6   *Centennial Record,* 218; University of California, *General Catalogue, 1922–23* (Berkeley, 1923), 384.

7   Edwin C. Voorhies, "Autobiography and History of Davis Campus" (1955), 67–68 (unpublished typescript, Bancroft Library of the University of California, Berkeley).

8   Assembly Bill 174, in California, Legislature, *Assembly Bills* (1935), Vol. I.

9   Santa Barbara *News-Press,* September 10, 1944, D–1, D–2. The legislature's authorization of this change influenced the Regents' decision to expand instruction at their Southern Branch to the third- and fourth-year levels.

10   *Ibid.,* D–2.

11   *La Cumbre,* 1940, as quoted in William H. Ellison, "Antecedents of the University of California, Santa Barbara, 1891–1944," 167 (unpublished typescript, University of California archives, Santa Barbara).

12   *Ibid.*

13   Ellison, 169.

14   Letter from E. S. Conner, secretary manager, Santa Barbara County Chamber of Commerce, to Robert Gordon Sproul, September 21, 1943, in President, "Correspondence and Papers" (University of California archives, Berkeley).

15   Ellison, 171.

16   Clipping, Santa Barbara *Free Press,* in President, "Correspondence and Papers."

17   "Report of the State Council of Educational Planning and Coordination to the Legislature of the State of California," March 24, 1941, 1 (in President, "Correspondence and Papers").

18   *Ibid.,* 2.

19   *Ibid.*

20   Assembly Bill 1931, in California, Legislature, *Assembly Bills* (1941), Vol. XI.

21   Clipping, San Jose *News,* April 11, 1943 (in President, "Correspondence and Papers").

22   Memorandum from Ernest J. Jaqua "To the Members of the Committee of Inquiry Appointed August 21, 1942 by Dr. Dexter and President Sproul to Make Recommendations Respecting the Administration of Public Education in California, More Particularly Higher Education," September 7, 1942 (in President, "Correspondence and Papers").

23   Minutes of the Regents Committee on Educational Policies and Relations, March 26, 1943 (University of California archives, Santa Barbara).

24   *Ibid.*

25   *Ibid.*

26   *Ibid.*

27   Letter from Robert Gordon Sproul to Governor Earl Warren, May 13, 1943, 2–3 (in President, "Correspondence and Papers").

28   California, *Journal of the Assembly* (1943), Vol. I, p. 1902; Vol. II, pp. 3345–6.

29   Letter from Sproul to Warren, May 13, 1943, 3.

30   *Ibid.,* 4.

31   California, *Statutes* (1943), c. MCXXX, Sec. 3, p. 3073.

32   Report of the University of California Academic Committee to Study Santa Barbara State College and Community, Part II, 20–21 (in President, "Correspondence and Papers").

33   Proceedings of the Regents Committee on Educational Policies and Relations, September 23, 1943 (Office of the Secretary of the Regents, University of California, Berkeley).

34   Minutes of the Regents Committee on Educational Policies and Relations, October 21, 1943 (Office of the Secretary of the Regents, Berkeley).

35   *Ibid.*

36   *Ibid.*

37   James H. Corley, interview with the author, June 15, 1967.

38   *Ibid.*

39   California, Constitution, Article IX, Sec. 6.

40   Monroe E. Deutsch, "Memorandum," October 15, 1943 (in President "Correspondence and Papers").

41   *Ibid.*

42   *Ibid.* Monroe Deutsch estimated the Santa Barbara College library collection at 39,000 volumes. However, Donald Davidson, the current Santa Barbara librarian, says the collection was closer to 30,000 volumes.

43   Letter from Robert Gordon Sproul to President Clarence L. Phelps, December 10, 1943 (in President, "Correspondence and Papers").

44   The degrees actually given were the A.B. and Ed.B.

45   Announcement by Robert Gordon Sproul at a meeting of the Academic Senate, Northern Section, June 5, 1944 (in *University of California Faculty Bulletin*, June 15, 1944, 4–5).

46   University of California, *Directory of Officers, 1945–1946* (Berkeley, 1946), 23 (University of California archives, Berkeley).

47   Robert Underhill, interview with the author, September 1, 1967.

48   Gordon P. Hagbert, "Seaside Campus," *California Monthly,* October, 1949, 18.

49   Minutes of the Regents Committee on Teacher Training Institutes, February 23, 1948 (Office of the Secretary of the Regents, Berkeley). This was formerly the Committee on Educational Policies and Relations. The name changed at the same time Santa Barbara State College was accepted into the University and suggests that the Regents were planning to handle other institutions of a similar kind.

50   Hagbert, *loc. cit.*

51   *Centennial Record,* 222–23.

52   *Ibid.*

53   The peak year was 1948–1949.

54   *Centennial Record,* 222–23.

55   *University of California Faculty Bulletin,* September, 1946, 2; *Centennial Record,* 62.

56   *UCLA Alumni Magazine,* November, 1949, 9.

57   *California Monthly,* December, 1949, 15, 17.

58   *UCLA Alumni Magazine,* November, 1949, 9.

59   University of California, *Financial Report for the Eighty-first Fiscal Year Ended June 20, 1949* (Berkeley, 1949), 28 University of California archives, Berkeley).

60   *Ibid.,* 38.

61   *Ibid.,* 30.

62   *A Report of a Survey of the Needs of California Higher Education,* March 1, 1948, 53 (hereafter referred to as "Needs").

63   *Ibid.,* 81–83.

64   *Ibid.,* 48–49.

65   *Ibid.,* 40.

66   *Ibid.,* 100.

67   *Ibid.,* 101–3.

68   *Ibid.,* 44.

69   *Ibid.,* 107.

70   *Ibid.,* 108.

71   Notes on *"New Business,"* President's Advisory Conference, January 30, 1948 (in President, "Correspondence and Papers").

72   "Needs," 108.

73   *Centennial Record,* 223.

74   "Needs," 74.

75   *Ibid.*

76   University of California, "Proceedings of the Second All-University Faculty Conference" (1947), 12 (University of California archives, Berkeley).

77   Letter from Robert Gordon Sproul to Robert Underhill, June 18, 1948 (in President, "Correspondence and Papers"). This committee actually superseded an earlier committee appointed by Sproul on March 20, 1947, under Walker's chairmanship. The earlier committee's work was more or less incorporated into the final report of the committee appointed in June, 1948.

78   The committee's members were Walker; James H. Corley, comptroller; Robert M. Underhill, secretary of the Regents; George P. Adams, professor of philosophy at Berkeley; A. M. Boyce, chairman, Division of Entomology, Riverside; Homer D. Chapman, chairman, Division of Soils and Plant Nutrition, Riverside; Alva Davis, dean of the College of Letters and Science, Berkeley; George H. Hart, dean, School of Veterinary Medicine, Davis; Martin Huberty, chairman of the Division of Irrigation and Soils, UCLA; Gordon S. Watkins, professor of economics, UCLA; and Henry R. Wellman, director of the Giannini Foundation and chairman of the Department of Agricultural Economics, Berkeley. Dean Hutchison sat in on the first meeting of the committee.

79   Letter from the Statewide Committee on University Expansion, Riverside and Davis campuses, to Robert Gordon Sproul, September 7, 1948, 3–4 (in George D. Louderback, "Correspondence and Papers," Bancroft Library, University of California, Berkeley).

80   *Ibid.,* 14.

81   *University of California Faculty Bulletin,* February, 1949, 75.

82   *Centennial Record,* 434.

83   *Ibid.,* 154.

84   Minutes of the Academic Senate, Northern Section, April 30, 1951 (Office of the Academic Senate, University of California, Berkeley).

85   *Ibid.*

86   These statements on administrative organization in 1948 are based upon University of California, Office of the President, "A Progress Report on Administrative Changes and Developments at the University of California," April 23, 1965 (University of California archives, Berkeley).

87   *Ibid.*

88   Letter from Claude B. Hutchison to Robert Gordon Sproul, June 3, 1949 (in President, "Correspondence and Papers").

89   *Ibid.*

90   *University Bulletin,* May 12, 1952, 1.

91   *Centennial Record,* 276–78.

92   *University of California Faculty Bulletin,* May, 1952, 105.

93   University of California, "Manual of the Academic Senate" (January, 1956), 44–49 (University of California archives, Berkeley).

94   *Ibid.,* 51–56.

95   *University Bulletin,* November 21, 1955, 97.

96   Academic Senate Record, II, no. 8 (April 10, 1956), i (Office of the Academic Senate, University of California, Berkeley).

97   *University Bulletin,* July 30, 1956, 13.

98   University of California, "Proceedings of the Eighth All-University Faculty Conference" (1953), 26 (University of California archives, Berkeley).

99   *Ibid.,* 31.

Chapter 22

1   John C. Merriam, "The Functions of Educational Institutions in the Development of Research," *University of California Chronicle,* April, 1920, 141.

2   President's Report, 1921–1922, 182–88.

3   George A. Pettitt, *Twenty-Eight Years in the Life of a University President* (Berkeley, 1966), 57–58.

4   Letter, Raymond T. Birge to Robert Gordon Sproul, July 7, 1952, Minutes of Committee on Research, v. 88, budget material (University of California archives, Berkeley).

5   Letter from W. R. Dennes, dean of the Graduate Division, to Raymond T. Birge, May 2, 1949, in Minutes of the Committee on Research, Vol. 68, attached to minutes of May 10, 1949 (University of California archives, Berkeley).

6   Letter from Raymond T. Birge to Robert Gordon Sproul, November 26, 1948, in Minutes of the Committee on Research, Vol. 72, in Budget Section (University of California archives, Berkeley).

7   *Ibid.*

8   Letter from William R. Dennes to Raymond T. Birge, May 2, 1949, in Minutes of the Committee on Research, v. 68, attached to minutes of May 10, 1949 (University of California archives, Berkeley).

9   Letter from Alden H. Miller to Clark Kerr, April 26, 1955, in Minutes of the Committee on Research, v. 103 (University of California archives, Berkeley).

10   Letter from Henry N. Smith to Clark Kerr, March 30, 1956, in Minutes of the Committee on Research, v. 110 (University of California archives, Berkeley).

11   Daniel M. Wilkes, "Lawrence Radiation Laboratory," in University of California, *Centennial Record* (Berkeley, 1967), 324.

12   *Ibid.*

13   Frederick Betz and Carlos Kruytbosch, *The Growth of Organized Research at the Berkeley Campus* (Space Sciences Laboratory, University of California, Berkeley, Internal Working Paper no. 59, August, 1967), 76–77. (The author is greatly indebted to this concise and informative work in the preparation of this chapter.)

14   *Ibid.*, 77.

15   The exact number is difficult to ascertain. Some units were created and then disbanded with little fanfare. Others functioned within departments of instruction and research and had no identification of their own.

16   *Centennial Record,* 310.

17   *Ibid.*, 514.

18   *Ibid.*, 206–7.

19   *Ibid.*, 309.

20   *Ibid.*, 521.

21   *Ibid.*, 125–26.

22   *Ibid.*, 400–1.

23   University of California, *Statistical Summary,* 1966–1967, 84.

24   Betz and Kruytbosch, 11.

25   "General Statement Concerning Request for Physics Research #211, 1941–42," attached to a letter from Raymond T. Birge to Robert Gordon Sproul, April 11, 1941, in Minutes of the Committee on Research, Vol. 44, in section on Grant #211, physics.

26   Letter from Raymond T. Birge to Robert G. Sproul, March 30, 1940, in Minutes of the Committee on Research, v. 41 (University of California archives, Berkeley).

27   Betz and Kruytbosch, 61.

28   *Ibid.*, 64.

29   *Ibid.*, 65–66.

30   Ibid., 67; *University Bulletin,* January 10, 1966, 172; April 15, 1963, 151.

Chapter 23

1   *California Monthly,* February, 1954, 7.

2   Clark Kerr, interview with the author, June 13, 1967.

3   *Ibid.*

4   *University Bulletin,* April 1, 1957, 157.

5   *Ibid.,* July 31, 1961, 18.

6   *Ibid.*

7   As quoted by Mary Ellen Leary, "California's Lonely Secret Agent," Los Angeles *Times: West,* April 2, 1967, 36.

8   Clark Kerr, interview with the author, June 13, 1967.

9   *Ibid.*

10   University of California, *Long Range Development Plan for the Berkeley Campus* (1956).

11   *Ibid.*

12   *University Bulletin,* May 4, 1957, 177.

13   *Ibid.,* February 10, 1958, 113.

14   "Clark Kerr's Inauguration," *California Monthly,* December, 1958.

15   The enumeration of the University's campuses varies at different points in history because of changes in concepts. Mount Hamilton, or the Lick Observatory, was regarded as a "campus" throughout most of Sproul's administration. By 1968, however, its administration had been transferred to Santa Cruz. La Jolla, in 1958, consisted of the Scripps Institution of Oceanography and an Institute of Technology and Engineering offering only graduate instruction. Both units were administered by a director. The San Francisco "campus" was and is a specialized professional unit. In 1958 it was directed by a provost. In anticipation that a general campus would be developed in relation to the Medical Center, the chief campus officer was redesignated chancellor in 1964. Hastings College of the Law was regarded as a campus under the Sproul administration, but as an affiliate institution under Clark Kerr. Its chief officer is a dean. So the eight campuses of the Sproul administration included Hastings and La Jolla. The nine campuses of the Kerr administration did not include Hastings, included the La Jolla institutions as part of the new San Diego campus, and included the new campuses at Irvine and Santa Cruz.

16   University of California, *Centennial Record* (Berkeley, 1967), 225. The figures on Berkeley and Los Angeles cited in the text are at variance with figures cited in this source and are found in "Summary of Students," Fall semester, 1958, University of California, Berkeley, compiled by the Registrar, which the author in this case considers more reliable.

17   H. H. Semans and T. C. Holy, *A Study of the Need for Additional Centers of Public Higher Education in California* (Sacramento, 1957), 85.

18   *University Bulletin,* September 9, 1957, 26; October 28, 1957, 53.

19   *Quality of Education in Relation to Numbers: Proceedings of the University of California Twelfth All-University Faculty Conference, Carmel, April 4, 5, and 6, 1957,* 15.

20   University of California, Office of the President, "Administrative Changes and Developments at the University of California: Progress Report," April 23, 1965, 3 (Centennial Publications files, University of California).

21   *Ibid.,* 4.

22   *University Bulletin,* July 28, 1958, 5.

23   *Ibid.*

24   *Ibid.,* September 29, 1958, 35.

25   *Ibid.,* August 31, 1959, 26.

26   *Ibid.*

27   *Ibid.*

28   *Ibid.*

29   *Ibid.*

30   *Ibid.*

31   Liaison Committee of the State Board of Education and the Regents of the University of California, *A Master Plan for Higher Education in California, 1960–1975* (Sacramento, 1960), 46.

32   *Ibid.*

33   *Ibid.*

34   Joint Staff of the Liaison Committee of the Regents of the University of California and the California State Board of Education, *A Restudy of the Needs of California in Higher Education* (Sacramento, 1955), 19.

35   *Ibid.,* 40.

36   Assembly Bill 24, in California, Legislature, *Assembly Bills, Original and Amended* (1955).

37   Assembly Bill 881, *ibid.*

38   Senate Bill 1039, in California, Legislature, *Senate Bills, Original and Amended* (1955).

39   H. H. Semans and T. C. Holy, *Report of the Joint Staff on the Proposal for a Four-Year State College in the Modesto Area* (Sacramento and Berkeley, 1953) (mimeographed), as referred to in H. H. Semans and T. C. Holy, . . . *Additional Centers . . . ,* 56.

40   Semans and Holy, . . . *Additional Centers . . . ,* 1.

41   Senate Bill 1039, in California, Legislature, *Journal of the Senate* (1955), 3614.

42   Senate Bill 1981, *ibid.,* 4479.

43   Semans and Holy, . . . *Additional Centers . . . ,* 1, 2.

44   *Ibid.,* 3, 4.

45   *University Bulletin,* September 9, 1957, 26; October 28, 1957, 53.

46   Semans and Holy, . . . *Additional Centers . . . ,* 49, 56.

47   Assembly Bill 4, in *Assembly Bills, Original and Amended* (1957).

48   Semans and Holy, . . . *Additional Centers* . . . , 51, 52.

49   *Ibid.*, 63, 64, 65.

50   *University Bulletin,* February 9, 1959, 114.

51   The first chancellor-members were Stanley Freeborn, Davis; Vern O. Knudsen, UCLA; and Glenn T. Seaborg, UCLA. Later they were Samuel B. Gould, Santa Barbara; Emil M. Mrak, Davis; and Herman T. Spieth, Riverside.

52   Master Plan Survey Team, *A Master Plan for Higher Education in California, 1960–1975* (Sacramento, 1960), 20.

53   Assembly Concurrent Resolution 88, in California Legislature, *Assembly Concurrent Resolutions* (1959).

54   Minutes of a joint meeting of the State Board of Education and the Regents of the University of California, March 14, 1959, in Minutes of the Board of Regents, Vol. LVIV, p. 316 (Office of the Secretary of the Regents, University of California, Berkeley).

55   *Ibid.*

56   *Ibid.*

57   *Ibid.*, p. 317.

58   *Ibid.*, p. 318.

59   *Ibid.*

60   *Ibid.*, p. 319.

61   *Ibid.*, p. 320.

62   San Francisco *Chronicle,* April 12, 1959, 6.

63   *Ibid.*

64   *Ibid.*, April 15, 1959, 4.

65   *Master Plan,* 20.

66   Minutes of a joint meeting of the State Board of Education and the Regents of the University of California, April 15, 1959, in Minutes of the Board of Regents, Vol. LVIV, p. 343.

67   Arthur Browne succeeded H. H. Semans, who had, by this time, left the Department of Education for a junior college post in San Mateo.

68   "Year of Decision," *California Monthly,* February, 1960, 21.

69   *Ibid.*

70   *Master Plan,* 41.

71   *Ibid.*, 41, 42.

72   *Ibid.*, 42.

73   *Ibid.*, 42, 43.

74   *Ibid.*, 43, 44.

75   *Ibid.*, 73.

76   *Ibid.*, 89, 111, 112.

77   *Ibid.*, 112, 113.

78   *Ibid.*, 111, 113.

79   *Ibid.*, 96–99.

80   *Ibid.,* 174.

81   *Ibid.,* 79.

82   Minutes of a joint meeting of the State Board of Education and the Regents of the University of California, December 18, 1959, in Minutes of the Board of Regents, Vol. LX, 305–6.

83   His position is clear in a joint statement issued about this time by Louis H. Heilbron, president of the State Board of Education, Roy Simpson, state superintendent of public instruction, and Donald McLaughlin, chairman of the Regents. See *University Bulletin,* April 4, 1960, 164.

84   After some amendments.

85   *University Bulletin,* May 9, 1960, 187.

86   Clark Kerr, "Values and Visions," *California Monthly,* June, 1965, 18, 19.

87   *University Bulletin,* June 19, 1967, 181.

88   As originally proposed by the Survey Team, there were no "public" representatives.

89   James G. Paltridge, *California's Coordinating Council for Higher Education* (Berkeley, 1966), 56–57.

90   *Ibid.,* 114–16.

91   *Ibid.,* 61–67.

92   *Ibid.,* 67–79.

93   *Ibid.,* 131–33.

Chapter 24

1   University of California, *Centennial Record* (Berkeley, 1967), 224–25.

2   *University Bulletin,* July 1, 1957, 1.

3   Charles Luckman Associates, *University of California Site Selection Study: A Report on the Search for New Campus Sites, California Metropolitan Center Section, South Cross Section,* 1959 ((University of California Archives, Berkeley). Other members of the committee were John E. Canaday, Edward W. Carter, Mrs. Dorothy B. Chandler, Robert Gordon Sproul (replaced by Clark Kerr in July, 1958), Donald H. McLaughlin, William G. Merchant, Gus Olson, and Jess M. Steinhart. Robert J. Evans, chief architect of the University, was appointed supervisor of the study.

4   *University Bulletin,* July 28, 1959, 8.

5   *Ibid.*

6   *Centennial Record,* 333.

7   *University Bulletin,* September 29, 1958, 35.

8   *Ibid.,* December 15, 1958, 88.

9   He was elected in September, 1958, but remained at Antioch until the end of the academic year.

10   *Centennial Record,* 25.

11   Letter, George Obern to Verne A. Stadtman, May 31, 1968.

12   *Ibid.*

13   *Ibid.*

14   *University Bulletin,* September 29, 1958, 36.

15   *Ibid.*

16   *Ibid.*

17   *Centennial Record,* 461.

18   The College of Dentistry was renamed the School of Dentistry in 1956.

19   Robert A. Nisbet, dean of the College of Letters and Science, Riverside, 1953–1963, interview with the author, August 1, 1967.

20   *University Bulletin,* April 27, 1959, 156.

21   *Ibid.*

22   *Ibid.,* November 2, 1959, 67.

23   *Ibid.*

24   Liaison Committee of the State Board of Education and the Regents of the University of California, *A Master Plan for Higher Education in California, 1960–1975* (Sacramento, 1960), 11.

25   Table 10, "Distribution of Full-Time Enrollments by Segment, Modified Projections—1975," in *A Master Plan . . . ,* 63.

26   *University Bulletin,* July 5, 1960, 1, 2.

27   *Ibid.*

28   Carl Eckart, interview with the author, July 28, 1967.

29   *University Bulletin,* September 10, 1956, 30.

30   *Ibid.,* August 26, 1957, 22.

31   *Ibid.*

32   *Ibid.*

33   *Ibid.,* May 2, 1960, 184.

34   *Ibid.,* July 28, 1958, 8, 9.

35   *Ibid.,* November 17, 1958, 71.

36   *Ibid.,* April 25, 1960, 173, 174.

37   *Ibid.,* August 1, 1960, 13.

38   *Centennial Record,* 452.

39   *Long Range Development Plan, University of California, San Diego* (October, 1963), 3, 4.

40   *Centennial Record,* 452.

41   Urey received this honor in chemistry in 1934; Mrs. Mayer shared the prize in physics in 1963.

42   Carl Eckart interview.

43   Letter from Roger Revelle to Verne A. Stadtman, May 25, 1968.

44   *Centennial Record,* 452–53.

45   *Catalog, University of California, San Diego, 1967–1968,* 25.

46   *University Bulletin,* September 9, 1957, 26.

47   *Ibid.,* January 4, 1960, 99.

48   *Long Range Development Plan, University of California, Santa Cruz* (September, 1963).

49   Santa Cruz *Sentinel,* October 14, 1965, 2.

50   *Ibid.*

51   *University of California, Santa Cruz, Undergraduate and Graduate Bulletin, 1966–1967,* 9.

52   *University of California, Santa Cruz, Undergraduate Bulletin, 1965–1966,* 2.

53   William L. Pereira & Associates, *Long Range Development Plan, University of California, Irvine* (June, 1963), 4.

54   *Ibid.*

55   Minutes of the Board of Regents, July 22, 1960 (Office of the Secretary of the Regents, University of California, Berkeley).

56   *Ibid.,* June 21, 1963.

57   Daniel Aldrich, interview with the author, July 31, 1967.

58   *University Bulletin,* January 29, 1962, 117.

59   *Ibid.,* January 2, 1962, 103.

60   Daniel Aldrich interview.

61   *Centennial Record,* 316.

62   *Ibid.*

63   Daniel Aldrich interview.

64   *Centennial Record,* 315, 316.

65   *Ibid.,* 314.

66   *Ibid.*

67   *Unity and Diversity, The Academic Plan of the University of California, 1965–1975,* 42.

68   *University Bulletin,* February 19, 1968, 114.

69   *Centennial Record,* 295.

70   *University of California, Budget for Current Operations, 1967–68,* 39.

71   Computed from data in Office of the Vice-President—Physical Planning and Construction, University of California, *Summary Report, 1966–1967,* 2.

72   *Centennial Record,* 295.

73   *Budget for Current Operations, 1967–68,* 46.

74   *Summary Report, 1966–1967,* 7.

75   *University Bulletin,* October 15, 1956, 55; October 29, 1956, 61; October 20, 1958, 51; May 28, 1962, 213; October 1, 1962, 44; October 5, 1964, 45.

76   *Ibid.,* February 28, 1966, 159–66.

77   *Ibid.,* 164.

78   *Ibid.,* June 1, 1965, 239.

79   *Ibid.*

80   *Ibid.*, January 3, 1966, 117–18.

81   Clark Kerr, *The Uses of the University* (Cambridge, 1963), 6.

82   *Ibid.*, 103–4.

Chapter 25

1   University of California, *Centennial Record* (Berkeley, 1967), 44; *California Monthly*, September, 1948, 11.

2   *Centennial Record*, 34, 41.

3   *Ibid.*, 34, 37.

4   *Ibid.*, 36–37.

5   *Ibid.*, 33.

6   *Ibid.*, 300–1.

7   *Ibid.*, 300–1, 59.

8   *Daily Bruin*, March 2, 1966, 9.

9   *Centennial Record*, 501.

10   *Ibid.*, 460.

11   *Daily Californian*, December 16, 1964, 8.

12   A Housing Office survey in the fall of 1954 showed that 69 per cent of UCLA's students traveled to campus by automobile. Seven thousand one hundred, the largest number, lived with family, relatives, or friends. The next largest number, 2922, lived in apartments. The third largest number, 1669, lived in fraternities and sororities (*UCLA Alumni Magazine*, January, 1955, 4).

13   *Ibid.*, June, 1954, 18.

14   *Centennial Record*, 223, 225.

15   Office of Analytical Studies, University of California, Berkeley.

16   Figures based on University of California, *Statistical Addenda for the Year 1955–56*, 48 (University of California archives, Berkeley).

17   Figures cited by Max Heirich show that, in 1956, 25 per cent of the students at Berkeley not living at home lived in apartments, and 27 per cent in fraternities and sororities. By 1964, 41 per cent of the students living away from home lived in apartments, and only 15 per cent lived in fraternities or sororities. (Max Heirich, "Demonstrations at Berkeley: Collective Behavior during the Free Speech Movement of 1964–1965," unpublished dissertation, Berkeley, 1967.)

18   "Responsibility and the Student Press," *California Monthly*, February, 1952, 8.

19   *Ibid.*, 9.

20   *Ibid.*, 8, 9.

21   *Ibid.*

22   *UCLA Alumni Magazine*, February, 1955, 9.

23   *Daily Bruin,* December 11, 1956, 1.

24   Clark Kerr, "The Student Riots of May 16," *California Monthly,* June–July, 1956, i.

25   *Ibid.,* iii.

26   *Ibid.,* i.

27   *Ibid.,* iv.

28   *Ibid.,* v.

29   *Ibid.,* vii.

30   A student organizer of Slate interviewed by the author in 1961 and quoted in "Is There a Student Movement at Berkeley?" *California Monthly,* April, 1961, 10.

31   *Ibid.,* 54.

32   *Ibid.*

33   Minutes of the Board of Regents, May 18, 1962 (Office of the Secretary of the Regents, University of California, Berkeley).

34   *University Bulletin,* November 2, 1959, 69.

35   *Ibid.,* 70.

36   *UCR Highlander,* December 2, 1959, 2.

37   *University Bulletin,* February 14, 1961, 111.

38   *Ibid.,* August 28, 1961, 30.

39   "Student Government Showdown," *California Monthly,* June–July, 1960, 30–32.

40   *UCR Highlander,* March 26, 1965, 1.

41   *Ibid.,* April 27, 1965, 1.

42   "Echoes of Last May," *California Monthly,* April, 1961, 40.

43   *Ibid.*

44   *Ibid.*

45   *UCR Highlander,* April 11, 1962, 1.

46   Negative votes were cast by State Superintendent of Public Instruction Max Rafferty and John Canaday. ("The Regents make some major changes in off-campus speaker policy," *California Monthly,* October, 1963, 6–8.)

47   *Ibid.*

48   "The Students," *California Monthly,* December, 1962, 32.

49   *The Untold Story: The Constructive Student, a Special Report to the Board of Regents of the University of California* (A special report to the Board of Regents, Office of the President, University of California, Berkeley, October, 1966).

50   *Ibid.*

51   *Ibid.*

52   *Daily Bruin,* May 3, 1960.

53   *California Monthly,* June–July, 1960, 33–34.

54   *Daily Bruin,* December 13, 1961, 1.

55 *Ibid.,* February 16, 1962, 1.

56 *Ibid.,* March 9, 1962, 1.

57 *Ibid.,* March 15, 1962, 1.

58 *Ibid.,* March 19, 1962, 1, 2.

59 *California Monthly,* July–August, 1964, 6.

60 *Ibid.,* 8.

61 *Ibid.,* 9, 10.

62 *Ibid.,* 11.

63 *University Bulletin,* June 8, 1964, 213.

64 *Ibid.,* April 20, 1964, 184.

65 *Ibid.,* May 25, 1964, 209.

66 Clark Kerr, interview with the author, September 18, 1967.

Chapter 26

1 Max A. Heirich, "Demonstrations at Berkeley: Collective Behavior During the Free Speech Movement of 1964–1965" (unpublished dissertation, University of California, Berkeley, 1967), 155; Clark Kerr, interview with the author, September 18, 1967.

2 *Ibid.,* 159.

3 This is almost verbatim language of the so-called Kerr directives of October, 1959.

4 Clark Kerr, interview with the author, September 18, 1967.

5 Meeting with Clark Kerr, Memorandum of K. C. Malloy, September 18, 1964 (copy in Centennial Publications files, University of California archives, Berkeley).

6 *Ibid.*

7 *Ibid.*

8 Clark Kerr interview.

9 "Three Months of Crisis: Chronology of Events," *California Monthly,* February, 1965, 37.

10 *Daily Californian,* September 22, 1964, 1.

11 "Three Months of Crisis . . . ," 37.

12 *Daily Californian,* September 23, 1964, 1.

13 *Ibid.*

14 Memorandum, Clark Kerr to Chief Campus Officers, October 2, 1964 (copy in Centennial Publications files, University of California archives, Berkeley).

15 "Three Months of Crisis . . . ," 38.

16 Heirich, 190.

17 *Daily Californian,* September 30, 1964, 1.

18   *Ibid.*, October 1, 1964, 1.

19   *Ibid.*

20   Heirich, 197.

21   *Daily Californian,* October 1, 1964, 1.

22   *Ibid.*

23   *Ibid.*

24   *California Monthly,* February, 1965, 39.

25   Clark Kerr, interview with the author, September 26, 1967.

26   "Three Months of Crisis . . . ," 41.

27   *Ibid.,* 43.

28   Heirich, 302.

29   Clark Kerr, interview with the author, September 26, 1967.

30   An organization called the Ad Hoc Committee to end discrimination announced on September 15 its plans to demonstrate against the Oakland *Tribune* to improve job opportunities for Negroes there. Many FSM members believed that the *Tribune* had brought pressure upon the University to prevent student participation in those demonstrations (Heirich, p. 167). A member of SNCC is also quoted as saying, "Obviously this ruling [to close the Bancroft strip] was directed against the civil rights movement. . . ." (Heirich, p. 170.)

31   Clark Kerr, interview with the author, September 26, 1967.

32   *Ibid.*

33   *Ibid.*

34   "Three Months of Crisis . . . ," 43.

35   *Ibid.*

36   *Ibid.,* 43, 44.

37   *Ibid.,* 44.

38   *Daily Californian,* October 6, 1964, 2.

39   *Ibid.,* October 8, 1964, 1, 3.

40   *Ibid.,* October 16, 1964, 1.

41   "Three Months of Crisis . . . ," 52.

42   *Daily Californian,* November 9, 1964, 1.

43   *Ibid.,* November 10, 1964, 1.

44   *Ibid.*

45   *Ibid.,* 1.

46   In ballots cast April 17, 1963, 420 faculty members at Berkeley voted for the *status quo* and 349 for year-round operations. On this same ballot, of three year-round plans the four-term calendar received 362 votes, a three-term calendar with a twelve-week summer term received 296 votes, and a three-term calendar with equal-length terms received 114 votes. *University Bulletin,* May 27, 1963, 191.

47   "Report of the Ad Hoc Committee on Student Conduct," *California Monthly,* February, 1965, 82–87.

48   *Daily Californian,* November 23, 1964, 1.

49   *Ibid.*

50   *Ibid.*

51   "Three Months of Crisis . . . ," 58.

52   Heirich, 408.

53   "Three Months of Crisis . . . ," 59.

54   *Daily Californian,* December 2, 1964, 1.

55   "Three Months of Crisis . . . ," 60.

56   Clark Kerr, interview with the author, September 26, 1967.

57   *Ibid.*

58   "Three Months of Crisis . . . ," 62–63.

59   *Ibid.,* 63.

60   *Ibid.*

61   *Ibid.,* 64–65.

62   "Three Months of Crisis . . . ," 67.

63   Clark Kerr, interview with the author, September 26, 1967. This is a widely quoted version of Savio's remarks. Professor Scalapino, who stood beside Savio while he spoke, does not remember these words. Another version is that he announced the Sproul Steps rally and said simply "That's all I wanted to say." Unfortunately, the tape of the episode played for the author by station KPFA in Berkeley covered Savio's behind-stage remarks and not his actual announcement.

64   *Daily Californian,* December 8, 1967, 1.

65   *Ibid.*

66   At a meeting earlier in the day, a professor heard a remark to the effect that serious trouble at the Greek Theatre was planned at 11 A.M. Police were alerted and responded by hiding themselves backstage. This warning, of course, made Savio's move seem less innocent to policemen than it was to the audience.

67   Clark Kerr, interview with the author, June 26, 1967.

68   *Daily Californian,* December 8, 1967, 3; "Three Months of Crisis . . . ," 67; Heirich, 473.

69   *Daily Californian,* December 8, 1967, 3.

70   "Three Months of Crisis . . . ," 68.

71   *Ibid,* 69.

72   *Ibid.*

73   As quoted in the *Daily Californian,* December 10, 1964, p. 1.

74   Edward A. Strong, "Student Demonstrations at Berkeley," a report to the Regents dated December 16, 1964, and reprinted in the San Francisco *Examiner,* March 13, 1965, 8.

75   *Ibid.,* 8, 10.

76   "Three Months of Crisis . . . ," 72–73.

77   Minutes of the Board of Regents, executive session, December 18, 1964 (Office of the Secretary of the Regents, University of California, Berkeley).

78   "Three Months of Crisis . . . ," 73.

79   Minutes of the Board of Regents, December 18, 1964 (Office of the Secretary of the Regents, University of California, Berkeley).

80   Berkeley *Daily Gazette,* December 31, 1964, 1.

81   *Ibid.,* January 1, 1965, 1.

82   *Daily Californian,* January 4, 1965, 6.

83   There is disagreement as to whether all of these activities were conducted according to the spirit and letter of regulations. Former Chancellor Strong, among others, has said they were not.

84   Clark Kerr, interview with the author, September 26, 1967.

85   *Daily Californian,* March 10, 1965, 1.

86   *California Monthly,* April, 1965, 14.

87   *Daily Californian,* March 15, 1965, 1.

88   Minutes of the Academic Senate, Berkeley Division, March 12, 1965.

89   *Daily Californian,* March 15, 1965, 12.

90   Report of Special Committee to Review University Policies, April 23, 1965, as published in *University Bulletin,* May 3, 1965, 221.

91   The Byrne Report was published in full in the Los Angeles *Times,* May 12, 1965.

92   One of the other reasons was that several Regents were strongly opposed to the report's recommendations.

93   *University Bulletin,* June 29, 1965, 271.

Chapter 27

1   Almost two-thirds of Berkeley's classes with fewer than thirty students actually were taught by teaching assistants. University of California, Berkeley, Academic Senate, *Education at Berkeley: Report of the Select Committee on Education* (March, 1966), 175.

2   University of California, Office of the President, *Unity and Diversity: The Academic Plan of the University of California, 1965–1967,* 3. The plan was approved by the Regents in December, 1964.

3   University of California, Office of the President, *New Calendar, New Directions* (1966), 11.

4   *Ibid.*

5   *Ibid.*

6   *Ibid.,* 12.

7   *Ibid.*

8   College of Letters and Science, Executive Committee Report . . . [on] the Experimental College Program, September 20, 1966 (University of California archives, Berkeley).

9   *Ibid.,* 14.

10   *Daily Californian,* February 17, 1965, 9.

11   Minutes of the Academic Senate, Berkeley Division, Secretary's Papers, March 1, 1965 (Office of the Academic Senate, University of California, Berkeley).

12   *Education at Berkeley,* iii.

13   *Ibid.,* 4.

14   *Ibid.,* 4, 5.

15   *Ibid.,* 6.

16   *Ibid.,* 5.

17   *Ibid.,* 6.

18   *Ibid.,* 36.

19   *Daily Californian,* March 18, 1966, 1; March 22, 1966, 1.

20   Michael Rossman, "Break the Habit, or, Son of Son of Consensus at Berkeley," *Ibid.,* May 3, 1966, 7.

21   Martin Trow, "Bell, Book, and Berkeley: Reflections Occasioned by a Reading of Daniel Bell's *The Reforming of General Education," Experiment and Innovation,* January, 1968, 7.

22   Academic Senate, University of California, Los Angeles, "Report of the Committee on Academic Innovation and Development," (December, 1967), iii.

23   *Ibid.*

24   *Ibid.,* iv.

25   *Ibid.,* 1.

26   *Ibid.,* 3.

27   *Ibid.,* 6.

28   From the text of Heyns' address as printed in the *Daily Californian,* September 23, 1965, 8.

29   *UCR Highlander,* February 26, 1965, 1.

30   *El Gaucho,* March 10, 1965, 1.

31   *UCLA Daily Bruin,* March 10, 1965, 2.

32   *UCR Highlander,* March 26, 1965, 1.

33   *Daily Californian,* March 17, 1965, 1.

34   *Ibid.,* March 24, 1965, 1.

35   *UCLA Daily Bruin,* February 9, 1966, 1.

36   San Francisco *Chronicle,* May 22, 1965, 4.

37   *UCLA Daily Bruin,* October 18, 1965, 3.

38   *UCR Highlander,* October 20, 1965, 1.

39   *UCLA Daily Bruin,* November 15, 1965, 1.

40   *Daily Californian,* March 16, 1966, 1.

41   *El Gaucho,* March 24, 1966, 1.

42   *Ibid.,* February 15, 1967, 1.

43   University of California, Berkeley, Study Commission on University Governance, "Summary of Graduate Student Voting Rights," from files of the Commission.

44   *Ibid.*

45   *Daily Californian,* March 29, 1965.

46   *Ibid.,* April 5, 1965, 1; April 9, 1965, 1.

47   *Ibid.,* April 8, 1965, 1.

48   *Ibid.,* April 28, 1965, 1.

49   *Ibid.,* April 26, 1966, 1; April 27, 1966, 1.

50   *Ibid.,* May 2, 1966, 1.

51   Oakland *Tribune,* March 10, 1965, 1.

52   Report of the Senate Factfinding Subcommittee on Un-American Activities to the 1965 Regular California Legislature, Sacramento, California.

53   Clark Kerr, interview with the author, September 26, 1967.

54   *California Monthly,* December, 1965, 44.

55   *Daily Californian,* March 28, 1966, 1.

56   *Ibid.,* 3.

57   San Francisco *Chronicle,* April 19, 1966, 11.

58   *Ibid.*

59   *California Monthly,* June, 1966, 14.

60   *Ibid.,* 15.

61   San Francisco *Chronicle,* August 7, 1966, 1.

62   Minutes of the Board of Regents, September 16, 1966 (Office of the Secretary of the Regents, University of California, Berkeley).

63   *University Bulletin,* October 31, 1966, 54.

64   *Ibid.*

65   *Ibid.,* 55.

66   *Daily Californian,* October 24, 1966, 12.

67   San Francisco *Chronicle,* September 10, 1966, 1.

68   Berkeley *Gazette,* September 28, 1966.

69   *University Bulletin,* November 14, 1966, 63.

70   *Ibid.,* December 12, 1966, 81.

71   Los Angeles *Times,* January 5, 1967, 1.

72   Berkeley *Gazette,* January 10, 1967, 1, 2; San Francisco *Chronicle,* January 10, 1967, 1, 6; Los Angeles *Times,* January 10, 1967, 1, 6.

73   Indeed, Mr. Grant originally made the formal motion that Kerr be fired that day but later withdrew it, and Regent Lawrence Kennedy, who had been on the Board longer, made the motion that actually passed.

74   Transcript of the tape-recorded remarks of Regent Theodore Meyer at Press Conference, January 20, 1967.

75   Clark Kerr, prepared remarks for the press on January 20, 1967 (Centennial Publications files, University of California archives, Berkeley).

76   From transcript of tape of press questions and responses of Clark Kerr, January 20, 1967 (Centennial files, University of California archives, Berkeley).

77   The California Poll, according to a report in the San Francisco *Chronicle,* February 3, 1967, 1, 10.

78   Berkeley *Gazette,* February 13, 1967, 1.

79   *University Bulletin,* February 27, 1967, 123.

80   *Ibid.*

81   *Ibid.*

82   *Ibid.*

83   Berkeley *Gazette,* March 1, 1967, 1.

84   *Ibid.,* March 22, 1967, 2.

85   *University Bulletin,* July 24, 1967, 15. (The Governor requested $252,000,000, but the legislature restored $6,000,000).

86   *Ibid.,* 14, 15, 16.

87   *Ibid.,* July 24, 1967, 18.

88   *Ibid.,* September 11, 1967, 137.

89   *Ibid.*

90   *Ibid.*

91   *Ibid.*

92   *Science,* September 3, 1965, 1074–75.

93   *University Bulletin,* August 1, 1966, 13.

94   In February, 1968, Franklin Murphy announced his intention to resign to become Chairman of the Board and Chief Executive Officer of the Times Mirror Company, which publishes the Los Angeles *Times* (*University Bulletin,* February 26, 1968).

95   *University Bulletin,* September 25, 1967, 44.

96   *Ibid.,* 43.

97   Los Angeles *Times,* September 23, 1967, 15.

98   *University Bulletin,* October 2, 1967, 49.

99   *Ibid.*

100   *Ibid.,* January 2, 1968, 85.

101   *Ibid.*

102   *Ibid.*

103   *Ibid.*

104   *Ibid.*

Chapter 28

1   University of California, Office of the President, Long Range Fiscal Program, 1966/67–1975/76, Appendix A-1.

2   *Ibid.,* Appendix A–2.

3   *Ibid.,* 10.

4   *Ibid.,* 5.

5   *Ibid.*

6   *University Bulletin,* December 11, 1967, 79. Originally, the Regents requested $306,000,000, but increased their request on the basis of larger-than-anticipated enrollment projections.

7   *Ibid.,* February 13, 1968, 97.

8   *Ibid.,* March 25, 1968, 127.

9   *Ibid.,* February 26, 1968, 115.

10   *Ibid.,* March 25, 1968, 127.

11   Berkeley *Gazette,* April 25, 1968.

12   *Ibid.,* March 27, 1968.

13   *University Bulletin,* July 24, 1967, 17.

14   *Ibid.,* May 20, 1968, 161.

15   *Ibid.*

16   *Ibid.*

17   California, Constitution, Article IX, Sec. 9.

18   The Donohoe Act enacted the Master Plan for Higher Education in California.

19   Organic Act, Sec. 15, in *California Statutes 1867–68,* 248–62.

20   Clark Kerr, *The Uses of the University* (Cambridge, 1963), 36.

21   *Ibid.,* 36–37.

22   University of California Annual Report of the Secretary to the Board of Regents for the year ending June 30, 1884, 27.

23   Letter from Roger W. Heyns to Dick Beahrs, ASUC president, and Ken Stahl, ASUC first vice-president, as reprinted in the *Daily Californian,* November 30, 1967, 9.

24   "The Culture of the University: Governance and Education," Report of the Study Commission on University Governance, University of California, Berkeley, January 15, 1968, 49.

25   *Ibid.,* 49, 51.

26   *Daily Californian,* May 20, 1968, 1.

27   Organic Act, Sec. 1.

28   Daniel C. Gilman, *The Building of the University: An Inaugural Address Delivered at Oakland, November 7, 1872* (San Francisco, 1872), 6 (in the University of California archives, Berkeley).

29   *Ibid.*

30   University of California, *The Inauguration of Benjamin Ide Wheeler as President of the University* (Berkeley, 1899), 27 (University of California archives, Berkeley).

31   *Ibid.*

32   George A. Pettitt, *Twenty-eight Years in the Life of a University President* (Berkeley, 1966), 202.

33   Kerr, 38.

34   Minutes of the Board of Regents, February 17, 1967 (Office of the Secretary of the Regents, University of California, Berkeley).

35   Charles J. Hitch, Inaugural Address, May 23, 1968 (manuscript), 7.

Index